W9-DIH-591

Regions at risk

UNU Studies on Critical Environmental Regions

Edited by Jeanne X. Kasperson, Roger E. Kasperson, and B.L. Turner II

Note from the editors

This book launches a series from the United Nations University (UNU) research project, Critical Zones in Global Environmental Change, itself part of the UNU programme on the Human and Policy Dimensions of Global Change. Both endeavours explore the complex linkages between human activities and the environment.

The project views the human causes of and responses to major changes in biogeochemical systems – global environmental change broadly defined – as consequences of cumulative and synergistic actions (or inactions) of individuals, groups, and states, occurring in their local and regional settings. The study examines and compares nine regional cases in which large-scale, human-induced environmental changes portend to threaten the sustainability of an existing system. The aim is to define common lessons about regional trajectories and dynamics of change as well as the types of human actions that breed environmental criticality and endangerment, thereby contributing to global environmental change. This volume, which provides an overview of the project, presents the overall results of the comparative analysis.

Regions at Risk draws upon the nine regional case-studies – Amazonia, the Aral Sea basin, the Nepal middle mountains, the Ukambani region of Kenya, the Llano Estacado of the North American Southern High Plains, the Basin of Mexico, the North Sea, the Ordos Plateau of China, and the eastern Sundaland region of South-East Asia – to explore the concept of environmental criticality. Shunning narrow "geocentric" and "anthropogenic" approaches in favour of a more integrative assessment of the trajectories of threat attendant on environmental change over time, the authors have refined the concept of criticality. A classification of environmental threat, replete with definitions, includes four categories: criticality, endangerment, impoverishment, and sustainability.

This fourfold classification guides the nine case-studies, each conducted according to a common research protocol, and informs the development of a theoretical framework for analysing the human dimensions of global environmental change. The analysis focuses on cumulative long-term changes and addresses the "regional dynamics" that are shaping the trajectories of change within each region at risk.

Titles currently available:

- Regions at Risk: Comparisons of Threatened Environments
- In Place of the Forest: Environmental and Socio-economic Transformation in Borneo and the Eastern Malay Peninsula
- Amazonia: Resiliency and Dynamism of the Land and Its People

Regions at risk: Comparisons of threatened environments

Edited by Jeanne X. Kasperson,
Roger E. Kasperson, and B. L. Turner II

TOKYO • NEW YORK • PARIS

The views expressed in this publication are those of the authors and do not necessarily reflect the views of the United Nations University.

This book has been published in cooperation with the Commission on Critical Environmental Situations and Regions, the International Geographical Union.

United Nations University Press
The United Nations University, 53-70, Jingumae 5-chome, Shibuya-ku, Tokyo 150, Japan
Tel: (03) 3499-2811 Fax: (03) 3406-7345
Telex: J25442 Cable: UNATUNIV TOKYO

UNU Office in North America
2 United Nations Plaza, Room DC2-1462, New York, NY 10017
Tel: (212) 963-6387 Fax: (212) 371-9454 Telex: 422311 UN UI

United Nations University Press is the publishing division of the United Nations University.

Typeset by Asco Trade Typesetting Limited, Hong Kong
Printed by Permanent Typesetting and Printing Co., Ltd., Hong Kong
Cover design by Joyce C. Weston

UNUP-848
ISBN 92-808-0848-6
03800 P

Contents

Acknowledgements

This volume is the interim report of the Project on Critical Environmental Zones (ProCEZ), based at Clark University, Worcester, MA, but involving teams of researchers from six continents in a remarkable collaboration. As editors of this book and its companion series, Critical Environmental Regions, we know all too well our indebtedness to our various collaborators and supporters.

The United States National Science Foundation set ProCEZ in motion in 1989 and even gambled on a second phase a year later. In 1991, the United Nations University (UNU) provided funds to continue the project and support the publication of this volume as well as a monograph series and a final report. We are extremely grateful to former vice-rector Roland Fuchs, academic officer Juha I. Uitto, and UNU Press director Amadio A. Arboleda for enabling us to proceed with our work. And we salute the patience and professionalism of the people at the Press, who suffered overdue manuscripts, missing artwork, and numerous excuses with unflappable good will.

From the outset, the project has benefited from sage counsel. The advisory committee included William Clark (Harvard University), Robert W. Kates (Brown University), Vernon Ruttan (University of Minnesota), and Barbara Boyle Torrey (US Bureau of the Census). A fifth adviser, Nikita Glazovsky of the Institute of Geography, Russian Academy of Sciences, played a dual role and wrote the chapter on the Aral Sea. Two colleagues from the Institute of Geography, Galina Sdasyuk and Larissa Mamayeva, also provided guidance. We appreciate immensely the rigorous and constructive criticism that we received from our advisers. We also thank David Kummer, a geographer at Clark University, for his insightful commentary on the introductory and concluding chapters. Finally, we wish that we could acknowledge personally the anonymous reviewers, enlisted by the UNU, who took time to read and evaluate our penultimate pages.

Here at Clark University, many people have earned more than their salaries reflect. Mimi Berberian, project administrator, has once again turned her flawless hand to keeping the books and her sharp eyes to copy-editing numerous drafts of all eleven chapters. Lu Ann Pacenka, our indefatigable word-processor and by now an old hand at producing books, has seen us through yet another volume with characteristic perfection, humour, and grace. Rishab Punjabi, a relatively new hand, has taken to producing books as though he were accustomed to it. Joining in the typing of innumerable drafts that included unfamiliar words and names in Chinese, Portuguese, Russian, and Spanish (as well as some unintelligible handwritten English!) were Susan Gemmel, Donna Martin, Dawn McCart, and Maureen Shaughnessy. We owe them dinner! We also owe dinner to Anne Gibson, director of Clark University's cartographic laboratory, and her assistant, Anne Garren, for their expert rendering of numerous maps and complex figures.

As the editors turned to the final editing, much of their usual routine landed on others. Heather Henderson deftly managed more than her share of duties at the George Perkins Marsh Institute, Mimi Berberian juggled numerous demands at the Center for Technology, Environment, and Development (CENTED), and B. J. Perkins and Kavita Iyengar kept the Marsh Research Library open and user-friendly. A sterling staff has made all the difference.

And so has the opportunity to work with an extraordinary group of colleagues, whose intellectual commitment held sway over more lucrative opportunities. That commitment brought many of them to Mexico City in the spring of 1993 to launch the monograph series, Critical Environmental Regions. For that gathering, we are indebted to the UNU for its continued sponsorship as well as to the Centro de Ecología, Universidad Autónoma de México, for the local arrangements and unmatched hospitality overseen by Alejandra Cedallos.

For our part, we look forward to more collaboration with this remarkable team. The ProCEZ experience has demonstrated that large interdisciplinary, and international, research projects can flourish.

Jeanne X. Kasperson
Roger E. Kasperson
B. L. Turner II
Worcester, Massachusetts

1

Critical environmental regions: Concepts, distinctions, and issues

Roger E. Kasperson, Jeanne X. Kasperson, B. L. Turner II, Kirstin Dow, and William B. Meyer

The causes and consequences of human-induced environmental change are not evenly distributed over the earth. They converge in certain regions and places where their impacts may threaten the long-term or even the short-term sustainability of human–environmental relationships. Designating such areas "critical environmental situations," Russian geographers have developed "red data maps" showing their locations (Mather and Sdasyuk 1991). Recognition of such situations has reached the public through the likes of the 1989 National Geographic Society map of "environmentally endangered areas" (NGS 1989). Yet, despite the currency of these notions, no fully developed conceptualizations now exist of environmental criticality or of the criteria by which environmentally threatened regions can be identified, although a 1991 meeting at McGill University suggested some useful approaches (Meredith, Marley, and Smith 1991). Determination of what constitutes a state of criticality has been largely subjective and judgemental, with no searching exploration of the associated conceptual and methodological issues.

In this first chapter, we examine in detail the concepts of environmental criticality and endangerment and provide more formal definitions. An examination of the relevant recent literature identifies differences between what we term *geocentric* and *anthropocentric* approaches to the study of criticality. We next investigate and elaborate concepts fundamental to the notions of endangerment and criticality, place them within the context of nature–society relations, and propose an integrative approach that structures the analyses that follow in this volume. Finally, we explore at greater length the regional dynamics of change that determines trajectories toward various levels of endangerment and criticality, suggesting potentially useful approaches for analysing such dynamics.

Previous studies

Human activities have always changed the physical environment, of course, but the scale and rate of impact have grown enormously during the past century. Human activities range from diverting rivers, clearing forests, and depleting soils to magnifying the natural chemical flows of the biosphere and introducing new synthetic substances. Such changes have caused widespread alarm as they threaten to damage valued environments, deplete essential resources, or reduce the productivity of agriculture and other human activities. The perception of severe problems of these sorts may prompt the judgement that a state of environmental criticality has been reached and the human use of the environment put in jeopardy. As we use the term, "criticality" denotes a state of both environmental degradation and associated socio-economic deterioration, however measured or identified. "Critical region" denotes an area that has reached such a state of interactive degradation. Such meanings are broadly consistent with various recent studies, ranging from global to local assessments (e.g. Turner et al. 1990a, 1990b).

Global approaches

Criticality and related terms, though often without a clear or carefully reasoned definition, have been used at a variety of spatial scales. Some assessments view criticality as reflecting a scope of impact sufficiently wide to merit global concern. *Man's Impact on the Global Environment: Report of the Study of Critical Environmental Problems* (SCEP 1970) focused on those environmental problems "whose cumulative effects on ecological systems are so large and prevalent that they have worldwide significance" (SCEP 1970, 5). The study concludes that individual problems of pollution, such as the persistence and spread of DDT, oil spills in the oceans, and atmospheric pollution, and change occurring across places comprise global changes that present new problems in research, monitoring, and response.

General models have been developed to forecast environmental criticality on a global level by assessing the interaction of multiple elements in human systems, such as population, economic growth, pollution, and resource depletion. Some modellers conclude that technology and socio-economic restructuring will ward off critical situations; others foresee doomsday outcomes. *The Limits to Growth* (Meadows et al. 1972) and its successor, *Beyond the Limits* (Meadows, Meadows, and Randers 1992), report on ambitious computer-modelling attempts to simulate the reaction of the global system when withdrawal exceeds carrying capacity. The model simulated the reactions among five factors – population, agricultural production, natural resources, industrial production, and pollution – and associated trends that the modellers believed determine and ultimately limit growth on this planet. Criticality, in this context of limiting growth, occurs when either basic human needs (such as food and energy) exceed available supply or environmental deterioration overwhelms existing environmental sinks and pollution inhibits continued human use. Such approaches reflect what are often referred to as Malthusian, neo-Malthusian, or Cassandra views of environmental crisis (e.g. Ehrlich and Holdren 1988).

The Global 2000 Report (CEQ 1980) draws on the databases and models of US federal government agencies and derives its predictions from trend extrapolation, assuming no major changes in public policy, institutions, or rates of technological change, and no wars or other disruptions. Its pessimistic conclusions, which align it with the neo-Malthusian school, are challenged by *The Resourceful Earth* (Simon and Kahn 1984) on the grounds of inaccurate extrapolation, inadequate data sets, and other shortcomings. *The Resourceful Earth* is unabashedly optimistic in seeing improvement rather than deterioration of environmental quality. It maintains that, although serious local and temporary large-scale problems may arise, "the nature of the world's physical conditions and the resilience in a well-functioning economic and social system enable us to overcome such problems" (Simon and Kahn 1984, 3). Finally, *The Global Possible* notes that, although "disturbing visions of the human condition early in the next century are not difficult to imagine from the present situation" (Repetto 1985, 7), known technologies and regulatory strategies are capable of improving the outlook. This perspective rests heavily on the capacity to detect change and to mobilize human response. The author identifies many technologies that could improve resource-use efficiency if widely used and if the network for diffusion of these technologies were in place. Similar views of environmental change are often classified as optimist, technological fix, or Pollyanna perspective.

Regional approaches

Whatever the validity of their specific findings, global-level approaches are valuable in raising many key issues around the conceptualization of environmental criticality. Other approaches have focused on the identification of criticality at the regional scale, at which, presumably, uncertainties are smaller than those at the global scale (Turner et al. 1990b). But the linkages among regions in an open global system introduce a different set of complications.

The red data maps developed by Soviet geographers indicate critical areas where "normal" human activities are threatened or deemed no longer possible, but they do not reflect a systematic definition and assessment (Kochurov 1991; Mather and Sdasyuk 1991). Similarly, the US Water Resources Council's (1978) assessment of national water resources developed a "water-supply adequacy analysis model" based on the concept of a balance between use and supply to identify "critical" water problems. Some of these problems are attributable to poor distribution, use conflicts and competition, or physical scarcity. Here "criticality" suggests that existing and long-term water-based uses are threatened. The Food and Agriculture Organization (FAO) of the United Nations has identified "critical zones" and "critical countries" based upon the capacity of the land resources to support, or carry, current and projected populations (FAO 1984). Blaikie and Brookfield (1987) have sought to develop, for regions experiencing severe land degradation, a multidimensional analysis focused on human-induced land transformations. Other research on such diverse topics as photochemical smog, acid precipitation, desertification, and famine has also sought to identify "endangered" or "problem" regions.

Local approaches

Those regional approaches that focus on a specific locale become local approaches as well. The local scale, however, is also the arena of a different approach, in which "criticality" and "critical areas" are used to designate areas of critical importance or value, rather than areas in critical condition. For example, the Conservation Foundation (1984, 172) defines ecologically critical areas as "special ecosystems that serve unique functions and are small in area or are unusually fragile relative to others." Accordingly, the Foundation identifies a broad spectrum of wetlands as "critical" areas, based on their high level of biological productivity, their importance to a wide variety of wildlife, and their role in various physical processes. Similarly, the Endangered Species Act (1973) in the United States requires the development of a list of critical habitats that are necessary for the normal needs and survival of endangered or threatened species. Such areas and habitats are termed critical because their loss would be irreparable, they are particularly vulnerable to human-induced changes, and their degradation or loss may have wider implications, including loss of biodiversity and increased ecosystem instability. The US Bureau of Land Management's Areas of Critical Environmental Concern programme assesses those areas in need of "special management attention ... to protect and prevent irreparable damage to their inportant historic, cultural, or scenic values, fish and wildlife resources, or other natural systems or processes" (Campbell and Wald 1989; FLPMA 1976). Such a definition of criticality need not be restricted to the local scale, of course; it might well serve to identify Amazonia as a globally critical zone because of its importance to the rest of the world as a reservoir of carbon and genetic diversity. In any case, however, referring as it does to the importance of an area rather than the degree to which it is currently threatened, it is not criticality in the sense in which we shall be using the term in this volume.

Regardless of the scale employed, a literature dealing explicitly or implicitly with criticality and endangerment exists. This work has developed in an ad hoc fashion, with no discernible movement toward a full-fledged conception of environmental endangerment or criticality. A more precise and systematic approach is needed to move beyond individual treatments and undertake comparative analyses.

Geocentric and anthropocentric approaches

Conceptualizing "critical" environmental areas is a challenging task because of the wide range of perspectives, many of them conflicting, from which the environmental threat or regional outcomes can be viewed. To simplify, we identify two polar positions – the geocentric and the anthropocentric – that appear to undergird some assessments of criticality or endangerment. These positions are similar to the extreme forms of what O'Riordan (1976) defines as "ecocentrism" and "technocentrism."

The geocentric perspective defines criticality in terms of changes in physical attributes or ecological dimensions. Criticality is reached when human-induced perturbations have so altered the biophysical system that a different system, substantially less diverse and more ecologically "degraded," results. Examples include the creation of a new vegetation complex with fewer species or less biomass, or the conversion of wetlands, involving a loss of water and a transformation of the surface biomass–nutrient–fauna complex. The Soviet studies of "red data situations" have taken this geocentric approach, emphasizing the alteration of multiple environmental resource components and projecting such biophysical change as detrimental to long-term human uses of the environment (Kochurov 1991; Mather and Sdasyuk 1991).

The use of a purely geocentric definition would require the designation of most urban–industrial complexes and most major farming regions as critical or endangered environmental areas because of the profound transformations in a variety of environmental components (species loss, land-cover replacement, changes in soil and water composition). Such an approach draws out important information on the extent of ecological change, but it is not necessarily directly relevant to the prospects for continued human occupancy or human well-being, or to the grounds on which managerial intervention is likely to be undertaken.

If the geocentric perspective focuses on the physical environment to the exclusion of its human inhabitants, the anthropocentric perspective does the opposite. In perhaps the extreme exposition of this view (Simon and Kahn 1984), environmental constraints on human activity are minimized or even assumed away, and technological or social change is seen as potentially sufficient to deal with natural or human-induced environmental threats. Environmental losses or catastrophes are blamed principally on social structures that block the innovations and adaptations that could have prevented them. Views that regard disasters as essentially social phenomena and employ primarily social measures also to some degree reflect this orientation (Hewitt 1983; Susman, O'Keefe, and Wisner 1983). Valuable in emphasizing the human dimensions of environmental degradation, this anthropocentric view typically underestimates or oversimplifies the varied ways in which the environment supports and sustains human life and well-being.

The valuable features of each approach and the contradictions between them suggest the need for an integrative, holistic approach to conceptualizing environmental threats. A judgement of criticality, in these perspectives, is typically based on the changes in either the physical or the human conditions of the zone, rather than on the details of their interaction. Experience suggests, however, that addressing rates and types of change in nature–society relations is essential to understanding environmental transformations, as is attention to both the fragility of the natural system and the societal ability to respond to environmental threats. A purely geocentric perspective can end up designating as "endangered" or "critical" a region that successfully maintains a large population and high standards of living and is likely to do so far into the future. This is a reality that will be repeatedly demonstrated in the chapters that follow in this volume. Correspondingly, a narrow anthropocentric perspective can easily offer unrealistic assessments based on assumptions about human ability to adapt to any environmental problem or to overcome any physical limits. Neither is adequate for the balanced approach to critical environmental situations needed to guide thoughtful analysis or judicious public policy.

Closely related to the concept of criticality is the notion of environmental degradation, and here again the geocentric and anthropocentric perspectives offer conflicting views. A geocentric definition of environmental degradation might equate such degradation with any human-induced change from the "natural" state; an anthropocentric one might see it as being at most an epiphenomenon of social maladjustment or conflate it with any form of social or economic decline. More useful is an interactive definition paralleling those offered by Blaikie and Brookfield (1987) and Turner and Benjamin (1993) for land degradation: environmental degradation is a decrease in the capacity of the environment as managed to meet its user demands. In a broad sense, of course, this definition, like our definition of criticality below, attaches central importance to the human significance of environmental change. It differs from the anthropocentric perspective discussed above, however, in recognizing the central place of the environment in gauging the costs, impacts, and limits of the societal responses.

A similarly integrative perspective on criticality is required. It must recognize the essential role of the environment in sustaining human life but recognize at the same time that not all elements of the environment are essential or equally important. It must also appreciate the essential role of human management and response. It should explicitly acknowledge continuing human adjustments and adaptations to environmental change, look beyond resource use to the broader realm of environmental interactions, take a long-term perspective, and place regions in their global context. It is to the construction of such an approach that we now turn, beginning with the key concepts upon which it must rest.

Key concepts and issues

An integrative and systematic approach to environmental criticality must not only view a particular human–environment situation within historical and spatial context but also examine attributes that have been identified as central to such situations. These attributes include sensitivity, fragility, resilience, and vulnerability; the nature of environmental change; threats and disaster; life-support systems; intergenerational export of damage; and societal response systems. From the reviews of these attributes we draw a number of lessons regarding the conceptualization and identification of environmental criticality.

Sensitivity, fragility, resilience, and vulnerability

Key considerations in criticality include the extent to which environmental stresses damage ecosystems and reduce their ability to maintain their basic structures under stress and recover from such damage. Similar considerations of the characteristics of social systems, groups, and individuals add to the set of processes that contribute to differential susceptibility to environmental changes. Indeed, it has long been recognized that environmental hazards are the joint product of stress and exposure on the one hand and fragility and vulnerability on the other. An array of often overlapping or conflicting terms – sensitivity, resistance, resilience, marginality, fragility, vulnerability – has arisen to address the latter term of this product.

The science of ecology, as Turner and Benjamin (1994) have pointed out, lacks a precise and accepted definition of ecosystem fragility. Ecologists (and some others) use "fragility" to denote a "system at risk," where the notion of "risk" is linked to ecological concepts of stability, instability, and susceptibility (e.g. Yodzis 1980, 545). The chain of linkages characterizing the system provides the ecological base for the notion of fragility. This complex internal structure of the ecological system, with its various pathways and differing sensitivities of species at risk, is receiving detailed analysis in the emerging field of ecological risk assessment (Travis and Morris 1992). Whether the notion of "system" or "land system" will ultimately prove too crude to capture the essential character of change and damage must await the results of these efforts by ecologists and ecological risk analysts.

According to Holling (1986, 296), "stability" is "the propensity of a system to attain or retain an equilibrium condition of steady state or stable oscillation," whereas "resilience" is "the ability of a system to maintain its structure and patterns of behavior in the face of disturbance." Increasingly, however, equilibrium-centred notions appear to be under challenge among ecologists, and linear views of stability and recovery are giving way to notions stressing the cyclic or irregular nature of ecosystem change and the spatio-temporal heterogeneity of landscapes and ecosystems (Turner 1987). Our approach to criticality is consistent with these emerging views.

"Sensitivity" is often used to measure the magnitude of negative impacts of environmental change. Change can have positive and negative impacts on human societies. Here the emphasis is on the degree of stress placed on the land or environmental system and on the identification of the important relationships and processes. Blaikie and Brookfield (1987) use the terms "sensitivity" and "resilience" to describe the quality of land systems. They use "sensitivity" to refer to "the degree to which a given land system undergoes changes due to natural forces, following human interference" and "resilience" to refer to "the ability of land to reproduce its capability after interference, and the measure of the need for human artifice to that end" (Blaikie and Brookfield 1987, 10). For its part, the concept of "fragility" combines two dimensions: the capacity to be wounded by a particular environmental perturbation (either nature- or human-induced), and the ability to maintain structure and essential functions and to recover.

From these discussions, we adopt the following definitions:

- *sensitivity* (or susceptibility): the degree of ecosystem or ecosystem component change associated with a given degree of human-induced stress;
- *resilience*: the ability of a particular ecosystem to maintain the basic structure essential to support human uses during perturbations and to recover from such (and especially damaging) changes.

"Fragility" reflects both of these basic properties of human–ecosystem interactions. In conceptions of criticality, we are particularly interested in human-induced stresses that erode irreversibly the abil-

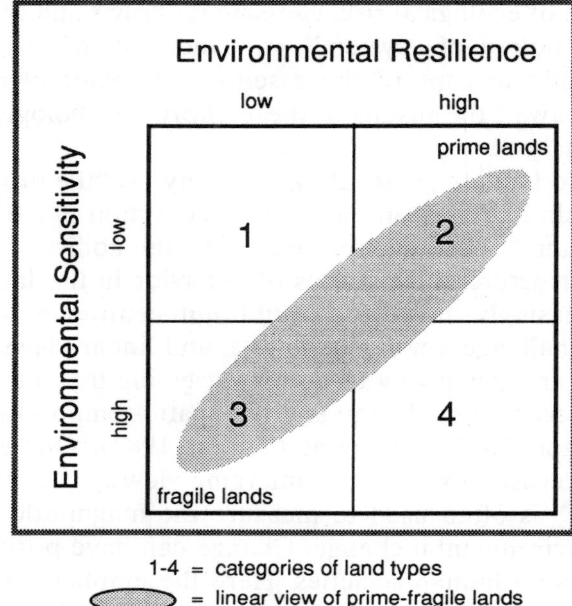

Fig. 1.1 **Environmental attributes of fragility and fragile land types (Source: Turner and Benjamin, 1994)**

ity of the ecosystem to support human productive systems or life itself. Accordingly, we adopt the following definition:

- *fragility*: the sensitivity of a particular ecosystem to human-induced perturbations and its resilience to such perturbations.

As Turner and Benjamin (1994) point out, these definitions indicate that four quadrants of fragility can be distinguished that represent different risk situations and different "buffering" to stresses (fig. 1.1). Some environments degrade rapidly but maintain themselves under stress and recover; others are sensitive to change and have low capabilities for maintenance and recovery; and so on.

Obviously, these different attributes are highly relevant to analysis of criticality in the face of human-induced environmental stresses. The physical properties of the environmental base matter. Fragile environments degrade more readily under mismanagement and exact higher societal costs for management or for substitution. More robust environments may not degrade so rapidly and may respond to substitutes more economically. It should be noted, however, that less fragile environments are almost invariably those under the most human stress and hence most subject to mismanagement.

Discussions of the differential susceptibility of social groups and individuals to losses from environmental changes have used diverse nomenclature, often paralleling discussions of ecosystems. Although "vulnerability" frequently refers to the differential susceptibility of both social and biophysical systems, it appears to be emerging as the most common term in the former context (Chambers 1989; Dow 1992; Downing 1991; Gleick 1990; Green 1990; Liverman 1990; Susman, O'Keefe, and Wisner 1983). At an abstract level, the social and ecological dimensions share concerns with the level of impact of a change and the ability to cope with the stress and to continue functioning. Throughout this volume, "vulnerability" refers mainly to the social dimension.

Vulnerability in this sense is a product of three dimensions: exposure, resistance (the ability to withstand impacts), and resilience (the ability to maintain basic structures and to recover from losses). These dimensions, slightly different from those applied above to ecosystems, incorporate the costs of recovery and the role of social relations and decision-making at a variety of social levels, from nation to household, in determining conditions of exposure as well as exposure itself. The distinction is an important one in relation to human activities leading to environmental change as well as the variety of adjustments or coping measures adopted in the face of environmental changes. For instance, the knowledge and resources that people bring to a new farming enterprise will affect the outcomes of that enterprise in that environment. Successful adjustments of farming techniques throughout a season can mitigate the impacts of unpredictable climatic conditions. The level of support that society gives to these farmers will also make a difference in the losses they experience in the case of poor harvest due to drought or declining land capability.

Green (1990, 14), in reference to flood hazards, expresses vulnerability as a relationship between changing conditions and normal use patterns. He defines vulnerability as a function of "*susceptibility* (the extent to which the presence of water will affect inputs or outputs of an activity); *dependency* (the degree to which an activity requires a particular good as an input to function normally); and *transferability* (the ability of an activity to respond by deferring demand, using substitutes or relocating)." Expanded to consider a broader set of relationships between nature and society, these characteristics become important dimensions in discussing the consequences of environmental changes.

Researchers have identified a broad variety of factors, including social relations (particularly race, ethnicity, class, and gender), institutional characteristics, demographic attributes (such as age and reproductive status), individual decision-making and perception, types of technology employed, and political–economic relations that may well contribute to vulnerability (Cannon 1994; Downing 1991; Liverman 1990). The scale of analysis differs among these factors; the appropriate scale for the analysis of vulnerability depends to a great extent on the type of event and the question of concern. The vulnerability of a country to declining agricultural productivity in a region will differ from that of farming households in the region.

The character of change

Discussions of environmental criticality often express particular concern with irreversible change. *Our Common Future*, for example, opens with a world of environmental stresses, the result of increasing interconnectedness in which "many regions face risks of irreversible damage to the human environment that threaten the basis for human progress" (WCED 1987, 27). The book usually specifies particular irreversible losses deemed as critical, such as species or particular vegetation systems that are unlikely to reappear, once lost or changed, regardless of socio-economic or technical response. Irreversibility is also linked to concerns over sustainable development through definitions that speak of societies that satisfy their needs without reducing the opportunities for future generations to satisfy theirs. Concerns with irreversible change or sustainability are often vague in specifying exactly what should be preserved for future generations, but quality of life, raw materials needed for innovation, and the store of capital assets and natural resources are commonly cited.

Rates of change are recognized as a second key aspect. Indeed, the definition of particular environmental changes as problems often rests less upon the magnitude than on the acceleration of change, as in concerns about exponential increases in Amazonian deforestation or the rapidity with which new chemical substances are introduced into the environment. In particular, the judged relationship between relative rates of environmental change and the estimated time needed for society to respond through prevention, adaptation, or adjustment has gained recognition as an important variable.

It is increasingly apparent that many environmental changes may be discontinuous. Threshold effects, non-linear relationships, surprises, and chaotic readjustments may thus be typical of society–environment relationships. Not only does this possibility have far-reaching implications for the construction of knowledge bases and assessment methodologies, but it suggests that human institutions and management strategies that assume linear change will face intrinsic difficulties in anticipating and interpreting environmental change. It also suggests that causality will often be elusive and that miscalculations and surprises will flourish. The recognition that essential parts of needed knowledge are unknowable and that threat situations involve moral and ethical issues has led Funtowicz and Ravetz (forthcoming) to argue for a "second order" science.

Hence not only the simple magnitude but other aspects of change must enter into concepts of environmental criticality. The reversibility of changes, their rates, and their possibly discontinuous and nonlinear character deserve particular attention, whereas past and possible future trajectories of change as well as magnitudes of change warrant consideration.

Threats and disaster

Notions of criticality embody assessments, often implicit, of losses and harm arising from alterations in nature–society relationships. Inevitably, such notions cannot be restricted to disruptions in productive systems or economic loss but involve broader effects on human values about nature. This is consistent with the definition of a "hazard" as a "threat to people and what they value" (Kates, Hohenemser, and Kasperson 1985, 21).

Societal capacities to respond and subjective human interpretation of events are important considerations in the regional context. Quarantelli (1985, 1987), for example, views disasters as a subset of studies addressing social crises (where crisis is assumed to refer to an unstable condition, a crucial turning point in the life-course of an individual, family, or nation). Thus disasters, whether the result of natural or of social events, are primarily social phenomena and can be assessed only in terms of society's capabilities to respond. Other researchers seek an intermediate ground and a more interactive definition. For instance, natural hazards are frequently described in terms of their duration, scope of impact, cause, and speed of onset – all measures that affect society's ability to predict, control, and give warnings (Wenger 1978). The ecologic–symbolic approach of Kroll-Smith and Couch (1990) conceptualizes disasters in terms of society–environment relationships.

Sociological research offers a further perspective on the effects of environmental change. An accepted list of needed social functions might include: (1) production–distribution–consumption; (2) socialization; (3) social participation; (4) social control; and (5) mutual support. One well-known definition of disaster is "an event, concentrated in time and space, in which a society or a relatively self-sufficient subdivision of a society undergoes severe danger and incurs such losses to its members and physical appurtenances that the social structure is disrupted and the fulfillment of all or some of essential functions of the society is prevented" (Fritz 1961, 655).

These perspectives introduce several considerations useful in conceptualizing environmental criticality. First, both changes to the environment and changes to society require assessment, particularly for establishing causal relationships. The degree of environmental change or social disruption will vary among events and among communities. Although some of the contributing factors will be environmental, others will be social, so that attributing a disaster to either environmental or social causes alone may be problematic. Relatively minor environmental changes can easily become disasters under unusually adverse social and economic circumstances. In short, environmental hazards are interactive phenomena.

Life-support systems

Among the varied threats to the environment, the most central (and most relevant to notions of criticality) is endangerment of the ability to sustain human life over the long term. Although no general agreement exists on this subject, discussions have treated such matters as basic functions, basic needs, and human well-being. These may be clustered under the general heading of "life-support systems," so long as that term is understood broadly to incorporate the environmental resources that sustain the economy as well as those – such as water and air – that support life in an immediate sense.

Some previous investigations of criticality have sought to assess the effects of environmental degradation on environmental life-support systems. A primary focus of the Soviet red-zone maps has been the long-term and potentially irreversible impacts on what are described as "life-support capabilities" (Mather and Sdasyuk 1991). A concern with "life-support" functions of the environment was also central to the arguments of *Our Common Future* (WCED 1987) and pervaded much of the rhetoric at the Earth Summit in Rio de Janeiro. Lacking a rigorous definition and means of measurement, however, this notion has thus far proven difficult to use in rigorous assessment, yet the concept strikes at an essential quality of human–environment interactions.

E. P. Odum (1989, 13) defines the "life-support environment" as "that part of the earth that provides physiological necessities of life, namely, food and other energy mineral nutrients, air and water," and a "life-support system" as the "functional term for the environment, organisms, processes, and resources interacting to provide these physical necessities." He sees these systems as under stress from pollution, poor management practices, and population pressure, with early warnings apparent in the erosion of prime agricultural soils and the death of trees in industrialized countries.

Social scientists have adapted and expanded Odum's fundamentally physiological definition of life-support systems. The "necessities of life" to which Odum refers have received extensive treatment in the social sciences under such umbrella terms as "basic human needs" – generally the likes of health, food, water, education, shelter, and sanitation (Haq and Burki 1980; World Bank 1980). Non-material attributes such as participation, political rights, cultural identity, and a sense of purpose in life are sometimes cited as basic needs (Stewart 1985; Streeten 1980). For others, basic needs are important largely because of their contributions to more fundamental aspects of human life, health, and education, and these goals are viewed as the primary objectives (Stewart 1985). The World Commission on Environment and Development argues that sustainable development requires meeting basic needs, however defined, and offering all an opportunity to achieve their aspirations for a better life (WCED 1987, 44).

Others would argue for "well-being" or "quality of life" as the appropriate term for the health of nature–society relationships. Appraisals addressing these concepts are unavoidably subjective (at least in part), embedded as they are in cultural values and perspectives. If endangerment is viewed as threats to human well-being or quality of life, both material and value-related attributes will need to be considered. Income, health, nutrition, and literacy are common such indicators. Economic growth measures, such as per capita GNP or GDP, are sometimes used as indicators of human well-being because of their general relationship with other desirable factors. They also are often criticized, however, because they fail to address issues or negative impacts of economic growth and do not accurately reflect such considerations as the importance of informal and unpaid work and costs not accounted for by market transactions. A broader and more integrative measure is the well-established "international human suffering index" (Population Crisis Committee 1987, 1992), which taps 10 measures: life expectancy, daily calorie supply, clean drinking water, infant immunization, secondary school enrolment, GNP per capita, rate of inflation, communications technology, political freedoms, and civil rights. The "human development index" (HDI) developed by the United Nations Development Programme combines indicators of life expectancy, educational attainment, and income to produce a composite measure of human development at both national and regional scales. Although the HDI has drawn fire for its ranking of countries, it is a useful tool, whose strength lies in its broad-based perspective: "Human development concerns all activities – from production processes, to institutional changes, to policy dialogues" (UNDP 1992, 13).

Assessments of these sorts need to address not only what is threatened by environmental degradation but also who. The most sensitive, vulnerable, marginal, or fragile typically experience impacts well before others and suffer greater harm. It is not unusual that risks are concentrated in particular regions or social groups. Notions of endangerment must discriminate and assess effects at different scales, with attention to variations by ethnicity, class, and gender. It is often these most vulnerable groups who are driven to erode their own (and their children's and grandchildren's) environmental life-support systems.

Basic measures of needs and quality of life assess the life-support capacities of the nature–society relationship from the social side. Beginning on the physical side, researchers have used various measures to indicate the degree of change in the environment or a consequent decline in productivity in order to identify areas whose life-support systems are threatened. The rangeland classification scheme of the US Bureau of Land Management ranks the quality of rangelands according to the degree of departure of the present vegetation from the ecological potential of the area (BLM 1979). The variables measured include species composition, production, and ground cover. Similarly, classifications of desertification have been used to identify and to map the most degraded areas (Berry and Ford 1977; Reining 1978; UNSO 1992). Dregne (1983, 5), for example, maps global desertification according to four categories – very severe, severe, moderate, and slight – based on four indicators: plant cover as a measure of rangeland condition; erosion (by type of erosion rather than measures of soil loss); amount of salinization or waterlogging; and the percentage reduction in crop yields. According to this definition and these indicators, very severe instances of desertification are those in which the ecological changes reduce agricultural or livestock production, a reduction likely to translate into a decline in human wealth or well-being.

Although human welfare and the environment are fundamentally related, the relationship is complex. Declines in human well-being often occur for reasons entirely unrelated to environmental degradation. Taken alone, falling indices of human welfare would be as inadequate to underpin a judgement of environmental criticality as would be purely physical measures of change. The exclusive use of the latter would fly in the face of the fact that societies typically tolerate some level of environmental degradation, and that even serious ecological or environmental degradation, as we shall see repeatedly in this volume, often is accompanied by improvements in human well-being and standard of living. The concept of life-support systems, by focusing attention on those aspects of the environment critical to sustaining human occupancy, avoids the extreme geocentric position of equating large or rapid ecological transformation of any sort with significant environmental degradation.

Environmental degradation can undermine life-support systems in a variety of ways. Consider three different regional situations with different resource bases and productive systems. The first, and the most simple, involves the mining of a finite resource, such as coal or oil. Criticality is reached when the resource becomes scarce as a result of resource depletion, limited knowledge of the resource base, market constraints, or technological limitations. In the second case, criticality occurs after the rate of exploitation of an otherwise renewable resource (e.g. soils, groundwater, fisheries) exceeds the rate of renewal. For instance, from the perspective of resource analysis, the section of the sustainable-yield curve for fisheries resources where the population has been depleted beyond its ability to reproduce itself is the "critical zone" (Rees 1985). The third case reaches criticality when the demand for disposal exceeds the assimilative capacity of the environment. For example, toxic emissions may result in high levels of air pollution and adverse health effects, and sewage disposal into a river may increase the biological oxygen demand to the point that flora and fauna die.

In looking at these problems as rates of replacement and issues of assimilation, Daly (1990) finds the basis to begin to operationalize notions of sustainable development using three guidelines: (1) rates of harvest should not exceed regeneration rates (sustained yield); (2) rates of waste emissions should not exceed the rates of the assimilative capacity of the environment; and (3) for quasi-sustainable use of non-renewable resources, the harvest of these resources should be paired with compensating investment in a renewable substitute. Gaps in these relationships suggest differing situations in which trajectories in human–environment relations may lead to criticality or some similar condition.

It is possible, however, to deplete resources within an area without major social consequences as long as the deficit can be made up from elsewhere. Hence, the external linkages of an area with other regions are of no small importance. Most regions are sustained to some degree by inputs from elsewhere. For a region whose economic base is substantially disconnected from local physical resources, even substantial transformation of the environment may pose little threat to life support, as long as pollution sinks are not seriously overburdened. For a regional economy that depends closely on regional natural resources, on the other hand, rates of depletion considerably in excess of rates of natural replenishment may progress to criticality if the costs of resource substitution through imports become so high as to make the linkage unsustainable. A region would enter a state of criticality if environmental change undermined the productive activities that sustain its population to the point that the costs of substitution for essential inputs from outside can no longer be sustained and no feasible societal responses exist that are capable of mitigating the ongoing degradation or sustaining the same level or quality of habitation (as indicated by size of population and level of human well-being).

Generally missing from these treatments of life-support systems and assessments of well-being are the spiritual dimensions of human–environment interactions. However much ecological crises are depicted and characterized in material terms, they are doubtless also spiritual, religious, and cultural in their roots. The ecocentric perspective to which O'Riordan (1976) refers finds its expression in ideas of stewardship, of human spirituality and development, of responsibility to future generations, and of respect for other species. Although basic-needs and life-support-systems approaches may inevitably need to focus on material conditions, it bears emphasizing that spiritual dimensions may be no less important, no matter how difficult they are to conceptualize and measure.

The literature on life-support systems, important as it is, strains definitional integrity by opening the interpretation of criticality and endangerment to cascading sets of issues that take us far afield from environment-based human needs. Many attributes cited as basic needs are virtually unmeasurable at this time, which questions the practical usefulness of such broader approaches. Life-support systems are a strong reminder, on the other hand, of what might be ignored in narrow interpretations of criticality and endangerment. Larger systemic relationships should not be lost from view in conceptualizing and analysing criticality.

The future

No approach to endangerment or criticality can escape issues of time orientation and connections between the past, present, and future. Future generations will experience many of the impacts of current environmental changes. An important dimension of environmental loss is what it forebodes for the future (Weiss 1989).

These impacts, alas, are murky, for we know little of the future's abilities, values, and needs. Present actions, even ones that appear exploitative, may – unintentionally or counter-intuitively as well as deliberately – add to rather than subtract from the wealth, resources, and options available to the future. We do, however, have some indications of potential degradation to be exported to the future by present actions, the costs of current interventions, and the uncertainties that characterize choices. In ecological terms, the impacts of current activities often have long latency periods. Adequate knowledge is often lacking to assess the implications of present actions and the levels of costs to export to future generations. But it is clear that present actions may draw down the "capital" held in nature, reducing the resources and the options available to future generations in meeting their needs and aspirations. Impositions on future generations occur in at least three major ways: (1) depletion of resources; (2) degradation of environmental quality; and (3) discriminatory access to the environmental resources and benefits enjoyed by previous generations (Weiss 1990). In proposing an innovative set of principles to guide intergenerational equity, Weiss argues that

> Every generation receives a natural and cultural legacy in trust from its ancestors and holds it in trust for its descendants. This trust imposes upon each

generation the obligation to conserve the environment and natural and cultural resources for future generations. The trust also gives each generation the right to use and benefit from the natural and cultural legacy of its ancestors. These rights and obligations, which may be called planetary rights and obligations, form the corpus of a proposed new doctrine of intergenerational equity in international environmental law. (Weiss 1990, 7)

Notions of security in the face of an uncertain world and future enter into assessments of endangerment. Threats occur in terms of both increased risk and reduced options for human responses. Environmental degradation and resource depletion reduce our abilities to cope with foreseen or unforeseen changes, increase our losses, place unacceptable burdens on future generations, and can exacerbate tensions among nation-states. Nature's capital includes both proven and potential assets, and it is enhanced by the human creation and maintenance of "landesque capital." Landesque capital refers to "any investment in land with an anticipated life well beyond that of the present crop, or crop cycle" and "involves substantial 'saving' of labour and other inputs for future production." It includes, for example, terracing, irrigation, and drainage (Blaikie and Brookfield 1987, 9). Depleting either potential or actual assets undermines the flexibility to respond to future challenges or surprises. Biodiversity, for example, may hold yet unrecognized potential for medical and agricultural development. The diversity and buffering capacity in the environment are a source of security for unknowable future impacts or demands.

Adding the dimension of the future complicates many of the issues surrounding criticality. Restricting the scope of impacts on human societies to the current generation fails to give adequate weight to accumulating deterioration and its ultimate impacts on the human condition (in future generations). Yet in many past cases in which hindsight reveals that degradation of essential resources had pointed inexorably toward an environmental catastrophe, that catastrophe was averted through economic or technological change – not necessarily undertaken for environmental reasons. Resources were substituted and environmental degradation was displaced or alleviated (e.g. Hagerstrand and Lohm 1990; Pfister and Messerli 1990; Riebsame 1990; Whitmore et al. 1990). The lessons are that seemingly severe degradation may ultimately prove to be ephemeral because of future adaptations and changes. On the other hand, even changes that do not directly threaten current or near-term uses may none the less be of great importance because of the costs that they are likely to exact from future users of the environment.

Response systems

Environmental threats, as we have already seen, are interactive phenomena. Similarly, environmental change can be assessed only by examination of the complex of interactive contributing factors at work in a particular landscape and culture. These factors include natural variability, human-induced stresses, the sensitivity and resilience of the ecosystem, the vulnerability of the population, and, not least, the goals and capacities of response and management systems.

These response systems are embedded in political economies and cultures and take on goals and structures consistent with those larger contexts. The state commonly lends its power to dominant groups and classes to support their accumulation while marginalizing others (Blaikie 1985; Blaikie and Brookfield 1987). Thus, scarce resources are typically not allocated to intervene in peripheral regions headed for criticality; indeed, conscious exploitation and extraction of resources often continue unabated in the face of warnings. In other cases, environmental degradation is less overtly driven by state policy but rather reflects a willingness to exploit nature's assets for short-term gain or to focus political resources on other societal priorities. In any event, political will and priorities are often the determining factors for intervention to deflect an approaching condition of environmental criticality, as the subsequent chapters on Amazonia and the Aral Sea will attest.

But capabilities and resources are also important. Delayed and ineffective responses to emerging environmental criticality across many capitalist and socialist societies suggest that the roots of inadequate response cut across, or extend beyond, political economies and state behaviour. Meadows and associates (1992) note that delayed response over lengthy periods toward accumulating environmental criticality is commonplace, not exceptional. It is apparent, as Blaikie and Brookfield (1987) argue, that grand theory will not provide satisfying explanations of particular regional situations, a recurrent observation from scholars of nature–society relationships. The response systems operating under both opportunities and constraints need detailed analysis conducted in regional context.

Such analysis will certainly assess political relations that characterize decision-making structures at various scales. But it will also need to address the adequacy of various knowledge systems – how alerting occurs, what catalysts for action occur, how problems and data are constructed, how interventions and management strategies evolve, and how social learning occurs (Glantz 1988; Lindblom and Cohen 1979; Ravetz 1986). Clearly the degree to which emerging environmental degradation in any situation is critical depends upon the resources and capabilities that can be brought to bear and the political will to allocate them to ameliorate damage. As Argent and O'Riordan argue in chapter 8, sea-level rise poses an extraordinary risk to the Netherlands, but the very high response capability of that society shrinks the degree to which criticality is likely to emerge.

Summary

From the foregoing discussion and the larger literature on which it draws, we derive several lessons for a sound approach to environmental criticality:

1. Environmental criticality is an interactive phenomenon that relates to types and rates of environmental change, the fragility of the ecosystem, the vulnerability of the population affected, and response capabilities.
2. Criticality must be assessed within the particular landscape and culture of occurrence and must be placed in historical and spatial context.
3. Human–environment trajectories appear particularly likely to lead to criticality in situations that have some combination of
   - economies of high sensitivity and low resilience to environmental change;
   - human societies with high social and economic vulnerability;
   - economies strongly dependent upon local environmental resources;
   - frontier areas exposed to new forms of use; and
   - close linkage with, and dependent position *vis-à-vis*, global markets or distant political authority.
4. Non-linear and discontinuous environmental change holds a high potential for exacerbating societal diagnosis and delayed responses.
5. Criticality refers to situations in which emerging environmental

degradation threatens to overtax the resources of the environment, leading to a loss of life-support capability.
6. The concept of a critical region alone does not adequately capture the range of identifiable situations. Additional categories identifying different kinds and degrees of criticality are required.
7. Much of the change inflicted by human pressures on the environment may impose costs on future generations that need to be included in approaches to endangerment and criticality. On the other hand, many of the perceived environmental threats of today may be dispelled in the near future.

Regions and the regional approach

We began by observing that environmental problems are not distributed uniformly across the earth and that environmentally critical situations are often concentrated in regions. We suggest also that the regional level offers advantages for the study of environmental criticality. The substantial variation in setting, process, impact, and ability to respond across the earth's surface makes a meaningful global aggregate assessment problematic if not impossible. Findings derived from local or micro-scale studies, on the other hand, may thwart generalization because of their particularity. Examples of criticality in small (local or micro-scale) areas of the world are not difficult to find: places suffering from severe erosion or soil impoverishment, from desertification, from pollution, or from resource depletion. In these cases, however, abandonment or relocation, or a change to a different livelihood system, may be costly for the local population but are not severely disruptive at the societal level and do not pose the difficult questions that regional criticality does. The persistence of the region as a middle level for geographic study seems to reflect "the recognition that it offers a meeting ground for the local and global poles of empirical research" (Meyer et al. 1992, 273). In such research, "vertical synthesis," or the close study of the interaction of processes within a region, can be usefully supplemented by "horizontal synthesis." The potential insights offered by such comparative study of regions are apparent in studies by geographers and others.

To use a regional approach, even a comparative one, to understanding criticality is to run the risk of ignoring significant aspects of the problem that transcend the region's boundaries. Many of the causes of regional environmental degradation cannot be understood without attention to processes occurring globally and in other regions, nor can the pool of responses available be gauged accurately. A cautionary tale in this regard is provided by the UN Food and Agriculture Organization's treatment of "critical zones" and "critical countries" (FAO 1984). This study assumes, unrealistically, that there is no movement of surplus food between regions in the country and it accordingly focuses on imbalances between population and food production from closed and static land resources. It estimates levels of inputs requisite to bring available food and population into balance and then maps "critical zones" in relation to estimated levels of needed inputs. These assumptions of spatially closed systems involve many problems (as this volume will make clear) and point to the need to consider regional linkages with other areas and global markets in any sub-global treatment of endangerment and criticality. The identification of the region as a reasonably homogeneous unit should also not be allowed to obscure the importance of differences across sub-areas and social groups within it. Finally, it is possible that disjunctures in the driving forces of change are identifiable at different spatial scales, with forces evident at the global level perhaps obscured at the regional and vice versa.

We define a "region" for the purposes of this investigation as a continuous portion of the earth's surface, characterized by a rough match between a distinct physical environment and a system or set of systems of human use. The term "region" as generally used implies a middle-level scale of study, spatially continuous and not smaller than, say, a large island or a megacity and its hinterland, but not larger than a subcontinent. It has long been recognized that the delineation of regions involves a degree of subjectivity because sharp boundaries in natural and social phenomena do not generally exist. The fuzziness of boundaries poses especially difficult problems where both natural and social processes are important. Different factors to be taken into account include national and subnational boundaries, climatic zones, topography, the economic base, and so on. Rarely do these features co-vary across space. Some degree of heterogeneity is unavoidable, but for our purposes some potential regional units exhibit too much diversity to be usable. The natural and social conditions and processes of transformation operating within the Amazon Basin, for example, make it a workable region for the assessment of criticality in a way that nation-states like India, Nigeria, and Chile – though smaller in area – would not because of the scale of their internal variety. (We recognize the variability within

Amazonia as well, but contend, on a comparative basis, that it is less than in the states noted.)

Definitions

Drawing upon the preceding discussion, we offer a set of definitions and concepts to guide an integrative approach to understanding environmental criticality. We begin by differentiating "criticality" from other states that denote lesser degrees of environmental threat. We recognize four conditions:

- *Environmental criticality* refers to situations in which the extent and/or rate of environmental degradation preclude the continuation of current human-use systems or levels of human well-being, given feasible adaptations and societal capabilities to respond.
- *Environmental endangerment* refers to situations in which the trajectory of environmental degradation threatens in the near term (this and the next generation) to preclude the continuation of current human-use systems or levels of human well-being, given feasible adaptations and societal capabilities to respond.
- *Environmental impoverishment* refers to situations in which the trajectory of environmental degradation threatens in the medium to longer term (beyond this and the next generations) to preclude the continuation of current human-use systems or levels of well-being and to narrow significantly the range of possibilities for different future uses.
- *Environmental sustainability* refers to situations in which nature–society relations are so structured that the environment can support the continuation of human-use systems, the level of human well-being, and the preservation of options for future generations over long time-periods.

Critical, endangered, impoverished, and sustainable regions are regions (as defined earlier) characterized by these situations.

Indicators that facilitate the application of these definitions are:

- *environmental degradation*: as indicated by, for example, water availability, water quality, air quality, soil fertility, biomass productivity;
- *wealth*: as indicated by, for example, gross national product, income per capita, savings;
- *well-being*: as indicated by, for example, longevity, mortality rates, infant mortality, nutrition, environmentally induced disease; and
- *economic and technological substitutability*: as indicated by, for ex-

ample, degree of cash-crop dependency, technological monocultures, technological innovation, specialization, and diversification of economic activity.

Henceforth, in discussing criticality or critical regions in a general sense (the three categories of non-sustainability), we will refer to impoverishment, endangerment, and criticality or to impoverished, endangered, or critical regions.

Regional dynamics and trajectories of change

Impoverished, endangered, or critical regions may reflect very different situations. In some cases, as in areas heavily dependent upon a single type of resource extraction (e.g. mining regions), a single environmental threat (resource depletion) may jeopardize sustained human occupancy. In other cases, as in the evolving Aral Sea catastrophe in Central Asia (see chapter 3), one primary human activity (the withdrawal of water for irrigation), augmented to be sure by use of fertilizers and pesticides, threatens multiple regional resources (water, fisheries, soil, vegetation, and so on). In yet other cases – South Florida comes to mind – wetland drainage, water withdrawals, urbanization, and widespread environmental pollution threaten one primary natural resource (freshwater). Finally, the most complex cases, such as that in the Basin of Mexico (chapter 7), involve diverse human activities that pose multiple threats to multiple environmental components and resources. A simple 2 × 2 matrix depicts these different examples (fig. 1.2).

Threatening Human Activities	Threatened Environmental Components or Resources: Single	Threatened Environmental Components or Resources: Multiple
Single	U.S. Southern High Plains	Aral Sea
Multiple	South Florida	North Sea Kenya Dry Hills

Fig. 1.2 **Four patterns of regional environmental threat**

Similarly, general treatment of the regional dynamics of environmental endangerment is needed if regional differences are to be taken seriously and comparative analysis and theory building are to move forward. By "regional dynamics of change," we refer to the relationships that exist among the factors that together shape the changing nature of human–environment relationships and their effects within a particular region. By "trajectories of change," we refer to the trends among these relationships over time. The analysis of regional dynamics requires successive examinations of relationships from different scales and vantage points, and over differing historical periods. Thus, it has much in common with the "regional political ecology" espoused by Blaikie and Brookfield (1987) but without axiomatically elevating political economy to primacy or focusing on the individual resource manager at the outset of the empirical analysis.

Trajectories of change

Our analyses suggest that the conditions of impoverishment, endangerment, and criticality and the regional dynamics that cause them take widely different forms and arise from different circumstances in different regional contexts. No simple evolutionary pattern or set of regional dynamics holds true across all regions. In particular, the relationship between growing environmental degradation and changes

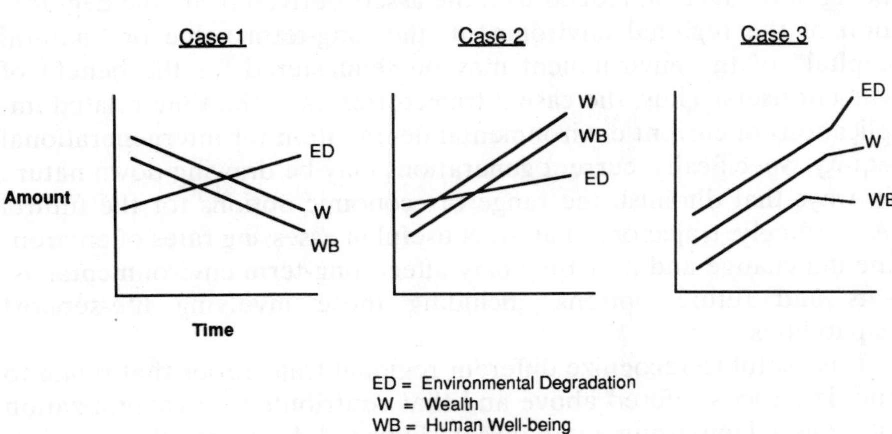

Fig. 1.3 **Contrasting regional trajectories of environmental change**

in the wealth and well-being of inhabitants varies markedly from region to region. Figure 1.3 suggests some cases, although many others are possible. Case 1 represents the situation often assumed in which increasing environmental degradation causes wealth and well-being to decline – in other words, the emergence of criticality. But in case 2, a shift from an agricultural to an industrial economy allows continuing increases in wealth and (most aspects of) well-being in the face of continuing environmental degradation (although, presumably, this cannot continue indefinitely). In case 3, continued resource exploitation supports increasing accumulation of wealth, but continued deterioration of environmental quality results in growing rates of environmentally induced disease and mortality and an eventual reversal in well-being trends.

In fact, case 2, however counter-intuitive, appears to be a very common pattern in the regional studies that follow in this volume. The reasons are several. First, much time typically elapses before natural resources are depleted or environmental sinks are overwhelmed. Even when portions of the environment are degraded, a significant time-lag is often involved in the induction of effects (as in the 20–30-year latency period for many cancers). So environmental degradation can stretch over lengthy time-periods during which the region's population becomes wealthier, healthier, and generally better off. Then, too, when a particular environmental component is degraded or exhausted, individuals and societies shift their activities to other productive systems and environmental assets that offer equal rewards.

In these common situations of increasing human wealth and well-being in the face of, indeed with the assets derived from, the degradation of the regional environment, the long-term value or "natural capital" of the environment may be sequestered for the benefit of current users. Thus, the case 2 trajectories have the time-related implications of current environmental degradation for intergenerational equity. Specifically, current generations may be drawing down nature in ways that diminish the range of economic options for the future. Accordingly, trajectory analysis is useful in assessing rates of environmental change and how they may affect long-term environmental assets and future options, including those involving life-support capabilities.

It is useful to recognize different regional trajectories that relate to the definitions offered above and that contribute to a categorization of regional environmental threat. Figure 1.4 depicts these trajectories as regions move to greater or less sustainability in human–en-

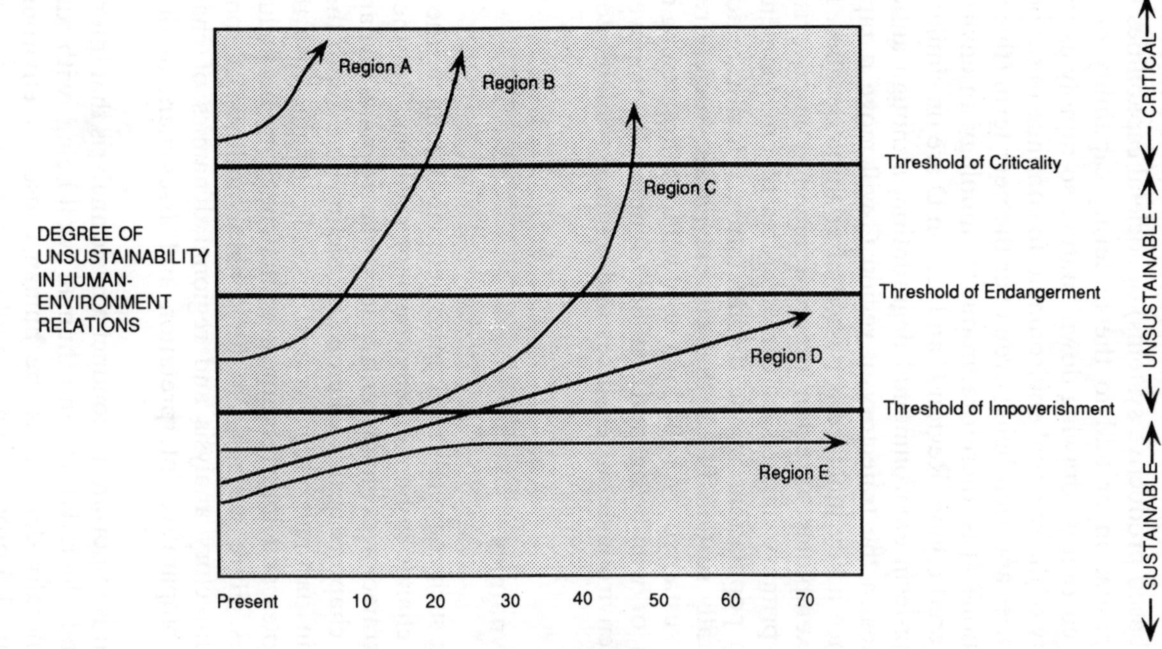

Fig. 1.4 **Hypothetical regional nature–society trajectories**

vironment relations. Region A is an environmentally critical region because overall environmental degradation has reached the level at which current systems of human use and levels of human well-being cannot be sustained, given feasible adaptations (often to other environmentally based productive systems) or societal capabilities to mitigate the degradation or add to the buffering capability of nature. Region B is currently "drawing down" nature so rapidly as to threaten the ability of the regional environment to continue to support current human uses and well-being even over the near term (this and the next generation). It is, therefore, in our terminology an environmentally endangered region. Region C and region D are on similar trajectories of long-term environmental degradation, although anticipated non-linearities in the trajectory of region C will move it rapidly to criticality once a key juncture is passed after three decades. Region D, which exemplifies a region of environmental impoverishment, exports the primary impacts of current rates of environmental degradation to populations in the distant future. Finally, region E is environmentally sustainable in that current nature–society relationships can be sustained over the long term without threatening current human uses or well-being and without significantly impoverishing the base of environmental resources and options available to future generations.

Regional dynamics

Constructing such regional trajectories helps to illuminate the nature and rates of change in human–environment relations. But the analysis of such trajectories must centre upon the regional dynamics of change. The chapters in this volume explore in some depth these dynamics within particular regions and provide insights into the key causal variables and interrelationships that need to be included in such analyses. Here we suggest the general outlines of some key aspects of trajectory analysis and regional dynamics of change as a guide to comparative interpretation and assessment of the case-studies.

To begin, it is important to conduct a basic analysis that interrelates environmental degradation and human well-being with the key variables generally defined as the human causes of environmental change. Figure 1.5 provides an example of such a set of trajectories. The selection of key driving forces of change for analysis will vary from region to region and should reflect their relative importance to environmental change and human well-being within a particular re-

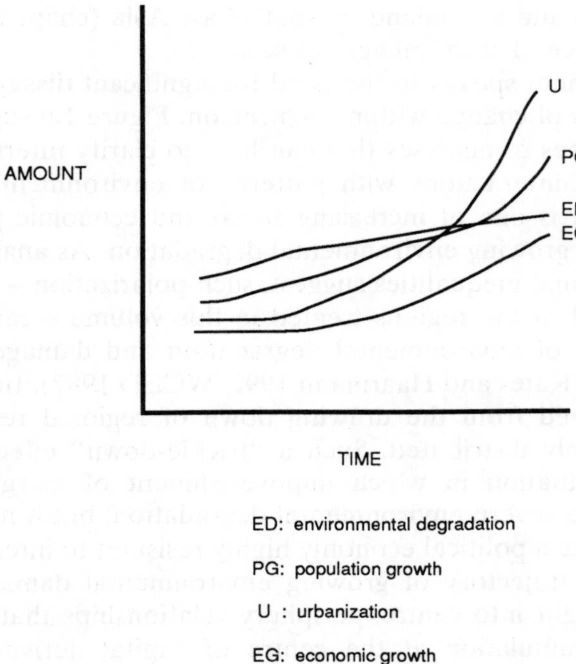

Fig. 1.5 **Trajectories of human driving forces of regional environmental change**

gion. The analysis itself should seek to explain not only the trajectory of each of these variables but the causal relationships among them. At minimum, this should include an interpretation of the relative importance of different human driving forces at different times as well as the relationship between environmental change and various measures of social impacts and human well-being.

As noted above, the degree of spatial linkage that exists between the region and various other regions as well as the global economy is a major attribute of regional context that structures the impact of external driving forces and changing regional vulnerabilities. Much evidence suggests, for example, the growing dependence of many agricultural economies on fluctuations in world market prices and shifting demand in distant markets (Turner 1989; Watts 1983; WCED 1987). In such cases, environmental degradation and emerging overall regional risk can be explained only with detailed attention to the restructuring of such economies over time and the way in which such changes interact with differential patterns of human vulnerability and well-being in the region. The case-studies that follow in this volume, and especially those of the middle mountains of Nepal (chap. 4) and Sundaland in South-East Asia (chap. 10), indicate the importance of such linkages of scale.

This argument speaks to the need for significant disaggregation of the dynamics of change within each region. Figure 1.6 suggests models of the types of analyses that can help to clarify internal regional changes and interactions with patterns of environmental degradation. Case A is one of increasing social and economic polarization attendant on growing environmental degradation. As analyses of global and national inequalities suggest, such polarization – which turns up in several of the regions treated in this volume – can become a major driver of environmental degradation and damage to human populations (Kates and Haarmann 1992; WCED 1987). In case B, the benefits reaped from the drawing down of regional resources are more equitably distributed. Such a "trickle-down" effect may help avoid the situation in which impoverishment of marginal groups helps to drive severe environmental degradation, but it may simultaneously create a political economy highly resistant to interventions to mitigate the trajectory of growing environmental damage. Case C provides insight into centre–periphery relationships that may structure the accumulation at the centre of capital derived from environmental or natural resource exploitation in the periphery. This pattern is apparent in some of the regional studies in this volume.

Finally, the nature of societal responses in the face of emerging trajectories of environmental change requires careful attention as an element of the regional dynamics. One key aspect of this analysis will centre upon the differential responses at various scales or managerial loci. Such assessments can characterize the types, number, and effectiveness of responses undertaken at these various levels as well as the options and constraints under which they operate. This analysis may, as political ecologists would advocate, put the environmental manager closest to the situation at "centre stage" (the "farmer first" approach) or, alternatively, begin with state policies and actions. Risk analysts would more likely begin with the structure of the hazard or the consequences of environmental change and work backwards, or upstream, to the driving forces of change (Kates, Hohenemser, and Kasperson 1985). Various analytical starting points are equally viable as long as the analysis is comprehensive enough to address the complexity of factors shaping the trajectories of change and the range of societal response that occurs.

A key consideration will be the comparison between trajectories of growing environmental damage and changing societal capability to

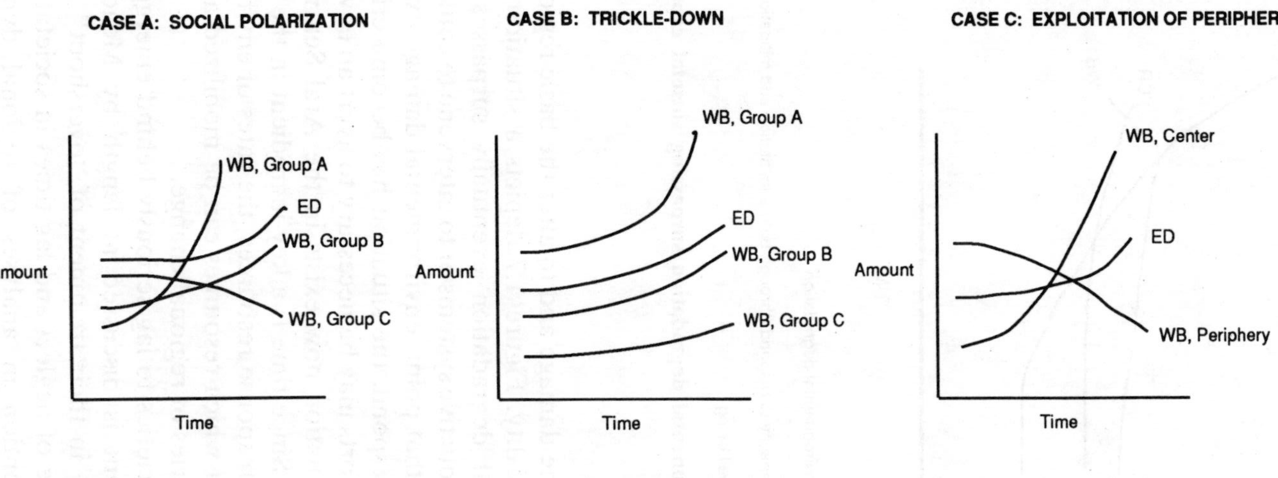

Fig. 1.6 **Three cases of regional social processes causing or interacting with environmental degradation**

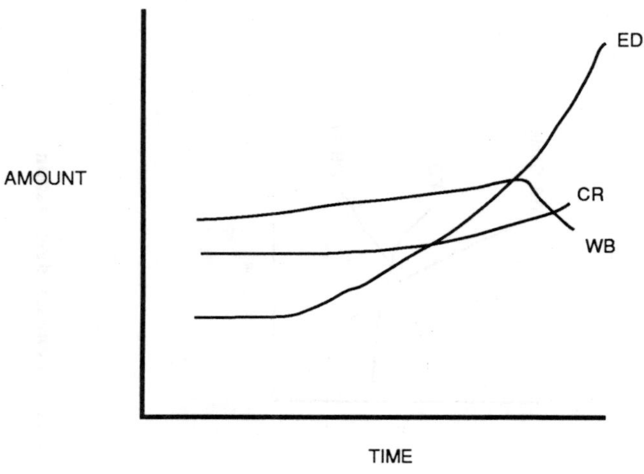

Fig. 1.7 **Regional environmental degradation surpassing societal capacity to respond**

intervene to mitigate the damage and to alter the basic regional trend to environmental criticality. Figure 1.7 depicts a situation in which growing environmental degradation eventually surpasses society's ability to substitute productive systems or to intervene to control or mitigate the damage. At that point, environmental damage exceeds the societal capability to respond, the situation has become critical, and international rescue efforts may be necessary to avert an environmental disaster. Such a situation now exists in the Aral Sea region, as chapter 3 makes clear. Since time is a key ingredient in the mobilization of society's latent response resources, the rates of environmental change and the rates at which resources can be mobilized are important aspects of trajectories of regional change.

The tendency for societies to lag seriously behind emerging environmental endangerment is discussed at length by Meadows and associates (1972, 1992) in their treatment of "overshoot" and "collapse." The importance of neglect and lag times in societal response deserves detailed attention in analyses of regional dynamics of change. The regional trajectory to environmental criticality will not

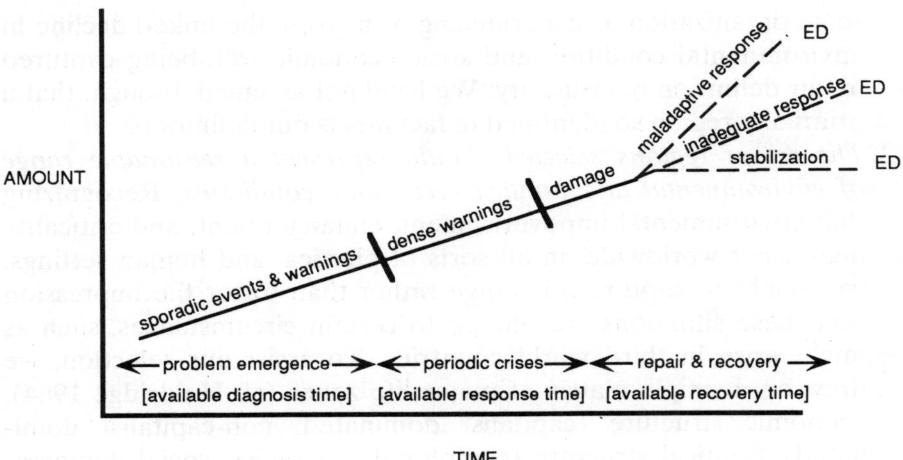

Fig. 1.8 **Emerging criticality and societal response**

occur without warning, of course. As environmental degradation proceeds, various events and indicators of change will prefigure the movement to greater damage and greater future risk (fig. 1.8). Such events and indicators will constitute a stream of "signals" that may alert society and various managers to impending damage. How such warning systems work, how they connect to management systems, and how and why appropriate responses do or do not occur are questions fundamental to understanding trajectories of regional change and diagnosing the outcomes that emerge along the trajectories.

This discussion of regional trajectories and dynamics of change, as noted above, seeks only to set the broad framework of analysis used in the various regional case-studies that follow. Chapter 11 returns to these issues in assessing the generic findings that emerge from the various regional assessments.

Case-study selection and protocol

Any empirical investigation of environmentally threatened regions is subject to the question: Why these particular regions and not others? We made our choices not on an ad hoc basis but according to a set of selection criteria:

1. *The region must have been identified in the literature as one experiencing environmental crisis*. The number of candidates is large. Many areas around the world have been identified by someone or

some organization as experiencing or nearing the linked decline in environmental condition and socio-economic well-being captured in our definition of criticality. We have not assumed, though, that a priori any region so identified in fact meets our definition.

2. *The set of regions selected should represent a reasonable range of environmental and political–economic conditions*. Recognizing that environmental impoverishment, endangerment, and criticality may occur worldwide, in all sorts of physical and human settings, we sought to capture this range rather than foster the impression that these situations are limited to certain circumstances, such as might arise in third world countries. To assist our selection, we drew on a simple matrix of major life zones (cf. Holdridge 1964), economic structure (capitalist dominated, non-capitalist dominated), political structure (complex democracies, social democracies, centrally planned states), affluence (advanced industrial, industrial agrarian), and population density (frontiers to megalopolises). We attempted, with only nine case-studies, to cover a substantial measure of this range (but not all combinations, obviously).
3. *The regions chosen should be ones in which ongoing research could provide a base from which the case-studies could draw*. Although research has been carried out in most candidate regions, we favoured regions in which individuals or teams of researchers were already engaged in the kind of work that would facilitate our study.

These guidelines led us to select the following regional candidates:

- **Amazonia** – a region of frontier agricultural and pasture development in a third world country that has experienced the loss of old-growth tropical rain forest, soil degradation, and other related environmental change, with possible links to global climate change and associated international concern.
- **Eastern Sundaland** – another tropical frontier region in the third world, but marked as well by international logging in an old-growth forest zone with outcomes similar to those noted for Amazonia.
- **Ukambani** – a semi-arid region of eastern Kenya where agro-pastoralists in dry forest and savanna lands have experienced colonization, widespread displacement and resettlement, male out-migration, and a transition to sedentary, permanent agriculture accompanied by deforestation, soil and water degradation, recurring droughts, and continuing state intervention.
- **Nepal middle mountains** – a high-altitude, high-energy region in the third world long containing substantial populations of smallholders who are currently shifting to commercial production under condi-

tions of market development and rapid population growth, leading to major deforestation and soil loss.

- **Ordos Plateau of China** – an arid region of Inner Mongolia, targeted for commercial development in a centrally planned economy and invaded by large numbers of smallholder farmers, leading to massive soil erosion and sandification.
- **Aral Sea basin** – another arid region of a former centrally planned economy of the Central Asian republics in which one of the largest state-ordained irrigation schemes in the world, along with rapid population growth, has severely damaged the sea and the land around it, with evident impacts on human well-being.
- **Llano Estacado** – a semi-arid region of the Southern High Plains of the United States where large-scale irrigated agriculture by wealthy farmers has drawn down the aquifer, increased soil erosion, and moved the region inexorably to higher future risk.
- **Basin of Mexico** – one of the largest concentrations of people and of industrialization on earth, located within a geologically closed basin, with rapidly increasing contamination of water and air, stress on water supply, and dependence on surrounding regions.
- **North Sea** – in the mid–high latitudes, a common-pool resource, surrounded by one of the longest-industrialized and wealthiest areas in the world, which has become a sink for a mass-producing and consuming society.

Each study was undertaken by an interdisciplinary team of researchers following a common protocol developed through the cooperation of the Clark University study group and the case team leaders. The protocol provides guidelines for defining the region, the time-scale of analysis, the major questions and topics to be addressed, the means of organizing each study, and the common forms of documentation. Each study undertook an analysis of regional dynamics of change, involving assessment of human driving forces, trends and patterns of environmental change, human vulnerabilities, impacts on human well-being, and societal responses. Particular attention was given to the trajectories over time of each of these components of the regional dynamics of change. Within each of these categories of analysis, specific data needs were established with the aim of providing as much comparability as possible among the various case-studies. This aim proved difficult, in part because so many of these data required new or reformulated information that could not be generated within the constraints of the study and available funds. Even so, the various studies share a common focus and range of information that provide insights into emerging environmental threats. We return to comparisons and major findings in chapter 11.

References

Berry, Leonard, and Richard Ford. 1977. *Recommendations for a system to monitor critical indicators in areas prone to desertification*. Worcester, MA: Clark University.

Blaikie, Piers M. 1985. *The political economy of soil erosion in developing countries*. London: Longman.

Blaikie, Piers M., and Harold C. Brookfield. 1987. *Land degradation and society*. London: Methuen.

BLM (Bureau of Land Management), et al. 1979. *Interagency agreement for classifications and inventories of natural resources: Major natural resources inventories of the participants*. Washington DC: BLM.

Campbell, Faith T., and Johanna H. Wald. 1989. *Areas of critical environmental concern: Promise vs. reality*. Washington DC: Natural Resources Defense Council.

Cannon, Terry. 1994. Vulnerability analysis and the explanation of "natural" disasters. In *Disasters, development, and environment*, ed. Ann Varley, 13–30. Chichester, Sussex: Wiley.

CEQ (US Council on Environmental Quality). 1980. *The global 2000 report to the President*. Washington DC: Council on Environmental Quality.

Chambers, Robert. 1989. Editorial introduction: Vulnerability, coping and policy. *IDS Bulletin* 21: 1–7.

Conservation Foundation. 1984. *The state of the environment: An assessment at mid-decade*. Washington DC: The Conservation Foundation.

Daly, Herman E. 1990. *Carrying capacity as a tool of development policy: The Ecuadorian Amazon and the Paraguayan Chaco*. Amsterdam: Elsevier.

Dow, Kirstin. 1992. Exploring the differences in our common future(s): The meaning of vulnerability to global environmental change. *Geoforum* 23, no. 3: 417–436.

Downing, Thomas E. 1991. Vulnerability to hunger in Africa: A climate change perspective. *Global Environmental Change* 1, no. 5 (December): 365–380.

Dregne, Harold E. 1983. *Desertification of arid lands*. New York: Harwood Academic Publishers.

Ehrlich, Paul R., and John P. Holdren, eds. 1988. *The Cassandra conference: Resources for the human predicament*. College Station, TX: Texas A & M University Press.

Endangered Species Act. 1973. PL 93-205 (28 December 1973). 16 U.S.C. 1531 *et seq*.

FAO (Food and Agriculture Organization of the United Nations). 1984. *Land, food and people*. Rome: FAO.

FLPMA 1976. The Federal Land Policy and Management Act of 1976, Sections 103(a) and 202(c)(3); 43 U.S.C., 1702(a); 1712(c)(3).

Fritz, Charles E. 1961. Disaster. In *Contemporary social problems: An introduction to the sociology of deviant behavior and social disorganization*, ed. Robert K. Merton and Robert A. Nisbet, 651–694. New York: Harcourt, Brace & World.

Funtowicz, S. O., and J. R. Ravetz. Forthcoming. Global environmental issues and the emergence of second order science. In *Global environmental risk*, ed. Jeanne X. Kasperson and Roger E. Kasperson. Tokyo: United Nations University.

Glantz, Michael H. 1988. *Societal responses to regional climate change. Forecasting by analogy*. Boulder, CO: Westview Press.

Gleick, Peter H. 1990. Vulnerability of water systems. In *Climate change and water resources*, ed. Paul E. Waggoner, 223–240. New York: Wiley.

Green, Colin H. 1990. *Hazard and vulnerability analysis*. Enfield, England: Flood Hazard Research Centre, Middlesex Polytechnic.

Hagerstrand, Torsten, and Ulrik Lohm. 1990. Sweden. In *The earth as transformed by human action: Global and regional changes in the biosphere over the past 300 years*, ed. B. L. Turner II, William C. Clark, Robert W. Kates, John F. Richards, Jessica T. Mathews, and William B. Meyer, 605–622. Cambridge: Cambridge University Press with Clark University.

Haq, Mahbub ul, and Shahid Javed Burki. 1980. *Meeting basic needs: An overview*. Washington DC: World Bank.

Holdridge, L. R. 1964. *Life zone ecology*. San José, Costa Rica: Tropical Science Center.

Holling, C. S. 1986. The resilience of terrestrial ecosystems: Local surprise and global change. In *Sustainable development of the biosphere*, ed. William C. Clark and Ralph Munn, 292–316. Cambridge: Cambridge University Press.

Kates, Robert W., and Viola Haarmann. 1991. *Poor people and threatened environments: Global overviews, country comparisons, and local studies*. Research Report RR-91-2. Providence, RI: Alan Shawn Feinstein World Hunger Program, Brown University.

———. 1992. Where the poor live: Are the assumptions correct? *Environment* 34, no. 4 (May): 4–11, 25–28.

Kates, Robert W., Christoph Hohenemser, and Jeanne X. Kasperson, eds. 1985. *Perilous progress: Managing the hazards of technology*. Boulder, CO: Westview Press.

Kochurov, Boris. 1991. Methodological approaches to the creation of a map of critical environmental situations. In *Defining and mapping critical environmental zones for policy formulation and public awareness*, ed. Thomas C. Meredith, Carol Marley, and Wynet Smith, 63–73. Montreal: Geography Department, McGill University.

Kroll-Smith, J. Stephen, and Stephen R. Couch. 1990. *The real disaster is above ground: A mine fire and social conflict*. Lexington: University Press of Kentucky.

Lindblom, Charles E., and David K. Cohen. 1979. *Usable knowledge: Social science and social problem solving*. New Haven, CT: Yale University Press.

Liverman, Diana M. 1990. Vulnerability to global environmental change. In *Understanding global environmental change: The contributions of risk analysis and management*, ed. Roger E. Kasperson, Kirstin Dow, Dominic Golding, and Jeanne X. Kasperson, 27–44. Worcester, MA: Clark University, Center for Technology, Environment, and Development (CENTED).

Mather, John R., and Galina V. Sdasyuk. 1991. *Global change: Geographic approaches*. Tucson: University of Arizona Press.

Meadows, Donella H., et al. 1972. *The limits to growth: A report for the Club of Rome's project on the predicament of mankind*. New York: Universe Books.

Meadows, Donella H., Dennis L. Meadows, and Jørgen Randers. 1992. *Beyond the limits: Confronting global collapse, envisioning a sustainable future*. Mills, VT: Chelsea Green.

Meredith, Thomas C., Carol Marley, and Wynet Smith, eds. 1991. *Defining and mapping critical environmental zones for policy formulation and public awareness*.

Montreal: Geography Department, McGill University.

Meyer, William B., Derek Gregory, B. L. Turner II, and Patricia McDowell. 1992. The local–global continuum: Spatial scales in geographic research. In *Geography's inner worlds: Pervasive themes in contemporary American geography*, ed. Ronald F. Abler, Melvin G. Marcus, and Judy M. Olson, 255–279. New Brunswick, NJ: Rutgers University Press.

NGS (National Geographic Society). 1989. *Endangered earth* (map). Washington DC: NGS.

Odum, Eugene P. 1989. *Ecology and our endangered life-support systems*. Sunderland, MA: Sinauer Associates.

O'Riordan, Timothy. 1976. *Environmentalism*. London: Pion.

Pfister, Christian, and Paul Messerli. 1990. Switzerland. In *The earth as transformed by human action: Global and regional changes in the biosphere over the past 300 years*, ed. B. L. Turner II, William C. Clark, Robert W. Kates, John F. Richards, Jessica T. Mathews, and William B. Meyer, 641–652. Cambridge: Cambridge University Press with Clark University.

Population Crisis Committee. 1987. *International human suffering index* [wall chart], ed. Sharon L. Camp. Washington DC: The Committee.

———. 1992. *International human suffering index* [wall chart], ed. Sharon L. Camp. Washington DC: The Committee.

Quarantelli, Enrico L. 1985. What is a disaster? The need for clarification in definition and conceptualization in research. In *Disasters and mental health: Selected contemporary perspectives*, ed. Barbara Souder, 41–73. Washington DC: US Government Printing Office.

———. 1987. What should we study? Questions and suggestions for researchers about the concept of disasters. *International Journal of Mass Emergencies and Disasters* 5: 7–32.

Ravetz, Jerome. 1986. Usable knowledge, usable ignorance: Incomplete science with policy implications. In *Sustainable development of the biosphere*, ed. William C. Clark and Ralph W. Munn, 415–432. Cambridge: Cambridge University Press.

Rees, J. 1985. *Natural resources: Allocation, economics, and policy*. London: Methuen.

Reining, Priscilla. 1978. *Handbook on desertification indicators: Based on the Science Associations' Nairobi Seminar on Desertification*. Washington DC: American Association for the Advancement of Science.

Repetto, Robert J., ed. 1985. *The global possible: Resources, development, and the new century*. New Haven, CT: Yale University Press.

Riebsame, William E. 1990. The United States Great Plains. In *The earth as transformed by human action: Global and regional changes in the biosphere over the past 300 years*, ed. B. L. Turner II, William C. Clark, Robert W. Kates, John F. Richards, Jessica T. Mathews, and William B. Meyer, 561–575. Cambridge: Cambridge University Press with Clark University.

SCEP (Study of Critical Environmental Problems). 1970. *Man's impact on the global environment: Assessment and recommendations for action*. Cambridge, MA: MIT Press.

Simon, Julian L., and Herman Kahn. 1984. *The resourceful earth: A response to Global 2000*. Cambridge, MA: MIT Press.

Stewart, Frances. 1985. *Basic needs in developing countries*. Baltimore, MD: Johns Hopkins University Press.

Streeten, Paul P. 1980. Planning for basic human needs in developing countries.

Peter B. Andrews Memorial Lecture.

Susman, Paul, Philip O'Keefe, and Ben Wisner. 1983. Global disasters: A radical interpretation. In *Interpretations of calamity*, ed. Kenneth Hewitt, 264–283. Boston: Allen & Unwin.

Travis, C. C., and J. M. Morris. 1992. The emergence of ecological risk assessment. *Risk Analysis* 12, no. 2 (June): 167–168.

Turner, B. L., II. 1989. The specialist-synthesis approach: The case of cultural ecology. *Annals of the Association of American Geographers* 79: 88–100.

Turner, B. L., II, and Patricia Benjamin. 1994. Fragile lands and their management. In *Agriculture, environment, and health: Toward sustainable development into the 21st century*, ed. Vernon W. Ruttan, 101–145. Minneapolis: University of Minnesota Press, forthcoming.

Turner, B. L., II, William C. Clark, Robert W. Kates, John F. Richards, Jessica T. Mathews, and William B. Meyer, eds. 1990a. *The earth as transformed by human action*. Cambridge: Cambridge University Press with Clark University.

Turner, B. L., II, Roger E. Kasperson, William B. Meyer, Kirstin M. Dow, Dominic Golding, Jeanne X. Kasperson, Robert C. Mitchell, and Samuel J. Ratick. 1990b. Two types of global environmental change: Definitional and spatial-scale issues in their human dimensions. *Global environmental change: Human dimensions and policy* 1, no. 1 (December): 14–22.

Turner, M. G. 1987. *Landscape heterogeneity and disturbance*. New York: Springer.

UNDP (United Nations Development Programme). 1992. *Human development report 1992*. New York: Oxford University Press for UNDP.

UNSO (United Nations Sudano-Sahelian Office). 1992. *Assessment of desertification and drought in the Sudano-Sahelian region, 1985–1991*. New York: UNSO.

US Water Resources Council. 1978. *The nation's water resources, 1975–2000: The second national water assessment*. 4 vols. Washington DC: US Government Printing Office.

Watts, Michael. 1983. *Silent violence: Food, famine, and peasantry in northern Nigeria*. Berkeley: University of California Press.

WCED (World Commission on Environment and Development). 1987. *Our common future*. New York: Oxford University Press.

Weiss, Edith Brown. 1989. *In fairness to future generations: International law, common patrimony, and integrational equity*. Tokyo: United Nations University and Transnational Publishers.

———. 1990. In fairness to future generations. *Environment* 32, no. 3 (April): 6–11, 30–31.

Wenger, Dennis. 1978. Community response to disaster: Functional and structural alterations. In *Disasters: Theory and research*, ed. Enrico L. Quarantelli, 17–47. Beverly Hills, CA: Sage.

Whitmore, Thomas M., B. L. Turner II, Douglas L. Johnson, Robert W. Kates, and Thomas R. Gottschang. 1990. Long-term population change. In *The earth as transformed by human action: Global and regional changes in the biosphere over the past 300 years*, ed. B. L. Turner II, William C. Clark, Robert W. Kates, John F. Richards, Jessica T. Mathews, and William B. Meyer, 25–39. Cambridge: Cambridge University Press with Clark University.

World Bank. 1980. *Poverty and basic needs*. Washington DC: World Bank.

Yodzis, P. 1980. The connectance of real ecosystems. *Nature* 284: 544–545.

2

Amazonia

Nigel J. H. Smith, Paulo de T. Alvim,
Emanuel Adilson S. Serrão, and Italo C. Falesi

The Amazon Basin contains the largest remaining stretch of tropical forest in the world. Development pressures are mounting to integrate better the still largely untapped region with national economies and global markets. Pioneer highways are providing ready access to formerly isolated portions of Amazonia, and reservoirs are transforming the landscapes of some large and small river valleys (fig. 2.1). A drive for greater energy self-sufficiency has prompted the construction of hydroelectric dams, which often lead to extensive flooding of forests and to changes in the fish fauna. The cutting and burning of Amazonia's biologically rich forests have triggered widespread concern about global and regional climatic change, loss of biodiversity, and disruption of peasant and indigenous communities. Indeed, few regions of the world have received more attention as a "critical" or "endangered zone" than has Amazonia (Smith et al. 1991).

The environmental and social consequences of the current changes in Amazonia cannot be adequately assessed without attention to the longer-term occupation of the region and the history of interaction between people and the various natural and human-influenced habitats in the region. Hence, we begin with a historical backdrop, emphasizing the diversity of ecosystems in the region and the significance of different management strategies for harnessing natural resources.

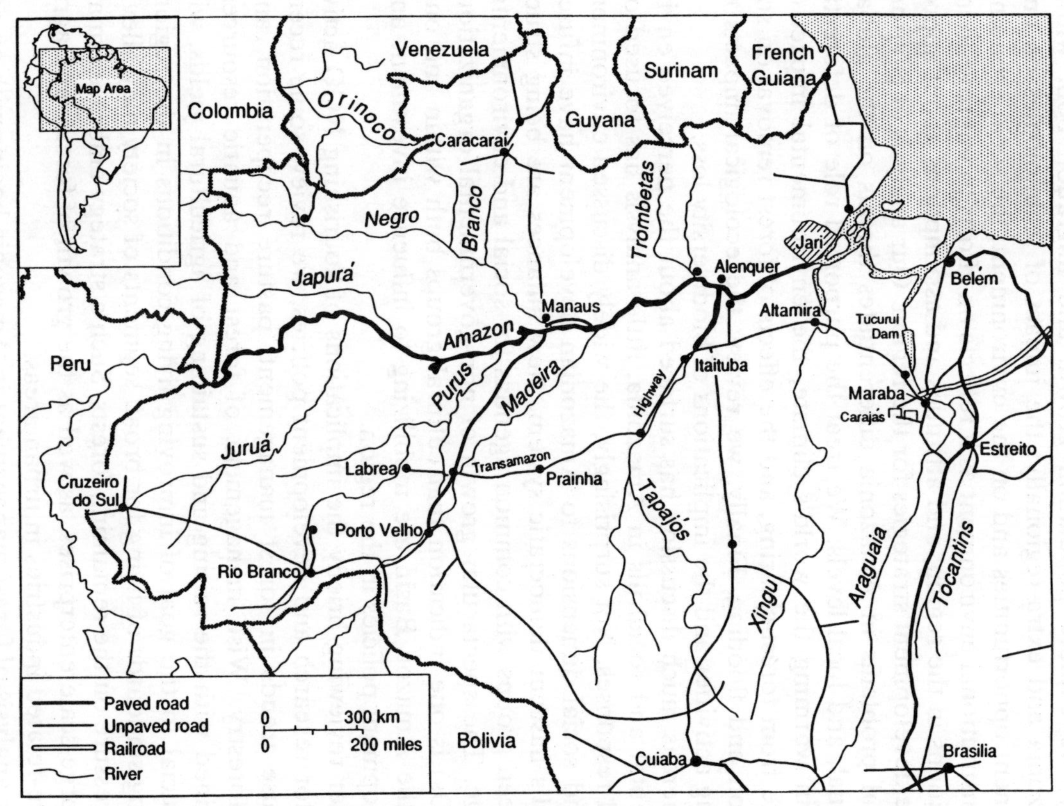

Fig. 2.1 **Major highways and some development projects in Amazonia**

Our treatment of human driving forces, consistent with the approach of this volume, focuses on changes in human populations, technologies, the policy framework and associated values for development, and issues surrounding the distribution of wealth. Specifically, we explore population growth and migration both within Amazonia and extra-regionally; the impact of technologies on employment opportunities and on the environment; the socio-economic and institutional environment as it reflects on efforts to improve living conditions in the region; and attitudes and assumptions about appropriate development strategies for the region. Our analysis of environmental problems in Amazonia differentiates threats on the global, regional, and local levels. We treat the purported role of deforestation in warming the world's climate, the environmental impact of smoke from forest-clearing, and the effects of forest removal on soil erosion and flooding. Finally, we review the ecological impacts of mining activities and the implications of biodiversity loss.

Whereas much discussion has surfaced about the perceived environmental and social ills in Amazonia, little analysis has focused on social responses. Not surprisingly, the widely discussed environmental and social dimensions to Amazonian development have infused Brazil's nascent democratic system. New alliances are being struck between groups with common agendas for social and environmental change. The spectacular growth of non-governmental organizations (NGOs) is one indication that cultural groups both within and outside the Amazon Basin are mobilizing to influence investment and development policies in the region.

After reviewing briefly the implications of flourishing NGO activities for research and development policies, we review some recent land-use trends in forest management, pasture recuperation, and agro-forestry. Wise management of forest and aquatic resources, combined with the raising and sustaining of agricultural yields, will be crucial to the goal of improving living conditions in the region. Raising standards of living for broad segments of society may alleviate pressure on the remaining forests. Such a strategy embraces small and large-scale enterprises, as well as the growth of forest- and agriculture-related industries in urban areas.

Our analysis of forest management in Amazonia begins with an assessment of the role of extractive reserves in the regional economy and the potential of such reserves for safeguarding forest environments. We also examine the management of Amazonian forests for timber production. The potential of agro-forestry and perennial cropping systems to generate food and industrial products as well as to protect the soil is also analysed. Pasture is often a major feature of Amazonian landscapes after clearing, but many ranches suffer from low productivity. Beef and dairy production in Amazonia could double if existing pastures were better managed. Thus, we review efforts to upgrade pastures and their policy implications.

Study sites

Not only is Amazonia a vast (5 million km^2) region, but, contrary to popular view, it is environmentally heterogeneous as well. It is not particularly useful, therefore, to address environmental change in Amazonia in terms of averages. Here we have broached this problem by focusing on several study sites or areas selected to represent a range of human activities in different forest and flood-plain ecosystems. A variety of land uses, ranging from mining to agro-forestry, extractive reserves, ranching, and small-scale farms in interfluvial areas, is examined. Another important criterion used in the selection of study areas is the duration of human occupation, which is particularly important in attempting to assess sustainability of land uses under different management systems. Some of the study sites have a relatively long history of settlement, whereas others have been penetrated by pioneer settlers only within the last 20 years.

We selected for closer scrutiny several main areas in the Brazilian Amazon, each of which contains a range of human activities, soil types, and vegetation. Although we concentrated our fieldwork in these study areas, we also incorporated relevant research findings from other sites. Figure 2.1 should be consulted for the locations of the main study areas described below.

Mining is emerging as a major development thrust in Amazonia, and a suite of associated development activities usually follows in the wake of mineral projects. Mining operations open up opportunities for spontaneous and planned settlement and plantations. Two multifaceted mining operations – the Carajás and Trombetas projects – are described and analysed.

The Carajás project in southern Pará, managed by the Brazilian firm Companhia Vale do Rio Doce (CVRD), mines the world's largest iron-ore deposit as well as several other strategically important minerals. An 890 km railroad was recently built between the Carajás range south-west of Marabá and the port of Itaqui in coastal Maranhão to serve smelters in the rich iron-ore field. A series of corollary development schemes, ranging from pioneer farms to agro-forestry projects and harvesting the forest to provide charcoal for pig-iron smelters, are under way. This multi-purpose development programme slices across a broad spectrum of Amazonian environments, some with long histories of human occupation.

Another mega-scale mining project that has begun operations within the last two decades is located along the clear-water Trombetas River, a northern affluent of the Amazon. The Trombetas project, operated by Mineração Rio do Norte, contains one of the world's largest deposits of bauxite and was a major factor in the Brazilian government's decision to build the Tucurui dam on the Tocantins River to supply hydroelectric power for smelting aluminium ore. The Trombetas project is removing large quantities of soil and vegetation.

The 1.6 million ha Jari project, formerly owned by Daniel Ludwig, is now managed by a consortium of Brazilian companies. Located in northern Pará and western Amapá, the Jari project includes plantations of eucalyptus, Caribbean pine, and Gmelina (*Gmelina arborea*) for pulp production, kaolin mining, and water buffalo ranching along the Amazon flood plain.

The environmental impacts and sustainability of some small-scale farmers and ranchers are reviewed in the Bragantina area, Tomé-Açu, Paragominas, and the Transamazon Highway. The Bragantina zone east of Belém encompasses some of the poorest soils in Amazonia and is also one of the most densely settled areas of the basin. The Bragantina zone comprises less than 1 per cent of the area of the Brazilian Amazon but contains close to one-third of the region's population. Sizeable shell mounds along Bragantina's brackish coast bear witness to the long history of human occupation in the area. A review of the history of farming efforts in this highly modified, formerly forested zone and an analysis of agricultural changes will highlight adaptive responses to ecological change and economic opportunities.

The Tomé-Açu area south of the Bragantina zone was settled by Japanese immigrants in the 1930s. After first trying their hand at cultivating upland rice, the newcomers soon turned to perennial crops that help conserve soil moisture, structure, and fertility. Black pepper proved highly profitable for several decades until a fungal disease provoked a search for alternative crops. How Japanese–Brazilian farmers have coped with this ecological surprise underscores the importance of resilience for sustainable agriculture.

The Altamira region of the Transamazon Highway is a good area to study pioneer farms two decades after they have been carved out of the forest. The dark-red alfisols of the Altamira region of the Transamazon Highway are some of the best soils of upland Amazonia and provide an opportunity to contrast farming systems with those found in the Bragantina zone. Perennial crops, particularly cacao (*Theobroma cacao*), robusta coffee (*Coffea canephora*), and citrus, are providing valuable alternatives to shifting cultivation for annual cash crops. The Transamazon landscape is evolving to agroforestry and improved pastures, with less environmental destruction than occurred in the earlier years.

Historical perspectives on environmental and social change

Boom-and-bust cycles characterize much of the history of Amazonian development. Poor planning, changes in world production patterns of certain commodities, ecological "surprises," and frequent shifts in policy at the national and regional level have all contributed to the demise of many extractive enterprises and settlement schemes. A brief historical review of major economic activities in Amazonia serves as a backdrop to current debates about appropriate models for development in the region.

From the seventeenth century to the early 1900s, extraction of forest products dominated economic activities in Amazonia. Dyes, woody and herbal essences, and certain highly prized timbers were obtained from the forests. Plantations of cacao and sugar cane were established, mainly along the Amazon flood plain and around Belém. The harvesting of turtle eggs and manatees for oil and meat were the principal activities in the region until the close of the eighteenth century (Domning 1982; Serrão and Homma 1993; Smith 1974). Creole cattle were introduced to spontaneous or fire-induced grasslands in Roraima and Marajó Island, but beef production was limited and destined almost exclusively for local consumption.

A rubber boom lasted from 1850 to 1912, until plantations of rubber trees (*Hevea brasiliensis*), based on seed taken out of the Brazilian Amazon by Henry Wickham in 1876, came into production. At the height of the rubber boom in Brazil, tens of thousands of northeasterners penetrated the myriad waterways of Amazonia to tap the wild trees. Rubber was once Brazil's third most important export commodity (Dean 1987; Weinstein 1983). Apart from the construction of some elaborate mansions, opera houses, and improved docking facilities in Belém and Manaus, the rubber boom did not sow the seeds of any long-lasting economic benefit. Profits were largely invested elsewhere.

Henry Ford's efforts to establish rubber plantations on uplands bordering the lower Tapajós in 1927 ultimately failed, mainly owing to attacks of South American leaf blight. The fungal pathogen, *Microcyclus ulei*, wreaked havoc in the large monocultural stands of rubber; attempts at double grafting to secure a resistant crown wedded to a highly productive bole proved too expensive in the face of competition from plantations in South-East Asia that still remain free of the disease. In 1945, Henry Ford pulled out of the rubber plantation business in the Amazon.

One of the most fertile environments for agriculture in Amazonia, the flood plain of the silt-laden Amazon, received a boost when Japanese immigrants introduced jute (*Corchorus* spp.) along the upper and middle Amazon in 1932. Although jute remains an important cash crop along the Amazon, competition from growers in Bangladesh and from synthetics is constraining further development of this fibrous crop in Amazonia. Recently, the Brazilian coffee industry, the largest customer for jute sacks in the country, has lobbied the government to allow the importation of less expensive jute sacks from Asia. The collapse of jute prices provoked a scramble for alternative crops on the Amazon flood plain.

Japanese immigrants also brought another important cash crop to Amazonia, black pepper (*Piper nigrum*), in 1933. Pepper was established in plantations at Tomé-Açu and, by the early 1950s, had become the leading agricultural export of Pará. Pepper is still a viable perennial crop in uplands of Amazonia today, but it is now planted as one of a sequence of crops that is replaced as *Fusarium* wilt takes its toll.

Rubber extraction surged in Amazonia briefly during the Second World War as a result of the Washington Agreement, signed in 1942. This accord was designed to develop alternative sources of rubber in response to the Japanese cut-off of supplies from South-East Asia. In 1954 a decree promulgated by the Brazilian government required tyre companies to set up some rubber plantations and, in 1966, the Brazilian government's Superintendency for the Development of Rubber Culture (SUDHEVEA) launched a programme, PROBOR (Programa da Boracha), to plant more rubber trees and to tap both wild and planted trees more rationally (Dean 1987, 131). In spite of such efforts, Brazil still imports most of its natural rubber needs.

The 1960s witnessed two major land-use changes in Amazonia: the rapid opening of forest for pasture development, and the ambitious silvicultural operation at Jari for pulp production. Fuelled by fiscal incentives that allowed corporations to invest half of their tax liabilities in approved development projects in Amazonia, massive deforestation for cattle pasture began in 1966. Initially concentrated along the recently opened Belém–Brasília highway, particularly in Paragominas, large tracts of forest began falling for planted pasture in other parts of the Brazilian Amazon, such as southern Pará and northern Mato Grosso. Many of these ranches were established for purely speculative purposes, and, lacking proper upkeep, extensive areas of pasture are now degraded. Efforts to recuperate such pastures, and the economic and policy constraints to renovation of cattle-raising areas, are discussed later.

The huge Jari operation is often portrayed as a failure. Many mistakes were made in setting up plantations of Gmelina (*Gmelina arborea*), Caribbean pine, and eucalyptus, but many of these initial ecological and managerial problems have now been addressed. Only about one-tenth of the property (totalling 1.6 million ha) is slated for plantations, and the pulp operation is finally making a profit. Conservation of the environment is a high priority at Jari. Ludwig's US$1 billion experiment seems to be paying off, mainly because of sophisticated silvicultural know-how generated by Brazilian firms and scientists.

The 1970s was the decade for launching colonization schemes, sponsored by federal governments and, in the case of Brazil, private companies as well (Fearnside 1986; Kleinpenning 1975; Moran 1981; Smith 1982). Brazil's national integration plan called for thousands of kilometres of pioneer roads to criss-cross the region, creating access to settlers and natural resources. The colonization schemes were designed originally for small-scale settlers, but many of the original colonists have sold out and moved to other frontiers, often leading to conflicts with other claimants to the land, including Indians (Barbira-Scazzocchio 1980; Hemming 1985a,b; Schmink and Wood 1984). Some colonists remaining along pioneer highways are thriving after establishing good-quality pasture and a mix of perennial crops for cash income. A trend towards better management of already cleared areas, rather than opening new fields, is well pronounced along the 20-year-old Transamazon Highway.

Another major development of the 1970s and 1980s was the push to develop more of the mineral resources of Amazonia. The export value of gold, manganese, aluminium, and pig-iron now far exceeds the value of agricultural exports in Amazonia. Mineral exploitation and associated development projects, particularly the Grande Carajás programme, are likely to continue to play a leading role in regional development for the foreseeable future.

In the 1980s and early 1990s, timber extraction accelerated markedly, particularly in Pará. Initially, only about 10 species were logged in any quantity, but now the sawmills are handling close to 100 species in the case of Paragominas. Much of the production is for domestic construction, although high-quality timbers, such as ipê (*Tabebuia* spp.), angelim pedra (*Diniza excelsa*), maçaranduba (*Manilkara* spp.), cumaru (*Dipteryx* spp.), and mahogany (*Swietenia macrophylla*), are also exported, mainly through Belém and Manaus.

This recent history of resource use in Amazonia has taken place in the context of a "frontier," one in which there was extremely sparse occupation at least since the sixteenth century. The evidence is mounting, however, that previous to the European penetration of Amazonia large concentrations of Amerindians were present in different areas and different times (Smith 1995). The activities of people surely had an effect on the environments of the Amazon Basin, if only as a result of the considerable clearing of the forest that took place. The point here is that the Amazon experienced a lull of close to four centuries after indigenous populations crashed shortly after 1500 and that, once again, wider-scale environmental changes are under way.

Resource-use systems in Amazonia have been and remain highly dynamic. As population density increases in the region, the intensity of land management is likely to increase (fig. 2.2). Environmental issues vary along the spectrum of land-management intensity; for example, efforts to raise and sustain agricultural productivity pose a new set of environmental issues, such as the impact of pesticides on human health and the effects of continual use of a field on soil structure. After exploring some of the environmental concerns of Amazonian development, we analyse attempts to improve forest management, agro-forestry, and perennial crop management, and to recuperate pastures.

Human driving forces

A major preoccupation with environmental change in Amazonia hinges on deforestation and the loss of plant and animal resources,

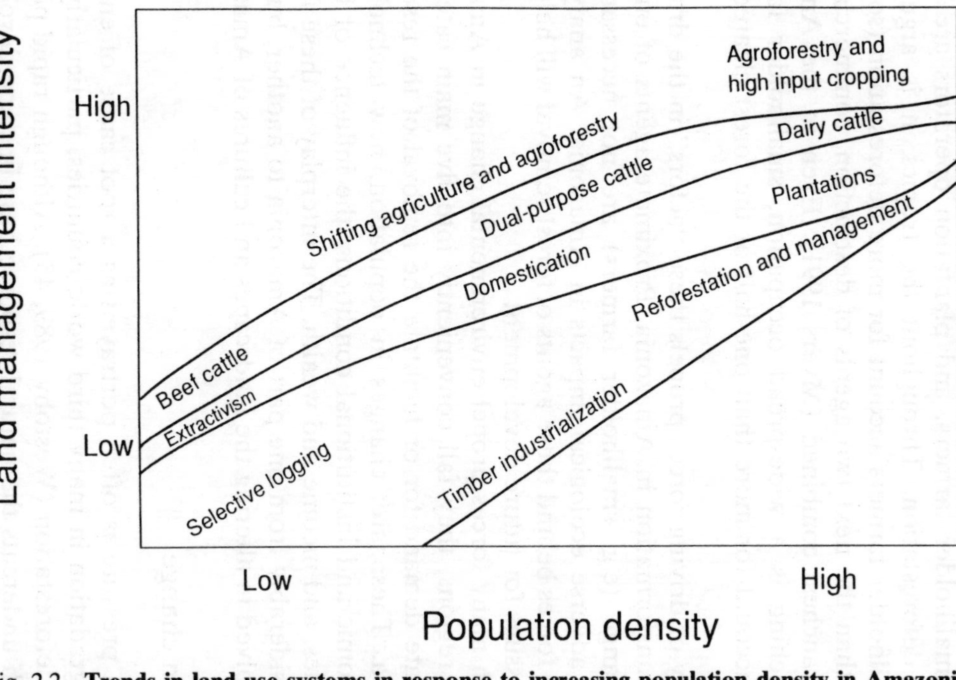

Fig. 2.2 **Trends in land-use systems in response to increasing population density in Amazonia (Source: adapted from Serrão and Homma, 1993)**

including fisheries. Much attention currently focuses on how to arrest this destruction. A confluence of forces is implicated in the destruction of habitat in the region, and the preponderance of forces responsible for the retreat of forest and disruption of other environments varies widely according to such factors as access to markets, road infrastructure, and fiscal incentives. Loggers, cattle ranchers, dam builders, smallholder farmers, and plantation operators are all involved in deforestation. Throughout the tropics, it is argued by some, smallholder farmers account for more deforestation (some 60 per cent) than the next two agents of destruction, commercial loggers and ranches, combined (Myers 1991). Even in the Amazon, where ranching is a widespread occupation, smallholder farmers probably account for more than one-half of the forest cleared each year.

A variety of driving forces propels these "actors" in the drama of regional transformation in Amazonia. Proximate agents of environmental change (e.g. smallholder farmers) are not necessarily to blame for adverse ecological impacts in Amazonia. An analysis of the driving forces behind these agents of forest removal will help clarify policy issues for future development.

Although many forces propel environmental change in Amazonia and other regions, they fall conveniently into five main categories that generate demand for or facilitate the removal of the resources in the area. These are: changes in population, new technologies, socio-economic and institutional conditions, the influence of beliefs and attitudes, and income and wealth. The interplay of these factors varies considerably from one part of Amazonia to another, but they are all involved in altering the landscapes and cultures of Amazonia.

Population change

Population pressure is often portrayed as a root cause of environmental degradation in many third world countries, particularly with regard to deforestation (Westoby 1989, 45). Although rapid population growth undercuts the natural resource base in some developing regions, it is hard to conceive of Amazonia having a population problem *per se*. The pre-contact population of Amazonia was denser in many rural parts of the basin than it is today (Smith 1980; Smith 1995), but the environmental impacts of the prehistoric population are poorly understood. Forests recovered, albeit in altered form. Even in regions perceived as suffering from overpopulation, though, overtaxing of the land may occur owing to inappropriate technologies or highly skewed patterns of land ownership, among other socio-economic factors.

Except in a few restricted areas, such as south-western and south-eastern Amazonia, population growth is a relatively minor force behind environmental change in the region. This growth is not internal to Amazonia, but exogenous, in so far as farmers, itinerant miners, and ranchers migrate to the region (Schmink 1988). There, new waves of settlers and speculators are mainly responsible for the retreat of forest and other ecological changes in Amazonia. Population growth in Amazonia is concentrated in Rondônia and southern Pará as incoming settlers from Paraná, Rio Grande do Sul, São Paulo, and Minas Gerais flood these areas.

When coupled with environmental hazards or overcrowding in environmentally sensitive areas, such as the Andean *altiplano*, migrants pour out from their hard-pressed source areas. Periodic droughts in the north-east of Brazil, for example, have pushed victims into Amazonia for over a century. Substantial proportions of the inhabitants of the Brazilian Amazon trace their roots to the arid backlands of the north-east. The impact of droughts in the north-east is exacerbated by the skewed land distribution pattern; the poor majority suffer most when the rains fail because they generally till marginal lands.

Two main migration currents are discernible in countries embracing Amazonia: a substantial rural exodus to towns and cities, and settlers penetrating the Amazon Basin along pioneer roads. For every migrant heading for Amazonia, though, many more have opted to settle in towns and cities. During the 1970s, some 766,000 people migrated to the Brazilian Amazon, accounting for only 5 per cent of the flow of people moving from the countryside to urban areas (Wood and Carvalho 1988, 234). Amazonia, therefore, is clearly not serving as a convenient safety-valve for population growth and socio-economic problems in other regions.

In Latin America, urban population growth is generally much higher than growth in rural areas, and this holds for countries with territories in Amazonia. Throngs of sharecroppers, unsuccessful or dispossessed farmers, and grown children of rural families have caught buses or trucks in search of new livelihoods in Latin America's swelling cities. Rural–urban migration has severely stretched the ability of rapidly growing cities to provide services for newcomers, and many settle in slums. Some shanty settlements around cities eventually improve, or people move out into better neighbourhoods after a few years if they have acquired some savings, but urban migrants rarely return to live or even work in their source areas.

Cities are a magnet to prospective migrants. Urban areas, in spite of their higher living costs, crime, and pollution, offer better opportunities for jobs, schooling, and health care. In contrast, pioneer areas of Amazonia have fewer health and educational facilities, and roads that become impassable in the rainy season can isolate farmers from markets, hospitals and clinics, schools, and needed supplies. This impressive sponge effect of cities has undoubtedly saved the Amazon from even more extensive deforestation.

The Andes and southern Brazil are currently the main source regions for Amazonian migrants. The crowded Andean valleys of Peru, Bolivia, Ecuador, and Colombia have sent aspiring landowners down into western and south-western Amazonia for several decades (Crist 1967; Eidt 1962; Hicks et al. 1990, 2; Hiraoka 1980; Rudel 1983; Stearman 1978). In the Brazilian Amazon, the north-east has long served as an important source of migrants for much of the basin, but the growing throng of settlers from southern Brazil has eclipsed their numbers.

The greatest influx of settlers into the Brazilian Amazon since the 1970s has come from such states as Paraná, Rio Grande do Sul, São Paulo, Minas Gerais, and Espírito Santo. Population growth is partly responsible for the flow of migrants to Amazonia, particularly in Paraná and Rio Grande do Sul, where small farms are divided up among sons and have, in some cases, become too small to be economically viable. *Minifundia*, rather than *latifundia*, are thus more of a problem in some parts of southern Brazil. In north-western Rio Grande do Sul, for example, areas pioneered in the 1940s had already become full by the early 1970s.

Other factors also account for out-migration from rural parts of southern Brazil to Amazonia and cities. Unequal distribution of land in some areas presses the landless in search of new lives and homesteads. Moreover, changes in farming methods (see below) can lead to redundancy for some farm labour.

In spite of more than two decades of intensive efforts to accelerate settlement and development and the influx of migrants, Amazonia remains relatively sparsely settled. The 3.8 million km^2 Brazilian Amazon contains only 10 million inhabitants, fewer than the megalopolis of São Paulo, and a density of population of less than 3 people/km^2. The Brazilian Amazon accounts for 45 per cent of Brazilian territory but less than 7 per cent of its population.

Overall, population pressure has clearly not reached any serious proportions in Amazonia, at least by comparison with the density of populations found elsewhere in tropical forest zones. Some rural areas of Amazonia have actually lost people to cities in the last two decades. A little over half of the population in Amazonia resides in urban areas, and Belém alone has over 1 million inhabitants. Population growth rates in Amazonian towns and cities far exceed those in rural areas (Godfrey 1990).

Growth in population has triggered environmental change, but the numbers are simply not sufficiently high to create large-scale environmental degradation in the region. Given that the rural poor and other land users in Amazonia tend to use "effective" technologies (i.e. practices that often require frequent and large-scale clearing of forest), any future population increases are likely to result in further clearing of forests.

Technological change

Changes in technology for agriculture, forestry, and mining, among other activities, can have adverse impacts on the environment. Few would deny that humankind's ability to alter the face of the earth and the atmosphere has increased dramatically with ever more potent technologies. The literature is replete with examples of technological changes that have wrought ecological destruction and social disruption (Bennett et al. 1974; Nelson 1973; Norman 1981; Turner et al. 1990), and this is so for Amazonia as well. But technologies can also be used to help manage resources more wisely, as is occurring in various parts of Amazonia.

Technological changes in agricultural areas elsewhere in Brazil may indirectly affect the environment of Amazonia. Such changes in southern Brazil have been cited as forcing people off the land, and some of them have moved to Amazonia. A switch to machine-intensive soybean production from more labour-intensive coffee production in parts of Paraná, for example, has allegedly contributed to the rural exodus (Wood and Carvalho 1988, 207). The widespread use of tractors on soybean farms has allegedly displaced labour, thereby contributing to migrants streaming into Amazonia (Muller 1988a).

Mechanization may have reduced on-farm labour needs, but it is not clear whether the increased use of tractors in southern Brazil has spurred migration to Amazonia or other parts of the country. The manufacture and servicing of agricultural machinery, combined with the impressive volume of soybean transportation and processing in Brazil, have undoubtedly created many new jobs. Some farm labourers are likely to have moved to the service sector in urban areas, rather than try their hand at farming in Amazonia.

Mechanization does not necessarily push small farmers off the land. In areas of Paraná settled by private land companies, or where farmers are members of efficient cooperatives, small landholdings remain viable in the face of mechanization and soybean cultivation (Muller 1988b). Rapid soil erosion and consolidation of landholdings by ranchers in Paraná, rather than technological change, have been mainly responsible for the demise of some small farms and an exodus of people from rural areas (Muller 1988b).

Sophisticated technologies are also not necessarily the major proximate sources of change in Amazonia. Small-scale farmers employing axes, machetes, and (in some cases) power saws are probably clearing more forest in Amazonia than any other agents. Even large landholders generally employ work gangs armed with power saws or axes to clear land. Indians formerly used stone axes to fell forest and, as has been argued previously, were quite capable of radically altering the plant geography of Amazonia.

Dam-building is radically altering the regimes of certain rivers (especially the Tocantins) and has flooded extensive areas of both upland and flood-plain forest. Thus far, the impact on fisheries appears to be minimal, but long-term loss of genetic resources of plants caused by the ensuing reservoirs could be appreciable. Along the Tocantins, for example, the Tucurui dam has inundated extensive populations of Brazil nut trees. A global recession and concern about environmental impacts on peasant and indigenous groups have slowed hydroelectric dam construction in Amazonia. As the world economy improves and fossil fuel prices climb, more dams are likely to be built in the region. An increased reliance on solar-based technologies and improved conservation measures could alleviate the demand for electricity. Some farmers on the Amazon flood-plain near Santarém, for example, have ordered water-pumps powered by photovoltaic cells from southern Brazil to irrigate their vegetable crops.

Introduced technologies can be a double-edged sword for the environment and society with respect to cattle-raising as well. African pasture grasses, particularly guinea grass (*Panicum maximum*) and jaraguá (*Hyparrhenia rufa*), helped make cattle-raising an attractive undertaking in Amazonia in the 1970s. The carpeting of substantial tracts of Amazonia with pasture grass stirred heated debate about appropriate land uses in the region. Now, both small and large ranchers are experimenting with "later generation" African pasture grasses, such as briachiarão (*Brachiaria brizantha*), in an effort to upgrade pastures and improve productivity. In this manner, pressure on the remaining forest is likely to be reduced, as will be explored in more detail later.

Socio-economic and institutional change

The fiscal and agrarian policies of the Brazilian government have significantly shaped land use in Amazonia since the late 1960s. Beginning in 1967, companies could invest up to one-half of their taxes in approved development projects in Amazonia. Administered by the Superintendency for Amazonian Development (Superintendência de Desenvolvimento da Amazônia, or SUDAM), projects supported by tax incentives were responsible for clearing over 10 million ha of forest, mostly for cattle pasture (Hecht and Cockburn 1989).

The large-scale conversion of forest to cattle pasture has proved to be the single most controversial aspect of fiscal policies in Amazonia during the 1960s and 1970s. As concern mounted about the ecological implications of such a rapid land transformation, and as the often disappointing productivity of many new ranches became apparent, the government suspended fiscal incentives for the development of cattle pasture in dense tropical forest in 1979. Nevertheless, many projects approved before 1979 were still being implemented in the 1980s. Furthermore, transitional forest skirting the basin was eligible for fiscal incentives to create pasture. SUDAM incentives accelerated pasture development in Amazonia, particularly in southern Pará and northern Mato Grosso, but overall they have accounted for less than 10 per cent of deforestation in the region (Mahar 1989, 15). On 25 June 1991, President Collor signed a decree removing fiscal incentives for cattle-ranching in any forested portion of the Amazon, including transitional forest.

Cattle-ranching remains one of the most common land uses in recently cleared areas of Amazonia, even without fiscal incentives. Cattle-ranching is a favoured occupation of large and small to medium-size holdings in the region because labour is scarce and a ready market exists for beef, particularly in the rapidly growing urban centres (Hicks et al. 1990, 14). If roads are impassable, cattle can still reach market. Cultural factors stemming from the tradition of cattle-raising in Iberia have sustained the conversion of formerly forested land to pasture in many parts of the region, including eastern Ecuador (Hiraoka and Yamamoto 1980).

Government-directed colonization schemes have opened up vast stretches of hinterland to settlers. In 1970, the Brazilian government announced the national integration plan, Programa de Integração Nacional (PIN), which called for a system of pioneer highways to criss-cross Amazonia, with the 3,000 km Transamazon Highway serving as the main east–west axis for the new highway system. PIN highways were initially designed to serve homesteads for drought victims in the north-east and the numerous large families of landless and small farmers from other parts of Brazil. The highways were further designed to create access to resources, such as minerals.

The road network in the Brazilian Amazon has grown spectacularly, from a total of 6,350 km in 1960 to 43,672 km by 1985 (Homma, Texeira Filho, and Magalhaès 1991). Tens of thousands of settlers have followed the bulldozers to take up lots in government-sponsored settlement schemes, to squat on unoccupied land, or to invade reserves and private holdings. By the mid to late 1970s, several private land companies were opening up substantial tracts of land in southern Pará and northern Mato Grosso to medium- and smallholder farmers.

Occupation of Amazonia would occur even without government incentives. A case can be made that certain government policies have accelerated rates of settlement and forest conversion, but they can hardly be blamed for widespread ecological change in Amazonia. Government policies have influenced the locations of such change, but many land-hungry settlers and investors are already motivated to try their luck in Amazonia. A desire to tap natural resources and seek new fortunes is a powerful enough incentive, and, as frontiers close in other parts of Brazil, eyes naturally turn to Amazonia, one of Brazil's last remaining frontiers.

Migration to and within Amazonia is sometimes attributed to a skewed distribution of land. Unequal access to land both within Amazonia and in other parts of Brazil, it is argued, uproots people and obliges them to seek a new life in frontier zones. Debate on whether drought, population growth, or latifundia are responsible for the long history of out-migration from north-eastern Brazil has continued for a long time (Hall 1978). All three factors are responsible in varying degrees, depending on the area in question. Without stepping too far into this complex question, it suffices to say that land ownership patterns have undoubtedly caused social conflicts in some parts of

Brazil, particularly southern Pará, and are partly responsible for migration to and within Amazonia.

The need for some degree of land reform and the expediting of secure land titles has been recognized for a long time in parts of Brazil and other areas of Latin America. Confusion over land titling has fuelled deforestation, since one of the most visible ways to place a stamp of ownership on the land is to clear it, even if the opened space is not used productively (Schmink and Wood 1987). Historically, the politically more expedient solution to the greatly skewed land ownership pattern in Latin America has been to open up "unoccupied" land for the needy, rather than tackle powerful landowning interests or invest in technologies to boost productivity (Wood and Schmink 1978). But even if significant land reform were carried out in Brazil, it is debatable whether breaking up large estates would greatly alleviate the flow of people to Amazonia. Land reform can exacerbate social problems by reducing agricultural production and dismantling managerial expertise for certain agricultural enterprises.

Subdividing land is thus not necessarily a cure-all for sustainable development and for saving vast tracts of Amazonia. In southern Brazil, *minifundia* rather than large landholdings are a significant cause of out-migration to Amazonia. In western Paraná and Rio Grande do Sul, for example, areas opened up for settlement in the 1940s and 1950s are already crowded. Further subdivision of lots for future generations is not feasible in many areas, such as around Tenente Portela in Rio Grande do Sul. In Peru, land reform has been carried out for several decades, but thousands of migrants still pour out of the packed *altiplano* in search of jobs in cities, such as Lima, or to eke out a living in the forests carpeting the eastern flanks of the Andes.

National beliefs and manifest destiny

Amazonia has long been considered a cultural and economic backwater. Although still considered exotic and steeped in mystery, at least in public perception, Amazonia is rapidly being incorporated into the heartlands of countries with a stake in the sprawling region. Brazil has been the pace-setter in implementing projects to integrate the region better into national society. In the 1960s and 1970s, the Amazon was seen as a region of great potential that warranted massive investments, from both national governments and international agencies. Enormous investments were made to upgrade transportation, communications, and electric-power networks. New roads would carve avenues to El Dorados, long entombed under the mantle of forest.

Although heavy government investment in Amazonia continued in the 1980s, the prevailing attitude of national governments shifted to the idea that the region should start "paying for itself." The downturn in the global economy during the 1980s and mounting budget deficits prompted governments to perceive the region more as a fountain of revenue, rather than as a sinkhole for public investments. Attempts were also made to shift more of the burden for development to the private sector, in part because some of the public sector investments, such as in planned settlements, were expensive and often produced disappointing results.

The authoritarian governments that ruled Brazil from 1964 to 1985 laid down bold development strategies for the Brazilian Amazon. Several military strategists associated with the military academy (Escola Superior da Guerra) erected the intellectual girders of these development plans. Civilian scholars and scientists, such as the economists Delfim Neto and Mário Henrique Simonsen, were also involved in rationalizing development plans. Gifted civilian technocrats were thus a critical part of the "revolutionary" governments and often occupied key administrative posts.

The revolutionary military governments that steered Brazil for 21 years have been blamed for much of the rampant destruction in Amazonia (Bunker 1985; Hecht and Cockburn 1989). The World Bank has also been criticized for funding portions of the Polonoroeste project, which included asphalting the Cuiabá–Porto Velho Highway through Rondônia. The World Bank has since withdrawn support for development projects in Amazonia.

The process of incorporating Amazonia into the respective national orbits would have occurred without SUDAM-approved projects, government settlement schemes, or World Bank loans. The building of roads into Amazonia was inevitable. Before the road to Brasília was completed in 1964, Belém could be reached only by air or sea. Even asphalting highways does not necessarily speed up settlement; rather, all-weather roads increase land values and farmers may be more inclined to invest in more intensive farming methods.

No single ideology or belief system can be "blamed" for the environmental changes under way in Amazonia. Several governments with different organizational structures and ideologies have been involved over the last few decades, and all have sponsored development and settlement schemes in the region. Only Venezuela, and to a certain degree Colombia, have been relatively cautious with regard to opening up their Amazonian territories, but then those countries occupy comparatively small segments of the region. Trends towards cattle-ranching, increased gold-mining, petroleum exploration, and deforestation are common to all countries with stakes in Amazonia (Barbira-Scazzocchio 1980; Hemming 1985a,b; Hiraoka and Yamamoto 1980; Moran 1981; Schmink and Wood 1984).

The notion that authoritarian governments are more damaging to Amazonia than democratic regimes does not hold water. In Peru, the democratically elected government under Alan García (who held office until 1990) did not stem widespread deforestation in western Amazonia. Brazil now has a democratic government and development pressures on Amazonia are increasing.

A development ethic, suffusing particularly authoritarian governments and financial institutions, is sometimes thought to be responsible for the ravages of Amazonia. If only governments in Amazonia would turn away from economic growth models, the argument goes, the environmental balance would be restored and prosperity would ensue. Although there is room for debate about the merits of different development strategies, the tapping of natural resources will continue in any case.

The idea that forest-clearing in the region must be halted at all costs is also unrealistic. To many in the developing world, the connection between halting deforestation and national well-being is unclear. Most of Haiti is deforested and it is one of the poorest countries in the hemisphere, but over 90 per cent of Western Europe's forests have been cleared (Williams 1990), yet inhabitants of that region enjoy some of the highest standards of living in the world. A similar situation prevails in Japan, an economic superpower. The fastest-developing countries in the third world are along the Pacific Rim, and much of their forests have been or are being destroyed. A case for conserving forests and other environments in Amazonia is made later, but it should be tied to economic development and improved standards of living for people who live within the region.

Income and wealth issues

The mounting foreign debt of developing nations is sometimes depicted as one of the "root causes" of tropical deforestation (Bramble 1987; Gradwohl and Greenberg 1988, 45; Spitler 1987). Many third world governments, it is suggested, have plundered natural resources to help pay off bank loans. Recent governments in Brazil have been accused of exploiting the Amazon rain forest to solve foreign exchange problems (Moran 1988). Some political leaders complain that, in order to meet debt payments, they are "forced" to ravage their natural resources to generate foreign exchange (Wood 1990).

But the linkage between foreign debt and accelerated development efforts has not been clearly established. Although banks in developed countries and multinational corporations are sometimes cast as the "villains" with regard to Amazonia, investments from southern Brazil are much more significant than international capital. It is true that some Amazonian resources are directly linked to the export trade, such as iron ore from Serra dos Carajás, manganese from Serra do Navio in Amapá, and pulp from the Jari plantations, and domestic investment from the industrial heartland of Brazil is a major factor in many development schemes. Companies headquartered in São Paulo enjoy much greater investment exposure in Amazonia than do the World Bank or private banks in the United States, Europe, or Japan.

Investments in Amazonia from São Paulo can be viewed as a means to redistribute some of the wealth accumulated in the nerve-centre of Brazilian business. To others, the great disparity of wealth between São Paulo, with its diverse agricultural and industrial base, and relatively undeveloped Amazonia contributes to the latter's demise. São Paulo is seen as exporting pollution to Amazonia and exploiting its resources with little long-term benefit to the region. Given that forces of change in Amazonia, ranging from population growth and institutional and socio-economic factors to questions of attitudes and distribution of wealth, are likely to remain essentially the same for the foreseeable future, we focus our analysis on ways to promote the sustainable use of forests, plantations, and agricultural lands. This is not to deny the validity of efforts to change the driving forces, but rather to display options for development that can be used by societies guided by a variety of principles and forms of government.

Environmental impacts

A host of ecological issues surrounds the debate about development in Amazonia. Deforestation and its alleged role in global warming have received the most attention both in South America and around the world, but other less publicized impacts may ultimately prove more important. After reviewing the arguments for and against the role of deforestation in global warming and rainfall, we explore the environmental effects of soil erosion and floods, mining, loss of biodiversity, and hydroelectric dams.

Climatic change

Deforestation in Amazonia and other tropical regions is often claimed to contribute to the greenhouse effect, yet no firm evidence has yet emerged that the world is becoming significantly warmer (Smith et al. 1991). Even if such changes will soon be documented, it will be difficult to separate natural climatic cycles from any greenhouse effect (Mitchell, Senior, and Ingram 1989; Smith et al. 1991). In the event that the greenhouse effect takes hold, tropical deforestation will be only partly at fault (Radulovich 1990). Deforestation accounts for less than 20 per cent of greenhouse gas emissions (Flavin 1989, 13). Carbon dioxide from the burning of fossil fuels, which occurs mostly in temperate countries, is the largest component of greenhouse gases.

In addition to temperature changes, deforestation has the potential to produce adverse effects on rainfall regimes. Half of the rain that falls in Amazonia is thought to come from evapotranspiration, and continued deforestation might lead to a drier regional climate (Hecht and Cockburn 1989, 43). How much forest can be removed without affecting rainfall is not known. No evidence has yet emerged to define with any precision the role that deforestation in Amazonia has had in affecting rainfall.

Soil erosion and floods

Regardless of Amazonia's contribution to global climate change, environmental change in this basin has acute, regional implications, especially for soil and water. Soil erosion is one of the most serious threats to the sustainability of agriculture, silviculture, and forestry in Amazonia. The need to protect the soil is a major reason why perennial crops, silviculture, and properly managed pastures are among the more viable options for rural development in areas already cleared. Soil erosion and associated loss of nutrients are contributing factors in the decision of many farmers to abandon their fields and clear a fresh plot from the forest. Soil erosion can also aggravate floods. Some unusually heavy floods along the Amazon in the mid-1970s raised the spectre that deforestation in the foothills of the Andes was having a tangible impact downstream (Fowler and Mooney 1990, 106; Gentry and Lopez-Parodi 1980; Smith 1981, 122). But statistical analyses of flood peak levels do not reveal any trend to more intense flooding along the Amazon (Richey, Nobre, and Deser 1989; Sternberg 1987).

Destruction of forests along streams and some river banks is surely affecting water quality and flow on a local scale. But the vast scale of Amazonia's forests appears to be masking the impact of deforestation on smaller watersheds. Also, the variability of rainfall in different parts of the Amazon Basin can prompt premature conclusions that floods are more pronounced along the Amazon.

Corporate mining operations

Mining has become a major economic activity in Amazonia. The environmental impacts of mining operations by corporations are localized and largely insignificant since some earlier water-pollution concerns have been addressed. Settlement and development activities associated with the poles of growth generated by mining concerns can have more widespread impacts. A much publicized siltation of a lake as a result of bauxite-mining along the Trombetas River, a northern affluent of the Amazon, has been corrected. Bauxite-mining requires removal of large quantities of overlying soil, and failure to take precautions can result in sediment's washing away into nearby watercourses. At one point, 7 miles of Lake Batata near Mineração on the Trombetas had filled in with reddish-brown soil, thereby killing trees and destroying fish and wildlife habitats (Mee 1988, 279). Corrective measures have been taken by building a siltation pond, and Lake Batata is being restored.

Mineração do Norte, which operates the bauxite mine along the Trombetas, eventually replants areas scraped to gain access to the aluminium ore. Topsoil is stockpiled and then spread back once an area has been mined. Several native trees are planted to speed up restoration of the land (Gradwohl and Greenberg 1988, 173). Such recuperation efforts are costly, but Mineração do Norte is demonstrating leadership in environmental management, and technologies

Fig. 2.3 ***Brachiaria humidicola*** **grass planted along a railroad to reduce soil erosion, Serra dos Carajás, Pará, Brazil, February 1990 (photograph by N. Smith)**

developed there are likely to prove useful at many other mining sites in the humid tropics.

At Carajás, forest-clearing around mines is minimized, and road and rail sidings are planted to brachiaria (*Brachiaria humidicola*), a perennial grass from Africa (fig. 2.3). Holding ponds to deposit mining sediment have also been established by the Companhia Vale do Rio Doce (CVRD) at Carajás. Outside the 400,000 ha concession granted to CVRD at Carajás, forest-clearing is rampant, particularly along the 890 km railroad to Itaqui in Maranhão. Settlement is provoking a rapid retreat of the forest.

Itinerant gold-mining

In contrast to most corporate mining operations, small-scale gold-mining activities in Amazonia are causing widespread ecological damage. Mercury contamination of rivers, fish, and humans as a result of gold-mining is arguably the most serious current environmental issue in Amazonia, at least from the perspective of human health. Although small-scale mining of placer gold has gone on for decades, a major gold rush began in the region in 1980 when gold prices soared (Cleary 1990). Little information, however, is available on the dimensions of the problem. Scattered reports of alarmingly high levels of mercury in human hair and certain game fish in the Madeira River system and in parts of southern Pará suggest that quicksilver, used to amalgamate gold, is working its way into the region's food webs (Braunschweiler 1991; Hecht and Cockburn 1989, 143; Malm et al. 1990; Martinelli et al. 1988).

Approximately half a million gold-miners (*garimpeiros*) operate in Amazonia year round. By the late 1980s, about 100 metric tons of gold were being exported annually from the Brazilian Amazon, worth some US$1 billion. For every kilogram of gold produced, at least 1.32 kg of mercury is lost to the environment. More than 100 tons of mercury are thus finding their way in to the region's ecosystems every year.

Every state in the Brazilian Amazon is currently experiencing a rapid influx of fortune-seekers. Garimpeiros are penetrating Indian reserves, national forests, and biological preserves where they pollute waters with mercury and sediment and hunt out game. Some Kayapó Indians have generated dangerously high levels of mercury, presumably from eating fish and drinking water from polluted rivers and streams (Hecht and Cockburn 1989, 143). As mercury levels rise in fish, an important source of protein in the region, the poor are especially likely to suffer. If more of the region's fish become unsafe to eat, wealthier inhabitants can more easily turn to beef, chicken, or imported fish.

Loss of biodiversity

Species extinction and the shrinking of plant and animal populations are some of the most serious consequences of habitat disturbance in Amazonia, particularly over the long term. Amazonia's forests are among the richest biomes on earth and contain a wealth of plants that could be tapped for food, industry, and medicinal uses. They also contain wild populations of many perennial crops important for commerce and subsistence (Smith et al. 1992). Wild populations of crops and, in some cases, their near relatives are increasingly sought by plant breeders for desirable traits, such as resistance to pests and disease.

Development and settlement in Amazonia are eroding wild populations of dozens of perennial crop species (Smith and Schultes 1990). The Amazon contains wild gene pools of such commercially important crops as rubber and cacao, as well as regionally important food and beverage crops, such as peach palm (*Bactris gasipaes*) and guaraná (*Paullinia cupana*). Peach palm is increasingly grown for the export trade in heart-of-palm, particularly in Costa Rica, and guaraná is a popular soda in Brazil and is now exported to developed countries such as Japan and Canada. The ability of developing countries in the Amazon region as well as in other parts of Latin America, Africa, and South-East Asia to raise and sustain yields of several important cash and food crops will hinge to a large extent on their marshalling of genetic resources to overcome constraints on production. Potential crops are also being lost as forests recede.

Ironically, a clean and renewable source of energy is contributing to the loss of biodiversity. Brazil, in particular, has been tapping the enormous hydroelectric potential in Amazonia since the 1960s. When oil prices increased sharply after 1973, efforts to harness the power of rivers to generate electricity increased markedly. Although the existing hydroelectric dams in Amazonia are making a valuable contribution to the region's economy by providing reliable and relatively inexpensive electricity to some areas, particularly in eastern Pará, the environmental toll is yet to be fully assessed. The impact on fisheries is mixed, with some good fishing above dams but lower yields downstream in some cases (Smith et al. 1991). The loss of forest biodiversity as a result of dam construction is even more difficult to gauge. One difficulty with implementing hydroelectric projects in Amazonia is the relative flatness of much of the basin, which leaves vast areas of forest permanently inundated.

Forests contain pollinators and dispersal agents of wild populations of many crop plants as well as their near relatives (fig. 2.4). Intricate and often fine-tuned relationships between plants and animals need to be maintained if the integrity of many wild populations of our

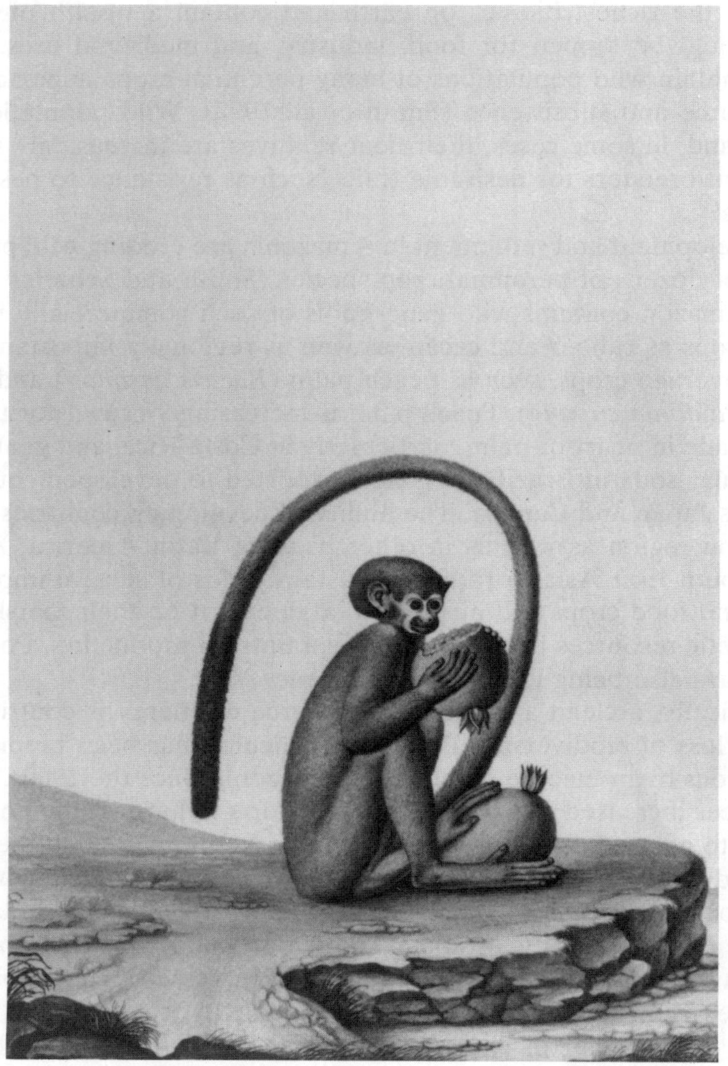

Fig. 2.4 **An 18th-century artist's rendition of a squirrel monkey (*Saimiri sciureus*) feeding on a guava fruit (*Psidium* sp.) in the Brazilian Amazon (Source: Alexandre Rodrigues Ferreira's *Viagem Filósofica*, Vol. 2, Plate 126, Conselho Federal de Cultura, Rio de Janeiro, 1971)**

crop plants is to be ensured. Conservation of forest environments, as well as of field gene banks, is thus essential for the long-term viability of many crops important for subsistence and commerce.

Another salient lesson from global efforts to conserve crop genetic resources is the need to maintain the cultural integrity of indigenous groups. People with a long history of interaction with the forest have much to teach us about sustainable agricultural practices. Rural folk are particularly knowledgeable about the location and natural history of wild populations of crops and their near relatives. Biodiversity and cultural heterogeneity are vital to sustainable development.

Societal responses

Many government organizations involved in development now recognize the importance of the environmental impacts of projects they promote and the need to conserve various ecosystems in Amazonia. Recent publications of the regional development agency for the Brazilian Amazon, SUDAM (Superintendência de Desenvolvimento da Amazônia), underscore the importance of conserving the environment and the ecological sustainability of economic activities (SUDAM 1990). At a May 1989 meeting of the Amazon Pact countries in Manaus, the heads of state of Bolivia, Brazil, Colombia, Ecuador, Guyana, Peru, Suriname, and Venezuela endorsed the need to use and protect natural and cultural resources, and highlighted the value of maintaining biodiversity.

Some may well argue that utterances from political leaders and development agencies may amount to little more than lip-service, but genuine concern does prevail about the ecological and social dimensions to Amazonian development among a broad range of government and development agencies. How much of this concern is translated into concrete action is debatable, but a change in values and attitudes is always a precursor to policy shifts. Some indicators that the "green positions" adopted by politicians and development agencies are more than mere window-dressing include evidence of changes in priorities for research and development in the region. Indeed, regional research and development bodies have approached various international organizations, such as the Food and Agriculture Organization (FAO) in Rome and CIAT (Centro Internacional de Agricultura Tropical), based in Cali, Colombia, for guidance and technical assistance in sustainable agriculture.

Until recently, Brazilian government authorities rejected the notion of debt-for-nature swaps on the grounds that such deals would compromise national sovereignty. In 1991, the federal government decided to authorize the conversion of US$100 million of the

US$123 billion external debt for environmental projects. These debt-for-nature dollars will be used mainly to demarcate national parks and reserves and to compensate landowners or settlers in protected areas for leaving their claims. Although effective protection and management of reserves and parks in Brazil will cost an estimated US$2 billion, the relinquished funds will certainly help.

Resources liberated by this debt-for-nature swap will be administered as a "patrimonial fund" under the control of the federal government. This adroit move allows the Brazilian government to avoid relinquishing any of its sovereignty while reducing, albeit slightly, its debt burden. At the same time, the availability of sizeable grants for certain worthwhile environmental causes permits the government to achieve a public relations coup at virtually no cost.

The growing influence of NGOs

Another response to the perceived need to tackle environmental and social problems in Amazonia is the striking growth in the number of non-governmental organizations (NGOs) operating in the region. More than 1,000 NGOs are currently operating in Brazil, and many of them focus on environmental concerns. This blossoming of NGOs seems to be a global trend; tens of thousands of grass-roots environmental groups have sprung up to raise public awareness of ecological problems and to press for policy (Brown 1991). About three-quarters of the NGOs in Brazil arose in the 1980s in response to increasing awareness among various levels of society about contentious development and environmental issues. A sense emerged in many quarters that prevailing models of economic development were not adequately addressing issues of social equity or sustainability and that more "extra-official" channels were needed for development assistance (Montecinos and Altieri 1991).

Many NGOs have targeted international media and organizations, rather than local, regional, or national governments. The primary mission of many NGOs is to promote the cause of disenfranchised groups, such as Indians, rubber tappers, and women, but they have skilfully "piggybacked" their agenda on the global preoccupation with the environment. Some groups advocating rights of rubber tappers and Indians have seized the growing concern about the environmental impacts of development in Amazonia as an opportunity to strengthen their hand and obtain greater media coverage and leverage with government and donor agencies.

Indigenous-rights groups, such as União das Nações Indígenas (UNI), and organizations attempting to organize rubber tappers, such as the National Council of Rubber Tappers (Conselho Nacional dos Seringueiros), have lobbied aggressively for land rights and for the defence of nature in Amazonia. Maria Allegretti's Institute for Amazon Studies has coordinated efforts to pressure authorities in Brazil to safeguard rubber groves against outside developers (Revkin 1990).

Although some NGOs are jockeying for position as saviours of the forest, particularly in the eyes of the media, this confluence of environmental and social concerns may turn out to be an ephemeral marriage of convenience. NGOs promoting the cause of disenfranchised groups have mixed agendas, and environmental concerns may well be peripheral in some instances.

Extractive reserves and forest management for timber

Extractive reserves have elicited considerable interest both within Brazil and abroad. The main idea behind extractive reserves is that local communities own and control the harvesting of forest products. The push to set up extractive reserves in Amazonia began in Acre in the mid-1980s under the leadership of Chico Mendes. Mendes was attempting to organize rubber tappers to defend the forest against encroaching development, particularly cattle ranches, until he was killed in December 1988. The rubber tappers' movement was envisaged as a dual-purpose cause to improve living conditions and to preserve the forest. Although Mendes has been portrayed as a saviour of Amazonian nature, his struggle was primarily for the social rights of a poor and relatively disenfranchised group of people.

Although the notion of extractive reserves has some appealing aspects, their ability to wrest rubber tappers from poverty and to safeguard the forest from wanton destruction is by no means assured (Homma 1989a,b). It is difficult to raise the standard of living of people by depending exclusively on tropical forest products (Lavelle 1987). The economics of extractive reserves needs further work. One hectare of forest near the village of Mishana on the Nanay River in the Peruvian Amazon can purportedly generate US$650 a year on a sustainable basis from the sale of fruits, nuts, and latex (Peters, Gentry, and Mendelsohn 1989). The Mishana study suggests that sustainable exploitation of rain forests can produce several times the income derived from cutting down the forest for agriculture, silviculture, or pasture. Whereas the Mishana study indicates that Amazon forests have untapped potential, the ecological heterogeneity of the region makes it difficult to extrapolate findings from one area to another. The Mishana site is near Iquitos, the largest town in the Peruvian Amazon. Also, it is doubtful that all patches of the Amazonian rain forest could generate several times as much income as alternative uses; if that were so, then forests would surely be less threatened.

Extractive reserves might better be regarded as supplements to the diet and income of people living in them. To raise living standards, communities will have to undertake other activities, such as farming. The problem is that legislation on extractive reserves specifically prohibits cutting of the forest beyond small patches for subsistence needs. Cultivation of crops for food and income will mean clearing parts of extractive reserves. To prohibit cutting more than the current limit of 5 ha of forest per family may condemn rubber tappers to poverty, at least for the foreseeable future.

In the case of extractive reserves in Acre, rubber and Brazil nuts are the main economic products, a poor prescription to elevate local communities to new levels of prosperity. Three-quarters of Brazil's demand for rubber is met by imports from South-East Asia. Rubber tapped from forests cannot compete in the market-place with rubber derived from plantations in South-East Asia, a lesson learned in the 1920s. Natural rubber produced in Brazil has been subsidized at approximately three times the world price since 1967 (Lei Federal No. 5227); even greater subsidies would be required to bring significant profits to rubber tappers working in the forest. In 1989, President Sarney abolished the Superintendency for promoting natural rubber (SUDHEVEA) and, in March 1990, the federal government reduced much of the subsidy for rubber as part of a policy of reducing import tariffs, thereby further weakening the economic prospects for extractive reserves in Acre. Subsidies will be needed to help extractive reserves survive, at least for the near term (Homma 1989a, 1991).

Although rubber tapped from wild trees in Amazonia still accounts for most of the natural rubber produced in Brazil, the contribution from plantations, mainly in Mato Grosso, Mato Grosso do Sul, Minas Gerais, São Paulo, Espírito Santo, and Bahia, is increasing. In the latter states, South American leaf blight is less prevalent because of the well-defined dry season, and high-yielding material has generally been planted.

Brazil nuts will undoubtedly prove a valuable source of cash income to people living in extractive reserves. Local processing of

Brazil nuts, particularly to extract oil, will add value to the product, thereby generating more income. Cultural Survival in Cambridge, Massachusetts, has helped find markets for Brazil nuts gathered in extractive reserves in Acre, such as Ben and Jerry's Rainforest Crunch ice cream (Pearce 1990). It is not clear, though, how much income Brazil nuts will generate for communities living in extractive reserves. The main producing area for Brazil nuts is Pará, from which transportation of nuts is easier to such deepwater ports as Belém, and established firms have been operating for decades. Also, the Brazil nut is being domesticated and plantations of the crop may eventually produce most of the world's Brazil nuts.

Another concern about extractive reserves is their alleged role in forest conservation. As a means to conserve the forest, extractive reserves could help preserve wild gene pools of certain crop plants as well as potential economic plants. On the other hand, people living in extractive reserves hunt dispersal agents for tropical fruit and nut trees. Several species of monkey, such as capuchin (*Cebus* spp.) and titi monkeys (*Callicebus*), disperse wild cacao, whereas guans and curassows (*Cracidae*) swallow fruits and later defecate seeds. Agoutis (*Dasyprocta* spp.) bury Brazil nuts and the fruits of other forest species.

Given hard economic choices, communities living in extractive reserves may opt to cut down substantial tracts of forest for pasture, plantations, or field crops. A limited amount of clearing for pasture and other agricultural activities has already taken place in at least one of the four extractive reserves established thus far in Acre. Or these activities could be largely abandoned if they do not generate sufficient income; after all, the young are likely to seek better educational and employment opportunities in towns and cities.

Casting extractive reserves as multi-purpose resources that would include the freedom to farm, to set up plantations, and even to rear livestock would render them more likely to contribute to the region's welfare. Each extractive reserve would have a different mix and density of economic plant species. Sustained harvesting of forest products would need more botanical and faunal inventories coupled with natural history studies. Such studies should combine scientific expertise and folk knowledge and involve locals, particularly indigenous groups, in the research effort.

As in the case of extractive reserves, attempts to manage forests in Amazonia for timber production are in their infancy. Current wood-harvesting practices in the region for timber generally damage the recuperative capacity of the forests and are largely unsustainable. Traditionally, most of the lumbering in Amazonia has been concentrated along rivers where access to timber is easier. As more pioneer highways were built in the 1970s, however, timber extraction penetrated deeper into the forest, such as around Itacoatiara near Manaus (Wesche and Bruneau 1990, 59). The tempo of timber extraction in Amazonia continues to increase as the regional network of roads expands. Between 1975 and 1984, log production nearly quadrupled in the Brazilian Amazon (Anderson 1987). Close to half of the timber production comes from the state of Pará. In a study of a logging operation near Paragominas, Pará, for example, one-quarter of the trees with a diameter at breast height of at least 10 cm were killed or severely damaged by logging activities (Uhl and Vieira 1989). The canopy cover was allegedly reduced by half at the study site. At current logging rates, Pará's extensive forests could be stripped of valuable timber within 80 years.

Logging does not always destroy half the canopy, however. If only a few desirable species are removed, as is typically the case, perhaps only a quarter of the canopy is opened. During a 40-minute overflight of forest patches on heavily logged ranches near Paragominas in April 1991, only 10–30 per cent of the canopy appeared to be significantly damaged. Light gaps are important for generating many commercially important timber trees, such as mahogany.

Loggers largely ignore regulations designed to conserve timber resources and protect valuable fruit and nut trees. Sawmills avidly seek Brazil nut trees because of their durable and lustrous red-brown wood. Although it is illegal to cut down Brazil nut trees, landowners, particularly if they are in need of cash, frequently allow loggers to remove the trees. A Brazil nut tree can be legally cut down if it is dead or dying, or in the way of urban expansion. Along the Transamazon, some colonists in the early 1970s deliberately set hot fires at the base of Brazil nut trees so that a cash windfall could be obtained by inviting loggers to remove the damaged trees. In the late 1980s, some loggers in parts of northern Mato Grosso obtained permits to fell Brazil nut trees deemed in the way of urban expansion, even though some of the trees were several kilometres from the nearest house.

Few models for sustained management of tropical forests for timber production are available to guide policy makers in Amazonia. In one part of Suriname, selective logging with carefully planned skid trails and the poisoning of non-commercial trees can produce timber harvests of 20 m^3 per hectare every two decades (Graaf 1982). Given the dispersed nature of desirable timber trees, sustained management of forests in Amazonia would appear to be a low-yield operation. Markets could be developed for some of the lesser-known timber trees, but dealers like reliable supplies in order to cultivate a new product. Considerable research is needed on potential timber trees and rational harvesting methods that offer reasonable economic returns. Of the more than 700 promising timber species in Amazonian forests, only 10 species accounted for more than 60 per cent of the region's saw and veneer log production in the 1980s (Anderson 1987).

As the more desirable species become scarce in heavily logged areas, however, sawmills shift increasing attention to second- and third-tier species. Sawmills in the Paragominas area, for example, send a substantial proportion of their production for the Brazilian market. In spite of the recession, demand is growing for lower-quality timber for general construction purposes, such as moulds for concrete. The Rosa Madeireira sawmill in Paragominas, for instance, was working with 58 timber trees in the early 1990s.

The increased logging activity may ironically help save some forest stands. In the vicinity of Paragominas, for example, several ranchers have halted deforestation on their properties, typically in the 1,000–10,000 ha range, because of the income derived from selling their forest stands to sawmills. The owner of Fazenda São João, which has 600 ha of pasture, sold logging rights to his 400 ha of forest to sawmill operators in 1982, 1986, and 1988. Although the forest on the São João ranch is unlikely to yield sufficiently valuable timber to justify logging three more times in the 1990s, the shift to less desirable species means that a reasonable income can be achieved by permitting logging cycles shorter than the several decades typically required for the premier timber species. Income derived from logging has been reinvested in some cases to upgrade pastures.

Pasture restoration, savannas, and flood-plain ranching

Domestic beef markets are a major driving force in Amazonian deforestation. Most existing or proposed extractive reserves are under pressure from surrounding ranchers. In the short term at least, it often makes economic sense to convert forest to pasture.

Pasture development in Amazonia is mired in controversy. From the social standpoint, ranches provide minimal employment and have contributed to some conflicts over land ownership, particularly in southern Pará. Ecologists have expressed alarm at the virtual biological deserts created by pastures planted to African grasses. Much of the heated debate about pastures in the region stems from the push, from the mid-1960s to the early 1980s, to open up artificial pastures in mature forest. Cattle-raising in Amazonia, however, is centuries old. Furthermore, cattle ranches can be sustainable operations, if properly managed.

Traditionally, most cattle in Amazonia have been raised on pastures along white-water rivers, such as the Amazon proper, and on isolated pockets of savanna. The big push to open up new cattle pastures in Amazonian forests started in the late 1960s. Spurred by generous fiscal incentives, corporations started investing up to half their taxes in development projects in Amazonia. A "grass rush" of major proportions ensued in eastern and southern Amazonia (Sternberg 1973). Some 10 million ha of forest, mostly in southern Pará and northern Mato Grosso, were felled and planted to such imported species as guinea grass (*Panicum maximum*), brachiaria (*Brachiaria decumbens*), and, in areas with a more pronounced dry season, jaraguá (*Hyparrhenia rufa*). Within about five years, weeds, resprouting trees, and compacted soils depressed the productivity of many of these new pastures. By the mid-1970s, brachiaria pastures were being severely attacked by several species of spittlebugs, especially *Deois incompleta*, which withered the grass and allowed weeds to proliferate (Penny and Arias 1982, 65). Close to half of the artificial pastures in Amazonia are degraded (Hecht 1985; Serrão and Toledo 1988).

After it became apparent that incentives for cattle pasture were being used primarily for land speculation and timber extraction, the federal government withdrew subsidies for pasture development in forested areas of Amazonia in the early 1980s. But, even without fiscal incentives, cattle pastures remain the predominant use of land in pioneer areas of Amazonia. In the vicinity of Parauapebas, at the base of the Carajás range in southern Pará, cattle pasture accounts for about 90 per cent of the cleared land in production after only 10 years of settlement (Nigel J. H. Smith, field notes).

Given that cattle pastures are likely to remain an important part of the agricultural economy of Amazonia, technologies and management practices must be sought to improve their productivity. As in Central America, improvement of existing pastures and livestock, rather than trying to "re-educate" people not to eat beef, is likely to prove more fruitful (Nations and Kromer 1983). Far from providing an incentive to cut more forest, viable pastures will help relieve pressure to clear more land (Serrão 1990). With proper management, artificial pastures in Amazonia can be productive and sustainable (Falesi 1976; Falesi et al. 1980). In Central America, fencing and rotation of pastures planted in former rainforest areas can substantially increase the yield and sustainability of cattle operations (Parsons 1989). Unless such pastures are managed correctly from the start, however, they soon degrade.

An investment up to US$300 per hectare is necessary to restore degraded pastures in Amazonia (Serrão and Toledo 1988; Uhl and Vieira 1989). In spite of the relatively high cost, between 700,000 and 1 million ha of artificial pasture had been rehabilitated in the Brazilian Amazon by the late 1980s (Serrão 1990; Serrão and Homma 1989). Although only a small fraction of the pastures cleared from forest in the Brazilian Amazon have been upgraded, ranchers will likely turn to pasture improvement as growing urban centres create ever more attractive markets for beef, milk, butter, and cheese.

Small- to medium-holder ranchers appear to be the most active in upgrading artificial pastures throughout Amazonia. In 1991, ranches with restored pastures were observed along the Manaus–Itacoatiara road; the Transamazon Highway from the Altamira area to km 80 of the Altamira–Itaituba stretch; the highway linking Tomé-Açu and Paragominas (PA 256); the Belém–Brasília highway from Paragominas to Belém; the road from the Belém–Brasília highway to Capitão Poço, Pará. At least a quarter of the ranches observed along these roads had all or some of their pastures under improved management.

Technologies for upgrading pastures are relatively well developed, but their use depends on cost and degree of degradation. Methods for improving artificial pastures in the Amazon include the use of fertilizers, particularly phosphorus (fig. 2.5); replanting with more productive and pest-resistant grasses; interplanting legumes for improved ground cover and nitrogen fixation; intercropping with fruit trees; removal of weeds; and, in heavily compacted sites, mechanically raking the soil (Serrão 1986a,b).

In the case of pastures damaged by spittlebugs, ranchers started turning to quicuio da Amazonia (*Brachiaria humidicola*), a fast-growing grass with moderate resistance to the pests, in 1976. This species is also widely used for erosion control along roads, railways, and electrical transmission lines. By 1982, however, spittlebugs were severely attacking some pastures of *B. humidicola* in the Paragominas area, thereby rendering pastures more susceptible to weed invasion. In

Fig. 2.5 **A 20-year-old pasture planted with *Brachiaria humidicola* fertilized in 1985 with superphosphate and rock phosphate. Fazenda Itaqui, km 54 of the Belém –Brasília highway, Pará, Brazil, January 1990 (photograph by N. Smith)**

wetter areas of Amazonia, *B. humidicola* apparently still resists the pests. Many ranchers have been planting brachiarão (*Brachiaria brizantha* cv. Marandu) since 1983. Also known as brizantão, *B. brizantha* is more vigorous than *B. humidicola*, provides better ground cover to suppress weeds, and currently resists spittlebugs.

Restoration of pastures is not a one-shot affair. Inevitably, rehabilitated pastures will require more fertilization as well as new forage species or varieties. How soon a pasture needs restoration depends on its management history and soil. Some first-generation pastures of guinea grass on alfisols (terra roxa) in the Altamira area of the Transamazon Highway are still reasonably productive after 20 years without fertilizer, provided that they are periodically weeded and fenced to allow rotation. On the other hand, a regularly weeded and fenced guinea grass pasture on yellow oxisol near Paragominas had to be replaced with brachiarão after 12 years.

Another way to help brake conversion of forest to pasture would be to make better use of natural grasslands or pockets of savanna in various parts of Amazonia (Serrão 1986b). Between 50 and 75 million ha of grassland occur in the region: well-drained savannas; poorly drained grasslands, such as in eastern Marajó Island; and seasonally inundated flood plains of silt-laden rivers, such as the Amazon. Well-drained savannas, particularly in Roraima, account for much of these unplanted grasslands, which have expanded from core areas as a result of repeated burning. Each category of "natural" grassland would require different management strategies, but stocking rates in such areas could increase from about 6 million head of cattle to at least 30 million head without felling any more trees (Serrão 1990).

Better utilization of grazing opportunities along flood plains of silt-laden rivers would also help alleviate pressure to clear forest on uplands. Water buffalo, introduced to Brazil in the late nineteenth century, now exceed 800,000 head, mostly in the lower Amazon (Alvim 1990; NRC 1981, 2). Only a small fraction of the estimated 11 million ha of flood-plain pasture available in the Amazon is effectively utilized by livestock, about the area cleared for artificial pastures in upland areas. Water buffalo take an average of three years to reach 350 kg, whereas cattle take four years to reach the same weight in Amazonia. Water buffalo can feed under flooded conditions, whereas cattle have to be transferred to upland pasture or crowded into floating corrals during the flood stage. How greater numbers of cattle can be accommodated on flood plains without further disruption of crop production remains an unsolved question.

Agro-forestry

As the forest is peeled further and further back from pioneer roads, pastures, second growth, and perennial crops eventually dominate the landscape in cleared areas. Several years are typically required to establish perennial crops, but they can provide a reliable source of food and income. Woody crops have the additional benefit of helping to protect the soil and provide more diverse agro-ecosystems for flora and fauna than annual cropping.

The Bragantina zone exemplifies the trend towards agro-forestry in upland areas. During the colonial period, Portuguese entrepreneurs established cacao and sugarcane plantations in the Bragantina zone most of which fell into disuse by the nineteenth century. In 1908, a new railroad between Belém and Bragança carried a large influx of settlers from the drought-plagued north-east who set up homesteads near the new transportation link. The government of Pará also encouraged foreigners to settle in the Bragantina zone and by 1902 had brought in 1,726 Europeans, mainly from Spain, Germany, France, Italy, Belgium, and Switzerland. At that time, over 8,000 north-easterners had also settled on Bragantina's infertile oxisols and entisols. Cropping with maize, manioc, and sugar cane quickly exhausted the naturally infertile sandy clays of Tertiary and Quaternary age. By the 1950s, many of the farms in the vicinity of the 293 km railroad had failed owing to short fallow periods and increasingly exhausted soils.

In the 1950s, Japanese immigrants set up intensively managed black pepper plantations in parts of the Bragantina zone. By the early 1960s, however, Fusarium wilt severely attacked these highly productive pepper plantations. Instead of abandoning their farms, Japanese–Brazilians and many locals switched to other cash crops, particularly perennials. In the 1980s, numerous small- and medium-scale farmers experimented successfully with a medley of perennial crops, such as Sunrise Solo papaya (*Carica papaya*), passion fruit (*Passiflora edulis*), and vitamin C-rich Barbados cherry (*Malpighia glabra*), which are less demanding of the soil and provide a valuable cash income. Also, some medium-scale plantations of oil palm (*Elaeis guineensis*), coconut (*Cocos nucifera*), and rubber have been established in the Bragantina zone.

Sometimes perennial crops are grown in agro-forestry systems or in relay fashion. As black pepper plantations succumb to Fusarium fungal attacks after about seven or eight years, for example, other perennials, such as oil palm or passion fruit, are interplanted so that they can take advantage of residual fertilizer. Some farmers are experimenting with new perennial species, such as Brazil nut, and expanding production of hitherto minor crops, particularly cupuaçu (*Theobroma grandiflorum*), a relative of cacao that produces a much-appreciated pulp used to make juice, ice cream, cakes, and puddings. Recently, several farmers have established small plantations of mangosteen (*Garcinia mangostana*), one of the premier fruits of South-East Asia. Mangosteen fruits were selling for US$1 each in Belém in April 1991, and growers are investigating the feasibility of air-freighting the fruit to Japan.

One of the reasons that farmers are having success with cash-cropping in the Bragantina zone is that the region is served by a relatively good network of all-weather roads. But other areas are benefiting from agro-forestry with cash and food crops. In Tom-Au, for example, farmers are interplanting native and exotic fruit and nut trees to supply regional and international markets. Even along the Transamazon, which is often impassable for short periods during the rainy season, some farmers are prospering with a mix of perennial crops. Cacao (*Theobroma cacao*), black pepper, and robusta coffee (*Coffea canephora*) are among the more important sources of cash income for farmers along the Transamazon. Given unpredictable swings in the world price of cacao and coffee, farmers are learning to diversify their operations by including some annual food crops and pasture.

The trajectory of change and regional dynamics

A case cannot be made at this time that Amazonia is heading inexorably for criticality. This overall statement should not be taken to mean that environmental trends in the region are all positive and that no action is required to avert potentially serious environmental damage. The vast area encompassed by the basin, coupled with the extraordinary variation in cultures, economic conditions, and habitats, invites caution when discussing the overall situation. In some areas, environmental conditions are clearly becoming worse and the plight of some social groups, particularly Indians, appears to be worsening. Yet in other parts of Amazonia, an improvement in both living conditions and ecosystem health is evident.

Although the impact of environmental changes under way in Amazonia appears to be confined to the regional or local levels, forces of destruction are likely to increase in the future. Brazil's population is growing by some 3 million people a year, and efforts to open up Amazonia for settlement and development will inevitably intensify. With a return to a democratic form of government in Brazil, pent-up social pressures for land reform and more jobs will surely lead to greater currents of migration and the opening of forest to settlement and development projects. Indeed, threats to parks and reserves are increasing during the transition to full democracy, as politicians seek to curry favour with voters, both poor and rich, by "liberating" forest areas for occupation.

Many of the environmental issues related to development in Amazonia hinge on the scale and rates of deforestation. The period spanning the late 1960s to the mid-1980s witnessed a spurt in forest removal, associated in part with the opening of pioneer highways and investments in cattle-raising (Malingreau and Tucker 1988). The mid-1980s surge in deforestation in the Brazilian Amazon may have been connected with the formulation of Brazil's new constitution, which was passed in 1988 and calls for land reform and stricter environmental controls. Landowners' fears that unoccupied land might be confiscated may have triggered a clearing frenzy (Revkin 1990, 180). This widespread effort to tame Amazonia's wilderness and integrate the region into the national economy, particularly noticeable in Brazil, stirred concern about the future of the forest and raised the spectre of deleterious regional and global environmental change.

Considerable controversy has characterized the debate about deforestation rates in Amazonia (Bonalume 1989a). Different definitions of forest, the difficulty of separating advanced second growth from forest, and whether temporary or permanent forest removal figures in the equation have contributed to different scenarios and conclusions about the dangers of deforestation. Some groups may have exaggerated deforestation rates to further political aims, whereas others may have downplayed figures in order to encourage further development of the region. No attempt will be made here to sort out all the claims and counter-claims as to how much of the Amazonian forest has been truly "lost." Three main points, however, are worth emphasizing: the notion of virgin Amazonian forests is a myth; considerable areas of Amazonia are still in mature forest (particularly in the western and northern parts of the basin); and rates of deforestation appear to be declining (Bonalume 1989b, 1991).

Deforestation since 1985 has slowed in Rondônia, an acknowledged "hot spot" for forest destruction (Fearnside 1989). Satellite imagery reveals a drop of approximately 27 per cent in deforestation in the Brazilian Amazon from 1989 to 1990 alone. The precise causes of this slow-down are unclear, but the severe recession gripping Brazil, the blocking of substantial portions of savings accounts by the government, and the desire of farmers and ranchers to put second growth back into production or to upgrade weed-choked pastures are partly responsible. Forests have waxed and waned in the face of economic cycles in other regions, such as the Mediterranean (Westoby 1989, 64). Farmers and ranchers in the Altamira area of the Transamazon Highway, for example, are cutting more second growth than forest. A similar pattern prevails among middle-scale ranchers in the Paragominas area.

Increased pressures to protect parks and reserves and to enforce environmental regulations in Amazonia have probably had negligible impacts. The notion that the removal of fiscal incentives for cattle-ranching in the Brazilian Amazon has slowed deforestation is implausible. The implications that the recession is a major factor in the slow-down in forest destruction, if correct, are worrisome. When the economy resumes growth on any significant scale, deforestation rates could pick up again. Only by adequately raising living standards for broad segments of society and taking a more systematic approach to environmental protection will ecological problems in the region be alleviated.

Unless alternatives to deforestation are offered, any widespread effort to halt forest-clearing could lead to lowered food production and more unemployment. Because of depletion of soil nutrients, weed invasion, and the build-up of pests and diseases, many farmers periodically clear new fields from forest. Farming methods that minimize forest-clearing, such as agro-forestry, thus need to be perfected for various soil and other environmental conditions.

Environmental degradation, such as soil erosion and the loss of fisheries and genetic resources, has not progressed on a scale sufficiently large to undercut economic development at this point. Poverty in the region is still largely a problem of access to better roads, schooling, and medical care, rather than putting out environmental brushfires. In the aggregate, wealth in the Amazon region is increasing. Cities are growing with new industries, and the middle class has expanded substantially in the last 25 years. It is true that a large proportion of the rural and urban population remains poor, but people today are probably better off in absolute terms than before 1960. The proportion of poor may have actually shrunk as new opportunities have arisen for land ownership or employment.

Progress towards improved well-being declined in the 1980s in response to inflationary pressures in Brazil and a downturn in rates of growth in the global economy. When inflation reached over 1,000 per cent a year by the close of the 1980s, very few segments of the economy were expanding. Inflation slowed considerably with the change in government in March 1990, but it has since headed up. Unless the management of national and international economies improves, it will be difficult to secure gains in living standards.

Not all segments of Amazonian society have benefited from the impressive investments in improving infrastructure and services in the region. Overall, indigenous groups have reaped few rewards from economic development in the region. And new proprietors have driven some smallholder farmers with no land titles off the land. But both rural and urban poor undoubtedly have better access to services and to educational and job opportunities than their parents had when they were young. Except in a few isolated areas, environmental degradation has not yet seriously undermined the long-term capacity of the landscape to cater to the needs of this and future generations.

Although environmental deterioration is not so alarming as is often portrayed in the media, and well-being and incomes are generally improving in the region, the stakes are ever higher. As more Amazonian ecosystems are altered to make room for people and development projects, nutrient recycling pathways are interrupted, heat and water fluxes may change, and other unseen ecological chain reactions may be taking place. The assumption here is that, as forest and aquatic environments are increasingly altered, human activities could become increasingly vulnerable to ecological surprises.

As Amazonia is increasingly occupied and the tempo of resource extraction accelerates, management input will have to increase accordingly. As farmers switch from extensive slash-and-burn systems to more intensive cropping patterns in response to population pressure and increasing land values, even more sophisticated management is needed. Traditional agro-forestry systems are certainly complex, but modern mixed-cropping patterns must also make adjustments to market conditions as well as shifting biotic pressures. Modern farms are characterized by a more rapid turnover of crop varieties and other technologies, all of which require a finely tuned agricultural research and development system. Farmers could become vulnerable to serious production shortfalls if the R&D pipeline becomes inefficient (Plucknett and Smith 1986).

Thus far, only 2 per cent of the Brazilian Amazon is in parks, reserves, or national forests. Even the inclusion of Indian reserves leaves less than 4 per cent of the region nominally protected. Sizeable tracts of forest will survive into the next century only if forests can be managed on an economically and ecologically sustainable basis and farms, pastures, and plantations are made more productive. Sustainable agriculture and forestry that provide cash income will be crucial to the survival of substantial tracts of forest in the next century. Poverty is arguably the greatest enemy of Amazonian forests.

Given the inevitable pressure to develop and occupy the Amazon, careful management of forest resources and agricultural activities will become ever more urgent. Although research is under way on many fronts to further our understanding of Amazonian ecosystems and socio-economic processes, much more needs to be learned if the region's resources are to be managed on a sound basis. The Amazonian flood plain, in particular, could be a major food-producing area for South America if more were known about how to tap its natural and cultural resources.

A better integration of research efforts across the many institutions conducting research within and outside of Amazonia would also help further our understanding of biodiversity patterns, sustainable agricultural practices, and the potential and impact of new technologies. Networking is poorly developed among Amazonian research institutions, ranging from basic and applied science to university centres. Networking can help avoid redundancy and can make more efficient use of resources, which is particularly important in countries with limited resources (Plucknett, Smith, and Ozgediz 1990). Fortunately, innovative farmers and ranchers and skilled researchers are adopting and developing new technologies to help overcome constraints to raising and sustaining agricultural and silvicultural yields in Amazonia. Although much more research and testing of agricultural technologies developed at scientific institutes and in farmers' fields is needed, ongoing efforts offer hope that many tracts of Amazonia's unique forests will survive.

If properly managed, a wide range of agricultural and silvicultural activities is possible in the region. Both smallholder farmers and corporate operations are achieving sustainable yields in various parts of the basin. The continued vitality of Amazonian agriculture will rest on controlling inflation, a deeper understanding of the natural history of Amazonian ecosystems, including man-made environments, and greater support for research at agricultural research stations, institutes for basic and applied research, and growing universities in the region.

This chapter has made an argument that some promising trends are under way in Amazonia that could help save more forest from the power saw and axe as well as provide more sustainable livelihoods for small-, medium-, and large-scale producers. Furthermore, the case suggests that the Amazon is not yet at a stage of criticality, although the definitions used in this volume would place the region in the endangered category. Amazonia is also an important environmental region, both regionally and globally, because of two main facets: its enormous biodiversity, and the fragility of many of its ecosystems.

The region's enormous wealth in species and genetic resources has already been pointed out. Policy makers may remain unimpressed. After all, some of the world's poorest people live in the world's richest biomass. In the short term, many land users in the region clear and burn wilderness for a variety of motives, with little thought to the genetic treasures and potential new plant and animal species that could be domesticated. How much will the Amazon be impoverished for future generations? Current economic models can hardly tackle this issue. Let us be honest at this point. We simply do not know the worth of forest currently being destroyed; all we can do is work hard to mitigate deforestation, primarily by raising standards of living and improving productivity, and by supporting research into this biological wonderland. And conservation? Unless the social needs of local people are met, most of the elaborate plans for parks and reserves will founder.

Research is essential for averting large-scale environmental catastrophes in Amazonia for two reasons. In comparison with its biological riches, little is yet known about Amazonian ecosystems and how they can be wisely managed. Second, heavily leached, infertile soils underlie vast stretches of Amazonian forests and other plant communities. More research needs to address how to manage these "problem" soils so that they remain productive without relying excessively on expensive and environmentally damaging inputs. Many farmers are already experimenting with novel crop combinations and land-management techniques, and stronger links among scientists, farmers, and NGOs are necessary to encourage this process. Ultimately, local people will decide the fate of the forest, and international policy makers should always address their needs and not impose solutions acceptable only to the first world.

References

Alvim, Paulo. 1990. Agricultura apropriada para uso contínuo dos solos da região Amazonica. Espaço, *Ambiente e Planejamento* 2, no. 11: 3–71.

Anderson, A. B. 1987. *Forest management issues in the Brazilian Amazon*. Report to the Ford Foundation. New York: Ford Foundation.

Barbira-Scazzocchio, Françoise, ed. 1980. *Land, people and planning in contemporary Amazonia: Proceedings of the Conference on the Development of Amazonia in Seven Countries, Cambridge, 23–26 September, 1979*. Centre of Latin American Studies, Occasional Publication no. 3. Cambridge: Cambridge University.

Bennett, C., G. Budowski, H. Daugherty, L. Harris, J. Milton, H. Popenoe, N. Smith, V. Urrutia, and E. Beltrán. 1974. Interaction of man and tropical environments. In *Fragile ecosystems: Evaluation of research and applications in the neotropics*, ed. Edward G. Farnworth and Frank B. Golley, 139–182. New York: Springer-Verlag.

Bonalume, R. 1989a. Rainforests: Destruction area disputed. *Nature* 339: 86.

———. 1989b. Amazonian forests: Burning continues, slightly abated. *Nature* 339: 569.

———. 1991. Deforestation rate is falling. *Nature* 350: 368.

Bramble, B. J. 1987. The debt crisis: The opportunities. *Ecologist* 17, no. 4/5: 192–199.

Braunschweiler, H. 1991. Provisional report for the Conselho Nacional de Desenvolvimento Científico e Tecnológico-CNPq about the Project of Mercury Load in the Tucurui Lake and Surrounding Areas. Belém, Brazil: Instituto de Pesquisas Ecológicas da Amazonia.

Brown, Lester R. 1991. The new world order. In *State of the World: A Worldwatch Institute Report on Progress Toward a Sustainable Society*, ed. Lester R. Brown et al., 3–20. New York: W. W. Norton.

Bunker, Stephen G. 1985. *Underdeveloping the Amazon: Extraction, unequal exchange, and the failure of the modern state*. Urbana, IL: University of Illinois Press.

Cleary, David. 1990. *Anatomy of the Amazon gold rush*. Iowa City: University of Iowa Press.

Crist, R. E. 1967. Quelques aspects des migrations humaines et de la colonisation en Amérique Latine. In *Les problèmes agraires des Amériques Latines, Paris, 11–16 octobre 1965*, 501–510. Colloques Internationaux du Centre National de la Recherche Scientifique. Paris: Éditions Centre.

Dean, Warren. 1987. *Brazil and the struggle for rubber: A study in environmental history*. Cambridge: Cambridge University Press.

Domning, D. P. 1982. Commercial exploitation of manatees *Trichechus* in Brazil c. 1785–1973. *Biological Conservation* 22: 101–126.

Eidt, R. C. 1962. Pioneer settlement in eastern Peru. *Annals of the Association of American Geographers* 52: 255–278.

Falesi, Italo Claudio. 1976. *Ecosystema de pastagem cultivada na Amazônia brasileira*. Boletim Técnico no. 1. Belém, Brazil: Empresa Brasileira de Pesquisa Agropecuária (EMBRAPA).

Falesi, Italo Claudio, Antônio Ronald Camacho Baena, and Saturnino Dutra. 1980. *Consequências do exploração agropecuária sobre as condições des físicas e químicas dos solos microregiões de Nordeste Paraense*. Boletim de Pesquisa no. 14. Belém, Brazil: EMBRAPA, Centro de Pesquisa Agropecuária do Trópico Úmido.

Fearnside, Phillip M. 1986. *Human carrying capacity of the Brazilian rainforest*. New York: Columbia University Press.

———. 1989. Deforestation in Brazilian Amazonia: The rates and causes of forest destruction. *Ecologist* 19: 214–218.

Ferreira, Alexandre Rodrigues. 1971. *Viagem filosófica pelas capitanias do Grão Para, Rio Negro, Mato Groso e Cuiaba. Vol. 2. Zoología, Botânica*. Rio de Janeiro: Conselho federal de cultura.

Flavin, Christopher. 1989. *Slowing global warming: A worldwide strategy*. Worldwatch Paper 91. Washington DC: Worldwatch Institute.

Fowler, Cary, and Patrick R. Mooney. 1990. *Shattering: Food, politics, and the loss of genetic diversity*. Tucson, AZ: University of Arizona Press.

Gentry, A. H., and J. Lopez-Parodi, 1980. Deforestation and increased flooding of the Upper Amazon. *Science* 210: 1354–1356.

Godfrey, B. 1990. Boom towns of the Amazon. *Geographical Review* 80: 103–117.

Graaf, N. R. 1982. Sustained timber production in the tropical rainforest of Suriname. In *Proceedings of the Joint Workshop on Management of Low Fertility Acid Soils of the American Humid Tropics*, Paramaribo, Suriname, 23–26 November 1981, ed. J. F. Wienk and H. A. de Wit. San José, Costa Rica: Inter-American Institute for Cooperation in Agriculture (IICA).

Gradwohl, Judith, and Russell Greenberg. 1988. *Saving the tropical forests*. Washington DC: Island Press.

Hall, Anthony L. 1978. *Drought and irrigation in north-east Brazil*. Cambridge: Cambridge University Press.

Hecht, Susanna. 1985. Environment, development and politics: Capital accumulation and the livestock sector in eastern Amazonia. *World Development* 13, no. 6: 663–684.

Hecht, Susanna, and Alexander Cockburn. 1989. *The fate of the forest: Developers, destroyers, and defenders of the Amazon*. London: Verso.

Hemming, John, ed. 1985a. *Change in the Amazon basin. Vol. 1, Man's impact on forests and rivers*. Manchester: Manchester University Press.

———. 1985b. *Change in the Amazon basin. Vol. 2, The frontier after a decade of colonisation*. Manchester: Manchester University Press.

Hicks, James F., Herman E. Daly, Shelton H. Davis, and Maria de Lourdes de Freitas. 1990. *Ecuador's Amazon region: Development issues and options*. World Bank Discussion Papers 75. Washington DC: World Bank.

Hiraoka, M. 1980. Settlement and development of the Upper Amazon: The East Bolivian example. *Journal of Developing Areas* 14: 327–347.

Hiraoka, M., and S. Yamamoto. 1980. Agricultural development in the Upper Amazon of Ecuador. *Geographical Review* 70: 423–445.

Homma, Alfredo Kingo Oyama. 1989a. A extração de recursos naturais renováveis: O caso do extrativismo vegetal na Amazônia. Ph.D. dissertation. Viosa, Minas Gerais: Universidade Federal de Viosa.

———. 1989b. Perspectivas da economia extrativista vegetal na Amazônia. Belém, Brazil: EMBRAPA, unpublished report.

———. 1991. A desmistificação do extrativismo vegetal na Amazonia. Paper presented at the Seminario Grandes Projetos, Desorganização e Reorganização do Espaco, Belém, 3–5 April.

Homma, Alfredo Kingo Oyama, A. R. Teixeira Filho, and E. P. Magalhaès. 1991. Análise do preço da terra como recurso natural durável: O caso da Amazônia. *Revista de economía e sociología rural* (Brasília) 29, no. 2: 103–116.

Kleinpenning, J. M. G. 1975. *The integration and colonisation of the Brazilian portion of the Amazon basin*. Nijmeegse Geografische Cahiers 4, Geografisch en Planologisch Instituut. Nijmegen, Netherlands: Katholieke Universiteit.

Lavelle, P. 1987. Biological processes and productivity of soils in the humid tropics. In *The geophysiology of Amazonia: Vegetation and climate interactions*, ed. Robert E. Dickinson, 175–214. New York: J. Wiley, for the United Nations University.

Ledec, George, and Robert Goodland. 1988. *Wildlands: Their protection and management in economic development*. Washington DC: World Bank.

Mahar, Dennis J. 1989. *Government policies and deforestation in Brazil's Amazon region*. Washington DC: World Bank.

Malingreau, J., and C. J. Tucker. 1988. Large-scale deforestation in the southeastern Amazon basin of Brazil. *Ambio* 17: 49–55.

Malm, O., W. C. Pfeiffer, C. M. M. Souza, and R. Reuther. 1990. Mercury pollution due to gold mining in the Madeira River basin, Brazil. *Ambio* 19: 11–15.

Martinelli, L. A., J. R. Ferreira, B. R. Forsberg, and R. L. Victoria. 1988. Mercury contamination in the Amazon: A gold rush consequence. *Ambio* 17, no. 4: 252–254.

Mee, Margaret. 1988. *Margaret Mee: In search of flowers of the Amazon forests*. Woodbridge, Suffolk, UK: Nonesuch Expeditions.

Mitchell, J. F. B., C. A. Senior, and W. J. Ingram. 1989. CO_2 and climate: A missing feedback? *Nature* 341: 132–134.

Montecinos, C., and Michael A. Altieri. 1991. *Status and trends in grass-roots crop genetic conservation efforts in Latin America*. Berkeley, CA: Consorcio Latino Americano sobre Agroecologia y Desarrollo.

Moran, Emilio F. 1981. *Developing the Amazon*. Bloomington: Indiana University Press.

———. 1988. Following the Amazon highways. In *People of the tropical rain forest*, ed. Julie Sloan Denslow and Christine Padoch, 155–162. Berkeley: University of California Press.

Muller, Keith D. 1988a. The impact of agricultural mechanization on population and migration in South Brazil: The example of West Paraná. *Latin American Studies* (University of Tsukuba) 9: 59–86.

———. 1988b. The impact of agricultural mechanization on land tenancy and farm size in South Brazil: The example of West Paraná. *Latin American Studies* (University of Tsukuba) 10: 181–210.

Myers, Norman. 1991. Tropical deforestation: The latest situation. *Biotropica* 41, no. 5: 282.

Nations, J. D., and D. I. Kromer. 1983. Central America's tropical rainforests: Positive steps for survival. *Ambio* 12, no. 5: 232–238.

Nelson, Michael. 1973. *The development of tropical lands: Policy issues in Latin America*. Baltimore, MD: Johns Hopkins University Press.

Norman, Colin. 1981. *The god that limps: Science and technology in the eighties*. New York: W. W. Norton.

NRC (National Reseach Council). 1981. *The water buffalo: New prospects for an underutilized animal*. Washington DC: National Research Council, National Academy Press.

Parsons, J. J. 1989. Forest to pasture: Development or destruction. In *Hispanic lands and peoples: Selected writings of James J. Parsons*, ed. William M. Denevan, 275–295. Dellplain Latin American Studies 23. Boulder, CO: Westview Press.

Pearce, F. 1990. Brazil, where the ice cream comes from. *New Scientist* 127, no. 1724: 45–48.

Penny, Norman D., and Jorge R. Arias. 1982. *Insects of an Amazon forest*. New York: Columbia University Press.

Peters, C. M., A. H. Gentry, and R. O. Mendelsohn. 1989. Valuation of an Amazonian rainforest. *Nature* 399: 655–656.

Plucknett, Donald L., and Nigel J. H. Smith. 1986. Sustaining agricultural yields: As productivity rises, maintenance research is needed to uphold the gains. *Bioscience* 36: 40–45.

Plucknett, Donald L., Nigel J. H. Smith, and Selcuk O. Ozgediz. 1990. *Networking in international agricultural research*. Ithaca, NY: Cornell University Press.

Radulovich, R. 1990. A view on tropical deforestation. *Nature* 346: 214.

Revkin, Andrew. 1990. *The burning season: The murder of Chico Mendes and the fight for the Amazon rain forest*. Boston: Houghton Mifflin.

Richey, J. E., C. Nobre, and C. Deser. 1989. Amazon River discharge and climate variability. *Science* 246: 101–103.

Rudel, T. K. 1983. Roads, speculators, and colonization in the Ecuadorian Amazon. *Human Ecology* 11, no. 4: 385–403.

Schmink, Marianne. 1988. A case study of the closing frontier in Brazil. In *Power and poverty: Development and development projects in the Third World*, ed. Donald W. Attwood, Thomas C. Bruneau, and John G. Galaty, 135–153. Boulder, CO: Westview Press.

Schmink, Marianne, and Charles H. Wood, eds. 1984. *Frontier expansion in Amazonia*. Gainesville, FL: University of Florida Press.

———. 1987. The "political ecology" of Amazonia. In *Lands at risk in the Third World: Local level perspectives*, ed. Peter D. Little and Michael M. Horowitz, 38–57. Boulder, CO: Westview Press.

Serrão, Emanuel Adilson S. 1986a. Pastagem em ârea de floresta no trópico úmido brasileiro: conhecimentos atuais. In *Anais do Primeiro Simpósio do Trópico Umido, Belém, Pará, 12 a 17 de novembro de 1984*, vol. 5: 147–174.

———. 1986b. Pastagens nativas do trópico úmido brasileiro: Conhecimentos atuais. In *Anais do Primeiro Simpósio do Trópico Úmido, Belém, Pará, 12 a 17 de novembro de 1984*, vol. 5: 183–205.

———. 1990. Pasture development and carbon emission/accumulation in the Amazon. Paper presented at the Intergovernmental Panel on Climate Change (IPCC) Meeting on Gas Emission from Conversion of Tropical Forests. São Paulo: Universidade de São Paulo.

Serrão, Emanuel Adilson S., and A. K. O. Homma. 1989. A questão da sustentabilidade da pecuária substituindo florestas na Amazônia: A influencia de variveis agronómicas, ecológicas, económicas, e sociais. Unpublished manuscript.

———. 1993. Brazil. In *Sustainable agriculture and the environment in the humid tropics*. Report for the Committee on Agriculture Sustainability and the Environment in the Humid Tropics, National Research Council. Washington DC: National Academy Press.

Serrão, Emanuel Adilson S., and J. M. Toledo. 1988. Sustaining pasture-based production systems for the humid tropics. Paper presented at the Man and the Biosphere (MAB) Conference on Conversion of Tropical Forests to Pasture in Latin America, 4–7 October 1988, Oaxaca, Mexico.

Smith, Nigel J. H. 1974. Destructive exploitation of the South American river turtle. *Yearbook of the Pacific Coast Geographers* 36: 85–102.

———. 1980. Anthrosols and human carrying capacity in Amazonia. *Annals of the Association of American Geographers* 70, no. 4: 553–566.

———. 1981. *Man, fishes, and the Amazon*. New York: Columbia University Press.

———. 1982. *Rainforest corridors: The transamazon colonization scheme*. Berkeley: University of California Press.

———. 1995 (forthcoming). Human-induced landscape change in Amazonia and implications for development. In *Principles, patterns, and processes: Some legacies of the Columbian exchange*, ed. B. L. Turner II. Madrid: Consejo Superior de Investigaciones Científicas (CSIC).

Smith, Nigel J. H., and R. E. Schultes. 1990. Deforestation and shrinking crop gene-pools in Amazonia. *Environmental Conservation* 17, no. 3: 227–234.

Smith, Nigel J. H., Paulo Alvim, Alfredo K. O. Homma, Emanuel Adilson S. Serrão, and Italo C. Falesi. 1991. Human-induced environmental changes in Amazonia. *Global Environmental Change* 1, no. 4 (September): 313–320.

Smith, Nigel J. H., J. T. Williams, Donald L. Plucknett, and J. P. Talbot. 1992. *Tropical forests and their plants*. Ithaca, NY: Comstock.

Spitler, A. 1987. Exchanging debt for conservation. *Bioscience* 37: 781.

Stearman, A. M. 1978. The highland migrant in lowland Bolivia: Multiple resource migration and the horizontal archipelago. *Human Organization* 37, no. 2: 180–185.

Sternberg, H. O'R. 1973. Development and conservation. *Erdkunde* 27, no. 4: 253–265.

———. 1987. Aggravation of floods in the Amazon River as a consequence of deforestation? *Geografiska Annaler* (Series A, Physical Geography) 69A, no. 1: 201–219.

SUDAM (Superintendência de Desenvolvimento da Amazônia). 1990. *Ação governamental na Amazônia: Subsídios ao zoneamento ecológico-econômico e ao plano de desenvolvimento da Amazônia*. Belém: Sudam.

Turner, B. L., II, William C. Clark, Robert W. Kates, John F. Richards, Jessica T. Mathews, and William B. Meyer, eds. 1990. *The earth as transformed by human action: Global and regional changes in the biosphere over the past 300 years*. Cambridge: Cambridge University Press with Clark University.

Uhl, Christopher, and I. C. G. Vieira. 1989. Ecological impacts of selective logging in the Brazilian Amazon: A case study from the Paragominas region of the state of Pará. *Biotropica* 21, no. 2: 98–106.

Weinstein, Barbara. 1983. *The Amazon rubber boom 1850–1920*. Stanford, CA: Stanford University Press.

Wesche, Rolf, and Thomas Bruneau. 1990. *Integration and change in Brazil's middle Amazon*. Development International vol. 7. Ottawa: University of Ottawa Press.

Westoby, Jack C. 1989. *Introduction to world forestry: People and their trees*. Oxford: Basil Blackwell.

Williams, Michael. 1990. Forests. In *The earth as transformed by human action: Global and regional changes in the biosphere over the past 300 years*, ed. B. L. Turner II, William C. Clark, Robert W. Kates, John F. Richards, Jessica T. Mathews, and William B. Meyer, 179–201. Cambridge: Cambridge University Press with Clark University.

Wood, Charles H., and José Alberto Magro de Carvalho. 1988. *The demography of inequality in Brazil*. Cambridge Latin American Studies, vol. 67. Cambridge: Cambridge University Press.

Wood, Charles H., and Marianne Schmink. 1978. Blaming the victim: Small farmer production in an Amazon colonization project. In *Changing agricultural systems in Latin America*, ed. Emilio Moran, 77–93. Studies in Third World Societies, Publication No. 7. Williamsburg, VA: Department of Anthropology, College of William and Mary.

Wood, W. B. 1990. Tropical deforestation: Balancing regional development demands and global environmental concerns. *Global Environmental Change* 1, no. 1 (December): 23–41.

3

The Aral Sea basin

Nikita F. Glazovsky

The ecological situation in the Aral Sea basin is one of the most complex in Central Asia. The situation is aggravated by the fact that environmental degradation is accompanied by a deterioration in economic and social conditions. Many of the problems of the Aral basin, however, are typical of many other arid and semi-arid regions of the world.

An analysis of the Aral Sea ecological crisis shows that any reliable estimate must address the whole Aral Sea basin, and the sea itself should also be the subject of surveys. The Aral Sea basin includes the basins of the Syr Darya and Amu Darya rivers, which flow into the sea, and also the Tedzhen and Murgabi rivers, the Karakum canal, and shallow rivers flowing from Kopet Dag and western Tien-Shan, as well as the areas with no runoff among these rivers and around the Aral Sea (fig. 3.1). Administratively, the region covers all of Uzbekistan and Tadzhikistan, portions of Kazakhstan (the Kzyl Orda and Chemkent areas and the southern part of the Aktyubinsk area), Kirghizstan (the Osh and Narym areas), and Turkmenistan (without the Krasnovodsk area), and also part of north Afghanistan and north-eastern Iran. The area of the whole basin amounts to about 2 million km^2. Special attention in this chapter is paid to the so-called Priaralye (the Aral area), a territory that lies in immediate proximity to the Aral Sea shores and includes the Amu Darya and Syr Darya deltas.

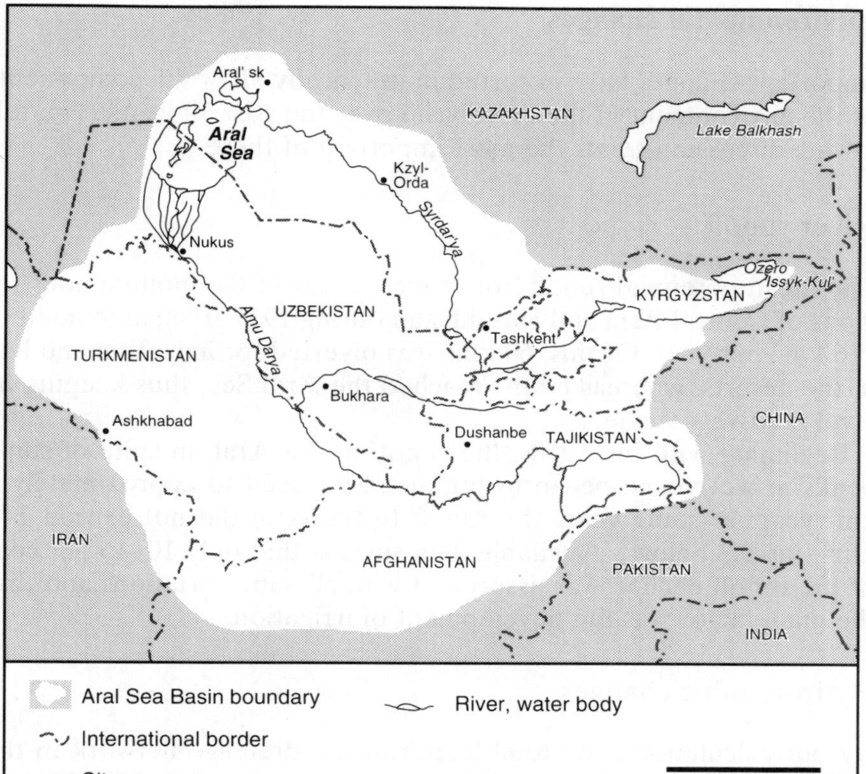

Fig. 3.1 **The Aral Sea basin**

Landscapes of arid and semi-arid regions are known to be very sensitive to global climatic changes and to tectonic events and other physical processes. The Aral region is one of the centres of origin of civilizations and farming, and primitive forms of artificial irrigation have existed here for more than 2,000 years.

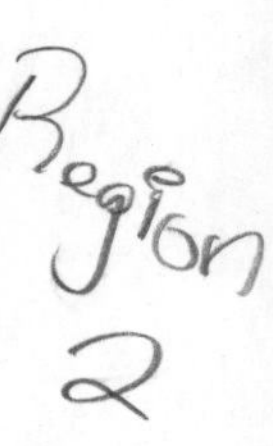

Natural variations and human activity led to significant ecological changes in the Aral basin during historical time. The sea itself often rose and fell considerably. During the Quaternary period, variations in the level of the Aral Sea evidently reached 36 metres. But in spite of such important earlier variations in the level of the sea, fluctuations during the first half of the twentieth century did not exceed 1 metre, and the ecological situation was quite stable up to the end of the 1950s. Substantial variations have taken place during the last 30 years, however, and this chapter focuses on this time-period.

Environmental changes

Important changes have occurred in practically all of the components of the environment in the Aral basin over the past 30 years. The following discussion treats the most important of these.

River runoff

The mean perennial runoff from source areas in the mountainous regions of Central Asia and Kazakhstan during 1911–1960 amounted to 116 km^3 per year. Of this, 60 km^3 was diverted for irrigation and lost in the deserts, whereas 6 km^3 reached the Aral Sea, thus keeping its level relatively stable.

Beginning with the 1960s, the runoff to the Aral, in spite of some peaks in wet years, began to fall and decreased to approximately 4 km^3/year. In some years the runoff to the Aral did not exceed 1–2 km^3 (fig. 3.2 below). Available data suggest that only 10–15 per cent of the runoff decline was associated with climatic variations and that the main factor was the development of irrigation.

Hydrographic changes

By our calculations, the total length of the drainage network in the arid zone of the former USSR stretches to 150,000–200,000 km, which is 10–15 times longer than the main rivers in this region. As a result of the discharge of drainage waters to the desert, vast new water basins without outflow have been formed, of which the Sarykamysh and Arnasai lakes are the largest.

The Sarykamysh lake in the south-eastern portion of the Usturt plateaux was formed as a result of discharging the drainage runoff from the left-bank irrigated massifs to the lower reaches of the Amu Darya river. These discharges started early in the 1960s. Currently, the lake covers an area of about 3,000 km^2 and has a volume of 26 km^3. Mineralization of the lake waters is continuously increasing: from 3–4 grams/litre (g/l) in the early 1960s to 12–13 g/l in 1987 (Shaporenko 1987). Annual increases in mineralization amount to 0.5–0.6 g/l.

The Arnasai lake (and, more precisely, the Arnasai lacustrine system) was formed on the site of the Aidar solonchak northward of the Nuratau ridge as a result of the diversion of discharge waters from irrigated massifs on the left bank of the middle reaches of the Syr

Table 3.1 **Changes in the number and area of natural lakes in the Amu Darya and Syr Darya deltas, 1936–1980**

Region	Period	No. of lakes	Area of lakes (km^2)
Amu Darya delta	1936	346	2,330
	1950–1960	490	840
	1972		630
	1980		76.3 (excluding Sudochye lake)
Syr Darya delta	1936	558	1,490
	1950–1960	2,080	833
	1967		789
	1976		400

Sources: Nikitin (1977) and Chebanov (1989).

Darya river. The area of this water basin has varied from 2,330 km^2 to 1,750 km^2, the water volume from 20 km^3 to 12.5 km^3, and mineralization in different parts of the lacustrine system from 4 g/l to 13 g/l (Nikitin and Lesnik 1982). As a result of a discharge of drainage waters into Karakum, swamps emerged that cover an area of over 200,000 (and perhaps 250,000) ha (Rozanov 1986).

Reduction in runoff has led to changes in the number and area of lakes in the Amu Darya and Syr Darya deltas. The area of natural lakes has continuously shrunk while the number of lakes during the first period of water-basin drying increased owing to the fragmentation of large lakes (table 3.1).

Variations in the Aral Sea

Prior to the 1960s, the Aral Sea area amounted to 68,300 km^2, comprising a water surface area of 66,100 km^2 and islands of 2,200 km^2. The volume of the sea water amounted to 1,066 km^3 (Nikolayeva 1969). The maximum sea depth was 69 m, but depths of less than 30 m were common over much of the sea. The sea level, meanwhile, fluctuated in the 52–53 m range.

Mineralization of the Aral waters during the past 100 years of instrumental observations has varied within a range of 10–12 g/l, and constant salinity has been sustained owing to two main processes – sedimentation of poorly soluble components owing to water evaporation and salt accumulation in narrow bays often connected only peri-

Table 3.2 **Water budgets of the Aral Sea prior to the 1960s (km^3/year)**

Inflow		Outflow	
River runoff	56	Evaporation	58–65
Groundwater runoff	0.7–0.3	Filtration to the banks and diversion to the lagoons	1–2
Atmospheric precipitation	5–8		

odically with the Aral Sea (especially in the south-eastern part of the sea) and in depressions without outflow near the seashore.

River runoff and evaporation were key factors in the water budget (table 3.2). Two rivers – the Amu Darya and Syr Darya – maintain river runoff. Some 20 fish species (including commercial ones), 266 species of invertebrates, and 94 species of superior and inferior plants existed in the sea.

With decreased river inflow beginning about the early 1960s, the water budget of the sea changed. The sea area decreased to 34,800 km^2 and the volume to 304 km^3 by 1990. Over the same period, the level of the sea fell to 37.8 m, a drop of more than 15 m from the preceding period (fig. 3.2). A significant part (about 33,000 km^2) of the sea floor dried up, the configuration of the shoreline changed, and water mineralization increased to 33 g/l. As water mineralization increased, the spawning sites of fish disappeared and a deterioration in the forage reserve led to a decline in fish, with only five species remaining. Nearly all limnoplankton and numerous haloplankton became extinct (Aladin and Khlebovich 1989; Williams and Aladin 1991).

Climate change

Owing to the recession of the sea, the climate in the Aral area has changed (Molosnova, Subbotina, and Chanysheva 1987). Summer and winter air temperatures at stations near the shore increased by 1.5–2.5°C, whereas diurnal temperatures increased by 0.5–3.3°C. At coastal stations the mean annual relative air humidity decreased by 2–3 per cent, reaching 9 per cent in spring and summer. Recurrence of drought days increased by 300 per cent. Spring now comes 7 days later and autumn 12–13 days later (the date on which the mean diurnal temperature passes the zero value) than previously. The last spring frosts shifted to later dates and the first autumn ones occurred some 10–12

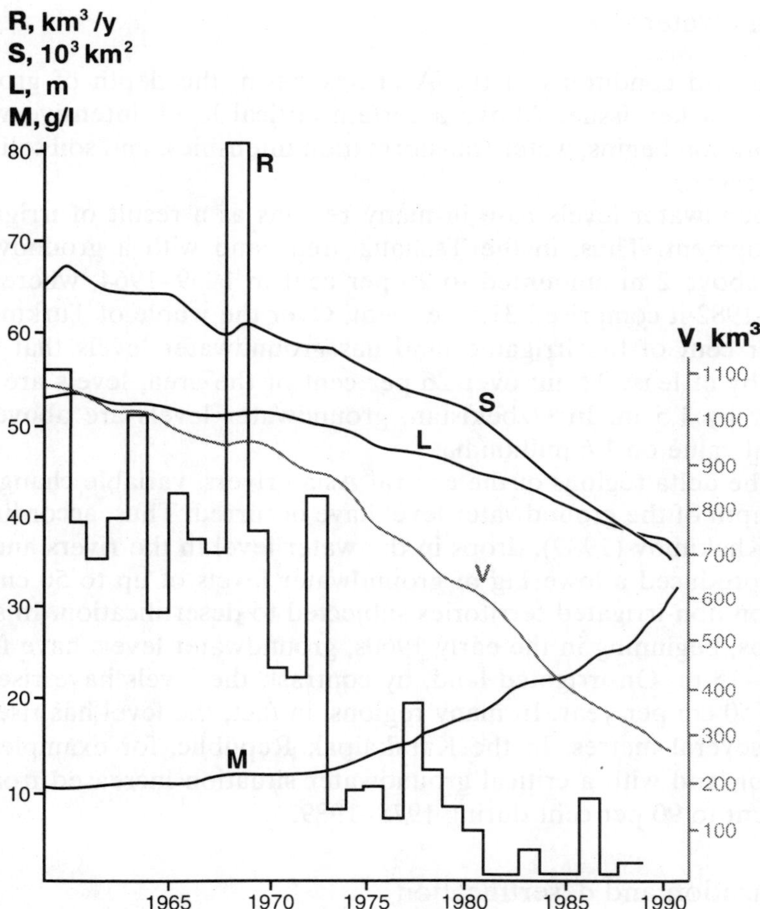

Fig. 3.2 **Changes in river water inflow to the Aral Sea, 1960–1990 (Key: R = change in river water inflow [km^3 per year]; S = sea area ['000 km^2]; L = sea level [m]; V = sea volume [km^3]; M = mineralization of sea waters [g/l])**

days earlier. The annual cycle of precipitation also changed. In 1959 the maximum precipitation fell during February–March and the minimum during September, whereas in 1970–1979 the maximum was observed in April and the minimum in July. A three-fold increase in reflected solar radiation in the Aral area due to a sevenfold rise in the albedo of the area previously occupied by the Aral Sea has contributed to an increase in the continentality of the climate (Kondratyev, Grigoryev, and Zhvalev 1986).

Groundwater

In the arid conditions of the Aral Sea basin, the depth of groundwater is a key issue. Above a certain critical level, intensive water evaporation begins, water transformation intensifies, and soil salinization occurs.

Groundwater levels rose in many regions as a result of irrigation development. Thus, in the Tashauz area, land with a groundwater level above 2 m amounted to 20 per cent in 1959–1964, whereas in 1978–1982 it comprised 31.5 per cent. Over the whole of Turkmenia, 87 per cent of the irrigated land has groundwater levels that have risen by at least 2.5 m; over 26 per cent of the area, levels are now higher by 1.5 m. In Uzbekistan, groundwater levels are above the critical value on 1.6 million ha.

In the delta regions of the central Asian rivers, variable changes in the depth of the groundwater level have occurred. Thus, according to F. I. Khakimov (1989), drops in the water level in the rivers and sea have produced a lowering of groundwater levels of up to 50 cm per year on non-irrigated territories subjected to desertification. In some regions, beginning in the early 1960s, groundwater levels have fallen by 10–15 m. On irrigated land, by contrast, the levels have risen by up to 50 cm per year. In many regions, in fact, the level has risen by fully several metres. In the Karakalpak Republic, for example, the area of land with a critical groundwater situation increased from 72 per cent to 90 per cent during 1975–1989.

Salinization and desertification

Rises in the groundwater level and water evaporation cause intensive soil salinization. Thus, in the newly irrigated areas of the Murghab oasis of Turkmenistan, the area of slightly salinized and unsalinized land decreased from 50 per cent to 25 per cent over eight years, and that of salinized land grew from 50 per cent to 75 per cent. In the Tedzhen oasis, 48,000 out of 70,000 ha of irrigated land are salinized. And in Turkmenia, 86.7 per cent of all irrigated land is salinized. In Uzbekistan, moderately and severely salinized soils constitute 60 per cent of all irrigated land. In some regions, the areas of salinized land are even larger; in Central Feigana, for example, they amount to 83.9 per cent, including 7.1 per cent of severely salinized and 31.3 per cent of moderately salinized irrigated lands (Popov 1988). In the Karakalpak Republic, 377,000 ha out of the

485,000 ha of irrigated land are salinized. A similar situation prevails in other republics of the Aral basin: 35 per cent of irrigated land is salinized in Tadzhikistan, 40 per cent in Kirghizia, and 60–70 per cent in Kazakhstan (Khakimov 1989).

As a result of decreases in river runoff and falling river water levels, and also owing to the fall in the Aral Sea level, the Syr Darya and Amu Darya river-beds have begun to function as drains, leading to even more rapid desertification of the coastal band.

According to F. I. Khakimov (1989), alluvial-meadow and swamp-meadow soils are shifting into meadow-takyr and meadow-deserts. Meanwhile, the humus content of soils has decreased, and sodium and magnesium levels in the soil have risen. V. A. Popov (1988) has predicted that, if the desertification trend continues, the area of hydromorphic geosystems in the southern Aral area will decrease by 2,000 ha, but the area of the xeromorphic geosystems will more than double. The area of halomorphic geosystems, which increased almost sixfold from 1965 to 1985, will likely remain at the current level.

Biota

In the cultivation and inundation of land a number of animal species have perished. The total number of animals is decreasing, but the population density is increasing on the unploughed sites on the banks of canals. Thus, L. A. Persianova, Yadgarov, and Saraeva (1986) found that on irrigated land in the Dzhizak area 9 out of 27 species had disappeared and 4 more were endangered. Of 21 reptile species, 2 will probably perish completely.

As a result of the Syr Darya delta drainage, flocks of waterfowl have been displaced during migration from the lower reaches of the Syr Darya river to the lakes of Turgai. Accumulations of white and Dalmatian pelicans have been observed beyond the northern boundary of the former Aral Sea (Novikova and Zaletayev 1985). Accumulations of migrating waterfowl have also appeared both in water reservoirs and in filtrational lakes formed in Central Asia (Zaletayev 1976). Meanwhile, newly formed wastewater basins have created conditions for large hibernation sites for waterfowl in a number of regions. Overall, the diversity of mammals inhabiting the Aral area has decreased from 70 to 30 species and the number of bird species from 319 to 168. The disappearance of nesting sites for many bird species has led to the disappearance of 38 of the 173 bird species nesting in the lower reaches of the Syr Darya.

Tugai communities in the deltas are also endangered. These tugais were extremely rich florally since they had 576 superior plants, including 29 endemic to Central Asia. Currently, owing to desertification, 54 species are on the verge of extinction (Novikova 1985; Sagitov, personal communication). Reed thickets, meanwhile, have perished in the Karakalpak Republic in the Amu Darya delta, and the relict tugai forests are also becoming extinct.

Pollution

Data on environmental pollution at the beginning of the study period are practically absent; therefore, only data on current pollution levels can be provided.

Soil pollution in the Aral region is observed throughout the agricultural zones. In almost all regions the DDT content in soils is about 2–7 times above the maximum permissible concentration (MPC) and in some regions it is 46 times higher (Izrael and Rovinski 1990). Territories with polluted soils amount to about 30–66 per cent of the surveyed areas. These soil pollutants end up in water sources. Organochlorine pesticides are recorded along the entire length of the Amu Darya and Syr Darya, and at some sampling stations their content exceeds MPC values. A specific peculiarity of the Aral basin is the increase in river-water mineralization owing to the discharge of drainage waters from irrigated massifs.

Mineralization of drainage runoff from irrigated massifs reaches 20 g/l, usually amounting to 2–8 g/l. The value of salt removal from irrigated massifs with drainage runoff reaches 60–70 t/ha. A significant part of the drainage runoff is discharged to rivers, leading to increased river-water mineralization. Thus, Syr Darya water mineralization increased in the lower reaches from 0.8 g/l in 1960 to 1.8 g/l in 1985 (fig. 3.3). A similar process is observed in the Amu Darya, where river-water mineralization has reached 1.7 g/l.

As a result of extensive irrigation, the ion content of river runoff has changed. Salt removal from the irrigated massifs has exceeded that from land in areas of river runoff formation (table 3.3). In spite of the reduction in the volume of river runoff, the inflow of salts to large lakes has increased. The Caspian Sea has experienced similar impacts. New lakes of ion surface runoff have also appeared, the largest of which are the Arsanai lake in the Syr Darya basin and the Sarykamysh lake in the Amu Darya basin.

Salt flow to land has also increased, owing to water filtration, the

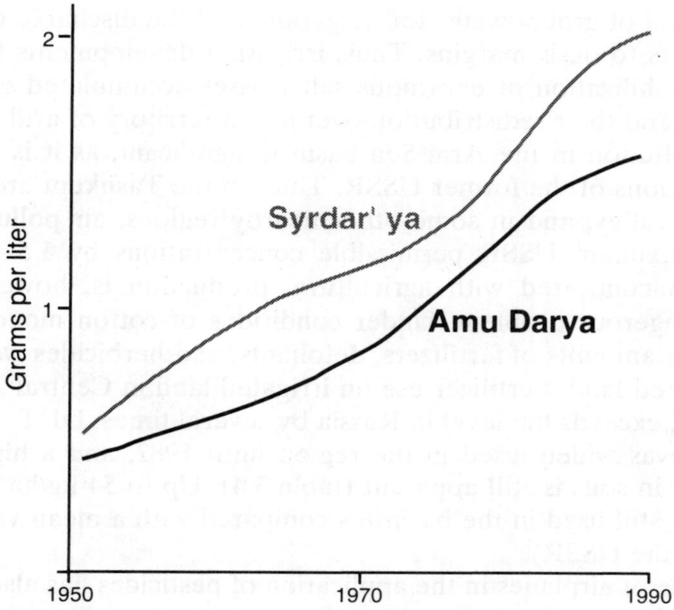

Fig. 3.3 **River water mineralization in the Syr Darya, 1950–1990**

Table 3.3 **Ionic surface runoff in the Aral region (millions of tons per year)**

Process	Ionic runoff[a]: Prior to the last stage of irrigation development	At the present stage
Inflow from outside the region	13	13
Removal from land in the areas of runoff formation	41	38
Removal from irrigated land	–	67
Total runoff	54	118
Supply to land and to small salt lakes	25	76–66
Runoff to Sarykamysh and Arnasai salt-receiving lakes	–	32
Runoff to the Aral Sea	29	10–20

a. Data on ionic runoff are not precise, since continuous transformation of ionic runoff is still proceeding.

withdrawal of groundwater for irrigation, and the discharge of drainage waters to oasis margins. Thus, irrigation developments have led to the mobilization of enormous salt masses accumulated earlier in the land and their redistribution over a vast territory of arid areas.

Air pollution in the Aral Sea basin is significant, as it is in many other regions of the former USSR. Thus, in the Tashkent area in the Fergana valley, and in some other nearby regions, air pollution exceeds maximum USSR permissible concentrations by 1.5–6 times. Pollution connected with agricultural production is, however, the most dangerous problem. Under conditions of cotton monoculture, extensive amounts of fertilizers, defoliants, and herbicides were used on irrigated land. Fertilizer use on irrigated land in Central Asia, for example, exceeds the level in Russia by several times. DDT, now forbidden, was widely used in the region until 1982, and a high DDT presence in soils is still apparent (table 3.4). Up to 54 kg/ha of pesticides are still used in the basin (as compared with a mean value of 3 kg/ha in the USSR).

The use of airplanes in the application of pesticides has also caused air pollution and has led to direct human exposures. Pesticides have also entered the food chain through fodder and drinking water. Up to 13 per cent of water samples from open reservoirs and 37 per cent of food products have contained pesticides.

Human driving forces

A number of human factors have interacted to create the widespread environmental changes described above.

Population

First, population changes are clearly important. Between 1950 and 1988, the population of the Aral Sea basin grew dramatically – from 13.8 to 33.2 million people, comprising increases from 8.1 to 19.9 million in Uzbekistan, 1.0 to 2.2 million in Kirghizstan, 2.0 to 5.1 million in Tadzhikistan, 1.5 to 3.5 million in Turkmenistan, and 1.2 to 2.4 million in Kazakhstan (all within the sea-basin limits).

In 1990, the population of the Aral Sea basin numbered 34 million. Very high natural population increases typify this region. This was true throughout the period 1950–1989. Mean annual rates of population increase in the late 1980s amounted to 2.85 per cent in Uzbeki-

Table 3.4 **Average content, expressed as fractions of maximum permissible concentration (MPC), of DDT and hexachlorocyclohexane (HCCH)***

Republic area	DDT (MPC = 0.1)[a]	HCCH (MPC = 0.1)[a]
Uzbekistan	3.70/3.55	0.18/0.14
Andizhan	4.11/4.83	0/0
Bukhara	3.20/2.09	0.17/0.07
Karakalpakia	3.18/1.44	0.47/0.10
Kashka Darya	8.37/9.26	0.39/0.20
Namangan	2.13/2.08	0.28/0.04
Samarkand	2.74/3.33	0.25/0.22
Sukhan Darya	5.56/5.49	0.25/0.22
Tashkent	2.14/1.61	0.11/0.08
Fergana	3.88/3.60	0.07/0.04
Khorezm	7.72/4.82	0.22/0.17
Tadzhikistan	8.76/8.85	0.24/0.26
Gorno-Badakhshan autonomous area	1.28/1.64	0.03/0.43
Kulyab	6.01/6.26	0.32/0.18
Leninabad	20.28/16.84	0.18/0.45
Garm	1.99/1.65	0.17/0
Buissar	1.27/2.84	0.17/0.17
Turkmenistan	1.28/–	0.30/–
Ashkhabad	0.63/–	0.48/–

Table 3.4 (*continued*)

Republic area	DDT (MPC = 0.1)[a]	HCCH (MPC = 0.1)[a]
Mariyskaya	0.46 / –	0.15 / –
Tashauz	5.40 / –	0.38 / –
Kazakhstan (Chimkent and Kzyl Orda)	0.10 / 0.08	0.07 / 0.03

Source: Unpublished data provided by Republican Agricultural Services, 1988.

a. Numerator refers to the spring levels; the denominator to autumn levels. MPC expressed as mg/kg.

stan, 2.60 per cent in Kirghizstan, 3.2 per cent in Tadzhikistan, 2.65 per cent in Turkmenistan, and 1.06 per cent in southern Kazakhstan (as compared with 0.95 per cent in the USSR as a whole).

Population growth is connected not with immigration but with natural increase, which amounted to 18.1 per cent in the Kazakhstan part of the basin, less than 5.5 per cent in Kirghizstan, less than 8.5 per cent in Turkmenistan, 30.8 per cent in Uzbekistan, and 35.2 per cent in Tadzhikistan (as compared with 6.8 per cent in Russia). The inhabitants of the Aral Sea basin have the largest families – ranging from 5.51 members for Kazakhs to 6.48 for Tadzhiks in the former USSR (where the mean figure in 1990 was 3.51).

Children and young people occupy a significant place in the age structure owing to the high natural increase of population. Children and teenagers up to 15 years of age comprise 42.5 per cent of the population in the Aral region (as compared with 26.8 per cent in the former USSR). Therefore, there are fewer people of working age here than in the USSR (49.2 per cent against 56.7 per cent). Thus more than half of the population is outside the age-limits of an able-bodied population. This circumstance aggravates the complex social situation in the region.

This age structure of the population also has a partial bearing on some of the medical problems. Because schoolchildren were extensively involved in cotton raising, environmental risks associated with the use of herbicides and defoliants affected children more than might ordinarily be expected.

Most of those professing religious belief are adherents of Islam, chiefly of Aryan and (to a lesser extent) of Shiite persuasion. Believ-

Table 3.5 **Use of the water resources of the Aral Sea basin at the level of the mid-1980s (km³/year)**

Economic sector	Water intake	Water diversion	Water consumption
Municipal economy	3.1	1.6	1.5
Industry and power generation	8.3	6.4	1.9
Fisheries	2.0	1.0	1.0
Agricultural water supply	0.86	no data	no data
Irrigated farming	114.0	26–39	75–88
Total	127	35–49	79–94

ers among the Pamir belong mainly to the Shiite group of Ismailites. In addition, other religions exist within the region. The multinational and multireligious character of the Aral Sea basin population needs to be taken into account when considering impacts and potential solutions.

Over the same period, both industrial and agricultural production also increased. Variations in river runoff and environmental pollution caused the principal environmental changes in the Aral region. Though water consumption in industry and municipal economies increased during this period, water consumption in these branches of the economy never exceeded 4–5 km³ per year (table 3.5). Clearly, the development of agriculture and, more specifically, the growth of irrigation have been the main engines of environmental change.

Irrigation

The area of irrigated land has increased since the early 1960s by 1.5 times in Uzbekistan and Tadzhikistan, 1.7 times in Kazakhstan, and 2.4 times in Turkmenistan. Significant capital investment in agriculture has accompanied this growth in irrigation. Thus, the funds to support agricultural production have increased 5–7 times, power generation capacities in agriculture have grown by up to 6 times, the number of tractors by 3.2 times, and tractor engine power by 7.6 times. Meanwhile, use of chemical fertilizers has grown two- to sixfold (table 3.6). Particularly noteworthy is the fact that fertilizer consumption per hectare is 2–3 times higher in the Central Asian republics than in the Russian republics. Thus, the growth of irrigation in the Aral Sea basin has been accompanied by enormous invest-

Table 3.6 **Use of chemical fertilizers in the Aral Sea basin, 1960–1985 (calculated for 100% of nutrients; kg/ha)**

Republic	1960	1965	1970	1975	1980	1985
Russia	6.7	19.8	32.9	58.5	67.5	96.0
Uzbekistan	111.1	146.9	197.2	238.3	263.1	285.6
Tadzhikistan	78.2	120.2	165.0	220.3	225.3	249.0
Turkmenistan	100.2	186.7	205.3	241.3	248.0	251.0

Table 3.7 **Capital investment in agriculture in Uzbekistan, 1956–1987 (million roubles)**

Period	For agriculture as a whole (excluding forestry and timber)	Including reclamation construction
1956–1960	1,729	459[a]
1961–1965	3,120	1,091[a]
1966–1970	5,441	2,042[a]
1971–1975	9,226	5,428
1976–1980	12,513	7,227
1981–1985	14,877	7,726
1986	2,738	1,420
1987	2,767	1,393

Source: Uzbekistan (1988).

a. For construction of the water economy only.

ments in agricultural production (table 3.7). At the same time, one should note that the basic capital investments were made almost solely for water-reclamation projects.

Whereas irrigation is generally necessary in arid regions, the design, construction, and exploitation of irrigation systems in the Aral Sea basin have involved far-reaching and serious drawbacks. The extensive development of irrigation paid attention primarily not to increasing productive output on existing land but to expanding irrigated areas. Frequent cultivation of severely salinized lands required substantial reclamation efforts but yielded only very modest harvests. All too often, unprepared land was used for irrigation. At the same time, the quality of many irrigation systems was very poor. Irrigation canals and drainage collectors, for example, were often constructed without filtration linings. Thus, the efficiency of irrigation systems is extremely low; some 30–45 per cent of all water is estimated to be lost.

Irrigation techniques are also extremely primitive. Thus, in Uzbekistan, 89.5 per cent of the irrigated area in 1977 was watered by means of furrows and only 1.5 per cent by means of sprinklers (USSR 1984). In the Tashauz area of Turkmenistan, 95 per cent of land was irrigated manually along furrows in 1984 (Batyrov et al. 1984). Systems of continuous control of soil and air humidity and plants are virtually non-existent.

Increased water saving could be achieved by instituting changes in rice cultivation. Irrigation levels for rice in the Aral region amount to 26,000–34,000 m^3/ha (USSR 1984), and water intake has reached at least 80,000 m^3/ha in the lower reaches of the Syr Darya (Voropayev, Ismaiylov, and Fedorov 1984). A primary reason for this large discharge of water is the irrational choice of rice cultivation, with its numerous embayments and operational losses of water.

Water demands for irrigation currently take little or no account of soil attributes. Water budget and water thermobudget methods take into account only the thermal–physical properties of soil (USSR 1984). The possibility of short-term droughts, mineralization, and the composition of irrigation waters have also not usually been considered. Indeed, irrigation practices were developed assuming maximum possible harvests (USSR 1984); this is often unreasonable both economically and ecologically.

Current water demand for cotton in the Aral region amounts to 7,500–12,500 m^3 per hectare. At the same time, farming data in the Karakalpak Republic suggest that optimal irrigation standards for cotton may be 3,500–4,400 m^3/ha (with yields of 2.5–3.0 tonnes/ha). One species cultivated requires 2,500–3,000 m^3/ha of water for the growing period, with a yield of 2.2 tonnes/ha. An irrationality attendant on water use is also apparent in the fact that the growth in water consumption in irrigated farming has greatly outstripped the increments to irrigated areas (fig. 3.4). Comparison of human-induced (anthropogenic) runoff expenditures with natural expenditures (evaporation and transpiration in river-beds, flood plains, and deltas) shows that the former are largely responsible for water deficits in the region (table 3.8).

As mentioned above, large amounts of fertilizers and herbicides have been used on irrigated land. In fact, fertilizer use in the Aral basin exceeds the average use in Russia by 10–15 times, and the amount of herbicides, defoliants, and other pesticides applied reaches 54 kg/ha (whereas, in the former USSR, 3 kg/ha was the average). These fertilizers eventually reach the rivers through drainage

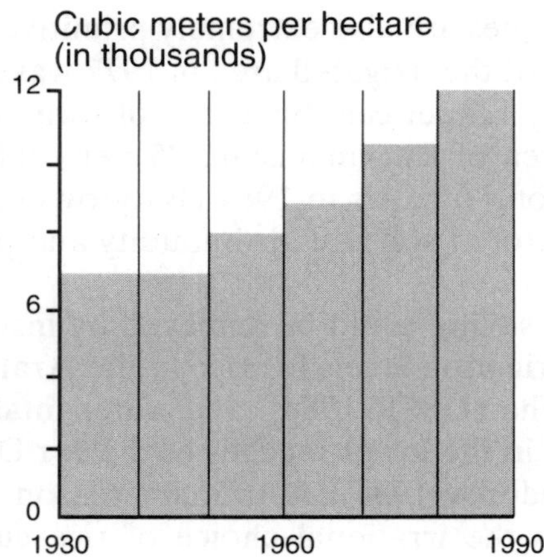

Fig. 3.4 **Growth of water consumption for irrigated farming in the Aral Sea basin, 1930–1990**

Table 3.8 **Changes in runoff, caused by natural and anthropogenic effects, from the main rivers of the Aral Sea basin, 1932–1985 (km³/year)**

	Syr Darya basin		Amu Darya basin	
Period	Natural	Anthropogenic	Natural	Anthropogenic
1932–1940	15.1	6.3–14.0	6.7	12.1–14.7
1941–1950	10.3	14.5–17.2	6.0	14.9–19.8
1951–1960	9.7	18.7–21.5	3.7	18.9–24.9
1961–1970	8.2	24.7–26.3	2.9	24.0–34.8
1971–1980	3.3	29.4–30.2	1.7	36.1–51.8
1981–1985	2.5	31.0–35.0	1.6	51.0–63.6

Source: Data provided by the State Hydrological Institute.

runoff, which is often used for the drinking-water supply. Many food products are also contaminated with pesticides, and their concentrations sometimes exceed the maximum permissible concentration for air.

The use of drainage runoff also reflects irrationality. In the first half of the 1980s, the drainage runoff (i.e. the runoff of drainage and discharge waters) amounted to 29–46 km^3 per year. It should be emphasized that the existing accounting system does not allow a precise determination of the volume of drainage runoff, part of which is discharged by relatively small drains to the desert and is not taken into account. Also, diversions in large main drains are not measured adequately. Part of the drainage waters, for example, is secretly pumped to irrigation canals. All figures for drainage runoff, therefore, need to be more precise. In recent years, drainage runoff has increased owing to the expansion of irrigation areas; it apparently now amounts to at least 45–50 km^3 per year, of which 25–26 km^3 is discharged into rivers, 10–12 km^3 to lakes, and 10–15 km^3 to the desert.

A solution to the drainage runoff problem is needed for several reasons. First, drainage runoff is one type of water resource that could contribute to reducing water deficits. Second, drainage waters in a desert often result in salinization of soils and groundwater, whereas discharges to rivers often produce increased mineralization and toxicity of river water.

Social and economic changes

Increases in morbidity

Deteriorating environmental quality as a result of irrigation development and the chemicalization of agriculture has contributed to increased sickness in the population. The overall illness trends are not encouraging. In Uzbekistan, for the period 1980–1987, for example, the number of hospitalized people increased from 21.8 to 26.3 per 100 people, including a change from 20.2 to 24.9 in the Karakalpak Republic.

The data on medical examinations reveal a growing number of cases of gall-bladder and gallstone disease, chronic gastritis, nephritis, and oesophageal cancer. According to V. Selyunin (1989), paratyphoid morbidity in the Karakalpak Republic is 23 times higher than the average in other republics of the USSR. Since the middle of the 1970s in some regions, the mortality rate has increased 15 times, cardiovascular morbidity 6 times, tuberculosis 6 times, gall-bladder and gallstone disease 5 times, and oesophageal cancer 7–10 times. Between 1984 and 1989 in the Kzyl Orda area on the lower reaches of the Syr Darya river, typhoid morbidity increased 20 times. Although a precise allocation of disease causation, including that attributable to ecological degradation, is not possible at this time, it is likely that child mortality rates reflect not only inadequate medical attention but environmental deterioration as well.

In certain regions of the Aral Sea area, and particularly in the Bozataus region of the Karakalpak Republic, infant mortality rates

Table 3.9 **Infant mortality, 1960–1987 (the number of children who died at age 1 or less per 1,000 of newborn)**

Country/republic	1960	1970	1980	1985	1986	1987
USSR	–	24.7	27.3	26.0	25.4	25.5
Russian Federation	–	23.0	22.1	20.7	19.3	–
Uzbekistan	–	31.0	47.0	45.3	46.2	–
Kazakhstan	–	25.9	32.7	30.1	29.0	–
Kirghizstan	–	45.4	43.3	41.9	38.2	–
Tadzhikistan	–	45.9	58.1	46.8	46.7	–
Turkmenistan	–	46.1	53.6	52.4	58.2	–
Bulgaria	45.1	27.3	20.2	15.4	14.6	–
Hungary	47.6	35.9	23.2	20.4	19.0	–
GDR	38.8	18.5	12.1	9.6	9.2	–
Cuba	–	38.7	19.6	16.5	13.6	–
Poland	54.8	33.4	21.3	18.4	17.3	–
Czechoslovakia	23.5	22.1	18.4	14.0	13.9	–

Source: Uzbekistan (1988).

exceed 110 per 1,000 newborn, a rate higher than that of Thailand (88), Mexico (82), Costa Rica (78), Jordan (75), Colombia (74), Syria (73), and many other countries (*Novy Mir* 1989). At the 1989 seminar "Problems of the Aral Sea and Aral Area," it was noted that 60 per cent of the children examined in Nukus and 64 per cent in Karakalpak Republic showed some health problems. In Uzbekistan, 280,000 cases of infectious hepatitis were recorded in 1987 (*Novy Mir* 1989). The Central Asian republics of Kazakhstan and Kirghizia have the highest level of infant mortality observed in the USSR. In most of these republics an absolute growth in the infant death rate was apparent between 1970 and 1985 (table 3.9). In all the other republics (with the exception of Moldavia), infant mortality rates declined during this same period. One might assume that an increased level of infant mortality is connected with insufficient medical examination of mothers and children and worsening medical service, but analyses do not confirm this assumption.

The inadequate development of the water supply and sewerage systems has greatly aggravated ecological criticality in the Aral Sea basin. Thus the centralized water supply in the lower reaches of the Syr Darya in the Kzyl Orda area of Kazakhstan provides water for only 65 per cent of the population, and in Karakalpakia for only 33 per cent. Sampling of water sources in the Aral Sea basin reveals that the quality of piped water does not meet state bacterial standards

Table 3.10 **Number of hospital beds for pregnant women and those in childbirth, 1960–1987 (per 1,000 women)**

Republic	1960	1970	1980	1987
Russian Federation	1.73	1.56	1.53	1.53
Uzbekistan	2.06	2.21	2.45	2.53
Tadzhikistan	1.38	1.97	2.08	2.39
Turkmenistan	2.16	2.55	2.71	2.70

Source: Uzbekistan (1988).

Table 3.11 **Number of births per year per bed in hospitals for pregnant women and those in childbirth, 1965–1986**

Republic	1965	1970	1986
Russian Federation	16.9	17.2	21.0
Uzbekistan	32.8	29.6	29.5
Tadzhikistan	43.7	34.8	34.8
Turkmenistan	37.4	27.1	27.0

in 25–47 per cent of cases. About 90 per cent of the rural population of the Aral Sea basin obtain their spring and summer water from the irrigation network. Only the largest cities of the basin have sewage systems, and these cover only an insignificant part of the territory in these cities.

The supply of hospital beds for pregnant women and those in childbirth in the Central Asian republics is higher than that in Russia, and this supply has been increasing in comparison with Russia (table 3.10). The pressure represented by number of births per bed in maternity homes, though higher than in Russia, abated during 1965 to 1986 (table 3.11). Meanwhile, the number of children's clinics grew 2.6 times in Turkmenia between 1970 and 1986, 2.9 times in Tadzhikistan, and 3.5 times in Uzbekistan.

Changes in agricultural production

Environmental deterioration negatively affects agricultural production, including that on irrigated land, much of which becomes salinized. Irrigation experience over many years suggests that even slight soil salinization decreases cotton yields by 10–15 per cent, moderate salinization by 30–40 per cent, and severe salinization by 50–60 per cent (Kurbanov 1988). B. G. Rozanov (1984) shows that increases of up to 1 per cent in the salt content of the ploughed-up layer of irrigated soil decreases crop production by one-third. When the salt content reaches 2–3 per cent, the crop is completely damaged. Estimates suggest that agricultural production is 30 per cent lower in Uzbekistan, 18 per cent lower in Tadzhikistan, and 20 per cent lower in Kirghizia as a result of soil salinization (Khakimov 1989).

Reductions in agricultural production are also connected with desertification, which arises in delta regions with changes in runoff associated with irrigation development. Climatic changes in the Aral area have also affected agricultural output. Environmental deterioration has led to direct losses. The productivity of irrigated lands in the Bostanlyk region in the middle part of the Syr Darya basin, for example, first increased during 1966–1988, from 536 to 1,126 roubles/ha, but later decreased to 951 roubles/ha. Meanwhile, governmental expenditures grew from 380 to 720 roubles/ha. Indeed, increases in costs exceeded production gains (Voropayev, Ismaiylov, and Fedorov 1984). In the Gyaur region of Turkmenia, production from a hectare of irrigated land declined from 2,000–2,500 roubles to 1,500 roubles (and less) between 1978 and 1984 (Kuleshov 1985). In the Karakalpak Republic, labour productivity in agriculture decreased by 11 per cent, while the gross product per hectare of irrigated fields plummeted between 1970 and 1985. This trend is typical of many regions in the Aral Sea area.

Increases in mineralization and changes in the composition of irrigation water affect both the amount and quality of the product. Thus, increases in the sulphate-ion content in irrigation waters affect the composition of protein in the grain. As a result, the gross production of raw cotton in the Central Asian republics has not (with the exception of Tadzhikistan) grown in recent years and in most republics has even decreased since 1980 (fig. 3.5) in spite of an expansion of irrigation. Cotton production initially increased in Turkmenia but by 1986 had declined to 1950 levels.

Cotton quality has also deteriorated. From the late 1950s to the early 1980s the specific gravity of the first and second qualities of raw cotton decreased from 70 per cent to 40 per cent in the total volume of production (Safayev 1982, 77). Decreases in yields are typical of other crops that are cultivated on irrigated land in the Aral Sea area (see, for example, fig. 3.6). Economic indices of agricultural production also reveal significant decreases (table 3.12).

In the Syr Darya and Amu Darya deltas, desertification began as a

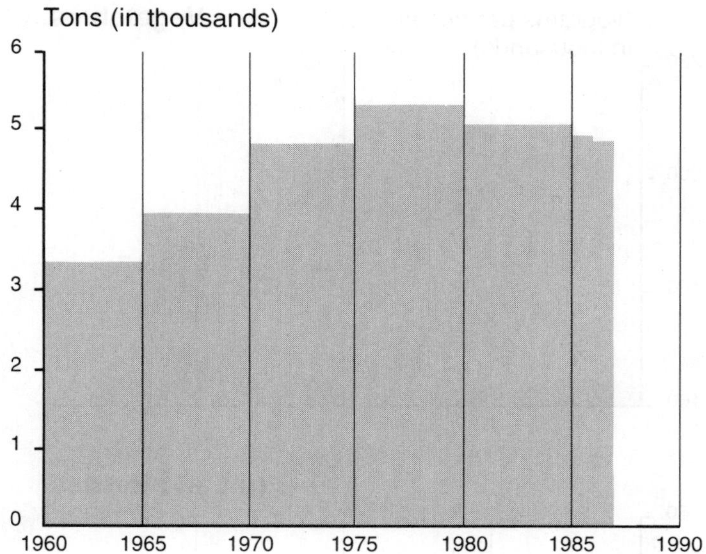

Fig. 3.5 **Cotton production in Uzbekistan, 1960–1987 (Source: Uzbekistan, 1988, and author's own estimates)**

result of decreases in runoff. Reed thickets became dry in shallow lakes, and more than 1 million hectares of flood plains dried up, including 280,000 ha in the lower reaches of the Amu Darya and 20,000 ha in the lower reaches of the Syr Darya river. The crop capacity of reed communities decreased from 3–4 tonnes/ha to 0.007–0.13 tonnes/ha (Novikova 1985). In the lower reaches of the Syr Darya, 114,000 ha of alluvial-meadow soils were desertified by 1978 and became solonchaks, 552,000 ha of swamp and meadow-swamp soils dried up, 31,000 ha were desertified, and 55,000 ha were transformed into solonchaks. Thus, about 752,000 ha in total were withdrawn from agricultural rotation (Gerasimov et al. 1983), while the productivity of pastures and hay areas shrank from 3–4 to 1.3–1.5 t/ha.

Total fodder reserves, meanwhile, declined by 1,200 tons and the productivity of cereal-forb and forb meadows decreased threefold. Reserves of medicinal plants also decreased, including licorice and sweet root (Novikova 1985). Muskrat production has largely disappeared in the Aral area: from 70,000–230,000 skins in 1950–1960, to 9,000 in 1968, and to 72 in 1978.

As a result of growing airborne salt transport, salt sedimentation on plants, including mulberry, has occurred. This may explain the reduc-

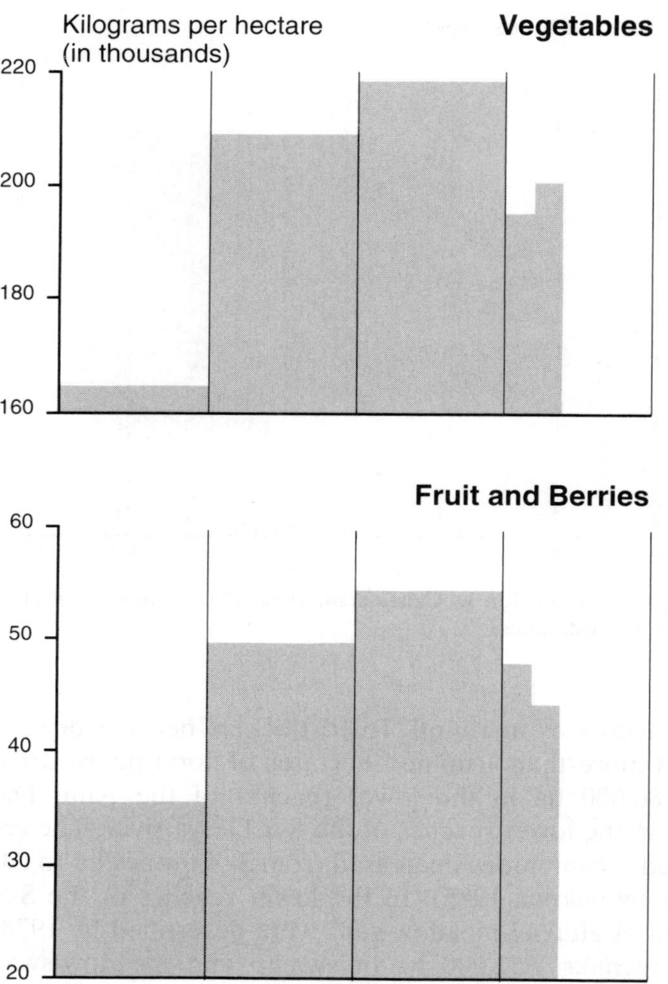

Fig. 3.6 **Vegetable and fruit/berry production in Uzbekistan, 1970–1987 (Source: Uzbekistan, 1988, and author's own estimates)**

tion in purchases of mulberry cocoons in the Karakalpak Republic. In 1981–1985, 1,005 cocoons were purchased annually; by 1985–1987 the figure had dropped to 915–941 (Uzbekistan 1988).

Reduced pasture lands and declining pasture productivity have negatively affected the number of sheep and goats and, correspondingly, the production of wool and astrakhan (tables 3.13 and 3.14).

Fisheries, meanwhile, have ceased to exist in the Aral area. Formerly about 40,000–60,000 tons of fish per year were taken. In the

Table 3.12 **Change in agricultural prices, 1965–1986 (roubles per ton)**

	Raw cotton			Vegetables		
Republic	1965	1975	1986	1965	1975	1986
Kazakhstan	309	352	480	115	143	185
Kirghizstan	199	432	651	97	108	152
Uzbekistan	288	447	550	83	98	130
Tadzhikistan	275	453	624	56	109	127
Turkmenistan	381	483	650	120	166	180

Source: Uzbekistan (1988).

Table 3.13 **Number of sheep and goats in Uzbekistan, 1971–1988 (for all categories of farms; '000 head)**

Type	Republic	1971	1981	1986	1987	1988
All sheep and goats	Uzbekistan	7,977.7	8,961.9	9,256.3	8,832.1	8,539.9
	Karakalpak	470.4	587.1	606.9	523.9	478.3
	Khorezmenia	257.1	100.2	163.9	151.6	138.4
Astrakhan sheep	Uzbekistan	5,072.1	5,312.9	5,245.5	4,914.1	4,751.2
	Karakalpak	288.7	467.2	463.9	378.5	342.8
	Khorezmenia	253.4	93.9	162.0	150.0	128.8

Source: Uzbekistan (1988).

Table 3.14 **Average annual wool and astrakhan production in Uzbekistan, 1971–1987**

Type	Republic	1971–1975	1976–1980	1981–1985	1986	1987
Wool production (tons)	Uzbekistan	16,085	19,047	24,097	23,541	24,347
	Karakalpak	1,215	1,488	2,172	1,827	1,730
	Khorezmenia	484	324	495	506	477
Astrakhan production ('000 skins)	Uzbekistan	2,274.1	2,329.6	2,308.8	1,640.6	1,380.5
	Karakalpak	111.0	166.8	163.4	132.5	125.2
	Khorezmenia	63.2	8.7	8.2	11.9	10.5

Source: Uzbekistan (1988).

Kazakhstan area of the Aral Sea and in the delta of Syr Darya, there were formerly 2 fishery bases, 1 Aral fish enterprise, 8 fish plants, and 19 collective fish farms. Earlier, 61,000 workers were involved in the production and processing of fish. Currently only 1,800 people still work in the fish industry (on both imported and lake fish). A similar picture prevails in the Karakalpak part of the Aral Sea basin, where the Muinak fish cannery continues to operate on imported ocean fish of low grade. Currently, fisheries operate only on the remaining lakes and deltas. Since the waters of these wastewater lakes are polluted, the quality of fish products is often unsatisfactory.

Finally, because of rising groundwater and salinization of soils, flooding of the foundations of buildings has occurred, accompanied by a rise of capillary water along the foundations and walls, salt sedimentation, and even the destruction of buildings. A number of cultural monuments are also threatened in Karakalpakia, Uzbekistan (Khiva), and Turkmenia.

Economic losses

Various estimates exist of economic losses in the Aral Sea basin connected with irrigation development and declines in sea levels. Researchers at the Institute of Water Problems, USSR Academy of Sciences (*Problems of the Aral Sea* 1973), project a decrease in annual gross income of 15–30 million roubles as a result of changes in the Aral Sea. The researchers conclude that comparison of these losses with irrigation effects shows the contradictions between using the Syr Darya and Amu Darya waters for irrigation and maintaining the inflow to the Aral Sea, thereby protecting economic uses of the sea. At 1980 levels, the annual losses in only the lower reaches of Amu Darya amounted to at least 92.6 million roubles (Gerasimov et al. 1983).

In our view, the total damage to nature and the regional economy should also include the cost of measures taken to mitigate the consequences of the Aral crisis. By current estimates, the cost of these measures is at least 37 billion roubles. This figure, and not 30–100 million roubles, should be recognized as the overall economic damage to the region. Real economic losses are likely to be even higher, because of lost agricultural production and losses connected with the deterioration in human health and associated medical compensation.

Reasons for the Aral ecological crisis

The geosystems of the Aral Sea region, which were in a state of dynamic equilibrium up to the 1960s, have become destabilized owing to the new, extensive development of irrigation and the intensive chemicalization of agriculture. Natural systems have been subjected to significant changes that have led, on the whole, to decreases in their biological productivity and to negative effects on environmental quality. As a result, population morbidity and child mortality have increased and agricultural production has declined. In some respects (e.g. gross output and crop areas), the economy has remained stable, but this stability has been achieved only through the continuing expansion of irrigated land. Thus, a peculiar "creeping stability" of the economic systems has occurred, supported by the continuing degradation or "draw-down" of the natural environment described in chapter 1. This stability is, thus, illusory.

One may distinguish the following reasons for the Aral Sea crisis:

1. *An inapt strategy of dislocating productive forces.* This is the most important cause of the long-term negative effects on the environment, economy, and social relations. The strategy of dislocating productive forces oriented to a water economy has led to extremely negative consequences and to the creation of an ecological crisis in the Aral Sea basin.
2. *Cultivation of low-productivity, marginal lands.* Extensive irrigation development has led to the cultivation of land whose productivity is difficult to sustain owing to high salinization, heavy soils, and unfavourable hydrogeological and geomorphological conditions. It is on such land that irrigation has demonstrated such negative ecological consequences, particularly secondary soil salinization and the formation of great salt drainage runoff. The Adyrs of the Fergana valley are an example of such land.
3. *An ill-conceived locational strategy for agricultural crops.* The most serious error has been the enormous expansion of fields with water-based crops, rice in particular. The introduction of monocultures (and in particular cotton) has also caused much damage, since monocultural agriculture requires heavy use of chemical fertilizers and herbicides.
4. *The poor quality of the design, construction, and operation of irrigation systems.* This is the primary reason for the negative ecological consequences.
5. *Approval of higher irrigation and water diversion standards.* In all republics of the Aral Sea region, and especially in Kazakhstan, a significant over-discharge of water for irrigation has occurred.
6. *Insufficient scientific substantiation of the irrigation standards.* Existing standards fail to take into account the peculiarities of soils and agricultural crops, often while aiming at maximum but not necessarily most productive uses.

7. *Lack of scientific assessment of alternative development strategies.* This has occurred for both the regional economy and its potential effects on the natural environment.
8. *Insufficient discussion of problems arising in the Aral Sea region.* A deficiency that is apparent among both scientists and the public. (Glazovsky 1990b)

Environmental deterioration, population change, and economic developments in the Aral Sea region have important spatial differentiation in their effects. Here we focus on only the very general features of this differentiation. The dynamics of nature and the economy in different parts of the Aral region show the ecological situation to be better in the upper reaches of the river basins of Central Asia than in the lower ones. Decreases in runoff, environmental pollution, and the degradation of natural ecosystems are most apparent in the Syr Darya and Amu Darya deltas. Social and economic indicators reveal a similar distribution. Infant mortality in Kirghizia and Tadzhikistan and in the upper parts of river basins of Central Asia is low, whereas in Uzbekistan and Turkmenia, and especially in the middle and upper parts of the river basins, it is much higher. Crop fields for cotton, vegetables, and cereals in Tadzhikistan, and to a lesser extent in Uzbekistan and Turkmenia, have developed in recent years. Judging from G. V. Voropayev's data (1984), specific expenditures on the use of irrigated land during 1966–1978 for the irrigation system increased in the middle reaches of the Syr Darya river by 47 per cent and in the lower reaches by 79–102 per cent. The cost of cotton production, meanwhile, has increased in this system by 1.3–1.7 times and in the lower reaches by 2–3 times.

It is evident that environmental management in the upper parts of the river basins greatly affects the state of the environment and human well-being in the lower parts of the basins. Thus, we can speak of the existence of a nature–social systems cascade, in which variations in the upper links of the system progressively affect changes in the lower links.

One of the serious causes of the Aral ecological crisis and many other problems of the former USSR was the organization of the production system. The main economic defects of this system were planning and the detailed regulation of all economic life through a system of ministries, and also the fact that payment for labour was not according to final results but according to various intermediate indices.

Up to 1985, the USSR had about 250 different ministries at the union level (i.e. ministries of the whole USSR), not including the numerous ministries in each of the 15 republics within the USSR. These ministries received from the state budget funds that were often not connected with each other in financial goals. A certain economic integrity, however, was ensured by various administrative mechanisms. Therefore, each ministry was motivated to get as much money as possible from the state budget and, at the same time, acted as a monopolist in its branch of economy. These ministries were unconcerned about the final results and quality of their work. Thus, the USSR Ministry of Reclamation and Water Management was primarily interested in expanding its construction activity (and not in maximizing agricultural production). It acted to secure the largest construction projects, such as large-scale development of irrigation works or the territorial redistribution of river runoff. The size of financing depended not on the assumed growth of agricultural production that would result from this irrigation, but on the planned scale of the reclamation work itself. In practice, this orientation led to the creation of gigantic projects, the economic and social effectiveness of which was not assessed. Strange as it may seem, the ministries advocating these large projects at different bureaucratic levels found support among the local authorities in the regions. The reason for this paradox was as follows. The budgets of individual regions and districts were often much lower than those of the ministries and their subdivisions. Therefore, local authorities often approved many billions of roubles in unneeded projects for their regions in the hope that some small sums of money would find their way to them and would be used for the development of the social sector – roads, hospitals, housing.

The fallacy of this economic approach is also apparent at lower levels of production. Thus, in cotton-growing areas on irrigated land, the financing of collective and state farms depended not on the amount of cotton grown but on the volume of technological operations planned (e.g. irrigation volumes, use of fertilizers, cotton processing with defoliants, etc.). Therefore, the producer was not interested in increasing final production and in decreasing production expenditures. Moreover, upon securing funds for certain technological operations, this system frequently fulfilled its operations only on paper, often supported by fictitious documents and significant sums of misappropriated money. This is why it was so difficult to introduce less water-consuming types of cotton in Central Asia – because they demanded less water, they reduced the financial awards made by the state.

In the future, a detailed zoning of the Aral Sea region should be undertaken, based on critical indices of the nature–society situation and trajectory. The integrated character, depth, and extent of the irreversibility of nature, social indices, the economy, and needed expenditures on mitigation and compensation should be used as criteria for this zoning. This could be of great practical value, since it would distinguish the priority regions for mitigatory measures.

Societal recognition of the Aral Sea problem

The extensive development of irrigation in the Aral Sea region began on the premise of promising economic advances to support a sharp increase in the living standard of the population. An improved supply of meat and rice, transformation of the region into an all-union flower and vegetable garden, and significant increases in hard currency receipts by the USSR from the sale of cotton and clothing were all envisioned. Against this background of heady optimistic prognoses of agricultural development based on the expansion of irrigated areas, the emergent problems of the Aral Sea and their environmental consequences have been a secondary priority.

In the 1960s and early 1970s, a viewpoint prevailed, initially set forth by A. I. Voiyeikov (1908), that the Aral Sea itself was a blunder of nature and that its existence was absolutely unjustified from the point of view of a rational economy. S. Yu. Geller, a well-known researcher of Central Asia, argued that the use of river waters for irrigation promised higher economic returns than allowing the runoff to proceed to the Aral (Geller 1969). A number of other scientists agreed with him. It should also be noted that water experts from Central Asia proposed a project in the mid-1920s to lower the level of the Aral Sea, with the aim of developing irrigation on the dry sea bed (Buniyatov and Mustafaev 1989). This recommendation was not based on physical–geographical, economic, or sociological studies, or on any special analysis of predicted changes in natural–social interactions in different parts of the Aral region.

Early in the 1970s, works began to appear that suggested that changes in the natural environment of the Aral area were significant and that recommended that several cubic kilometres of river water be supplied to preserve the deltas (Kliukanova and Kuznetsov 1971). The first projects for the partial salvation of the Aral Sea proposed disaggregation of the sea into individual water basins, with manageable water and salt regimes (L'vovich and Tsigel'naya 1978). By the middle of the 1970s, many scientists were concerned about the future of the Aral Sea and its region. This was reflected in the papers presented to the All-Union Working Meeting, organized by the Institute of Geography of the (then) USSR Academy of Sciences, addressing the impacts of inter-basin transfers of river runoff (Gerasimov 1975). Headed by I. P. Gerasimov, the Ad Hoc Scientific–Technical Commission of the USSR State Committee on Science and Technology worked in 1975 to assess the impacts of changes in the level of the Aral Sea on the environment and economy of the surrounding region. The Commission noted two opposing viewpoints on the Aral problem: (1) a fall in the sea level was unavoidable and would not have any serious negative consequences; (2) a fall in the sea level would be accompanied by important ecological and economic losses, and therefore stabilization of the sea level at the highest possible level was necessary.

In December 1975, the Bureau of the Interdepartmental Scientific–Technical Council on Complex Problems of Environmental Protection, USSR State Committee on Science and Technology, considered the report of this Commission in which a decline in the sea level was linked with irretrievable consumption of water on newly irrigated land. The report stated that far-reaching adverse changes in the environment and regional economy should be expected if mitigatory measures were not undertaken. Still it is apparent that, at that time, most researchers did not comprehend the possible consequences of further irrigation developments and sealevel fall.

Early in the 1980s, more and more scientists began to recognize the urgency and complexity of the situation and tried to identify possible solutions. Taking part in the work of an Expert Commission, the USSR State Planning Committee examined the complex use of water resources in the Syr Darya river basin. The unpublished report concluded that the ecological and water problems of the region were serious and that the quality of the design, construction, and operation of the irrigation systems was unsatisfactory. Other scientists also protested against the unrestrained expansion of irrigation and cotton monoculture and the widespread use of pesticides. During the work of the Commission, headed by A. L. Yanshin, the Central Asian situation was thoroughly discussed, although most attention focused on the problems associated with irrigation in the southern European territory of the USSR.

At the first recognition of the problems associated with irrigation, and especially with the territorial redistribution of runoff, all open discussion of these problems was forbidden. Publications addressing these problems were few and were allowed only in the classified press. Critical comments on the developing economic situation in the Aral region emerged in the 1970s and early 1980s from members of the Council on the Study of Productive Forces, the State Planning Committee of the USSR, and the Council on the Study of Productive Forces, Academy of Sciences of the Uzbek Soviet Socialist Republic. Specialists from the Ministry of Public Health of the Kazakh Soviet Socialist Republic also worked assiduously to assess the medical and sanitary situation in a number of Aral regions.

As a result of the studies performed in 1983, the Soviet Institute of Geography, jointly with the Council on the Study of Productive Forces, the State Planning Committee of the USSR, and the Soyuzgiprovodkhoz, prepared and submitted to the planning bodies and the CPSU Central Committee a special report entitled "Degradation of the Ecosystems of the Aral Sea, the Amu Darya and Syr Darya Deltas, and the Anthropogenous Desertification of the Aral Area Caused by the Irretrievable Withdrawals of Central Asian Rivers' Runoff with the Aim of Intensification of Irrigated Farming." This report analysed environmental changes and, to a lesser extent, the Aral Sea regional economy. It attempted to assess the economic damage and the social consequences of anthropogenic desertification of the Aral Sea area and the fall in the Aral Sea level. It also proposed a number of priority measures to save the region. Viewing this document from the vantage point of the present, we must emphasize that, in spite of the limited range of questions considered and the controversial character of certain statements, the report was the first complete and searching discussion of the essence of problems arising in the Aral Sea area. Unfortunately, only N. F. Vasilyev, the Minister of Reclamation and Water Economy, responded. It was a negative comment, supplemented by a statement signed by a number of academicians and corresponding members of the All-Union Agricultural Academy engaged in water reclamation and water economy, who argued for the further expansion of irrigation in the region.

In April 1987, the Governmental Commission on the Ecological Situation in the Aral Sea Basin was created, headed by Yuriiz A. Izrael. This Commission undertook certain necessary efforts but unfortunately the findings of the Commission were not widely discussed in the scientific community. It is difficult to share the view of the Commission chairman that, owing to the extremely acute ecological and social situation, the Commission members should deliberately avoid wide dissemination of their work. The Commission prepared a report, on the basis of which the CPSU Central Committee (CC) and the USSR Council of Ministers (CM) adopted the Resolution "On Measures of Radical Improvement in the Ecological and Sanitary Situation in the Aral Sea Region, Increase of Effective Uses, and Strengthening the Protection of Water and Land Resources in the Basin." This Resolution stated the serious effects of the use of the water and land resources of the Aral Sea basin and the development of new areas of irrigated lands without taking due account of the ecological and social consequences. A brief characterization of the state of nature and economy of the region was provided, along with proposals to change the natural environment, to restore the ecological balance in the Aral area, and to stimulate the growth of productive forces, including increasing the inflow of river water to the deltas, reconstructing irrigation systems, constructing new water supply facilities, and improving regional medical services.

We should note, however, that the Resolution also suffered from several serious shortcomings. It set forth the reasons for the Aral crisis in only a vague and general form that did not permit the formulation of a clear priority solution for the ecological, social, and economic problems of the region. The Resolution also authorized further growth of irrigated land, and the water volumes envisioned for discharge to the deltas and to the Aral Sea were completely insufficient to solve the ecological problems. Whether even this small amount of water would arrive is doubtful because the Resolution failed to specify the sources from which this water should be obtained. It also failed to make any water assignments to different regions of the basin to ensure an ecological flush.

Social democratization after 1985, and the abrogation of restrictions on scientific works analysing ecological, social, and economic problems, encouraged more extensive discussions of the Aral Sea problems. The Uzbek and Kazakh Committees for Saving the Aral were created, and numerous scientific and public conferences were held annually in different cities in the region. Public recognition of the problem occurred with the Aral-88 Expedition, organized by the *Novy Mir* and *Pamir* magazines. Participants in the expedition – writers, scientists, journalists – travelled throughout the Aral region and met with the public authorities of republics, districts, and regions, the local population, ministers, agricultural and water economy specialists, physicians, and representatives of grass-roots ecological movements. As a result of this expedition, an address was prepared and sent to the government which contained an analysis of the critical situation in the Aral area. It was accompanied by an appeal for urgent action to solve the ecological and social problems of the region. The indisputable authority of the well-known scientists, writers, and journalists who took part in the expedition and signed the appeal drew governmental attention to the Aral problem once again. An important result of the expedition was to alert public officials to the real situation and its causes.

"Aral Days" were held in the Central Club of Writers and in the editorial offices of some magazines and newspapers in Moscow where writers, scientists, and public figures voiced concern. The "Days" were organized by the Uzbek Public Committee for Saving the Aral, by the Kazakh Public Committee on Aral and Balkhash Problems, and by the International Movement of Poets "20th Century, World, and Ecology."

Late in 1989 a group of participants in the popular Aral movement addressed the Second Congress of People's Deputies of the USSR and also the Politbureau of the CPSU CC, the USSR Supreme Soviet, and the USSR Council of Ministers with an appeal to confront the Aral ecological crisis. The number of popular articles on the Aral problem had also sharply increased (Kaipbergenov 1989; Kotlyakov 1991; Selyunin 1989). Meanwhile, the Aral Sea problem began to attract the attention of foreign researchers. The most complete review of the problem using Soviet sources is that of Micklin (1988).

The Aral problem has been discussed at numerous meetings, including "Problems of the Aral Sea and the Aral Area" (June 1989), the meeting of the Uzbek "Man and Biosphere" National Committee (Bakhretdinov and Chembarisov 1989), the scientific symposium, "Working Out a Conception of Social-Economic Development of the Amu Darya Lower Reaches (the Aral Area) as a Special Economic Zone," in Shavat (1989), the International Symposium in Nukus (1990), and a number of other subsequent conferences and meetings. In the USSR Academy of Sciences, the Aral Sea problems were also discussed in depth by scientific councils of the Institute of Geography and the Institute of Water Problems at the end of 1989.

In the 1988 Resolution of the CPSU CC and USSR CM, a decision was taken to create an Institute of Water and Ecological Problems of the Aral Basin, USSR Academy of Sciences, in the city of Nukus. During 1988–1991 an international project was established by the United Nations Environment Programme, the Institute of Geography of the USSR Academy of Sciences, and the Centre for International Projects of the USSR Ministry of the Environment. The goal of the project was to analyse the situation in the Aral Sea region and to consider the possibility of undertaking other international projects. Meanwhile, several proposals have appeared for solving the Aral Sea problem (Glazovsky 1990b; Osnovnye ... 1991). The Aral Sea and basin, with Chernobyl, are now recognized in Russia and the Commonwealth of Independent States as zones of ecological calamity.

Thus, at least three periods can be distinguished in the history of growing societal awareness of the Aral problem. The first period (the 1960s to mid-1970s) involved a lack of attention to the problems associated with the widespread development of irrigation in the region. The Aral Sea was, in short, to be sacrificed. The second period (the early 1970s to mid-1980s) saw a gradually growing perception by scientists of the acute ecological situation arising in the Aral Sea area. These scientists identified initiatives to improve the situation. The roots of the crisis, however, were not assessed even in the most objective works. Only the Aral Sea area proper was considered, and the measures suggested pertained only to relatively specific problems. In fact, hydrotechnical construction continued to aim at the maximum expansion of irrigation. Objective analysis of the problem by the press was limited and often forbidden. The third period (the mid-1980s to the present) witnessed growing scientific recognition of both the general and the specific causes of the Aral crisis and broad public discussion of the Aral problems. Public committees for the salvation of the Aral Sea were created. Continuous changes in the positions of some political representatives and public authorities of the Central Asian republics, ministers, ministries, agencies, and reclamation bureaux occurred during this time. Although emphasis initially focused on the further development of irrigation, more recent communications and statements have recognized the necessity of restricting irrigation.

Despite the recognized value of the wide and open public discussion of the Aral Sea crisis, some negative features have accompanied the growing popularity of the issue. Unfortunately the Aral Sea crisis is sometimes used for political purposes. With social democratization, some people have used this problem to enunciate nationalistic demands. Others have sought to make political capital by discussing the Aral problem, while failing to suggest any constructive proposals. Also, numerous solutions of a technocratic nature have been proposed by people who lack the necessary expertise. Unfortunately, the authors of these ideas have often done their best to avoid searching discussion while seeking the support of incompetent authorities for immediate action. One final negative phenomenon, which could be called a "leader's fear syndrome," has involved the adoption of a series of hasty and unsubstantiated scientific decisions, including superficial, if prompt, solutions to this problem aimed at mobilizing public opinion.

Possible solutions and rescue scenarios

The future development of the Aral Sea situation depends on how successfully we manage to solve existing problems and to address the basic causes. An analysis of the essence of the problems that have arisen in the Aral Sea basin reveals two key aspects: (1) the need to solve the social, ecological, and economic problems of the Aral region, and (2) the need to preserve the Aral Sea (Glazovsky 1990a,b). These two aspects are interconnected, of course, but to our mind the problems of preserving the Aral Sea are secondary in both significance and prospective solutions as compared with the more pressing problems of the Aral Sea basin.

Proposed solutions differ in their scientific substance, the character and scope of problems, and the possible time limits for their realization. The top-priority measures should contribute to improving the ecological and life-support conditions of the population in the shortest time possible. Measures that are urgently needed include:

1. The development of a drinking and municipal water supply, first in the Karakalpak autonomous republic and the Kzyl Orda area and later in all other areas of the Aral Sea region. These systems may be based on different water sources: purified groundwater and surface rainfeed waters. Optimal systems of water supply should be designed, depending on such conditions as the presence of potential water sources, the volume and regime of required water consumption, and the quality of natural waters.
2. The construction of sewage systems and sewage-disposal facilities.
3. The cessation of pesticide use, beginning with defoliants and moving to more judicious use of chemical fertilizers. With the existing high inputs of manual labour in cotton harvesting, a solution to this problem should help to reduce human health impacts.
4. The creation of a network of modern medical institutions.

...plying high-quality food products to the populations through ...eased product-quality control and improved organization of ...d assistance.

6. More effective information on sanitary, hygienic, and ecological issues.

Implementation of these measures would do much to stabilize the population's health.

A solution to the Aral problems will require, at least during the first stage, the introduction of modern technologies and methods. To this end, an international fund(s) to rescue the Aral Sea region should be created. Such a fund, with the participation of international, state, and public organizations, private companies, and individual persons, is possible if two conditions are met: the tasks to be solved must be clearly defined, and the political will must be present. These measures would facilitate the solution of a number of important problems existing in the Aral Sea region but would not eliminate the deep-seated causes of the crisis. Therefore, strategic long-term measures are also necessary.

If most scientists and practitioners agree on the necessity of short-term measures to improve ecological conditions, mid-term and long-term measures can be subjected to differing assessments. To define scenarios for the further development of the situation, we must briefly address the basic strategic proposals for solutions to the Aral Sea crisis. The greatest bone of contention concerns the strategy of economic development of the Aral Sea basin. There are two main viewpoints, which differ in principle. The first conception assumes that the future development of the Aral region should be based on the expansion of irrigated farming. The proponents of this view point to what they regard as favourable climatic conditions (warm climate, abundance of sunny days, a long growing season), which, together with water, allow irrigated land to yield a great biological productivity. Crops such as cotton, rice, and subtropical varieties are possible that cannot be cultivated in more northerly regions of the former Soviet Union. This scenario of development corresponds to the traditions of the Aral Sea regional economy where, as emphasized above, irrigated farming developed over several thousand years and has been an important long-term component of the economy. It is presumed that, in the future, irrigated farming will absorb the surplus labour resources of the region. It is also argued that irrigated farming would feed the rapidly growing population of the Aral Sea basin. Many water experts and a number of regional political leaders, especially in Uzbek, support this point of view.

To this author, such a developmental path would aggravate many existing ecological, social, and economic problems and would prove ultimately to be a blind alley. Most of the potentially productive land in the Aral Sea basin is already cultivated. Therefore, new irrigation development would bring into production land with less favourable soil conditions, much of it located at long distances from water sources. Therefore, capital investments to construct irrigation systems and expenditures for their operation would be even higher. Thus, the cost of the products from this newly irrigated land could be much higher than present costs. This tendency was observed at earlier stages of irrigation development. The extensive development of irrigation would also intensify existing environmental problems since this new irrigated land would introduce millions of tons of currently immobile salts. As shown above, irrigation development has already led to an intensification of regional salt migration and a change in the salt budget in the region. What is to be done with the immense mass of salts that would be removed from irrigated lands by drainage runoff?

Finally, since the water resources of the basin are practically exhausted owing to extensive irrigation, further expansion of irrigated land would be possible (with existing irrigation technologies) only by importing water into the basin, perhaps from the runoff of Siberian rivers. The issue of river reversals has stimulated much debate in Russia. The main arguments of the opponents are still germane:

- the economic and social effectiveness of river reversal has not been proved,
- there is no scientifically substantiated prediction of environmental changes, both in the regions of water withdrawal and in those to which the water would flow.

In particular, the proposed withdrawal of 25 km^3/year (and the prospect of up to 60 km^3/year) of water from the Ob river would change the expanse and duration of flood-plain inundation. This, in turn, would affect commercial fish reserves and the thermal and ice regime of the Ob river. The boundary of mixed river and sea water would be displaced, and the glacial situation in the southern part of the Kara Sea would also change. Water filtration from the reversal canal would cause landscape transformation in the zone near the canal. At the same time, extensive irrigation development in the Aral region would predetermine the further development of raw materials sources in the region, an important issue because the available large reserves for agricultural intensification have not thus far been used.

Cultivation of new irrigated land and the runoff from reversal of the Siberian rivers would require enormous capital expenditure, in the order of 100 billion roubles according to 1991 estimates. In fact, as the experience of implementing large projects in Russia has shown, several times this amount should be expected. Given the present economic state of these countries, such enormous expenditure of material resources is foolish. Such a development would pre-empt necessary investments in the social sphere, in the reconstruction of the water economy and agriculture, and in the creation of a processing industry in the Aral Sea region. This strategy also presumes the disappearance of the Aral Sea, since nearly all additional water arriving in the region would be allocated to irrigation. Assumptions that irrigated farming would provide jobs for the growing population of the Aral region are also not justified. Analysis shows that, during recent years, in spite of an expansion in irrigated lands, the numbers of those working in agriculture has not increased, while the share of agricultural employment has declined (fig. 3.7). The existing outmoded irrigation technologies assumed by this strategy do not allow for human progress and the well-being of those working in agriculture.

The Aral Sea basin trajectory

This volume has a central concern with regional environmental trajectories. Trajectories of the Aral Sea region are presented in figure 3.8. With intensified, irrigated agriculture, the ecological and economic situation will certainly continue to deteriorate. Human health could improve, however, with imported food products, water, and a better system of medical care. As an alternative, we propose a different strategy to solve the Aral problem (Glazovsky 1990b), one that appears to be gaining supporters. It is, however, not widely recognized, and many scientists and politicians prefer the traditional approach.

We believe that a long-term plan for a change in the strategy for developing productive forces in the Aral Sea basin is the most efficient approach to solving the social, economic, and ecological problems in an integrated way. The economic efficiency of water reclamation has often been overestimated. Thus, calculations of efficiency have not taken into account the prior hydro-reclamation and crop yields (i.e. calculations have been based not on marginal increases in productivity but on overall gross productivity). Priority needs for natural resources, better technology, and fertilizers for irrigated land have not been taken into account. Efficiency estimates have been distorted because they have been based on overall costs and not on incremental gains in productivity. Thus, real data do not confirm the prevailing

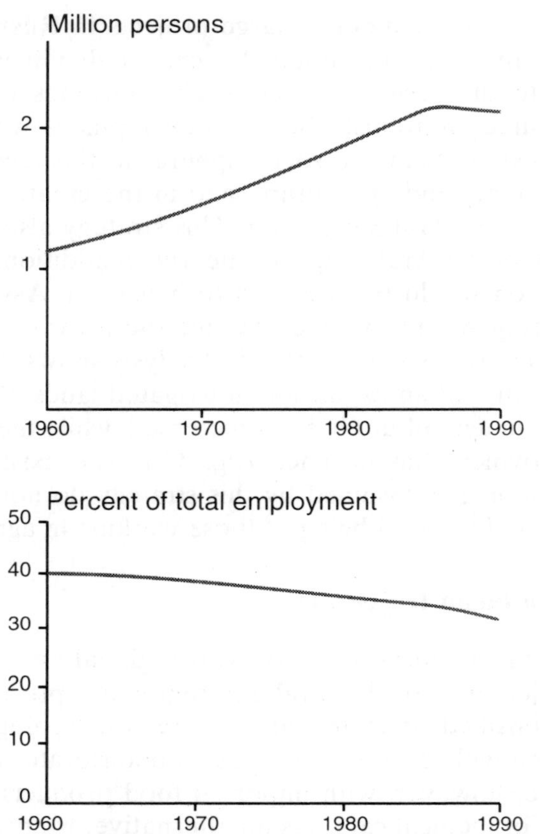

Fig. 3.7 **Persons engaged in agriculture in Uzbekistan, 1960–1990 (Source: Uzbekistan, 1988, and author's own estimates)**

view of the high efficiency of farming in Central Asia. The real cost of grain in Russia, the Ukraine, and Byelorussia is 2–3 times lower than that in Central Asia; the cost of vegetables in Russia is about the same, while the Ukraine and (especially) Byelorussia have much lower costs than does Central Asia.

One of the important arguments favouring a new extensive development of irrigation in Central Asia turns on the necessity of cotton production and its effectiveness. Is it possible to decrease cotton production without damaging the regional economy? Part of the cotton production goes to meet military needs. With the dramatic changes in the international political situation and the replacement of cotton with synthetic materials, cotton production for military purposes could be significantly reduced. Recent estimates suggest that 30–80

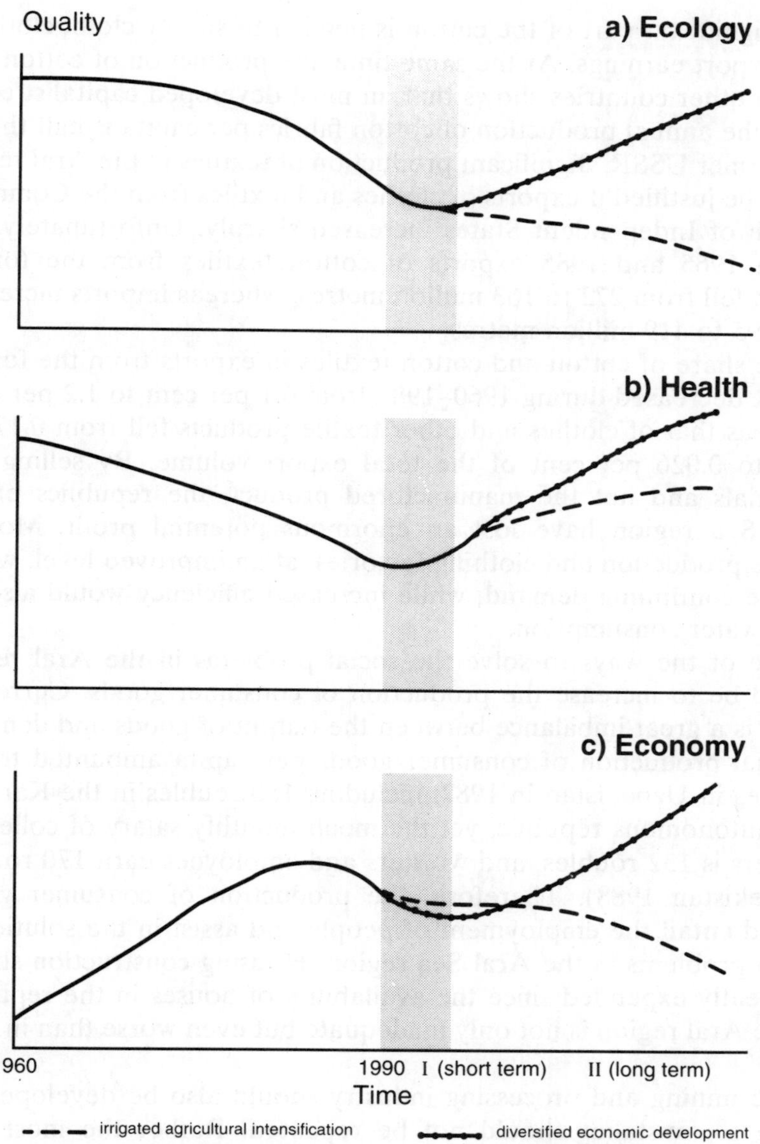

Fig. 3.8 Trajectories of nature–society relationships in the Aral Sea basin

per cent of the cotton consumed in the former USSR for industrial and household uses could be replaced by synthetic fibres. The United States has traditionally spent 4–5 times less on cotton for these purposes than has the former USSR (Safayev 1982).

A significant part of the cotton is needed to supply cloth, clothing, and export earnings. At the same time, the production of cotton fabrics in other countries shows that, in most developed capitalist countries, the annual production of cotton fabrics per capita is half that of the former USSR. Significant production of textiles in the Aral region could be justified if exports of clothes and textiles from the Commonwealth of Independent States increased sharply. Unfortunately, between 1965 and 1985 exports of cotton textiles from the former USSR fell from 272 to 163 million metres, whereas imports increased from 95 to 419 million metres.

The share of cotton and cotton textiles in exports from the former USSR decreased during 1960–1985 from 6.1 per cent to 1.2 per cent, whereas that of clothes and other textile products fell from 0.17 per cent to 0.026 per cent of the total export volume. By selling raw materials and not the manufactured product, the republics of the Aral Sea region have lost an enormous potential profit. Modern textile production and clothing factories, at an improved level, would ensure continuing demand, while increased efficiency would also reduce water consumption.

One of the ways to solve the social problems in the Aral region would be to increase the production of consumer goods. Currently, there is a great imbalance between the output of goods and demand. Annual production of consumer goods per capita amounted to 472 roubles in Uzbekistan in 1987, including 180 roubles in the Karakalpak autonomous republic, yet the mean monthly salary of collective farmers is 132 roubles, and workers and employees earn 170 roubles (Uzbekistan 1988). Therefore, the production of consumer goods should entail the employment of people and assist in the solution of social problems in the Aral Sea region. Housing construction should be greatly expanded since the availability of houses in the republics of the Aral region is not only inadequate but even worse than in Russia.

The mining and processing industry should also be developed. In doing so, mistakes should not be repeated. Rather the most profitable processing of raw materials should be undertaken but with care for ecological requirements. The development of an electronics industry should also be considered. Development of these important branches of industry would be important since they would guarantee increases in the professional and cultural level of the workers. Such initiatives should also ensure structural and technological diversity in agriculture.

Unproductive salinized land that entails immense water use should be withdrawn from irrigation. Even if only 5 per cent of the least suitable land were withdrawn, water consumption savings would reach 7 km^3 per year. It might be advisable to withdraw even larger areas on the basis of ecological and economic considerations, because about 15 per cent of irrigated land in the Aral basin is in an extremely unsatisfactory condition. This could lead to savings in the order of 15–20 km^3 of water per year or more.

It should be emphasized that withdrawing land from irrigation should proceed hand-in-hand with the solution of social problems. New work places should be created, while the most ecologically unfavourable sites should be eliminated. People and enterprises should be compensated for losses connected with the cessation of irrigation and the restructuring of the regional economy. Without this withdrawal of land from irrigation, difficulties will continue. It will also be necessary to develop new uses for land where irrigation is terminated.

Irrigation systems on the remaining land will need to be reconstructed and their efficiency improved. Reducing the filtration of water from canals would make it possible to free at least 10–20 km^3 of water. Improvements in land use would make it possible to decrease the washing standards, and thus to obtain several additional cubic km of water per year. Irrigation reconstruction should also cause land productivity to rise. About 3 km^3 of water could be gained by replacing rice with other crops. Revising irrigation standards in accordance with scientific recommendations and the experience of advanced economies with improved irrigation technologies could deliver between 10 and 20 km^3 of water per year. The introduction of modern methods of watering and systems of water management could increase this figure by 20–30 km^3. Implementation of all these measures would save about another 40 km^3 of water per year.

The most promising means of drainage runoff utilization is re-use of the water for irrigation or discharge after biological improvement of rivers and creation of a cascade system of farming. These utilizations of drainage runoff could be combined. Salt is a very serious problem. The possibility of using salts as a raw material for a chemical industry and also to develop a technology of residual brines should be explored.

A solution to the problem of water conservation in agriculture in Central Asia depends, of course, not only on water management and reclamation measures. The introduction of less water-consuming agricultural plants is essential. Water saving is also necessary in other branches of the economy. To improve agricultural productivity, conserve soil fertility, and reduce the use of pesticides and chemical fertilizers, crop rotation is necessary. Some increases in water consumption may occur since some crops (e.g. alfalfa) that are usually necessarily present in crop rotation on irrigated land in Central Asia require more water than cotton. And certainly vegetable and grape production on irrigated lands of the Aral Sea basin should be increased.

Concerning the preservation of the Aral Sea, two basic points of view prevail. Some politicians, heads of ministries, and scientists believe that the Aral Sea is not needed. As an argument, they provide calculations of the economic efficiency of Aral Sea use (for fisheries, other bioresources, transport development, and recreation) and also an estimate of losses connected with the environmental changes (e.g. climate, salt transportation, groundwater). They then compare the economic profit to be gained by capturing the Amu Darya and Syr Darya runoff to the Aral Sea for irrigation with adverse environmental impacts. What are the drawbacks of such an assessment approach?

First, it is difficult to evaluate losses connected with environmental impacts, because this question has been little studied in the Commonwealth of Independent States. To preserve the Aral as a single water basin at a sea level of 40+ metres and an area of about 40,000 km^2, and allowing for a water discharge for evaporation of about 35 km^3/year, stabilization of the sea level requires that 35–38 km^3 of water per year arrive in the sea. With a developmental strategy for the regional economy based on advanced development of industrial processing and reconstruction of the water economy, these volumes of water appear possible. Since not all the proposed measures can be implemented, one must assume that some fall in the level of the Aral Sea is unavoidable. Therefore, a general strategy for rescuing the Aral should aim at stabilizing the level and then restoring the necessary long-term level.

According to recent estimates, the cost of restoring environmental quality will amount to several tens of billions of roubles (in 1990 prices). The approximate distribution of the necessary investment is as follows:

- reconstruction of irrigation systems — 25–30 billion roubles
- measures to prevent the inflow of polluted drainage water to rivers — 1.6–3 billion roubles

- introduction of new irrigation technologies and new kinds of plants — 6–10 billion roubles
- stabilization of the desiccated sea floor — 0.5–1 billion roubles

If we also take into account the measures necessary to improve the sanitary/hygienic and communal conditions of life and the medical services, and the need for new work places and changes in the structure of the economy, the required expenditure would exceed 100 billion roubles.

Thus, a sound strategy for the Aral Sea region will take account of potential trajectories of the situation (fig. 3.8). These trajectories are, we emphasize, hypothetical and in the spirit of the discussion in chapter 1 and like those of chapter 5. They are not based upon quantitative assessments or projections.

Saving the Aral Sea

The Aral Sea crisis is a disaster that involves the degradation of ecosystems in the Aral basin, a deterioration in human health, economic decline, a growth in social tensions, and a drying up of the Aral Sea itself, with an increase in its salinity and a degradation of its formerly integrated water ecosystem. It is the clearest example of a "critical region" presented in this volume. Among the reasons for the crisis are blunders in the choice of the developmental strategy for the region's productive forces, serious errors in designing, constructing, and operating irrigation systems, and the ill-considered chemicalization of agriculture. Societal reaction to the crisis has evolved over time, at first halting and repressed but growing to a crescendo in recent years.

A portfolio of measures of varying scope and priority is required. First, it is necessary to elaborate and implement priority measures to improve life expectancy and human health, and municipal water supply systems must also be constructed. Sewage-treatment facilities are also desperately needed. Pesticide use should be curtailed, and the discharge of contaminated drainage waters should cease. Medical services must be greatly improved and a secure food supply developed for the population. To ensure the supply of medical items and high-quality food for the population, to introduce modern technologies, and to improve scientific research, funds must be created to rescue the Aral Sea region.

Mid-term measures (2–10 years) should include the reconstruction of irrigation systems, water supply, better use of drainage runoff, the introduction of new agricultural methods and technologies, changes in the structure of agricultural production, and the introduction of new special and free-trade economic zones. Long-term measures (designed for 10–15 years) should include a change in the developmental strategy for productive forces, economic diversification, and governmental improvements. The long-term period is defined largely by the scope of the proposed changes, the scale of the capital investment required, and the necessity for in-depth scientific investigations.

An acceptable approach to the preservation of the Aral Sea is impossible without a detailed assessment of the ecological requirements of the Aral Sea, a precise understanding of the salt sea budget, sound predictions of regional climatic changes, and assessments of the various schemes put forth for saving the Aral Sea. Any specification of social and economic requirements for the Aral Sea should be made only after wide discussion of these problems and full consideration of the aspirations of the various peoples of the Aral Sea area, whose history and ways of life are intimately linked with the sea, and the expenditures needed to realize their hopes.

References

Aladin, N. V., and Vladislav V. Khlebovich, eds. 1989. *Gidrobiologicheskye problemy Aralskogo morya* [Hydrobiological problems of the Aral Sea]. Trudy Zoologicheskogo Instituta, v. 199. Leningrad: Zoologicheskii institut Akademiia Nauk SSSR.

Bakhretdinov, B., and E. Chembarisov. 1989. Razpabat'ivaetcya kontseptsiya po Araly [Developing the Aral concept]. *Sel'skaya Pravda*, 14 October.

Batyrov, A., G. Muradov, T. M. Morozova, and L. Kh. Prikhod'ko. 1984. *Social'no-economicheskie problemy pazvitiya proizvoditel'nykh sil Tashauzskogo oazisa* [Social and economic problems of the development of productive forces in the Tashauz oases]. Ashgabad.

Buniyatov, Z. M., and I. O. Mustafaev. 1989. Prochess sredneaziatskikh vodnikov [Legal proceedings of Central Asian water planners]. *Izvestiya AN Azerbaidzhanskoi SSR, seriya istorii, filosofii i prava* no. 1.

Chebanov, Mikhail S. 1989. *Sistemnyi analiz vodnogo i teplovogo rezhima del'tovykh ozer* [Systems analysis of water and thermal regime of lakes in the deltas]. Leningrad: Gidrometeoizdat.

Geller, S. Yu. 1969. Nekotor'ye aspecti problemi Arals'kogo Morya [Selected aspects of the Aral Sea problem]. In *Problema Arals'kogo Morya* [The Aral Sea problem], ed. S. Yu. Geller, 5–24. Moscow: Nauka.

Gerasimov, I. P., ed. 1975. *The impact of interbasin redistribution of river runoff on the environment of the European territories and middle region of the USSR: Proceedings of the Workshop (April 1975)*. Moscow: Institute of Water Problems.

Gerasimov, I. P., N. T. Kuznetsov, A. S. Kes, and M. E. Gorodetskaya. 1983. Problemy Arals'kogo morya i antropogennogo opust'ynvaniya Priaral'ya [Problems of the Aral Sea and anthropogenic desertification of the Aral region]. *Problemy osvoeniya pustyn'* 6: 22–33.

Glazovsky, Nikita F. 1990a. *Aralskii krizis* [The Aral crisis]. Moscow: Akademiia Nauk.

———. 1990b. Kontseptsiya vykhoda iz "Aralskogo Krizisa" [Ideas on an escape from the "Aral Crisis"]. *Izvestiya AN SSSR: Seriya geograficheskaya* no. 4: 28–41; *Soviet Geography* 32, no. 2: 73–89.

Izrael, Yurii A., and Feliks I. Rovinski, eds. 1990. *Obzor sostoyaniya okruzayushchei prirodnoi sredy v SSSR* [Survey of the state of the natural environment in the USSR]. Moscow: Gidrometeoizdat.

Kaipbergenov, A. 1989. Prokuror ziya zashcity Arala [Procurator for protection of the Aral]. *Pravda*, 18 March: 3.

Khakimov, Fikki I. 1989. *Pochvenno-meliorativnye usloviya opustynivahyuschikhshya del't: Tendentsii izmenii prostrant'svennaya differentsiatsia* [Soil reclamation conditions of delta desertification: Tendencies of transformation and spatial differentiation]. Pushchino: Nauchnyi Tsentr biologicheskikh isseldovaniy AN SSSR.

Kliukanova, I. A., and N. T. Kuznetzov. 1971. Soderzhanie elementov pitaniya rastenii v noviyezhik otlozheniyakh v delt' Amudar'; i razvivayuzhikhoya na nikh pochvakh [Composition of plant nutrients in the newest sediments of the Amudar delta and soils that are developing there]. *Izvestiya AN SSSR: Seriya geograficheskaya* no. 3.

Kondratyev, K. Ya, A. A. Grigoryev, and V. F. Zhvalev. 1986. Vliyaniye moschnykh pylevykh bur' na radiatsionnuyu energetiku atmosphery i pustyn' [The influence of powerful dust storms on the radiation power capacity of the atmosphere and deserts]. *Prirodnye resursy pustyn' i ikh osvoyeniye Ashkhyabad*: 27–31.

Kotlyakov, V. M. 1991. The Aral Sea basin: A critical environmental zone. *Environment* 33, no. 1 (January/February): 4–9, 36–38.

Kuleshov, V. 1985. Sachem pustyne [Why a desert needs swamps]. *Bolota Izvestiya*, 6 December.

Kurbanov, Kamal. 1988. *Territorial'naya organizatsiya sel'skogo* [The spatial structure of agriculture]. Tashkent: FAN.

L'vovich, M. I., and I. D. Tsigel'naya. 1978. Control of the water balance of the Aral Sea. *Izvestiya AN SSR: Seriya geograficheskaya* no. 1: 42–54.

Micklin, Philip P. 1988. Desiccation of the Aral Sea: A water management disaster in the Soviet Union. *Science* 241, no. 4870 (2 September): 1170–1176.

Molosnova, T. I., O. I. Subbotina, and S. G. Chanysheva. 1987. *Klimaticheskiye posledstviya khozyaistvennoi deyatelnosti v zone aral'skogo morya* [Climatic consequences of economic activity in the zone of the Aral Sea]. Leningrad: Gidrometeoizdat.

Nikitin, A. M. 1977. O dinamike ozer srednego i niznego techeniya reki Syrdaryi [On the dynamics of the lakes in the middle and low reaches of the Syrdarya River]. *Trudy SARNIGMI* [Central Asian Research Institute of Hydromelioration] 56, no. 131: 22–30.

Nikitin, A. M., and Yu N. Lesnik. 1982. Otsenka dinamiki ravninnykh ozer Srednei Azii po materialam kosmofotosnimkov [Utilizing remote sensing in an analysis of the dynamics of lowland lakes in Central Asia]. In *Gidrometeorologiya ozer i vo-*

dokhranilishch, ed. Yu N. Ivanov and A. M. Nikitin. Trudy Sredneaziatskogo regional'nogo nauchno-issledovatel'skogo instituta im. V. A. Bugaeva 87, no. 168: 49–55.

Nikolayeva, R. V. 1969. *Osnovnoye morfologicheskoye kharakteristiki aral'-skogo morya. Problemy Aral'skogo morya* [The main morphological characteristics of the Aral Sea. The problems of the Aral Sea]. Moscow: Nauka, 25–38.

Novikova, N. M. 1985. Dinamika rastitelnosti del'tovykh ravnin aridnykh rajonov vsledstvii antropogennogo preobrazovaniya rechnogo stoka [Vegetation dynamics of the delta plains of arid regions caused by anthropogenic transformation of river runoff]. In *Biogeograficheskiye aspekty opustynivaniya* [Biogeographical aspects of desertification], ed. Oleg A. Kibal'chich, Anatolii G. Voronov, and D. D. Vishyvkin. Moscow: Moskoviskii filial Geograficheskoe obshchestvo SSSR.

Novikova, N. M., and V. S. Zaletayev. 1985. Vodnoye khozyaistvo kak faktor transformatsii prirodnykh ekosistem [Water economics as a factor in the transformation of natural ecosystems]. In *Biogeograficheskiye aspekty opustynivaniya* [Biogeographical aspects of desertification], ed. Oleg A. Kibal'chich, Anatolii G. Voronov, and D. D. Vishyvkin, 4–12. Moscow: Moskoviskii filial Geograficheskoe obshchestvo SSSR.

Novy Mir. 1989. Aral'skaia katastrofa [Aral catastrophe]. *Novy Mir* no. 5: 182–241.

Osnovnye polozheniya kontseptsii sokhraneniya i vosstanovleniiya Aralskogo morya normalizatsii ekologicheskoi, sanitarno-gigienicheskoi, medico-biologicheskoi i sotsialno ekonomicheskoi situatsii v priaralye. 1991. [The main statements of a concept of preservation and restoration of the Aral Sea, normalization of ecological, sanitary, hygienic, medico-biological and socio-economic situation in the Aral area]. *Izvestiya AN SSSR: Seriya geograficheskaya* no. 4: 8–21.

Persianova, L. A., T. Yadgarov, and Kh. M. Saraeva. 1986. Zakonomernosti izmeneniya sostava miekopirayushschikh i presmykayushchikhsya v svyazi s obvodneniem zasushlivykh territorii [Patterns in the changes of fauna due to watering of arid territories]. In *Prirodnye resursy pustyn' i ikh osvoenie*, 336–340. Ashgabad: Ilim.

Popov, V. A. 1988. *Opustyunivaniye v Uzbekistane i bor'ba s nim* [Desertification in Uzbekistan and its prevention]. Tashkent: FAN.

Problems of the Aral Sea. 1973. Moscow: Nauka.

Rozanov, Boris G. 1984. *Osnovy ucheniya ob okruzhayushchei srede* [Basic ideas of the theory of the environment]. Moscow: Moscow State University.

———. 1986. Zemelnye resursy aridnogo poyasa SSSR, ikh ratsional'-noye ispozovaniye i okhrana [Lands of the arid belt of the USSR, their rational use, and protection]. *Problemy osvoyeniya puistyn* 5: 22–28.

Safayev, A. 1982. Problemy compleksnoy narodochozyaistrennoi programmi "Khlopok" [The problems of the comprehensive national economic programme "Cotton"]. *Kommunist* 7: 76–87.

Selyunin, V. 1989. Vremya deiistviy [Time for action]. *Novy Mir* no. 5: 213–241.

Shaporenko, S. I. 1987. Vliyaniy gidrologicheskogo rezhima na ryboropoduktivnost' osolonyayushikhsya vodoyemov (na primere Aralskogo morya, ozer Arsanajskoi sistemy i Sarykamysh) [The effect of hydrological regime on fish productivity of salinized water bodies (using the example of the Aral Sea, lakes of the Arnasai system and Sarykamysh)]. *Avtoref na soisk uch. step.k.g.n.* (Moscow).

USSR. 1984. *Ukrupnennye normy vodopotrebnosti diya orosheniya po prirodno-kli-*

maticheskim zonam SSSR [Generalized standards of water needs for irrigation according to natural-climatic zones of the USSR]. Moscow: Gidrometeoizdat.

Uzbekistan. 1988. Narodnoye khozyaye Uzbekskoye SSR v 1987 [The national economy of the Uzbek Soviet Socialist Republic in 1987]. In *Statisticheskie ezhegodmik* [Statistical Yearbook]. Tashkent: Izd-vo "Uzbekistan."

Voiyeikov, A. I. 1908. Oroshenie zakaspiyskoye oblasti s tochki zreniya geografii i klimatologii [The irrigation of the Transcaspian region from the viewpoint of geography and climatology]. *Izvestiya imperatorskogo russkogo geograficheskogo obshchestva* 44, no. 3: 131–160.

Voropayev, G. V., G. Kh. Ismaiylov, and V. M. Fedorov. 1984. *Modelirovanie vodokhozyaistvennykh sistem aridnoi zony SSSR* [Modelling of water-usage systems in the arid zone of the USSR]. Moscow: Nauka.

Williams, W. D., and N. V. Aladin. 1991. The Aral Sea: Recent limnological changes and their conservation significance. *Aquatic Conservation* 1, no. 1 (September): 3–24.

Zaletayev, Vladimir S. 1976. *Zhizn' v pustyne* [Life in the desert]. Moscow: Mysl.

4

The Nepal middle mountains

N. S. Jodha

The Himalayas are one of the youngest mountain systems in the world. A product of geological and climatic conditions, the resource degradation and associated environmental consequences are a part of the natural process of mass wasting in the region (Ives 1987). Hence it is argued that changes in the Himalayan ecosystem are inevitable and the recent outcry accusing mountain people of environmental degradation is misplaced. Without questioning the role of natural processes affecting the Himalayan environment, however, it is noteworthy that human interference has greatly accentuated the process of change. At both macro and micro levels, vast differences in comparable environmental parameters, in areas with and without human intervention, would confirm this. The situation is approaching a critical level of irreversible changes in some parts of the region. An investigation of strategies for sustainable mountain agriculture in selected areas of this region alerted researchers to emerging negative trends in several relevant variables (Jodha 1990). These changes relate to biophysical variables, production flows, patterns of resource use, and people's economic conditions.

An enquiry into these negative changes and their causal factors and processes constitutes the background to this chapter. This discussion, which is focused on the middle mountains of Nepal, also draws on the evidence and understanding generated by other studies covering larger areas of Nepal. The focus of this chapter is environmental change as a product of interaction between the specific resource characteristics of mountain areas and the attributes of human activities designed to use mountain resources. A paucity of relevant, disaggregated data severely constrains the analysis of human driving forces and their impact on the environment in the middle mountains of Nepal. Hence, a mixed approach begins with macro- and micro-level evidence from different locations, inferences from qualitative insights generated by field observations, and some quantitative details based on oral history. The next section describes the choice of area and time-frame for which to report the changes. A focus on environmental changes gives way to a discussion of attendant factors and processes. The chapter then turns to the impacts and consequences of these environmental changes, as well as human awareness of and responses to the changes, and concludes with a brief commentary on the trajectory towards greater endangerment and criticality.

The area chosen for examining environmental change, its causes and its consequences, is the Nepal Himalayas. Within the overall mountain areas of the country the focus will be on the middle mountains, more specifically the area referred to as the Bagmati zone in the central development region of the country. At a lower level we refer to Nuwakot district, one of the five hill districts in Nepal with the status of a heavily degraded watershed (Shrestha et al. 1983). The village-level evidence relates to Nuwakot as well as to other districts in the Bagmati zone.

Figure 4.1 indicates the geographical location of the areas, and table 4.1 presents some relevant statistics on them. The evidence and analysis presented relate to micro-level situations generated through interactions between mountain specificities and attributes of resource-use patterns. However, such situations are fairly common to micro-environments within the overall mountain areas, especially the middle mountains.

The middle mountains – a broad strip of sharply dissected and highly variable hill country – occupy some 30 per cent of Nepal's land area and cover about 42,000 km^2. About 48 per cent of Nepal's population lives in this area, which includes the broad shallow basin of the Kathmandu Valley. Beyond this relatively small basin the topography is consistently rugged, with less than 5 per cent of flat land. It is generally well watered, with characteristically intensive monsoon rainfall of 2,000 mm or more in the middle-western region, but decreasing

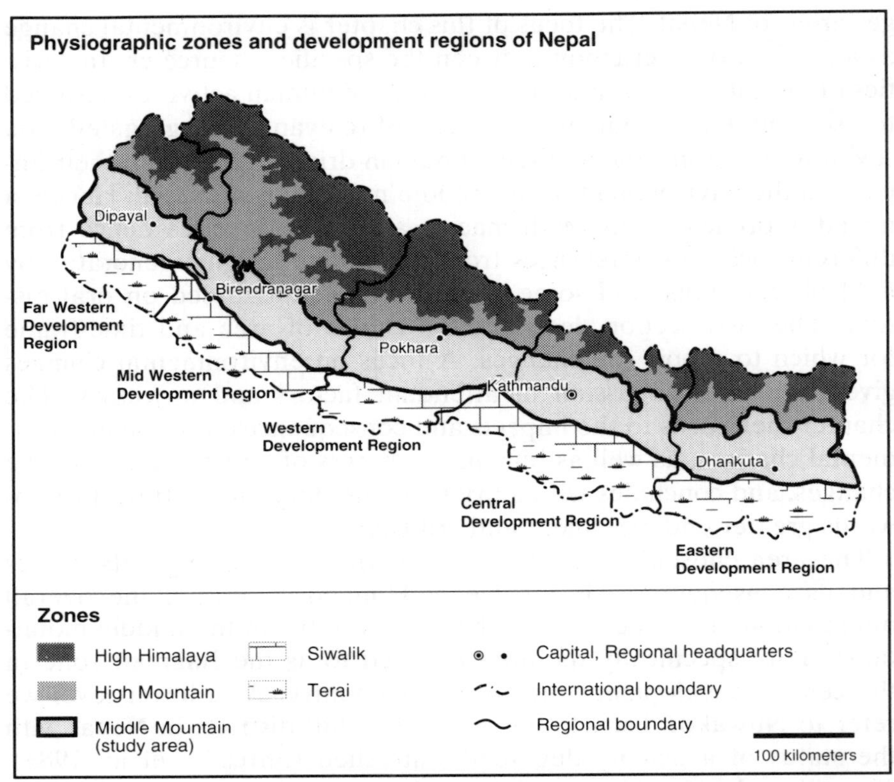

Fig. 4.1 **Physiographic zones and development regions of Nepal (Source: Clark Labs)**

to about 1,000 mm of more evenly distributed rainfall in the far western region. With warm summers and cool but mild winters, this middle mountain division has been the historical focus of national development, and has already acquired a hill population of over 5 million. This is Nepal's major problem area for which a coherent development strategy is required. The bulk of the subsistence agriculture depends directly on the productivity of both wild and cultivated plants. The terraced arable areas of the middle mountains have already been cropped continuously to a state so near to exhaustion of mineral nutrients that farmers do not risk committing seed unless they are able to apply manure. The many abandoned terraces throughout the hills demonstrate that the supply of nutrients is often inadequate for continuous cropping (World Bank 1984).

Table 4.1 **Some statistical details of the middle mountains of Nepal**

Details	Middle mountains (districts)	Bagmati zone[a]	Nuwakot district	Six study villages
General				
Area ('000 ha)	13,611	9,428	1,121	1.2
Population density (per '000 ha)	122	189	181	178
Family size (no.)	6.3	–	5.7	6.0
Annual pop. growth, 1951–1981 (%)	–	1.87	1.54	1.74[b]
Agricultural details				
Proportion of cultivated area (%)	23.9	22.0	32.6	34.3
Farm size (ha)	0.71	–	0.95	0.84
Man/land ratio on farms (no./ha)	8.9	–	6.0	6.9
Fully irrigated area (%)	11	–	14	9
Livestock units per farm	8.9	–	3.6	4.2
Cropping intensity (%)	153	–	148	151
Average animal holding (no./farm)				
Cattle	3.1	–	–	3.7
Buffalo	1.5	–	–	1.8
Goat	9.5	–	–	8.8
Food crop yield (mt/ha)				
Paddy	2.33	–	–	2.81
Maize	1.66	–	–	2.10
Wheat	1.17	–	–	1.12
Details by farm size				
Small farm (mean size 0.25 ha):				
Man/land ratio (no./ha)	21.6			23.3
Cropping intensity (%)	170			182
Large farm (mean size 1.91 ha):				
Man/land ratio (no./ha)	4.3	–	–	4.8
Cropping intensity (%)	142	–	–	157
Seasonal fodder deficit				
(quantity total digestible nutrients per farm)				
November–February	−40	–	–	–
March–June	−199	–	–	–
July–October	−134	–	–	–

Sources: Middle mountains and Nuwakot district – DFAMS (1986); Bagmati zone – Nepal (1984); 6 study villages – quick studies using Rapid Rural Appraisal methods.

a. The nine districts of the Bagmati zone are Nuwakot, Sindhuli, Tanahu, Ilam, Gulmi, Sallyan, Baitadi, Dailekh, and Okhaldhunga.

b. Based on number of households.

Geographical delimitation and time-frame

Apart from the importance of the area and the severity of the problems it faces, several factors guided the choice of the middle mountains and the Bagmati zone for study. First, the area has both major types of situation characterizing mountain regions of the Himalayas. In addition to vast areas of stagnant production systems and rapid population growth, it also has dynamic areas in which market forces and public intervention are contributing to transformations with visible negative environmental effects. Second, past studies and evidence are available for these areas. Finally, some logistical considerations (e.g. the nearness of the Bagmati zone to Kathmandu) were also relevant. One special feature of the Bagmati zone is that the Greater Kathmandu Valley (GKV) forms a part of this zone.

The time-scale to assess environmental changes may vary, of course, depending on the variables being considered. Guided by the experience of earlier studies and conforming to the general approach in this volume, a period of around 50 years has been chosen as a benchmark. This is the period during which relatively faster changes occurred through public intervention, market forces, and population growth. Furthermore, oral history, an important tool for understanding and recording the past, also suggests 50 years as an appropriate period for assessing environmental change. In 1951, Nepal passed through a major institutional change with the transfer of power from the Ranas to the king. This important milestone in the country's history helped in activating people's memories (for recall information) on the status of resources and the environment they had seen in the past, about 40–50 years ago. Wherever necessary, however, the benchmark period may exceed 50 years.

Environmental changes and emerging indicators of unsustainability

Before discussing the environmental changes in mountain areas, a word on some conceptual issues is required. The environment is a joint product generated by the composition and interactions of different biophysical variables in a given ecological context. Socio-economic factors play their own role in influencing interactive patterns of biophysical variables. Depending on the tangible, as against the abstract, nature of the "product," environmental change can be quantified or measured. More important, the biophysical factors generating "environment as a joint product" are not only contributors to but products of the environment. Environmental change, then, can be seen in terms of: (1) changes in its parameters (i.e. status and interaction of biophysical variables such as land, water, plants, etc.), and (2) changes in the tangible (as against abstract or difficult to measure) impacts of (1) above.

Furthermore, some of the changes mentioned above may manifest themselves as "impacts" or "consequences," whereas others form a part of certain ongoing processes. Another important aspect of these changes is that they may differ in terms of their degree of visibility (Jodha 1990). Although some (e.g. the extent of soil erosion) are directly visible, others may be concealed by human responses to the change (e.g. replacement of cattle by small ruminants following the decline in carrying capacity of mountain pastures). Similarly, depending on whether change takes the form of an impact or a component of a process, the nature of its visibility will differ (e.g. the reduced extent of irrigation following the reduction in natural water flow is immediately visible; the impact of the reduced diversity of mountain agriculture as a process may become visible after a time-lag). Methodological approaches to assess the change will also differ according to the choice of indicators of change.

Using this framework, I assess a number of observed or documented negative changes in the middle mountains of Nepal. These persistent negative changes are described as indicators of the unsustainability of mountain agriculture and associated patterns of resource use. Table 4.2 summarizes these changes. Various studies (APROSC 1990; Banskota 1989; Banskota and Jodha 1992a; ICIMOD 1990; and Yadav 1992) record and (in some cases) quantify some of these changes. In the context of the overall framework of this chapter, this table includes changes that may represent awareness, responses to environmental change, and impacts of adjustments.

Village-level evidence

Focused enquiries at the village level can capture most of the indicators of change listed in table 4.2. The existing statistical system, based on too much standardization of data-gathering procedures and listing of variables, often fails to record such changes. Nevertheless, some proxies for the above changes (i.e. changes in land-use pattern, cropping pattern, occupational structure, etc.) at macro levels can be identified from the formal statistical records at two points in time. A few

Table 4.2 **Classification of negative changes as indicators of the unsustainability of mountain agriculture**

Visibility of change	Changes related to:[a] Resource base	Production flows	Resource-use/management practices
Directly visible changes	Increased landslides and other forms of land degradation; abandoned terraces; per capita reduced availability and fragmentation of land; changed botanical composition of forest/pasture. Reduced water flows for irrigation, domestic uses, and grinding mills.	Prolonged negative trend in yields of crops, livestock, etc.; increased input need per unit production; increased time and distance involved in food, fodder, fuel gathering; reduced capacity and period of grinding/saw mills operated on water flow; lower per capita availability of agricultural products.	Reduced extent of: fallowing, crop rotation, intercropping, diversified resource-management practices; extension of plough to submarginal lands; replacement of social sanctions for resource use by legal measures; unbalanced and high intensity of input use.
Changes concealed by responses to changes	Substitution of: cattle by sheep/goats; deep-rooted crops by shallow-rooted ones; shift to non-local inputs. Substitution of water flow by fossil fuel for grinding mills; of manure by chemical fertilizers.[b]	Increased seasonal migration; introduction of externally supported public distribution systems (food, inputs);[b] intensive cash-cropping on limited areas.[b]	Shifts in cropping pattern and composition of livestock; reduced diversity, increased specialization in monocropping; promotion of policies/programmes with successful record outside, without evaluation.[b]

Table 4.2 (*continued*)

Visibility of change	Changes related to:[a] Resource base	Production flows	Resource-use/management practices
Potentially negative changes[c] (processes) due to development initiatives	New systems without linkages to other diversified activities; generating excessive dependence on outside resource (fertilizer/pesticide-based technologies) ignoring traditional adaptation experiences (e.g. new irrigation structure).	Agricultural measures directed to short-term quick results; primarily product- (as against resource-) centred approaches to agricultural development.	Indifference of programme policies to mountain specificities; focus on short-term gains; high centralization; excessive, crucial dependence on external advice, ignoring wisdom; technology, trade geared to overextraction.

Source: Adapted from Jodha (1990; 1992, 66).

a. Most of the changes are interrelated and could fit into more than one block.

b. Since a number of changes might occur for reasons other than unsustainability, a fuller understanding of the underlying circumstances of a change will be necessary.

c. Changes under this category differ from those in the above two categories in the sense that they are yet to take place, and their potential emergence could be understood by examining the involved resource-use practices in relation to specific mountain characteristics.

such changes can be inferred from table 4.1, which presents statistical profiles of the study areas. Micro-level details from selected villages supplement these data.

Quick but focused enquiries verified the changes indicated in table 4.2 for six villages from different parts of the Bagmati zone. These enquiries used the Rapid Rural Appraisal (RRA) methods developed and used in different contexts (Conway, McCracken, and Pretty 1987). Besides field observations, research examined people's perceptions and oral histories. For the latter, the benchmark period chosen was the early 1950s, when major institutional and political changes took place in Nepal. Reference to these changes helped to activate people's memories about the status of their environment and resource situation at that time. In the study villages, most of the changes summarized in table 4.2 were verified. For understandable reasons, however, a quantification of changes was not possible for all variables. Table 4.3 presents some broad quantified estimates based on discussions with village elders, physical verification of changes, and discussions with members of households affected by these changes.

The table presents information at two points in time (prior to or around 1950–1952 and 1988–1990) and shows considerable negative changes in different variables grouped under four environmental parameters: (1) land/topsoil fertility; (2) vegetation/carrying capacity, (3) water flows and seasonal stresses, and (4) regenerative processes. The first section of table 4.3 covers variables (e.g. loss of topsoil) that directly or indirectly suggest declines in resource productivity and their impacts on food deficits and people's inability to sustain their livelihood. Replacement of deep-rooted crops like maize by shallow-rooted minor millets is also an indicator of the loss of topsoil.

"Vegetation-related changes" covers the impact of declines in vegetative resources. The increased time and distance involved in collecting the same quantity of fodder and fuel from non-cropped lands and the greater emphasis on small ruminants owing to the reduced carrying capacity of grazing lands are visible impacts of vegetative degradation. Villagers and researchers observed first-hand a decline in the vegetative composition of pastures and village forests, but it was difficult to quantify. Faced with a shortage of fuelwood, villagers started using inferior plants such as *banmara* (*Eupatorium* sp.), a product traditionally seldom used as fuel.

Changes in waterflow are difficult to measure unless one uses an experimental mode of investigation. In the present case, however, indicators of decline or instability of water flows were recorded in terms of the status of waterflow-based activities (e.g. grinding mills). A number of them, unlike in the past, do not operate at full capacity during part of the year. The reduced water supplies are reflected in community irrigation systems and drinking water points. The increased frequency of flash floods on the one hand and moisture stress for crops on the other hand indicate the increased instability of the moisture situation.

The last section of table 4.3 covers some of the practices that are crucial components of the processes that help resource regeneration and that interlink diversified systems of land uses. The changes reported in the table adversely affect these processes. In fact, people reported many more changes, but only those that could be easily quantified are reported in the table.

Table 4.3 **Extent of change in selected variables in the study villages in Bagmati zone, middle mountains of Nepal**

Items of change	Situation during 1950–52	1988–90
A. *Land-related changes*		
Land/mud slide (no.)	1	4
Land area affected (ha)	<1	5.0
Abandoned terraces (ha)	nil	4.3
Pasture/forest land put to crops (ha)	nil	6.7
Minor millets replacing maize (ha)	nil	3.8
Maize yield (mt/ha)	1.8	1.3
Households with food deficit, period exceeding 1 month per year (%)	2	26
Households permanently out-migrated (no.)	nil	7
B. *Vegetation-related changes*		
Time required for one head-load of:		
Fuel (hr)	4	7
Fodder (hr)	1.5	3
Distance covered for one head-load of:		
Fuel (km)	<1	6
Fodder (km)	<1	4
Proportion in animal holding:		
Cattle (%)	47	36
Sheep/goats (%)	31	38
C. *Waterflow-related changes*		
Number of water points (kuwa) with full flow/ supply during dry season	13	8
Water mills running full time (no.)	18	10
Flash floods (no./5 yrs)	nil	2
Moisture stress for crops (no./5 yrs)	nil	3
Undependability of full supply in community irrigation channel (no./5 yrs)	nil	2
D. *Regenerative process-related changes*		
Land area put to intercropping (%)	80	36
High-value cash crops (%)	2	21
Manure use (mt/ha)	6	3.5
Duration of land fallowing in crop/ fallow rotations (yrs)	7/4	3/1
Area of common property lands (%)	38	21

Source: Based on village-level investigations using Rapid Rural Appraisal methods in six villages; total number of households 148, total area of landholdings 135 hectares. Some of these changes were also recorded by detailed field studies sponsored by the International Centre for Integrated Mountain Development (ICIMOD) in the selected hill areas of China, India, and Pakistan (Sharma and Jodha 1992).

More important, the impacts of different changes on each other and, consequently, their further accentuation formed the major part of people's assessments of regenerative processes. They were not easy to quantify. By using some weighted opinion assessment of different aspects, however, some idea of the severity of the changes was obtained. However, one should be fully aware of the possible degree of subjectivity associated with such exercises.

Criticality or severity of emerging scenarios

Despite the widespread emergence of indicators of environmental degradation (tables 4.2 and 4.3), and their greatly felt impacts, it is difficult to identify precisely the degree of severity or criticality of the situation. Yardsticks are needed by which to gauge the degree of severity.

One such yardstick is the number of negative changes that are taking place simultaneously at a given location. The greater the number of such changes at a location, the nearer it should be to a critical level. In several areas of the Bagmati zone, most of the change indicators listed in the above tables are clearly visible. The relevant information for the study villages is summarized in table 4.4. This shows that 10–15 of the changes listed in table 4.2 are simultaneously visible in all six villages. But, since a single change need not extend to every household or every land parcel in the same village, the degree of seriousness of the change in terms of its coverage of people and land area needs to be examined – 10–15 changes are simultaneously visible in the case of 51 per cent of farm households and 63 per cent of the farm area in the study villages. There are only 10 per cent of

Table 4.4 **Extent of simultaneous occurrence of indicators of environmental change as listed in table 4.2**

	Occurrences of negative changes[a] (%)		
	10–15	5–10	<5
Villages affected	100	–	–
Farm households affected	51	39	10
Farm area affected	63	32	5

Source: Data based on investigations in six villages in the Bagmati zone, middle mountains of Nepal. Total number of households 148; area of landholdings 135 ha.

a. See table 4.2 for details of negative changes.

households and 5 per cent of the land area where fewer than five of the change indicators are simultaneously visible. Thus, according to table 4.4, the situation in the six villages is fairly critical. But this approach to measuring criticality does not distinguish among the different types of changes in terms of their relative importance and potential role in accentuating other negative changes. Hence, a better approach could be to judge the situation in terms of direct or indirect impacts of individual negative changes on the environmental parameters. The yardsticks to facilitate this are described below.

The criticality-assessment yardsticks fall into four categories. The first relates to the current status of a specific negative change (e.g. elimination of vegetative cover on hill slopes), in terms of its severity, spread, and irreversibility. The remaining categories relate to the potential or actual adverse effects of a negative change on: (1) the biophysical resource base or environmental parameters and their interaction patterns (e.g. decline of natural vegetation affecting regenerative processes, nutrient and moisture cycles, and the whole hydrology of a region); (2) societal conditions, including the availability of productive resources, production flows from resources, and the resilience of the economy and society (e.g. reduced diversity of agriculture influencing resilience of farming system); (3) the usage patterns of a resource base, which tend to accentuate further the vicious circle of "resource degradation–overextraction." For instance, any negative change (e.g. reduced resource productivity, slackened regenerative process) that further compels people towards greater resource extraction and use of desperate measures (e.g. unseasonal and frequent lopping of trees, cropping on steeper slopes) will be an important symptom of the criticality of the situation.

Using this framework to identify the severity of changes, however, is constrained by the lack of relevant data. Nevertheless, based on the general assessment of cause-and-effect relations and patterns of interactions among different variables (as inferred from circumstantial evidence, oral history, and the present status of farming systems and people surviving in degraded environments), some assessment of the emerging critical situation in the middle mountain areas of Nepal is possible.

Our focus is on people's perceptions in terms of the relative severity, spread, and impacts of the specific negative changes covered by table 4.3. The impacts, both current and potential, again relate to the biophysical resource base (or environmental parameters), societal conditions, and the acceleration of forces causing environmental degradation. People's perceptions are not just their opinions but views that emerged after discussions of physically observed situations in the study villages. The procedures used in the Rapid Rural Appraisal approach involved physical observation of specific changes, followed by discussions with knowledgeable groups of village elders or others directly contributing to or affected by the change.

This approach reduced the coverage of investigations in terms of the number of villages but contributed to the depth of the information collected. One feature of the information gathered is the identification of just one dominant view per village for each of the aspects covered by RRA. This became possible because physical verifications helped in reducing the scope for a multiplicity of views on the same issue in the same village. The perceptions based on physical observation and discussion were pooled for all the villages using weighting systems. Accordingly, individual villages rated each change on a scale of 1 to 4 (the greater the significance of the change, the higher the score it received). In pooling these scores, the overall value given to specific variables involved the summation of the score multiplied by the number of villages giving the same scores. For instance, if three villages considered reduced water flows as the most severe problem (thus getting a score of 4), the weighted rank value would be $4 \times 3 = 12$. If only two villages subscribed to the above view, the final value would be $4 \times 2 = 8$.

The values elicited in this way for each of the aspects covered by table 4.5 were pooled to reflect people's perceptions of the changes and their impacts and severity. The values presented in table 4.5 can again be divided by 6 (i.e. the total number of villages) to conform to the usual weighting procedures, but that will not alter the structure of opinions on the degree of environmental change.

According to table 4.5, any score with values of 20 and higher should be considered as a dominant situation as regards the villagers who have seen and are living with the environmental changes. Thus, in terms of both severity and spread, the decline in measures and practices contributing to regenerative processes in the mountains is the most important change approaching a critical situation. The degradation of vegetation, with all its consequences, is also widespread.

The changes in individual environmental parameters have a second-level influence on each other (i.e. on biophysical resource variables and processes), on socio-economic conditions, and on the very process of change already initiated. Viewing the degree of criticality of environmental change in terms of such impacts and interactions, a

Table 4.5 **Assessment of the degree of severity of environmental change through people's perceptions in middle mountains of Nepal**

Parameters of environmental change	Degree of severity indicated by people's perception				
	Current status of change indicator		Impacts on current position of:		
	Severe	Wide-spread	Biophysical parameters[a]	Societal condition[b]	Severity trends[c]
Land-resource decline (landslide, topsoil erosion)	12	10	16	20	22
Degradation of vegetation (composition/ carrying capacity)	16	22	15	18	20
Reduced water flows (seasonal scarcity)	10	5	15	12	10
Shrinking regenerative processes (interlinked, self-sustained activities)	22	23	18	20	22

Source: Based on village-level investigations in six villages in the Bagmati zone, middle mountains of Nepal, using Rapid Rural Appraisal methods. The procedure used for calculating the values reported involved weighted opinion assessments. Accordingly, each change was judged in terms of its severity, spread, and impacts on a scale of 1 to 4. The higher the rank, the higher the value (from 1 to 4). The ranking of each variable was weighted by the number of villages (i.e. collective opinion of village elders, etc.) giving specific rank. For instance, if three villages considered reduced water flows as the most severe problem (getting rank 4), the weighted rank would be 4 × 3 = 12. If only two villages subscribed to the above rank, the weighted rank value would be 4 × 2 = 8. The pooled value of such weighted ranks is presented in the table to give some idea of the severity of the situation indicated by each change as perceived by the villagers. To conform to the usual procedure of a weighting system, one could divide each of the values in the table by 6, but that would not change the structure of opinions revealed by the table.

a. Topsoil, vegetation, water flows, microclimate, seasonality.
b. Productive resource availability, production flows, resilience.
c. Push for inferior options, desperation in resource use, accentuation of resource-extractive tendencies.

value of 20+ in table 4.5 suggests that the decline of regenerative processes and decline of the land resource base are two major indicators of the severity of the situation. These indicators greatly contribute to further deterioration in societal conditions in terms of productive resource availability, production flows, and the traditional resilience of mountain communities. More importantly, these changes further accelerate the processes of resource degradation based on the vicious cycle of resource degradation/resource extraction. In other words, people are pushed to accept inferior options, resort to more desperate measures, and increasingly adopt resource-extractive strategies to maintain their survival. All environmental changes, except those related to water flows, accentuate the severity of negative changes. Yet, villagers viewed changes in water flow as the most critical facet of environmental change in the villages.

Human driving forces of environmental change

In the debate on environmental degradation in the Himalayas, it is not difficult to see two relatively extreme views. As discussed during the Mohonk Mountain Conference reported in Ives and Ives (1987), the conventional view blames subsistence hill farmers for deforestation, soil erosion, and associated resource degradation. The other view, instead of blaming humans, projects resource degradation as a consequence of the natural process of mass wasting. The reality lies somewhere in between. Various studies report an accentuation of resource degradation with increased human interference in the Himalayas. In assessing the role of human interventions in environmental change, it should be stated that a society's inability to live within the usable limits of the biophysical resource base of its habitat is the major cause of environmental degradation. The tolerance limits of any habitat *vis-à-vis* the intensity and variety of human interventions differ according to specific characteristics of an ecosystem. In fragile resource zones like mountains, such limits are narrower than in relatively stable zones of high productivity.

Hence, resource-use patterns considered normal and non-extractive in the latter case may prove environmentally degrading in the mountain areas. To elaborate on this and to identify some of the human driving forces causing environmental changes in the middle mountains of Nepal, we may discuss their specific characteristics and their "critical imperatives" for the environmental or ecological health of the region. The same can then be related to public and private interventions (or their attributes) to facilitate the assessment of factors and processes associated with negative changes.

The relationships between resource characteristics and the attributes of resource-centred activities can be understood conceptually. But it may be difficult to determine causal relationships between environmental changes and specific factors. The lack of comparable information on benchmarks, differences in lead-times for fuller reflection of the impacts of interventions, and the difficulty of controlling the impacts of additional (compounding) factors emerging in the intervening period are among the complicating factors. Consequently, in relating negative changes to different human driving forces, we shall focus on "processes of change" and some contextual evidence.

Mountain specificities

Specific conditions or characteristics of mountain areas separate them from plains. We call these "mountain specificities" (Jodha 1990). The important ones considered here are: inaccessibility, fragility, marginality, diversity, ecological and other niches (products or activities with natural suitability and comparative advantage in mountain regions), and human adaptation mechanisms in mountain habitats. Most of the specificities are not only interrelated owing to common causes (like edaphic and terrain conditions, etc.) but share the consequences of disturbance to each other through human interventions. The operational implications of these mountain characteristics generate constraints and prospects for specific activities and products in mountains. They also condition and shape the patterns of activities based on mountain resources. As long as these activities are well adapted to mountain specificities, human interventions do not harm the environmental situation. However, the mismatch between mountain conditions and human activities insensitive to the limitations of the resource base leads to environmental degradation (Jodha 1995).

Table 4.6 presents the key imperatives of mountain specificities in terms of objective circumstances that, in association with specific human driving forces, may result in environmental degradation. The table is fairly self-explanatory. Its key purpose is to highlight the "critical" importance of some of the mountain features in the whole process of maintaining the health and stability of the environment as well as mountain production systems. Any disregard of these imperatives for short-term considerations would mean a definite step towards environmental degradation and long-term unsustainability of mountain resources and associated activities.

In the context of the foregoing discussion, the role of human driving forces in environmental changes in mountain areas can be understood in terms of how they handle or mishandle the critical imperatives indicated in table 4.6. The issues can be framed in terms of the following concrete questions.

Table 4.6 **Mountain specificities and their critical imperatives relating to environmental protection/degradation**

Mountain specificity	Imperatives
Inaccessibility	Relatively closed system with limited (and unequal) external linkages; limited scope for siphoning off local pressure on resources, compulsion and limits to local absorption of rising pressure. Improved accessibility tends to bring additional pressure on fragile resources.
Fragility	Low carrying capacity, vulnerability to irreversible damage under high use intensity. Forces of market, state intervention, and demographic pressures tend to ignore fragility and its implications.
Marginality	Marginal resources and marginal people prone to neglect and overexploitation by mainstream decision makers as and when it suits the latter. Owing to "marginality," interests/concerns and contributions of mountain area/people have high invisibility for the mainstream.
Diversity	Sources of diversified, interlinked, self-sustaining activities as true indicators of pressure-bearing capacities of resource base; liable to be disregarded under production patterns encouraged by public intervention and demographic and market pressures. If understood and harnessed, they serve as a basis of "regenerative/sustainable processes."
Niches	Special activities/products with comparative advantage to mountains, serving as basis of links with other areas; usually overextracted and depleted (on unequal terms) by the mainstream; attractive basis for public intervention.
Adaptation mechanisms	Traditional technological and institutional methods of resource management that help in balancing pressure on resources; inability of traditional mechanisms to withstand new forces of change (population, market, and public intervention) brings about degradation.

1. What are the factors and processes contributing to increased pressure (demand) on mountain resources?
2. In view of inaccessibility and low carrying capacity (owing to characteristics of fragility and marginality), how is the increased pressure absorbed or managed without straining and damaging the local resource base?
3. In the face of fragility and marginality, what are the means by which the use intensity and input-absorption capacity of land re-

sources are enhanced without negative side-effects in terms of resource degradation?

4. How are the niche- and diversity-based potentialities conceived of and harnessed (or overextracted) to enhance the pressure-absorption capacity of mountain resources? As a side-effect, how does the pressure on resources become accentuated?
5. What are the traditional mechanisms that have evolved over time to ensure a match between human activities and the attributes of mountain resources? And how have the forces identified in question 1 above affected their feasibility and effectiveness?

Answers to these questions may reveal the composition and role of different human forces causing environmental changes in mountains. The three basic forces in this context are: (1) population growth, (2) market mechanism and commercialization, and (3) public intervention in mountain areas. During different phases of growth and effectiveness of these forces, different mechanisms and strategies are consciously or unconsciously developed to respond to the issues implied by the questions. Tables 4.7, 4.8, and 4.9 summarize the relevant details. For each of the three categories of forces, historically specific phases are noted. For each phase, key features of the driving force are indicated. Similarly, for each phase, strategies for stress management (e.g. controlling or regulating demand and enhancing supplies) are indicated. Next, the implications of these strategies for environmental changes are examined. In some cases the discussion may go far beyond 50 years (the reference period used for reporting changes summarized in tables 4.2 and 4.3). This is unavoidable if the dynamics of change are examined in a historical context. Furthermore, for reasons stated earlier, it is difficult to relate these forces precisely to the specific changes noted in tables 4.2 and 4.3. However, the two could be linked as parts of resource-use/resource-degradation processes.

Accordingly, the process of environmental change can be presented as a rate and pattern of deforestation, soil erosion, disruption in water movements, reduction in biodiversity, and interdependence of various biophysical variables as a part of "regenerative processes." The immediate causative factors – the use of the plough in submarginal lands hitherto kept under natural vegetation, the push for monoculture in place of polyculture, a slackening of the social sanctions and traditional folk agronomic practices that helped to regulate the intensity of resource use – are rooted in basic driving forces. Tables 4.7 to 4.9 present major phases in these basic forces and their implications in terms of societal responses (strategies) and impacts on environmental parameters. Although the tables summarize information on different periods and phases of change, our main focus for elaborating human driving forces and their implications/impacts is on the past 40–50 years.

Furthermore, the processes of change discussed below cover the Himalayas or middle mountains in general, of which the Bagmati zone and the study villages are part. It may not be possible to capture fully all the specific causative factors and to relate them to the degree of environmental change, but some can be inferred from the data presented in tables 4.1 and 4.3. Some additional information relevant to these issues is presented in table 4.10, which indicates for the study villages significant demographic, technological, and economic changes that have a direct bearing on the environmental changes discussed above. In the following discussion, the focus will be on processes of change at the macro level, although similar changes occur in the study villages.

Demographic factors

As shown by table 4.7, during the different phases of history, population spurts have taken place in the Nepal Himalayas. In the recent past (over the last 50 years or so), mountain areas, like the rest of the developing world, have experienced an unprecedented rate of population growth (Sharma and Banskota 1992). This is interpreted as an outcome of the health revolution and some governmental welfare programmes. The quality and spread of health facilities in the mountains are nowhere comparable to those in the accessible and productive plains. The inaccessibility and marginality of distant areas and their inhabitants obstruct the spread of health facilities, as both welfare and wealth programmes betray a tendency to follow tarmac roads (Chambers 1983). Certain health interventions, such as smallpox eradication, which required a single inoculation or infrequent contact with distant communities, were less obstructed by these constraints. Demographic data from different studies summarized by Poffenberger (1980) reflect the impact of the health revolution in the post-1950 period. The crude death rate in Nepal declined from 30–37 per 1,000 population in 1951 to 22 in 1971. The corresponding infant mortality figures are 250–260 and 172. The life expectancy for the same period increased from 27.1 to 42.9 years for males and 28.5 to 38.9 years for females. Health and welfare programmes, as well as the development activities (including foreign aid) that have contrib-

Table 4.7 **Population growth and environmental changes in middle mountain areas of Nepala**[a]

Population change: phases and features	Pressure (demand/ supply) management strategies	Environmental implications
Migration-induced population growth		
12th century onwards • migration from Indian plain following Muslim invasions • transformation from semi-nomadic to sedentarized population	Resource upgrading by ethno-engineering (terraces, irrigation), folk agronomy; mixed farming, diversified interlinked land-based activities; demand rationed by social sanctions on resource use, etc.; population–food balanced.	Increased use intensity of land, balanced land-use pattern; limited excess/ extractive burden on resources.
Food surplus-induced population growth		
Late 18th to early 19th century • introduction of maize and potato eased food situation, induced population growth	Facilitated use of uplands; surplus production, no (supply) constraints; greater use of resource diversity	Increased replacement of perennial (natural) vegetation by annual crops; higher land-use intensity; gradual resource erosion
Health revolution-induced population growth		
Post-1950 • welfare programmes, health improvements, control of epidemics; development programmes; changes in number and quality (in terms of attitude, enterprise, etc.) of population; reduced migration possibilities	Collapse of institutional arrangements; infeasibility of land-extensive practices; overstocking and overgrazing; production and supply fail to keep pace with demand; dependency on external supplies (of products/inputs); recourse to inferior/ marginal options; enhanced extraction capacities	Decline of resource conservation measures; increased resource extraction; environmental degradation, leading to more severe situation

a. For details on different issues covered by the table, see Blaikie, Cameron, and Seddon (1979), Fürer-Haimendorf (1974), Hitchcock (1963), Mahat et al. (1987), Poffenberger (1980), Price (1981), Rana et al. (1973), Sharma and Banskota (1992), and Upadhyaya and Abueva (1974).

uted to these demographic trends, have yet to succeed in raising the living standards of the people to a level that could help reduce population growth. The obvious consequence is increased pressure on mountain resources. And changed expectations further accentuate the heightened subsistence needs attendant on the increased number of people. The rise in people's expectations, a product of increased commercialization, public intervention, improved accessibility, exposure, and also persistent economic inequities, has increased the average level of demand on resources.

The broad overview of demographic changes and the responses of communities (in terms of out-migration and upgrading resources and their productivity) shows that earlier strategies no longer work. The pressure on mountain resources due to increased subsistence and "beyond-subsistence" needs has not enjoyed any concomitant development of human skills or increase in resource productivity through technological innovations. On the contrary, constraints imposed by inaccessibility, fragility, and marginality put a high premium on larger family size, thereby inducing further population growth (Sharma and Banskota 1992). As a consequence, high pressure on the stagnant production system has produced changes in the resource-use pattern, with adverse effects on the environment. Intensity of resource use, even without significant technological and institutional innovations, has increased. Submarginal lands hitherto kept under natural vegetation (forest and pasture) have gone over to annual crops. Cropping has extended to steeper and more fragile slopes. Overstocking and overgrazing have emerged as dominant patterns of livestock management.

Wherever permitted by agroclimatic conditions or improved market linkages, cropping intensity has increased. Land-use and overall agricultural activity patterns have changed. The area of forest and pasture has declined. The increased demand for food and consequent changes in the resource-use pattern have eroded the traditional resource-regenerative processes based on diversified, interlinked, land-extensive practices.

This has happened despite people's awareness of the situation. Helpless in the present serious demand–supply imbalance, people are aware but lack the means to combat the situation. A focus on short-term, inferior, and desperate options forms part of their forced adaptation to new changes. Options in terms of off-farm employment and migration are insufficient to syphon off the pressure from local resources (Banskota 1989). Inadequate improvements in human skills and an absence of non-agricultural activities reduce the potential for sizeable migration. Migration as a means to relax local population pressure is less feasible now, owing to the lack of resource opportunities in proximity to the mountains and to the increased border rigidities over recent decades.

Other mechanisms for managing the stress on mountain resources also have not had much impact. The options could include resource upgrading through infrastructural works (e.g. irrigation, slope stabilization), raising the carrying capacities of resources through resource-centred technologies, and yield-raising production technologies (Jodha 1991). In the public sector, more efforts have occurred since 1950 than at any time in past history. In limited pockets, at least in the short term, they have had some effect, but their general weakness, as in the case of other interventions in mountain areas, is their inability to internalize the mountain perspective – i.e. the conscious consideration of mountain specificities while conceiving, designing, and implementing the measures (Jodha 1992). Interventions are often based on the experiences of non-mountain areas and so are completely indifferent to the rationale of traditional systems that help match resource characteristics and resource-use practices. Consequently, we have huge infrastructural works that are not only indifferent to the diversified development needs of mountains but also insensitive to their side-effects (Banskota and Jodha 1992a). There are resource-centred projects with a dominance of "technique"-oriented activities with little concern for "user perspective." Production technologies have focused on use intensity, with a high dependence on external inputs (e.g. high-yield varieties with fertilizers and plant-protection chemicals) and little sensitivity to diversity and interlinkages of other land-based activities (Jodha 1991). Moreover, access to such technologies is restricted to those who have the resources to use them. In the absence of appropriate technology, efforts at more intensive use of resources to secure a higher volume of production amount to mining the resource base.

Market forces and commercialization

Despite problems of high transport costs, poor mobility, and inaccessibility, mountain areas have never been completely isolated from other regions. Petty trading based on harnessing local niches, transhumance, and migration had always linked the mountain with the plains. Rarely self-sufficient in food supplies, the areas needed me-

Table 4.8 **Market forces and environmental changes in middle mountain areas of Nepal**[a]

Market forces: phases and features	Pressure (demand/supply) management strategies	Environmental implications
Early 20th century		
a. Focus on state revenue by timber trade	a. Forests treated as "inexhaustible" resource; timber trade without productive reinvestment	a. Heavy extraction of permanent vegetation in accessible locations
b. Local need-based exchange and upland/lowland linkages, petty trading, transhumance, etc.	b. Niche/comparative advantage as basis of petty trade; exchange-based supplies supplemented local requirements; inaccessibility restrained overextraction	b. Resource exploitation within limits
Latter half of 20th century: Commercialization as a part of transformation process		
a. Selective opening of areas, infrastructure, linkages with mainstream markets	a. Accessibility encouraging one-way flow of resources; unequal exchange for mountains; distant markets insensitive to local resources and local demand	a–c. Unregulated, overexploitation of resources; negative side-effects of infrastructure and large-scale programmes to harness niches; reduced diversity of production activities; weakened regenerative processes, environmental backlash.
b. Development-induced commercialization (institutions, technologies for cash crops, etc.)	b. Focus on cash crops, pushing food crops to marginal areas; highly extractive and inegalitarian development	
c. Concentration on mountain niches (timber, power, horticulture, tourism)	c. Heavy extraction of mountain niches with unequal terms of trade, indifference to side-effects	

a. For details on issues covered by the table, see Banskota and Jodha (1992a,b), Hitchcock (1963), and Jodha (1990).

chanisms for balancing demand for and supplies of food. Yet, markets traditionally served as the "servant" of the system. Exchange was largely local needs centred. Linkages and exchange activities fluctuated with changes in demand for mountain products and people (e.g. recruits for outside armies) as well as changes in trading patterns, partners, and routes.

Since the early 1950s, mountain areas have become better integrated with external markets. Upland–lowland linkages have also become stronger and more varied. The subsistence hill economy has become rapidly integrated with wider market economies (Banskota 1989). Linkages with external systems provide some means to enhance the sustainability of a hitherto closed system with high pressure on resources (Jodha 1990). In the present phase of transformation of mountain areas, however, market integration has several negative side-effects, most of which also adversely affect the environment.

The issue of market and mountain economy interactions can be discussed at two interrelated levels: commercialization of production systems within mountains, and linkage of the mountain economy with the mainstream market.

Commercialization of mountain agriculture

Monetization of the mountain economy, or of agriculture as its dominant sector, can be judged in terms of the increasing role of the cash nexus (i.e. the cash economy). Following improved accessibility, technological and institutional interventions, and a rise in people's expectation levels, even extremely subsistence-oriented communities have slowly moved towards cash transactions (Banskota 1989). A rising proportion of external inputs, in both consumption and production activities, has accelerated the process. Domination of a cash nexus reduces the importance of other considerations (e.g. resource conservation, regeneration, interdependence of multiple activities) in farming decisions.

An increase in the extent of high-value cash crops (vegetables, fruits), supported by new technologies and state patronage, has been a major factor encouraging commercialization of agriculture in relatively accessible areas. This helps mountain areas in harnessing their comparative advantage. But commercialization of mountain areas with complete disregard for mountain specificities has serious negative consequences. First, its impact in terms of internal inequities and changed human attitudes has led to a rapid erosion of social sanctions and informal collective arrangements for the protection and sustainable use of resources. Secondly, the commercial orientation has introduced imbalances in land-use patterns. Relatively better land is put under profitable cash crops (especially vegetables), and staple food crops (e.g. maize) are pushed to submarginal land with low productivity, compelling the extension of crops to still more submarginal lands. An emphasis on both vegetables and fruit crops and high-yielding food crops in some areas has led to reduced diversity of mountain agriculture and a decline in the interdependence of different land-based activities (Mahat et al. 1987; Yadav 1992). This sort of narrow specialization has eroded the resource-regenerative processes mentioned earlier. Finally, "servicing" of cash crops (e.g. the provision of wooden packaging for fruits and wrapping material for vegetables, and the use of ecologically harmful chemicals) has negative side-effects on the environment.

Links with external markets

The environmental consequences of the market forces discussed above are accentuated by the side-effects of external linkages of mountain areas. The promotion of external market linkages is a part of the formal state approach to mountain areas. The guiding considerations are the transformation or development of these areas, and the need to harness the mountains' comparative advantages in some products and activities. Horticulture, tourism, irrigation, and hydropower production are the major areas attracting the attention of both the state and the market.

But the new market links produce an exchange between unequals, at least in the transitional phase. Because of their natural and man-made handicaps, mountain areas tend to interact with mainstream markets on unequal terms. External markets often treat mountain niches as virgin opportunities ripe for plundering. The whole process amounts to overextraction of mountain resources with adverse environmental and economic consequences. Resource extraction, even by the local communities, becomes a function of signals from distant markets that are not sensitive to local needs and resource problems. Several products and activities that contribute to diversity and sustainability of mountain farming systems become marginal and extinct if they do not fit into market-determined processes. Moreover, not even a small fraction of the economic revenue ultimately generated by mountain products (e.g. timber price in the final market) is ploughed back into mountain areas. The approaches to harnessing mountain niches (through investment, technology, support services) are guided by norms and procedures that are incapable of incorporating long-term environmental consequences (Jodha 1992).

Public intervention

State intervention in mountain areas is as old as the governance of these areas by the nation-state. Mountains, by providing refuge to political or religious dissidents, had in the past helped many who formed new states. Until the early 1950s, however, the state's intervention (under both colonial and other modes of rule) was largely for resource extraction to sustain the state apparatus with all its hierarchies. The last four to five decades have witnessed a new phase, which has involved the state in activities beyond resource extraction and administration. Welfare concerns, relief activities, and development needs have induced public intervention in mountain areas, including Nepal (Banskota and Jodha 1992a,b).

The interventions have also included the legal and institutional measures that affect people's access to natural resources. In mountain areas of Nepal, especially since the early 1950s, the compulsion to manage pressure on resources and the need to harness mountain niches set the stage for various public policies and programmes (ERL 1988; Shrestha 1988). Public intervention has had little impact on balancing supplies with demands on mountain resources. In fact, increasing development efforts and declining trends in performance (when seen in terms of the total impact on the economy and environment) have operated simultaneously (ICIMOD 1990).

The principal reason for the prevailing situation, which is applicable to the Himalayas as a whole, is the lack of a mountain perspective while designing and implementing welfare and development interventions in mountain areas. Most of the development interventions (technological or institutional) entail a transfer from outside without a full understanding of the objective circumstances of mountains (Banskota and Jodha 1992a; Jodha 1992). We can briefly illustrate this with a focus on issues bearing on environmental changes.

Policies affecting resource and resource-user relations

A major policy intervention in the mountain areas of Nepal addresses people's access to natural resources. Such access could be examined at two levels: community access to common resources and private land and users' relation to them.

Regarding the former, the usurpation of people's traditional rights to natural resources has been a part of state policies in the Himalayas for a very long time (Guha 1989). Historically, in the Nepal Hima-

Table 4.9 **Public intervention and environmental changes in middle mountain areas of Nepal**[a]

Public intervention: phases and features	Pressure (demand/ supply) management strategies	Environmental implications
State acquisition of community resources		
a. Mid-18th century Money value on land, private tenure replacing community ownership	a. Land alienation/ insecurity; money (not land characteristics) dominated management and use	a. Inducement to neglect or overexploit resource
b. Latter half of 20th century Nationalization for conservation/development and revenue	b. Same as the above; reduced access to land, forest, water; promotion of pressure on remaining accessible resources	b. High resource-use intensity; people's indifference to and neglect of resources
Welfare programmes		
Latter half of 20th century Health facility, relief, subsidies, etc.	Promotion of pressure on resources without resource development	Higher use intensity, depletion of land, vegetation, water resources; protection in selected pockets
Development interventions		
Latter half of 20th century Infrastructure, technology, institutional measures, management–economic policies focused on increased resource extraction, short-term gains	Focus on supply, upgrading resources and their productivity; focus on short-term goals; imposition of options evolved elsewhere; effort–performance gaps; demand–supply gap widened; demand side not managed, greater focus on promotion of supplies	Negative side-effects of development interventions, because they lack mountain perspective; infrastructure ignores fragility, technology ignores need for diversity; niches harnessed in "extractive" mode, high environmental cost of development projects

a. For details on issues covered by the table, see Banskota and Jodha (1992b), Blaikie et al. (1979), DFAMS (1986), Poffenberger (1980), Rana et al. (1973), and Zaman (1973).

layas it happened gradually as the society moved from nomadism to sedentary living and the feudal system of rule took hold. In recent decades, however, interventions such as the nationalization of forests, the establishment of conservation areas or national parks, the transfer of land to public institutions, the acquisition of land for industries and public utilities, and the privatization of community pasture and forest land have reduced people's access to natural resources. Other interventions include marketing and price regulations on natural-resource products collected by the people. The introduction of state monopoly or specific trading arrangements on medicinal plants and herbs is one example. Another way of affecting people's relation to resources is through the introduction of new species, which do not fit into people's diversified production and usage systems, to upgrade these resources. The *Nepal Miscellaneous Series*, periodically published by the Regmi Research Institute, has documented most of these interventions, the effective implementation and impacts of which are not uniform over the middle mountains or total mountain areas of Nepal. Yet in a number of areas negative side-effects have occurred. Besides alienating people from resources, some policies have encouraged indifference and a tendency to overexploit resources, thereby accentuating pressure on the resources that are still easily accessible to the people. The traditional linkages between production and resource-use systems based on common property resources and private property resources have broken down. This collapse has several environmental implications.

Regarding access to private land resources, Nepal has slowly tried to create an equitable system of land ownership. Here again, however, owing to the long time-lag between the declaration of state intentions and legislation or between legislation and implementation, the impact of the change is pre-empted by vested interests (Regmi 1971; Zaman 1973). Consequently, land inequity, landlessness, and land hunger continue to feature in mountain areas in Nepal. The security of formal or informal tenancy (which is quite widespread) is also affected by the inequity of power associated with land inequity. One of the major implications of this inequity is a higher use intensity of small landholdings and a tendency to grab and convert submarginal common lands into private lands for cropping (tables 4.2 and 4.3).

Production programmes

The focus of production programmes in mountain areas is primarily on resource-use intensification and extraction. These considerations guide other aspects of public interventions – be they infrastructural, development, or investment strategies (Banskota and Jodha 1992a). Consequently, the focus of production programmes is on mountain niches such as irrigation and hydropower potential, mining, tourism, or horticultural production. These are largely guided by external demand and the revenue needs of the state. The environmentally relevant implications of these initiatives include a high rate of resource extraction, reduced diversification of resource-centred activities, and negative side-effects on fragile mountain resources (Jodha 1995).

Even in the case of agriculture, the dominant sector of the mountain economy, the key focus of these programmes is on raising the productivity of crops and livestock. Learning from the past history of agricultural transformation elsewhere, the emphasis has been on selected crops and their seed, fertilizer, and irrigation-based technologies. The whole approach, based as it is on the experiences of the plains, frequently disregards the need for diversity and interlinkages, constraints on resource-use intensity, and the problems attendant on inaccessibility. This applies to both annual and perennial plant-based activities. Environmentally, a more alarming side-effect of this approach is reduced diversity and a consequent increase in the risk and unsustainability of the system (Jodha 1991).

Resource-centred programmes in agricultural sectors related to watershed development, afforestation, and pasture development bear a more direct relationship to environmental health and stability. A fairly large number of programmes of this type are scattered all over the middle mountains of Nepal (ERL 1988). Most programmes take a sectoral approach and do not fully consider interlinkages between mountain specificities. Moreover, given a strong focus on "techniques" rather than a user perspective, they are largely sustained by government subsidy or donor support. Some initiatives of non-governmental organizations (NGOs), however, are exceptions.

Investment and subsidy

An outstanding feature of most of the production- or resource-related interventions is their heavy dependence on public investment and subsidy. Given the low level of development and widespread poverty, this seems unavoidable. At the same time, however, mountain areas in Nepal (and elsewhere) are faced with underinvestment. This becomes clear in comparing the magnitude of investment with overall needs of diversified activities and the high fixed and operational costs of activities in the inaccessible, fragile mountain areas (Banskota and Jodha 1992a). Underinvestment leads to underdevelopment, which, in turn, initiates overexploitation of resources and environmental degradation. More important, the investment priorities (focused on extraction of mountain potential and building of infrastructure, such as roads and bridges) generally ignore the diversified, ancillary activities (Banskota and Jodha 1992a). Thus the investment strategies for mountains bypass diversification, the regeneration of local resources, and other activities so conducive to environmental stability.

"Subsidy" is another important feature of public sector investment in mountain areas. Instead of subsidies being used as inducements for diversified and sustainable resource use, they often promote more extractive use of resources and narrow specializations. Thus, in most cases, so-called "perverse incentives" cause environmental degradation.

Infrastructural development

Constructing irrigation and communication systems is an important step in the development of resources and the integration of mountain economies with the rest of the world. However, this step has two important side-effects relating to environmental questions. First, the norms and yardsticks for designing such systems and calculating their worth, borrowed as they are from non-mountain situations, prove very short-sighted and narrow in the mountain context (Jodha 1992). The negative externalities, in terms of environmental degradation or reduced resilience of production systems in mountains, seldom receive due consideration. Moreover, most infrastructural works have a sectoral focus, and their positive or negative impacts on related activities or resources do not get sufficient consideration. In short, overextraction of resources is quite widespread in mountain areas.

Welfare schemes

Mountain areas also enjoy their share of state patronage reflected in various welfare and relief schemes. Without denying their utility, it may be stated that they play an important role in sustaining high pressure on mountain resources without building the carrying capacity of resources.

Finally, most of the public interventions in mountain areas are directed to dealing with the supply aspects of the situation (e.g. raising productivity, upgrading the resource base, providing welfare support). Their negative impacts (through intensification and overextraction of a resource use) are accentuated by the absence of any measures to control or regulate the demand on mountain resources (Sharma and Banskota 1992).

Synthesis

The preceding pages have presented a broad account of the factors and processes associated with environmental changes in the mountain areas of Nepal. Precise separation of the roles and relative importance of different human driving forces is quite difficult. In the last four to five decades most of the forces of change – namely population growth, market integration, and technological and institutional interventions – not only have operated simultaneously, but some have reinforced the impacts of others. For instance, new technologies enhanced resource extraction capacities and accelerated the population pressure, leading to overexploitation of mountain resources. Population-induced poverty prompted increased state intervention through welfare and development activities; these in turn focused on infrastructure and the market integration of mountains with other regions. As a next step, state policies and market forces helped each other to produce higher resource extraction, with its adverse environmental consequences.

In most cases, environmental change has occurred as a result of the disregard of specific mountain conditions such as fragility, diversity, and inaccessibility. These mountain characteristics are interrelated in terms of common biophysical causes or shared consequences, which obstruct a clear separation of the relative roles of forces leading to environmental degradation.

The final problem stems from the scale of operation or consequence of forces behind the change. Owing partly to the interrelationships of mountain specificities and partly to temporal and spatial lags between causes and effects, the events of "cause and effect" in macro or micro contexts are not scattered in any systematic way. Consequently, a precise one-to-one association between the driving force of change and its impacts is difficult to capture. Yet some idea of the relative role of different driving forces emerges from the distribution of proximate causes of environmental changes. This can be attempted in the macro context more easily than in the micro (village) level context (table 4.10), because the operation of various proximate causes and basic driving forces is more visible at the macro level.

Table 4.11 summarizes different proximate factors and the driving

Table 4.10 **Changes indicating transformation of study villages over time**

Feature	Range of situation during: 1950–52	1988–90
Households	36–44	41–52
Adults with education up to 7th class	3–7	12–25
Households with one or more member working outside in town	4–7	15–18
Shops in village/neighbouring villages	0–2	8–12
Radios in villages	0–0	4–7
Government programme/facilities in village/ neighbouring village[a]	0–2	5–11
Households using external inputs (fertilizer, diesel, seed, etc.)	0–0	8–15
Households with some area under multiple cropping	0–0	11–15

Source: Based on enquiries in six villages in the Bagmati zone, middle mountains of Nepal, using the Rapid Rural Appraisal method.

a. Includes credit facility, extension agency, health facility, employment and development programme, communication point, etc.

forces. The proximate causes listed disregard, in one way or the other, the imperatives of mountain specificities. Some primarily cause disruption of the resource-use system that is conducive to environmental stability; others largely contribute to resource-use intensification or extraction of resources and disregard the side-effects. As the table shows, most proximate causes are linked to more than one driving force. Looking at the fairly even distribution of proximate causes *vis-à-vis* driving forces, it is not easy to identify the relative role of different driving forces. In a rather broad sense, however, one can single out market forces as key factors underlying most of the proximate causes of environmental changes. This is quite understandable in so far as inducements for resource extraction, as facilitated by infrastructure, technology, and state facilities, operate through market mechanisms. Yet, population pressure and public intervention reinforce the role of the market. The distribution of proximate causes, under different driving forces, broadly illustrates these possibilities.

An important limitation of the formulation indicated by table 4.11 relates to the uncertainty about the magnitude of impact of different causative factors. For instance, it is difficult to judge whether reduced diversity of land-based activities affects mountain environments more than the overextraction of mountain niches, or vice versa.

Table 4.11 **Proximate causes and human driving forces behind environmental change[a] in the middle mountain areas of Nepal**

	Population	Market forces		State intervention		
Proximate cause	Health care, accessibility-induced population growth	Market linkage, cash nexus	Profit motive, attitude change	Legal, administrative, institutional changes	Development, welfare activities	Technology, infrastructure, etc.
Overcropping, overgrazing	×					
Deforestation, narrow specialization, external input-intensive agriculture		×	×			×
Reduced diversity, interlinkages in agriculture	×	×	×		×	
Disruption of traditional resource management, collective regulations; local control, access, etc.	×	×	×	×	×	
Overextraction of mountain niches, other resources		×		×		×
Side-effects of massive infrastructure, scale, technology of operation				×	×	×
Distant demand-induced resource extraction			×			×
Focus on short-term gains, application of external experiences, disregard of mountain specificities	×	×	×		×	×

a. For details see tables 4.7, 4.8, and 4.9.

Socio-economic vulnerabilities and impacts

The foregoing discussion of the indicators of environmental change and human driving forces has already alluded to some socio-economic impacts of environmental changes. In fact, some of the second- or third-order changes in the status of environmental resources are manifestations of impacts of people's adjustment to environmental changes. For such reasons, at times it is difficult to separate precisely the impacts of environmental changes as causes of socio-economic disruptions from the environmental changes as consequences of socio-economic adjustment. Similarly, at times it is difficult to separate the socio-economic impacts resulting from environmental changes and those resulting from the forces underlying environmental change.

Such dilemmas prevail because socio-economic impacts are products of overall transformation processes, which involve simultaneously both the environmental variables and the factors affecting them. Hence, we may talk more comfortably about the socio-economic impacts of change (i.e. transformation process) with a special focus on the environmental components of this transformation.

Accordingly, in the first place, the transformation processes have disrupted the overall production base and interlinkages of land-based activities, which evolved through adaptations to specific conditions of mountain habitats (tables 4.7–4.10). Ineffectiveness or infeasibility of several traditional production and resource-management practices due to the above changes may be treated as manifestations of socio-economic vulnerabilities. The changed status and productivity of environmental resources are important factors behind such vulnerabilities.

As a consequence of the marginalization of age-old and well-tested components of traditional farming systems, the mountain communities (most of which depend on agriculture) are under serious pressures. Mountain farmers must: (a) produce more, owing to the increased number of people, increased market demands, and increased inducements by the state; (b) produce more from a qualitatively degraded and quantitatively (per capita) reduced resource base; (c) perform the above tasks without any viable technologies, since their traditional resource-extensive technologies are incompatible with required resource-intensive production systems and new substitute technologies are either not available or not accessible to the bulk of the farmers.

The second impact of transformation processes via environmental changes relates to the diversity of mountain habitats and mountain communities. Accordingly, the impacts (and related socio-economic vulnerabilities) vary according to the resource endowments of different areas and people within a given area. Some sort of duality created in the process can be indicated through (a) progressive and rapidly commercializing areas, and (b) stagnant areas still dominated by subsistence agriculture. The former include the physically and economically better-endowed areas that benefit from the development interventions and that do better despite the marginalization of their traditional farming systems. Relatively better, accessible areas with market linkages covered by special projects focused on mountain niches (e.g. horticulture) fall into this category.

The second category, accounting for the bulk of the areas, represents a decaying situation, in which the overall range and efficacy of options are reduced. Table 4.12 reflects the vulnerability of such areas and groups to environmental degradation. The breakdown and infeasibility of traditional diversified, resource-regenerative practices and the degradation of the resource base have reduced the range, flexibility, dependability, and payoffs of production or resource-use options. The slackening or disruption of collective risk-sharing arrangements and resource-management systems (such as for common property resources) and the introduction of formal, legalistic arrangements to regulate the relationship of people to their natural resources also reflect a deteriorating environmental situation.

In the case of progressively commercializing areas, the scenario is quite different: they are economically better off; environmental degradation does not influence their high payoff options (at least in the short term); they are in a much better position to absorb investment and other facilities offered by public intervention. At the same time, their potential vulnerability is associated with their market linkages. First, market-induced narrow specialization and overextraction may expose them to serious problems in the future. Second, despite their comparative advantage in certain products (e.g. fruits, vegetables), in the mainstream markets (in the plains) they interact with the other party as unequals. This makes them vulnerable to unequal terms of exchange.

The above phenomenon can be seen at the macro level with reference to other mountain products, such as timber and hydroelectricity. These resources are extracted extensively, but their trade often proceeds on highly unequal terms of exchange. The socio-economic im-

Table 4.12 **Environmental change and socio-economic impacts/vulnerabilities in mountain areas**

	Socio-economic impacts[a]			
Environmental changes and underlying processes of transformation	Infeasibility of traditional production systems, regeneration	Reduced range of options, inferior options	Increased dependency on external resources, unequal exchange, subsidy	Reduced collective sharing systems, resilience
Physical degradation of land resources	×	×		
Reduced variability, flexibility of production factors	×	×	×[b]	
Increased "ecological" subsidization through chemical, physical, biological inputs			×[b]	×[b]
Vicious cycle of resource degradation—overextraction—degradation		×	×	×
Niche, technology, market-induced overextraction, reduced resource availability/access		×	×[b]	×[b]

a. For vulnerabilities at the macro level see the text.
b. The details presented in the table largely relate to agriculture dominated by stagnant production systems, but these items apply to progressive agricultural areas as well.

pacts or vulnerabilities at a macro level can be understood in terms of a growing food deficit in most of the hill districts of the country, increased seasonal migration, the absence of visible success of several development interventions to satisfy people's basic needs, and the state's inability to balance priorities between food self-sufficiency and environmental stability (Banskota and Jodha 1992a,b; HMG 1981; ICIMOD 1990; Shrestha 1988).

Environmental change, emerging awareness, and responses

The environmental awareness of and responses to negative changes differ greatly between the micro (farm/village community) and macro (policy, planning) levels. These differences are a product of the variations in perception, time-horizon, capabilities, and mechanisms of information collection and communication. An important factor that differentiates farmers and policy makers is the degree of closeness to the phenomenon of change and their stakes in its consequences. Accordingly, a farmer whose survival strategy is closely linked with the environmental resource would exhibit perspectives markedly different from those of the chief of the environment department in any government, whose professional concerns for the environment may not converge with personal priorities. In keeping with such differences, the type of response and the time-lag between awareness and response would also differ. The discussion to follow takes up awareness and response issues separately for the two groups (i.e. farmers and policy makers). Table 4.13 summarizes the major issues in terms of identification of environmental concern, expression of awareness and concern, signals of environmental change, and responses.

Awareness/response of farmers and the village community

Mountain people become aware of environmental degradation the hard way, when they are faced with the fast disappearance of production options that sustained them in the past. Accordingly, environmental change emerges as a felt reality reflected through changes in the resource base and production performance as well as changes in the quality and quantity of inputs and products harnessed from non-crop lands. Villagers rarely articulate awareness unless induced to do so through some focused investigations or NGO activities or tempted by the possibility of government relief or development projects linked to the environmental situation.

An easier way to understand people's awareness of environmental change is to monitor their responses to such change as reflected through alterations in their resource-use practices, which are attempts to adjust to environmental changes. The time-lag between environmental awareness and response at the farm level is often too short or too imperceptible for meaningful simultaneous examination. Tables 4.2 and 4.3 have already listed a number of changes in resource-management practices and choices of activities that illustrate the point. These details could also be rearranged according to the categories (e.g. signals of environmental change, responses, impacts) as indicated by table 4.13. At the village level, however, one can easily

Table 4.13 **Environmental change: Emerging awareness and responses**

Awareness/ response impacts	Group responding: Mountain people at village level[a]	Group responding: National/international macro-level policy makers, researchers, donors, development agencies[b]
Identification of environmental concerns	Felt production constraints; scarcity of resources, products; infeasibility of traditional practices	A recent phenomenon; different from village communities; aggregated view on deforestation, etc.
Expression of awareness and concern	In terms of changed resource use, farming practices (as responses to change); expression rarely articulated unless induced by factors like possibility of grant/ relief or NGO activities	Media coverage, official circulars, evaluation reports; concern expressed following severe events, e.g. floods; international (donors') reports
Signals of environmental change	Decline of resource-centred options, traditional survival strategies; reduced (number and type of) product, input availabilities	Changes in land-use pattern, deforestation, floods; changes revealed by sophisticated means, e.g. remote sensing; failure of development interventions
Responses (adjustment to change)	Overextraction of resources; focus on alternative options (high-payoff, market-oriented options); rich–poor differences in adjustment (responses); community living with the degradation; slow revival of traditional group action (community forestry, etc.)	Research and evaluation studies, resource conservation projects, seminars, publicity; donor-induced initiatives (conservation strategy, conservation parks); grass-roots-level programmes
Impacts	Push for survival under scarcity situation; alternative options limited to some areas/groups; slow revival of community action	Focus on supply side of issues; demand pressures (driving forces) ignored

a. For details see tables 4.2 and 4.3, APROSC (1990), Yadav (1992).
b. For some details see Bass (1983), ERL (1988), World Bank (1984).

notice differences between rich and poor farmers with reference to most of the above variables. Whereas the rich may adopt high-pay-off options to withstand environmental change, the poor have to live with the marginalization of traditional mechanisms and attempt through overextraction of environmental resources to manage survival.

At the community level in several districts of the middle mountains, community forestry and user-group initiatives reflect the "awareness/response" situation. Supported by NGOs and multilateral and bilateral aid programmes, such initiatives also cover watershed development and private planting. Most are initiated as development activities but have strong environmental contents (Fisher 1991).

Awareness/response at the policy-making level

First, some features of awareness and response to environmental changes in the mountains (not confined to the middle mountains alone) may be noted. Policy makers' environmental concern or awareness is a relatively recent phenomenon in Nepal. Second, although routine discourses on environmental issues continue internationally, policy makers become seriously aware of them during periodic crises (e.g. the Bangladesh floods a few years ago activated the international debate/attention to deforestation in the Himalayas). Third, for the reasons stated above, awareness of environmental change and responses to it at macro levels are quite different from those at the village level.

The environmental concerns can be identified in terms of policy pronouncements and other political discourses focusing on deforestation, soil erosion, and other changes at the macro level. Media attention, concerns expressed by international agencies and donors, and research reports offer different channels through which environmental awareness is generated and expressed. More focused work, using both manual methods and more sophisticated means (e.g. remote sensing), presents environmental changes in more concrete terms. The responses include projects to acquire more information or analysis to treat specific environmental resources (often through sectoral focus), to mobilize resources, and to induce villages to practise resource conservation. This applies to macro-level situations in practically all mountain areas in the Himalayas. The specific issues relating to environmental awareness/response in the case of Nepal may be briefly summarized.

First, owing to Nepal's very liberal approach and easy access by researchers and other international experts, one finds more documentation and discussion of various aspects of environmental change in Nepal than in any other parts of the Himalayas. This awareness induces considerable internationally supported initiatives for further research as well as action. Hence activities ranging from strategies for nature conservation to community forestry programmes are in progress in different parts of the Nepal hills (Bass 1983; Fisher 1991).

Second, for want of a substantial hinterland to produce surplus food to meet the increasing demands of the hill population, Nepal, despite an awareness of environmental degradation, has to emphasize current production. This involves both intensification of resource use and acceleration of resource extraction, with environmental degradation as a side-effect. In Nepal, agricultural development policies have oscillated between food self-sufficiency and environmental protection (Banskota and Jodha 1992a; HMG 1981; Shrestha 1988).

Third, owing to its small size, land-locked situation, and generally stagnant and underdeveloped economy, the country has to focus on the activities that can help generate maximum current revenue. Consequently, activities range from overexploitation of timber to promotion of tourism and other ventures (e.g. large-scale irrigation systems) that may have adverse environmental effects. Thus, despite the awareness of environmental change, in practice it is difficult to formulate appropriate responses. The country simply does not have enough financial resources. Hence the greater proportion of donor-driven environmental projects in the country.

Fourth, most of the environmental protection and conservation initiatives (including the ones supported by donors) are not only sectoral, but confined to a few selected environmental resources. Watershed development and conservation parks are no exception. Most of the initiatives neglect the totality of the situation, including balancing conservation and production needs. This results in the poor response of village communities to such programmes (Fisher 1991).

Lastly, as does the rest of the world, Nepal attempts to handle environmental issues largely from the supply side of the problem, without effectively controlling the demand-side variables. This is particularly true of the basic driving forces that put increasingly higher pressure on mountain resources and that cause environmental degradation.

Is the situation critical?

The discussion above portrays a rather discouraging picture of the middle mountains in Nepal. But is the situation critical or alarming enough to require immediate attention and changes? A valid response to this question can be made only on the basis of selected indicators that relate not only to the environment and physical resource base of the area but also to the socio-economic conditions and quality of life of mountain people. For this purpose, table 4.14 lists different variables under the categories of (a) environmental degradation, (b) wealth, (c) well-being, (d) economic and technological possibilities (substitutability), (e) spatial and market linkages, and (f) capacity to respond to environmental changes (and new opportunities). These are consistent with the general approach of this volume and the definitions of criticality set forth in chapter 1. The trends in different variables and their desirability are indicated in the table, which permits a series of inferences:

- all the variables characterizing environmental degradation (quantity/quality of water, soil fertility, biomass productivity, etc.) show declines and this is an undesirable trend.
- the variables under wealth show a mixed picture in which overall GNP is increasing but per capita GNP is declining. Indebtedness is on the increase but savings and investment in progressive pockets are on the rise. This has equity implications, too.
- Largely owing to the "health revolution" and improved accessibility, human well-being, as judged by longevity, a reduced mortality rate, food availability, and education, is improving. Economic and technological possibilities are limited but in some pockets they have succeeded. Technologies conducive to regeneration and environmental stability are lacking.
- Spatial and market linkages are increasing, and access to mainstream markets has helped some activities. But unequal terms of trade for mountains leads to the accentuation of resource extraction.
- The capacity to respond to changes or to generate and use new opportunities is lacking. The development of human skills is limited and the institutional frameworks to strengthen these skills are scarce. This is also responsible for the limited substitutability of technology.

Overall, one may say that human well-being is increasing but largely because of external subsidization in cash or kind. Both the unfavourable terms of trade and the limited capacity to respond to

Table 4.14 **Details indicating the criticality of the situation in the middle mountain areas of Nepal**

Variables/categories	Status of the variable and its spread	Desirability	Remark: primary reasons; long-term prospects/implications
Environmental degradation			
Quantity/quality of water	Decline (W)	(−)	Overextraction disregarding resource limitations, and interlinked activities; indicator of long-term unsustainability
Soil fertility	Decline (W)	(−)	
Biomass productivity/ availability	Decline (W)	(−)	
Regenerative processes, material, energy flows	Decline (W)	(−)	
Wealth			
Gross national product	Increase (W)	(+)	Increased high-value activities, external linkages caused all (+) entries; population growth and institutional problems caused all (−) entries
Per capita	Decline (W)	(−)	
Saving/investment	Increase (P)	(+)	
Indebtedness	Increase (W)	(−)	
Wealth/income inequality	Increase	(−)	
Well-being			
Longevity	Increase (W)	(+)	Improved accessibility, linkages, infrastructure; public distribution system, health services, schooling, etc.
Mortality/infant mortality	Decline (W)	(+)	
Nutrition level	Stagnant (increased in pockets) (W)	(+)	
Environment-induced disease	Decline (W)	(+)	Externally supported, need internal self-sustaining capacity
Access to natural resources	Decline (W)	(−)	
Food availability	Improved (W)	(+)	
Dependence on inferior options/opportunities	Increase in poor areas (W)	(−)	
Education, health care	Increase (P)	(+)	
Economic–technological substitutability (availability of options)			
High-intensity/extraction options	Increase (P)	(−)	New technology, economic options with high-extraction orientation, limited regeneration
High-payoff cash crop, monoculture, external input	Increase (P)	(+)	

Table 4.14 (*continued*)

Variables/categories	Status of the variable and its spread	Desirability	Remark: primary reasons; long-term prospects/implications
Rapid regeneration, diversification	Decline (W)	(–)	
New skills, human resource development	Stagnant (W)	(–)	
Spatial/market linkages			
Accessibility, market integration	Increase (P)	(+)	Market linkage, trade usually on unfavourable terms of exchange; external aid promoting excess dependency and insensitivity to mountain specificities
Regional/interregional trade flows	Increase (P)	(+)	
International concern, aid, indebtedness	Increase (W)	(+)	
Commercial capital flows	Stagnant (W)	(–)	
Capacity to respond to environmental degradation and negative side-effects of new options, market links, external assistance, etc.			
Folk knowledge	Present but not harnessed (W)		Human capital formation is the weakest component of development strategies
Scientific expertise/skills	Limited (W)		
Institutional infrastructure	Limited (W)		
Physical information	Limited (W)		
Political/economy capacity	Limited (W)		

W = widespread and general situation; P = in limited pockets or groups of population

change render mountain areas in Nepal unable to use market and technology for their betterment. Finally, the biophysical resource base, which is degrading rapidly, tends to discount all the positive things, including the rapid transformation of limited pockets. Viewed this way, the situation in the middle mountains tends to be critical. Possible approaches to respond to the situation require:

1. a greater focus on controlling or regulating human driving forces, and
2. designing and implementing interventions with greater sensitivity to mountain specificities (Banskota and Jodha 1992a,b; Jodha 1992).

References

APROSC (Agricultural Projects Service Centre). 1990. *Farmers' strategies and sustainability of mountain agriculture (Nepal)*. A report of the study sponsored by ICIMOD. Kathmandu: APROSC.

Banskota, Mahesh. 1989. *Hill agriculture and the wider market economy: Transformation processes and experience of the Bagmati Zone in Nepal*. Occasional Paper no. 18. Kathmandu: International Centre for Integrated Mountain Development.

Banskota, Mahesh, and Narpat S. Jodha. 1992a. Investment, subsidies, and resource transfer dynamics: Issues for sustainable mountain agriculture. In *Sustainable mountain agriculture. Vol. 1, Perspectives and issues*, ed. Narpat S. Jodha, Mahesh Banskota, and Tej Partap, 185–203. New Delhi: Oxford and IBH Publishers.

———. 1992b. Mountain agricultural development strategies: Comparative perspectives from the countries of the Hindu Kush–Himalayan region. In *Sustainable mountain agriculture. Vol. 1, Perspectives and issues*, ed. Narpat S. Jodha, Mahesh Banskota, and Tej Partap, 83–114. New Delhi: Oxford and IBH Publishers.

Bass, S. 1983. *The national conservation strategy for Nepal: A prospectus*. Kathmandu: NPC/IUCN, His Majesty's Government, Nepal.

Blaikie, Piers M., John Cameron, and David Seddon. 1979. *The struggle for basic needs in Nepal*. Paris: Development Centre of the OECD.

Chambers, Robert. 1983. *Rural development: Putting the last first*. London: Longman.

Conway, Gordon R., Jennifer A. McCracken, and Jules N. Pretty. 1987. *Training notes for agroecosystem analysis and rapid rural appraisal*. London: Sustainable Agriculture Programme, International Institute for Environment and Development.

DFAMS. 1986. *Main report on National Farm Management Study, Nepal 1983–1985*. Lalitpur, Nepal: His Majesty's Government of Nepal, Ministry of Agriculture, Dept. of Food and Agricultural Marketing Services.

ERL. 1988. *National resource management for sustainable development: A study of feasibility policies, institutions and investment activities in Nepal with special emphasis on hills*. London: Environment Resource Limited.

Fisher, R. J. 1991. *Studying indigenous forest management systems in Nepal: Towards a more systematic approach*. Honolulu: Environment and Policy Institute, East–West Center.

Fürer-Haimendorf, Christoph von, ed. 1974. *Contributions to the anthropology of Nepal: Proceedings of a symposium held at the School of Oriental and African Studies, University of London, June/July 1973*. Warminster, England: Aris & Phillips.

Guha, Ramachandra. 1989. *The unquiet woods: Ecological change and peasant resistance in the Himalaya*. Delhi: Oxford University Press.

Hitchcock, J. T. 1963. Some effects of recent change in rural Nepal. *Human Organization* 22, no. 1 (Spring): 75–82.

HMG (His Majesty's Government of Nepal). 1981. *Nepal's experience in hill agricultural development*. Kathmandu: Ministry of Agriculture, HMG.

ICIMOD (International Centre for Integrated Mountain Development). 1990. *Agricultural development experiences in Nepal*. MFS Workshop Report no. 3. Kathmandu: ICIMOD.

Ives, Jack D. 1987. The theory of Himalayan environmental degradation: Its validity and application challenged by recent research. *Mountain Research and Development* 7, no. 3 (August): 189–199.

Ives, Jack D., and Pauline Ives, eds. 1987. The Himala–Ganges problem: Proceedings of a conference, Mohonk Mountain House, New Paltz, New York, U.S.A., 6–11 April 1986. *Mountain Research and Development* 7, no. 3 (August).

Ives, Jack D., Bruno Messerli, and Michael Thompson. 1987. Research strategy for the Himalayan region: Conference conclusions and overview. *Mountain Research and Development* 7, no. 3 (August): 332–344.

Jodha, Narpat S. 1990. Mountain farming systems: Search for sustainability. *Journal of Farming Systems Research Extension* 1, no. 1: 55–75.

———. 1991. Sustainable agriculture in fragile resource zones: Technological imperatives. *Economic and Political Weekly (Quarterly review of agriculture)* 26, no. 13 (30 March): A15–A30.

———. 1992. Mountain perspective and sustainability: A framework for development strategies. In *Sustainable mountain agriculture. Vol. 1, Perspectives and issues*, ed. Narpat S. Jodha, Mahesh Banskota, and Tej Partap, 41–82. New Delhi: Oxford and IBH Publishers.

———. 1995 (forthcoming). Global change and environmental risks in mountain ecosystems. In *Global environmental risk*, ed. Jeanne X. Kasperson and Roger E. Kasperson. Tokyo: United Nations University Press.

Mahat, T. B. S., D. M. Griffin, and K. R. Shepherd. 1987. Human impacts on some forests of middle hills of Nepal: Part 4, A detailed study in southeast Sindhu Palchok and north east Kabhre Palchok. *Mountain Research and Development* 7, no. 2 (May): 111–134.

Nepal, Kendrīya Tathyānka Vibhāga. 1984. *Statistical pocket book, Nepal.* Kathmandu: Kendrīya Tathyānka Vibhāga.

Poffenberger, Mark. 1980. *Patterns of change in the Nepal Himalaya.* Delhi: Macmillan Company of India.

Price, Larry W. 1981. *Mountains and man: A study of process and environment.* Berkeley: University of California Press.

Rana, Pashupati, J. B. Shumshere, and Kamal P. Malla, eds. 1973. *Nepal in perspective.* Kathmandu: Centre for Economic Development and Administration.

Regmi, Mahesh C. 1971. *A study in Nepali economic history 1768–1846.* New Delhi: Manjusri Publishing House.

Sharma, Pitamber, and Mahesh Banskota. 1992. Population dynamics and sustainable agricultural development in mountain areas. In *Sustainable mountain agriculture. Vol. 1, Perspectives and issues*, ed. Narpat S. Jodha, Mahesh Banskota, and Tej Partap, 165–184. New Delhi: Oxford and IBH Publishers.

Sharma, S., and Narpat S. Jodha. 1992. Mountain farmers' response to development efforts: Comparative perspectives from the countries of the Hindu Kush–Himalayan region. In *Sustainable mountain agriculture. Vol. 1, Perspectives and issues*, ed. Narpat S. Jodha, Mahesh Banskota, and Tej Partap, 129–140. New Delhi: Oxford and IBH Publishers.

Shrestha, B. D., et al. 1983. *Watershed conditions of the districts of Nepal.* Kathmandu: Department of Soil Conservation and Watershed Management, HMG.

Shrestha, B. P. 1988. *Review of policies, strategies and programme of mountain agriculture in Nepal.* Kathmandu: Workshop on Nepalese experience in mountain agriculture – policies and strategies, ICIMOD.

Upadhyaya, Daya Chandra, and Jose Velaso Abueva, eds. 1974. *Population and development in Nepal: A collection of papers presented in the Population and Devel-*

opment Seminar, August 1–2, 1974. Kathmandu: University Press, Tribhuvan University.

World Bank. 1984. *Strategy for development of hill agriculture: A review*. Report No. 5182-NEP (limited circulation). Washington DC: World Bank.

Yadav, Y. 1992. Farming–forestry–livestock linkages: A component of mountain farmers' strategies (Nepal). In *Sustainable mountain agriculture. Vol. 1, Perspectives and issues*, ed. Narpat S. Jodha, Mahesh Banskota, and Tej Partap, 141–161. New Delhi: Oxford and IBH Publishers.

Zaman, Mohammad Asaduz. 1973. *Evaluation of land reform in Nepal*. Kathmandu: His Majesty's Government Press.

5

The Ukambani region of Kenya

Dianne Rocheleau, Patricia Benjamin, and Alex Diang'a

Regional environmental change in the dry farmlands of Kenya represents a microcosm of the processes at work in the savanna and dry forest landscapes of East Africa (and much of southern Africa as well). For global-change studies in particular, Kenya's dry farmlands provide a valuable lesson for the future of the larger region and the planet. Many other nations are encouraged to strive for the economic and resource-management standards that Kenya has already attained, yet the arid and semi-arid farmlands of Kenya suffer from multiple environmental problems associated with land-use change and development itself (Darkoh 1989; Deacon and Darkoh 1987; Mbithi and Wisner 1973). These problems, in turn, will affect and be affected by larger global processes. The dryland farming regions throughout Kenya epitomize the codetermination of economic and ecological change within and among local, regional, and global systems.

The well-documented case of the Akamba people in eastern Kenya provides particular insight into both the substance and process of regional environmental change. Ukambani, the traditional home of the Akamba, is now largely contained within the borders of Machakos and Kitui districts in Kenya (fig. 5.1).[1] The combined area of the two districts is approximately 45,000 km^2, although one-fifth of Kitui, some 6,300 km^2, lies within Tsavo National Park and is therefore unavailable for use by the Akamba. More than 95 per cent of the

Fig. 5.1 **The Ukambani area of Kenya**

Machakos/Kitui population is Akamba (Porter in prep.; Republic of Kenya 1980; Tiffen 1991a,b,c), and approximately 85 per cent of all Kamba speakers reside in Ukambani (Porter in prep.).

The region regularly recurs as a "classic example" of land degradation in accounts dating back to the 1930s (e.g. Dregne, 1990, 434; Hall 1938, 396; Matheson and Bovill 1950, 218), and state policies have continuously been devised to address this concern. Rural residents report frequent crop failures and water shortages, and food relief has become a permanent feature of rural life (Porter in prep.). A community leader in a semi-arid part of Kitui District, for example, classified 51 per cent of the years from 1947 to 1979 as "bad" or "very bad" famine years (Jaetzold and Schmidt 1983, C213). The Machakos District was a net importer of maize for 14 of the years between 1942 and 1962 for which data are available, and for 8 of the years from 1974 to 1985 (Mbogoh 1991). The ever-present need for food relief has been variously attributed to overpopulation and environmental degradation, to colonization and development, or to insufficient development.

The story of the Akamba people and their lands provides important lessons about the interaction of environmental change with state policy, especially the impacts of sedentarization, privatization, and the commercialization of agriculture, on rapid demographic change (numbers, composition, and distribution of population within the region). The most significant changes in land use at regional scale have included: the movements of highland Akamba to dryland areas, an ongoing land survey and tenure reform, a gradual shift from agro-pastoral to mixed farming production systems, the continuing conversion of dry forest and savannas to agriculture, the progressive replacement of subsistence by commercial production from household to regional level, the "mining" of dry forest and savanna trees for commercial charcoal markets in the city, and the quarrying of sand from dry river-beds and channels to construct new housing and commercial buildings in the city.

Both intensive gardens and frontier expansion constitute increasingly important features in the landscape of Ukambani. Concurrent with these visible changes in the landscape, a restructuring of labour has brought many people into the wage labour force, resulting in a new spatial division of labour between men and women in households with rural roots and urban branches. These processes have converged to make the land and people of the region more vulnerable to economic and ecological stress, or more dependent on external market forces and the state. Throughout the drier zones of the region in particular, people describe the degradation of soil, water, flora, and fauna and report crop failures due to drought or pests in four to six seasons out of every ten.

Ukambani constitutes an endangered region as defined in chapter 1, assuming that the area remains non-industrial and rural for the foreseeable future. That is, under the current and foreseeable circumstances of nature–society interaction, land and water degradation threatens the health and livelihoods of the people of the region, and some of the degradation that has already occurred is irreversible. It is important in this case to note the striking variability in the conditions within the region and the very high uncertainty about the future directions and magnitude of environmental change. The central lessons of Ukambani over the last 100 years combine the changing nature and perception of environmental change over time with the distinct experience of those changes across different scales of analysis and between different groups of people.

The more detailed geography and history of environmental change in Ukambani presented below is derived from a combination of literature review, in-depth fieldwork at selected sites, and periodic field visits and discussions with fieldworkers and residents in communities throughout the region. The review of the literature summarizes an extensive and rich record of land-use, development, conservation, and ethnographic studies and activities in the region, from the 1890s to the present, including the major works of geographers, anthropologists, and sociologists. The field research that informs this study was part of a series of research and development projects in Machakos District to promote sustainable production and resource-management systems, with most of the fieldwork conducted between 1983 and 1992 in affiliation with the International Centre for Research in Agroforestry, or ICRAF (Nairobi), the Kenya National Environment Secretariat, the Institute for Development Studies of the University of Nairobi, and Wageningen University (the Netherlands).

In addition to participation in field trials of agro-forestry technologies and land-use planning exercises, field research included: land-use and resource mapping at the watershed and farm level; participant observation in individual and group work in agriculture, conservation, and related subsistence activities; focus group interviews, group interviews, and household interviews; key informant interviews; individual oral histories; questionnaire surveys (two sites), and participatory rural appraisal (PRA) exercises. The qualitative information from fieldwork, particularly concerning the drought and famine of 1984–1985 and current trends in migration, has substantially influenced the interpretation of census, survey, and inventory data from other sources. In addition to direct observation in regular and periodic visits to numerous sites, the discussion below also reflects the experience and analyses of technical and research staff working throughout the region, based on frequent discussion and consultation in the field and in national technical and policy forums.

The Ukambani study area

The physical setting

Ukambani is situated on a predominantly semi-arid, eastward-facing slope, which becomes progressively lower and drier to the east. It is part of Kenya's Eastern Foreland Plateau, an eroded basement complex broken by residual hill masses and occasionally overlain by Tertiary volcanics (Bernard, Campbell, and Thom 1989; Wisner 1977). Moore (1979a) describes the Machakos Hills area as hills dropping down to a series of plains, separated by steep slopes.

This part of Kenya forms an environmental gradient of decreasing altitude (from 2,100 m to 440 m), increasing temperatures, and decreasing moisture (from 1,270 to 381 mm average annual rainfall) from west to east (Ojany and Ogendo 1973; Owako 1971; Porter 1965). Elevation controls the quantity of rainfall at the regional scale, whereas topography strongly influences rainfall distribution at the local scale. Rainfall, except in the hill regions, is low and unreliable (Bernard, Campbell, and Thom 1989). The precipitation pattern is bimodal, with long rains falling between March and May and short rains from October to December (Moore 1979b; Porter 1965), as illustrated by the rainfall and cropping calendar for one site in Machakos (fig. 5.2).

The soils of Machakos and Kitui reflect the largely metamorphic parent material and the rainfall regimes that contribute to their formation (Barber, Thomas, and Moore 1981; Ojany and Ogendo 1973). In Machakos, the dominant soil groups are alfisols, ultisols, oxisols, and lithic soils (Barber, Thomas, and Moore 1981; Lezberg 1988; Porter in prep.).

These soils are all generally of low fertility, and many are highly erodible (Barber, Thomas, and Moore 1981). The ultisols and alfisols are also susceptible to sealing (capping), which increases runoff and makes the clay soils hard to plough by the end of the dry season (Barber, Thomas, and Moore 1981). A rough estimate of the agricultural quality of the region's soils indicates that less than 20 per cent of Kitui and Machakos has well-drained, deep, friable red and brown clays of good fertility; more than 60 per cent of the region has very erodible, relatively shallow, sticky, red, black, and brown clays of variable fertility, on steep slopes; 20 per cent has poorly drained, shallow, stoney soils of low fertility (Bernard, Campbell, and Thom 1989, based on Jaetzold and Schmidt 1983).

The dominant vegetation of this part of Kenya is dry bush with trees, and, in the higher areas, savanna with scattered trees (Ominde 1968). The hills were once forested, but by the beginning of the colonial period most of the "desirable" agricultural land had been cleared (Harroy 1949; Owako 1971; Silberfein 1984), leaving patches and corridors of forest along ranges, rivers, ravines, and hilltops, as well as dry forest in large expanses of grazing land. Characteristic vegetation at the higher altitudes (above 1,700 m) includes remnant evergreen forest (*Podocarpus* spp.) and bracken, mist forest, and evergreen thicket clumps in grassland. Elevations at 1,200–1,700 m are dominated by *Combretum* species, with particular plant associations correlated with topography and moisture. The most widespread

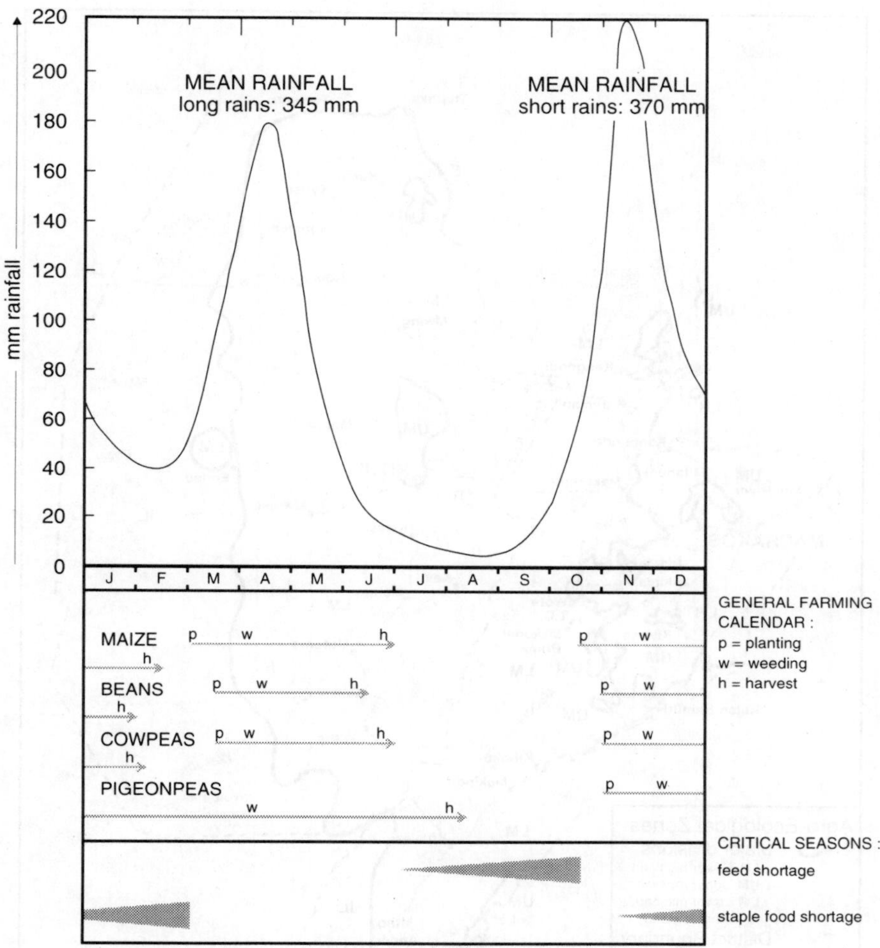

Fig. 5.2 **Rainfall and agricultural calendar for Mbiuni location, Machakos (Source: adapted from Darnhofer, 1985)**

vegetation type in Ukambani, and especially in Kitui, is semi-arid deciduous thicket and bushland, particularly *Acacia/Commiphora* associations in the 800–1,200 m elevation range. In the dry areas below 900 m, *Commiphora/Sanseveria* thorn bush grades into semi-desert vegetation (Ojany and Ogendo 1973; Owako 1971; Porter in prep.).

The forest zone is now largely under cultivation, with shrubby secondary growth dominating non-cultivated areas. The soils characteristic of the moist *Combretum* areas are fairly productive for

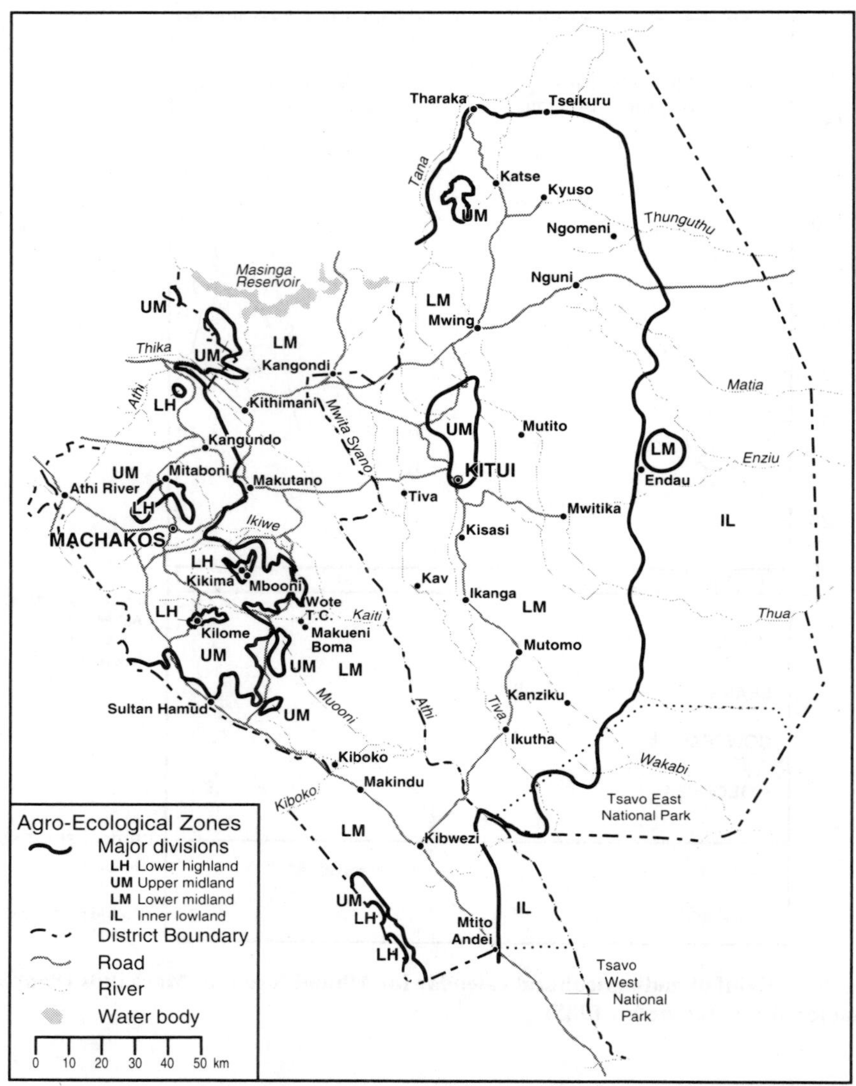

Fig. 5.3 **Agro-ecological zones of Ukambani (Source: Jaetzold and Schmidt, 1983)**

agriculture, but the dry *Combretum* zones have sandy soils of limited fertility. The *Acacia/Commiphora* zone includes perennial grasses valued for grazing (Porter in prep.), but even in these areas forest and shrubland are increasingly being converted to cropland.

Biophysical agricultural potential in Ukambani is a function of soil

Table 5.1 **Classification of agricultural land in agro-ecological zones (%)**

District	Zone 2	3, 3/4	4	5	5/6	6
Machakos	1.2	5.1	26.2	53.5	4.3	9.7
Kitui	–	0.5	14.0	50.7	–	34.9

Zones: 2, 3 Suitable for banana and coffee
4 Semi-humid to semi-arid transition; suitable for maize
5 Semi-arid; suitable for livestock, millet, and sorghum
6 Arid; suitable for ranchng

Source: Jaetzold and Schmidt (1983), Vol. 2: *Natural conditions and farm management information*, Part C, *East Kenya (eastern and central provinces)*.

characteristics and moisture availability, both of which are largely controlled by elevation and topography. Jaetzold and Schmidt (1983) mapped agricultural potential in Kenya using a modified version of the FAO Agro-ecological Zone system (fig. 5.3, table 5.1). Downing and colleagues (1987, cited by Lezberg 1988) calculated that 76 per cent of the Machakos District falls into agro-ecological zones 4 (semi-humid to semi-arid) and 5, with fully 58 per cent falling in zone 5 (suitable for livestock, sorghum, and millet). The 1980 development plan for Kitui classifies 2 per cent of the district as high potential, 37 per cent as medium potential, and 61 per cent as low potential (Republic of Kenya 1980).

Population, settlement, and land-use practices

Preliminary results from the 1989 census indicate that the current population of Machakos and Kitui districts is approximately 2 million people. The vast majority (90 per cent) of the population live in rural villages and rely on a combination of subsistence and commercial agriculture, with some wage labour (Ondiege 1992). According to a 1982/83 survey of rural households in the Machakos District, agriculture accounted for 50 per cent of income, off-farm enterprises for 17 per cent, salaries and wages for 24 per cent, and other sources for 9 per cent (Ondiege 1992).

Men's employment outside the region has a long history. For the last 50 years many Akamba men have served as soldiers and policemen, as well as wage labourers in nearby factories, plantations, and urban areas (mainly Nairobi and Mombasa, but also Machakos and Kitui towns). As sex ratios (table 5.2) and local case-studies

Table 5.2 **Ukambani population: Sex ratios (adult males per 100 adult females), 1948–1979**

District	1948	1962	1969	1979
Machakos	71	74	82	86
Agro-ecological zones 2/3	64	69	72	
Agro-ecological zone 4	65	68	76	
Agro-ecological zones 5/6	119	85	94	
Urban	424	247	190	
Kitui			89	76

Sources: Tiffen (1991b), Republic of Kenya (1980).

(e.g. Mwaria 1985; O'Leary 1984; Ondiege 1992; Van Ginneken and Muller 1984) make clear, this out-migration continues to form an important part of household livelihood strategies. It is, however, increasingly common for younger people to earn wages locally for labour on other people's farms.

The density of population throughout much of Ukambani has exceeded the number of people that can be supported by subsistence or commercial agriculture under present technology (see Bernard, Campbell, and Thom 1989). Out-migration of men and partial remittance of wages to rural communities, from World War II up until recently, seems to have slowed the pace of land-use intensification in response to higher population densities. This pre-empted or postponed the impact of population density on technology innovation and agricultural intensification as postulated by several authors for agrarian systems elsewhere (Boserup 1965; Lagemann 1977; Ruthenberg 1980; Turner, Hanham, and Portararo 1977).

Intensification has lagged behind local population growth and, in drier areas, behind in-migration of new families from crowded upland farming communities. This has not been an obstacle for the people of the region so long as wages from outside employment could offset the deficits in production. The differential ability of households to deal with this problem has resulted in widespread movements of population and changes in land use.

Rural settlement patterns in Ukambani reflect the productive potential of the agro-ecological zones noted earlier. The higher-potential upland areas are much more densely populated than the dry lowlands (table 5.3). In Kitui, for instance, approximately 60 per cent of the population occupies only 20 per cent of the district's

Table 5.3 **Population density in 1979 by agro-ecological zone (persons per km²)**

Zone	Machakos	Kitui
2/3	285	
3		231
4	110	103
5/6	40	
5		26
6		3

Sources: Machakos – Tiffen (1991b), Republic of Kenya (1980); Kitui – Downing (1988).

land area outside of Tsavo National Park, and the population density ratio of highland to lowland divisions is approximately five to one (Republic of Kenya 1980). Using 1969 census data, for example, O'Leary (1984) found highland sublocation population densities ranging from 24 to 113 people/km^2 and lowland densities from 6 to 22 people/km^2. He also found local highland densities as high as 240 people/km^2.

Although district-level population figures (table 5.4) are the most accessible and the most often used, it is the movement between agro-ecological zones, and between urban and rural areas, that best reflects the dynamics of population, economy, and environment in Ukambani and neighbouring regions (Bernard 1985; Bernard and Thom 1981; Bernard, Campbell, and Thom 1989; Campbell 1990; Downing et al. 1989; Lezberg 1988; Tiffen 1991a,b). These complex patterns of movement may be obscured by district-level data, making these figures somewhat difficult to interpret. In Machakos District, for example, net increases in any given period result from a combination of natural increase, out-migration to Nairobi, Mombasa, and settlement frontiers in coastal or dry upland sites in Kitui and other districts. The district-level data are "blind" to the widespread migration from the hills to drier frontier areas within Machakos District.

Overall, population has risen steadily from the 1930s to the present (table 5.5), but rates of change have been uneven across agro-ecological zones. As table 5.5 indicates, growth rates in the high-potential areas of Machakos District declined from the 1930s to the 1960s, whereas those of the low-potential areas have remained high (Tiffen 1991b). The latter is due primarily to migration of highland Akamba

Table 5.4 **Population estimates for Ukambani, 1890–1989 ('000)**[a]

Year	Machakos	Kitui	Total
1890	–	–	200–400[b]
1902	102	–	–
1910	–	87	[190]
1918	120	104	224
1931	239	140	379
1948	358	211	569
1962	551	285	836
1969	707	343	1,050
1979	1,023	457	1,480
1989	1,382	–	[1,990]

Sources: pre-1948 – based on district tax censuses and estimates reported in Owako (1971), Mwaria (1985), Tiffen (1991b); 1948–1979 – based on census figures reproduced in Republic of Kenya (1980), O'Leary (1980), Tiffen (1991b); 1989 – preliminary census figures for Machakos, reported by Tiffen (1991b), Ondiege (1993).

a. Formal census figures are not available before 1948, and district and tax figures are notoriously inaccurate. In addition, the boundaries of administrative units have changed, making raw census figures non-comparable through time. The figures given here are approximate and should be taken as indicators of relative magnitude and trend directions.

b. Based on 1902/1910 reports on estimates of 50% mortality during famine and on conflicting reports on population prior to famine.

Table 5.5 **Machakos population by agro-ecological zone, 1932–1979**

Zone	1932	1948	1962	1969	1979
Population ('000 persons)					
2/3	86	132	175	196	225
4	132	184	265	305	377
5/6	21	47	116	191	355
Urban	–	2	10	15	66
Total	239	365	566	707	1,023
Population distribution (%)					
2/3	36	36	31	28	22
4	55	50	47	43	37
5/6	9	13	20	27	35
Urban	0	1	2	2	6
Population density (persons per km²)					
2/3	82	127	189	211	285
4	56	78	85	97	110
5/6	2	5		20	40

Source: Tiffen (1991b).

into the dry agricultural frontiers of the district. O'Leary (1984) reports a similar dynamic, albeit somewhat later, for Kitui District. The imposition and lifting of barriers to movement during the colonial and immediate post-colonial periods have heavily influenced population changes through time in both districts.

Land-use change

As urban and civil service opportunities contract, or fail to keep pace with the growing demand from Ukambani and other regions, many men have returned home to farm and young people are increasingly choosing not to leave. This has spurred a new cycle of agricultural intensification and experimentation in many communities since the beginning of the 1990s. The current process of land-use intensification represents a delayed response to higher population density overall and to progressive displacement of population into the drier portions of Ukambani. The changes in land use and settlement also reflect a changing pattern of land tenure, in both the character and the distribution of land rights.

Landholdings range from 0 to 1000's of hectares (ha), with most households in agro-ecological zone 4 owning 2–10 ha and in zone 5 owning 2–15 ha (Hoekstra 1984; Ondiege 1992; Rocheleau, Baumer, and Depommier 1985). As land is subdivided and allocated or sold to the rising generation, however, farm sizes of 0.5–1 ha have become commonplace in zone 4. Among all holdings in Machakos District (all zones), 30 per cent are less than 0.9 ha in size; the figure for Kitui is 17 per cent (Ondiege 1992). Increasing numbers of people in zone 4 have been rendered landless, or forced to migrate to urban areas (mostly men), to plantations (mostly women), or to zone 5 frontier areas (whole families and clusters of brothers, sisters, and friends with families). In Machakos, as migrants from zone 4 and resident young people subdivide the available land in zone 5, the landholding size there is also shrinking rapidly (Hoekstra 1984; Porter in prep.; Rocheleau 1985, 1992; Rocheleau, Baumer, and Depommier 1985; Tiffen 1991a,b). New settlers to these areas often purchase plots of 5–10 ha.

In Kitui, westward migration from the crowded central highlands toward Yatta Plateau had virtually ceased by the early 1980s, resulting in increased fragmentation of highland holdings to non-viable dimensions (O'Leary 1984). Meanwhile, manipulation of land markets and state development schemes allowed the wealthy to accumulate sizeable holdings in both highland and lowland areas of Kitui (Mutiso 1975). By the late 1980s, an estimated 6 per cent of Kitui households were landless (Ondiege 1992). In the dry areas, in which shifting cultivation and "bush fallow" systems have been widely practised, the current "land rush" (*Weekly Review* 1991a,b,c,d) is rapidly filling in the dry forest, "fallow," and grazing lands between cropped fields in established farming communities.

Most households (with an average of eight persons) keep both cattle and goats, with an average of two cattle and eight goats or sheep in Machakos and somewhat higher numbers in Kitui (Ackello-Ogutu 1991). The most common food crops are maize, beans, cowpeas, pigeon peas, pumpkins, sweet potatoes, green gram, and bananas. Farmers intercrop maize, beans, bananas, potatoes, sweet potatoes, pumpkins, and sometimes coffee in the wet uplands of Ukambani. Many upland coffee farmers also grow other tree crops, including macadamia nuts, mango, papaya, timber, and fuelwood. Cabbages, tomatoes, onions, red peppers, and greens are usually limited to river flood plains or poorly drained valley sites. In the drier parts of the region most farmers grow maize, beans (on moister sites), cowpeas, pigeon peas, and sometimes green gram and cotton. Sorghum and millet, once the staple grains, are found in small patches in croplands, but have been largely replaced by maize. Sweet potatoes, pumpkins, and bananas are fitted into the wetter sites in the field, along the base of terrace walls, in deep pits (1 m^3) with fruit trees, on termite mounds, or in gardens near the home. Increasingly, farmers in zone 4 are also intercropping papaya, citrus, and some fodder or timber trees with their field crops.

The typical crop mix raised by a farm household still varies substantially between eco-zones but increasingly also varies within eco-zones between households and between more localized landscape niches determined by topographic location, soil type, soil moisture, and proximity to water points and to forest. Whereas single households (usually extended families sharing production and consumption) once maintained a number of fields, across eco-zones, most farm households are now reduced to nuclear families or smaller extended family units cultivating a single plot or a cluster of similar plots in one eco-zone. Moreover, most households in the past relied on a regular supplement of food supply from wild and semi-domesticated plants in forests, hedgerows, rangelands, and fallows.

The resulting paradox is that, although new food and commercial crops may have increased and the total number of crops in individual fields may be greater, the total number of crops raised and the variety of plants used by any given household may be fewer than 20 years ago. The exceptions are small home gardens and the orchard-like mixed-cropping systems of some largeholders, based on tree crops such as citrus, papaya, banana, and other fruits. Even there, the loss of many wild and semi-domesticated plants has resulted in a net loss of diversity in locally available foods. For the wealthiest this is compensated by purchased foods, whereas for the poorest it represents a deterioration in nutritional quality, seasonal distribution, and reliability of food supply (Rocheleau et al. 1985; Van Ginneken and Muller 1984).

Environmental hazards and environmental degradation

For most of Machakos and Kitui, the main limiting factors for settlement and agriculture are the lack of rainfall and of reliable sources of surface water (Owako 1971). The latter has been further exacerbated by disruption of streamflow due to deforestation. Most streams are intermittent and deeply incised (Moore 1979a). In some areas, ticks and tsetse here limited livestock development into the 1970s (Owako 1971). Since these disease vectors are vegetation dependent, their presence was once marked by clear boundaries, well known to the Akamba people (Porter 1965). There is less certainty under present conditions in complex, finely divided mosaics of bush, cropland, and pasture, and tsetse flies have been reported in settled areas along the Athi River and the Yatta Plateau (J. Kyengo, L. Kyongo, and M. Musyoki personal communication). Crop environmental limits have always been less clear (Porter 1965), tempting government and international agencies to push agricultural settlement into dry or hilly areas not capable of supporting intensive maize cultivation under existing levels of technology (Bernard, Campbell, and Thom 1989).

One underestimated and underreported constraint on crop mix and management is proximity to forest, particularly in dry forest frontier plots. Large and small herbivores, from rhinoceros and elephant (in the 1950s and 1960s), to monkeys, baboons, wild hogs, squirrels, and antelope (at present), cause serious but selective damage to field crops. Herbivory by mammals causes farmers to change the composition of intercropping systems as well as their management practice, not to mention their own sleep habits. Many farmers keep all-night vigils in their fields just prior to harvest to protect grain and roots from marauding nocturnal animals (field interviews, Machakos and Kitui 1991; Lelo 1994).

Land degradation by cropping and overgrazing has been a recurring theme throughout the last 70 years of colonial and later national agricultural and resource-management programmes. In this region, the high susceptibility of cropland to erosion derives from a combination of factors: concentrated settlement in fertile and well-watered hilly terrain; the tendency of the soils to "cap"; and the fact that 70 per cent of the most erosive rainstorms occur in the first month of the rainy season, before crops can establish an effective cover (Barber, Thomas, and Moore 1981; Moore 1979a,b). Cattle, goats, and sheep also have pronounced effects on those Ukambani soils that have a propensity to form a pavement-like surface when denuded by overgrazing and physically compacted by trampling. The resulting land degradation, in turn, reduces future crop and livestock production.

Although the climate, soil, and topography of Ukambani make the region susceptible to erosion, compaction, and denudation, crop and livestock management practices can exacerbate, prevent, or even reverse land degradation. Figure 5.4 illustrates the complex interaction of causal relations between agricultural production and environmental degradation at the farm level as derived from surveys in Mbiuni location, Machakos (Raintree 1984; Rocheleau 1985; Vonk 1983b). Several points of technical intervention could reverse or at least ameliorate land-degradation and production problems.

In reality, both regional and local variation in physical characteristics and cultural practices determines the potential for crop and livestock production and the condition of land and water resources in Ukambani. The state has tended to work primarily from regional-level differentiation of agricultural potential, whereas farmers and herders tended to focus more on local-level variations. Rural people in the region have often been thwarted by settlement, tenure, and agricultural development policies that force them into single "consolidated" holdings. There, they are expected to pursue a single land use, with household heads as single points of ownership and control. Land allocation has also tended to treat all local land as equivalent in inherent characteristics, current condition, productive potential, and vulnerability to damage. Likewise, many agricultural production and conservation programmes have promoted single-technology packages to achieve "sustainable production."

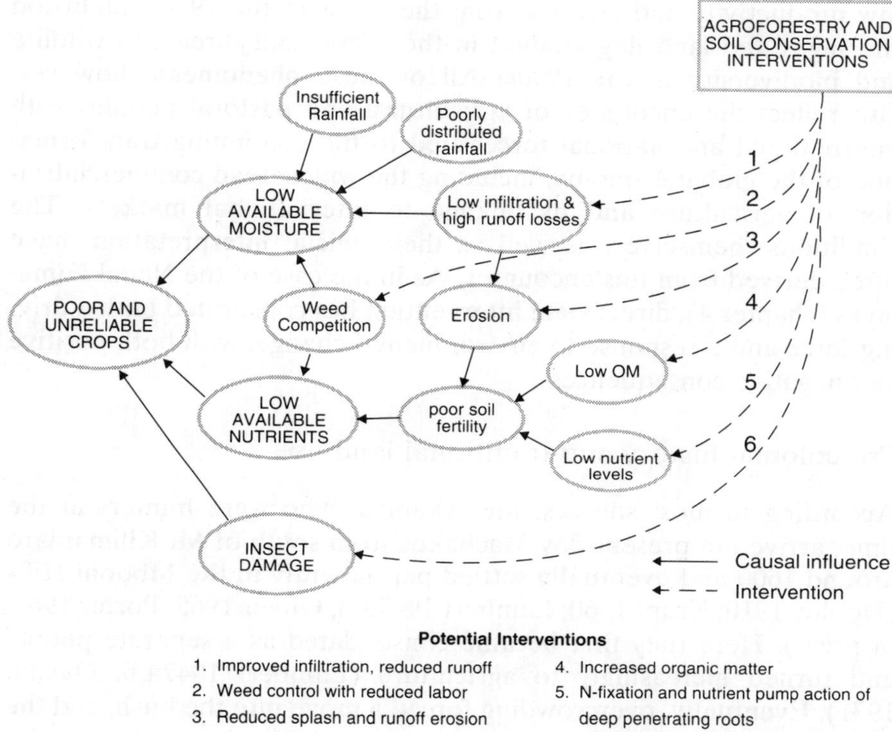

Fig. 5.4 **Causal relations between agricultural production and environmental degradation at the farm level (Source: adapted from Raintree, 1984)**

The history of settlement, land use, and environment (1890–1990)

The 100-year story of environmental and economic changes in Ukambani places current concerns and conditions within a broader context, informed by history as well as multiple perspectives on singular places and events. During this period, both land use and cropping systems changed rapidly in response to new markets, new property relations, population growth, and large-scale migration and resettlement. Many of the conditions that outsiders see as intrinsic to the region or its people are, in fact, results of specific colonial, national, and international policies and interventions. Outsiders noted famines and disease in the 1890s, severe land degradation in the 1920s and 1930s, low productivity and poverty from the 1950s to the 1970s, fuelwood shortages and land degradation in the 1980s, and threats to wildlife and biodiversity in the 1990s. All of these phenomena, however, also reflect the encounter of agricultural and pastoral peoples with international and national forces tied to the continuing transformation of the global economy, including the widespread commercialization of agriculture and its linkage to international markets. The conditions themselves, as well as their official interpretation, have often derived from this encounter. As in the case of the Nepal Himalayas (chapter 4), direct state intervention has constituted both a driving force and a response to environmental change, with both positive and negative consequences.

Pre-colonial history and traditional land use

According to most sources, the Akamba, who were hunters at the time, arrived in present-day Machakos from south of Mt Kilimanjaro around 1600 and eventually settled permanently in the Mbooni Hills (Hobley 1910; Krapf 1860; Lambert 1947a,b; Oliver 1965; Porter 1965, in prep.). Here they first became consolidated as a separate people and turned increasingly to agriculture (Lambert 1947a,b; Owako 1971). Eventually, overcrowding forced a move into the bush, and the traditional land-use system of integrating highland agriculture with lowland cattle-grazing came into being (Lambert 1947a,b). The land-tenure system of *ng'undu* (nearby grazing lands), *utui* (small clan-based settlements or small villages with permanent household cultivated plots and fallows), *kisese* (household grazing plots and paddocks), and *weu* (large tracts of common pastureland) developed in conjunction with this new subsistence system (Lambert 1947a,b; Wamalwa 1989).

Cattle owners led the settlement of dry frontier lands, attracted to the superior grazing on the plains. They began these settlements as cattle posts (with permanent residences retained in the hills) but later established permanent villages (Owako, 1971). From Mbooni, the first major move, occurring about 150–200 years ago, was across the Athi River to Kitui (Lindblom 1920, 15). In this and other moves, the Akamba retained integrated highland/lowland, crop/livestock systems of land use. The chief aim of the land-tenure system was to spread risk and ensure group survival. The system was flexible, equitable, and geared to the community as a whole (Wamalwa 1989).

The mobility of the Akamba can be taken as an indicator of a frontier culture (Lambert 1947a,b; Oliver 1965; Owako 1971), although their successful adaptations in place at specific sites of sedentary farming and intensive land use suggest otherwise (Porter 1965, in prep.). Some authors depict an optimally adapted pre-colonial land-use system disrupted by external forces (Muthiani 1973; Wamalwa 1989; for adjacent areas, see also Deacon and Darkoh 1987; Sindiga 1984). On one point – that the traditional land-use system was well adapted to the vagaries of the physical environment – most authors agree. Integrated crop/livestock systems, spatially separated holdings, and mutual reciprocity arrangements served to spread risk and to provide mechanisms for coping with drought (Bernard and Thom 1981; Mutiso 1975; Porter 1965; Silberfein 1989; Waller 1985; Wamalwa 1989).

Akamba adaptability can also be seen as the very core of a stable nature–society relationship based on flexibility of movement and technology change. The traditional land-use system may be conceptualized as a coherent repertoire of diverse strategies, including both expansion and intensification of settlement, agriculture, and livestock production. Akamba farmers and agro-pastoralists cultivated a readiness to expand, intensify, relocate, or supplement their farming and livestock production activities in response to the changing economic and ecological conditions at local and national level (Gupta 1973).

Colonial contact (1890s)

In the 1890s, the Akamba experienced the first significant contact with colonial settlers and administration. The British Crown took over the administration of East Africa from the private International British East Africa company. The high cost of the Uganda Railroad was one impetus for this change, and making the railroad pay was the major reason behind the decision to try to entice white settlers to the Kenyan highlands (Bates 1987; Bradshaw 1990). Unfortunately, the railroad also seems to have been the means by which rinderpest invaded Ukambani in 1898 (Hardinge 1899). Also in 1898–1899, foreigners brought smallpox to the region and a severe drought occurred (Ambler 1988; Wamalwa 1989). These forces coalesced into the great famine of 1897–1901 (Ambler 1988). Since cattle normally served as the main drought insurance, the results were devastating. Kitui was especially hard hit (Hardinge 1899). Tate (1904) and Lindblom (1920) estimated the mortality rate in Ukambani during the famine at 50 per cent.

The devastation brought by this famine had lasting social effects (Ambler 1988). Depopulation weakened community bonds, differential survival rates of rich and poor caused tension, and in some places a total social breakdown occurred. Refugee urban migration brought growth to the "Swahili towns." Relief camps located at missions and government posts drew people into wage labour and served to "entrench the increasingly dominant position of these centers in commercial, political, and ideological terms" (Ambler 1988, 139). These trends also weakened the Akamba people's ecological control over their environment (Wamalwa 1989).

Land alienation (1900–World War I)

Among the various regional case-studies in this volume, Ukambani was influenced more than most (except perhaps the Southern Plains of the United States; see chap. 6) by the extent of land alienation for settlement of European farmers and ranchers. This led to large-scale displacement and relocation of rural people and dramatic changes in land-tenure systems, a legacy that continues to affect land use and migration in the region.

The first settler came to Machakos in 1894, but most of the district's land alienation and settlement occurred between 1901 and 1914 (Porter in prep.; Wisner 1977). Ignorance of indigenous land-use practice, combined with a rinderpest-depressed cattle population, caused an underestimation of Akamba land needs (Morgan 1963; Munro 1975; Silberfein 1984; Spencer 1983). Approximately 1 million acres were alienated in Ukambani between 1901 and 1914, and large tracts were placed "off limits" (Gupta 1973). The Akamba lost effective access to about two-thirds of the land that they had formerly controlled (Porter in prep.), including their most fertile lands, half of all their pasture (including their best grazing land), and their freedom to migrate (Munro 1975; Spencer 1983; Wisner 1977).

The Akamba, and their animals, were confined to "Native Reserves" in Machakos and Kitui. Colonial policy was directed at maximizing export crops, which Africans were forbidden to grow in order not to threaten the white monopoly. The state generally ignored "native" agriculture, while livestock activities were actively curtailed. The veterinary service was preoccupied with quarantining African cattle ostensibly to avoid contaminating European cattle, and an almost continuous quarantine existed from 1901 onward. These quarantines inhibited movement (perhaps exacerbating health problems), contributed to overcrowding of cattle on the reserves, and made it very difficult to sell cattle (Spencer 1983).

From the very beginning, the Akamba focused their dispute with the colonial government on the loss of land (Tignor 1976). Their entire land-tenure system had depended on seasonal and periodic access to large tracts of grazing land (Wamalwa 1989). Like many other Kenyan societies, Akamba social organization was based on conditions of abundant land and scarce labour and freedom of movement. Colonialism, by curtailing movement, closing the frontier, taking over existing settled lands, and forestalling the option of opening new lands, reversed these conditions. Land became scarce and labour abundant within a reduced, rigidly bounded area (Bates 1987), a situation that led many Akamba men to serve in the Carrier Corps of the British Colonial Army in World War I. Some recruits were coerced directly (Lelo 1994), whereas others responded to the new relations of land and labour established by land and livestock policy.

Land degradation in the 1920s and 1930s

By 1920, European expansion in Machakos had ended, and the colonial government continued to facilitate the transfer of resources from the reserves to the settlers. On the reserves, population increased, and the economy became more commercial. Land scarcity stimulated settlement in the plains, but poor land, tsetse, lack of water, and the 1924–1925 famine forced an exodus back to the hills, resulting in the virtual depopulation of parts of the plains and increased crowding in the hills (Owako 1971; Wisner 1977).

Relatively few Akamba engaged in wage labour through the 1920s, but this began to change by the end of the decade (Tignor 1976). The retrenchment of population from the plains, coupled with government hostility toward the pastoral sector, led the Akamba to pursue several agricultural innovations on the Machakos Reserve. These included the use of teams of oxen for ploughing and cart transport (allowing acreage increases), new crops, and intensive market gardening, all initiated without government aid (Munro 1975). Livestock production did not fare well. Disease outbreaks and fear of Akamba pressure for a reinstatement of grazing rights in Machakos and Yatta inspired continued official repression of the pastoral sector, including strict quarantines (Spencer 1983).

During this period, colonial officials and the settlers became increasingly aware of land degradation on the Native Reserves and linked this to cattle. State policy focused on conserving grazing land rather than developing African cattle resources (Spencer 1983). Although a few outlets for Akamba pastoral expansion existed in the 1920s, in the 1930s all external options were closed, and any hope for cooperation gave way to increasing regulation, compulsion, and monopoly (Munro 1975, 178; Spencer 1983).

In 1929, the highly publicized Hall Commission report elevated erosion in Machakos to the status of one of the most serious problems in all of Kenya, defining it as a major hazard (Myrick 1975; Spencer 1983). Contemporary accounts suggested that parts of Kitui were barren and depopulated (Champion 1933), that Machakos was eroded down to subsoil over 37 per cent of its area (Harroy 1949), and that over 1 million acres of the Akamba reserve were damaged and might never recover (Stockdale 1937, 290). The actual extent of damage is difficult to estimate because of official tendencies to exaggerate and the lack of systematic analyses (Munro 1975). The visibility of erosion was increased by the effects of locust invasions in 1929–1931 and a drought from 1931 to 1935 (Jacks and Whyte 1939).

Various agricultural changes, including intensification, contributed to land degradation (Munro 1975). Land scarcity led to decreased fallow and more continuous cropping, which, combined with the concurrent replacement of millet with maize, resulted in soil exhaustion and reduced yields. The remaining commonage (in both *ng'undu* and *weu*) was under severe strain as a source of forage and wood, particularly because many farmers began cash-cropping, ploughing up their grazing land, and exerting increased pressure on the *weu* and the shared grazing and fallow lands nearer to settlements. Erosion of pastureland and cropland resulted from overuse as well as expansion to steeper lands and more marginal soils. Colonial officers reported overgrazing (by goats on deforested slopes); grass fires; shifting cultivation on steep slopes without conservation measures; extensive deforestation to plant maize, coffee, and other cash crops; and parallel ploughing on 70 per cent slopes (Harroy 1949; Stockdale 1937).

In the densely populated Machakos Hills, land scarcity resulted, by the early 1930s, in permanent use of land and enclosure with fences or sisal hedges (Munro 1975). Land sales, tenancy, and, for the first time, landlessness became features of Akamba life (Silberfein 1984). Ready access to common lands had provided the basis of egalitarian Akamba society, but land scarcity and a market in land prompted the emergence of social stratification based on landholdings, and land disputes became common (Munro 1975; Mutiso 1975). Earlier traditions of multiple, functionally based tenure rights were replaced with individual-landowner rights, and formerly temporary usufructs were solidified into permanent, exclusive rights (Lambert 1947a,b; Wamalwa 1989), assimilated into "informed" reciprocity arrangements, or lost. Scarcity of pastureland along with other financial and administrative pressures resulted in an overall decrease in Akamba cattle wealth and a drastic decline, for most households, in livestock holdings. By the beginning of World War II, in contrast with the period just after World War I, significant numbers of Akamba were peasant cultivators instead of pastoralists, and crops had become a significant source of income (Munro 1975).

In spite of their own substantial soil degradation problems, the settlers waged a successful campaign to portray African agriculture as a kind of infectious disease, spreading insidiously across the landscape and contaminating productive European lands. Colonial policy throughout the 1930s was one of direct intervention in African land use. For the Akamba, the resulting policies served "to defend the European community by throwing a *cordon sanitaire* around the Akamba inhabited areas and intervening directly in the management of their land" (Munro 1975, 214).

In Machakos, the poor condition of the reserves, political fears of settlers, the global anti-erosion movement, and the new professionalism of the colonial agricultural bureaucracy (McCracken 1982) all coalesced in 1935 in the policies that emanated from the Kenya Land Commission. Aside from the minor changes in reserve boundaries, the Commission's major recommendations for Machakos were "destocking" and "reconditioning." When destocking began in 1938 (Moseley 1983), resistance erupted (Myrick 1975; Tignor 1971). More than 2,000 Akamba marched to Nairobi and petitioned the governor (Munro 1975), who returned the cattle and ended destocking (Moseley 1983).

Concurrently, agricultural officials focused with renewed vigour on reconditioning, actively encouraging the enclosure and seeding of grazing lands as well as the enclosure of homestead lands. By the end of 1939, 407,000 acres had been enclosed. In 1939–1940, the organizations created to oppose destocking also worked against enclosure, which they cited as a means to create cheap labour for Europeans by causing landlessness. Resistance included the sporadic destruction of hedges and continued challenges to several restrictive policies and practices. With the outbreak of war, this resistance was suppressed, but the call-up of agricultural officers also brought a virtual halt to reconditioning.

Whether all the activity that followed the Commission's recommendations was effective in improving the condition of the land is questionable. In 1944, a district agricultural officer concluded that the campaign of the previous six years had been ineffective and that only the compulsory closure of grazing lands, not individual fencing or ownership, had made any difference to the condition of the range (Lambert 1947a,b). Agricultural intensification and innovation did occur on the reserves during this time-period, but the agricultural services did little to assist innovative farmers (Munro 1975).

World War II and Kenyan independence

With the advent of World War II, colonial officials all but abandoned the quest for soil conservation in favour of campaigns to recruit Akamba men, both voluntarily and under coercion (Lelo 1994), into the army and to increase wartime production of grain crops. Nairobi and London officials sought to transform the rural landscape of Ukambani into an efficient and specialized production unit for grain crops during the war and for cash crops in the post-war period. The resulting soil depletion, combined with grain exports and unfavourable weather, contributed to severe food shortages and famines on the reserves in 1946, 1951–1952, and 1961. The colonial administration and the 2,000 settler families worked throughout the war years to promote commercial, settler-run enterprises with African wage labourers (Spencer 1980, 216).

Initially, the settlers were to intensify, specialize, and commercialize agriculture with Africans as wage labourers on their farms throughout Kenya. The 2,000 settler families took advantage of the war to recover from the depression and to gain control over the economic planning machinery of the colony (Spencer 1980, 513). Unlike the colonists, the reserves did not profit much from the war.

After the war, the government assisted demobilized British officers to "claim" or to buy land in Kenya (Lelo 1994), which intensified land use and increased pressure to evict "squatters," including Kenyan war veterans (Bates 1987). Combined with other pressures, this eventually led to the "MauMau rebellion" of the early 1950s (Bates 1987). The persistent low productivity on the reserves and a growing political insurrection in some parts of Kenya led to a liberal proposal for land-tenure reform, which continues to shape the evolving landscape in Ukambani and all of Kenya.

The Swynnerton Plan of 1954 was supposed to address African land problems by reforming land tenure, consolidating fragmented holdings, issuing freehold title, intensifying and developing African agriculture, providing access to credit, and removing restrictions on growing crops for export (Bradshaw 1990). It consisted of a three-phase programme: (1) land adjudication to "phase out" customary tenure; (2) land consolidation into one block per household to eliminate small, dispersed parcels, to allow greater specialization, and to realize economies of scale in cash crop production; and (3) land registration to provide for security of ownership and to establish a land market. Overall, the aim was to facilitate increased investment and employment in agriculture and to increase rural incomes and the "productivity" of land (Okoth-Ogendo 1976, 1981, 1991; Wangari 1991). The plan was predicated on an assumption that explicitly "successful" or wealthy African farmers would "be able to acquire more land and bad or poor farmers less, creating a landed and a landless class" (Swynnerton 1955, 10, cited in Wangari 1991).

The Swynnerton Plan created the basis for a market-oriented class of African farmers to work within a commercial-farming export sector and was credited with tripling agricultural output between 1955 and 1964 (Bradshaw 1990; Shipton 1988). It also succeeded in fostering land concentration (Shipton 1988) and social stratification, as foreseen by those who drafted the policy.

The simultaneous creation of a successful largeholder class and a landless and near-landless class in the highlands did not have the economic effect desired by Swynnerton and caused unforeseen environmental problems. The people who found themselves pushed off the best lands in their home areas did not all stay to work on the farms of others or to establish non-farm enterprises. Many went to work in the cities, the army, and the police force, and a large number went to drier frontier areas in search of new settlement opportunities.

Some migrants moved to resettlement areas opened up by the state in the late 1940s and the 1950s to alleviate the land shortage. Once independence was nearly at hand, many people prepared to move or risked illegal squatter settlements in anticipation of the reallocation of Crown Lands and large private holdings underutilized or abandoned by settlers (Mbithi and Barnes 1975). Thus, land hunger was often displaced to another more fragile area, rather than diverted into pursuit of wage labour in the same area. The simple equation envisioned by the Swynnerton Plan to describe a local zero-sum game was multiplied into a cascading effect that shook all of Ukambani and continues to the present.

Class formation and stratification, fuelled by the land-tenure reform, also affected livestock holdings, grazing practices, and land degradation. Colonial officials blamed overgrazing on the people most dependent on herding, yet the most overstocked areas of Ukambani in 1961 were the densely populated commercial farming areas in the hills (Porter in prep.). Although fodder grasses grown on farm may have altered carrying capacity somewhat, the degree of land degradation suggests that animals were overstocked relative to technology and management practice at the time. The wealthiest landholders often accumulated large herds and sent them to graze on whatever land was available – that is, "no man's land" under the new property regime. The overstocking problem attributed to the "tragedy of the commons" seems, in retrospect, to have followed the destruction of the commons and communal control and the concentration of private property.

Throughout this period, the conservation programmes of the 1930s continued with less visibility and lower priority than before. Considerable terracing and grass planting were carried out on private land during the period 1937–1944 (DeWilde 1967). Enclosure of grazing land and croplands gave way to the promotion of communal terracing (Munro 1975), and afforestation programmes fell off markedly (Harroy 1949).

The Akamba continued to view "reconditioning" with suspicion; they anticipated that these lands would be turned over to Europeans and that forced labour on settler farms and stock reductions were imminent (DeWilde 1967). In response to the Matungulu Betterment Scheme of 1946, which entailed the introduction of tractors to make terraces on broad tracts of land in a large-scale project, people threw themselves in front of the tractors (Bernard, Campbell, and Thom 1989; DeWilde 1967). Ironically, private soil-conservation efforts in Machakos, in spite of less government support than before, peaked in the mid-1950s amidst many reports of "startling recoveries" (DeWilde 1967, 94).

The response of Akamba farming and agro-pastoral communities to declining yields, the redefinition of property, and the continuing concern over land degradation was not uniform. Negotiation of specific responses played out in a middle region somewhere between the dramatic resistance against the Matungulu Betterment Scheme and the apparent success of government terracing programmes on private cropland. The widespread adoption of terracing in the 1950s did not reflect eventual acquiescence to government conservation interests, nor did resistance constitute rejection of terraces as such. Rather, farmers responded to the perceived risks and opportunities of specific programmes within their own production systems and political context.

For example, the increasing shift from sorghum and millet to maize as a staple crop throughout much of Ukambani accounts in large part for the willingness to terrace, since maize requires more water and responds well to the moister soil profile created by improved water storage on terraced croplands. Farmers switched to maize in response to strong market incentives and the removal of children's labour from the fields (a strong component of sorghum production). That maize was less drought resistant made farmers in the region far more vulnerable to drought. Terraces allowed them to maintain their link to the grain market, while also ensuring a greater supply of available water to the staple crop. On balance, the shift to maize still placed farmers at greater risk of losing their grain crop and reduced the food-production capacity of Machakos and Kitui districts over the long term (Bernard and Thom 1981).

By the time Kenya won independence, the people of Ukambani had experienced a restructuring of their livelihoods as well as their landscape. They had also witnessed the transformation of the property regime that had governed the ecological and spatial order of their homeland (Bernard and Thom 1981; Mutiso 1975; see also Sindiga 1984). Frequent crop loss due to drought, like sedentary life and land registration, constrained the livelihoods of most residents of Machakos and many Kitui farmers as well (Porter 1965, in prep.). Akamba farmers anticipated independence and perhaps restoration of the grazing lands and the freedom of movement lost during the colonial period.

Independence and development (1961–1978)

Independence brought new hope and a change in the definition of national and regional problems, if not in the proposed solutions. In spite of dramatic increases in national agricultural productivity, particularly of export crops, Ukambani continued to experience food shortages and land degradation. Independence came hard on the heels of a severe drought followed by flooding, which produced a major famine in the region in 1961. The new nation identified poverty and hunger as the two most pressing problems of the rural majority – for the country as a whole and for the region in particular. Government sources reported that 46 per cent of small-farm families in Kitui and 38 per cent of those in Machakos fell below minimum food consumption standards during the late 1970s (Republic of Kenya 1979, 66). Environmental concerns were identified as a legacy of the colonial past. Economic development remained the first-priority response of the national government, but the control and distribution of benefits changed.

Redistribution of land, coupled with increasing commercialization of smallholder agriculture, was seen by many as the solution to both poverty and hunger at local and national levels. In the drylands, many smallholders owned plots too degraded or too small to constitute viable production units under prevailing technology and cropping systems. Akamba demands for land were tied to the decades-old battle with the colonial government for the restoration of their grazing lands. Kenyan government policy from 1961 onward, however, extended the logic of the Swynnerton Plan (Migot-Adholla 1984; Wangari 1991). The National Development Plans of 1970, 1974, and 1978 referred explicitly to the need to extend the benefits of this programme to the semi-arid lands (Johnston 1989; Roe and Lewis 1989). Agricultural research followed a parallel route, focusing on the development of a high-yielding, fertilizer-responsive variety of hybrid maize with a short growing season for Akamba farmers (John Gerhart, personal communication). The dry farming areas of agro-ecological zones 4 and 5 were largely left out of this process until the 1970s. Most of zone 5 in Machakos and Kitui districts was not surveyed until much later, although the anticipation of legal demarcation and land title set in motion a process of land sales, land clearing, and consolidation of claims.

The land-tenure reform, as enacted in Ukambani during this period, bought off land hunger for some at the expense of others. It strengthened the private property of some men but left many men and most women with a shrinking commons, a frontier closed to free settlement, and less secure terms of access to resources in the communities in which they lived.

Widespread intensive cultivation increasingly displaced common grazing and gathering areas essential to poor smallholders. Those without capital, savings, or investments other than livestock were often not able to maintain medium-sized or even small farms under such conditions, and they sold out or abandoned their holdings. Women lost many of their rights of use and access, and most retained no legal authority over the land they occupied and even managed. They lost rather than gained, relative to men and even relative to their prior terms of access to resources under customary law.

The new government also promoted cash crops, increasing specialization, and the opening of government rangelands as frontiers for settlement. These were viewed as the main engines of growth and as sources of income, including income for purchasing food. This led to simultaneous, separate, and often conflicting policies to increase the land area planted to export cash crops and to increase food security and income among the rural poor.

Between 1961 and 1980, Machakos farmers doubled the land area under cultivation, while keeping more than 80 per cent of this area in food crop production, especially maize, beans, and peas (Mbogoh 1991). From independence to 1988, food crop area per capita stayed nearly constant (although it has declined slightly since 1982) and cash crop area per capita more than doubled (Mbogoh 1991), while non-cultivated area per capita decreased dramatically. The cash crop area represented primarily the commercial expansion of prosperous largeholders. The decrease in non-cultivated area selectively affected those most dependent on off-farm resources (wood, fodder, food, and herbs).

As a counterpoint to its substantial support for privatization of land and the consequent polarization of rich and poor, the state promoted "harambee" or community and group efforts to improve public infrastructure and social welfare, and to provide relief under special circumstances to particular regions or groups of people in need (Hill 1991). This approach appealed to traditional values and practices of self-help and communal solidarity and was widely adopted in Ukambani (Bahemuka and Tiffen 1992; Hill 1991; Mbithi and Rasmusson 1977; Mutiso 1975).

By the 1960s, land hunger was acute throughout much of Ukambani. The dramatic migration of people within the region at this time has been described in part as a response to increased population density and overtaxed carrying capacity (Bernard, Campbell, and Thom 1989; Bernard and Thom 1981). But the impetus for migration had built up over many decades through land alienation, crowding, and reduced mobility. The timing and direction of the 1960s migrations were tied to Independence and the opening, through both formal and informal initiatives, of vast tracts of state land and former estates to individual and cooperative settlement. For example, the government developed planned irrigation settlements and group ranches and also declared some areas, such as the Yatta Plateau and North Yatta, to be "open" for independent settlement and subsequent land claims. Landless and near-landless farmers from crowded high- and medium-potential areas hastened to occupy other well-situated tracts near water and roads on "unused" state or private lands (Mbithi and Barnes 1975; Migot-Adholla 1984; Okoth-Ogendo 1991; Tiffen 1992b; Wangari 1991). Although much former settler land was turned over to African small farmers (Ojany and Ogendo 1973) under a variety of government programmes, land concentration continued. Even cooperative ranches established on former private and public lands in Machakos and Kitui were dominated by wealthy absentee landowners (DeWilde 1967; Mutiso 1975, 1977). For Kenya as a whole, by the end of the 1980s, less than 0.2 per cent of farms (large farms, plantations, and ranches) controlled more than 40 per cent of farmland (Bradshaw 1990). Some scholars (Hunt 1984; Wasserman 1976) have viewed this policy of dryland resettlement specifically as a means of controlling the force of land hunger in the better sites.

Environment and development (1978–1990)

During the late 1970s, land degradation and resource management in Kenya once again attracted national and international attention. The major environmental concerns of the Kenyan government were sedimentation of dams at major hydroelectric facilities, soil erosion in cropland, declining crop yields, deforestation, and fuelwood shortages. The state focused on the national energy, water, and soil resources needed to increase agricultural production and to support the further development of urban services and industrial production in a developing economy. The national government, as well as its international advisers, identified the rural poor, particularly farmers and herders in semi-arid lands, as the major cause of the problem. This was often explicitly linked to Kenya's population growth rate – at that time approaching 4 per cent per annum – one of the highest in the world.

Over the course of the 1980s, environmental concern shifted from soil erosion to deforestation, and the related concerns about rural poverty shifted toward hunger in response to the famine of 1984–1985. The national agencies did, however, maintain a continuity of concern over issues of energy, food, and water for national needs and rural subsistence. By the close of the 1980s, development and conservation priorities had once again splintered. Development agencies focused on food and cash crop production in the well-watered farmlands at higher elevations. Conservation agencies reverted to the preservation of savannas and wildlife in national parks, as the mainstay of the country's new main industry, tourism. Special agencies focused on the livelihoods of the rural poor in arid and semi-arid lands. The perception that the rural poor, their increasing numbers, and their land-use practices were the causes of environmental degradation and food deficits remained constant, albeit with a change in tone to accommodate the recognition of the pressures and constraints propelling them toward destructive use of natural resources.

Soil erosion and watershed degradation

A new generation of soil-conservation programmes in Ukambani began with research on the erosive effects of rainfall, soil erodibility, stream sediment levels, erosion rates, and sediment delivery rates in small watersheds. Researchers in Machakos measured erosion rates in cropland ranging from 2 to 109 tons per hectare per year (Moore 1979a) and sediment delivery rates of 10–20,000 tons per km^2 per year (Dunne 1979; Dunne, Dietrich, and Brunengo 1978). With no historical comparison of erosion and production at the same sites and without a large sample of different sites at any given time, however, they could not predict the impact of erosion on current and future crop yields. The conservation efforts were driven not so much by concern over soil loss as by worries about the sedimentation of dams downstream.

The national and international agencies in Kenya returned to the colonial strategy of erecting physical structures, somewhat modified from the drainage works and terraces of the colonial period. Smallholder farmers in Ukambani, motivated by the need to intensify production on permanent sites, engaged in widespread construction and repair of modified terraces on their cropland. The new, less labour-intensive terraces were cheaper to build than the bench terraces of earlier campaigns, yet still harvested and stored runoff water, increasing soil moisture and crop yields. They also reduced nutrient loss and facilitated concentration of organic debris, compost, and water in new niches within the cropland.

The agricultural extension service successfully spread the practice of planting bananas in deep, composted holes along the base of terrace risers. Independently, farmers dramatically increased the acreage in other horticultural crops, particularly citrus, papaya, mango, and guava. They also expanded production of vegetables tenfold from the 1970s to the 1980s (Mbogoh 1991, 9). Thus, farmers' interests in increasing soil moisture and fertility for more intensive maize and horticulture production on fixed plots coincided with national soil-conservation interests.

Meanwhile, the state also took steps to integrate conservation, food production, and other elements of rural development in semi-arid farmlands. The Machakos Integrated Development Project (MIDP) was one of the first major national development efforts of this type. The initiative was limited to Machakos District but was to serve as a pilot programme to guide government policy in Kitui District and other semi-arid farming districts in eastern Kenya. Production farming and conservation were both included but were treated as separate activities.

Although MIDP and related soil-conservation programmes focused nearly all of their efforts on croplands (including already terraced croplands), researchers found that the overwhelming majority of the sediments in Machakos streams originated in grazing lands (table 5.6; Dunne 1979; Moore 1979a). The proportional contribution of grazing versus croplands reflected the much larger area in grazing land as compared with cropland, as well as a higher rate of soil loss per unit area for grazing land (Moore 1979a). Absentee landowners, large herds of livestock, and poorly maintained tracts of grazing land caused much of the problem. In addition, rural roads were found to contribute 1.2–2.2 times as much sediment as croplands to the total sediment yield at district level (EcoSystems Ltd. 1981, 1986; see also Dunne 1979). Although the need for preventive, protective, and re-

Table 5.6 **Estimated annual soil-erosion losses[a] from Machakos area soils under different land-use systems**

	Tons/ha	Millimetres/yr equivalent
Cultivated land under maize	49.0	4.9
Overgrazed bare soil	109.0	9.0
Recently ploughed and grassed land	6.1	0.5
Old pasture	2.4	0.2

Source: Moore (1979a, 425).

a. Calculated using Universal Soil Loss Equation.

habilitative measures was greatest for grazing lands and roads, bureaucratic perceptions of smallholder farmers as the causal agents of soil erosion prompted a response directed almost exclusively toward croplands.

This is not to say that cropland conservation was not useful or necessary. As conversion to cropland proceeds, the expected erosion rate from "marginal" pasture plots, once under cultivation, may be substantially higher than the previous rates under grazing or the average cropland rates on better-quality land. The initial procedure of clearing and tillage, and the first season's rains on the newly exposed topsoil, may also result in substantially higher (10 to 100 times higher) soil losses on new croplands than the average rate for cropland (Lal 1976; Rocheleau 1984).

Although this would presumably indicate the need for proportionately more effort to avoid and slow the conversion of forest and pasture to cropland, or to terrace new fields, MIDP focused soil-conservation activities on the terracing of established croplands, the repair of active gullies, and the physical rehabilitation of severely degraded grazing lands. MIDP paid community work groups to construct hillside drains and to check dams and other watershed rehabilitation structures. On-farm terracing was left mostly to individual farmers or their own self-help groups with technical assistance (terrace contour markings) from MIDP soil-conservation extension agents.

Unfortunately, private terracing of cropland tended to proceed from the best lands to the worst, following the progress of the land survey and land adjudication teams from higher-potential, densely populated, and valuable lands outward into more marginal lands. New croplands were often terraced well after the heavy losses of topsoil in the initial cropping season. Thus a wave of intensified conservation practice lagged behind the growing wave of land conversion to cropland and soil erosion in new plots.

As soil erosion preoccupied district, national, and international conservation and development agencies, soil harvesting became a serious problem in "sand rivers" (seasonally dry stream-beds) downstream. Deforestation and erosion in semi-arid watersheds often change streamflow from permanent to seasonal regimes, but the sand deposits in stream-beds partially compensate for the disruption of streamflow, helping to maintain water points well into and even through the dry season. During the 1980s, highway and building contractors sent large trucks and work crews to mine sand from dry river-beds in rural communities (Diang'a 1991; Thomas 1988). Although the practice of "sand scooping" attained some notoriety in the national press, it was treated as a law-enforcement problem rather than as an environmental issue.

In many communities with no piped water supplies these sand deposits store and filter water and often constitute the closest, cleanest, or only sources of water during the dry season. The destruction of one of these water points may add 4–10 km per day to the water-gathering journeys of rural women and children, which is especially significant for those who carry the water on their backs. It also increases the daily journey to water for cattle and goats, increasing the stress on the animals themselves as well as producing physical damage to roads, paths, river banks, and drainage systems.

Although some legal provisions exist for regulation at district and national level, the scale, timing, and nomadic nature of sand-scooping activity require enforcement at the local level. The community-level institutions that formerly governed access to land and other resources, however, have lost much of their former authority and enjoy no binding legal powers of enforcement, even where local community leadership does take a stand on such issues. Although national and district soil-conservation programmes did support infrastructural development at selected sand river water points in Ukambani, they did not address the protection of existing sites from outside, commercial interests. This partial treatment of the sand-scooping issue derived from the poor definition of rights and responsibilities with respect to shared resources and the segmentation of expertise and authority between local and national institutions.

Meanwhile, beyond the confines of Ukambani, the national development plan for 1980–1985 placed a high priority on Kenya's arid and semi-arid lands, with a view toward expanding land under cultivation further into the dry frontier zones and intensifying existing dryland cultivation. The same five-year plan sought to protect the forest, soil, and water resources of national importance from further damage. The impetus for this national initiative owed much to a decade of intensive research on poverty and environmental issues in Machakos District (Mbithi and Barnes 1975; Mbithi and Rasmusson 1977; Migot-Adholla 1984; Mutiso 1975; Muzaale and Leonard 1985) as well as to intensive research efforts on soil erosion (Barber, Thomas, and Moore 1981; Dunne 1979; Moore 1979a; Thomas, Barber, and Moore 1981) and agricultural technology (Collinson 1979; Gielen 1982; Lynam Gerhart, personal communication). Arid and semi-arid land programmes in Kitui (Louis Berger Inc. 1985), Baringo (Thomas and Barber 1983; Thomas et al. 1982), and other districts also emphasized the rehabilitation of degraded hillslopes and water sources. These new initiatives all included soil-conservation activities, with the addition of a strong concern for water supply, dry forests, savanna trees, fuelwood supplies, and charcoal.

Deforestation and energy

During the 1970s, energy supply emerged as a major issue in development planning and environmental management. Surveys of energy use and sources in Africa revealed that most people depended on wood fuel (firewood or charcoal) for cooking and other domestic uses, as well as for many commercial uses. The magnitude of fuelwood demand in both urban and rural households raised serious concerns over future energy supplies in countries in which the annual harvest of wood far outstripped the rate of replacement in forests and savannas. As of 1979, the forest reserves of Kenya produced enough wood to meet 4.4 per cent of national energy needs, leaving trees on private lands and uncontrolled woodlands and scrubland to meet the remainder of the demand (Adams 1979). As with soil conservation, Machakos District served as a research laboratory for the dryland farming districts of the nation and the larger region.

Energy consumption, fuelwood sales, charcoal trade, and agro-forestry surveys identified Machakos District as a wood-fuel deficit area (Barnes, Ensminger, and O'Keefe 1984; Bradley 1991; Buck 1981; Mung'ala and Openshaw 1984; O'Keefe, Raskin, and Bernow 1984; Raintree 1984; Rocheleau 1985; Vonk 1983a). The district also exported charcoal to Nairobi, particularly during the drought of 1984, though the trade was illegal and mostly undocumented. Charcoal-selling was ubiquitous along roadsides as well as at markets (Van Buren 1983). Mung'ala and Openshaw (1984) predicted, on the basis of local consumption alone, that fuelwood harvesting would deplete the stock of wood in plantations, dry forests, and savannas in Machakos District between 1986 and 2000.

Many rural people in both districts cited charcoal production and sale as the alternative of first resort when crops failed. It was equated with "starvation" or "reserve" crops (such as cassava) grown as a hedge against failure of more vulnerable crops (such as maize) during drought (Van Buren 1983; J. Kyengo and R. Vonk, personal communication). The deforestation problems in the drier parts of Ukambani resulted more from the widespread reliance on charcoal from dry forest trees as a "cash crop" than from the harvesting of fuelwood for local use (Wisner 1985).

Many research and rural development programmes at the time assumed that local use of fuelwood and urban charcoal markets (e.g. increases in local population and the commercialization of charcoal) caused deforestation in dry forests. Field research conducted in some districts (DeWees 1989) contradicted this prevailing assumption and suggested that, over the long term, land-clearing for agriculture was often the main "engine" of deforestation, with charcoal as a by-product. Even in the case of agricultural expansion and land conversion, however, the existence of the urban charcoal market facilitated more and larger land-conversion efforts by many farmers in dry forests in Machakos and Kitui. Some farmers harvested the standing trees on their land as assets that they "liquidated" (sold off) to subsidize the establishment of new croplands and home compounds. One farmer in a frontier zone in Machakos reported clearing over 10 ha of dry forest for charcoal in order to subsidize the establishment of 2 ha of cropland and a home compound (field interviews, 1991).

Frontier expansion into the dry forests was driven by a combination of population growth, commercial agriculture, and land markets in the densely populated farmlands in the region. The depletion of trees and forests in Ukambani, in both crowded and frontier zones, was driven by more than a simple process of population growth and escalating per capita energy demand. The rise in landlessness, owing to land consolidation and increased local and national market demand for food and cash crops, led to an even higher opportunity cost for keeping land in dry forest (Adams 1979).

Although many assumed that the depletion of forests and trees was a classic case of the tragedy of the commons, increasing privatization of land during the 1970s and 1980s may actually have accelerated the process of deforestation on the remaining common and state lands. In dry-forest frontiers, individual landholders hastened to clear-cut and cultivate as much land as possible in order to legitimize their claims through recognized use and "improvement," which did not include management of woodland and savanna. As noted above, the existence of a commercial charcoal market further encouraged deforestation of entire holdings as farmers "liquidated" wood-fuel assets to subsidize investments in new homesteads and cropland. The remaining commons came under ever greater pressure from the landless and smallholders, as well as from the livestock herds of largeholder farmers.

Not only the cause, but the very nature and awareness of the fuelwood shortage, proved to be quite complex. In Ukambani the shortage was perceived relative to prior conditions, preferred species, and existing practices of brick-making, charcoal production, and home cooking. Perceptions of the nature and importance of the shortage also varied between men and women, since women were responsible for domestic fuelwood collection and use in most households, whereas men controlled charcoal production and trade. The experience and perception of shortage at the household level varied even more substantially according to the terms of access rather than supply in the surrounding landscape (B. Wisner, personal communication). Poor women reported severe hardship imposed by dwindling fuelwood supply in landscapes in which some households enjoyed an abundant supply of wood from their own property or purchased charcoal from local producers (Rhoda Kisusu and others; self-help groups in Mbiuni and Katangi locations, personal communication, 1984).

Regardless of the severity and distribution of the fuelwood shortage, in-depth field studies revealed it to be one small part of a far more complex situation, which included a diversity of local-level responses that were "invisible" to national sectoral surveys. It seems that forest and energy planners may well have been looking in all of the wrong places for trees. Using satellite imagery, land-use surveys, and thematic maps of land cover, they could not see the growing numbers of trees and other woody plants on cropland, grazing land, boundaries, and homesteads, for the shrinking forests on state and county council land. Yet, whereas forests accounted for only 1 per cent of the area of Machakos District in 1985, hedgerows and boundary plantings in the landscape covered 1.7 per cent of the land area in some parts of the district and were major sources of fuelwood for household use (EcoSystems Ltd. 1981, 1986; Mortimore 1992; Rocheleau and Hoek 1984).

Not only were many existing woody plants invisible to wood-fuel surveys, but the potential for new planting sites on farms had escaped the notice of many energy programmes. On-farm tree-planting efforts far surpassed any of the plantations on public sites and state reserves (Mortimore 1992). In fact, the farmers of Ukambani had already planted and selectively protected several woody species in cropland, grazing land, home compounds, and boundary lines (Fliervoet 1981; Gielen 1982; KENGO 1985; Poulsen 1981; Rocheleau 1985). They responded rapidly and enthusiastically to the availability of seed and seedlings for a diversity of tree species suited to multiple uses in a variety of niches in the landscape (Getahun 1989; Hoekstra 1984; Hoekstra and Kuguru 1983; KENGO 1989a,b; Rocheleau 1985, 1992).

As with soil conservation, the most successful programmes to protect and replace trees and forests were those that addressed a wide range of environmental and economic concerns, including food, water, fodder, small timber, and cash, as well as fuelwood supplies (Getahun 1989; Mortimore 1992; Rocheleau 1985). Independently, and with the help of the more flexible sources of technical assistance, many Akamba farmers began to integrate fuelwood planting into the land-use system over a much longer time-horizon. Tree-planting on farm resulted in a higher density of trees in the densely settled uplands (including very small farms) than in the more sparsely settled areas downslope. Farmers in the drier parts of the region were still depleting the wood stocks in the surrounding savanna and dry forest, while planting new fruit and timber and fencing trees on their own farms.

The national- and district-scale sectoral focus on energy also masked the multiple uses and values of trees and forests in Ukambani and elsewhere. The Akamba perceived fuelwood largely as a by-product of trees and shrubs serving other "higher" purposes (timber, poles, fodder, food, medicine, boundary markers, fencing), or looked to weedy species growing in fencerows and grazing lands as a source (Raintree 1984; Rocheleau 1985; Vonk 1983a,b). The loss of trees and dry forests as fodder reserves and sources of timber, poles, food, and medicine mattered to many Akamba as much as or more than the loss of future fuelwood supply or convenient sources of high-quality fuelwood. Although less direct and obvious, the impacts of deforestation on local water supplies were a significant hardship for rural peoples throughout the region. For most people the quality, reliability, and proximity of water sources were of higher priority than fuelwood. Moreover, water-supply improvements eventually proved to be a crucial prerequisite for tree propagation and on-farm planting, as well as for protection of existing trees from trampling and browsing by livestock en route to distant water points (Rocheleau 1985, 1992; Jama et al. 1992).

During the 1980s, the Ministry of Energy, the Forestry Department, and the Ministry of Agriculture, as well as MIDP and several special projects, provided technical assistance and millions of tree seedlings and seeds each year to farmers in Ukambani. Through the efforts of the Kenya Rural Energy Development Project and other multi-purpose tree-planting efforts, the availability of seedlings expanded from two species of Cypress and Eucalyptus in forest nurseries and a few exotic fruits in agricultural nurseries in 1978 to over 85 species (28 of them indigenous), stocked in large numbers in nurseries and seed centres throughout the country by 1988.

Biodiversity

The preservation of Kenya's wildlife loomed large on the international agenda during the 1980s (Anderson and Grove 1987; Myers 1982). Over the course of the decade, both scientific and activist environmental programmes paid increasing attention to the habitat of endangered animals, and they identified plant species and finally whole ecosystems as worthy of preservation (Anderson and Grove 1987; Yeager and Miller 1986). However, little national or international attention focused on biological impoverishment (loss of biodiversity) and the homogenization of landscape (loss of ecodiversity) in predominantly agrarian and pastoral landscapes. Official policy and practice sought effective exclusion of neighbouring people from the national parks, rather than the integration of local livelihoods with biodiversity, inside and outside the boundaries of the nation's parks.

Meanwhile, local communities in Ukambani experienced a substantial loss of biodiversity in their immediate surroundings and in their crop and livestock production systems. Their concerns reflected subsistence and drought preparedness as well as religious and cultural values. For poor farmers and herders, biodiversity concerns were intimately linked with livelihood and survival. Many Akamba people shared a practical interest in the continuing availability of medicinal herbs, wild and semi-domesticated foods, and a variety of fibres, dyes, wood products, and fodder sources within agrarian landscapes. The diversity of flora and fauna, with their attendant products for human use and their invisible services to the ecosystem (nutrient fixation and cycling, seed dispersal and plant pollination, water retention and regulation), depended, in turn, on the complexity and diversity of the landscape itself. But little research and discussion addressed the price of agricultural land-use intensification from the point of view of landscape complexity and biodiversity and even less took up the relation of biodiversity to the diversity of livelihood options and the preservation of culture (Oldfield and Alcorn 1991; Richards 1985).

In spite of the prevailing separation of production and biodiversity concerns in national and international institutions, the settlers of dry agricultural frontiers dealt with the integration of both concerns daily. Recent migrants noted the persistence of many large mammals as pests or simply as coexisting residents in landscapes characterized by a mosaic of cropland, pasture, and forest (Jama et al. 1992; Malaret 1991). Active hunting and concerted expulsion of wildlife emptied many frontier farming and herding communities of rhinoceroses, elephants, and large carnivores in the 1950s and 1960s. The surviving fauna in many areas in the 1980s included large and diverse populations of antelope (several species), primates, rodents, wild pigs, and warthogs, as well as amphibians, reptiles, birds, a multitude of insects (including pests, food sources, pollinators, and nutrient cyclers), and the less visible, but crucial, microfauna (field observations and interviews at sites throughout Machakos and Kitui, 1983–1991).

Throughout the drier zones of Machakos and Kitui, rural people tolerated, protected, and even fostered the growth of a multitude of wild plants, including many characterized as "weeds" by colonial, national, and international agricultural scientists. These grew in interstitial spaces such as fencerows, field boundaries, and drainage channels, as well as between row crops, in fallow croplands, in grazing lands, and in forest remnants and patches. The maintenance of complex patterns of land use and cover was essential to the survival of many plant and animal communities within agrarian landscapes that had already been largely deforested. Agricultural intensification and expansion directly threatened this landscape complexity.

An invisible (and irreversible) loss of genetic, species, and cultural diversity proceeded as the landscape was increasingly brought under cultivation, yet farmers initiated many counter-efforts to restore diversity by encouraging the survival of specific plants and animals in the remaining "spaces between." Even so, scores of plants and animal species and locally adapted varieties disappeared from the landscape and local land-use systems, diminishing the biological basis of future land-use options and rural livelihoods. As species and varieties vanished from the daily experience of local people, an attendant loss of knowledge and skill occurred (Rocheleau 1992).

Land-conservation and rural-production initiatives both tended to ignore the issue of biodiversity, in spite of the importance of wild plants to the diet, health, economy, and ecology of rural farming communities in Ukambani. Conservation efforts likewise overlooked the importance of both plants and animals in agrarian landscapes in favour of the concentrations of large mammal populations of global scientific and economic (touristic) interest. The 1984–1985 drought and famine brought renewed interest in indigenous plants and "minor" forest products (KENGO 1989a,b; Rocheleau et al. 1985; Wachira 1987), which attracted some national and international recognition. The connection between biodiversity and local livelihoods in agrarian landscapes, however, remained tenuous in official circles beyond the community level, and the issue was relegated to activist groups and indigenous non-government organizations (NGOs) as in many other parts of the globe (Altieri and Merrick 1988; Fowler and Mooney 1990; Oldfield and Alcorn 1991). The maintenance of diverse landscapes with a variety of wild plants and small animals persisted as a matter of local concern (IFPP 1991; Rocheleau 1992; see Juma 1989a on a parallel process in Bungoma district and Richards 1985 on West Africa), but was not yet recognized as a subject of national and global significance.

Drought and famine

In the midst of renewed national and international concern over vanishing wildlife, deforestation, soil erosion, and threatened energy and water supplies, the people of Machakos and Kitui districts experienced one of the most devastating events of the century, the drought and famine of 1984–1985. Over the course of two crop failures in 1983–1984 and the nearly total disappearance of green fodder sources during the dry seasons of 1984–1985, the Akamba suffered up to 60 per cent reductions in livestock and liquidated many of their hard-won assets in order to purchase food. Many farmers lost their draught animals (oxen), which hampered their recovery from the drought and reduced their ability to cultivate their croplands for years after (residents of Machakos and Kitui, personal communications; Kamau 1989). Some people, particularly children and the elderly, died; widespread acute and chronic malnutrition in Machakos, Kitui, and neighbouring districts left lasting effects on infants and young children deprived of adequate nutrition at crucial stages of mental and physical development (S. Saito, personal communication; Ndegwa, 1989; Neumann et al. 1989).

In Ukambani the drought began with the failure of the 1983 October–December rains, which resulted in crop failure as well as stress on livestock during the subsequent dry season. By the failure of the March–June rains (which affected most of the country), the moister zones of Machakos and Kitui districts were experiencing serious and widespread food shortage and income losses, while people in the drylands suffered from food, water, and fodder shortages.

Many communities in the drier parts of Ukambani were accustomed to losing one crop in three, or even one of every two crops. They had normally offset this loss through livestock sales and the purchase of food at "normal" prices from the cities or the neighbouring highlands. In the case of this severe drought (the worst since 1930), however, the livestock were dying for lack of fodder. In eastern and central Kenya (which includes Ukambani), stock reductions in agroecological zones 4 and 5 ranged from 26 to 51 per cent of cattle and 23 to 57 per cent of goats, with most of Machakos and Kitui toward the high end of that range since they had already experienced crop failure and poor rains the year before (Anyango et al. 1989). Since the drought was also national in scope, livestock prices were depressed in a nationally glutted market. For the same reason (for a time) virtually no food was available for purchase, except at vastly inflated prices beyond the means of most rural people (Anyango et al. 1989; Borton 1989; Downing et al. 1989).

By August 1984, many normally "permanent" water points went dry, forcing already overburdened and weakened women and children to trek longer distances for water. In the drier parts of Kitui, men and women began to rotate water-collection and livestock-watering journeys, and some people made the long treks at night to conserve energy and to avoid the midday heat. In response to the low prices and lack of transportation for livestock, Akamba men and boys began long livestock drives on foot to deliver large herds of cattle and goats to Nairobi and the nearby Kenya Meat Commission plant at Athi River. Rotting carcasses lay on the roadsides of the major arteries linking Kitui and Machakos villages to Nairobi, attesting to the prior condition of the livestock and the stress of the journey (*Weekly Review* 1984).

In spite of their experience with periodic drought, the Akamba were hard hit. Many experienced famine because of their distance from the centre, their peripheral status relative to other affected districts, and the erosion of their prior self-sufficiency in responding to drought under extreme conditions. In Machakos, 1984 was known as the famine "I Shall Die with the Money in my Hand" – *Nikw'a Ngwete* – (Alice Mwau, Japheth Kyengo, and Francis Lelo, personal communication), reflecting the painful irony of changing times. Eventually people were forced to fall back on their traditional practices in local space, or to wait for the state to bring relief. Although a large body of knowledge persisted, the people had lost much of their local knowledge about famine foods and fodder reserves (Rocheleau 1992; Rocheleau et al. 1989).

In 60 per cent of households, women were left (with or without cash remittances) to fend for themselves, their children, and their livestock. Thus in 1984 the feminization of poverty in Ukambani expanded to include the feminization of famine and of response to famine. Women sought the advice of older men and experimented widely to determine which plants could serve as fodder reserves for livestock; this was previously part of the knowledge and responsibility of men (Rocheleau 1992). Even when they discovered the traditional drought-coping strategies, women often learned that the land-tenure reform process had converted special fodder and famine food reserves in the plains to cropland for new settlers. Land-tenure reform had also constrained (but not completely restricted) local and regional mobility for both people and livestock.

In fact, individual migration prompted by drought provided some indication of the relative impact of this event in different agro-ecological zones of the region. In eastern and central Kenya one or more persons moved away owing to the drought in 38 per cent of all households in zone 5, as compared with only 7 per cent in the upland coffee zone (zone 2), 21 per cent in zone 3, and 26 per cent in zone 4 (Anyango et al. 1989). Overall, reliance on migration and remittances was greater in the drier zones, reflecting less wealth and the differential vulnerability of cattle in zone 5 versus tree-crop and non-farm assets in the wetter uplands.

As with the neighbouring pastoral Maasai, the differential impact of the drought among communities was determined by: ecozone; population density; prior conditions of people, livestock, and land; wealth; and the extent and strength of social support networks (Grandin, de Leeuw, and Lembuya 1989). At the household and individual level, the depth of the crisis depended upon the diversity of income streams; the stock and fluidity of assets; the strength, complexity, and geographical range of social networks; and mobility within those networks. Prior to the colonization and sedentarization of the Akamba, the whole community, as a group, might have moved or sent its large herds to distant, well-watered sites. Although that option no longer existed at the community scale, the principle still held at the household level during the 1984 drought. Many farm families in the dry savanna zones sent livestock, and sometimes family members, to stay with relatives in more well-watered areas. Likewise, many rural families sent some of their members to stay with relatives in towns and cities. Others relied heavily, and more than usual, on cash from family members working in urban centres. At a more local scale, many people shifted their focus of activity from cropland to herding, or from both cropland and grazing land to dry woodlands and in-between spaces (Rocheleau et al. 1989). For the more vulnerable members of the population, however, these options were often either unavailable or insufficient to stave off hunger, illness, livestock loss, or distress sales of household and personal assets.

The differential vulnerability has been distinguished as *food shortage* (less than 66 per cent food self-sufficiency on farm), *food poverty* (insufficient income to purchase food and/or inability to acquire food through kin and other social networks), and *food deprivation* (food shortage serious enough to cause wasting, stunting, and vulnerability to disease, or to force migration) (Anyango et al. 1989, 186–187; Kates et al. 1988). According to the figures compiled by Anyango and colleagues (1989, 187 and 208), in the six districts of eastern and central Kenya the proportion of the population that was both food short and food poor was 10 per cent in average years and 30 per cent in drought years. The figures are even higher for Machakos and Kitui owing to the relatively higher proportion of semi-arid land. By January 1985, a survey found that, throughout the six-district region, 50 per cent of children were malnourished, 14 per cent severely. In zone 4, only 14 per cent of children were healthy and 64 per cent were malnourished. In an earlier background survey, 30 per cent of the children in Kitui and 23 per cent in Machakos showed signs of stunted growth, indicating widespread food deprivation (CBS 1983). Overall, the studies point to a high and growing vulnerability to severe malnutrition among children in zones 4 and 5, owing to rising population densities and inadequate diversification of household access to food among the poor (Anyango et al. 1989; Downing 1988).

At least 300,000 people in Kitui and as many in Machakos received food aid from the Government of Kenya relief programme in 1984–1985 (Deloitte, Haskins, and Sells Management Consultants 1985). District-level figures indicate that 35 per cent of the population in Machakos and 95 per cent of that in Kitui received food aid (Anyango et al. 1989, 184). Many others moved, relied on assistance from family members, or received assistance from church and other non-government organizations outside of the main food programme. Imported food was distributed as direct food relief (15 per cent), through market channels (62 per cent), and through a variety of post-relief programmes (23 per cent) (Borton 1989, 27). Much of the relief and post-relief food was dispersed in "food-for-work" programmes, which in Machakos and Kitui often involved construction and rehabilitation of soil- and water-conservation structures as well as tree planting. By the end of 1985 most households and large tracts of barren landscape in Machakos and Kitui were on the way to varying degrees of recovery.

In retrospect, most analysts attributed the avoidance of widespread famine throughout Kenya to the simultaneous use of market channels (primarily in the wetter uplands) and relief programmes (mainly in the drylands) to distribute food imports and to the flexible collaboration of national, international, and non-government organizations in food delivery and distribution. Some analysts noted an unnecessary national vulnerability to drought owing to: (1) overdependence on maize; (2) the extension of maize cropping (and expanding populations of farmers) in areas of uncertain and irregular rainfall; (3) the failure of livestock marketing mechanisms to allow for rapid (and remunerative) offtake at the onset of drought; and (4) lack of infrastructure for small-scale water storage and irrigation (Wyckoff 1989, 366–367).

At the local level, rural people in Ukambani attribute their successful survival of the famine to:

- reliance on their indigenous plants (and their knowledge of them) for food, fodder, and medicine;
- reliance on cash remittances from family members already earning wages (and perhaps residing) elsewhere;
- migration of one or more resident household members in search of employment or simply alternative sources of food and support in another household;
- use of group work and group contacts to secure access to official and external sources of relief aid; and
- mobilization of family, clan, church, and other networks of mutual support to secure employment, loans, outside relief, or temporary residence and food for both people and livestock.

Field observations, interviews, and published accounts all support the importance of political and social networks in gaining access to the relief food in direct aid programmes. This was true for church and NGO sources as well as for deliveries channelled through district and local officials (Borton 1989). In many cases, social networks served as crucial information links to connect centres of supply and specific communities or households in serious need of aid.

Self-help responses to environmental crisis

During the 1980s, the people of Ukambani, and women in particular, attracted national attention for the scale and degree of commitment of their (apparently) communal self-help group efforts in soil and water conservation, reforestation, and on-farm tree planting. The government had encouraged local groups (*mwethya* and other similar groups) of traditional origin (Mbithi and Rasmusson 1977; Mutiso 1975) to register as official organizations and to take responsibility for development and conservation efforts in rural communities (Bahemuka and Tiffen 1992). At the time of registration by the government in the early 1980s, most of the active self-help groups were women's groups that functioned as associations of individuals engaged in reciprocal work for mutual benefit at individual and household level. They were engaged primarily not in communal or public works but rather in shared work on private land or in small group enterprises (Rocheleau 1992).

Most of the groups focused on rotational group labour to weed croplands, thatch houses, make bricks, build and repair terraces, gather fuelwood, and construct and repair fences for members. Some groups specialized in marketing crafts and produce and provided rotating credit to members (Bahemuka and Tiffen 1992; Muzaale and Leonard 1985; Rocheleau 1985; Wijngaarden 1983). During the 1980s, government demands expanded the mandates of these groups to public works, including up to three days per week on road repair, gully repair, land rehabilitation at degraded sites, construction and maintenance of water impoundments, tree propagation and planting, and construction of primary school classrooms (Rocheleau 1985). A recent survey documented 115 groups in Machakos alone engaged in conservation activities and 345 involved in income-generation projects (Bahemuka and Tiffen 1992; Ondiege 1992).

The self-help groups played a crucial role in procuring, maintaining, and protecting resources for the households of members, and they conducted much of the soil-conservation and land-rehabilitation work at community level during the 1980s. During the drought and famine of 1984–1985, the women's self-help groups connected many of the rural poor in the drier parts of Ukambani to local sources of food, fodder, fuelwood, and employment as well as to sources of relief food (both government and NGO). Although the groups provide leverage for women to gain access to resources otherwise beyond their reach, it should be noted that they often do not represent or serve the very poorest women. Lack of time, child care, and membership dues may keep the poorest and most isolated women from participating as members (Bahemuka and Tiffen 1992; Rocheleau 1985). Owing to the very visible nature of their soil-conservation and tree-planting work and the strong government and international support for those initiatives, many groups secured needed relief assistance for their entire communities as well as for their neediest members (Rocheleau 1992). They also attracted development assistance for many long-term endeavours in forestry, agriculture, water management, and income generation. In the process, women's groups acquired technical resource management and production skills and strengthened their political leverage to gain and maintain rights of use and access to shared resources on both public and private lands (Rocheleau 1992).

In spite of substantial state support for group activity at the community level, these groups were not linked to planning and policy decisions at the regional and national levels, although Tiffen and Mortimore (1992, 381) report that groups in Machakos "have learnt to pull in capital and expertise from national and international sources." Support for specific activities was contingent on the coincidence of state and local objectives, particularly with respect to watershed protection and rehabilitation. National government responses to soil and water degradation of national concern (sedimentation of dams) affected the timing and nature of local conservation activities. Strong incentives (financial reward, food for work, access to government services) promoted group work on gullies and highly degraded hillslopes, rather than on private farms. In contrast, local self-help responses to land degradation integrated farm- and community-level concerns for food security, water supply, fodder, fuelwood, commercial production, and environmental quality. Nevertheless, these priorities did not directly affect national-level programmes. The 100-year history ends, as it began, with a region caught between two worlds, in this case the distinct realms of state and local power, experience and perception.

The trajectory of change in Ukambani

What does this 100-year story tell us about Ukambani and regional environmental change? Is Ukambani a critical zone? What lessons does it hold for understanding the regional dynamics of environmental change? Clearly, if "critical" implies that environmental degradation has so eroded life-support systems as to preclude the

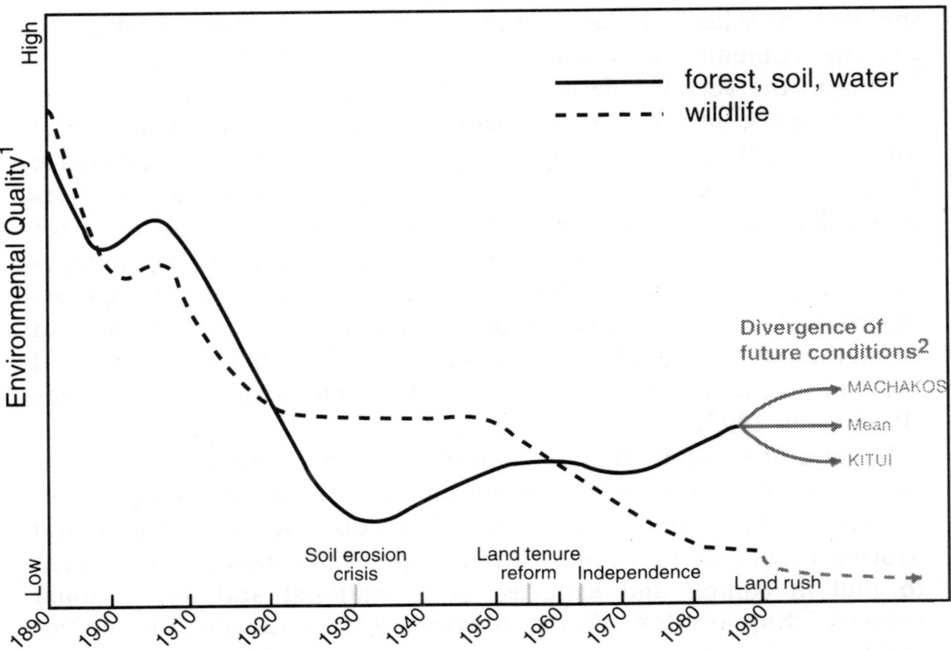

[1] Differential environmental quality based on projected migration from Machakos to Kitui and on agricultural expansion in Kitui.
[2] Multiple lines indicate divergent paths for Machakos and Kitui (around the mean) - not actual values.

Fig. 5.5 **Environmental quality trends as derived from oral histories**

continuation of current land-use systems and lifeways, then critical it is not. Along the continuum from criticality to sustainability (see chap. 1) the region falls best into the category "endangered" – that is, Ukambani is susceptible to a critical situation within the next generation.

In this case, the trajectories of land degradation, environmental quality, wealth, and population (figs. 5.5 and 5.6) are particularly ambiguous and unpredictable, with a wide range of possible outcomes, both in the aggregate and for distinct groups and subregions (fig. 5.7).

In figure 5.5, regional environmental quality is expressed in qualitative terms as (1) the condition and quantity of resources available for people, and (2) the numbers and diversity of wildlife. The graph depicts a sharp downturn in both wildlife and other natural resources (forest, soil, water) during the drought and plagues of the 1890s, a partial recovery at the turn of the century, followed by serious deterioration in forests, soils, and water resources from 1910 to 1920, owing to the sedentarization and concentration of growing (recovering) populations in ecological zones 4 and 5. Although wildlife stabilized to some extent after the establishment of parks and ranches in large tracts (albeit limited in extent and subject to legal hunting and poaching), the processes of deforestation and soil erosion continued at an accelerated rate within the limited confines of the "African reserve" farming areas. A moderate recovery began in the 1930s and continued into the 1950s, with a combination of local agricultural innovation and soil-conservation and rehabilitation measures promoted by the state.

The land-tenure reforms and settlement programmes that began in the mid-1950s brought a new wave of agricultural expansion into marginal lands, including deforestation of many areas of wildlife habitat (Yatta Plateau and dry plains). During the last two decades, the wildlife has continued to decline, more slowly, while environmental recovery due to agricultural intensification, soil conservation, and reforestation in some parts of the Machakos has contributed to further recovery of ecosystems in the upland and moister parts of the region (Tiffen and Mortimore 1992). The current land rush and settlement in Kitui may well bring a sharp divergence in the futures of Machakos and Kitui districts and in the wetter upland versus dry lowland sites within the region.

The trajectories of wealth, population, and environmental degradation illustrated in figure 5.6 suggest that land-use intensification and soil-conservation measures counteracted population and other production pressures on the land at particular points in history. During the land-rush and settlement periods, however, the land degradation in newly opened regions outstripped the counter-effects of intensive resource management in the more densely settled regions. Once again, the divergence between Machakos and Kitui figures prominently in the projected future of population, wealth, and land degradation in the region. Figure 5.7 indicates a similar divergence in the environmental quality and wealth of specific groups within both districts. Frontier farmers (group 3), defined by a mix of class and age, consist mainly of young and relatively poor (often near-landless) people who still have enough capital or labour to sell or trade for land in drier areas, in combination with some entrepreneurs from more densely settled areas. The near-landless and landless people (group

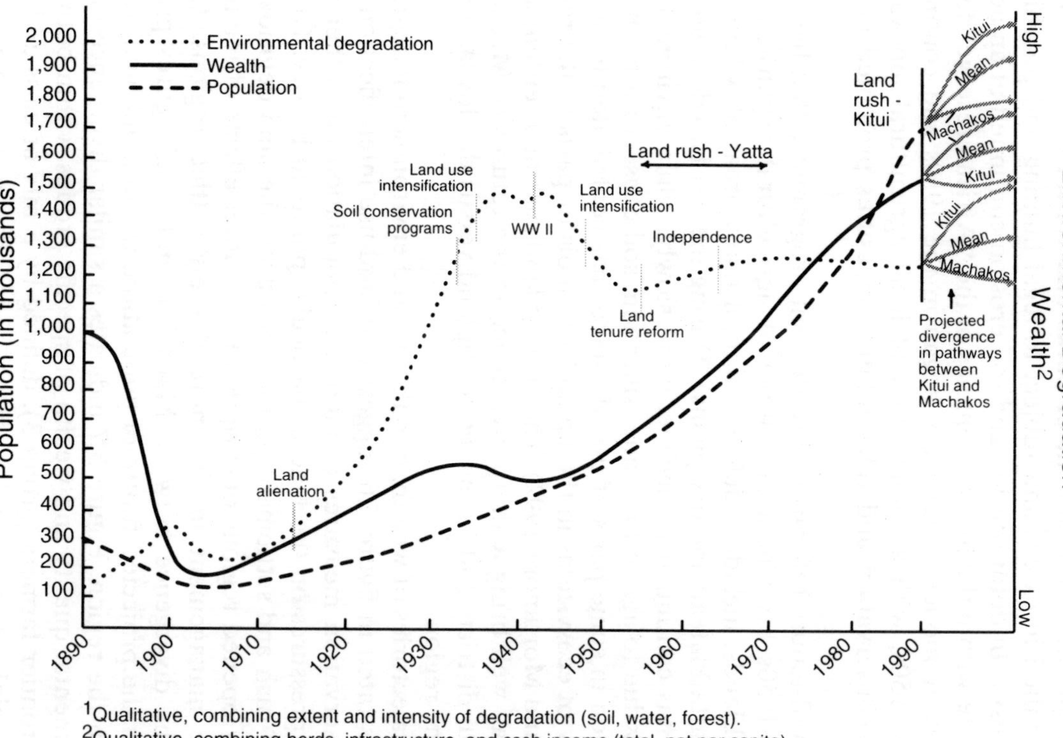

[1]Qualitative, combining extent and intensity of degradation (soil, water, forest).
[2]Qualitative, combining herds, infrastructure, and cash income (total, not per capita).

Fig. 5.6 **Trends in population, wealth, and environmental degradation**

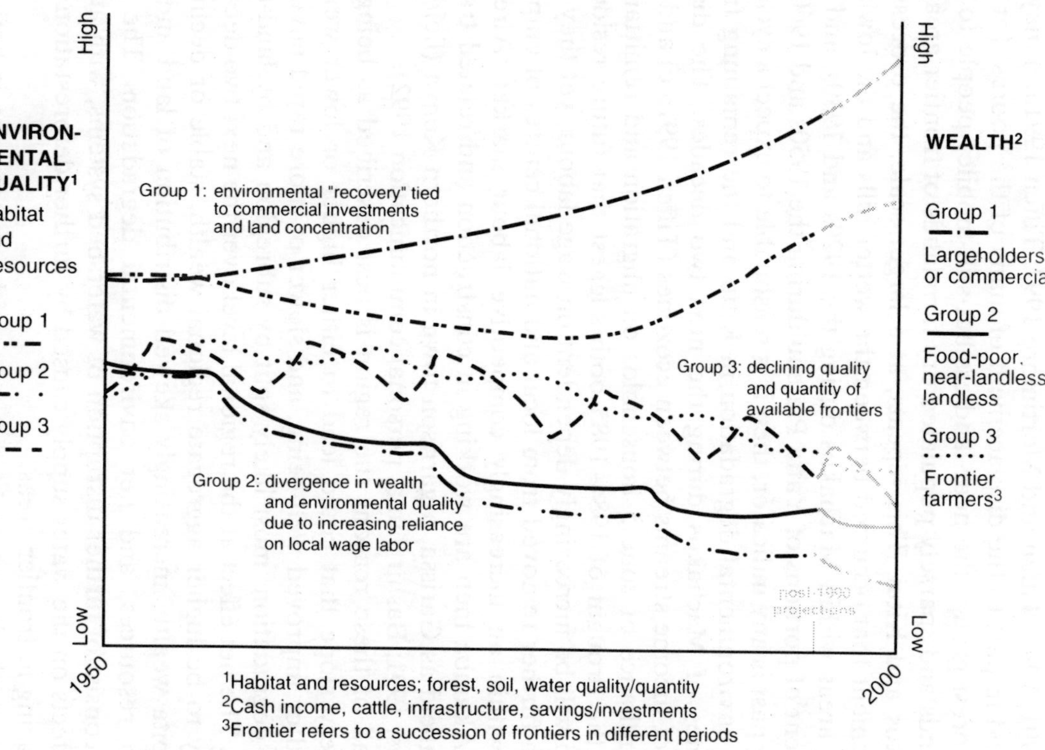

Fig. 5.7 **Divergences in environmental quality and wealth: Trends among social groups**

2) who remain in the established farming areas are primarily the poorest households of the prior and rising generations as well as many single (or widowed, abandoned, or divorced) women.

The apparent stability of Machakos over the last decade (Mortimore 1991, 1992; Tiffen and Mortimore 1992; Tiffen 1991a,c) may be attributed in part to the displacement of many of the poorest (or the next-poorest group, the near-landless-but-still-mobile) people to the rangelands and sparsely populated dry farmlands of frontier areas in Machakos and Kitui. This repeats, at a larger scale, the process of displacement that occurred between the wetter hills and the lowland grazing areas within Machakos during the 1920s and 1930s, and the settlement of portions of Yatta Plateau during the 1950s and 1960s.

If the past is any indicator, then it is reasonable to expect a cycle of serious environmental degradation in Kitui and the remaining frontier zones of Machakos during the next two decades. The distribution of income streams between ecozones (Tiffen 1991a,c) and the higher reliance of zone 5 households on migration and remittances during the drought of 1984–1985 both suggest that future residents of Kitui will be increasingly dependent on wage labour, yet they will be even further removed from local and national centres of employment, within an increasingly competitive labour market. Already young Akamba men are working in construction and related trades as far afield as Garissa, a garrison town in northern Kenya (field interviews, 1991; Bashir Jama, personal communication 1992).

For all of these reasons the region is best described as being on a slippery slope that could lead to either higher or lower wealth, reduced or improved well-being, and slower or more rapid environmental degradation, most likely split by subregion and by land-user groups. The net effect at the regional level over the next two decades is likely to be higher aggregate regional wealth, stable or declining per capita wealth, increasingly skewed distribution of land and access to resources, and net environmental degradation. The last would consist of further disruption of watershed systems, with attendant effects on the water supply caused by further deforestation and overgrazing in frontier areas.

The hydrologic system in this semi-arid environment is both the linchpin and the "Achilles heel" of the regional ecosystem. Water is a scarce resource, crucial to life support and livelihoods, and yet it is the single most sensitive element within the system in its responses to land-use change, reductions in forest cover, and increasing compaction by near-sedentary cattle. This translates into a major criterion for judging land-use options in degraded areas. For example, intensification of agriculture in a deforested, degraded area could well restore partial tree cover through on-farm and boundary planting of trees. Although it is quite possible that this could substitute for forest products (such as fodder and wood fuel), the replacement water-storage and distribution functions of the forest would require elaborate physical structures and management systems.

An effective response to offset deforestation and watershed disruption would require major labour, management, and capital inputs from the farmers of Ukambani. This is a high expectation given the increasing proportion of smallholders and near-landless people who will either clear new plots from forest and range elsewhere, colonize marginal and fragile spaces within their local landscapes, or deplete the remaining resources in their existing plots in order to compensate for the shrinking size of holdings as plots are subdivided to children. Eventual outcomes depend on a host of contingencies in the national and international systems in which the region is embedded, as well as on the vagaries of local and regional weather and internal social and political processes.

Mortimore (1992) points out the folly of the dire predictions of imminent desertification of the 1930s. After six decades and a five-fold increase in population, not only is Ukambani not a desert, but soil condition and tree cover are improved in much of Machakos District. Likewise, Downing (1991, 379) concludes that "visions of eco-catastrophe in the 21st century are not warranted!" Yet fear of eco-tragedy is not unrealistic for the "bottom" 20–30 per cent in Ukambani who are food short and food poor, and who are likely to experience food deprivation in future droughts and displacement over the long term. The region may sustain livelihoods and life support for some, as well as contribute to national production, at the expense of excluding an ever-larger number of Akamba from access to home, workplace, and habitat within its borders, and by relegating many of those who remain to a precarious and vulnerable status with respect to ecological and economic perturbations. That 30 per cent of the children in Kitui were stunted from malnutrition in a "normal" year (Anyango et al. 1989; CBS 1983) suggests that a large segment of the population in the drier parts of Ukambani is highly vulnerable to future fluctuations in local weather as well as in local and national markets for staple foods. Biological impoverishment of the otherwise "stable", "recovered" landscape in the higher-potential lands (mostly in Machakos) may also narrow future livelihood and life-support options for all those who remain in Ukambani.

If the region is not critical in the absolute sense, is it, on one of its potential trajectories (figs. 5.5 and 5.6), sustainable? Sustainable development postulates the reconciliation of "environment" with "development." Development worth sustaining will need to incorporate and reconcile a multiplicity of views on environment and development as experienced by those who would be "sustained." The 100-year history of ecological and economic crises in Ukambani suggests several themes that focus the concerns and experiences of a multiplicity of groups among the Akamba, including the poor and the displaced whose fortunes and futures are not apparent in the greening landscape and the financial ledgers of the region (fig. 5.7).

The question of regional sustainability is transformed when the focus is on the people of the region, on those who call it home. Population then becomes a question of difference and distribution, rather than sheer numbers. The question of poverty broadens, as noted in chapter 1, to include the changing well-being, quality of life, and range of options for the poor in Ukambani, including their livelihoods and use of natural resources. Land degradation expands from physical degradation of the "resource base" for national production to encompass the life-support and livelihood needs of the rural poor and the paradox of land-use intensification as a solution to poverty and land degradation (fig. 5.8). The degradation of water resources extends beyond national hydropower supply to encompass the amount, timing, and quality of local water sources for domestic, agricultural, and livestock uses. In the history of Ukambani, all of these issues intersect in the continuing and deepening problems of drought, water shortage, poverty, and hunger with the changing nature of land cover, property regimes, mobility of people, and the level and terms of integration of economic and ecological systems from local to international scale.

Two major indicators of the "stability and health" of the region and the trajectory for the future are the status of water resources and the vulnerability of the region as a whole to drought. The savannas and the ranges of wooded hills that cover much of East Africa, and Ukambani in particular, are susceptible to natural hazards, which can become disasters as population densities, production pressures, or both, increase, and as traditional drought response and famine prevention measures are pre-empted by changes in land cover,

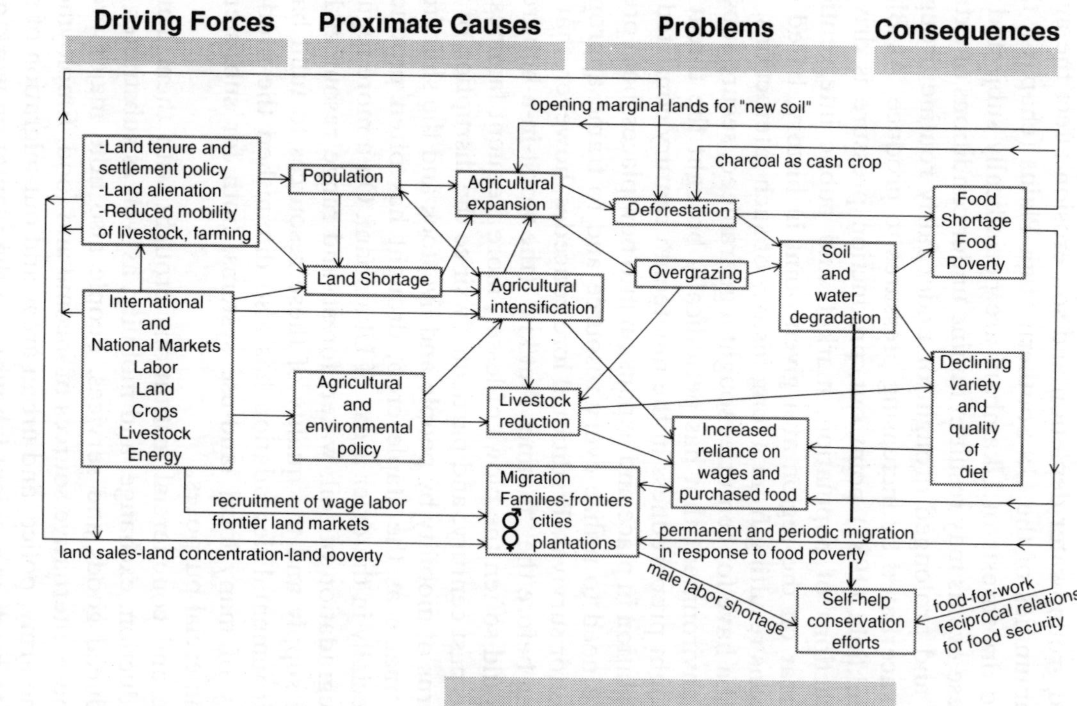

Fig. 5.8 **Regional environmental degradation in Ukambani: Linkages among driving forces, proximate causes, problems, and consequences**

land use, livelihood, and land tenure. All of these proximate causes are driven by a combination of national and international development and environmental policy, commercialization of rural production, and, increasingly, rapid population growth. Whereas mass wasting of hillslopes is a major issue in the Nepal middle mountains (chap. 4) and groundwater depletion and soil erosion affect the agricultural communities of the US Southern High Plains (chap. 6), the savannas and dry forests of Ukambani are periodically subjected to drought. These events may result in famine under conditions of extremely severe and prolonged drought or under fairly routine drought conditions exacerbated by increasing pressures to produce. As Blaikie and Brookfield (1987) point out, production pressure is driven by the interactions of population, market, and public intervention brought to bear on the region at a given point in history, based on prior conditions resulting from a long history of such interactions.

The Akamba have for centuries sought a guaranteed, secure subsistence in an environment that has periodically brought the threat of famine. Drought preparedness in the nineteenth century consisted of a mix of adaptation in place and expansion into new places, both predicated on the need to utilize every resource and to frame appropriate strategies for survival. Traditional lore concedes, however, that all this is nothing before the "famines that kill" (the worst-in-a-hundred-years) but could soften the blows of lesser, more frequent famines.

During the past century, and particularly since the disruption of regional patterns of mobility by people and livestock and the shift from sorghum to maize as the staple crop, drought has often produced famine, especially in the drier areas of Ukambani. On a more regular basis, the degradation of soil, water, forest, and range resources has reduced the supply and the quality of these resources to fulfil basic needs. Environmental degradation has also diminished the productive capacity of many local land-use systems, both for subsistence and for commercial purposes.

New state and commercial institutions brought with them a new logic of production, exchange, and mobility, as well as substitutes for locally produced goods and services. People also note major problems with these alternative sources of income and food. Employment of men in the army, police, and urban areas and out-migration of single women to work as resident labourers in the plantation workforce have all become less viable options during the last decade. Recent moves to diversify the ethnic composition of the army and police force have left less "space" for Akamba men. Saturation of the urban job market has also resulted in many men returning unemployed from job-seeking forays and short-term stints in the capital city. Women in the plantation workforce regard it as a last resort from which they often cannot return to their home villages.

The rising generation of young people in Ukambani confronts a resource base that has been largely circumscribed by encroachment of commercial interests into the best agricultural lands and the removal of valuable trees (timber, fuelwood, and fodder resources) from the less productive "marginal" lands. Their parents have settled or used the remaining area, with limited scope for subdivision in the most densely settled agricultural communities. The youth are caught between two forces: population pressure, land concentration, and declining resources from within juxtaposed with a declining capability of urban centres to absorb migrants and a growing return flow of migrants.

Added to this is the constant pressure from government and commercial interests to provide raw materials to the city and export cash crops to earn foreign exchange. The result is likely radically to alter life as the Akamba people have known it. Alternatively, land-use systems may change slowly and incrementally, stabilizing through land-use intensification and conservation measures as described in several recent studies (Mortimore 1992; Porter in prep.; Tiffen 1992a,b). The latter trend, however, will most likely exclude increasing numbers of people from that experience, by relegating "surplus" people to permanent residence elsewhere, and rendering them homeless (in the sense that home has been understood in their culture). Alternatively, the migrants from Machakos District may continue to stream into the dry forests and rangelands of neighbouring Kitui District, thus achieving apparent sustainability in one part of Ukambani (Machakos), at the expense of the land and the people (including the new migrants) in the drier half of the region (Kitui).

In terms of the physical resource base, it is the disruption of hydrological cycles that will do the most damage to both biological and economic productivity. The story of land-use change in Ukambani is a story of people maximizing returns to water (Tiffen 1991a) under changing economic and ecological conditions, at different scales, and with varying degrees of control over their own and other people's use of the resource. Whereas people formerly concentrated around permanent groundwater sources or along perennial streams, widespread deforestation and soil compaction have led to the transformation of many permanent groundwater sources to seasonal supplies and have reduced perennial streams to intermittent flow. This has changed water quantity and quality and has radically altered the timing and terms of water availability for agriculture, livestock, and domestic use. Moreover, the changes in use pattern engendered by these effects has in turn caused further damage and disruption in watershed systems (fig. 5.9).

Soil erosion is the single most visible and notorious form of environmental degradation in Ukambani (Dunne, Dietrich, and Brunengo 1978; Moore 1979a,b). Ironically, it is also probably the most reversible – that is, the most responsive to restoration and rehabilitation. Past experiments in range management and land rehabilitation (e.g. research and project reports from Baringo, from Machakos and Kitui districts, 1930s to present) suggest that many of the degraded sites, if fenced and protected, are likely to recover rather quickly and dramatically. Until such measures are taken, however, many areas will produce less fodder, food, and other goods and services essential to rural life.

Although none of the damage is irreversible at the local scale with major investments of labour, management, and capital, no structure or process is currently in place that is poised to effect such a reversal at the regional level. Overall, the regional disruption of hydrologic systems caused by the interaction of state policy, national markets, and individual farm households is now left to a process of intensification and recovery on a farm-by-farm basis. This is true for land cover and condition as well as for intensification of water use and management, with major water-supply infrastructure being developed at community level in scattered locales throughout the region. Not all households and communities are in the same position to invest in or to take advantage of new water-supply and drainage infrastructure. Consequently, the process of watershed degradation is likely to persist, concurrent with water resource development and watershed rehabilitation at dispersed sites throughout Ukambani (as in the case of deforestation and reforestation). In both cases a sustainable future rests on a dramatic and widespread intensification of the current land-use system, under changing and somewhat unpredictable policy and market developments and a growing population.

Equally important in the long run is the biological impoverishment that attends loss of genetic and species diversity. This includes the loss of genetic resources in the form of locally adapted varieties, as well as the loss of entire species from the region, along with the knowledge of their ecology and economic use. Local varieties of crop plants, as well as wild relatives of local cultivars, have been

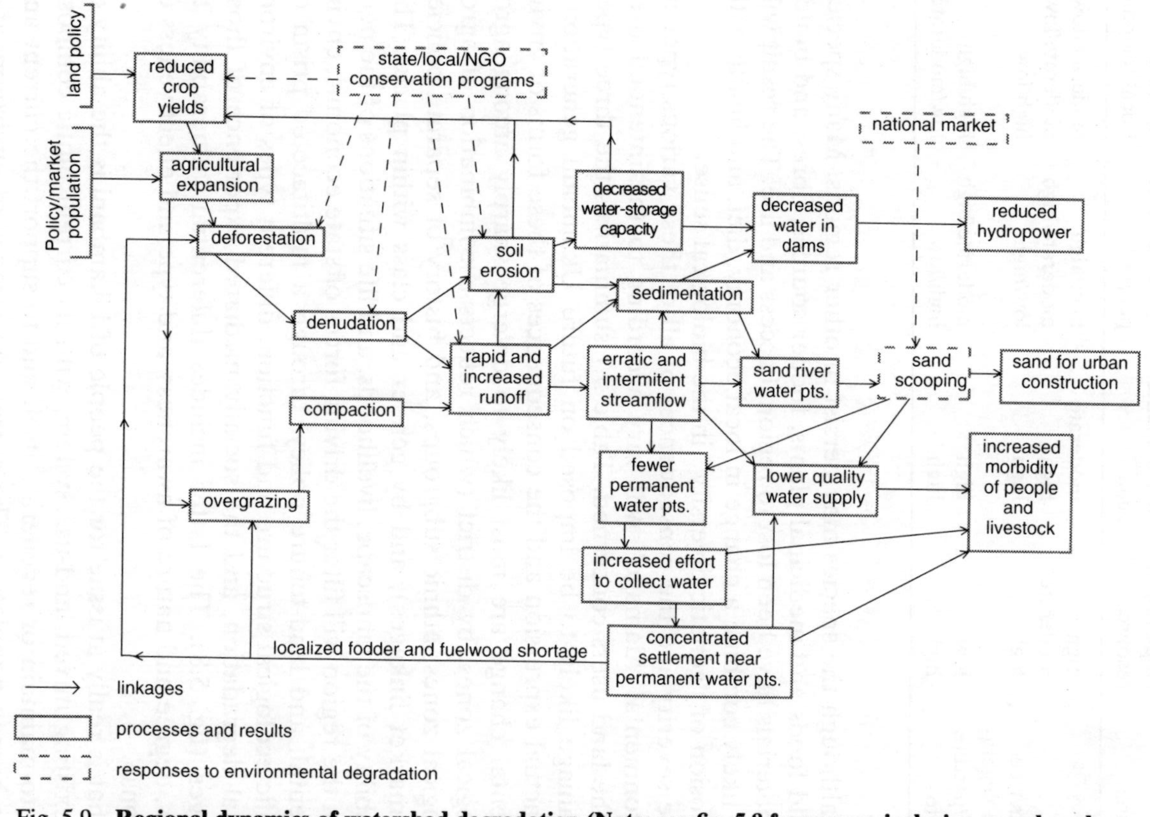

Fig. 5.9 **Regional dynamics of watershed degradation (Note: see fig. 5.8 for a more inclusive causal analysis of environmental degradation)**

Table 5.7 **Three types of "impositions" on the future generations of Ukambani**

Resource	Depletion of resource	Degradation of environmental quality	Vulnerability Of resource/of people	Prospects for reversal Local/regional
Water	high	moderate	high/high	moderate/low
Soil	moderate	high	moderate/high	moderate/low
Forests/trees	high	high	low/high	high/low
Range vegetation/pasture	low	high	moderate/high	high/high
Wildlife	high	high	high/low	low/moderate

lost, although the species may persist in other regions. Many species of wild foods and medicinal plants, fodder sources, fibres, and building materials have been lost to regional access and use. The result will most likely combine a change in local economy, diet, and health with an erosion of "genetic diversity" in the biological sense.

The severity and the consequences of all of these various types of environmental "damage" will vary according to the intended uses and the land users concerned. Table 5.7 summarizes the three types of damage likely to be imposed on future Ukambani generations. The actual expression and the consequences of these forms of environmental change are most likely to diverge sharply among agro-ecological zones, by district (which reflects a combination of agro-ecological zones, ethnic subgroups, and history of separate policies and market linkages), and by gender and class within places. The variability of the landscape, livelihoods, and life situations of the people in the region will filter the driving forces of state economic, environmental, and land-tenure policy, through a multifaceted prism of specific ecological structure and function, different types of environmental degradation, and the socially mediated experience of those changes (fig. 5.8). The latter includes differential vulnerability to stress, degree and nature of awareness, and type and effectiveness of response.

What is really at issue for the people of Ukambani is the ability of the existing mixed land-use system, with its current biotic composition, to maintain or regenerate itself and to support the current and rising human population. The current divergence of environmental, economic, and social indicators between Machakos and Kitui, and between distinct groups (by gender, class, and generation), is illustrated in figures 5.5, 5.6, and 5.7. The future trajectory of the region will ultimately depend on whose home, habitat, and workplace it will be and on the ability of affected groups to moderate state and market influences to serve their own interests, to reconcile population and production growth, and to negotiate a new basis for integrating ecology and economy in Ukambani as a region.

Note

1. Since 1991, these two districts have been subdivided into four separate districts; all records contained in this chapter refer to district boundaries that defined Machakos and Kitui, and Ukambani up until that time.

References

Ackello-Ogutu, C. 1991. Livestock production. In *Environmental change and dryland management in Machakos District, Kenya, 1930–1990: Production profile*, ed. Mary Tiffen. ODI Working Paper 55. London: Overseas Development Institute.

Adams, P. 1979. Deforestation in Kenya: A case of "over-exploitation" of the common property resource? M.A. thesis, University of Sussex, UK.

Altieri, Miguel A., and Laura C. Merrick. 1988. Agroecology and in situ conservation of native crop diversity in the Third World. In *Biodiversity*, ed. Edward O. Wilson, 361–369. Washington DC: National Academy Press.

Ambler, Charles H. 1988. *Kenya communities in the age of imperialism: The central region in the late nineteenth century*. New Haven, CT: Yale University Press.

Anderson, David, and Richard H. Grove. 1987. *Conservation in Africa: People, policies and practice*. Cambridge: Cambridge University Press.

Anyango, G., et al. 1989. Drought vulnerability in Central and Eastern Kenya. In *Coping with drought in Kenya: National and local strategies*, ed. Thomas E. Downing, Kangethe W. Gitu, and Crispin M. Kamau, 169–210. Boulder, CO: Lynne Rienner.

Bahemuka, J., and Mary Tiffen. 1992. Akamba institutions and development, 1930–1900. In *Environmental change and dryland management in Machakos District, Kenya, 1930–1990: Institutional profile*, ed. Mary Tiffen, 3–51. ODI Working Paper, Draft. London: Overseas Development Institute.

Barber, R. G., D. B. Thomas, and T. R. Moore. 1981. Studies on soil erosion and runoff and proposed design procedures for terraces in the cultivated, semi-arid areas of Machakos District, Kenya. In *Soil conservation: Problems and prospects (Proceedings of Conservation 80, the International Conference on Soil Conservation held at the National College of Agricultural Engineering, Silsoe, Bedford, UK, 21st–25th July, 1980)*, ed. Royston P. C. Morgan, 219–237. New York: Wiley.

Barnes, Carolyn, Jean Ensminger, and Phil O'Keefe, eds. 1984. *Wood, energy and households: Perspectives on rural Kenya*. Stockholm: Beijer Institute; Uppsala: Scandinavian Institute of African Studies.

Bates, R. 1987. The agrarian origins of Mau Mau. *Agricultural History* 61: 1–28.

Bernard, F. E. 1985. Planning and environmental risk in Kenyan drylands. *Geographical Review* 75, no. 1: 58–70.

Bernard, F. E., and D. J. Thom. 1981. Population pressure and human carrying capacity in selected locations of Machakos and Kitui Districts. *Journal of Developing Areas* 15: 381–496.

Bernard, F. E., D. J. Campbell, and D. J. Thom. 1989. Carrying capacity of the eastern ecological gradient of Kenya. *National Geographic Research* 5, no. 4: 399–421.

Blaikie, Piers M., and Harold Brookfield. 1987. *Land degradation and society*. London: Methuen.

Borton, J. 1989. Overview of the 1984/85 National Drought Relief Program. In *Coping with drought in Kenya: National and local strategies*, ed. Thomas E. Downing, Kangethe W. Gitu, and Crispin M. Kamau, 24–64. Boulder, CO: Lynne Rienner.

Boserup, Ester. 1965. *The conditions of agricultural growth: The economics of agrarian change under population pressure*. Chicago: Aldine.

Bradley, Phillip N. 1991. *Woodfuel, women and woodlots*. London: Macmillan.

Bradshaw, Y. W. 1990. Perpetuating underdevelopment in Kenya: The link between agriculture, class and state. *African Studies Review* 33, no. 1: 1–28.

Buck, L. 1981. *Proceedings of the Kenya National Seminar on Agroforestry*. Nairobi: International Council for Research in Agroforestry (ICRAF).

Campbell, D. J. 1990. Community-based strategies for coping with food scarcity: A role in African early-warning systems. *GeoJournal* 20, no. 3: 231–242.

CBS (Central Bureau of Statistics). 1983. *Third rural child nutrition survey 1982*. Nairobi: CBS, Government of Kenya.

Champion, A. M. 1933. Soil erosion in Africa. *Geographical Journal* 82, no. 2: 130–138.

Collinson, Michael P. 1979. *Research planning study, Data presentation: Parts of lower, drier areas of Northern Division, Machakos*. Nairobi: CIMMYT/Medical Research Center.

Darkoh, M. B. K. 1989. Desertification in Africa. *Journal of Eastern African Research and Development* 19: 1–50.

Darnhofer, Till. 1985. *Meteorological elements and their observation*. Working Paper no. 14. Nairobi: International Council for Research in Agroforestry (ICRAF).

Deacon, P. J., and M. B. K. Darkoh. 1987. The policies and practices behind the degradation of Kenya's land resources: Preliminary review. *Journal of Eastern African Research and Development* 17: 34–51.

Deloitte, Haskins, and Sells Management Consultants. 1985. *Final report on the USAID/GOK food relief monitoring and evaluation*. Nairobi: USAID/Kenya.

DeWees, P. A. 1989. The woodfuel crisis reconsidered: Observations on the dynamics of abundance and scarcity. *World Development* 17, no. 8: 1159–1172.

DeWilde, J. C. 1967. *Experiences with agricultural development in tropical Africa. Vol. 2, The case studies*. Baltimore, MD: Johns Hopkins University Press.

Diang'a, Alex. 1991. *Report on sand-scooping in Machakos District*. Nairobi: African Centre for Technology Studies (ACTS).

Downing, Jeanne, Leonard Berry, Lesley Downing, Thomas Downing, and Richard Ford. 1987. *Drought and famine in Africa, 1981–1986: The U.S. response*. 2 vols. Worcester, MA: Cooperative Agreement on Settlement and Resource Systems Analysis (SARSA), Clark University.

Downing, Thomas E. 1988. Climatic variability, food security and smallholder agriculturalists in six districts of Eastern and Central Kenya. Ph.D. dissertation, Graduate School of Geography, Clark University, Worcester, MA.

———. 1991. Vulnerability to hunger in Africa: A climate change perspective. *Global Environmental Change* 1, no. 5 (December): 365–380.

Downing, Thomas E., Kangethe W. Gitu, Crispin M. Kamau, and John Borton. 1989. Drought in Kenya. In *Coping with drought in Kenya: National and local strategies*, ed. Thomas E. Downing, Kangethe W. Gitu, and Crispin M. Kamau, 3–23. Boulder, CO: Lynne Rienner.

Dregne, H. E. 1990. Erosion and soil productivity in Africa. *Journal of Soil and Water Conservation* 45, no. 4: 431–436.

Dunne, T. 1979. Sediment yield and landuse in tropical catchments. *Journal of Hydrology* 42: 281–300.

Dunne, T., W. E. Dietrich, and M. J. Brunengo. 1978. Recent and past erosion rates in semi-arid Kenya. *Zeitschrift für Geomorphologie* NF. Suppl. Bd. 29: 130–140.

EcoSystems Ltd. 1981. *Survey of agriculture and land use, Machakos District, Kenya*. Nairobi: Ecosystems Ltd.

———. 1986. *Baseline survey of Machakos District: 1985 and land use changes in Machakos District: 1981–1985*. Report no. 4 for MIDP. Nairobi: EcoSystems Ltd.

Fliervoet, E. 1981. *An inventory of trees and shrubs in the Northern Division of Machakos District, Kenya*. Wageningen, the Netherlands: Wageningen Agricultural University; Nairobi: International Council for Research in Agroforestry (ICRAF).

Fowler, Cary, and Pat Mooney. 1990. *Shattering: Food, politics, and the loss of genetic diversity*. Tucson: University of Arizona Press.

Getahun, A. 1989. Agroforestry for development in Kenya. In *Agroforestry development in Kenya: Proceedings of the Second Kenya National Seminar on Agroforestry held in Nairobi, Kenya, 7–16 November 1988*, ed. A. M. Kilewe, K. M. Kealey, and K. K. Kebaara, 85–109. Nairobi: International Council for Research in Agroforestry (ICRAF).

Gielen, Hans. 1982. *Report on an agroforestry survey in three villages of Northern Machakos, Kenya*. Nairobi: International Council for Research in Agroforestry (ICRAF); Wageningen, the Netherlands: Wageningen Agricultural University.

Grandin, Barbara E., Peter N. de Leeuw, and P. Lembuya. 1989. Drought, resource distribution and mobility in two Maasai group ranches, Southeastern Kajiado District. In *Coping with drought in Kenya: National and local strategies*, ed. Thomas E. Downing, Kangathe W. Gitu, and Crispin M. Kamau, 245–263. Boulder, CO: Lynne Rienner.

Gupta, D. 1973. A brief economic history of the Akamba, with particular reference to labour supplies. *Journal of Eastern African Research and Development* 3, no. 1: 65–74.

Hall, D. 1938. Soil erosion: The growth of the desert in Africa and elsewhere. *Nature* 141: 394–397.

Hardinge, A. [*c*.1899] 1971. Report on the British East Africa Protectorate for the year 1897–98. In *British Parliamentary Papers. (Vol. 69: Reports and correspondence on British Protectorates in East and Central Africa, 1890–1899)*, 397–427. Shannon: Irish University Press.

Harroy, Jean-Paul. 1949. *Afrique, terre qui meurt: La dégradation des sols africains sous l'influence de la colonisation*. 2nd edn. Brussels: Marcel Hayez.

Hill, Martin J. D. 1991. *The Harambee movement in Kenya: Self-help, development and education among the Kamba of Kitui District*. London: Athlone.

Hobley, Charles W. [1910] 1971. *Ethnology of A-Kamba and other East African tribes*. Reprint of 1st edn. (Cambridge University). London: Frank Cass.

Hoekstra, Dirk A. 1984. *Agroforestry systems for the semi-arid areas of Machakos District, Kenya*. Working Paper no. 19. Nairobi: International Council for Research in Agroforestry (ICRAF).

Hoekstra, Dirk A., and F. M. Kuguru. 1983. *Agroforestry systems for small-scale farmers: Proceedings of a workshop held in Nairobi in September 1982*. Nairobi: International Council for Research in Agroforestry (ICRAF).

Hunt, Diana. 1984. *The impending crisis in Kenya: The case for land reform*. Aldershot, UK: Gower.

IFPP. 1991. *Indigenous Food Plants Program Newsletter*. Kenya Freedom from Hunger, National Museums of Kenya and Worldview International.

Jacks, Graham V., and Robert O. Whyte. 1939. *Vanishing lands: A world survey of soil erosion*. New York: Doubleday, Doran and Company.

Jaetzold, Ralph, and Helmut Schmidt. 1983. *Farm management handbook of Kenya*. 4 vols. Nairobi: Kenya Ministry of Agriculture.

Jama, M., L. Malaret, D. Rocheleau, and I. Jondiko. 1992. *Farmer/researcher collaborative approach to rural development: Final project report*. Nairobi: IDRC.

Johnston, B. F. 1989. The political economy of agricultural development in Kenya and Tanzania. *Food Research Institute Studies* 21, no. 3: 205–264.

Juma, Calestous. 1989a. *Biological diversity and innovation: Conserving and utilizing genetic resources in Kenya*. Nairobi: African Centre for Technology Studies (ACTS).

———. 1989b. *The gene hunters: Biotechnology and the scramble for seeds*. Princeton, NJ: Princeton University Press.

Kamau, Crispin M. 1989. Case studies of drought impacts and responses in Central and Eastern Kenya. In *Coping with drought in Kenya: National and local strategies*, ed. Thomas E. Downing, Kangethe W. Gitu, and Crispin M. Kamau, 211–230. Boulder, CO: Lynne Rienner.

Kates, Robert W., Robert S. Chen, Thomas E. Downing, Jeanne X. Kasperson, Ellen Messer, and Sara R. Millman. 1988. *The hunger report: 1988*. Providence, RI: Alan Shawn Feinstein World Hunger Program, Brown University.

KENGO. 1985. *Kitui District energy profile and workshop*. Nairobi: Kenya Energy and Environment Organization.

———. 1989a. *Seeds and genetic resources in Kenya*. Nairobi: Kenya Energy and Environment Organization.

———. 1989b. Survey of trees and seeds in Kenya's semi arid lands. Draft manuscript.

Krapf, Johann L. [1860] 1968. *Travels, researches, and missionary labors during an eighteen years' residence in Eastern Africa*. Reprint of 1860 edn. (London: Trübner). London: Frank Cass.

Lagemann, Johannes. 1977. *Traditional African farming systems in eastern Nigeria*. Afrika-Studien v. 98. Munich: Weltforum Verlag.

Lal, R. 1976. *Soil erosion problems on an alfisol in western Nigeria and their control*. IITA Monograph no. 1. Ibadan: International Institute of Tropical Agriculture (IITA).

Lambert, H. E. 1947a. Land tenure among the Akamba (Part I). *African Studies* (Johannesburg) 6, no. 3: 131–147.

———. 1947b. Land tenure among the Akamba (Part II). *African Studies* (Johannesburg) 6, no. 4: 157–175.

Lelo, Francis. 1994. Human dimensions in wildlife management: A case study of Ol Donyo Sabuk National Park, Kenya. Ph.D. dissertation proposal, Graduate School of Geography, Clark University, Worcester, MA.

Lezberg, Sharon. 1988. Political ecology and resource management: An examination of response to soil erosion in Machakos District, Kenya. M.A. thesis, Clark University, Worcester, MA.

Lindblom, Gerhard. [1920] 1969. *The Akamba in British East Africa: An ethnological monograph*. 2nd edn. New York: Negro University Press.

Louis Berger, Inc. 1985. *Planning and design for soil and water conservation in Kitui District*. Nairobi: Ministry of Finance and Planning.

Lusigi, W. 1981. New approaches to wildlife conservation in Kenya. *Ambio* 10, no. 2–3: 87–92.

McCracken, J. 1982. Experts and expertise in colonial Malawi. *African Affairs* 81, no. 322: 110–114.

Malaret, Luis. 1991. Biodiversity, rural landscape pattern and land use change in a semi-arid farming community. Planning grant proposal funded by National Science Foundation, Washington, DC.

Matheson, J. K., and E. W. Bovill, eds. 1950. *East African agriculture: A short survey of the agriculture of Kenya, Uganda, Tanganyika, and Zanzibar, and of its principal products*. New York: Oxford University Press.

Mbithi, Philip, and Carolyn Barnes. 1975. *The spontaneous settlement problem in Kenya*. Nairobi: East African Literature Bureau.

Mbithi, Philip M., and Rasmus Rasmusson. 1977. *Self-reliance in Kenya: The case of Harambee*. Uppsala: Scandinavian Institute of African Studies.

Mbithi, Philip M., and Ben Wisner. 1973. Drought and famine in Kenya: Magnitude and attempted solutions. *Journal of East African Research and Development* 3: 95–143.

Mbogoh, S. G. 1991. Crop production. In *Environmental change and dryland management in Machakos District, Kenya, 1930–1990: Production profile*, ed. Mary Tiffen, 1–44. ODI Working Paper 55. London: Overseas Development Institute.

Migot-Adholla, S. E. 1984. Rural development policy and equality. In *Politics and public policy in Kenya and Tanzania*, ed. Joel D. Barkhan, 199–232. New York: Praeger.

Moore, T. R. 1979a. Land use and erosion in the Machakos Hills. *Annals of the Association of American Geographers* 69, no. 3: 419–431.

———. 1979b. Rainfall erosivity in East Africa. *Geografiska Annaler* 61A, no. 3–4 (Physical Geography): 147–156.

Morgan, W. T. W. 1963. The "White Highlands" of Kenya. *Geographical Journal* 129: 140–155.

Mortimore, Michael. 1991. *Environmental change and dryland management in Machakos District, Kenya, 1930–1990: Environmental profile*. ODI Working Paper 53. London: Overseas Development Institute.

———. 1992. *Environmental change and dryland management in Machakos District, Kenya, 1930–1990: Forestry profile*. ODI Working Paper 63. London: Overseas Development Institute.

Moseley, P. 1983. *The settler economies: Studies in the economic history of Kenya and Southern Rhodesia, 1900–1963*. Cambridge: Cambridge University Press.

Mung'ala, P. M., and K. Openshaw. 1984. Estimation of present and future demand for woodfuel in Machakos District. In *Wood, energy and households: Perspectives on rural Kenya*, ed. Carolyn Barnes, Jean Ensminger, and Phil O'Keefe, 102–123. Stockholm: Beijer Institute.

Munro, J. Forbes. 1975. *Colonial rule and the Kamba: Social change in the Kenya highlands, 1889–1939*. Oxford: Clarendon Press.

Muthiani, Joseph. 1973. *Akamba from within: Egalitarianism in social relations*. New York: Exposition Press.

Mutiso, Gideon-Cyrus M. 1975. *Kenya: Politics, policy and society*. Kampala: East African Literature Bureau.

———. 1977. *Kitui, the ecosystem, integration, and change: An overall approach*. IDS Working Paper no. 303. Nairobi: Institute for Development Studies, University of Nairobi.

Muzaale, P., and D. K. Leonard. 1985. Women's groups in agricultural extension and nutrition in Africa: Kenya's case. *Agricultural Administration* 19, no. 1: 13–25.

Mwaria, Cheryl B. 1985. The changing conditions of social production and reproduction among the Kitui Akamba, 1800–1976. Ph.D. dissertation, Columbia University, New York.

Myers, Norman. 1982. Forest refuges and conservation in Africa with some appraisal of survival prospects for tropical moist forests throughout the biome. In *Biological diversification in the tropics: Proceedings of the fifth annual symposium of the Association for Tropical Biology, held at Macuto Beach, Caracas, Venezuela, February 8–13, 1979*, ed. Ghillean T. Prance, 658–672. New York: Columbia University Press.

Myrick, B. 1975. Colonial initiatives and Kamba reaction in Machakos District: The destocking issue, 1930–1938. In *Three aspects of crisis in colonial Kenya*, ed. Bismark Myrick, David L. Easterbrook, and Jack R. Roelker. Foreign and Comparative Studies, Eastern Africa, 21. 1–26. Syracuse, NY: Maxwell School of Citizenship and Public Affairs, Syracuse University.

Ndegwa, Philip. 1989. Drought and food policy in the African context. In *Coping with drought in Kenya: National and local strategies*, ed. Thomas E. Downing, Kangethe W. Gitu, and Crispin Kamau, 369–378. Boulder, CO: Lynne Rienner.

Neumann, C. G., N. O. Bwibo, E. Carter, S. Weinberg, A. A. Jensen, D. Cattle, D. Ngare, M. Baksh, M. Paolisso, and A. H. Coulson. 1989. Impact of the 1984 drought on food intake, nutritional status, and household response in Embu district. In *Coping with drought in Kenya: National and local strategies*, ed. Thomas E. Downing, Kangethe W. Gitu, and Crispin Kamau, 231–244. Boulder, CO: Lynne Rienner.

Ojany, Francis, and Reuben B. Ogendo. 1973. *Kenya: A study in physical and human geography*. Nairobi: Longman.

O'Keefe, Phil, Paul Raskin, and Steve Bernow, eds. 1984. *Energy and development in Kenya: Opportunities and constraints*. Stockholm: Beijer Institute; Uppsala: Scandinavian Institute of African Studies.

Okoth-Ogendo, H. W. O. 1976. African land tenure reform. In *Agricultural development in Kenya: An economic assessment*, ed. Judith Heyer, J. K. Maitha, and W. M. Senga, 152–186. Nairobi: Oxford University Press.

———. 1981. Land ownership and land distribution in Kenya's large-farm areas. In *Papers on the Kenyan economy: Performance, problems, and policies*, ed. Tony

Killick, 329–338. Nairobi: Heinemann Educational Books.
———. 1991. *Tenants of the crown: Evolution of agrarian law and institutions in Kenya*. ACTS Legal Studies Series no. 2. Nairobi: African Centre for Technology Studies (ACTS).

Oldfield, Margery L., and Janis B. Alcorn, eds. 1991. *Biodiversity: Culture, conservation, and ecodevelopment*. Boulder, CO: Westview Press.

O'Leary, M. 1980. Responses to drought in Kitui District, Kenya. *Disasters* 4: 315–327.

———. 1984. *The Kitui Akamba: Economic and social change in semi-arid Kenya*. Nairobi: Heinemann Educational.

Oliver, S. C. 1965. Individuality, freedom of choice and cultural flexibility of the Kamba. *American Anthropologist* 67: 421–428.

Ominde, Simeon H. 1968. *Land and population movements in Kenya*. London: Heinemann Educational Books.

Ondiege, P. O. 1992. Local coping strategies in Machakos District, Kenya. In *Development from within: Survival in rural Africa*, ed. David R. F. Taylor and Fiona Mackenzie, 125–147. London: Routledge.

———. 1993. *Population and employment levels and trends in Machakos and Kitui Districts*. Nairobi: African Centre for Technology Studies (ACTS), derived from Republic of Kenya 1989 Census, District and National Summaries.

Owako, F. N. 1971. Machakos land and population problems. In *Studies in East African geography and development*, ed. Simeon H. Ominde, 177–192. London: Heinemann Educational Books.

Penwill, D. J. 1951. *Kamba customary law: Notes taken in the Machakos District of Kenya Colony*. London: Macmillan.

Porter, Phil W. 1965. Environmental potentials and economic opportunities: A background for cultural adaptation. *American Anthropologist* 67, no. 2: 409–420.

———. In prep. The Kamba. In *Adaptation in ecological context: Studies of east African societies*. Berkeley: University of California Press.

Poulsen, Gunnar. 1981. *Malawi: The function of trees in small farmer production systems*. Rome: Food and Agriculture Organization of the United Nations.

Raintree, J. B. 1984. A diagnostic approach to agroforestry design. In *Strategies and designs for afforestation, reforestation, and tree planting: Proceedings of an international symposium on the occasion of 100 years of forestry education and research in the Netherlands, Wageningen, 19–23 September 1983*, ed. K. F. Wiersum. Wageningen: PUDOC.

———. 1987. The state of the art of agroforestry diagnosis and design. *Agroforestry Systems* 5: 229–250.

Republic of Kenya. 1979. *Arid and semi-arid lands development in Kenya: The framework for implementation, programme planning, and evaluation*. Nairobi: Prudential Printers Ltd.

———. 1980. *Kitui District development plan, 1979–1983*. Nairobi: Ministry of Economic Planning and Development.

Richards, Paul. 1985. *Indigenous agricultural revolution: Ecology and food production in West Africa*. London: Hutchinson.

Rocheleau, Dianne E. 1984. An ecological analysis of soil and water conservation in hillslope farming systems: Plan Sierra, Dominican Republic. Ph.D. dissertation, University of Florida, Gainesville, FL.

———. 1985. *Criteria for re-appraisal and re-design: Intrahousehold and between-household aspects of FSRE in three Kenyan agroforestry projects.* ICRAF Working Paper no. 37. Nairobi: International Council for Research in Agroforestry (ICRAF).

——. 1992. *Gender, ecology and agroforestry: Science and survival in Kathama.* Ecogen Case Study Series. Worcester, MA: Clark University.

Rocheleau, Dianne E., and Annet van den Hoek. 1984. *The application of ecosystems and landscape analysis in agroforestry diagnosis and design: A case study from Machakos District, Kenya.* Working Paper no. 11. Nairobi: International Council for Research in Agroforestry (ICRAF).

Rocheleau, Dianne E., et al. 1985. *Women's use of off-farm lands: Implications for agroforestry research.* Nairobi: International Council for Research in Agroforestry (ICRAF).

Rocheleau, Dianne E., M. Baumer, and D. Depommier. 1985. *Consultancy report and project proposals for SIDA/Kenya soil conservation programme.* Nairobi: International Council for Research in Agroforestry (ICRAF).

Rocheleau, Dianne E., Kamoji Wachira, Luis Malaret, and Bernard M. Wanjohi. 1989. Local knowledge for agroforestry and native plants. In *Farmer first: Farmer innovation and agricultural research*, ed. Arnold Pacey, Robert Chambers, and Lori A. Thrupp, 14–24. London: Intermediate Technology Publications.

Roe, Emery, and David B. Lewis. 1989. *Report of the Cornell University Workshop on the arid and semi-arid lands of Kenya.* Ithaca, NY: Institute of African Development, Cornell University.

Ruthenberg, Hans. 1980. *Farming systems in the tropics.* 3rd edn. Oxford: Clarendon Press.

Shipton, P. 1988. The Kenyan land tenure reform: Misunderstandings in the public creation of private property. In *Land and society in contemporary Africa*, ed. R. E. Downs and Stephen P. Reyna, 91–135. Hanover, NH: University Press of New England for University of New Hampshire.

Silberfein, Marilyn. 1984. Differential development in Machakos District, Kenya. In *Life before the drought*, ed. Earl Scott, 101–123. Boston, MA: Allen & Unwin.

———. 1989. *Rural change in Machakos, Kenya: A historical geography perspective.* Lanham, MD: University Press of America.

Sindiga, I. 1984. Land: Population problems in Kajiado and Narok, Kenya. *African Studies Review* 27: 23–39.

Spencer, I. 1980. Settler dominance, agricultural production and the Second World War in Kenya. *Journal of African History* 21, no. 4: 497–514.

———. 1983. Pastoralism and colonial policy in Kenya, 1895–1929. In *Imperialism, colonialism, and hunger: East and Central Africa*, ed. Robert I. Rotberg, 113–140. Lexington, MA: Lexington Books.

Stockdale, F. 1937. Soil erosion in the colonial empire. *Empire Journal of Experimental Agriculture* 5, no. 20: 281–297.

Swynnerton, R. J. M. 1955. *A plan to intensify the development of African agriculture in Kenya.* Nairobi: Government Printer.

Tate, H. R. 1904. Notes on the Kikuyu and Kamba tribes of British East Africa. *Journal of the Royal Anthropological Institute* 34: 130–148.

Thomas, B. P. 1988. Household strategies for adaptation and change: Participation in Kenyan rural women's associations. *Africa* 58, no. 4: 401–422.

Thomas, D. B., and R. G. Barber. 1983. The control of soil and water losses in semi-arid areas: some problems and possibilities. *The Kenyan Geographer* 5, no. 1&2: 72–79.

Thomas, D. B., R. G. Barber, and T. R. Moore. 1981. Terracing of cropland in low rainfall areas of Machakos District, Kenya. *Journal of Agricultural Engineering Research* 25: 57–63.

Thomas, D. B., et al. 1982. *Review of soil and water conservation research in the semi-arid areas of Eastern Kenya: Report of a consultancy carried out at the request of the Government of Kenya.* FAO and USAID No. 30.

Tiffen, Mary. 1991a. *Machakos longitudinal study* (Draft). London: Overseas Development Institute.

——— ed. 1991b. *Environmental change and dryland management in Machakos District, Kenya, 1930–1990: Population profile.* ODI Working Paper 54. London: Overseas Development Institute.

——— ed. 1991c. *Environmental change and dryland management in Machakos District, Kenya, 1930–1990: Production profile.* ODI Working Paper 55. London: Overseas Development Institute.

——— ed. 1992a. *Environmental change and dryland management in Machakos District, Kenya, 1930–1990: Institutional profile.* ODI Working Paper, Draft. London: Overseas Development Institute.

———. 1992b. *Environmental change and dryland management in Machakos District, Kenya, 1930–1990: Farming and incomes systems.* ODI Working Paper 59. London: Overseas Development Institute.

Tiffen, Mary, and Michael Mortimore. 1992. Environment, population growth and productivity in Kenya: A case study of Machakos district. *Development Policy Review*, 10: 359–387.

Tignor, R. L. 1971. Kamba political protest: The destocking controversy of 1938. *International Journal of African Historical Studies* 4, no. 2: 237–251.

———. 1976. *The colonial transformation of Kenya: The Kamba, Kikuyu, and Maasai from 1900 to 1939.* Princeton, NJ: Princeton University Press.

Turner, B. L., II, R. Q. Hanham, and A. V. Portararo. 1977. Population pressure and agricultural intensity. *Annals of the Association of American Geographers* 67: 384–396.

Van Buren, E. 1983. *Patterns of woodfuel scarcity and commercialization: The case of Kenya.* London: International Institute for Environment and Development (IIED).

Van Ginneken, J. K., and A. S. Muller. 1984. *Maternal and child health in rural Kenya: An epidemiological study.* London: Croom Helm.

Vonk, Remko B. 1983a. The effect of different mulch treatments on the growth of maize and beans in a mixed cropping system. M.Sc. thesis (Tropical Crop Science), Wageningen Agricultural University, Wageningen, the Netherlands.

———. 1983b. Report on a technology-generation and diagnostic exercise in the Kathama area. M.Sc. thesis, Wageningen Agricultural University, Wageningen, the Netherlands.

Wachira, Kamoji K. 1987. *Women's use of off-farm and boundary lands: Agroforestry potentials: Final report.* Nairobi: International Council for Research in Agroforestry (ICRAF).

Waller, R. D. 1985. Ecology, migration and expansion in East Africa. *African Affairs* 84: 347–370.

Wamalwa, B. N. 1989. Indigenous knowledge and natural resources. In *Gaining ground: Institutional innovations in land-use management in Kenya*, ed. Amos Kiriro and Calestous Juma, 45–65. Nairobi: ACTS (African Centre for Technology Studies) Press.

Wangari, Esther. 1991. Effects of land registration on small-scale farming in Kenya: The case of Mbeere in Embu District. Ph.D. dissertation, New School for Social Research, New York.

Wasserman, Gary. 1976. *Politics of decolonization: Kenya Europeans and the land issue, 1960–1965*. Cambridge: Cambridge University Press.

Weekly Review. 1984. Economy performed well despite drought. 21 December: 46–47.

———. 1991a. Land questions. 24 May: 6–11.

———. 1991b. The MPs and the land. 14 June: 9–10.

———. 1991c. Maku: Too vocal on land grabbing. 21 June: 17.

———. 1991d. Masongaleni deals nullified. 26 July: 16–17.

Wijngaarden, J. van. 1983. Patterns of fuel gathering and use. M.Sc. thesis, Wageningen Agricultural University, Wageningen, the Netherlands.

Wisner, Ben. 1977. Man-made famine in eastern Kenya: The interrelationship of environment and development. In *Landuse and development*, ed. Phil O'Keefe and Ben Wisner. African Environment Special Report 5, 194–215. London: International African Institute.

———. 1985. Fuelscape process: Modelling socio-environmental stress with a matrix approach in Kenya. Paper presented to the International Conference on Management of Rural Resources, International Geographical Union Commission on Changing Rural Systems, The University of Guelph, Canada. 14–20 July 1985.

Wyckoff, J. B. 1989. Drought and food policy in Kenya. In *Coping with drought in Kenya: National and local strategies*, ed. Thomas E. Downing, Kangethe W. Gitu, and Crispin M. Kamau, 355–368. Boulder, CO: Lynne Rienner.

Yeager, Rodger, and Norman N. Miller. 1986. *Wildlife, wild death: Land use and survival in eastern Africa*. Albany, NY: State University of New York Press.

6

The Llano Estacado of the American Southern High Plains

Elizabeth Brooks and Jacque Emel

The Southern High Plains have been called "heaven's tableland," the "dust bowl," the "land of enchantment," and the "land of exploitation." Outsiders argue that the land should be allowed to return to a "buffalo commons" (Popper and Popper 1991). Insiders insist that it is "God's country" – the only place they could call home. Whether these views are consonant or conflicting, one thing is certain: the region is undergoing irreversible decline. In fewer than 50 years, human activities, with extensive institutional support, have succeeded in fully replacing the complex grassland ecosystem with a highly mechanized monocrop agriculture dependent upon non-renewable groundwater. Is the region on the threshold of "criticality" as defined in chapter 1 of this volume? For the original grassland ecology, the transformation has been extensive. For the definition of "criticality" as environmental change that threatens human well-being, future systems, and life-support or production capacity, the current regional economy is approaching such a condition.

In this chapter, we outline the environmental changes that have occurred in the region: the institutional, technological, and market forces that have facilitated and encouraged environmental transformation; the vulnerabilities and resulting social and economic impacts; and the social responses to those impacts. Finally, we address the possible futures of the region in terms of the conceptualizations of environmental "endangerment" and "criticality."

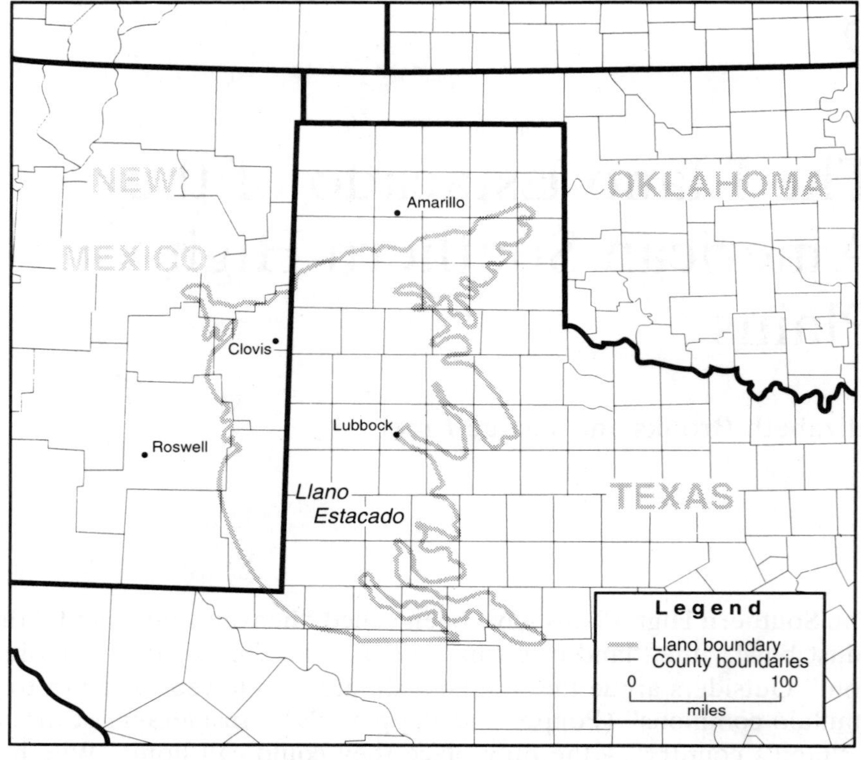

Fig. 6.1 **The Llano Estacado**

The Llano Estacado

The Southern High Plains are a region along the eastern face of the Rocky Mountain system underlain by the High Plains regional (or Ogallala) aquifer. We focus specifically upon a portion of the Southern High Plains known as the *Llano Estacado* or "Staked Plain," an area spanning the Texas–New Mexico border, bounded on the north by the Canadian River in the Panhandle of Texas, on the east and south by the Caprock Escarpment, and on the west by the Pecos River Valley in New Mexico (see fig. 6.1). Physiographically, the Llano Estacado is a region distinct from the neighbouring areas: the Rolling Plains, the Edwards Plateau, and the Central High Plains (E. Johnson 1931). Characterized by a westward rise in elevation from about 610 m to about 1,200 m above sea level, the Llano was formed by alluvial deposits from ancient rivers of glacial runoff. A clay-like stratum (caliche) known as the Caprock forms the southern and eastern boundary to the region, giving way to the more eastern Rolling Plains and the southern Edwards Plateau.

Climatically, the Llano Estacado is marked by low rainfall, a high percentage of sunny days, a relatively long killing-frost-free season, and high winds. Rainfall averages, over the area, from about 560 mm annually along the eastern edge of the Caprock to about 360 mm annually along the eastern edge of the Pecos Valley, the western boundary of the study area. Rainfall amounts typically peak in May and September, with very dry conditions prevailing from October through April, a critical period for enhancing the storage of soil moisture. The 510 mm isohyet (20 inches annually), which has generally been used as the boundary dividing sub-humid and semi-arid conditions (W. Johnson 1894), runs slightly east of the region's centre, denoting an area of generally deficient rainfall. In the period 1930–1960, the 510 mm isohyet moved considerably eastward across the Southern High Plains (Texas Agricultural Experiment Station 1968).

Temperatures are fairly moderate, with the first killing frosts occurring by the first of November, and the last by mid-April at the latest. The soil warms to 10 degrees Celsius at 10 cm by the end of March, with an average depth of frost penetration about 20 cm. Overall, this results in a growing season that ranges from 225 days along the eastern margin to about 185 days along the western edge. Another important factor that affects the length of a growing season is the quantity of sunshine an area receives. In the study area, the average is well over 70 per cent annually (Potts, Lewis, and Dorries 1966; Texas Agricultural Experiment Station 1968). Relative humidity increases through the spring to peak in the midsummer months, with average pan evaporation rates from 10 to 12 mm daily (Texas Agricultural Experiment Station 1968).

Wind is an important climatic factor on the Llano Estacado, chiefly owing to its desiccating effects on young plants and the potential for devastating soil erosion. The Lubbock recording station (roughly the geographical centre of the study area) reports the windiest period in the spring, with calm conditions only 1.8 per cent of the time from March to May, with predominantly southwest, south, and southeast winds blowing at 14 knots and higher 45 per cent of the time. In the summer, the winds shift almost entirely to south winds with speeds above 11 knots nearly 25 per cent of the time (Griffiths 1981). These winds are a major factor in soil erosion, as described below.

The soils of this region tend to be dark brown to reddish-brown neutral sandy loams and clay loams. Also, there are some small areas with slightly clayey loams (Arbingast and Kennamer 1973). The less sandy soils are fine-textured and high in organic material. These rich soils are quite susceptible to wind erosion when the natural vegetative cover is removed (Tharp 1952). The sandier soils in the southern and western margins of the South Plains are prone to "disastrous" wind erosion when disturbed (Tharp 1952).

"Regional social contracts" or distinct social relationships of production, which include particular configurations of social norms, and forms of social organization around labour, transportation, capital availability, and marketing structures, also demarcate this region (FitzSimmons 1990). The specific pattern of human use of the area exists on a continuum with the neighbouring regions, but represents a unique mix of commodity specialization in cotton and, to a much lesser extent, cattle-ranching and oil and gas production. This pattern of commodity specialization has arisen from the social and ecological history of the region, in particular in its relationship to the spatial and temporal trajectories of the international and national economies of cotton, cattle, and other commodities. The following sections develop the history and form of this regional social contract.

Changes in the pre-European ecosystem

Prior to agricultural development in the second half of the nineteenth century by colonizers of European descent, a vegetation–wildlife complex had existed for centuries in the region. Sites excavated around an ancient lake-bed northwest of Lubbock, Texas, indicate hunter/gatherer settlements dating back to AD 1100 (*Lubbock Avalanche-Journal* 1990). Lush grasslands provided food and shelter for a wide variety of animals, and offered seeds and fruits to the paleogatherers. Relict prairie communities found in the foothills of the Colorado Rockies in the 1950s provide some clues to the complexity of those ancient grasslands (Livingston 1952).

This pre-European ecosystem of the Llano does not exist to any appreciable extent anywhere in the area. Studies such as Livingston's (1952) and reports from explorers and later settlers from the early part of this century help to re-create an idea of the plant and wildlife complexes that once covered the region. Assessments of the contemporary ecological definition of the Llano necessarily focus on the replacement ecologies of monocrop agriculture (predominantly cotton) and domestic range animals (mostly cattle and some sheep).

Vegetation

Prior to the 1870s, complex climax grasslands ecosystems existed throughout the area. In 1876, the first large-scale organized ranching operation began the steady, and eventually complete, replacement of the short-grass prairies. The plant complex had been dominated by blue grama (*Bouteloua gracilis*) and hairy grama (*Bouteloua hirsuta*), and secondarily by buffalo grass (*Buchloe dactyloides*). Tharp (1952) reports that buffalo-grazing in the mid-eighteenth century reduced the grama grasses to secondary importance over time; the pre-European/cattle range complex has been re-created as: buffalo grass (1st rank), blue grama (2nd rank), hairy grama (3rd rank), plains, Reverchon's and Wright's three-awn and three-awn grama (*Bouteloua* sp.) (4th rank), and 37 other short grasses and forbs sharing 5th rank (Tharp 1952). Even a plain as uniform as the Southern High Plains had micro-environments, chief among which were the buffalo wallows or "sinkholes," canyon floors, and dune areas. One-metre-tall western wheat grass hay blanketed the buffalo wallows. The occasional canyon floor (cutting back from the escarpment), with less sandy soils and more rolling surfaces, had fairly widespread hair-leaved sand sage (*Artemisia filifolia*) mixed in with the more commonly occurring grama grasses, including side oats (*Avena* sp.) and sweet blue stem (*Andropogon* sp. [Tharp 1952]). The sandiest, more dune-prone areas had less extensive grass cover; under grazing pressure the grass cover was even more stressed. Some of the more drought-resistant, soil-stabilizing plants in these areas include thread leaf sage (*Artemisia* sp.), catclaw (*Mimosa borealis*), and covered spike drop-seed (*Sporobolus* sp.), none of which dominates (Higgins and Barker 1982; Odum 1971; Tharp 1952). Increased pressure on the grass complexes from intensified cattle-grazing and the ploughing under of vast areas resulted in the increase in "weed" species and forbs such as sunflowers (*Helionthus* sp.) and tumbleweed (*Salsola* sp.).

Wildlife

Of the animals that lived on the Llano, most are permanently displaced, some are extinct, and a very few are actually regaining a niche, although not in the numbers of a century ago. The story of the Llano Estacado and the Southern High Plains in general is one of resource extraction and exploitation. This pattern reached its fullest expression early, when the buffalo hunters eliminated the bison from the area, and has recurred numerous times throughout the recent history of the Llano.

The buffalo were the first commodity of the Southern High Plains. Millions of bison were killed for their hides, one of the most massive slaughters ever recorded by historians, travellers, and Native Americans (Gard 1959). As has often been the case with resource use on the Southern High Plains, the bison were thought at first to be in endless supply to meet the demands of the newly developing hide industry in the eastern United States. This perception was understandable; early buffalo hunters saw hundreds of thousands of buffalo on the plains. In the early 1800s, people crossing the Great Plains between the Rocky Mountains and the Missouri River had bison in view nearly the entire distance. Wagon trains were stopped for days, blocked by huge herds. Major Richard Irving Dodge (1876) observed one great herd, some 50 miles deep, that took five days to pass. Wayne Gard (1959), a noted historian of the western United States, suggests that a conservative estimate of the number of bison that roamed North America before Europeans arrived would be 60–75 million head. Few of the animals remained on the Southern High Plains or in the nation by the early 1880s.

In addition to bison, the area was also home to grey wolves, cougars, bobcats, prairie dogs, black-footed ferrets, sharp-tailed grouse, coyotes, and jaguars. All of these species are now extinct or threatened. The major species of large animals now in the area are range cattle. The grey wolf (*Canis lupus*) was exterminated chiefly to protect the cattle. Cowboys killed the wolves in the winter for bounties. Some 34,000 grey wolves were killed between the 1870s and 1920s, and, by 1926, state statistics stopped reporting grey wolves (Doughty and Parmenter 1989). Jaguars (*Felix onca*), though never abundant, were killed off for their pelts; only four were reported by 1905. Prairie dogs (*Cynomys ludovicionus*) were targeted by ranchers and state and federal authorities in a poisoning campaign launched on the strength of a government study reporting that prairie dogs ate too much grass and hurt the cattle industry (Doughty and Parmenter 1989). The Predator and Rodent Control Act of 1931 targeted dozens of other animal species and nearly devastated coyote, rabbit, fox, and multiple bird populations throughout the Plains and western states – a policy still in effect today (Ryden 1989).

Across the United States, grasslands have suffered more destruction than other major ecosystems. For example, an estimated 45 per cent of the grama–buffalo grass and 65 per cent of the bluestem–grama type prairies have been destroyed, compared with 1 per cent of juniper–pinyon forest or 3 per cent of western ponderosa pine forest (Graul 1980). The United States has only 1,618,800 hectares (ha) of protected grassland, but 73,655,400 ha of protected forest land, most of which was severely abused prior to its incorporation into the national grassland system. No pristine grassland ecosystems still exist, and many characteristic species are already gone.

Apart from the wholesale elimination of ecosystems, other human-induced changes in the regional ecosystem have occurred. Grazing, browsing, and barking by cattle and sheep have affected plant growth and spacing, altered species composition, and induced evolution. Grazing has also affected the growth forms of plants. Hedging has occurred in some places; shrubs and young trees have grown bushier through removal of terminal buds, which stimulates more lateral branching. This may have actually encouraged some bird populations because hedging provides better concealment, more nesting sites, and more insects for food (Graul 1980). In response to grazing, some plants may have evolved chemicals that stimulate growth by reaction with the saliva of herbivores (French 1979). Also, plants have evolved other chemicals, toxins, spines, and thorns to ward off grazing (Rosenthal and Janzen 1979). Other plants, particularly those most preferred by livestock and those more susceptible to grazing injury, have decreased or disappeared.

Some species have adapted, at least partially, to the transformations wrought by agriculturalists. In shortgrass prairies, removal of vegetative cover as well as trampling have exposed soils to increased wind and water erosion. Although the habitats for species of birds (such as meadowlarks and lark buntings) that require taller grasses for nesting and young-rearing have been reduced, the increased erosion has created gullies that provide new nesting habitats for rock wrens, rough-winged swallows, Say's phoebes, and barn owls (Ryder 1980). Sandhill cranes have adapted to the replacement ecology and farming practices (particularly grain farming), and have steadily regained their niche after near-extinction in the first quarter of this century from hunting.

Mid-continent flocks of crane winter in the Southern High Plains, particularly around the Muleshoe National Wildlife Refuge. Their adaptations include roosting on the large alkaline lakes of the Llano and feeding on field-grain waste and cottonseed from picked cotton fields. Some farmers have experienced serious crop depredation, however, when the cranes feed on green winter wheat or sprouting corn in the spring and they have tried to institute hunting programmes as a solution. The creation of other wildlife refuge areas has returned to the rattlesnakes, jackrabbits, cottontails, burrowing owls, and prairie dogs that formerly populated the Llano a small part of their former habitat.

In short, within 50 years, both the vegetative and animal ecologies of the Southern High Plains were either extirpated or replaced by agriculture and range animals. "Just varmints," "just bad," and "just nasty" are how Doughty and Parmenter (1989, 29, 33, and 34) describe the justifications behind the slaughter of the animals of the region. The "wild" was carefully separated from the cultivated. In regard to the grasslands complex, Odum (1971, 388) states that no biome type has been abused to a greater degree by humans. The determination to farm, graze, and urbanize the area has resulted in the extinction of multiple animal species, loss of habitat for many others, and nearly complete replacement of the pre-European vegetative cover.

Development of the Southern High Plains: A social and agricultural history

Removal of the Native Americans and their buffalo

The Llano Estacado was the final refuge not only for the great bison herds but also for the Comanches, who relied upon the bison for food and shelter and "might be found scattered over a region that stretched from western Oklahoma and the central part of Texas westward to the vicinity of the Rio Grande. They seldom were seen north of the Arkansas [River], but south to the Mexican border and even beyond if they held sway as the 'Lords of the Southern Plains.' Others, white or red, entered this region at their peril" (Hagan 1976, 12).

Realizing that reservations and buffalo hunters spelled an end to their way of life, the Comanches attacked the buffalo hunters and the would-be settlers who together desired their removal. The federal government placed these Native Americans on a reservation near Fort Sill, Oklahoma. They were given inadequate rations and were expected to farm. Some of the often-hungry nomadic warriors left the reservations to raid colonizing farmers and ranchers. In the fall of 1874, the army campaigned against the remaining Comanches who had refused the reservation and taken refuge in the wild canyons and breaks along the eastern edge of the Llano (Richardson, Wallace, and Anderson 1970). By the following spring, their removal to the reservation was completed, after relentless pursuit by superiorly mounted and armed government troops. As soon as the warriors were removed, buffalo hunters swarmed into the area and began their slaughter. The extinction of the buffalo on the Llano guaranteed the full dependency of the Comanches upon the government. These Native Americans were forced to adopt farming and cattle-raising practices. Many did not survive the transition:

> What actually had been accomplished was to strip the Comanches of virtually all their land and much of the basis of their culture. Some individuals, usually mixed-bloods, had for all practical purposes relinquished their Indian identity. Most, however, had been pauperized by the system and had developed a painful dependence on the Bureau of Indian Affairs. Resentful of the control exercised by the government over even the smallest details of their lives, yet believing that only by continued association with it could they maintain their status as Comanches, they found themselves in the dilemma that still confronts them today. (Hagan 1976, 294)

Removal of the Native Americans and extermination of the bison from the region coincided with the boom in the range cattle industry following the Civil War. Some enterprising thinkers ascertained that what was good for bison could be good for cattle and, by the 1880s, cattle ranches were scattered throughout the region. According to Richardson, Wallace, and Anderson (1970), three factors encouraged the rapid occupation of the ranges in the area: (1) the extension of railroads into West Texas, (2) the invention and sale of barbed wire, which made it possible to fence vast tracts of land for containing cattle, and (3) the discovery of an adequate supply of water. The windmill provided water from the shallow aquifers of portions of the Llano (see also Webb 1931). The range cattle industry expanded rapidly until the mid-1880s. Land was easily acquired – land laws at this time favoured the large landholder – and beef prices were relatively high (Gordon 1961).

The first permanent European settlement in the Southern High Plains, in addition to the ranches' headquarters established below the escarpment on the valley floors of the Canadian and Red Rivers, was a small Quaker community, founded in 1879 by Paris Cox in what is now Crosby County, Texas. Only two or three people survived the first winter, but after a few years of good weather the colony grew to 10 families by 1882. By 1890, approximately 400 people were living in the area. This population increase can be attributed directly to two factors, one environmental and the other institutional. First, several years of better-than-average rainfall during the 1880s led to good crops. Secondly, land laws were instituted that discouraged amassing huge landholdings for ranching and encouraged small family farms. For example, the price of land was legislatively raised from US$0.25 per acre (approximately 0.4 ha) to US$2.00 and US$3.00 per acre. In addition, the statute of 1 April 1887, commonly referred to as the "Four Sections Act," represented a victory for the small homesteader. All sales were restricted to actual settlers and no individual could purchase more than four sections of land. Terms of payment were one-fortieth down and the remainder in 40 annual payments (Gordon 1961).

In 1889, a great influx of homesteaders began coming over the Caprock into the northern and central portion of the Plains. Floyd, Crosby, Hale, and Lubbock counties in Texas were the most heavily populated. By the end of 1890, 1,700 people were living in the Southern High Plains in several dozen communities, a social pattern that would become more prominent over time. The region is still primarily one of small urban communities, the vast majority of which are agriculturally based. Some of the oldest towns and cities in the area are just over 100 years old: Amarillo and Plainview were founded in 1887, Lockney in 1888, and Lubbock in 1891.

In a matter of a few years, more than 1,000 persons applied for and settled upon the land of their choice. Over 90 per cent of those applications resulted in forfeiture due to the drought, accompanied by severe winters, that began in 1885 and lasted nearly a decade. Hundreds of thousands of cattle died as a consequence of the drought or the overgrazing of the ranges. Many large investors were ruined and the herds were reduced by as much as 20 per cent (Gordon 1961). The disaster encouraged the expansion of farming. Supplemental feeds, grown on the ranch (rather than imported), were used to sustain the animals through winter months. Thus began a considerable amount of experimentation with feed crops in the area, once the drought abated. Sorghum and milomaize did very well, as did Johnson grass, millet, oats, and corn; alfalfa and rice-corn, by comparison, were failures (Gordon 1961). Nevertheless, settlers by the hundreds loaded their wagons and headed eastward (V. Johnson 1947). After the drought ended in the mid-1890s, farmers headed back to the region.

The return of "good" weather renewed the settlers' belief that the Southern High Plains would be a lush agricultural area. The ranges had been successfully reduced, through environmental and (more important) institutional measures, and the stage set for agricultural expansion, anchoring a boom in population across the Llano.

The boom years and the "Dust Bowl"

Agriculture exploded on the Southern High Plains with the onset of World War I, and the European demand for food intensified after the war. The high prices and strong demand led many farmers to overexpand their operations and to overuse their land. Not only were good farmlands overtaxed with endless cropping, but, with the refinement of mechanized farm machinery, marginal land susceptible to severe erosion and gullying was also cultivated (GPDAC 1936). By the end of the 1920s, land under cultivation had nearly doubled on the Llano from fewer than 3,237,600 acres (13,100 ha) to more than 6,475,200 acres (26,200 ha) (see table 6.1). The amount of unimproved land (scrubland, woodland, or just unploughed land) steadily decreased from 1900 to 1930 (US Bureau of the Census 1900–1935). As Gibson (1932, 11) remarked at the peak of the agricultural boom in 1932: "Believing firmly in the potentialities of the new land through successive trials resulting occasionally in success but more frequently in failure, man has triumphed ... And the large scale system of agriculture now in vogue on the High Plains is producing and maintaining a thriving civilization with a newness and color all its own."

The 30 years of expansion were in large part due to the wetter-than-average weather, together with the institutional and market-driven forces, but the exuberance of the 1920s was to end abruptly with the start of the new decade.

The "Dust Bowl" era of the 1930s – an environmental and social catastrophe – resulted from the confluence of at least three factors: higher production demand, enormous agricultural capacity, and extremely low annual rainfall from 1929 to 1941. Drought had set in from the mid-Atlantic states to the Mississippi Valley in 1930. In

Table 6.1 **Land-use history**

Year	Land area of counties (acres)	Land in farms (acres)	% total land	Cropland (acres)	Pasture, woodland, non-crop (acres)
1900	20,160,800	8,833,224	43.81	–[a]	–[a]
1910	24,419,846	12,764,016	52.27	–[a]	–[a]
1920	25,656,966	16,544,517	64.48	–[a]	–[a]
1925	25,656,966	14,604,409	56.92	2,747,852	9,403,203
1930	31,564,320	20,249,833	64.15	9,975,748	11,209,085
1935	31,564,320	22,090,187	69.98	9,593,152	14,674,061
1940	31,152,640	24,859,547	79.80	9,066,218	–[a]
1945	31,152,640	28,308,587	90.87	7,774,248	20,725,700
1950	31,149,440	25,289,741	81.19	8,511,086	18,264,392
1954	31,149,440	26,576,735	85.32	8,848,601	18,299,224
1959	31,149,440	26,213,960	84.15	8,988,287	16,778,679
1964	31,149,440	26,363,500	84.64	9,204,792	16,716,138
1969	31,149,440	26,321,878	84.50	9,173,958	16,554,551
1974	31,149,440	25,536,087	81.98	9,143,124	16,392,963
1979	31,093,689	26,072,016	83.85	8,958,196	28,875,762
1982	31,093,689	25,250,873	81.21	8,596,308	26,516,614

Source: US Bureau of the Census (1900–1982).

a. Incomplete data (Texas and New Mexico).

1931, the drought spread west to the Great Plains (see fig. 6.2). By 1936, every state in the country, with the exception of Maine and Vermont, was experiencing drought (Worster 1979). The drought deepened in 1933, and no spring rains arrived in 1934. In the Dust Bowl, people abandoned their farms at alarming rates. Farm tenancy, for example, dropped by 20 per cent in 15 years (Potts, Lewis, and Dorries 1966). Two and a half million people on the High Plains received relief from the American Red Cross in the winter of 1934, the year in which the dust storms demonstrated their ultimate capacity for devastation (Paradis 1969).

The dust storms started, localized and infrequent, in 1932; 1933 brought 179, the worst of which, starting 9 May, blew dust to New York and Georgia (Worster 1979). Winds blowing up to 100 miles per hour caught up 350 million tons of topsoil. After two days, the dust, some of which originated in Wyoming and Montana, settled on Boston and Washington, D.C. Four and five days later, ships nearly 500 km out in the Atlantic Ocean reported dust covering their decks (Worster 1979, 13, 14).

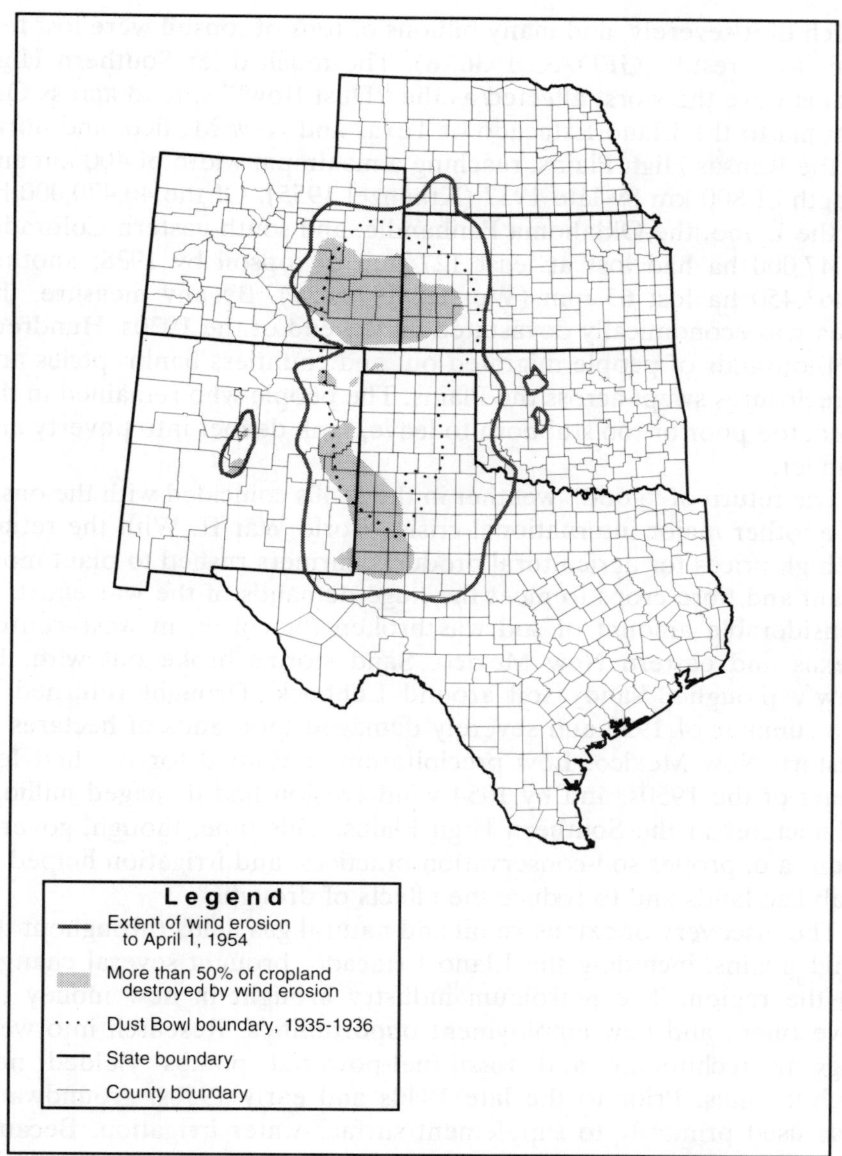

Fig. 6.2 **Dust Bowl boundaries (Source: Hurt, 1981)**

By 1935, approximately 150,000 people had migrated away from the Plains (GPDAC 1936, 8). Disastrous wind erosion had damaged 162 million ha of land (roughly 80 per cent of the High Plains), much of it severely, and many billions of tons of topsoil were lost forever as a result (GPDAC 1936, 8). The much drier Southern High Plains were the worst affected as the "Dust Bowl" spread across Oklahoma to the Llano Estacado of Texas and New Mexico, and north to the Kansas High Plains, reaching a maximum width of 400 km and length of 800 km by late 1937 (Kraenzel 1955). Of the 40,470,000 ha of the Llano, the Oklahoma Panhandle, and south-eastern Colorado, 4,047,000 ha had lost at least 127 mm of topsoil by 1938; another 5,463,450 ha lost 65 mm (Worster 1979, 29). By any measure, the area was economically devastated by the end of the 1930s. Hundreds of thousands of people migrated out and countless bankruptcies and foreclosures swept across the Plains. The people who remained in the area, too poor or too stubborn to leave, sank deeper into poverty and hunger.

The return of "good" weather in the 1940s coincided with the onset of another major international crisis, World War II. With the return of high prices for agricultural products, farmers rushed to plant more grain and fibre crops to meet the huge demands of the war effort. A considerable amount of sod was broken for cotton in west–central Texas and eastern New Mexico. Sand storms broke out with the newly ploughed sandy soil around Lubbock. Drought returned in the summer of 1950 and severely damaged thousands of hectares in eastern New Mexico. Low precipitation continued for the first few years of the 1950s, and by 1954 wind erosion had damaged millions of hectares in the Southern High Plains. This time, though, government aid, proper soil-conservation practices, and irrigation helped to stabilize lands and to reduce the effects of drought.

The discovery of extensive oil and natural gas fields throughout the High Plains, including the Llano Estacado, brought several changes to the region. The petroleum industry brought in new money for investment and new employment opportunities. Research into well-digging technology and fossil-fuel-powered pumps yielded new technologies. Prior to the late 1940s and early 1950s, groundwater was used primarily to supplement surface-water irrigation. Because very little of the subsurface water was artesian, most had to be drawn to the surface with pumps powered by windmills. The gas and oil drillers brought the new technology to drill wells and to pump from greater depths. Thus, farmers continued to "dust out," but not in the numbers of the earlier decades. Irrigation was proving to be the reliable supply of rainfall that nature could not provide. With the introduction of centre pivot irrigation, ever vaster areas could be brought into permanent production. It seemed for farmers on the Southern High Plains, and for all their communities dependent on agriculture, that a reliable and apparently endless supply of water had been tapped.

Wind-driven soil erosion was severe again in 1977 as storms blew top soil from more than 240,000 ha in New Mexico and nearly 900,000 ha in Texas (Hurt 1981). The sandy cotton lands of West Texas continued to blow during the winter. Early in the morning on 16 December, a strong wind rose from the south-west in the vicinity of Lubbock. Heavy dust was blowing at sunrise, and by 10.00 a.m. wind gusts reached 97 km per hour. The storm blew all day. Motorists turned on headlights, dust-laden air filled homes and office buildings, swimming pools turned to muddy water, and, on the Texas Tech University campus, "the soil drifted curb deep" (Hurt 1981, 159). Since then, the US Environmental Protection Agency (EPA) has designated Lubbock a non-attainment area in violation of federal air-pollution standards. Too many particles were found in the city's air on three occasions during a four-year span, causing Lubbock to fail federal Clean Air Act standards. In May of 1991, however, the city convinced EPA that the air-quality problems resulted from natural causes and not from industrial activity (*Lubbock Avalanche-Journal* 1991, 1).

The "naturalness" of the dust storms is contestable. Soil transport experts at Texas Tech University found rather low correlations between the Palmer Drought Index and high wind speeds and dust flux for the period between 1947 and 1990 (Lee and Sturgis 1991). Their analysis suggests that land-use and cropping practices must play a large role in producing wind erosion (see also Argabright 1988). Cotton-growing, in particular, leaves the soil bare during the windiest part of the year in the study area. From February through May, the average wind speed is around 26 km per hour, but wind speeds up to 95 and 130 km per hour are not uncommon. Cotton is planted in late April or early May, leaving the soil exposed to the constant assault of the wind coming across the flatlands from the Rocky Mountains. Because cotton is a low residue crop, the exposure during the spring is exacerbated. Most fields on the Southern Plains are larger than 65 ha, which creates an unsheltered field width of at least 650 m. In addition, the young cotton plants get damaged by the wind as well as the hail that can accompany the local storms throughout the spring and summer. Where the soil is irrigated, contour ploughed, or terraced, less erosion generally occurs. Conservation tillage works only with irrigation in this area. Clod-forming tillage is one of the few practices in which every farmer can engage effectively.

In general, soil erosion appears to be under better control than in the past. Good managers can hold it to about 11 tons per hectare per year, and conservation programmes, irrigation, tillage practices, and other factors have reduced the amount of blowing soil. Some of the land – ploughed flat, and with no cover – that went into the recently established Conservation Reserve Program had potential erosion rates of 140–150 tons per hectare per year. Although 2–3 m drifts of soil at the end of fields do occur in the south-western part of the study area, they are uncommon. Residents of Lubbock say there are fewer days when the red traffic lights are invisible than 25 years ago (G. Underwood, personal communication, May 1991). The only irreversible soil erosion is in the south-western part of the study area, in small areas in Gaines and Cochran counties, Texas (H. Dregne, personal communication, May 1991). There the land has become hummocky. In the north-western portion of the study area, several sand-hills have blown out as a result of overgrazing. These blow-outs may be reversible with irrigation and time, but the economic level of the farming operations in those locations does not encourage that likelihood.

Experts disagree on the productivity losses associated with wind erosion (cf. Dregne 1988 and Sears 1941), but both on- and off-site costs associated with blowing sand increase production costs for farmers, require the cleaning of roads and buildings – similar to snow removal – and produce mental and health stresses for both rural and urban dwellers (Davis and Condra 1988; Huszar 1988).

Human driving forces: Commodity specialization in cotton

The contemporary landscape of the Llano Estacado is one of cotton, grazing cattle, and grain. Cotton dominates the agricultural scene, both economically and in land area. As early as 1932, a number of counties had devoted to cotton more than 50 per cent of the total cultivated land; in the cotton belt, the area planted ranged from 50 to 70 per cent (Gibson 1932, 253). By 1958, approximately 17 per cent of the cotton grown in the United States was produced in the area (Gordon 1961). This had increased to 30 per cent by 1980 (Bednarz and Ethridge 1990, 390). Most of the crop (60–70 per cent) is exported for use in making low-count yarns, thus making its production important not only to the region but to the US economy as well.

Economics drove the transition from ranching to cotton during the early decades of the twentieth century. A bale produced on 0.4 or 0.8 ha could bring US$50, the price of four or five yearlings, which might require 8–16 ha for grazing (Gordon 1961). Cotton also brought cash, a welcome addition to the largely barter economy of the early twentieth century. It was unclear to many growers in those days whether cotton would be as drought-resistant as the grain sorghum that was grown for feed. According to Gordon (1961), the Texas Agricultural Experiment Station at Lubbock was largely responsible for conducting studies that proved the comparable status of cotton *vis-à-vis* the time-tested sorghums. An abundant supply of pre-planting soil moisture was necessary to produce either a good cotton or grain sorghum crop; in-season rainfall was less important. For cotton, this meant leaving the soil bare from harvest to planting – a condition that exacerbated soil erosion. In both these respects, the climate is unforgiving – October through April are the driest months, and wind speeds are highest in the spring, prior to planting. The Experiment Station also conducted experiments in the improvement of cotton culture that solved the problems peculiar to the region and allowed for the rapid development of the cotton industry (Gordon 1961).

Don L. Jones, noted agronomist and superintendent of the Experiment Station at Lubbock from 1917 to 1957, suggested five factors to explain the success of cotton in the study area: good soil; introduction of the row-crop tractor; development of a cotton plant that could do well with a relatively short growing season, scant rainfall, and high winds; the presence of groundwater for irrigation; and the self-reliance and adaptability of the people who settled the area (Jones 1959, 34). Other factors that must be added to the list are the availability of credit to finance irrigation, land, and machinery; yearly inputs; and the government's special commodity-farm programmes. Without these last two, it would have been impossible to maintain cotton production in the Southern High Plains.

Prior to its introduction to the study region and the far western United States, cotton traditionally was grown under conditions of higher humidity, longer growing season, and lower altitude than those on the Llano. The plant had to be bred to withstand drought and still make reasonable yields. Other important considerations were the percentage of lint (the fibre around the seed of unginned cotton), length of lint, length of lint vs. yield, quality vs. price, and storm resistance (Gordon 1961, 114). With the exception of yield, length of lint was perhaps the most important factor, because, below a minimum length, the cotton was not marketable. Length of staple (degree of quality of fibre) is highly weather dependent; if the rainfall is insufficient during boll (the pod of the plant) development in September, the length will be inferior. Nearly all of the cotton varieties grown in the area, however, produce adequate length.

Breeding for storm resistance was one of the most difficult problems. The high winds of the Plains created conditions not experienced in more traditional cotton areas. Low humidity, high altitude, and wind tended to cause the burrs to shrivel and let the fibre hang out onto the ground. Although the cotton could be salvaged, its dirtiness lowered the quality. If a rainstorm beat the lint into the ground, it would be totally lost. What was needed was a plant that would hold on to the fibre in the face of windstorms, but would yield the fibre to the mechanical fingers of the harvesting machines. Gordon (1961) wrote that this problem consumed the energies of the State Department of Agriculture's Lubbock Experiment Station for over two decades.

By 1934, a cotton-production culture unique to the area had evolved through the ingenuity and experimentation of farmers, ginners (owners of de-seeding operations), and scientists. Farms were much larger than those of the older cotton belt (in Texas, Louisiana, Mississippi, and other areas of the South) and the large, level fields required much less labour in production. A US Department of Agriculture study conducted between 1924 and 1927 found that it took about 96 hours of labour to produce 1 ha of cotton in Lubbock, compared with 380 hours in North Carolina (Browne 1937). The net production costs were comparably lower as well. A Lubbock Chamber of Commerce survey of the area's cotton industry in 1924 revealed that 60 per cent of the improved land was in cotton and that a total of 121 gins were operating. Land was still available and the opinion was that a farmer could pay for his farm with one cotton crop (*Lubbock Morning Avalanche*, 21 September 1924, p. 1, as cited in Gordon 1961).

This extreme optimism was not without its alarmists, and in the end they were proved right. The economy and the weather coincidentally went "bad." High production had suppressed prices at a time when demand had declined following World War I. In 1926, the price of cotton dropped drastically. An adverse season resulted in a crop loss in excess of 60 per cent in some communities (Gordon 1961, 151). Thus, the cotton farmer joined the appeal for relief assistance from the federal government. These years brought to an end the initial phase of cotton culture development on the Southern High Plains – a phase in which the individual was pitted against the uncertainties of climate and competitive market (Gordon 1961, 151).

Passage of the Agricultural Adjustment Act (AAA) in 1933 began the long-term direct intervention of the federal government in the cotton-growing industry. The AAA authorized the federal government to enter into agreements with farmers to control production by reducing areas devoted to basic crops, to store crops on the farm and make payment advances on them, to enter into marketing agreements with producers and handlers in order to stabilize product prices, and to levy processing taxes as a means of financing the crop-reduction programme. A large number of growers voluntarily curtailed their planting. The drought of 1934 reduced output even further. When the dryness continued into the early part of 1935, it was clear that it was not just another "dry spell."

Many regarded irrigation as the solution to these recurrent droughts, but capital was exceedingly scarce for farmers who had barely survived the depression and the weather. Irrigation was not a new concept to the Southern High Plains; wells coupled with windmills had served the cattle ranchers since the 1880s. By 1900 the existence of subsurface water in the area was widely known and publicized by the US Geological Survey. The search for water was largely a search for the economically feasible technology to bring the water to the surface in quantities sufficient for irrigation purposes (Green 1973). The first significant irrigation wells, installed in 1910 and 1911 in the vicinities of Hereford and Plainview (in Texas), were powered by vertical centrifugal pumps powered by gasoline engines and oil engines (Green 1973). Nevertheless, the real boom in irrigation did not occur until the 1930s and 1940s. The 1935 Census of Agriculture reports 2,916 irrigated farms in the Llano (see table 6.2). These were largely within the areas of shallow water. In New Mexico, truck farmers were irrigating. In Texas, cotton was the most important irrigated crop because high profits could be realized in spite of low prices.

None of this would have been possible without the extensive credit that was made available for the installation of the pumps. Local bankers, pump companies, and other concerns aided by federal government loan agencies organized to install and finance irrigation plants, forging another government/capital link in the growing cotton industry.

During and after World War II, an increase in domestic and foreign

Table 6.2 **Farm size and irrigation profile**

	Study area		Irrigated land in study area			
Year	Number of farms	Average size (acres)	Number of farms	Acreage	% of farms	% cropland
1900	2,132	4,603 (N) 782.4 (T)	269	21,977	–[a]	–[a]
1910	12,345		1,336	103,205[a]	–[b]	–[a]
1920	12,357	817.9[a]	–[a]	–[a]	–[a]	–[a]
1925	19,510	1,144.1	–[a]	–[a]	–[a]	–[a]
1930	33,802	1,157.4	–[a]	–[a]	–[a]	–[a]
1935	35,880	1,119.3	2,916	116,872	8.13	1.22
1940	30,558	1,502.8	–[a]	–[a]	–[a]	–[a]
1945	29,526	1,665.6	–[a]	–[a]	–[a]	–[a]
1950	28,066	1,586.0	10,940	1,839,935	38.98	21.62
1954	26,290	1,745.7	14,536	3,096,291	55.29	34.99
1959	22,797	2,002.1	15,855	3,938,856	69.55	43.82
1964	20,018	2,207.5	14,648	4,099,247	72.27	44.53
1969	21,080	2,108.16	–[a]	–[a]	–[a]	–[a]
1974	16,843	2,471.08	10,721	3,956,035	63.65	43.26
1979	17,026	2,507.45	9,793	3,973,184	57.50	44.35
1984	15,741	2,422.86	8,134	3,090,880	51.67	35.96

Source: US Bureau of the Census (1900–1984).

a. Incomplete data.
b. No data.
N = New Mexico
T = Texas

demand for most commodities, including cotton, encouraged an increase in irrigation and cotton production. The new pumping technology made the deep-water reserves of the Ogallala accessible, opening what appeared at the time to be an endless source. With ample groundwater and a plentiful supply of natural gas, the number of irrigation wells increased at the rate of approximately 2,000 per year for the Southern Plains area (Gordon 1961, 169). But during the years immediately prior to World War II, irrigation expansion had to compete with other technological innovations for capital. The row-crop tractor, first produced by the McCormick Company in 1925, was ideally suited to the light, rock-free soil and flat terrain of the plains (Jones 1959). Efficient utilization of the new tractors required the lister-planter and cultivating equipment. Because the introduction of the tractor coincided with the depression, conversion to tractors did not occur until the latter part of the 1930s. One study, cited in Gordon (1961), showed that 44 per cent of all tractors engaged in cotton production were located in the state of Texas, with the highest concentration found in the Plains area. Mule teams in the fields were rare by 1945.

Another important technological change in cotton culture was the invention of mechanical harvesters. Mechanical harvesters were popular even before the labour shortage created by World War II. By 1951, approximately 21,000 were in operation, a sufficient number to harvest all the cotton grown (Jones 1954). In addition, improvements in gin machinery made machine-harvested cotton more practical. Mechanical stripping created problems of trash in the seed cotton as burrs, leaves, stem, and other material were gathered by the machine. Storage of cotton on the field prior to ginning exacerbated the problem. A local person, Ennis E. Moss of Lubbock, invented the lint cleaner in 1950 and began (in 1958) manufacturing machines to clean the lint after ginning.

The Korean War again created an escalated demand for American cotton, and existing surpluses were quickly exhausted. High market prices encouraged planting and irrigation expansion, so, by 1953, there were again surpluses and the Secretary of Agriculture announced marketing quotas for the 1954 crop. Marketing quotas have been in effect ever since. Planting allotments accompanied the marketing quotas and were particularly severe where the most recent development had occurred. The response was to increase fertilizer and other inputs, thus increasing yields on the allowed area. As a result, total yields were barely decreased (see table 6.3). Parity prices virtually guaranteed commercial farmers on the Llano favourable commodity prices for their crops and a substantial profit. Thus, a most productive and profitable agricultural industry developed. Lubbock became a major cotton market and a centre for the processing of cotton and cotton seed (Hill 1986). Cattle-feeding and meat-packing were booming industries, as were agricultural implement and equipment suppliers and manufacturers. The manufacture and installation of irrigation equipment also became big business in the area. The 1950s and 1960s, in short, were the heyday for agricultural producers.

The 1965 Food and Agriculture Act, which lowered levels of price support to world market levels, combined with increasing costs of production to begin a turnaround in the agricultural economy of the region. Cotton provisions of the 1973 Agriculture and Consumer Protection Act had little or no effect on the level and stability of farm

Table 6.3 **History of cotton production**

	Study area		
Year	Number of farms	Acreage	Bales
1925	12,976	907,697	325,362
1932	20,006	1,564,922	–
1935	16,152	777,264	181,311
1940	16,904	1,112,154	413,577
1945	12,024	1,057,395	584,426
1950	15,970	1,889,614	1,694,926
1955	16,521	2,193,384	1,483,058
1959	16,136	2,023,588	1,831,150
1964	14,306	1,998,591	1,875,863
1974	9,328	2,009,974	1,195,779
1978	9,225	3,416,940	1,910,728
1982	6,381	2,169,293	1,214,099

Source: US Bureau of the Census (1925–1982).

prices, consumer prices and supplies, or world markets. Cotton disaster payments were about the only provision of the Act that added to net farm income in 1974 and 1975. At the same time, farming costs and irrigation costs in particular were increasing. As groundwater levels fell, more energy was required to lift water to the surface, and specific yields declined. Energy costs increased by an order of magnitude between the late 1960s and the early 1980s. In several cases, irrigation costs constituted more than half of the variable costs of crop production on the South Plains of Texas. According to Hill (1986), the agricultural economy of the area continued to be sustained by the general inflation experienced in the United States from 1973 to 1981. Despite the temporarily inflated prices, inevitably the boom years were over – the limits of the water supply were slowly realized, credit was increasingly costly, government programmes were less supportive – and the slow erosion of prosperity on the Southern High Plains had begun.

The vulnerability of the cotton economy of the Llano Estacado

The economic risks in cotton production

During the late 1980s, the margin of profit decreased in cotton and only the good managers and operators have survived (Underwood, personal communication, May 1991). Many factors influence the returns on cotton production: selection of cotton seed varieties, planting dates, rainfall and availability of irrigation, accumulated heat units, fertilization and management systems, soil type, insects, weeds, hail and wind damage, first freeze date, cotton lint prices, machinery efficiency, processing costs, and agricultural support programmes (Segarra, Keeling, and Abernathy 1990). The climate is just barely suitable for cotton. The growing season is from 185 to 225 days long, which is considered comparatively short as growing seasons in some cotton areas around the world extend to nine months. Rainfall averages about 460 mm per year, also comparatively low (cotton is a monsoon crop in India), but, fortunately, approximately 75 per cent falls during the growing season from early May to mid-October. Nevertheless, rainfall is highly erratic temporally and spatially (the latter referring to the intensely local nature of storms). Irrigation relieves some of the risk of rainfall deficit, but it is expensive and the groundwater resource is non-renewable and depleting. In general, in years when precipitation is ample and timely, most producers do fairly well. When several years of bad weather occur, growers go under and lose their farms.

In addition to the weather and insects, growers are at the mercy of the international cotton market. Cotton has been traded internationally for over a century. In 1850, nearly 90 per cent of US cotton was exported, with earnings offsetting the costs of about two-thirds of all goods imported into the United States (Sanford 1990). In 1988, almost 40 per cent of US cotton was exported, with earnings offsetting the costs of less than 0.5 per cent of all goods imported into the United States. And yet, while the United States amassed a US$150 billion trade deficit, the US cotton trade generated a surplus of nearly US$2 billion. The profits of growers, once they have brought the cotton to market, depend upon the dollar exchange rate, cotton production in other countries, the import and export policies of other countries, existing surpluses or stocks worldwide, and the demand for cotton. When synthetic fibres are in fashion, demand for cotton declines, and farmers lose their market to big chemical fibre companies (e.g. Eastman Kodak and Fiber Industries). These are huge, well-financed, sophisticated, public and private corporations that develop, market, and technically support the products they produce. Demand is also age and income related, and is thus governed by changing demographics. Figure 6.3 illustrates the fluctuation of world cotton supply and demand during a recent 10-year period.

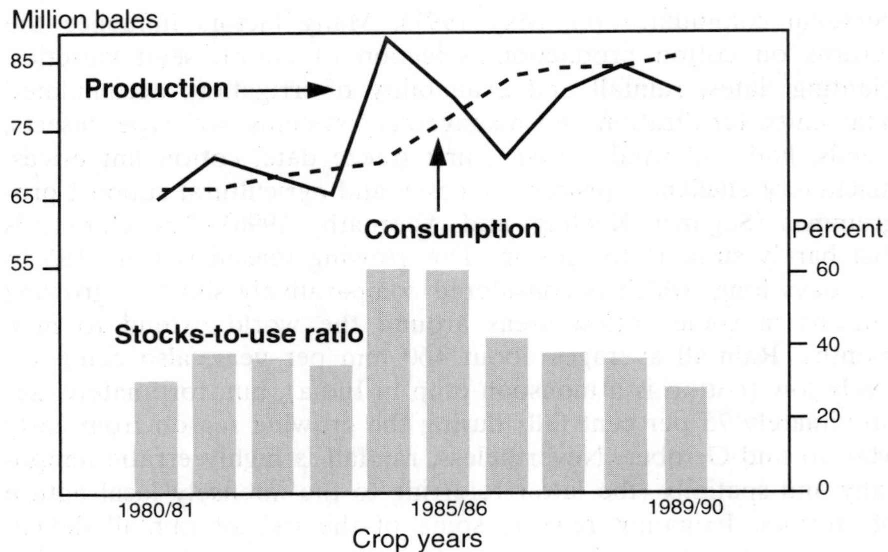

Fig. 6.3 **World cotton supply and demand (Source: Brown, 1990, 344)**

The United States produces over one-fourth of the world cotton crop. US cotton exports to Asia and Far Eastern countries have increased substantially during the past 10–15 years, whereas sales to Europe have declined (during the early 1960s Europe imported one-half of all US cotton exports). Most of the Llano cotton is grown for export. The international market trades in inferior-grade cotton more so than the domestic market. The US textile industry uses highly mechanized mills, which require superior-quality cotton, whereas most foreign mills, because they are more labour intensive, are able to use lower-quality fibre.

The industry has experienced several major market swings in the past decade, and the bottom fell out of the local agricultural economy in the early to mid-1980s. Sluggish regional and world economic growth, the heavy debt burden of many countries, the high value of the dollar, and the success of agricultural programmes elsewhere reduced domestic and export demand. Yields hit record levels and surpluses quickly accumulated despite planting-reduction programmes. Increased stocks depressed commodity prices and lowered farm income. Locally, irrigation costs continued to escalate and interest rates were phenomenally high. Costs of production in the south-west region (including the study area, Arizona, California, and the rest of

Texas) cotton industry rose from US$200 per planted hectare in 1974 to US$603 in 1985 (Bednarz and Ethridge 1990, 375). For the United States in general, production costs increased from US$164 to US$400 for the same period. On the Texas High Plains, variable costs of production per kilogram in 1985 were 12 per cent above the national average, and total costs of production per kilogram of cotton were 24 per cent above the national average (Bednarz and Ethridge 1990, 391). In other words, the study area went from being a relatively low-cost production area in the 1970s to a relatively high-cost area by 1985.

Increasing costs of production are a result of decreases in yields, not simply the increases in input costs. Cotton yields in the area declined at a rate of about 11 kg per hectare per year between 1965 and 1985, although increases were recorded in 1987 and 1988. Yield declines appear to be due to long-range soil fertility and management problems as well as increased input costs (and thereby lower use of inputs) (Bednarz and Ethridge 1990).

A major factor in maintaining the farming economy of the Llano has been, and still is, the US government's involvement in financial support and planting area controls. Under the Commodity Credit Corporation Charter Act (15 U.S.C. 714), the US Department of Agriculture (USDA) administers various farm price support programmes to stabilize agricultural commodity markets and to control agricultural surpluses. These programmes, administered through the Agricultural Stabilization and Conservation Service, provide for commodity loans and purchases as well as price support and production adjustment payments to farmers. Participation in these programmes is voluntary and available to producers of programme crops – wheat, feed grains (barley, corn, grain sorghum, and oats), rice, and cotton. Only producers who participate are eligible for the income and price supports offered by USDA. Through the early 1970s, producers were guaranteed a good income from these programmes if the market or the weather were to fail them.

Since the 1970s, the United States has moved closer to a deregulated and unrestricted cotton industry, but continues to provide these essential income supports. The 1985 Food Security Act was designed to enhance international competition, reduce stocks, provide safety-net protection of farm income, control budget costs, and protect land resources. Although direct government payments remained substantial from 1985 to 1990, they did decline. The 1990 Farm Bill continues to deregulate the industry, while attempting to maintain the competitiveness of US crops. For example, a quota on imported cotton goes into effect if US cotton is uncompetitive in world markets for 10 consecutive weeks.

Other requirements of the 1990 Act include paid land diversions (planting crops other than cotton), land idling, and various resource conservation programmes to protect highly erodible land (the Conservation Reserve Program or CRP), wetlands, and lands susceptible to water pollution caused by farming. The CRP was inaugurated in the 1985 legislation and continued in the 1990 Act. Nationwide, some 526,000 ha of cotton land were put into the reserve by the 1989/90 crop year (Chen and Anderson 1990). This elimination of land from production not only contributed to an increase in the price of cotton, but also had ecological effects. The Llano has experienced the highest sign-up rates in the country for the CRP, owing, at least in part, to the low margin of profit in agriculture in the area and the high susceptibility of much of the land to wind erosion.

Federal government support has continued to play an important stabilizing role. From 1980 to 1986 the farm value of cotton was insufficient to cover production costs. With government payments, however, cotton producers were able to earn a profit, after paying all costs, including returns to land and unpaid family labour. In fact, solvency of cotton farmers improved slightly during the late 1980s. On the other hand, income and cash flow deteriorated and a sizeable group of cotton farmers are facing negative net incomes (Chen and Anderson 1990).

The effects of changes in production costs (including higher irrigation outlays), greater competition in the global market, and government deregulation are a decline in the number of farms in the study area as well as declining farm income. Table 6.2 shows that the number of irrigated acres and the number of farms have declined since the 1960s. Figures 6.4 and 6.5 indicate the decline in value of crops sold in the study area after the mid-1970s.

Effects on the cities and towns

The declining agricultural base affects people in the cities and towns of the region in diverse ways. As farming families sink into poverty, multiplier effects spread throughout their communities. Substance abuse, crime, teenage pregnancy, and homelessness exist at rates frequently higher than national rates in the greater Lubbock, the largest city in the study area (Alliance for the Nineties 1989). According to

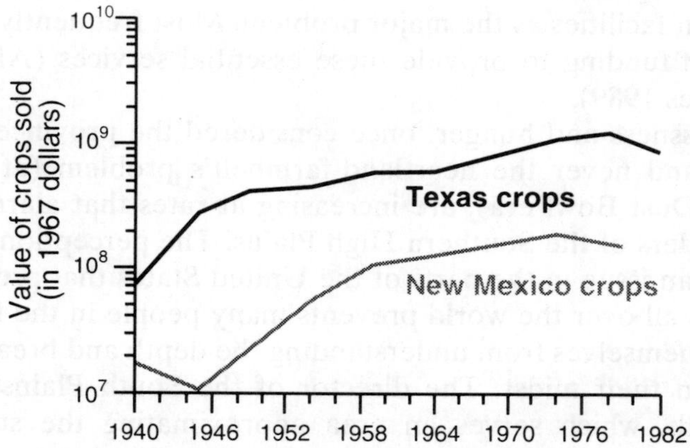

Fig. 6.4 **Dollar value of all crops sold (Source: based on data from US Bureau of the Census, Census of Agriculture)**

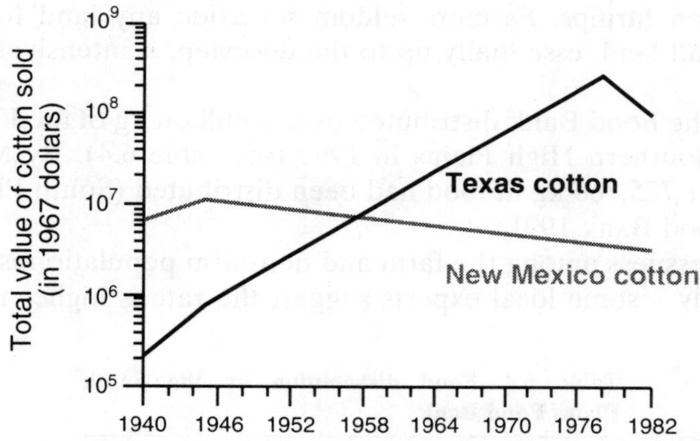

Fig. 6.5 **Dollar value of cotton sold (Source: based on data from US Bureau of the Census, Census of Agriculture)**

an extensive survey of the general public and civic leaders of Lubbock, nearly one-half of the help and support agencies of the greater Lubbock area reported an increase in need for their services (Alliance for the Nineties 1989). Moreover, nearly 55 per cent of those help and support agencies believed that the services they do provide are not meeting the full extent of need in the Lubbock area, clearly a result of inadequate financial resources (Alliance for the Nineties 1989). Survey respondents noted the sharp difference in the need for and the availability of alcohol and substance-abuse treatment and rehabilitation facilities as the major problem. Most frequently cited was the lack of funding to provide these essential services (Alliance for the Nineties 1989).

Homelessness and hunger, once considered the province of urban America and never the heartland-farmbelt's problem (at least not since the Dust Bowl era), are increasing at rates that alarm the service providers of the Southern High Plains. The perception that hunger is not an issue in the parts of the United States that provide food for people all over the world prevents many people in the farm communities themselves from understanding the depth and breadth of the problem in their midst. The director of the South Plains Regional Food Bank, which serves an area approximating the study area, reports ever-increasing numbers of farm families requesting daily meals (C. Lanier, personal communication, May 1991). In one episode, a farm couple came into the Food Bank, reluctant but determined to seek food assistance. Their family had survived as long as it could on turnips. Farmers seldom set aside any land for family gardens; all land, essentially up to the doorstep, is intensively monocropped.

In all, the Food Bank distributed over 3 million kg of food throughout the Southern High Plains in 1990 (see table 6.4). By March of 1991, over 725,760 kg of food had been distributed (South Plains Regional Food Bank 1991).

Homelessness among the farm and non-farm population is also rising rapidly – some local experts suggest the rate is higher than that

Table 6.4 **Food distribution by the South Plains Food Bank**

Year	Food distributed (lb)[a]
1984	1,000,000
1985	3,500,000
1986	5,800,000
1987	6,200,000
1988	6,400,000
1989	6,231,000
1990	7,200,000

Source: South Plains Regional Food Bank (1991).

a. Food Bank director estimates 1 lb of food per meal. Therefore, the figure for 1990, 7.2 million lb, represents 7.2 million meals.

nationally (C. Lanier, personal communication, May 1991). Again, the problem is greatly undercounted, officially. This undercounting is attributed in part to the transient nature of the homeless, and the large number of so-called "couch people," those extended family members, friends, and acquaintances who take up residence in already overcrowded homes. Additionally, many homeless are squatters in abandoned farmhouses, making them very difficult to count. One measure of the magnitude, however, is the number of calls received by the Lubbock Information and Referral service: requests for rent assistance, emergency shelter, and long-term shelter were the second-highest category of calls (D. Neugebauer, personal communication, May 1991).

A major contributor to homelessness, along with divorce, is unemployment and underemployment, whether in the farm or non-farm sectors (Office of Community Development 1990). Median household incomes in most of the Southern High Plains average about 60–70 per cent lower than the national average (see table 6.5). Economic

Table 6.5 **Income statistics**

County[a]	Median household income (US$)	Per capita income (US$)	As % of the US average (US$11,924)
Bailey	12,521	8,225	69.0
Cochran	12,650	8,566	71.8
Crosby	11,719	7,730	64.8
Dickens	8,917	7,119	59.7
Floyd	12,793	7,722	64.8
Garza	13,432	9,114	76.4
Hale	13,518	7,985	67.0
Hockley	15,604	8,281	69.4
King	12,566	8,102	67.9
Lamb	12,513	8,598	72.1
Lubbock	15,704	10,549	88.5
Lynn	11,761	10,172	85.3
Motley	9,656	8,744	75.3
Terry	14,332	8,066	67.6
Yoakum	17,697	8,822	74.0
SPAG region	13,026	8,520	
Texas	16,708		

Source: South Plains Association of Governments (1991).

a. Does not include New Mexico.

Table 6.6 **Principal economic activities as of 1987**

Activity	%
Agriculture-related	22.2
Grain/oil milling	
Fibre processing	
Food processing	
Manufacturing-related	25.9
Casting/foundry	
Light machinery	
Plastics	
Services	31.5
Health-related	
Public utilities	
Distribution/packaging	
Construction	3.7
Building	
Roads	
Mining/refining	11.1

Source: South Plains Association of Governments (1991).

activity in the region is weighted heavily in the traditionally low-paying service and light manufacturing sectors (see table 6.6). In terms of the non-agricultural wage base, retail/wholesale and services account for 53.6 per cent of earned income (Texas Employment Commission 1991). Further, the largest producers of income in the Lubbock area are health services and Texas Tech University. In terms of employment prospects, clearly the jobs increasingly are either in low-paying service positions or in highly skilled professional positions. This does not bode well for an increasingly displaced farming and agriculture-related workforce.

Research also indicates that, within the farming community, suicide is a growing response to the pressures of mounting debt, shrinking markets, and diminishing futures. A 1986 report chronicled the rise of suicide across the farm belt, focusing on the strong link between financial troubles and suicide among male farmers (Robbins 1986). A more detailed study, carried out over 10 years by the National Farm Medicine Center, found a suicide rate for farmers and ranchers 70 per cent higher than among adult white males in the general population (Gunderson 1991). Clearly there are far-reaching impacts of the shrinking agricultural community that are not captured by changes in yield data and market rates. The further impacts of the decline in agriculture also point to the increasing isolation of farm people, a troubling echo of the social concerns addressed by the Great Plains Drought Area Committee's Report of 1936. As the community shrinks, the support services available to a troubled family also shrink, and the growing loneliness and isolation can only exacerbate a difficult, and apparently more frequently overwhelming, situation.

Other data also point to the increasing need for social services in the farm communities. Records kept by an information and referral clearinghouse hotline reveal substantial increases in the number of calls seeking emergency income assistance, food, and housing information. This reflects a general increase in calls for all types of assistance (D. Neugebauer, personal communication, May 1991).

Members of racial and ethnic minorities, and women, have the most to lose with the erosion of the agricultural base. African-Americans, who represent less than 10 per cent of the Southern High Plains population, have traditionally been tenant farmers or field labourers if they are involved in agricultural activity at all. And unemployment rates for the non-farm populations hover at double the rates for Anglo men (Texas Employment Commission 1990). The likelihood that these people, already at the margins of society, will find a means of living in the area is small.

Southern High Plains communities were organized around a single activity, farming. With the diminishing importance of farming, a vacuum has developed in the regional economy. New capital to generate growth and employment is non-existent, since the banking crisis arrived in Texas and the Southwest several years prior to the rest of the nation. And so, as farming capital, both for investment and as profits, shrinks, the entire economy shrinks (see table 6.7). This means, in real terms, erosion of schools and hospitals, roads and public services, as well as greater isolation and increasing poverty. Some people have migrated, but most people cannot afford to leave the Southern High Plains at this time of national recession and local crisis.

Social responses to environmental change and economic vulnerability

Three social responses have resulted from the change-over to cotton-cropping as the predominant replacement ecology. These responses include attempts to (1) remedy the actual environmental impacts of

Table 6.7 **Bankruptcies in the South Plains (all businesses)**

Year	Number[a]
1980	108
1981	135
1982	211
1983	265
1984	328
1985	372
1986	756
1987	848
1988	689
1989	775
Total	4,487

Source: South Plains Association of Governments (1991).
a. Does not include New Mexico.

this dramatically altered landscape; (2) improve the resilience of the regional economy, anchored primarily on cotton production; and (3) better the health and other prospects for the region's dense network of cities and towns. In this final section, we explore these three areas.

Responses to environmental impacts

Soil erosion and groundwater depletion are the two most problematic environmental effects of development for local, regional, and national groups. Both the rain and the US Soil Conservation Service were responsible for reducing the amount of seriously eroded land following the tragedy of the 1930s. Congress appropriated thousands of dollars for lands granted emergency status in the spring of 1935. By the 1940s, proper tillage implements, contour ploughing, terracing, and other soil-management efforts were in wide use.

Viewing the Dust Bowl disaster strictly in terms of environmental damage, however, reveals only part of the story. The consequences are intertwined with various social and ecological institutions and factors. The vulnerability of the Southern High Plains to such complete devastation is a human artefact. Individual farmers using ill-considered farming practices with little thought to the possibility of massive erosion, the pressure from the larger society to produce more, and the support from government institutions in the form of loans and credit all contributed to the creation of the Dust Bowl. Underlying the environmental disaster was the widespread human toll. Whole communities, founded in agriculture but now the places of education, trade, communications, medical care, legal services, culture, and identity, were deeply shaken or destroyed. Farming brought these people to the Llano, but their homes, neighbours, and communities kept them there. Vulnerability developed and rested on a fragile environmental foundation.

The Great Plains Drought Area Committee (GPDAC), formed by President Franklin D. Roosevelt in 1935, created a series of reports recording and assessing the human and environmental toll of the "dirty thirties." The Committee also developed a series of proposals for the restoration and maintenance of some sort of ecological balance for the Plains as a region and for stabilizing the Southern High Plains. The Committee wrote, with remarkable clarity:

> Whether the drought condition is to be brief or protracted, the practical problems of the people and the land of the Great Plains will remain of the same character. Whatever is done now toward stabilizing the Great Plains economy will have its value, regardless of whether or not a continuance of dry years forces drastic action later on. We should adapt our policies to promote the welfare of the present inhabitants of the Plains under the conditions we can reasonably foresee. We are certain that under any conceivable climatic conditions the practices which have destroyed the sod and desiccated the soil are harmful and must, for the good of all concerned, be changed or abandoned. (GPDAC 1936, 9)

To this end, the Committee suggested eight objectives, which together formed a far-reaching comprehensive plan for maintaining environmental integrity and life and livelihoods for the millions who lived in the region. The first two objectives focused on sustainability of the highest possible standard of living and an economy capable of withstanding the "shocks of recurrent periods of drought." The Committee also sought programmes for relief and assistance designed to bring self-reliance and solvency to the people, and the local institutions and governments. Another objective focused on stabilizing land tenure and farmer occupancy to reduce out-migration. Furthermore, the Committee recommended reorganizing the community structure of the Plains, to distribute more efficiently social goods like education, health care, and court systems, with the added benefit of reducing "social isolation." Along with this, they recommended a new tax system to lower the tax burdens and bankruptcy rates of farmers. Finally, and most important to the Committee's way of thinking, they proposed to "[a]rrest the wastage of soil by erosion and make efficient use of the water resources of the region" (GPDAC 1936, 9).

To achieve this final objective – stopping soil erosion in the Dust Bowl – the Great Plains Drought Area Committee drew up several radical land-use reform proposals. Starting from a re-division of land into environmentally defined sub-areas, submarginal lands could be permanently taken out of "commercial production" and replanted as grasslands. Soil-conservation practices, including terracing, strip-cropping, and shelter belts, would be required on arable lands. Recognizing a link between ownership and conservation, the Committee recommended extending public credit to tenant farmers so that they might buy the land they farmed, on condition that the new owners operate their farms "according to rational principles of soil and water conservation" (GPDAC 1936, 15). A form of crop insurance was proposed to help mitigate the variability of rainfall.

The principal objectives of the Drought Area Committee have been echoed many times over the past 55 years, as the Plains endured the subsequent droughts of the mid-1970s and early 1980s. But the foundation of ecological understanding the Committee brought to its work has been missing. Noted ecologists such as Aldo Leopold, Frederic Clements, and Paul B. Sears have been invoked and, in the case of Sears, even appointed to head federal land-reform programmes (Worster 1979). Nevertheless, the far-reaching plans of the various agencies and administrations developed to mitigate and counter the conditions that contributed to the Dust Bowl era must not be over-idealized. Very few programmes were realized in their entirety, and certainly the cooperative spirit considered fundamental to the future of the Plains could not be mandated.

Currently, because of the highly erodible condition of much of the land in the Southern High Plains, over 20 per cent of the agricultural area has been placed under contract within the US Department of Agriculture Conservation Reserve Program (CRP). In some counties the sign-up rates are over 25 per cent. Only nine states in the entire country have more land in the CRP than does the study area. In the 20 county areas around the city of Lubbock, nearly 608,000 ha are out of production either voluntarily, as part of the CRP, or awaiting final approval for the CRP. The popularity of the CRP is due to erosion problems, of course, but also the weather was not conducive to dryland farming for the few years prior to the initial sign-up period. Some farmers went out of business (15–20 near the city of Lubbock alone), their land sold by loan institutions. Many more decided to farm fewer hectares (G. Underwood, personal communication, May 1991).

One could argue that the real reason the Dust Bowl has not re-emerged to the same extent as in the "dirty thirties" has been the incorporation of new technology, such as sprinkler irrigation, into agriculture. Irrigation has long been a response to the semi-arid climate of the study area. Coronado saw Indians irrigating crops in the south-west in 1541 and archaeological evidence suggests that irrigation existed long before that in the Trans-Pecos region. To the east, on the Southern High Plains, irrigation began only when the groundwater could be effectively lifted to the surface of the land. The history of irrigation in the study area is recounted in several texts, the most notable being Donald Green's *Land of the Underground Rain* (1973).

The Southern High Plains aquifer system is part of the High Plains regional aquifer that underlies about 450,660 km^2 of parts of Colorado, Kansas, Nebraska, New Mexico, Oklahoma, South Dakota, Texas, and Wyoming (Weeks 1986). The system consists mainly of near-surface deposits of late Tertiary or Quaternary age (Gutentag and Weeks 1980). The Ogallala Formation of the Tertiary age, the principal geologic unit, consists of heterogeneous sequences of clay, silt, sand, and gravel deposited by braided streams flowing eastward from the Rocky Mountains (Weeks 1986). Since the Ogallala rests primarily upon impervious shales ranging in age from Permian to Cretaceous, only those parts of the Plains in which the Ogallala is thick enough to supply reasonable yields have adequate groundwater for irrigation.

Prior to development in the late 1930s, saturated thicknesses of the aquifer ranged from 0 to 120 m in the study area (Cronin 1969). By 1980, the saturated thickness had been reduced by more than 30 m in some areas. Because of the high potential evapotranspiration and the relatively low precipitation in the area, potential recharge to the aquifer is quite low, areally averaging far fewer than 25 mm per year. This means that the aquifer is essentially non-recharging for all practical purposes and that regional declines will continue as long as irrigation occurs.

The problem of declining water levels in the High Plains regional aquifer began to attract the attention of the public in the early 1970s. The threat of exhausting the water supply in an area of heavily capitalized agriculture during a period of spiralling fuel costs and market expectations generated a congressional mandate to conduct an intensive study of the problem. The six states of the High Plains Ogallala Region and the Economic Development Administration of the United States Department of Commerce formed the High Plains Study Council to carry out the study.

The congressional effort was not the first concern over the depletion of the aquifer. Several researchers (e.g. Kennamer 1959) had remarked on the uncertainty of sustaining irrigated agriculture in the area. A 1957 study projected the end of the water supply by the mid-1980s (Persons 1957). Heightening awareness of the issue was the 1970s boom in wheat and corn exports that fuelled the expansion of irrigation northward into Kansas and Nebraska. Soon, every state in the High Plains was experiencing water-level declines and escalating production costs. Figure 6.6 depicts the net depletion of the Ogallala aquifer from 1963 to 1987.

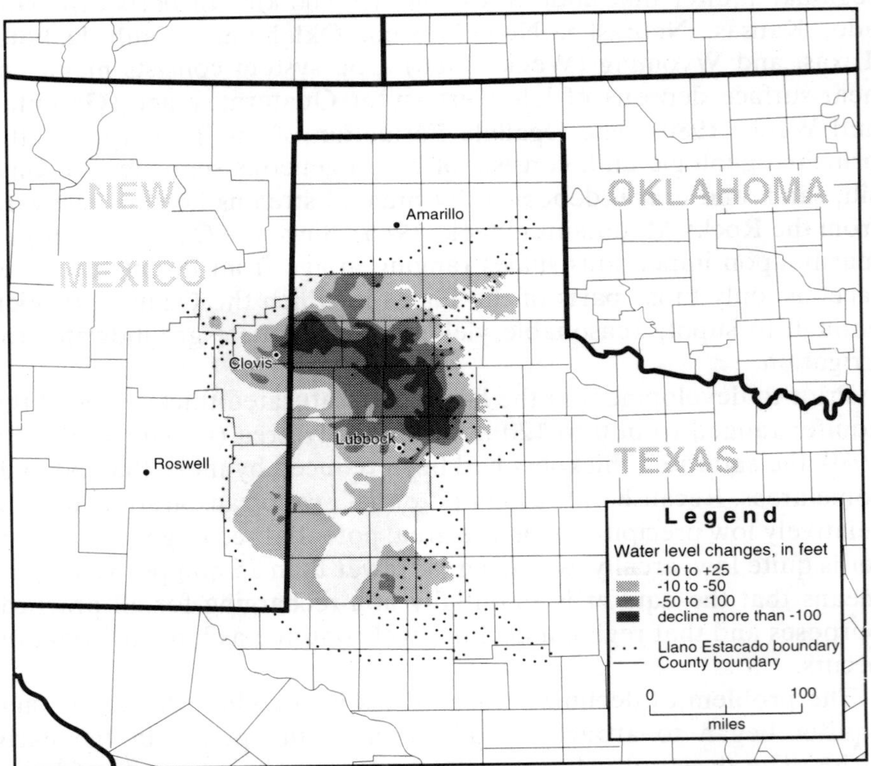

Fig. 6.6 **Net depletion of the Ogallala aquifer, 1963–1987 (Source: Wyatt, 1988, 2)**

Once again, however, the most popular solution to the problem (declining water levels, this time) in the Southern High Plains was institutional intervention. Rather than reduce dependence on irrigation, plans were devised in the Texas legislature to import water from east Texas, the Mississippi River, and even the Columbia River in the north-western United States. Such elaborate schemes of canals and pipelines over thousands of miles represented the type of technological fix the people of the Plains had come to expect for solving environmental problems. Even more recently, the US Army Corps of Engineers (1982) conducted analyses of water-transport schemes that would draw upon the Arkansas and other rivers to the east as part of the High Plains Regional Study. Because the estimated price tags of these transfers were in the billions of dollars, because farmers would increase their water costs by at least one order of magnitude, and because easterners were not inclined to support "mega-water projects" for western farmers, the plans were shelved. The only feasible response to the alarming rates of decline was an extensive water-conservation programme, at least in the Texas portion of the study area.

Groundwater-management institutions covering much of the study area were organized in the early 1950s. Most of the irrigated area in New Mexico was included in "controlled basins" supervised by the State Engineer's Office in Santa Fe. The State Engineer's Office then estimated the amount of water in storage and allocated water rights to ensure that the water would last several decades, long enough to amortize long-term capital loans. Texans, insisting on local control of resources, established a large district managed by a popularly elected board of directors. Over most of the Llano Estacado in Texas, water-users' associations of individual counties coalesced into the High Plains Underground Water Conservation District No. 1 through a series of local elections in the early 1950s. The use of demand management and well-spacing helped to reduce water use and inefficiency. The programmes, and especially the Texas programme, were strikingly successful.

In the early days of irrigation on the Llano Estacado, a well was drilled on the high point of a field and water was transported to the field in unlined, open, earthen ditches. Losses ranged from 10 to 30 per cent per 300 m (or about 1,000 ft) of ditch. It was common practice to irrigate rows slightly less than 1 km long in 12-hour sets. Considerable over-irrigation occurred at the low end of the field – runoff from the fields was usually about 20 per cent of the water pumped.

The installation of approximately 10,000 miles of underground pipeline and more than 3,000 tailwater return systems, plus reductions in the length and time of irrigation sets, resulted in nearly a one-third decrease in pumpage. Furrow dike installation and other land-management practices maximized the effective use of precipitation and helped to reduce further pumpage. Time-controlled surge valves and sprinkler systems reduced water pumpage by 10–40 per cent on many farms (Wyatt 1988).

In 1977, the 46 counties of the Texas High Plains had a total of 3,645 centre pivots. By 1988, 3,384 centre pivot sprinkler systems were operating within the 15-county High Plains Underground Water Conservation District No. 1 service area (Wyatt 1988). These sprinkler systems cost around US$30,000 each, representing over US$100 million dollars committed by farmers toward conserving (and using) the underground water resources of the Ogallala aquifer. Surge irrigation systems cost considerably less but still entail a significant financial investment.

Government commodity and conservation programmes, land and water resource-management practices, technology investments, high fuel costs, global market trends, and water depletion – all of these are responsible for reduced irrigation in the study area in the 1990s compared with the 1970s. Quantifying the effects of any one of these factors is not feasible in this study. Overall, however, the number of farmers and labourers has declined owing to this overdetermined ecological–economic dynamic, as has the wealth produced by the region. Almost 300,000 fewer hectares (about 700,000 acres) were irrigated in 1989 than in 1984 (*Cross Section*, 1991, 2).

Groundwater depletion exacerbates the riskiness of the cotton economy of the Southern High Plains. Yet most farmers believe it is the only crop capable of supporting them (Underwood, personal communication, May 1991). Vegetables have high water requirements, peanuts require contracts (although there are some "wildcat" growers in the area), and the corn grown for the local Frito-Lay plant is "maxed out." Corn also has fairly high water requirements. Some farmers have begun growing grapes in the last decade or so. These prime-quality grapes sell for US$400/ton, and, although production may increase, it is difficult to imagine that grapes will sustain the region to the extent that cotton has. Ultimately, no matter what crop is irrigated, the groundwater will be gone. The Ogallala portion of the High Plains regional aquifer is essentially non-renewable – all use is essentially mining. Careful conservation can extend the water supply that is the foundation of the existing economy of the Southern High Plains, but economic diversification and dry farming are the long-term solutions to sustainability.

Agricultural risk and economic diversity

Is change possible on the Southern High Plains? Can diversification of the agricultural economy lessen dependence on an inherently unstable foundation? Some believe that future livelihoods cannot be made here – they argue for a great parkland reservation, a "buffalo commons," with the removal of what they view as "unviable" communities (Popper and Popper 1991). As an alternative, attempts have been made to integrate less capital-intensive (and less water-intensive) crops into Llano Estacado agriculture, and also to broaden the manufacturing/industrial sector. Neither has been very successful.

The overwhelming dependence of Southern High Plains farmers on cotton as a cash crop has troubling implications for the regional economy. Attempts to diversify agriculture speak to the vulnerability of the economy, to fluctuations in the global and national markets, to yearly weather risks, and to the long-term environmental effects of monoculture.

In the aftermath of what was now unmistakably recurring drought, civic leaders in Lubbock, the largest city in the Southern High Plains, sought advice from outside experts on how to diversify and expand the Southern High Plains economy. In 1958, Cresap McCormick and Paget, a management consulting firm based in Chicago, released its extensive study on the prospects for the Southern High Plains economy, with Lubbock as its hub.

The study noted positive aspects of the Southern High Plains but deflated many projects favoured by the city leaders. For example, despite the many transportation links to east Texas and the West Coast, the consultants pointed out that the major consumer and industrial markets were east of the Mississippi River and that, practically speaking, the hinterland surrounding Lubbock extended chiefly to west Texas and eastern New Mexico, an area it already served. Likewise, on the positive side, a "sizeable, growing, relatively stable and productive supply of labor" existed that was, moreover, "largely non-union" (Cresap, McCormick, and Paget 1958, III-8). Detracting from this asset, though, were the largely unskilled nature of the labour and the relatively high wage rates. "Right to Work" laws notwithstanding, the higher wages were a major factor in the area's inability to attract spinning, knitting, or fabric mills, the most likely value-added manufacturing activity (given the local cotton crop). The mills were and are much less expensive to operate in the south-east United States and overseas.

Overall, the report concluded, the most likely path to success for the Southern High Plains economy was what it already had – irrigated agriculture, with minor transshipment activity aimed at the "Texico" region. All potential prospects raised by community leaders – fabric mills, food product manufacture, oil-seed mills, transportation and distribution centres – were all deemed largely infeasible. The Southern High Plains region was (and remains) simply too remote and too limited in natural resources and attributes to flourish as anything but an agricultural region (Cresap, McCormick, and Paget 1958).

A brief flurry of industrial influx during the prosperous 1960s brought some economic diversity to the area. A Holly Sugar plant located in Hereford, Texas, to mill the local sugar beet crop (Dunn 1986). Yet sugar beets have never really been established as a major crop on the South Plains; throughout the 1980s, sugar beet crops accounted for only a small percentage of the total agricultural production of the South Plains. A Hanes knitting mill announced construction plans (never realized) for a site in Lubbock County. Frito-Lay, Inc., which expanded its operations in the 1960s, remains one of the few major manufacturing employers in the region. The cottonseed-oil mill cooperative is also an important industry, although not a major employer. These efforts, however, are all agriculture based and are dependent on the future of farming on the Llano Estacado.

By and large, the consultants' report seems to have been accurate. Manufacturing currently provides a mere 8 per cent of employment in the Southern High Plains, whereas the service and retail sectors provide about 65 per cent. What this implies, unfortunately, in terms of diversification, is that value-added manufacturing and industrial activity represent a very small segment of the economy, with the further implication that the new capital necessary for investment to generate more growth is non-existent. The importance of value-added manufacturing, whether agriculture based or not, cannot be overstated. As the bedrock of a healthy economy, value-added enterprises offer the sole means of bringing private capital into a regional economy to continue the chain of economic investment and development. Federal investments in the region, other than shrinking farm subsidies, are limited to a few public-works projects, chiefly highway building. Opportunities to establish new non-agriculture-based businesses are thus very limited. Furthermore, as the Small Business Administration representative of the South Plains Association of Governments emphasized, the spectacular collapse of the savings and loan industry in Texas has essentially eliminated loans or credit for the establishment of new enterprises or businesses in the region (T. Pierce, personal communication, May 1991).

Community health and prospects for the future

Despite, or perhaps because of, technological advances, institutional innovations, and agricultural adaptations designed to make replacement of the cotton-culture ecology more permanent, the farming communities of the Southern High Plains are in many ways more at risk than ever (Farney 1989). Efforts to diversify the economic base have not been very successful, and smaller communities have continued to lose population, services, and revenue to the bigger, less agriculture-dependent cities. Nevertheless, these fragile small towns both support and rely on the larger urban centres for information, higher education, and medical care. Two-thirds of all hospital beds in the Southern High Plains, for example, are in Lubbock (South Plains Association of Governments 1991). The larger cities, in turn, need the people of the small towns to use their facilities (a recent hospital survey reported that 42 per cent of all patients at a major Lubbock hospital were not residents of Lubbock) and to create revenue through sales, restaurant, and entertainment taxes. As competition increases for continually decreasing capital, and as chances for new income-generating industries moving to the Southern High Plains diminish, all economic activity consists of "slicing the pie a little thinner" (T. Pierce, personal communication, May 1991).

These late-twentieth-century, fully articulated communities are slowly facing the reality of sustaining a complex way of life in a region that specializes in a single activity. The need to diversify is well understood, and over the past 40 years various interest groups on the Southern High Plains have sponsored feasibility studies on potential income-generating activities. For a variety of reasons, such as remote location, an unskilled labour force, and an uncertain water supply, very few actual value-adding operations have been created. The heavy dependence on agriculture has continued.

The erosion of the agricultural base has rippled through the Southern High Plains economy. One of the most important effects is the loss of jobs in the agricultural and agricultural-support sectors. The latter includes distribution of agricultural chemicals, supply of agricultural equipment, and maintenance, seed production, and processing and milling operations. These last two – processing and milling operations – employ many people and have the highest value-added impact. Another important effect of the diminishing role of agriculture for the communities of the Southern High Plains is the attrition of other economic sectors. As the capital generated by agriculture slowly shrinks, so does the attraction for investment in the region as a whole. Decisions to locate businesses in the Southern High Plains include assessments of the robustness of the economy prior to a move into the region. A steadily increasing pool of available unskilled labour does not offset the growing lack of cash circulating in the local economies. Unable to attract replacement industries, the communities of the area have nowhere to turn in the face of the predicted (and seemingly inevitable) shrinkage of agriculture.

Outside experts predict agricultural viability up to 50 years, basing their assumptions only on how long the water will last, given a free flow of technological innovations (Farney 1989). Various informed sources in the region, considering social viability, credit availability, limits on capital, markets, and water, estimate a 10–15-year horizon for agriculture's prominence (Lanier, personal communication, 1991; Pierce, personal communication, 1991; Steglich 1986). Given nearly a decade of relatively poor rainfall, even the near future appears ominous.

The future of the Southern High Plains

It is difficult, of course, to predict the future trajectory of the Southern High Plains. Clearly, however, the region will accommodate less irrigated land and more dryland farming. It is also unlikely that new land will be brought into cultivation (Riebsame 1990). The question remains as to what will become of the other lands, abandoned by farmers, either through bankruptcy, retirement, or lack of accessible (or affordable) water. Perhaps more land will be converted to wildlife refuges or other reserves.

A positive economic trajectory for the communities of the Llano Estacado depends upon achieving sufficient diversity to reduce the region's dependence on irrigated agriculture. One measure of possible futures is employment forecasts based on studies of economic growth, technological change, and industrial and occupational trends (Texas Employment Commission 1988). Overall, projections of employment prospects for the Lubbock to Amarillo region suggest little growth over the next five years (Texas Employment Commission 1988). Forecasts project a growth rate of 1.9 per cent (or 5,514 jobs) for all employment demand (growth plus replacement) across all job categories, from surgeons to unskilled day labourers. Only 1,915 of those jobs represent actual new jobs, and no single employment category is expected to experience actual growth (Texas Employment Commission 1988). Predictions for the Amarillo Standard Metropolitan Statistical Area (SMSA) are identical, with even fewer jobs in the new-job category. Zero demand is predicted for farmers and farm managers, with a growth prediction of a mere five jobs by 1995 for general farm labourers. And again, the largest sources of employment in the Southern High Plains economy of the near future are professional jobs, especially health related and sales and service. This is not an optimistic prospect for economic growth in the region, which lacks a manufacturing base to replace farming as a generator of wealth.

Efforts to diversify the agricultural economic base of the Southern High Plains are clearly limited. Expansion into other forms of agriculture simply reinforce the difficulty of maintaining farming in this windy, semi-arid former grasslands environment. Attempts to broaden the manufacturing–industrial sector have likewise stalled. Adding a layer of social expectations to this situation increases the challenge for diversification. Cotton has dominated the Southern High Plains for 50 years – most of living memory. And, despite the very high level of risk involved, cotton has promised the reward of a standard of living set in the 1950s and 1960s.

What must be understood is that this way of life on the Southern High Plains has been created and maintained by two outside factors – technological innovations and institutional arrangements, generally in the form of government interventions (both state and federal level), and financial arrangements, chiefly in the form of the extension of credit. In Texas, the state's Department of Agriculture, through its agricultural experiment stations and extension services, has provided invaluable research and support for farmers on the Plains from the turn of the century. Developments in irrigation technology were matched by credit arrangements to provide the capital essential to adopt that technology. Although this sort of cooperation has benefited farming throughout the United States, on the Southern High Plains it is clear that agriculture would not have flourished, or even survived as long as it has, without it.

The finite supply of water underscores reality and the future of the Llano Estacado. Increasing costs to pump water from ever-increasing depths will determine how long the water will "last." The scaling-back of government programmes, props really, throughout the farming sector has hit the Llano Estacado severely. The retreat of technological and institutional resources has returned the people of the Plains to essentially the situation encountered by the original European settlers – that of the individual pitted against the uncertainties of climate and competitive markets. The question becomes: What sort of life is possible with the environment as it now exists and with the resources that can be extracted? Many people believe that agriculture will not last long into the future. What, then, will the people of the Plains do?

Conclusions

Institutional support for maintaining the settlements of the Llano Estacado enjoys a long-standing tradition, dating from the earliest attempts to establish permanent agriculture-based communities. The social history of the Southern High Plains is essentially a history of institutional and technological devices to overcome what was environmentally untenable – rainfall-based agriculture. From the Four Sections Act in 1887, to the Agricultural Assistance Administration in 1933 and the price-support programmes and federal farm subsidies in the 1970s and 1980s, federal and state agencies have buttressed and enabled the process of environmental change. Farm credit programmes, with their beginnings in the farm relief programmes of the 1930s, have been especially critical for maintaining agriculture.

Farmers followed a fairly typical pattern of agriculturalists in the Great Plains. Their first attempts at sod-busting and crop production failed during every drought. Many left the area; some stayed. But, over time, irrigation, transportation, storage, production and marketing technologies, extension services, and credit formed the basis for economic success and market competitiveness. With higher fuel costs, less water, more competitors, smaller market shares, and lower soil fertility, that comparative advantage has slipped. The region is now one of the most technologically advanced agricultural systems in the United States. Many of the farmers have college degrees, and only the best managers have survived the 1980s. Even so, farm credit delinquencies, foreclosures, and bankruptcies are increasing. At the end of 1990, over 40 per cent of all Farmers Home Administration (FmHA) loans for the Southern High Plains were delinquent, and the majority of these were emergency loans (South Plains Association of Governments 1991). Meanwhile there is nowhere else to move, no extra margin for the moment.

The transformation of the environment from a complex mature grassland to a monocropped agricultural/social landscape on the verge of collapse took very little time. In less than a generation, the change has become evident. The transformation took vast amounts of capital, technological development, institutional support, and human endeavour. If the history of the pre-European settlement of the Southern High Plains is a portrait of a stable, evolved, plant–wildlife ecosystem, with and without human occupancy, then the history of post-European settlement is really a history of forced adjustment, transplantation, and extinction.

A major outcome of the Dust Bowl era is the full institutionalization of a way of life on the Llano Estacado. A policy and support infrastructure has propped up a farming-based culture, a regional economy, and a community network in an agriculturally marginal area. The environmental consequences, several of which are quite serious, serve to remind us that, despite all the human creativity and perseverance in building a life on the Southern High Plains, the effective curtailment of the technological inputs due to a dearth of investment capital and the scaling-back or outright removal of institutional interventions have propelled the region rapidly toward greater endangerment and risk of overall regional collapse.

References

Alliance for the Nineties. 1988 and 1989. *Alliance for the Nineties: Lubbock human needs assessment*, 2 vols. Lubbock, Texas: Alliance for the Nineties.

Arbingast, S., and L. Kennamer. 1973. *Atlas of Texas*. Austin: University of Texas Bureau of Business Research.

Argabright, M. S. 1988. History of wind erosion and the Soil Conservation Service. In *Proceedings of the ASAE Wind Erosion Conference, April 11–13, 1988, Lubbock, Texas*, 34–42. Lubbock: Texas Tech University.

Bednarz, M. S., and D. Ethridge. 1990. Sources of rising unit costs of producing cotton in the Texas High Plains. In *Beltwide Cotton Production Research Conferences: January 9–14, 1990, Las Vegas, Nevada: 1990 Proceedings*, ed. James M. Brown, 390–393. Memphis, TN: National Cotton Council of America.

Brown, J. M. ed. 1990. *Beltwide Cotton Production Research Conferences: January 9–14, 1990, Las Vegas, Nevada: 1990 proceedings*. Memphis, TN: National Cotton Council of America.

Browne, W. A. 1937. Agriculture in the *Llano Estacado*. *Economic Geography* 13: 156–174.

Chen, D. T., and C. Anderson. 1990. Cotton market responses to 1985 Food Security Act, dollar devaluation and U.S. weather disturbances. In *Beltwide Cotton Production Research Conferences: January 9–14, 1990, Las Vegas, Nevada: 1990 proceedings*, ed. James M. Brown, 464–469. Memphis, TN: National Cotton Council of America.

Cresap, McCormick, and Paget. 1958. *Industrial survey of Lubbock, Texas*. New York: Cresap, McCormick, and Paget.

Cronin, James G. 1969. *Ground water in the Ogallala formation in the southern high plains of Texas and New Mexico*. Hydrologic Investigations Atlas HA-330. Washington DC: US Geological Survey.

Cross Section. 1991. Texas Water Development Board survey shows less water applied to irrigated acreage. 39, no. 6 (June): 2, 4.

Davis, B., and G. Condra. 1988. The on-site costs of wind erosion on farms in New Mexico. In *Proceedings of the 1988 Wind Erosion Conference, April 11–13, 1988, Lubbock, Texas*, 7–13. Lubbock, TX: Texas Tech University.

Dodge, Richard I. 1876. *The plains of the great West*. New York: G. B. Putnam's Sons.

Doughty, R., and Parmenter, B. 1989. *Endangered species: Disappearing animals and plants in the Lone Star State*. Austin, TX: Texas Monthly Press.

Dregne, Harold E. 1988. Wind erosion: An international perspective. In *Proceedings of the 1988 Wind Erosion Conference, April 11–13, 1988, Lubbock, Texas*, 175–182. Lubbock, TX: Texas Tech University.

Dunn, Robin S. 1986. Agriculture builds a city. In *Lubbock: From town to city*, ed. Lawrence L. Graves, 11–19. The Museum Journal, v. 23. Lubbock, TX: West Texas Museum Association.

Farney, D. 1989. Abiding frontier: On the Great Plains, life becomes a fight for water and survival. *The Wall Street Journal*, 16 August, 1, A5.

FitzSimmons, M. 1990. The social and environment relations of U.S. agricultural regions. In *Technological change and the rural environment*, ed. Philip Lowe, Terry Marsden, and Sarah Whatmore, 8–32. London: David Fulton Publishers.

French, Norman R., ed. 1979. *Perspectives in grassland ecology: Results and applications of the US/IPP Grassland Biome study*. New York: Springer-Verlag.

Gard, Wayne 1959. *The great buffalo hunt: Its history and drama, and its role in the opening of the West*. Lincoln, NE: University of Nebraska Press.

Gibson, J. S. 1932. Agriculture of the southern high plains. *Economic Geography* 8: 245–261.

Gordon, Joseph F. 1961. The history and development of irrigated cotton on the high plains of Texas. Ph.D. thesis, Texas Technological College, Lubbock, Texas.

Graul, W. D. 1990. Grassland management practices and bird communities, Great Plains ecosystem. In *Management of western forests and grasslands for nongame birds: Workshop proceedings, February 11–14, 1980, Salt Lake City, Utah*, comp. Richard M. DeGraaf and Nancy G. Tilghman. USDA Forest Service Technical Bulletin INT-86. Ogden, Utah: Intermountain Forest and Range Experiment Station, US Department of Agriculture, Forest Service.

GPDAC (Great Plains Drought Area Committee). 1936. *Report of the Great Plains Drought Area Committee*. Washington DC: US Government Printing Office.

Green, Donald E. 1973. *Land of the underground rain: Irrigation in the Texas High Plains, 1910–1970*. Austin, TX: University of Texas Press.

Griffiths, John F. 1981. *One hundred years of Texas weather, 1880–1979*. College Station, TX: Dept. of Meteorology, Texas A & M University.

Gunderson, P. 1991. An epidemiologic study of suicide among farmers and its clinical implications. Draft. Marshfield, WI: National Farm Medicine Center.

Gutentag, Edwin D., and John B. Weeks. 1980. *Water table in the High Plains Aquifer in 1978 in parts of Colorado, Kansas, Nebraska, New Mexico, Oklahoma, South Dakota, Texas and Wyoming*. US Geological Survey Hydrologic Investigations Atlas HA-642. Washington DC: US Government Printing Office.

Hagan, William T. 1976. *United States–Comanche relations: The reservation years*. New Haven, CT: Yale University Press.

Higgins, Kenneth F., and Barker, William T. 1982. *Changes in vegetation structure in seeded nesting cover in the prairie pothole region*. Special Scientific Report no. 242: Wildlife. Washington DC: US Department of Interior, Fish and Wildlife Service.

Hill, R. 1986. Economic, environmental and policy factors affecting cotton yields in the Texas High Plains. Master's thesis, Texas Tech University, Lubbock, Texas.

Hurt, R. Douglas. 1981. *The Dust Bowl: An agricultural and social history*. Chicago: Nelson-Hall.

Huszar, P. C. 1988. Economics of off-site damages and control of wind erosion. In *Proceedings of the 1988 Wind Erosion Conference, April 11–13, 1988, Lubbock, Texas*, 47–53. Lubbock, TX: Texas Tech University.

Johnson, Elmer H. 1931. *The natural regions of Texas, 1893–1947*. University of Texas Bulletin no. 1113, 1 April. Austin, TX: University of Texas.

Johnson, Vance. 1947. *Heaven's tableland: The Dust Bowl story*. New York: Farrar, Strauss & Co.

Johnson, Willard D. 1894. *The High Plains and their utilization: 2d Annual report of the Geological Service, pt. 4*. Washington DC: US Government Printing Office.

Jones, D. L. 1954. Harvesting cotton with the mechanical stripper. *The Cotton Gin and Oil Mill Press* 3: 78–80.

———. 1959. Cotton on the Texas High Plains. *The Cotton Gin and Oil Mill Press* 10: 34–35.

Kennamer, Lorrin. 1959. Irrigation patterns in Texas. *Southwestern Social Science Quarterly* 40: 205–212.

Kraenzel, Carl F. 1955. *The Great Plains in transition*. Norman, OK: University of Oklahoma Press.

Lee, J., and J. Sturgis. 1991. Drought and blowing dust in the Southern High Plains, 1947–1990. Paper presented at the meeting of the Southwestern and Rocky Mountain Division, American Association for the Advancement of Science. 67th Annual Meeting, 15–18 May, Lubbock, Texas.

Livingston, R. B. 1952. Relict true prairie communities in central Colorado. *Ecology* 33: 72–86.

Lubbock Avalanche-Journal. 1990. Lubbock Lake site. 6 October, pull-out section.

———. 1991. City breathes easier after EPA action. 22 May, 1A, 7A.

Lubbock Committee for Women. 1990. *Women in Lubbock: A profile for the 90s*. Lubbock, Texas.

Odum, Eugene P. 1971. *Fundamentals of ecology*, 3rd edn. Philadelphia: W. B. Saunders.

Office of Community Development. 1990. *Comprehensive Homeless Assistance Plan 1990*. Lubbock, TX: Office of Community Development.

Paradis, Adrian A. 1969. *The hungry years: The story of the great American Depression*. Philadelphia: Chilton Books.

Persons, Robert H. 1957. Groundwater mining in the Great Plains environment: Agricultural land use in the South Plains of Texas. Ph.D. dissertation, Columbia University, New York, NY.

Popper, Frank J., and Deborah E. Popper. 1991. The reinvention of the American frontier. *Amicus Journal* 13, no. 3 (Summer): 4–7.

Potts, Frances P., John L. Lewis, and W. L. Dorries. 1966. *Texas in maps*. Commerce, TX: East Texas State University Research Publications.

Richardson, Rupert N., Ernest Wallace, and Adrian N. Anderson. 1970. *Texas: The lone star state*. 3rd edn. Englewood Cliffs, NJ: Prentice-Hall.

Riebsame, W. E. 1990. The United States Great Plains. In *The earth as transformed by human action: Global and regional changes in the biosphere over the past 300 years*, ed. B. L. Turner, William C. Clark, Robert W. Kates, John F. Richards, Jessica T. Mathews, and William B. Meyer, 561–576. Cambridge: Cambridge University Press with Clark University.

Robbins, W. 1986. Farm belt suicides reflect greater hardship and deepening despondency. *New York Times*, 14 January, A11.

Rosenthal, Gerald A., and Daniel H. Janzen, eds. 1979. *Herbivores: Their interaction with secondary plant metabolites*. New York: Academic Press.

Ryden, Hope. 1989. *God's dog: A celebration of the North American coyote*. New York: Lyons & Burford.

Ryder, R. 1980. Effects of grazing on bird habitat. In *Management of western forests and grasslands for nongame birds: Workshop proceedings, February 11–14, 1980, Salt Lake City, Utah*, comp. Richard M. DeGraaf and Nancy G. Tilghman, 51–65. USDA Forest Service General Technical Report INT-86. Ogden, Utah: Intermountain Forest and Range Experiment Station, US Department of Agriculture, Forest Service.

Sanford, S. O. 1990. Trends in upland cotton exports. In *Beltwide Cotton Production Research Conferences: January 9–14, 1990, Las Vegas, Nevada: 1990 proceedings*, ed. James M. Brown, 451–453. Memphis, TN: National Cotton Council of America.

Sears, A. B. 1941. The desert threat in the Southern Great Plains: The historical implication of soil erosion. *Agricultural History* 15, no. 10: 1–11.

Segarra, E., W. Keeling, and J. R. Abernathy. 1990. Analysis and evaluation of the impacts of cotton harvesting dates in the Southern High Plains of Texas. In *Beltwide Cotton Production Research Conferences: January 9–14, 1990, Las Vegas, Nevada: 1990 Proceedings*, ed. James M. Brown, 386–390. Memphis, TN: National Cotton Council of America.

South Plains Association of Governments. 1991. *Report of economic development.* Lubbock, TX: SPAG.

South Plains Regional Food Bank. 1991. *Report and proposal for funding*. Lubbock, TX: South Plains Regional Food Bank.

Steglich, X. 1986. Population trends. In *Lubbock: From town to city*, ed. Lawrence L. Graves. Lubbock, TX: West Texas Museum Association.

Texas Agricultural Experiment Station. 1968. *Agroclimatic atlas of Texas*. College Station, TX: Texas A & M University.

Texas Employment Commission. 1988. *Area jobs 1995: Employment by industry and occupation, vols. 1 and 2*. Austin, TX: Texas Employment Commission, Economic Research and Analysis Department.

———. 1990. *Population and employment estimates, July 1990*. Austin, TX: State Department of Labor.

———. 1991. *Lubbock labor force estimates*. Austin, TX: State Department of Labor.

Tharp, Benjamin C. 1952. *Texas range grasses*. Austin, TX: University of Texas Press.

US Army Corps of Engineers. 1982. *Six-state High Plains Ogallala Aquifer regional resources study: Water transfer element*. [Dallas]: US Army Corps of Engineers, Southwestern Division.

US Bureau of the Census. 1900–1982. *Agriculture Census*. Washington DC: US Government Printing Office.

Webb, W. P. 1931. *The Great Plains*. Boston: Ginn & Co.

Weeks, John B. 1986. High plains regional aquifer-system study. In *Regional aquifer-system analysis program of the U.S. Geological Survey: Summary of projects, 1978–84*, ed. Ren Jen Sun, 30–49. US Geological Survey Circular 1002. Washington DC: US Government Printing Office.

Worster, D. W. 1979. *Dust Bowl: The Southern Plains in the 1930s*. Oxford: Oxford University Press.

Wyatt, A. W. 1988. Estimated net depletion shown. *Cross Section* 34, no. 1 (January): 2.

Interviews

Dregne, H., May 1991. Arid Lands Institute, Texas Tech University, Lubbock TX.

Lanier, C., May 1991. Director, South Plains Regional Food Bank, Lubbock, TX.

Neugebauer, D., May 1991. Coordinator, Information and Referral Services, City of Lubbock, TX.

Pierce, T., May 1991. Director of Economic Development, South Plains Association of Governments/Caprock Local Development Co., Lubbock, TX.

Underwood, G., May 1991. Soil Conservation Service, Lubbock, TX.

7

The Basin of Mexico

Adrián Guillermo Aguilar, Exequiel Ezcurra, Teresa García, Marisa Mazari Hiriart, and Irene Pisanty

The Basin of Mexico lies on the southern edge of the Central Volcanic Axis, an upland formation of Late Tertiary origin. It is a naturally closed (but now artificially drained) hydrological unit of approximately 7,500 km^2 (fig. 7.1), the lowest part, a lacustrine plain, averaging about 2,240 m above mean sea level. The basin is surrounded on three sides by a succession of volcanic sierras (the Ajusco and Chichinautzin to the south, the Sierra Nevada to the east, and the Sierra de las Cruces to the west). To the north, it is bounded by a series of low ranges (Los Pitos, Tepotzotlán, Patlachique, Santa Catarina, and others). The highest and snowcapped peaks, Popocatepetl and Ixtaccihuatl (at 5,465 m and 5,230 m, respectively) lie south-east of the basin, but many other peaks reach elevations of around 4,000 m.

Prior to the Spanish conquest in 1519, the lacustrine system in the floor of the Basin of Mexico covered approximately 1,500 km^2 and was formed by five shallow lakes running in a north–south chain: Tzompanco (Zumpango), Xaltocan, Texcoco, Xochimilco, and Chalco. Texcoco was the largest and lowest-elevated of the lakes, so that the entire system drained toward it. During high water, the lakes were connected as a surface system, but during extreme drought they may have desiccated sufficiently to have separated. The northern three lakes were saline and the southern two were fresh water, owing to the greater amount of precipitation and springs located in that area of the basin. This drainage was altered somewhat during the fifteenth century by

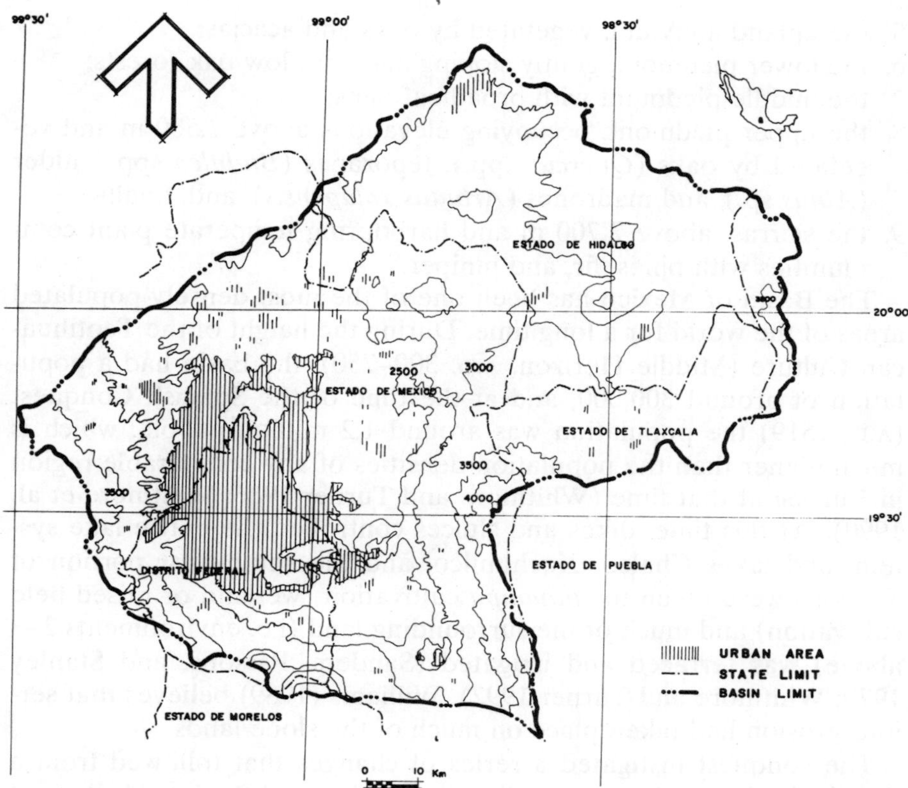

Fig. 7.1 **The Basin of Mexico: Political and geographical boundaries**

the Aztec state, which first diked the connection between lakes Xochimilco and Texcoco and then did the same within Texcoco to protect the south-western portion of that lake in which the island capital of Tenochtitlán was situated (Palerm 1973).

Sanders, Parsons, and Santley (1979) and Sanders (1976) recognize nine major environmental zones (seven located between 2,240 m and 2,500 m elevation) within the basin during its Amerindian occupation:

1. the lake system, which was an important habitat for migratory waterfowl;
2. the saline lakeshore, with halophyllous plants;
3. the deep-soil alluvium, covered by sedges and swamp cypresses (*Taxodium mucronatum*);
4. the thin-soil alluvium, dominated by grasses and agaves;

5. the upland alluvium, vegetated by oaks and acacias;
6. the lower piedmont, gently sloping and with low oak forests;
7. the middle piedmont with broadleaf oaks;
8. the upper piedmont, occupying elevations above 2,500 m and vegetated by oaks (*Quercus* spp.), tepozanes (*Buddlea* spp.), alder (*Alnus* sp.), and madrones (*Arbutus xalapensis*), and, finally,
9. the sierras, above 2,700 m and harbouring temperate plant communities with pines, fir, and juniper.

The Basin of Mexico has been one of the most densely populated areas of the world for a long time. During the height of the Teotihuacan Culture (Middle Horizon, A.D. 300–750), the basin had a population of around 300,000, and at the time of the Spanish Conquest (A.D. 1519) the population was around 1.2 million people, which is much higher than the population densities of any comparable region in Europe at that time (Whitmore and Turner 1986; Whitmore et al. 1990). At this time, dikes and sluices controlled the entire lake system, and lakes Chalco, Xochimilco, and the south-west portion of Texcoco were taken to *chinampa* cultivation (wetland or raised field cultivation) and much of the surrounding land (i.e. environments 2–8 above) was terraced and irrigated (Sanders, Parsons, and Stanley 1979; Whitmore and Turner 1992). Williams (1989) believes that serious erosion had taken place on much of the slope lands.

The conquest instigated a series of changes that followed from a drastic decline in the Amerindian population and the introduction of new biota and technologies from Europe (Whitmore and Turner 1992). Ultimately, the central lakes were drained as modern Mexico City expanded and land uses throughout the basin changed during colonial and post-colonial times. Today, metropolitan Mexico City, estimated to be the largest city in the world by the beginning of the next century, has completely transformed the basin (Ezcurra 1990a,b). The lakes are gone and much of the basin is paved or lies under structures of some type. The city's water must be partially pumped from elsewhere, and its effluent must be pumped out. The old basin floor is sinking under the enormous pressures of the city, and the air pollution is so bad that the surrounding mountains cannot be seen.

Although human-induced environmental change in the ancient basin was significant, this study focuses on the effects of the rapid change in the Basin of Mexico in recent times. Our study concentrates on the past 100 years, with particular emphasis on the period

Table 7.1 **Evolution of the urban area and population densities in Mexico City, 1600–1989**

Year	Area (km²)	Population ('000)	Urban density (persons/km²)
1600	5.5	58	10,584
1700	6.6	105	15,885
1800	10.8	137	12,732
1845	14.1	240	16,985
1900	27.5	541	19,673
1910	40.1	721	17,980
1921	46.4	906	19,534
1930	86.1	1,230	14,287
1940	17.5	1,760	14,974
1953	40.6	3,480	14,464
1980	80.0	13,800	14,082
1989[a]	1,371.0	19,200	14,000
1990[b]	1,050.0	14,700	14,000

Sources: DDF (1986); and projections by the authors.

a. Projected values.

b. Preliminary values of the 1990 population census.

1950–1990. This is the time marked by gigantic growth in population numbers and large-scale industrialization, as Mexico City changed from a relatively small third world capital city into the largest urban conglomeration in the world (table 7.1).

The socio-economic background

Mexico City is a spatially continuous urban area, originally contained within the boundaries of the Federal District, but during the 1950s spreading beyond into adjacent municipalities of the State of Mexico. The current urban area of Mexico City encompasses all 16 subunits or *delegaciones* of the Federal District and 21 *municipios* in the neighbouring State of Mexico (henceforth, both *delegaciones* and *municipios* are referred to as "municipalities"). The urban area, therefore, does not coincide with political administrative divisions. The Metropolitan Area of Mexico City (hereafter Mexico City) corresponds to the territorial extension of the old central city in the Federal District into the urbanized political–administrative units contiguous to it (fig. 7.2; see Negrete and Salazar 1986).

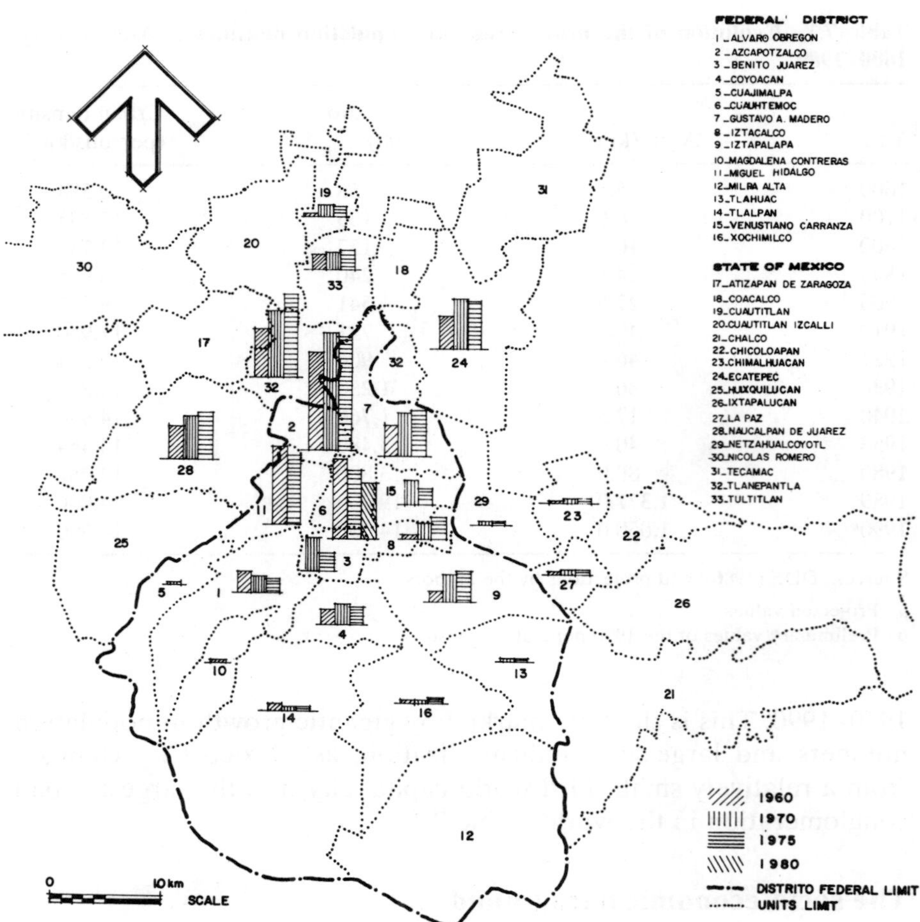

Fig. 7.2 **Municipalities and industrialization trends in Mexico City, 1960–1980 (Source: Garza, 1987, 103)**

In contrast, the Basin of Mexico is a larger, hydrologically defined unit integrated by 84 municipalities of four different political administrative units: the Federal District, and the states of Mexico, Hidalgo, and Puebla. Mexico City represents the most important social, economic, and spatial unit within the basin, concentrating 93 per cent of the basin's population. Thus, the Basin of Mexico and Mexico City are almost synonyms in demographic terms, but the latter is a subset of the former in geographic terms.

The economy of the basin

The Basin of Mexico concentrates almost 25 per cent of the country's total population, and an even greater percentage of the country's economic output. These circumstances were not always so. In the 1940s, Mexico City, being the seat of the federal government, had an extensive urban infrastructure, a concentrated market for industrial products, a variety of professional and financial services, and abundant facilities for administrative transactions. A flow of government investments and fiscal incentives stimulated the concentration of economic development in the area – maintaining a tradition of concentration that can be traced back to pre-Hispanic times. The basin contained, in 1940, 8 per cent of the nation's total population and its share of the national industrial output was 32 per cent; by 1980, however, it had grown to include 21 per cent of the national population and contributed 48 per cent of the industrial output. The Federal District alone contributed 35 per cent of the gross national product.

In the early 1950s, industrial activity in the basin became especially dynamic, and, at a national level, a clear trend appeared towards concentration in the capital city. In 1930, 6.8 per cent of all the industrial establishments of the country were located in Mexico City. This number increased without interruption: in 1970 the capital contained 27.9 per cent, and in 1980, 29.5 per cent of the industries in the nation. Between 1970 and 1980 the number of industries increased 15 per cent (from 33,185 to 38,492), and with it the investment of industrial capital also went up. This dramatic industrial concentration in the capital during the present century has created a situation in which the city produces almost half the total of the national industrial production.

To understand the economic dynamics of the basin, it is important to analyse the diversification and internal structure of industry in Mexico City. This structure is divided into two broad sectors (table 7.2), the means of production and consumer goods. The first sector represented 27.4 per cent of all industry in 1970, including capital goods (11.1 per cent) such as machinery and tools, and intermediate goods (16.3 per cent), which are basically raw materials for other industries. On the other hand, industries that produced consumer goods were the most important within the basin, representing 73 per cent of the total. This sector is in turn divided into two groups: immediate consumer goods (56 per cent; e.g. food, beverages, tobacco,

Table 7.2 **Industrial structure of Mexico City according to the type of value aggregated, 1950–1970**

Industrial groups and sectors	Percentage of total aggregated value 1950	1960	1970	Growth rate 1960–70 (%)
Production goods	25.25	22.61	27.37	12.2
Capital goods	7.37	5.58	11.06	17.2
Metallic products	6.02	4.22	7.85	16.5
Non-electric machinery	1.35	1.36	3.21	18.9
Intermediate goods	17.88	17.03	16.31	9.9
Wood	3.58	0.31	0.32	10.4
Cellulose and paper	2.78	3.35	3.20	9.9
Oil and coal products	3.84	3.61	3.55	10.2
Non-metallic minerals	4.47	4.68	4.25	9.4
Basic metals	3.21	5.08	4.99	10.2
Consumer goods	74.75	77.39	72.63	9.7
Immediate consumption goods	64.32	61.31	56.09	9.4
Foods	11.14	10.68	9.77	9.4
Beverages	8.67	8.43	4.48	4.0
Tobacco	2.27	0.99	0.90	9.3
Textiles	11.13	8.67	6.41	7.3
Shoes and clothing	5.38	3.24	4.60	13.8
Printers	3.91	5.35	4.38	8.8
Leathers	1.12	0.70	0.56	8.0
Rubber products	4.77	3.55	3.63	10.5
Chemicals	15.93	19.70	21.16	11.0
Durable consumption goods	10.43	16.08	16.54	10.6
Furniture	1.63	0.81	1.34	15.7
Electric appliances	2.18	6.01	8.02	13.2
Automobiles and parts	3.49	6.31	5.47	8.9
Other industries	3.13	2.95	1.71	4.9

Source: Garza (1984).

clothing) and durable goods (16.5 per cent; e.g. electric appliances, automobiles, furniture). As table 7.2 indicates, the durable goods and capital goods sectors showed the highest increases in the 1950–1970 period (Garza 1984).

The economic predominance of Mexico City over the rest of the country also shows up in other economic sectors. The city holds an enormous share of the major financial exchanges, private businesses, and central offices in the country; it also has the largest number of institutions of higher education and centres of culture. Indeed, compared with industry, services show an even higher trend to concentrate in Mexico City. Many industries have begun to relocate their manufacturing operations to outlying cities, although their administrative headquarters remain in the capital. In general and aggregate terms, the economic base of the city rests mainly on industry, construction, commerce, restaurants and hotels, and financial services. In 1980, 4.9 per cent of the active population were employed in the primary sector, 41.4 per cent were occupied in industrial activities, and 53.7 per cent were economically active in services.

Urban growth and social distribution

The spatial development of Mexico City until 1950 was characterized by a pattern of concentration in the four central municipalities of the Federal District, which contained around 70 per cent of the urban area at that time. Thereafter, the expansion of the city underwent a rapid process of suburbanization that affected the surrounding municipalities and finally produced a demographic spillover into the adjacent municipalities of the other states. In this process the city occupied agricultural land or, more frequently, land unsuited for urbanization, such as the desiccated lake-bed of Texcoco in the east, the unused open-cast mines and sand quarries to the west, and the mountain slopes of the south.

The period 1930–1950 witnessed an important process of decentralization of urban activities towards the south along two main avenues (Insurgentes and Calzada de Tlalpan). This process set in motion a commercial invasion of properties along those thoroughfares, with the establishment of service institutions. This, in turn, stimulated the appearance of low-density neighbourhoods to the south and west (Polanco, Del Valle, and Chapultepec Morales), occupied mostly by the upper social classes. Thus, the more affluent bourgeoisie left the historic centre of Mexico City and started moving towards the west and south of the basin, where the neighbourhoods with the highest standard of living are now located (figs. 7.3 and 7.4). The most impressive impact on the urbanization pattern, however, was that of the expansion of low-income neighbourhoods, induced by the location of industry in the north. The demand for labour in the newly established factories attracted migrants into working-class municipalities such as Azcapotzalco and Gustavo A. Madero: 70–80 per cent of their growth in the decade 1940–1950 was due to migration. The central part of city also absorbed part of the migrant population, which

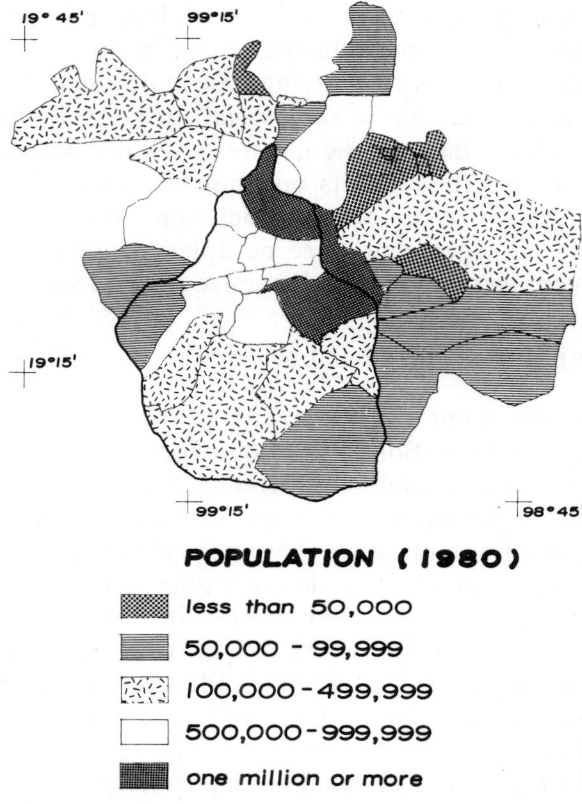

Fig. 7.3 **Population by municipalities in Mexico City, 1980 (Source: Tamayo, Valverde, and Aguilar, 1989)**

found accommodation in the old and dilapidated buildings (*vecindades*) that had been abandoned by the wealthy (on Mexico City urban expansion, see Aguilar 1986; Bataillon and Rivière d'Arc 1973; Garza and Schteingart 1978; Unikel 1974; Ward 1981, 1990).

Suburbanization was stimulated at the beginning of the 1950s by the government's ban on new residential developments within the Federal District. Tax incentives in the State of Mexico encouraged industrial zones to expand, especially to the north-east (Ecatepec) and north-west (Tlanepantla, Naucalpan), around railway terminals. This expansion was accompanied by new housing developments supported by significant improvements in the road system, such as the Mexico–Queretaro freeway, which reduced the travel time from the new suburban areas to either the city centre or the industrial zones.

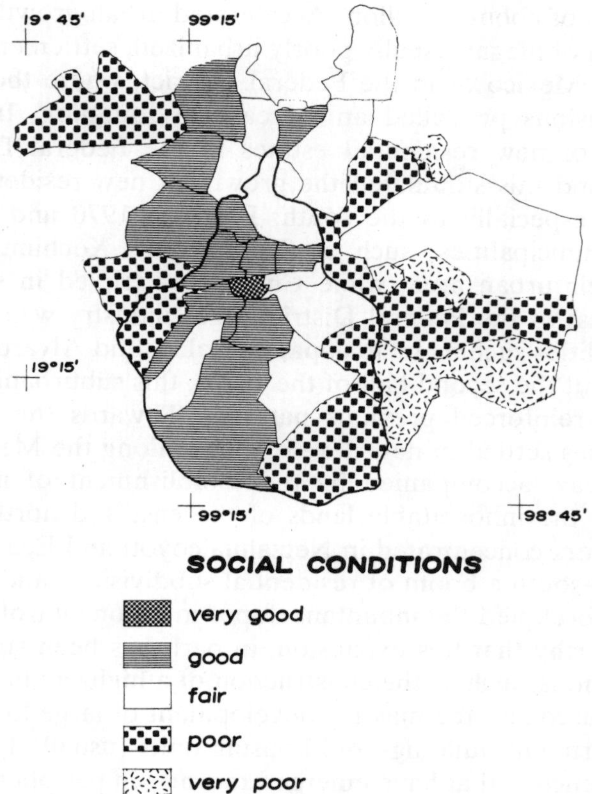

Fig. 7.4 **Social conditions as defined by a multivariate social indicator, by municipalities in Mexico City, 1980 (Source: Tamayo, Valverde, and Aguilar, 1989)**

This widely encouraged the middle and upper classes to settle towards the north-west in developments around Ciudad Satelite (which opened in 1957). In contrast, the low-income groups were segregated towards new, slum-like settlements in the east. These settlements occupied the salty, inhospitable land of the old Lake Texcoco and lacked the most basic urban services. Additionally, they were vulnerable to seasonal flooding and dust storms.

Increasing immigration and the flight of the poor from the city centre into the outer urban contours spawned the proliferation of settlements, most of them products of illegal land subdivision. Perhaps the most impressive example is that of Ciudad Nezahualcoyotl, established in large part on the former lake-bed, and which increased its population from 65,000 in 1960 to 650,000 in 1970; today it contains a population of about 2 million. Accelerated urban growth led to the proliferation of illegal, usually poorly urbanized, settlements either in the State of Mexico or in the Federal District, where the ban upon new subdivisions provoked an increase in squatting. In 1968 the prohibition of new residential estates in the Federal District was overruled, and this stimulated the growth of new residential neighbourhoods, especially to the south. Between 1970 and 1975 some southern municipalities, such as Tlalpan and Xochimilco, almost doubled their urban area, while Cuajimalpa tripled in size. In the east and west of the Federal District, light industry was established in municipalities such as Iztapalapa, Iztacalco, and Alvaro Obregón.

Throughout the second half of the 1970s, this suburbanization continued and reinforced previous patterns. Towards the north-west, middle classes settled in new developments along the Mexico–Queretaro highway, accompanied by the establishment of more heavy industry. In the inhospitable lands of the east and north-east, low-income sectors concentrated in Netzahualcoyotl and Ecatepec, while towards the south a boom of residential subdivisions and diverse social groups occupied the mountain slopes in an uncontrolled fashion. It is noteworthy that this expansion, in part, has been stimulated by public decisions, such as the construction of a highway between Picacho and Ajusco and the massive development of large lower-middle-income apartment buildings and housing units (usually built by government agencies) that have emerged recently in peripheral locations (fig. 7.3).

It is notorious that those municipalities located to the east represent the highest proportions of the active population that earn less than the minimum salary (fig. 7.4). In municipalities such as Chalco, Chimalhuacan, La Paz, or Ixtapalucan, this proportion is more than 50 per cent, whereas in central and western administrative units the poorer groups represent less than 30 per cent, and middle and upper classes reach percentages higher than 10 or 15 (as in, for example, Benito Juarez, Miguel Hidalgo, or Tlalpan). The high proportion of low-income population in peripheral municipalities follows from three principal factors. First, peripheral municipalities still include a large number of people engaged in agricultural occupations, and thus the populations represent the least industrialized of the city. Secondly, peripheral populations that have recently been incorporated into the urban economy are poorly qualified for higher-paying employment. And thirdly, these municipalities receive the poorer population from the centre who are looking for cheaper land or dwellings, as well as the incoming rural migrants (Aguilar Martínez and Godínez, 1989).

Recent environmental changes in the basin

Like many other Latin American countries, Mexico entered the twentieth century under a paternalistic, semi-feudal regime that was determined to incorporate the industrial revolution to the country, while maintaining the privileges of the ruling elite. Under the prolonged dictatorship of Porfirio Díaz from 1884 to 1911, factories and railroads were built, and Mexico City was modernized for the benefit of a small, centralist, and very powerful bourgeoisie whose aim was to transform the wealthier quarters of Mexico, copying the plan of contemporary European cities. The newly laid railroads brought peasants looking for employment in the new industries, and some of the smaller towns nearer the old city, like Tacuba, Tacubaya, and Azcapotzalco, were engulfed by the urban perimeter.

Between 1910 and 1920, the Mexican revolution brought a decade of ruthless confrontation between the old Porfirian bourgeoisie, which defended its privileges, and other social sectors demanding more participation in the distribution of the national wealth. This was one of the first social revolutions of modern times, and it marked the beginning of a series of large-scale social uprisings that shook the world in the twentieth century. Mexico City had at that time approximately 700,000 inhabitants and, unexpectedly, suffered little damage. The revolution was mostly a rural movement, and the city became a haven for middle-class provincial families, who flocked into the Basin of Mexico searching for protection under the new bureaucracy and the rising industries.

During the post-revolutionary period (1920–1940), and particularly after World War II, the industrial growth of Mexico developed at an increasing speed. Mexico City became an industrial complex, and a massive migration started from the country into the urban area. In less than 80 years the population of the urban conglomerate jumped from less than 1 million to nearly 18 million in 1987. Former peripheral towns, like Coyoacán, Tlalpan, and Xochimilco, were incorporated within the urban perimeter. A deep drainage system was built to remove the torrential surface runoff from the urban portion of the basin, while most of the old lake-beds dried up. The overexploitation of the aquifer system and the contraction of the expansive clays of the former lake-bed on which the modern city sits above the former Aztec capital of Tenochtitlán lowered the centre of the city by approximately 9 m between 1910 and 1987. The extremely low wind speeds in the high-altitude basin, together with intense industrial activity and the emissions of 3 million vehicles, have degraded the quality of the atmosphere in the basin to levels that are dangerous to human health. These and other changes are explored in detail below.

Vegetation and surface water

Several geographical characteristics influence the development of a diverse flora in the basin: its high altitude and inter-tropical location, the high mountain ridges that surround and isolate the valley bottom, and the fact that the Central Volcanic Axis of Mexico constitutes a boundary area between the Nearctic and the Neotropical biogeographic regions. Additionally, internal geological discontinuities create different patches originally covered with distinct vegetation types. Rzedowski (1986) remarked that in the 7,500 km^2 of the basin more species could be found than in several European countries. This vegetational diversity, however, is now heavily disrupted by human use and urban growth, continuing a process that began with the emergence of large populations in the basin over 2,000 years ago (Sanders 1972).

The different vegetation types in relation to the environment, described by Sanders (1976) and by Sanders, Parsons, and Santley (1979), were summarized in the introduction to this chapter. Several detailed classifications have been made of them. The most important ones are the studies of Miranda and Hernandez Xolocotzl (1963) and Rzedowski (1975). Table 7.3 summarizes Rzedowski's ecological zones, their main characteristics, and the vegetation associated with them.

During the long years of human occupation, the environment of the Basin of Mexico has changed drastically (Niederberger 1987), and probably irreversibly in many aspects. Changes range from transformations of the natural systems, without altering their main ecological structure, to radical elimination of whole ecosystems, with the concomitant extinction of species and lateral effects on the surroundings. One of the earlier and important changes in the landscape of the basin was associated with agricultural activities in its shallow lakes and wetlands. *Chinampas*, an extremely efficient form of wetland cultivation based on the construction of canals on the wetland and lake floors and platforms of earthen and vegetal materials between the canals, created an intricate network of water and fields (raised) on the surface. The effect was to lower the water table (via the canals) relative to the raised planting surface while maintaining subsurface irrigation at all times. The planting beds were held together with the roots of a willow (*Salix bomplandiana*, locally known as *ahuejotes*) planted along their periphery, the slender silhouette of which is characteristic of lakes Chalco and Xochimilco where this highly efficient agriculture developed and still persists.

Corn, beans, squash, chile, and flowers, among other species cultivated on these extremely rich soils, faced no water shortage. Their growth was not rainfall dependent, and aquatic muck from the canals provided a regular source of plant and soil nutrients. When the top soil was exhausted in one *chinampa*, it was thrown back into the lake or canals, and a new layer was taken out. During the apex period of *chinampa* use (Late Horizon), the *chinampa* system was protected from and expanded into the saline waters of Lake Texcoco by the use of hydraulic controls (Palerm 1973).

The arrival of the Spaniards and the succeeding conquest of the Aztec empire were turning points in the use of natural resources in the basin. Tenochtitlán was a lacustrine city, constructed in the western portion of Lake Texcoco. Most transportation to and within the city was by shallow-bottom canoes (*chalupas*) that moved across the lakes and through the network of *chinampa* and city canals. As power changed hands, a new view of the world was imposed, complete with a new version of landscape configuration and use. The introduction of Spanish preferences and European biota and technologies included a demand for wheat and livestock, the use of the plough, and the use of large animals for transport and ploughing (Whitmore and Turner 1992). These changes required open, dry land, not a lacustrine system. Tenochtitlán, now called Mexico, was appropriately transformed by converting the canal networks into roads and draining water away from the centre of the city. The alluvial plains and piedmonts were also transformed, first by the loss of Amerindians to keep up the ancient terrace systems, and secondly by Hispanic-controlled uses. Although the degree of change in these areas is unclear, apparently considerable deforestation on the upper slopes took place to construct the new, Hispanic Mexico City and to provide wood fuel (as much as 25,000 trees per year). Erosion on slope lands, perhaps well under way during the Late Horizon (Williams 1989), was exacerbated in some cases by overgrazing livestock but diminished in others owing to decreased land pressures attendant on the dramatic depopulation of the Amerindians and to their improved ability to control their own lands

Table 7.3 **Vegetation zones in the Basin of Mexico**

Vegetation	Main species	Zone/altitude/precipitation	Additional information
Aquatic and subaquatic	*Typha latifolia* *Scirpus* spp. *Lemna* spp. *Eichhornia crassipes* *Juncus* spp. *Cyperus* spp. *Echinochloa* spp. *Hydrocotyle* spp. *Eleocharis* spp. *Bidens* spp. *Sagittaria* spp.	Lake system	Drastic reduction of the lakes has caused the disappearance of many species, allowing exotic species, particularly *Eichhornia crassipes*, to become dominant. The revegetation of the dry bed of Lake Texcoco allowed the establishment of halophyllous grasses and herbs.
Halophytes	*Sporobolus* spp. *Distichlis* spp. *Typha* spp. *Atriplex* spp. *Eragrostis obtusiflora*	Saline and alkaline lakeshores and dry beds of former lakes. *c.* 2,200 m	These species are frequently found as low grasslands growing in highly saline and badly drained soils. Soils along the former lakeshores were used as salt sources in Aztec times.
Xerophyllous scrub	*Opuntia streptacantha* *Mimosa biuncifera* *Hechtia podantha* *Jatropha dioica* *Eysenhardtia polystachya* Some former low tree communities were probably present, interspersed with grasses and shrubs.	Lowlands, on deep and thin soils. They can be found in different regions. In the southern part, they are characteristic of Pedregal de San Angel. *c.* 2,250–2,700 m 400–700 mm	These are flat zones surrounding the lake system. They are relatively dry, and soils are more or less deep except in the northern region, where it is very thin. Agriculture in this zone needs irrigation.

Grasslands	*Hilaria cenchroides* *Buchloe dactyloides* *Aristida adscensionis* *Bouteloua simplex* *Potentilla candicans* *Calamagrostis tolucensis* *Festuca* spp.	Distributed through different environments with superficial or deep soils. 2,250–4,300 m 700–1,200 mm	In many cases, grasslands are secondary communities that can eventually be substituted by trees. In some cases they coexist with shrubs.
Scrub oak forest	*Quercus microphylla*	Found in the lower piedmont, on sandy loams. 2,300–3,100 m 700–1,200 m	Probably a fire-induced community. Soils in these slopes are very vulnerable to erosion.
Juniper forest	*Juniperus deppeana*	Grows in the first part of the upper piedmont, characterized by shallow clay soils. 2,400–2,800 m 600–800 mm 11–14°C	Juniper forests are open, probably secondary communities. Owing to the low cover values, under-story species are abundant.
Oak forests	*Quercus* spp.	Found from the upper piedmont to the sierra regions. Inadequate forestry has reduced their original distribution area. Soils are shallow or deep, and frosts frequent. 2,350–3,100 m 700–1,200 mm	

Table 7.3 (*continued*)

Vegetation	Main species	Zone/altitude/precipitation	Additional information
	Quercus laeta *Quercus deserticola* *Quercus crassipes* *Quercus obtusata*	Found at less than 2,500 m.	Low forests (5–10 m), with sparse canopies.
	Quercus rugosa *Quercus mexicana* *Quercus angustifolia*	Characteristic of the upper piedmont with deep or moderately shallow soils. 2,500–2,800 m 600–800 mm 11–14°C	Frequently the first species forms pure stands, but it can be found mingled with the other two.
Pine forests	*Pinus* spp.	Evergreen communities, growing in shallow, rocky, or deep soils, in the sierra region. 2,350–4,000 m 700–1,200 mm	Agriculture, grazing, and timber-logging have strongly disrupted these communities.
	Pinus leiophylla	This species coexists with several species of oaks, forming mixed communities. 2,350–2,600 mm	Deeply disturbed communities, with severely eroded soils.
	Pinus montezumae *Pinus patula*	Relatively high and almost pure stands. 2,500–3,100 m	

	Pinus hartwegii	This species can grow on steep slopes. 2,900–4,000 m	This forests marks the timberline in the higher part of the mountains.
Cloud forests	*Clethra mexicana* *Quercus laurina* *Prunus brachybotrya* *Alnus arguta* *Pinus* spp.	Upland alluvium. 2,500–3,000 m *c.* 1,000 mm	Found in restricted areas with deep soils and protected from strong winds and frosts. A high proportion of its original range has been transformed into agricultural areas.
Fir forests	*Abies religiosa*	Characteristic of the sierra region. It grows on deep, well-drained, rich soils. 2,700–3,500 m 1,000–1,500 mm 7.5–13°C	Dense, high, and evergreen forests. Together with *Pinus hartwegii*, this forest reaches the timberline. It is used for pasturing herds and for wood extraction.

Sources: Sanders (1972); Sanders, Parsons, and Santley (1979); Rzedowski (1975).

as formal colonial policy was better enforced (Butzer 1991; Butzer and Butzer 1995).

Major environmental changes took place in Mexico owing to the conquest, but the degrading nature of all or most of these may have been overstated. Major afforestation occurred initially because of the reduced native population. And, according to the Butzers (1995), the Spaniards and Amerindians readily adapted their livestock and other land-use practices to local environmental conditions. With the exception of the destruction of the lacustrine system in the Basin of Mexico, major environmental degradation, as opposed to change, perhaps waited for the nineteenth century.

Desiccation of the lakes and deforestation of the upper slopes of the basin continued through the colonial and independence period of Mexico and into the beginning of the present century. This included the construction of the canal to drain the lakes. In the 1930s, formal action was taken to protect the forests and the mountain catchment areas around the basin. Lázaro Cárdenas, President from 1934 to 1940, changed the official attitude towards the use of natural resources in the basin. Most of the basin's 20 national parks were established between 1936 and 1939. Only one national park, Desierto de los Leones, had been established previously, in 1917. Among the most recently created protected areas is a small part of the Pedregal de San Angel, a unique plant community that developed on a basalt outcrop in the southern part of the basin, mostly on the grounds of the National University.

Now 80,164 ha of land within the basin receive formal protection, but most of it suffers severe disruption by erosion and deforestation. Some of this land has completely lost its plant cover and is little more than part of the urbanized area of the basin. The deterioration of national parks set in shortly after their creation. For example, during 1946–1952, while Miguel Alemán was the President of Mexico, the Cumbres del Ajusco National Park was given in concession to one of Mexico's most important paper factories.

Mexico City inherited one of Tenochtitlán's main traits: the high density of its human population (see Whitmore et al. 1990). Since 1940, however, the population has increased constantly at rates of 4–5 per cent per year, so peripheral towns like Coyoacán, San Angel, Atizapan, and Tlatelolco have become an integrated part of the megalopolis. The agricultural lands that separated them have completely disappeared. Only a small proportion of the lakes has survived. Lake Chalco was drained in 1954, and only Xochimilco and Tlahuac subsist as *chinampa* areas. The remaining *chinampas* are withering because of the deteriorating quality of the water.

This urban and industrial growth has had enormous impacts on many aquatic, subaquatic, and halophyllous species, many of which have become extinct. Some vegetation types on the surrounding slopes are also on the verge of extinction, as is the case of some forests on the upper slopes of the southern mountains. The arboreal communities have been deeply damaged. More than 9,000 ha of trees have disappeared in only the past 10 years, and insect pests are fiercely attacking some of the protected zones, such as the Desierto de los Leones and the famous Chapultepec Park. Many introduced tree species have been used to reforest, resulting in a loss of the animal species that were associated with the native vegetation. In particular, eucalyptus was planted on a large-scale basis throughout the basin because its demand for water helped to dry up the lake system. Overall, monospecific communities have replaced the species-rich flora of the Basin of Mexico.

In addition to these changes, the plants that remain are affected significantly by air pollution. Little is known about the effects on plants of pollutants such as ozone and lead, both of which are a problem in the basin (see below). Hernández Tejeda, Bauer, and Krupa (1985) and Hernández Tejeda and Bauer (1986) have detected effects of specific pollutants on the growth and photosynthetic rates of trees.

Urbanization

The population of the metropolitan area of Mexico City has accelerated at a particularly rapid rate since the end of the Mexican revolution. From 1950 to 1986, the average annual growth rate was 4.8 per cent (table 7.4). The population has grown more quickly in the industrial area of the neighbouring State of Mexico, north of the Federal District, where the average rate of increase has been 13.6 per cent, compared with 3.3 per cent in the Federal District. Much of the high growth rate of the city is due to the continuous arrival of migrants from the economically depressed rural areas (Goldani 1977; Stern 1977; Unikel 1974). Between 1970 and 1980, for example, 3,248,000 immigrants arrived in Mexico City (Calderón and Hernández 1987). The intrinsic annual growth rate of the city, therefore, can be calculated as approximately 1.8 per cent, considerably lower than the na-

Table 7.4 **Population in Mexico City, 1519–1986 (millions)**

Year[a]	Federal District	State of Mexico	Total
1519 (conquest)	0.3	–	0.3
1620 (colony)	0.03	–	0.03
1810 (independence)	0.1	–	0.1
1910 (revolution)	0.5	–	0.5
1940 (Cardenist period)	1.8	–	1.8
1950	3.0	–	3.0
1960	4.8	0.4	5.2
1970	6.8	1.9	8.7
1980	8.8	5.0	13.8
1986	10.0	6.7	16.7
1989[b]	11.0	8.2	19.2
1990[c]	8.2	6.5	14.7
Estimated yearly growth rate (1950–86)	3.3%	13.6%	4.8%
Stand. error	0.3%	1.7%	0.2%

Sources: DDF (1987); and projections by the authors.

a. Pre-1950 dates have been chosen as approximate indicators, and correspond with the important historical dates indicated in parentheses.

b. Projected value.

c. Preliminary values of the 1990 population census.

tional average, which was around 3.0 per cent for the same period. In short, it is immigration more than reproductive growth that maintains the high rate of increase of the population of Mexico City.

Applying the 1980 growth rates to the 1987 population of 18 million, one can calculate that every day around 900 babies are born and 1,500 new immigrants arrive in the Basin of Mexico. Since many of the newborn are those of immigrants, migration further increases the growth rate of the population by elevating the natural birth rates (Goldani 1977).[1]

The growth rate of the city in spatial extent, estimated from the urban areas measured on aerial photographs, is close to that of the population (5.2 per cent, see fig. 7.5 and table 7.5). In 1953, the urban area covered 240 km^2 (8 per cent of the basin), whereas by 1980 it had increased to 980 km^2 (33 per cent of the basin). The expansion, however, has not kept the old style of urbanization. In many parts of the basin, especially in the poorer areas, the new developments are more dense and less planned and generally include fewer open spaces.

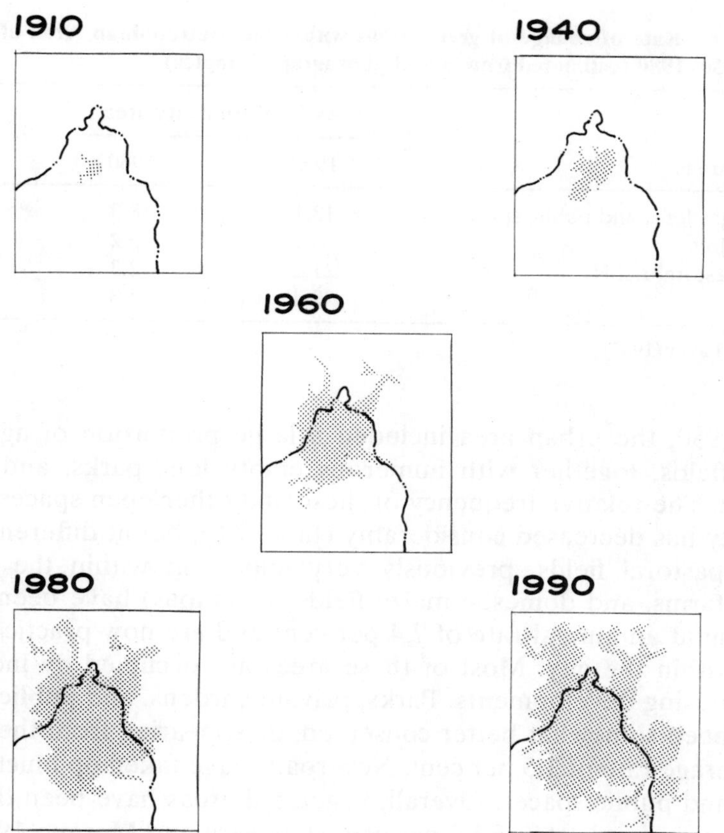

Fig. 7.5 **Growth of the urban area of Mexico City, 1910–1990 (Source: Macgregor, González-Sánchez, and Cervantes, 1989)**

Table 7.5 **Total urban area estimated from aerial photographs, 1953 and 1980**

Year	Area (km²)
1953	240.6
1980	980.0
Estimated average annual growth rate	5.2%

Sources: DDF (1986); and projections by the authors.

Many developments that are now built on hill slopes generate a considerable amount of soil erosion and a significant increase in flash floods after rainstorms (Galindo and Morales 1987).

Table 7.6 **Rate of change of green areas within the Metropolitan Area of Mexico City, 1950–1980 (estimated from aerial photograph samples)**

Green areas	As % of total city area		Yearly change
	1950	1980	
Parks, gardens, and public spaces	13.1	8.3	−1.5%
Empty lots	8.1	3.2	−3.1%
Agro-pastoral fields	21.2	2.3	−7.4%
Total	42.4	13.8	−3.7%

Source: Lavín (1983).

In 1950, the urban area included a large proportion of agro-pastoral fields, together with numerous empty lots, parks, and public spaces. The relative frequency of these and other open spaces within the city has decreased considerably (table 7.6), but at different rates. Agro-pastoral fields, previously very important within the city as dairy farms, and domestic maize fields (or milpas) have been disappearing at an annual rate of 7.4 per cent and are now practically absent within the city. Most of these areas are occupied by industrial and housing developments. Parks, private gardens, and public spaces have been somewhat better conserved, disappearing from the city at an average rate of 1.5 per cent. New roads have taken up much of the park and public spaces. Overall, vegetated areas have been decreasing at an annual rate of 3.7 per cent (Guevara and Moreno 1987).

Lavín (1983) conducted an analysis of the rate of change of vegetated ("green") areas within different sectors of Mexico City from 1950 to 1980. She found that the total rate of change of green areas varied considerably from one sector of the city to another. Among her key findings were:

- The east of Mexico City (in particular Ciudad Netzahualcoyotl, with some 2.5 million inhabitants), where the larger proletarian settlements lie, was changing most quickly. Nearly 6 per cent of its open space disappeared each year over the 30-year period (table 7.7).
- Open spaces were disappearing most slowly in the old centre of the city (−1.0 per cent).
- The rate of change within urbanized areas depends on the social status of their inhabitants and on the time of their establishment. In the poorer and more recently established areas, vacant land was quickly transformed into new houses, leaving less green area per person.
- Although some quarters have more than 10 m^2 of green land per per-

Table 7.7 **Rate of change of green areas within different sectors of the Metropolitan Area of Mexico City, 1950–1980 (estimated from aerial photograph samples)**

Sector	Green areas as % of area of sector		Yearly change
	1950	1980	
North	52.6	21.8	−2.9%
South	41.6	14.7	−3.5%
East	23.5	4.0	−5.9%
West	62.5	28.1	−2.7%
Centre	5.0	3.7	−1.0%

Source: Lavín (1983).

son, others have much less. Azcapotzalco, an industrial quarter with a population of some 700,000, has at present 0.9 m^2 of green area per inhabitant (Barradas and J-Seres 1987; Calvillo-Ortega 1978), whereas the United Nations Environmental Programme (UNEP) suggests a minimum of 9 m^2 per inhabitant.

The worst problem associated with urbanization in the Basin of Mexico is not so much the size of the city and the demands it generates, both of which create problems enough, but the phenomenal rates of urban growth. These rates generate enormous pressure on the capacities of the social and environmental systems. As the government struggles to meet existing demands, new demands are surfacing at an ever-increasing pace. The projection of present trends (understanding that this is an exercise only) shows that, by the year 2000, Mexico City will occupy around 2,700 km^2 with a population approaching 30 million (Ezcurra 1990a). Houses and roads will take up most (92 per cent) of the city surface, whereas parks, private gardens, and public spaces will cover a mere 6 per cent. The people living in the basin will enjoy only 5 m^2 of green area per capita. In the poorer parts of this future city, the inhabitants will have less than 1 m^2 of open public spaces for recreational use. Mexico City will have been transformed into pavements and roofs (Ezcurra 1990b; Ezcurra and Sarukhán 1990).

Water resources

Water supply

Water resources have always been an important component in the environmental-use history of the basin (Lara 1988; Serra Puche

1991). Before massive lake drainage and urbanization, runoff from the surrounding mountains filled the lower part of the basin during the rainy season, creating the basin's lacustrine system. During the dry season, evaporation and use conspired in the spatial fragmentation of this system (Bribiesca 1960). As noted above, this system has been destroyed, and the natural bodies of water have almost disappeared. At present, all that remains is a small section of Lake Texcoco and some of the old *chinampa* canals in Xochimilco; Lake Zumpango, which dried in the 1970s, has now been dredged and refilled.

Runoff flows through seasonal rivers (all small and localized) only during the rainy season. The aquifers that underlie the city, mainly in the northern and southern parts of the old lacustrine zone, had artesian pressure until the nineteenth century and even until 1920 in some areas. Today, pumping has reversed the gradients; natural flow in springs has ceased. Water tends to move downwards through the ancient lake sediments, from which it is heavily pumped (Marsal and Mazari 1969; Mazari and Alberro 1991; Ortega 1988).

Natural water infiltration has decreased in the basin as urbanization has advanced over what previously were water-recharge areas. The almost 1,000 km^2 of urbanized land generate massive runoff during the rainy season, but almost all this water is lost through the drainage system and does not infiltrate the soil. Various authors have estimated the recharge of the aquifer system to be some 23–27 m^3 per second, less than 50 per cent of the volume (50–52 m^3 per second) that is currently extracted (Ezcurra 1990a; Garza 1987; Murillo 1990).

Excessive groundwater extraction from the basin has significantly influenced the lacustrine clays and, in the lower strata of the basin sediments, particularly the soil mechanics involved. For the last century, the base level of the city has sunk continuously, and the progression of this subsidence has paralleled that of water extraction. From the beginning of the century until 1938, the rate of subsidence was 4.6 cm per year; in the early forties it increased to 16 cm per year. The greatest subsidence was registered during 1948–1956, a period in which the city sunk at a rate of 30 cm per year. This problem forced the closing of several extraction wells and their relocation north and south of the city in 1954. During the late 1950s, subsidence decreased to 7.5 cm per year, and in the eighties dropped to 4.5 cm per year (Mazari, Marsal, and Alberro 1984; Mazari and Alberro 1991).

A considerable volume of the water consumed in the Basin of Mexico is transported, at high expense, from other basins where it is also

Table 7.8 **Water supply systems for the Federal District, 1988**

Origin	Number of wells	Flow (m^3/s)
External sources		
Lerma basin	234	6.0
Cutzamala basin	(surface)	9.0
Internal sources		
North	62	2.1
South	143	6.4
Centre	96	3.0
East	41	1.1
West	18	0.5
Other wells	209	9.2
Río Magdalena and other surface sources	(surface)	0.8
Private wells	538	1.2
Treated water	–	1.3
State of Mexico[a]		18.4
Total	1,341	59.0

Sources: DGCOH (1989); Guerrero, Moreno, and Garduño (1982); SARH (1985).

a. Water systems in the State of Mexico, also supplying the urban area, are reported globally.

needed (table 7.8). In 1976, the city used 1.3 billion m^3 of water at an average rate of 41 m^3 per second; 30 per cent of this (12 m^3 per second) came from the Lerma basin (DDF 1977). At present, the city uses 57–64 m^3 per second (Alvarez 1985; DDF 1989; Herrera and Cortés 1989; Murillo 1990), of which 18 m^3 per second (about 570 million m^3 per year) are pumped from the Lerma and Cutzamala basins in the neighbouring states of Mexico, Michoacán, and Guerrero (DDF 1989). Increasing dependency on external sources of water is affecting the very basins from which the water is extracted.

The average daily supply of water in Mexico City is around 300 litres per person, more than in many European cities (Alvarez 1985). Even so, many parts of the city suffer from chronic water shortages, especially during the dry season. Industrial use is very inefficient, wastewater recycling is only about 6 per cent of the total used, and nearly 15 per cent of the water supply is lost through deficient piping systems (table 7.9). Pipe breakage in the muddy subsoil of the old lake-bed also represents a potential health hazard, since the migration of micro-organisms and chemicals from the sewer system could contaminate drinking water.

Water quality is also a controversial and poorly understood prob-

Table 7.9 **Distribution and consumption of water in the Federal District**

Use	Number of users	Flow[a] m³/s	%
Domestic	1,900,000 households	22	59
Industrial	30,000 industries	5	14
Services	60,000 institutions	4	11
Commercial	120,000 shops	1	2
Losses	–	5	14

Source: SARH (1985).

a. Water systems in the State of Mexico, also supplying the urban area, are not reported.

lem. For decades attention has focused on the bacteriological aspects of water quality. Infectious and parasitic diseases, partly related to poor-quality drinking water, continue to rank among the five most common causes of death in the country, especially for infants (CAE 1990; Martínez-Palomo and Sepúlveda 1990; WHO 1988). Inorganic compounds degrading water in the basin have been studied and are well defined in the drinking-water regulations. Mexico, like many other Latin American countries, is still out-dated in the analysis and regulation of organic chemicals in water. Organic pollutants, mostly in the form of synthetic products used by industry, represent an impending problem since untreated residues are dumped into the drainage system.

Drainage system

Mexico City uses a combined system that carries stormwater and untreated water through sewers, rivers, open canals, reservoirs, lagoons, pumping stations, and a deep drainage system (Guerrero, Moreno, and Garduño 1982). At present the wastewater-treatment capacity through 24 plants is 3.5 m^3 per second, which accounts for approximately 6 per cent of the water used in the basin (Murillo 1990; see table 7.10). Untreated wastewater flows to the north into the Tula River basin, before it flows to the Moctezuma–Pánuco river system, passing through the Zimapán Hydroelectric Project (currently under construction), and on to its final destination, the Gulf of Mexico.

Wastewater is discharged into the Tula basin through two systems: an open surface channel (the Gran Canal), which has been in operation since the beginning of the twentieth century, and a closed, deep underground drainage system (the Drenaje Profundo), which was

Table 7.10 **Sewage treatment plants in the Federal District, 1982**

Plant	Installed capacity (litres/s)	Present working capacity litres/s	%	Operating since:
Cerro de la Estrella	2,000	1,800	90	1971
Xochimilco	1,250	0	0	1959
San Juan de Aragón	500	300	60	1964
Ciudad Deportiva	230	230	100	1958
Chapultepec	160	160	100	1956
Acueducto de Guadalupe	80	0	0	1982
Bosques de las Lomas	55	22	40	1973
El Rosario	25	22	88	1981
Total, 1982	4,300	2,534	59	
Total, 1991 (24 plants)[a]	5,000	3,500	70	

Source: SARH (1985).

a. Since 1982, three new plants have been constructed in the Federal District, and 13 new plants in the State of Mexico, giving a total working capacity of approx. 3,500 litres/s in 1991 (Murillo 1990; Comisión Nacional del Agua, unpublished data).

built in the early 1970s. As the city subsided through overexploitation of the aquifer, the Gran Canal lost its slope and stopped functioning. At present, water has to be moved up slope through the channels by means of auxiliary pumping stations. The maximum drainage capacity of this system is 100 m^3 per second. The closed drainage system is composed of a network of underground tunnels 30–200 m deep. It operates mostly during the rainy season. Since it was built to account for subsidence, it does not require supplementary pumping. During the rainy season, it can carry a maximum flow of 200 m^3 per second (Guerrero, Moreno, and Garduño 1982).

Waste

Liquid waste

Untreated wastewater is eliminated from the basin by means of both drainage systems. The drainage water is used mostly in the State of Hidalgo to irrigate 580 km^2 of agricultural fields (Strauss 1988). The untreated wastewater used for irrigation is a significant source of soil and plant contamination in agricultural areas. For example, the mean concentration of surfactants in the water used for irrigation is around 13 mg/litre (Mazari Hiriart 1992). If a field is irrigated with about

2,000 mm per ha per year (i.e. 20,000 $m^3ha^{-1}y^{-1}$, a common volume for the area), it will receive around 260 kg of surfactants per hectare each year. Heavy metals as a group can show concentrations as high as 0.75 mg/litre in the wastewater used for irrigation. This means that as much as 16 kg of heavy metals can be incorporated every year into a hectare of irrigated agricultural land. A similar situation obtains with boron, which has mean concentrations of 1.1 mg/litre in the Gran Canal (DDF 1979), representing about 22 kg of boron incorporated into each hectare of agricultural fields every year. One of the main causes of water contamination is the dumping of industrial waste in the sewer system as a means to dispose of toxic substances. The basin urgently needs a waste-processing plant, for it currently has no disposal system for chemical and toxic waste other than the city sewers or transportation to distant landfills.

Irrigation with wastewater in Hidalgo has also generated a severe problem of microbiological contamination. Using most-probable-number (MPN) procedures, total coliform counts have been reported in the ranges of 6×10^6 to 2×10^8 MPN/100 ml in the Gran Canal waters, which are used directly for irrigation at Chiconautla. Very high densities of colibacteria have also been reported in vegetables grown at these sites. Median values of faecal coliform counts are 43 MPN/10 g within plant tissues and 96 MPN/10 g in plant surfaces. Some samples, however, have shown faecal coliform counts as high as 3,000 MPN/10 g (Strauss 1986). Additionally, viable amoebic cysts have been found in the Canal waters and in irrigation ditches (Rivera et al. 1980).

Solid waste

The city produces approximately 12,000 tons of domestic solid waste per day. Almost one-half (48 per cent) of the solid waste produced is of industrial origin, while the remaining 52 per cent is domestic waste (table 7.11). Around 50 per cent of the domestic waste is organic refuse, and the rest is paper (17 per cent), glass (10 per cent), textiles (6 per cent), plastics (6 per cent), metals (3 per cent), and other refuse (9 per cent). In contrast with developed countries, which generate garbage with a low proportion of organic residues, the waste of Mexico City is rich in vegetable and fruit waste (Restrepo and Phillips 1985). Until 1987, the disposal of most of these residues in open yards represented a public health hazard. These dump-yards have now been closed, but many smaller, and very often clandestine, disposal yards exist throughout Mexico City. In 1986, the inauguration

Table 7.11 **Concentration of industries and production of industrial waste in the different municipalities within Mexico City**

Municipality (*delegación*)	Number of industries	Industrial waste production (tons/day)
Alvaro Obregón	1,322	473
Azcapotzalco	2,324	917
Benito Juárez	2,879	497
Coyoacán	1,055	617
Cuajimalpa	190	67
Cuauhtémoc	5,948	557
Gustavo A. Madero	3,946	430
Iztacalco	1,897	410
Iztapalapa	3,751	590
Magdalena Contreras	202	7
Miguel Hidalgo	2,521	730
Milpa Alta	128	1
Tláhuac	468	47
Tlalpan	762	143
Venustiano Carranza	2,447	220
Xochimilco	22	87
Total	29,862	5,791

Source: Dirección General de Servicios Urbanos, Dirección de Desechos Sólidos, Departamento del Distrito Federal, unpublished data, 1990.

of a more modern system of landfills east of the city reflected an attempt to deal with, in part, the tremendous environmental problem posed by garbage disposal.

Air quality

One of the worst environmental problems associated with the uncontrolled growth of the city (and certainly the one that is most perceived by the population) is the high level of atmospheric pollution in the basin (SAHOP 1978; SMA 1978b,c). This problem is particularly severe during the winter season (December to February), during which the low temperatures stabilize the atmosphere above the basin and the air pollutants accumulate in the stationary mass of air that hovers over the city (SEDUE 1986; Velasco Levy 1983). Studies of the lead (Pb) and bromine (Br) content in the air particulate pollutants in Mexico City have shown that most of the air pollution originates from automobile exhaust (Barfoot et al. 1984; Sigler Andrade, Fuentes Gea, and Vargas Aburto 1982). Government esti-

Table 7.12 **Number of vehicles in Mexico City, 1978–1989**

Year	Vehicles ('000)	Population (million)	Urban area (km^2)
1978	1,600.0	12.8	949.9
1980	2,000.0	13.8	980.9
1983	2,800.0	15.5	1,104.4
1986	3,505.3	17.4	1,208.2
1989[a]	4,000.0	19.2	1,371.0

Sources: Legorreta (1988); and projections by the authors.

a. Projected.

mates show that motor vehicles are responsible for 85 per cent of all atmospheric pollutants in Mexico City. In some parts of the city, particularly towards the east central area, the concentration of total suspended particles exceeds the Mexican and the international air-quality standards more than 50 per cent of the time (Fuentes Gea and Hernández 1984).

Although air quality during the rainy season has remained more or less constant since the mid-1980s, the total of suspended particles during the dry season is increasing at approximately 6 per cent per year (calculated from Fuentes Gea and Hernández 1984). In agreement with the idea that most of the atmospheric pollution derives from automobile exhaust, the number of cars in the city is also increasing at a 7 per cent annual rate (more than 3 million cars in 1986; see table 7.12). According to these data, the deterioration in the air quality in the Basin of Mexico during the dry season outstrips the rates of population growth and urban expansion. If the trend continues, in a few years atmospheric pollution will exceed the acceptable air-quality standards most of the time, with very serious consequences for human health.

According to Bravo Alvarez's (1987) detailed report, vehicles produce most of the carbon monoxide and hydrocarbon residues in the basin, but fixed sources are responsible for most of the particles, sulphur dioxide, and nitrogen oxides (table 7.13). Particulate pollution is highest towards the east central part of the city, but sulphur dioxide is highest in the north, where most of the industries are located. Until 1986, lead was probably the worst pollutant in the atmosphere of the basin (Salazar, Bravo, and Falcón 1981). Only high-leaded gasoline was sold in Mexico City at that time, and the concentration of lead in the air increased steadily with the number of cars, reaching an

Table 7.13 **Atmospheric emissions estimated for the Metropolitan Area of Mexico City, 1983**

	Fixed sources		Vehicles		Total	
Pollutant	tons/year	%	tons/year	%	tons/year	%
Particles	141,000	2.9	12,800	0.3	153,800	3.1
Carbon monoxide	120,000	2.4	3,600,000	72.8	3,720,000	75.3
Hydrocarbons	140,000	2.8	385,000	7.8	525,000	10.6
Sulphur dioxide	400,000	8.1	11,000	0.2	411,000	8.3
Nitrogen oxides	93,000	1.9	39,000	0.8	132,000	2.7
Total	894,000	18.1	4,047,800	81.9	4,941,800	100.0

Source: Bravo Alvarez (1987).

Table 7.14 **Average concentration of lead in the atmosphere of Mexico City, compared with several cities in the United States, 1970**

City	Micrograms per m^3
Mexico	5.1
Cincinnati	1.4
Philadelphia	1.6
Los Angeles	2.5
New York	2.5

Source: Bravo Alvarez (1987).

average value of 5 $\mu g/m^3$ 1968 (Halffter and Ezcurra 1983) and around 6 $\mu g/m^3$ in 1986 (four times the Mexican standard of 1.5 $\mu g/m^3$, see table 7.14).

The problem became so critical that from 1980 on the national oil company (PEMEX) gradually decreased the concentration of lead in the gasolines sold in Mexico City (table 7.15). In September 1986, regular leaded gasoline in the basin was replaced by a low-lead fuel in which synthetic oxidizing additives replaced the action of leaded compounds. The change produced unexpected side-effects. Although the atmospheric concentration of lead indeed decreased, ozone concentrations rose quickly as a result of a reaction between ultraviolet solar radiation, atmospheric oxygen, and the oxidizing effect of the new gasoline additives (Bravo Alvarez et al. 1991). The present mean ozone concentration is, on average, around 0.15 ppm (300 $\mu g/m^3$), 10 times the normal atmospheric concentration, more than double

Table 7.15 **Concentration of lead tetra-ethyl in Mexican gasolines, 1978–1990 (ml/litre)**

	Type of gasoline	
Year	Regular	Extra
1978	0.77	0.770
1979	0.77	0.018
1980	0.77	0.018
1981	0.66	0.018
1982	0.48	0.018
1983	0.44	0.018
1984	0.22	0.018
1985	0.22	0.011
1986	0.14	0.011
1987	0.14	0.011
1988	0.14	0.011
1989	0.14	0.011
1990[a]	0.14	0.011
1991	0.14[b] 0.00[c]	

Source: Bravo Alvarez, Sosa, and Torres (1991).

a. Last year that Extra gasoline was sold.
b. For pre-1991 vehicles.
c. For 1991 vehicles with catalytic converters.

the maximum limit in the United States and Japan (Avediz Asnavourian 1984), and high enough to damage most of the urban vegetation (Skärby andSelldén 1984). Because of the time-lag involved in the formation of ozone, the highest ozone levels are registered towards the south-west of the city in the direction of the prevailing winds. During the winter of 1987–1988, the ozone levels in this area exceeded the maximum allowable standard (0.11 ppm) more than 50 per cent of the time and generated continuous health complaints from the population.

The distribution of air pollutants within the city is not uniform. Whereas suspended particles and sulphur dioxide tend to concentrate above the industrial sectors of the city (north and north-east) (fig. 7.6), carbon monoxide shows high concentrations near the centre of the city, where automobile emissions are greatest. Ozone, which is a result of photochemical reactions, is produced from pollutant precursors with a certain time-lag. Thus, ozone tends to concentrate towards the south-west, as the dominant winds usually blow

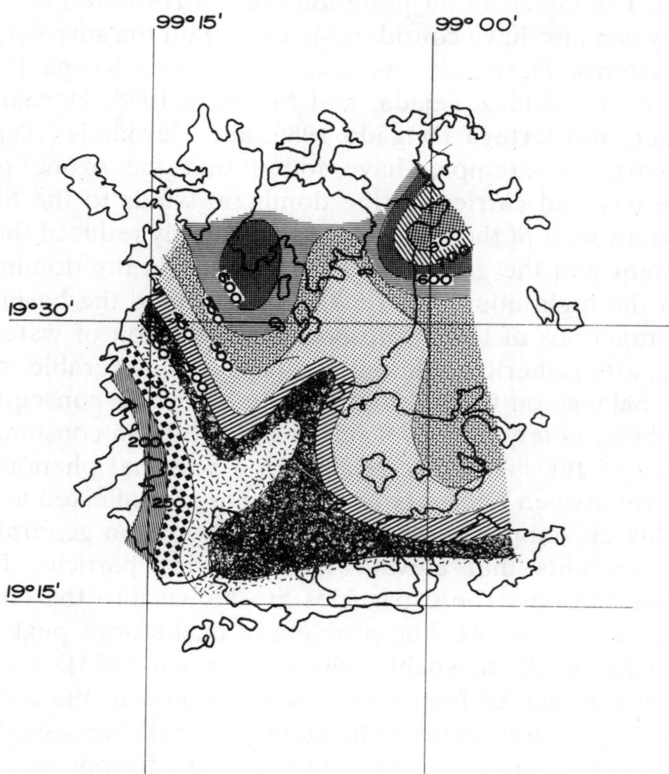

Fig. 7.6 **Concentration of suspended particles ($\mu g/m^3$), sulphur dioxide (ppm), carbon monoxide (ppm), and ozone (ppm) above Mexico City, 1990 (Source: Jáuregui, 1990)**

from the north-east. It is interesting to note that the south-west of the city is a residential area, with relatively open spaces and lower population densities. In spite of being one of the environmentally most benign areas of the city, it receives the highest concentrations of ozone, the worst pollutant during 1991.

Atmospheric pollution also has a considerable influence on the quality of rainwater. Páramo and colleagues (1987; see also Bravo Alvarez 1987) reported, for the 1983–1986 period, a significant decrease in the pH of incoming rainwater in Mexico City owing to the increasing concentration of sulphur and nitrogen oxides in the air. In the urban parts of the basin the average pH of rainwater is around 5.5, and a few rain events have been registered with pH values as low as 3.0. The effects of air pollution are not restricted to the urban areas; they can also have considerable impact on the surrounding natural ecosystems. Hernández Tejeda, Bauer, and Krupa (1985; see also Bauer, Hernández Tejeda, and Manning 1985; Hernández Tejeda, Bauer, and Ortega Delgado 1985; and Hernández Tejeda and Bauer 1986), for example, have found that the ozone produced above the city and carried by the dominant winds to the Sierra del Ajusco, south-west of the basin, have significantly reduced the chlorophyll content and the growth of *Pinus hartwegii*, the dominant pine species in the high mountains (*c*. 3,500 m) around the basin. One of the main functions of these forests is the collection of water for the city. Thus, atmospheric pollution may have a considerable impact on the water balance on the hillslopes of the basin and consequently on the availability and quality of water used for human consumption.

Drainage of the lake-beds, related to a seasonal phenomenon of dust storms between February and May, has also affected air quality. The midday air temperatures during the dry season generate strong advective currents that elevate salt and clay particles from the former lake bottom. These particles are blown into the city by the prevailing easterly winds. The problem of dust storms peaked in the 1970s and has declined slightly since (Jáuregui 1983). The decline (or at least the lack of increase) in soil particles in the atmosphere during the dry season seems to be associated with successful government efforts to vegetate the dry mud-bed of the former lake Texcoco (Jáuregi 1971, 1983), which has now become a pasture of halophyllous grasses and forbs. In spite of this moderate success, faecal contamination from wastewater is still common in the lake-beds, and the dust storms remain a potential source of infection. The concentration of faecal bacteria in the rainwater of Mexico City is 100–150 micro-organisms/litre (Soms García 1986). Gamboa (1983) sampled the micro-organisms suspended in the air of Mexico City and found a significantly high frequency of potential pathogens.

The driving forces of environmental change

The rapid rise and the enormous power of the Aztec state were based on the control of much of Mesoamerica and on the subordination of hundreds of different groups that paid tribute to the emperor. Aztec

Table 7.16 **Energy consumption in the Mexican Republic and in the Basin of Mexico, 1970–1975**

	Consumption (m³)[a]			
	1970		1975	
	Mexico	Basin of Mexico	Mexico	Basin of Mexico
Oil	34,060,003	9,215,600 (27.1%)	48,081,005	13,202,132 (27.5%)
Electricity	2,320,482	753,874 (32.5%)	3,708,698	1,065,554 (28.7%)
Coal	1,470,000	0	2,616,000	0
Total	37,850,485	9,969,474 (26.3%)	54,405,703	14,267,686 (26.2%)

Source: Ibarra, Saavedra, Fuente, and Schteingart (1986).

a. The numbers in parentheses indicate the proportion used by the Basin of Mexico with respect to the whole country.

wealth depended to some extent on the concentration of high-quality goods (e.g. metals, obsidian, tropical fruits, high protein food) and labour collected as tribute from conquered groups. Even with the highly productive *chinampa* system and dry-field and irrigated terraces throughout the slopes, the Basin of Mexico probably had to subsidize a sizeable portion of its food and fibre during Aztec times from elsewhere and took food from considerable distances during times of famine (Williams 1989).

This tradition of concentration persists today. Intensified by the Spaniards and during independence, it has now reached staggering proportions. Approaching 20 million residents and with most of its agricultural lands and water taken over by settlement, the basin generates only a small fraction of its resource needs (table 7.16) and must import vast amounts of food, energy, wood, water, building materials, and many other products. In effect, other ecosystems, often to their own economic and environmental detriment, subsidize the water and energy flows of the basin. This subsidization is possible because Mexico City is the hub of an immense concentration of economic and political power that permits it to concentrate resources as well.

Critical to understanding the driving forces of environmental change, then, is a system of subsidies, in terms of both natural (ecological subsidies) and financial resources (economic subsidies), underpinned by social institutions and organizations that legitimate and implement them. This system represents the "how" of sustaining the process of concentration, but it is its forces of demand and production that ultimately drive environmental changes in the basin. These integrative forces are population change, governmental policy, and technological capacity.

We are unable here to demonstrate quantitatively the linkage of each of these proposed driving forces to environmental change *per se*. We are stymied by the paucity of quantitative measures of these forces, save for population change. Our claims, therefore, reflect qualitative judgements regarding the major forces that shape demand for natural resources in the basin, including those that exacerbate demand by not dealing adequately with its environmental impacts.

Population change

The Mexican model of development has given priority to improving the quality of life in the large cities, in which demand and political power are more concentrated, at the expense of the rural areas, which have become comparatively poorer. As a result, from 1950 to 1980 the basin experienced marked improvements in demographic and domestic indicators of quality of life (table 7.17), exceeding those for the country as a whole and especially those of impoverished rural areas. Public services such as education, potable water, and sewerage are underdeveloped in the poorer areas of central and southern Mexico. In the Mixtec region south of the basin, for example, the proportion of houses with drinking water is less than 4 per cent, and most of the towns do not have sewerage systems. The rural

Table 7.17 **Evolution of the quality of life indicators for the Basin of Mexico, 1950–1980**

Indicator	Basin of Mexico 1950	Basin of Mexico 1960	Basin of Mexico 1970	Basin of Mexico 1980	Mexican Republic[a] 1980
Life expectancy at 1 year of age (years)	55.0	60.8	63.2	65.2	64.4
Infant mortality (%)	12.0	7.9	7.4	4.3	7.1
Adult literacy (%)	83.8	88.4	92.6	95.6	83.0
% of houses with running water	n.a.	35.0	53.0	67.0	n.a.
% of houses with drainage	n.a.	33.0	63.0	81.3	n.a.
% of houses owned by their residents	n.a.	34.0	50.0	52.7	n.a.

Source: Ibarra, Saavedra, Fuente, and Schteingart (1986).
n.a. = not available

a. Values for the Mexican Republic are given for comparison purposes.

poor, then, view the basin not only as a concentration of potential employment but as an improvement in the quality of life, at least in terms of education, health services, and so on. These push–pull factors drive rural migrants to the basin, generating most of the enormous population growth there.

Population growth cannot be ignored as a major driver of environmental change in the basin because of the overwhelming demands for resources and generation of effluents that follow from it. At the current growth rate, estimated at approximately 4 per cent, the population doubles every 15–18 years, and with it the demand for water, electricity, transportation, and housing more than doubles. For example, the number of automobiles grows at an annual rate of about 8 per cent, and doubles every decade. In turn, this increase in cars has enormous impacts on air quality in the basin. If the population levels of the basin were lower and growth rates smaller, the magnitude of environmental changes would surely have been less; comparisons with environmental conditions in the 1950s illustrate this claim.

Governmental policy

Governmental policy has acted as a driving force in at least three ways: it has promoted the concentration of employment and services in the basin, subsidized resources that sustain this employment, and aggravated the environmental impacts of demand through environmental policies.

Since Aztec times, the basin has been a "primate place" where all political and economic power rested. This primacy has fostered decisions to promote industrial, governmental, and service activities in the basin, providing employment and attracting population. Services are, in effect, underwritten by the country at large. For example, buses, trolley-buses, and the metro train now cost approximately US$0.10 per trip, a fixed tariff that is independent of the distance travelled. The metro train, which transports 3 million passengers per day (Bravo Alvarez 1986), generates a revenue of US$300,000 per day, but the real cost of operating the system is in the order of US$1.5 million per day (Bazdresch 1986). The difference is ultimately met by all taxpayers, many of whom reap no benefit from the service in any way. Other services, such as electricity, gas, garbage collection, and road maintenance, are subsidized for the whole country and not only for the Basin of Mexico. Because the city receives these services in a higher proportion than the rest of the nation, however, it also receives a higher share of the subsidy, as in the case of energy.

Having exceeded the resource base of the basin itself, policy makers have turned to subsidies from elsewhere. These need not be reiterated here, save for the example of water, noted above. Unable to meet the demand for water, officials have met chronic shortages in the basin by importing water from the Lerma and Cutzamala basins (Bazdresch 1986). At the same time, the export of sewage water into the Tula basin is contaminating that system. Water costs around US\$0.10/m^3 to distribute in Mexico City, largely owing to the high costs of pumping water into the basin (Bazdresch 1986). The government spends approximately US\$150 million per year to supply water to the Basin of Mexico, but the revenue collected is in the order of US\$42 million, less than 30 per cent of the total cost.

The official response to environmental deterioration in the Basin of Mexico has largely helped to sustain the problems. Solid waste, for example, was disposed of in open dump-yards surrounded by poor neighbourhoods until 1986 (Ezcurra 1990b). Only when government officials realized that the yards were infiltrating toxic leachates into the aquifer and contaminating the air – thus affecting the entire basin, not just the immediate neighbourhoods – did they make a decision to dump waste in confined trenches designed expressly for the purpose.

In another example, the Mexican Index of Air Quality (IMECA) has been copied almost verbatim from the National Ambient Air Quality Standard (NAAQS) of the United States (SEDUE 1985), which in turn was derived from an index proposed by Thom and Ott (1975). Table 7.18, which offers a comparison of the three indexes, reveals that IMECA minimizes the risks involved in different levels of atmospheric pollution. That is, for a similar concentration of air pollutants, the Mexican standard informs the population of risks much milder than those really involved. Similarly, during the winter season when atmospheric thermal inversions abound and render the air quality unacceptably poor almost every day, the health authorities inform the public to take care against influenza and other respiratory diseases, thereby implying that these diseases are related to seasonal ills rather than to pollution. In short, governmental policies have ignored environmental problems until they become dangerous to human occupation. Such disregard actually promotes the drivers of environmental change by not controlling them.

Table 7.18 **Comparison of the Mexican air-quality index (IMECA), against Ott and Thom's index and the National Ambient Air Quality Standard (NAAQS) of the United States, for similar pollution levels**

Index	IMECA description	Ott and Thom	NAAQS
0–50	Favourable environment for all sorts of physical activities	Good	Below NAAQS
51–100	Favourable environment for all sorts of physical activities	Satisfactory	Below NAAQS
101–200	Slight reaction in sensitive persons	Unhealthy	Above NAAQS
201–300	Reaction and relative intolerance towards physical exercise in persons with breathing or cardiovascular problems. Slight reaction in the population in general.	Dangerous	Alert
301–400	Diverse symptoms and intolerance towards physical exercise in healthy people.	Dangerous	Warning
401–500	Diverse symptoms and intolerance towards physical exercise in healthy people.	Dangerous	Emergency
501 +	(Not described)	Significant harm	Significant harm

Source: Thom and Ott (1975).

Technological capacity

Environmental problems have not been seen as such in part because of a "technological-fix" mentality that seeks solutions through technological change, largely on the supply side. After all, did not economic and technological growth from 1950 to 1980, on average, lead to increases in the material standard of living for the people of the basin during a time of major environmental change? This mind-set prevails in the case of coping with water shortages by enlisting the requisite technology for long-distance transport of the water. A plan developed in the early 1970s sought to serve the immediate water needs of the basin by using an even more extensive pumping system to import water from the states of Morelos, Tlaxcala, and Puebla

(Guerrero, Moreno, and Garduño 1982). An extreme faith in the technological capacity to handle the impacts of human actions on the environment has bred complacency and thwarted inclinations to deal with those actions themselves.

In another vein, technological capacity has acted as a direct agent of environmental change by enhancing people's access to and use of the resources of the basin. Increasing numbers of people are acquiring more and more ability to consume resources, be it through electrical and water systems or automobiles. Simply stated, the concentration of technology in the basin increases resource use and damage, especially compared with the country as a whole (but not with other major urban centres).

In summary, the driving forces of environmental change in the basin reflect a systemic relationship among long-term policies (institutions and organizations) to promote growth and concentrate wealth, the demographic and technological responses to these policies, and the specific mitigations to counter the impacts brought on by the "concentration" ethic. The entire system of causes, extending back at least to Aztec times, has been predicated on external subsidies of resources to the basin. These subsidies have subsequently grown in scale and expanded in kind to the point that the basin provides little more than a physical locale for a huge metropolitan complex.

The vulnerability of the basin

On the basis of open space, water availability, water and air quality, and sewage treatment, the Basin of Mexico may well be approaching the limits beyond which it will be economically infeasible to continue subsidizing these resources and facets of the environment at current levels. In this case, the likelihood of sustaining the current quality of life in the basin is questionable. Current indicators provide strong reasons to believe that these limits are being approached rapidly. Projections of present trends (table 7.19) show that Mexico City may well spread over 2,700 km^2 by the year 2000, possibly spilling over the boundaries of the basin into the adjacent basins and drainages of Toluca, Querétaro, Cuernavaca, and Puebla. Perhaps 30 million people will live in the basin, which will have changed from the patchy mixture of urban and rural environments typical of the first half of this century to a massive and overcrowded urban sprawl.

Table 7.19 **Population, total urban area, and vegetated areas per person for the Metropolitan Area of Mexico City, 1950 and 1980, and projected values for the year 2000**

	1950	1980	2000
Population (million)	3.0	13.8	32.7
Total urban area (km²)	215	980	2,700
Total urban green areas (m²/person)	29.0	9.9	5.6
Parks, gardens, and recreational areas (m²/person)	9.0	5.9	5.0

By that time, around 100 m³ per second of water will have to be extracted from inside and outside sources, unless new and more efficient wastewater treatment and recycling methods are adopted soon. The source for this future hydrological subsidy from other watersheds into the Basin of Mexico is not clear yet. Other basins have been mentioned as potential water sources, but it will require an enormous expenditure of energy (in the order of 3 million MW hours per year) to pump such huge volumes of water, as well as significant ecological alterations and water shortages in the supplier basins.

One cannot be optimistic about these prospects. The current system is viable only by enormous levels of subsidies, which would have to increase significantly to sustain continued growth under current resource uses. In this sense, the environmental and economic systems in the basin appear to be in a state of high vulnerability to perturbations of several kinds, all of which would affect the quality of life of the basin's inhabitants.

Factors of environmental endangerment

Vegetation and open space

The settlement and paving of the basin's last open lands is occurring at a rapid rate, creating conditions of exceptional crowding and little open space. At the current pace of change, 92 per cent of the basin will soon be houses and roads. Each person will have only 5 m² of green area (table 7.19), and in extremely poor areas this space will be reduced to 1 m². The few patches of "preserved" vegetation (e.g. reserves) will also be consumed. Hence, open spaces and "natural" vegetation are highly endangered in the basin.

Water quality and quantity

During this century, the Basin of Mexico has evolved from a high level of self-sufficiency in natural resources to a complete dependence on imports from other regions. Most of the lacustrine area, which represents the best soils of the basin, is now occupied by buildings; the aquifer level has been drawn down by more than 10 m in some areas, and water quality is degraded. This is particularly noticeable in the south in Xochimilco and Chalco. *Chinampa* agriculture still exists, but is fast disappearing owing to the declining water table and the inadequate recharge of canal waters with partially treated wastewater. Therefore, most of the vegetables consumed within the basin are imported from outside its boundaries. The main problems associated with water quality are its bacterial contamination and chemical pollution as well as the contamination of crops irrigated with wastewater.

The second important problem associated with water is the availability and renewability of the resource. If a daily quota of 300 litres per capita is considered, then the recharge rate of around 27 m^3 per second can supply water for 7–8 million people. In theory, this is a reasonable carrying capacity for the population of the basin. Any population density above this threshold will necessarily mean, in the long term, obtaining extra water from the catchment of rainwater during the wet season, recycling and treating wastewater, or importing water into the basin at very high cost. The basin surpassed this supply level in the 1960s.

Pumping from external sources into the Basin of Mexico is inefficient and expensive. The pumping system from the Cutzamala basin, for example, must elevate water flow some 1,100 m, and requires a constant energy input of 190 MW (SARH 1985). The whole water system in the basin, which includes the Cutzamala and Lerma basins, the deep-well pumps, and the drainage system, requires around 400 MW on average (i.e. the system uses 3–4 million MW hours per year; Castillo 1991). For comparison, this energy input is 53 per cent of the energy produced at peak operation (750 MW) by the thermoelectric generating plant of the Basin of Mexico which supplies energy to the city, 33 per cent of the energy produced at peak operation by Chicoasén, the largest (1,200 MW) hydroelectric dam in Mexico (García de Miranda and Falcón de Gyves 1972), and 31 per cent of the energy that the two nuclear generators at Laguna Verde will produce when they finally start full operations (1,280 MW). The energy costs involved in pumping water into, within, and out of the Basin of Mexico appear at present as one of the most limiting factors to the growth of Mexico City.

Waste

At present waste is not classified in Mexico City, and very little recycling occurs. Most of the waste that is recycled is processed by *pepenadores* (i.e. people who gather waste), but no official effort has been made to reduce the amount of waste dumped by the city. Most experts believe that solid waste disposal will remain a problem until a better disposal service is implemented and more regulations are applied (Aguilar Sahagún 1984) and, above all, until waste-processing plants are built to cope with the large output of garbage produced by the city (Monroy Hermosillo 1987; Trejo Vázquez 1987). Owing to its high content in organic residues, the garbage generated by Mexico City could be used for making compost at a relatively low cost if litter were classified according to its recycling characteristics. Solid waste of industrial origin, which forms 48 per cent of all the city waste, represents a potential problem since toxic waste may be combined with other types of refuse.

Air quality

As noted above, air quality is literally dangerous in some sections of the basin and at certain times of the year when thermal inversions trap pollutants within the basin. Automobile emissions, which account for 85 per cent of all atmospheric pollutants, cause much of the pollution. Automobiles are increasing at a 7 per cent annual rate of growth. Given a 10-year average life-span of a car in the basin, a 1991 measure requiring catalytic converters in new cars may not have a significant effect on air quality until the late 1990s. In addition, the Mexican standard for maximum allowable exhaust emissions in new vehicles is two to three times more permissive than that of, for example, the United States (tables 7.18, 7.20, and 7.21).

Despite a series of controls inserted to combat air pollution (see below), air quality has not improved much. Not only have some individual pollutants frequently exceeded what are considered to be healthy limits, as is the case with ozone, but globally the air quality index (IMECA) has surpassed 200 points during most of the recent years, indicating that at least one pollutant is well above the healthy limit. These levels of pollution represent a serious danger to human health.

Table 7.20 **Emission standards for new vehicles in Mexico and in the United States (g/km per vehicle)**

	1975		1985	
	Mexico	USA	Mexico	USA
Hydrocarbons	2.5	0.9	2.6	0.5
Carbon monoxide	29.2	9.4	24.2	9.4
Nitrogen oxides	(no standard)	1.93	2.2	0.62

Source: Bravo Alvarez (1987).

Table 7.21 **Lead content in regular gasoline for different countries, compared with Mexico (ml of lead tetra-ethyl per litre of gasoline)**

Country	1980	1987	1991
England	0.28	zero	zero
Germany	0.15	zero	zero
Mexico	0.77	0.14	0.14 (leaded) zero (unleaded)

Source: Bravo Alvarez (1987).

If the growth in automobiles continues, then the overall impacts on air quality may remain more or less the same, even with the increased use of catalytic converters. Mass transit, responsible for about 23–30 per cent of all vehicular emissions, already transports 81 per cent of all passengers in the basin (Bravo Alvarez 1986); it is doubtful, however, that major improvements will follow from major shifts in ridership on mass transit. The average emission of pollutants per passenger using private vehicles is 10 times higher than that of passengers using public transportation. Vulnerability associated with air quality, then, very much hinges on sustained controls on automobile exhaust and on reducing the number of cars on the road.

The response to the environmental problem

Government's response: New environmental policies

Since 1970 Mexican environmental policy has passed through two main phases. The first one, from 1970 to 1982, involved two presidential terms, those of J. López Portillo and L. Echeverría, whereas the second phase, from 1983 to 1990, involved the mandates of Miguel de la Madrid and Carlos Salinas de Gortari. In the first phase, the debate about environmental degradation started with the first Law of Environmental Protection (*Diario Oficial*, 23 March 1971) and the creation of the Subsecretaría de Mejoramiento del Ambiente (SMA; Subsecretary for Environmental Improvement) within the Ministry of Public Health. Although this stage produced the first institutional mechanisms of environmental protection, it also betrayed a lack both of specific actions to prevent pollution and of a comprehensive view to deal with the growing environmental problem. Even so, during this period people started to be conscious of the deteriorating environmental quality in Mexico City and its impacts on human health and living standards.

During the second phase (1983–1990), environmental policy obtained a higher political status through the creation of government agencies devoted exclusively to the environment and through an increase in specific regulations and programmes. In the first half of the 1980s, the coordination of all government actions to prevent and control pollution passed from the Subministry of Health Assistance of the Ministry of Public Health to the recently created Ministry of Urban Development and Ecology (SEDUE), where a Subsecretary of Ecology was created. Additionally, a National Commission of Ecology was established in 1985 to define priorities in environmental matters and to coordinate the different public institutions dealing with environmental actions. As a result of these changes in national policies came an administrative change in the government of Mexico City (i.e. the Department of the Federal District, or DDF), which incorporated a Commission of Ecology in 1984 and, a year later, a General Directorate of Urban Planning and Ecological Protection to deal with decision-making on environmental problems within the city.

Until the mid-1980s, however, very limited actions were carried out to prevent pollution, mainly owing to the deep economic crisis that the country had faced since 1982, a situation aggravated by the 1985 earthquake in Mexico City. In this context the environmental problem lost its priority in relation to financial constraints and living standards. From 1986 onwards, social pressure mounted owing to the lack of effective action to prevent environmental deterioration and to the ever-increasing levels of air pollution in the city, particularly during winter. As a result, in 1986 the government of the Federal District formulated new programmes and specific regulations defining stricter pollution-control measures.

At the beginning of 1986, SEDUE announced a set of 21 anti-pollution measures to be applied in Mexico City. Among these, the following were the most important:

1. 2,000 state-owned public service buses were converted to run on new, low-emission engines;
2. non-polluting urban electric transport was extended to include 4.7 km of new lines for underground trains and 116 km of new lines for tramways, trolley-buses, and light trains;
3. solid wastes were dumped in sanitary landfills and the old open-space dumps were covered;
4. a programme was begun gradually to substitute natural gas for oil as fuel in the thermoelectric generators in the basin;
5. the metropolitan zone of Mexico City was supplied with low-lead gasoline in 1986;
6. a programme was established gradually to incorporate anti-pollution devices in new automobiles (*Gaceta Oficial DDF*, March 1986).

For the first time these measures tried to quantify actions and to set specific time-periods for their implementation. Together with these measures, highly oriented to control air pollution, the Urban Development Plan for the Federal District was approved in 1987. The establishment of an ecological reserve of 85,554 ha to the south of the basin in the Ajusco and the Chichinautzin ranges, where urban expansion was to be contained, agricultural activities were to be stimulated, and forest areas were to be preserved and expanded, betrays a primary concern with preserving the southern forests of the basin, which are also the most important water catchment areas for the city.

In 1989, under the mandate of Salinas de Gortari, the definition of an official environmental policy continued, clearly becoming a political priority. At a national level, a new Law of Ecological Equilibrium and Environmental Protection (1989) was passed and a National Programme for Environmental Protection (1990–1994) appeared in the National Development Plan. Along these lines, and as part of a more direct political response to the serious pollution problem, a programme against atmospheric pollution in the Mexico City Metropolitan Zone was announced in 1990. This programme included four main policy decisions: (1) to rationalize the urban transport system; (2) to improve the quality of fuels used in the basin; (3) to install systems to control polluting emissions from vehicles, industries, and service facilities; (4) to regenerate natural areas with high ecological disturbance.

To a great extent, this new programme was a continuation of the "21 measures" of the previous government and, it is apparent, the strategies were more oriented towards controlling critical levels of air pollution. The main actions taken in this new programme included the following measures.

1. Emission of atmospheric pollutants was to be controlled in service facilities such as public baths, dry-cleaning shops, and laundries. These places frequently did not comply with technical standards owing to their old equipment and a notorious lack of maintenance.
2. Industries in the basin were to be inspected regularly and systematically in order to verify the correct functioning of their pollution-monitoring and emission-control equipment. The use of this type of equipment became mandatory for all industries.
3. Checking vehicular exhaust emissions every six months became mandatory in late 1989, for both official and private vehicles. From 1991 onwards, the regulation was changed to compulsory verification every six months for heavy-use vehicles only and yearly for all other vehicles.
4. The use of each car was banned one day of the week, according to the numbers on the licence plate. The programme, initiated in the 1989–1990 winter, was aimed at reducing the circulation of vehicles to approximately 500,000 cars on average during working days. Currently, it is still in force, although some people have tried to outwit the ban by purchasing second, or even third, vehicles (often older heavy polluters).
5. The levels of lead in gasoline were to decrease even more than in 1986, and in 1991 unleaded gasoline was introduced to the basin and the use of catalytic converters became obligatory in all new cars. The lower levels of lead, however, increased the amount of unburnt oil residues, which in turn increased the ozone formed in the air of the city during daylight hours.
6. The two thermoelectric generating plants that work in the basin of Mexico increased their consumption of natural gas as a substitute for oil.

Despite these measures, atmospheric pollution has remained at critical levels.

Many factors have contributed to the sluggish response of official environmental policy. First, a marked delay has occurred in the application of the technical norms that regulate atmospheric emissions. Although the atmospheric problem was clear to many experts by the mid-1970s, strict government control started only when air pollution was overwhelming in its magnitude, and substantial lag time separates the enforcement of control and the observation of environmental impacts.

Second, the political will to apply continuous and strict anti-pollution measures has been weak in relation to the economic interests of the main polluting industries. Such is the case of the automobile industry, which for years avoided the use of anti-pollution devices in new models, and of the industrial sector in Mexico City, which for many years avoided the installation of emission controls. Industries have enjoyed the protection of favourable treatment from government officers who did not wish to drive large companies away and found an excuse for not including industrial emissions in the financial costs of pollution control. It was not until the 1990–1991 winter that many industries faced formal closure and large penalties for not complying with the environmental legislation.

Lastly, for many years, government agencies consistently minimized the real danger posed by air pollution. They not only played down the real consequences of air pollution, but they used indices measuring air quality in a way that, by averaging over time and over different stations, hid local peaks in the concentration of pollutants. This self-deluding attitude was shared by many public officers who really believed that the problem was not so serious as some scientists and civil organizations contended.

Thus, the perception of the environmental situation by government decision makers has focused mainly on reducing air pollution and only secondarily on the regeneration of heavily disturbed or eroded natural areas. The current governmental approach does not include many other environmental problems and it does not address the more comprehensive issues of the causes of these problems and their differential impacts owing to poverty and social inequality.

The public administration has responded with strict measures to what it perceives as a potential source of political trouble, but the lack of a long-term vision of the problem may lead to rather ephemeral solutions. For example, the decrees that make car-exhaust checks mandatory and force citizens to stop using their cars one day during the week were aimed at reducing emissions by 10–20 per cent. With the number of cars growing at a rate of 6–8 per cent a year, however, the measures will have only limited effect in the short term, and the problem will continue and even worsen for several years.

The social response: Environmental activism

Environmental problems have acutely affected the Basin of Mexico for the last 15–20 years, but the inhabitants of the capital city have been relatively slow to respond. Lack of information about deteriorating environmental quality, basic ecological processes, and possible effects of increasing pollution levels has contributed to this slow reaction. For example, the government's attitude tended to belittle the importance of air and water pollution as a rapidly growing problem. In 1985 and 1986, however, a critical point was reached in public awareness; television and radio announcements exhorted people to lead an environmentally sound life, a "cleaner" and "greener" way of living. But these calls for action failed to provide reliable information about the prevailing situation or about what specifically one should do to improve it. With severe air and water pollution, plus a marked water shortage that resulted from the 1985 earthquake, new attitudes were demanded from citizens. The slogan "pollution is each one of us" ("la contaminación somos todos") seems, according to official policy, to hold every citizen individually at fault for the severe environmental crisis. The changes in school schedules imposed in 1987 to decrease activity during the early morning hours, when thermal inversions are more pronounced, and the restrictions on the use of automobiles imposed in 1989 drew everyone's attention to something serious being at stake.

Ecology entered the Mexican government's discourse formally in 1982. Although many ministries were involved in activities with ecological backgrounds (Fisheries, Agriculture and Hydraulic Resources), it was only in 1982 that ecology became part of the government's official worries – and, hence, open to public scrutiny. That year Miguel de la Madrid, as one of his first actions as President of Mexico, created a ministry called SEDUE, short for Secretaría de Desarrollo Urbano y Ecología, which curiously but symptomatically integrated urban development and ecology. During his campaign, de la Madrid had trumpeted an urgent need for a "national ecological awareness" to avoid the "historical immorality" represented by the destruction of nature as a consequence of modern development. Some 10 years later, ecology became an official issue, and a public issue.

It was during this period of transition from governmental indifference to, or lack of responsibility for, or both, the sudden decision to become "clean" that people organized and responded in different ways. The inhabitants of the Basin of Mexico, as well as some people living elsewhere, had certainly been conscious, in one way or another, of environmental changes prior to governmental pronouncements. The official framework, however, enhanced the social responses. Environmental activists, who had been considered radicals before 1986, suddenly became part of official discourse. In addition to urban-ecology activism, some academic groups had, since the early 1970s, developed political activities to protect natural zones outside Mexico City. Ecological activism had, for example, halted the construction of a nuclear reactor on Lake Patzcuaro, Michoacán. In this case, the inhabitants of the lake's shore, including Indian communities, gathered to oppose this project and finally succeeded in stopping it. The discussion around this issue aroused the environmental awareness of many people in different parts of Mexico.

In the deeply affected Basin of Mexico, however, organized reactions were sparse until the mid-1980s. Before this time, only a few groups of citizens had formed temporarily to oppose specific actions affecting the district in which they lived. The widening of avenues at the expense of parks, sidewalks, and green areas with trees sparked the Green Brigades in 1977, but their activities ended quite unsuccessfully in 1979. Both the importance and the weaknesses of this type of association become evident if we recall that, in the meantime, green movements and parties had become important in Western Europe as a reaction to nuclear energy, pollution, and environmental destruction in general. European ecological groups were heterogeneous in origins and aims, but none the less they had a strong influence in Mexico.

In 1983 the first ecological association with political aims was formed in Coyoacán under the name of Asociación Ecológica de Coyoacán (Coyoacan Ecological Association). Originally, Coyoacán was a small town some distance away from Mexico City, but urban growth incorporated it into the perimeter of Mexico City (as it incorporated many other surrounding places). Today, it still preserves many colonial buildings and is considered to be a trendy place, where middle- and upper-class intellectuals like to live. The group was worried about the protection and conservation of the so-called "ecological equilibrium" in the Basin of Mexico, and it identified itself as independent of any links with political, religious, government, or industrial organizations. Other similar groups were formed in succeeding years, such as the Alianza Ecologista Nacional, self-defined as a "free and natural human organization where individual and group efforts are gathered to improve, protect and restore the environment" (Sandoval and Semo 1985a). These associations acted successfully against some official decisions that would have degraded the basin's environment and several other ecosystems in the country.

Despite their success in specific actions, these groups lacked a comprehensive and general proposal for the environmental management of the basin and the growth policy of the city. Many other groups of this type, identified by Semo and Sandoval (1985) as "green romantics," formed in different districts of Mexico City, and in 1984 they all got together in the Red Alternativa de Ecocomunicación (Alternative Network of Eco-Communication). Eclectic from the start, the network gathered advocates of alternative technologies, anti-nuclear activists, "post-hippies" worried about nature, people engaged with oriental philosophies, disenchanted leftists, and other marginal/radical groups. As might be expected, this group did not last for long, nor did it produce any lasting results, but it was a starting point for many other social experiments working with environmental problems.

Groups of intellectuals (among whom the lack of scientists is remarkable) interested in environmental issues were also formed. Among them, the self-appointed Grupo de los 100 (Group of 100) had an important impact on public opinion. One hundred artists, including painters, musicians, poets, and writers, gathered around the motto "No crisis can justify our sacrifice. We have the right to live." As was the case with all the other groups mentioned, this group has opposed various policies without producing a comprehensive analysis or a general proposal about its own environmental objectives. Because members of the group are well known, however, their complaints and opinions have been well received by a large part of the Mexican middle class.

Other environmental associations formed during the 1980s with more practical goals, often with the help of technical supervisors. Included in this group are, for example, associations of land-squatters who have enlisted environmental arguments to protect their tenancy, and associations of *campesinos* (peasants) who defend their land against the encroachment posed by urban growth on environmental grounds. These groups tend to be local and their aims are very specific; they lack the political influence and communication capability that characterize, for example, the Grupo de los 100.

Quadri (1990) and Semo and Sandoval (1985) recognize that, by 1985, four major kinds of environmental groups could be identified at the Encuentro Nacional de Ecologistas (National Meeting of Ecological Activists):

1. a group of opponents to almost any governmental proposal, heirs of the European anti-nuclear movements and proponents of this movement in Mexico;
2. people worried about the extinction of species and the loss of ecosystems (usually conservative in political outlook, this group has a romantic view of conservation that none the less has helped to create an awareness of ecological deterioration);
3. groups searching for alternative, environmentally sound technologies (these groups inherit positions from the United States and West European countries, involving such measures as paper recycling, where ecologically oriented production and consumption are good business. Though the impact of environmentally sound production and consumption in Mexico is still to be evaluated, it does express itself through specific issues. For example, traditional resource use among Indians is respected throughout the country as a non-destructive way to utilize nature. This tradition has enriched the views and consolidated public respect for a people who think that the environment can be transformed and exploited successfully without irreversibly destroying it);
4. people whose main concern is the political side of the environmental crisis, because they believe that the solution to environmental degradation lies in political decisions (as might be expected, the range of political positions within this group is large, and disagreements are more frequent than agreements; for Quadri, 1990, the Grupo de los 100 is a typical example of this trend).

Ten years of social response have yet to have the kinds of impacts on environmental issues one might imagine, in part because the various groups have been fragmented and not coordinated in their activities. In 1986, the Movimiento Ecológico Mexicano (Mexican Ecological Movement) and the Pacto de Grupos Ecologistas (Pact of Ecological Groups) brought together many of the environmentally active organizations. A third group, the Federación de Conservacionista Mexicana (Mexican Conservationist Federation), also exists, but its primary focus is the conservation of natural ecosystems and it has had little impact within the Basin of Mexico.

The environmental problems of the basin appeared in the platforms of different political movements for the 1988 elections, motivated by the aftermath of the 1985 earthquake and by the new *organizaciones de barrios* (neighbourhood organizations). Public perception and awareness of these environmental problems seemed at that time to be changing very rapidly. The new political activism created a dynamic social situation, in which different groups were increasingly involved in environmental issues. The Convención del Anahuac, a centre–left, middle-class movement, was demanding an autonomous government for the Federal District, and also demanded stringent environmental protection measures (e.g. effective recycling of wastewater and protection of the remaining forests and *chinampa* fields). The Asamblea de Barrios, a popular working-class movement that arose after the 1985 earthquake, surprisingly expressed its support for these demands, and publicly attacked the official policy on public transport and the federal subsidy of the automobile industry.

This rather intense activism declined slowly after 1988, during the presidency of Carlos Salinas de Gortari. One of the most visible indications of this decline was the disintegration of the Pact of Ecological Groups. Its former members went in different directions: some remained as lone activists, some started to work within the new government administration, and others went back to their grass-roots organizations.

The reasons for these changes are still unclear. On the one hand, it seems that the ecological movement became disenchanted when some of its leaders accepted government posts. On the other, it seems that civil activism fluctuates with the presidential elections that occur every six years. Lastly, in 1991 the Partido Ecológico Mexicano, a political party, was registered to participate in the September 1991 elections, following the trend towards institutionalization of the European "greens."

What is currently clear is that: (1) the government is making a visible effort to meet some of the environmentally related demands of the people (even if the results are far from impressive); (2) the ecological movement has become institutionalized and has lost much of the dynamism that it displayed during the late 1980s; and (3) despite the undeniable effect that these organized efforts have had on societal attitudes towards environmental problems, ecological activism has not yet been able to halt or reverse the ongoing environmental crisis in the Basin of Mexico.

Review and conclusions

Although many of the environmental problems in the Basin of Mexico became severe in the late twentieth century, industrial development is not solely to blame. Urban primacy and political centralism have been a tradition in Mexican society at least since Aztec times. The Basin of Mexico, for nearly two millennia one of the most densely populated areas of the world, has used its pre-eminent administrative and political position to obtain advantages over other areas of the country. But modern industrialization, coupled with increasing technological capacity and political control, has dramatically exaggerated this historical trend and is responsible for the disproportionate urbanization and the biased distribution of population and wealth in the Basin of Mexico.

Since the revolution, a brand of economic development, which Sandbrook (1986) has called "conservative modernization," developed in Mexico through the alliance of three dominant sectors: the paternalistic post-revolutionary government, local private enterprises, and foreign capital. The goal of this alliance has been massive industrial development, often at the expense of social equality. The allocation of public resources, largely to the industrial sector, has accelerated urban growth. The Basin of Mexico concentrates government, public bureaucracy, a large middle class with a high capacity to consume, infrastructure such as electricity and roads, health services, and industries eager to profit from this growing market. These sectors have formed the "modern" part of the city, with its skyscrapers, large shopping centres, highways, and residential suburbs. Most of the city, however, consists of poor quarters inhabited by workers and underemployed persons who only a generation ago were peasants in rural Mexico and who migrated into the basin looking for a share in some of the services and goods that industrialization and urban development seem to promise. This migratory trend continues, and the metropolitan area is still expanding over forests and fields.

Unlike the past, current environmental change and resource constraints are not limited to those of the landscape or terrestrial ecology (e.g. draining the lacustrine system or deforestation). Now modern production and consumption have directly affected the biogeochemical flows that sustain air and water quality, and the pace and scale of environmental change are unprecedented. Importantly, the material standards of life in the basin, relative to impoverished rural areas, and as measured by common indicators (e.g. family income, health standards) have increased during the latter half of this century, a period that has witnessed some of the most rapid depletion of resources and a staggering array of environmental problems.

This circumstance occurred not from mining the basin's resources alone but from enormous levels of subsidies that brought (and still bring) critical resources to the basin and exported (and export) some of the environmental problems. The ability to continue this course in the face of the scale and pace of changes in demand seems highly unlikely, particularly in regard to water. The basin appears to be approaching, or has approached, a critical moment in its history in which a failure to address the problems associated with concentration may well trigger environmental biteback.

A strong decentralization policy promoting migration to smaller cities, promoting life in rural areas, and reducing the subsidies for the Basin of Mexico might stop the concentration process. But such a policy would cost hard currency in a country with a foreign debt of over US$100 billion, would go against the interests of both national and multinational industries, might also be disadvantageous in the short term for the workers of Mexico City, and could well create political problems for the party that supported it. People must be made aware of the seriousness of the environmental problem and provided with alternatives before demand-side actions are taken, such as those associated with decentralization.

Will awareness of the magnitude of the problem increase sufficiently to avert large-scale damage to the population? Or will the increasing incidence of health problems and the generalized deterioration in the standard of living trigger greater awareness and prospective solutions? We do not know, but almost every week during December 1991 and January 1992 air pollution levels reached levels considered dangerous under international standards. The booming automobile industry and the number of cars growing at a rate of around 8 per cent per year offer no reason to believe that the next few years will bring any improvements. Furthermore, the water shortage problem is likely to become more acute in the future, making the overall situation very difficult.

At a time of rapid change in the international arena, the future of the Basin of Mexico seems to be inextricably linked with the economic future that Latin America adopts and with the political and social model that the country adopts in the next decade. So far, the new winds of economic liberalization have had little or no impact on the general environmental problem. This, of course, may change in the future, but long-term government plans to deal with the problem are still lacking.

The long-term history of the basin is one of growth, collapse, and cultural rebirth, of catastrophic disintegration and cultural reorganization (Whitmore et al. 1990). Although more acute than ever before, centralism, resource dependence, and many of the other problems of the basin are not new. It is now in the hands of both government and society to find novel and original answers to the dramatic questions posed by the industrial development of the old Anahuac, the former capital of the Aztec empire.

Note

1. The preliminary results of the 1990 population census yielded a total population for the basin that is 4 million below the projected value, based on the 1980 census and on other official statistics from government sources (see tables 7.1 and 7.4). These differences could mean that the rate of migration into the basin is decreasing, but they could also mean that there is a large error in either or both the 1980 and 1990 censuses. As the 1990 statistics are still preliminary, it is not possible to speculate further on this subject until the official and definite data are released.

References

Aguilar Martínez, Adrián G. 1986. Contemporary urban planning in Mexico City. Its emergence, role and significance. Unpublished Ph.D. thesis, University of London.

Aguilar Martínez, Adrián G., and L. Godínez. 1989. *Desigualdad del ingreso y expansión metropolitana en México*. Vivienda 14, no. 2. Mexico: Instituto del Fondo Nacional de la Vivienda para los Trabajodores (INFONAVIT).

Aguilar Sahagún, G. 1984. Reglamentación en problemas de desechos solidos. In *Memorias de la I Reunión Regional sobre Legislación Ambiental, Monterrey, Nuevo León*, 35–45. Mexico: Secretaría de Desarrollo Urbano y Ecología.

Alvarez, Nogera José R., ed. 1985. *Imagen de la gran capital*. Mexico: Enciclopedia de México.

Aznavourian, A. 1984. Normas de calidad del aire en México. In *Memorias de la I Reunión Regional sobre Legislación Ambiental, Monterrey, Nuevo León*, 101–120. Mexico: Secretaría de Desarrollo Urbano y Ecología.

Barfoot, K. M., C. Vargas-Aburto, J. D. MacArthur, A. Jaidar, F. García-Santibáñez, and V. Fuentes-Gea. 1984. Multi-elemental measurements of air particulate pollution at a site in Mexico City. *Atmospheric Environment* 18: 467–451.

Barradas, V., and R. J-Seres. 1987. Los pulmones urbanos. *Ciencia y Desarrollo* 79: 61–72.

Bataillon, Claude, and Hélène Rivière d'Arc. 1973. *La ciudad de México*. Mexico, D.F.: SEP-Setentas.

Bauer, L. I. 1981. *Efectos de los gases tóxicos en la vegetación*. Seminario sobre administración y tecnología del medio ambiente. Chapingo, Mexico: Centro de Fitopatología, Colegio de Posgraduados.

Bauer, L. I., and S. V. Krupa. 1990. The Valley of Mexico: Summary of observational studies of air quality and effects on vegetation. *Environmental Pollution* 65: 109–118.

Bauer, L. I., T. Hernández Tejeda, and W. J. Manning. 1985. Ozone causes needle injury and tree decline in *Pinus hartwegii* at high altitudes in the mountains around Mexico City. *Journal of the Air Pollution Control Association* 35, no. 8: 838.

Bazdresch, C. 1986. Los subsidios y la concentración en la Ciudad de México. In *Descentralización y democracia en México*, ed. Blanca Torres, 205–218. Mexico, D.F.: El Colegio de México.

Bravo Alvarez, Humberto. 1986. La atmósfera de la Zona Metropolitana de la Ciudad de México. *Desarrollo y Medio Ambiente. Fundación Mex. Rest. Ambiental* 2: 2–3.

———. 1987. *La contaminación del aire en México*. Mexico. D.F: Fundación Universo Veintiuno.

Bravo Alvarez, Humberto, R. Sosa, and R. Torres. 1991. Ozono y lluvia ácida en la Ciudad de México. *Ciencias* 22: 33–40.

Bribiesca Castrejón, José L. 1960. *Hidrología histórica del Valle de México*. Mexico: Ingeniería Hidráulica en México, Jul–Sept.

Butzer, Karl W. 1991. Spanish colonization of the New World: Cultural continuity and change in Mexico. *Erdkunde* 45, no. 3: 205–219.

Butzer, Karl W., and Elizabeth K. Butzer. 1995 (forthcoming). Transfer of the Mediterranean livestock economy to New Spain: Adaptation and consequences. In *The Columbian encounter and global land-use/cover change*, ed. B. L. Turner II, A. Gomez Sal, and F. di Castri. Madrid: Consejo Superior de Investigaciones (CSI).

CAE (Consejo Asesor de Epidemiología). 1990. *Mexico: Información prioritaria en salud*. Mexico: Secretaría de Salud.

Calderón, E., and B. Hernández. 1987. Crecimiento actual de la población de México. *Ciencia y Desarrollo* 76: 49–66.

Calvillo-Ortega, M. T. 1978. Areas verdes de la ciudad de México. *Anuario de Geografía* 16: 377–382.

Castillo, H. 1991. Para salvar la ciudad. *Proceso* 793: 32–36.

DDF (Departamento del Distrito Federal). 1977. *Volumen de agua potable para la Ciudad de México, datos estimativos 1976*. Mexico: DDF, Dirección General de Obras Hidráulicas.

———. 1979. *Monitoreo de la calidad del agua del sistema de drenaje de la Ciudad de México*. Technical Report. Mexico: DDF, Dirección General de Construcción y Operación Hidráulicas.

———. 1986. *Manual de planeación, diseño y manejo de las áreas verdes urbanas del Distrito Federal*. Mexico: DDF.

———. 1987. Programas de desarrollo urbano del Distrito Federal. 1987–1988. Mexico. (Published in all Mexico City newspapers on 8 January 1987.)

———. 1989. *Estrategia Metropolitana para el Sistema Hidráulico del Valle de México*. Mexico: Gobierno del Estado de Mexico.

DGCOH (Dirección General de Construcción y Operación Hidráulicas). 1989. *El sistema Hidráulico del Distrito Federal. Estrategia para el periodo 1989–1994*. Internal report. Mexico: DGCOH and Departamento del Distrito Federal.

Ezcurra, Exequiel. 1990a. Basin of Mexico. In *The earth as transformed by human action: Global and regional changes in the biosphere over the past 300 years*, ed. B. L. Turner II, William C. Clark, Robert W. Kates, John F. Richards, Jessica T. Mathews, and William B. Meyer, 577–588. Cambridge: Cambridge University Press.

———. 1990b. *De las chinampas a la megalópolis: El medio ambiente en la Cuenca de México*. La Cienca desde México, 91. Mexico, D.F.: Fondo de Cultura Económica.

Ezcurra, Exequiel, and J. Sarukhán. 1990. Costos ecológicos del crecimiento y del mantenimiento de la Ciudad de México. In *Problemas de la Cuenca de México*, ed. J. Kumate and M. Mazari, 215–246. Mexico: El Colegio Nacional.

Fuentes Gea, V., and A. A. C. Hernández. 1984. Evaluación preliminar de la contaminación del aire por partículas en el Area Metropolitana del Valle de México. In *Memorias del IV Congreso Nacional de Ingeniería Sanitaria y Ambiental*, 523–526. Mexico: Sociedad Mexicana de Ingeniería Sanitaria y Ambiental.

Galindo, G., and J. Morales. 1987. El relieve y los asentamientos humanos en la Ciudad de México. *Ciencia y Desarrollo* 76: 67–80.

Gamboa, M. T. 1983. Identificación y cuantificación de microorganismos (bacterias y hongos) y su relación con la distribución del tamaño de partículas en cuatro sitios de la atmósfera de la Ciudad de México. Thesis, Facultad de Ciencias, UNAM, México.

García de Miranda, Enriqueta, and Zaida Falcón de Gyves. 1972. *Nuevo atlas Porrúa de la República Mexicana*. Mexico: Editorial Porrúa.

Garza, Gustavo. 1984. Concentración espacial de la industria en la Ciudad de México. *Revista de ciencias sociales y humanidades* 5, no. 11 (Mexico: Universidad Autónoma Metropolitana-Azcapotzalco).

———. ed. 1987. *Atlas de la Ciudad de Mexico*. Mexico: Departamento del Distrito Federal, El Colegio de México.

Garza, Gustavo, and M. Schteingart. 1978. México City: The emerging megalopolis. In *Metropolitan Latin America: The challenge and the response*, ed. Wayne A. Cornelius and Robert V. Kemper, Latin American Urban Research no. 6, 51–85. Beverly Hills, CA: Sage Publications.

Goldani, A. M. 1977. Impacto de los inmigrantes sobre la estructura y el crecimiento del área metropolitana. In *Migracíon y desigualdad social en la ciudad de México*, ed. Humberto Muñoz, Orlandina de Oliveira, and Claudio Stern, 129–137. Mexico: Instituto de Investigaciones Sociales, UNAM, and El Colegio de México.

Guerrero, G., A. Moreno, and H. Garduño. 1982. *El sistema hidráulico del Distrito Federal*. Mexico: Departamento del Distrito Federal, DGCOH.

Guevara, S., and P. Moreno. 1987. Areas verdes en la zona metropolitana de la ciudad de México. In *Atlas de la Ciudad de México*, ed. Gustavo Garza, 231–236. Mexico: Departamento del Distrito Federal and El Colegio de México.

Halffter, G., and E. Ezcurra. 1983. Diseño de una política ecológica para el valle de México. *Ciencia y Desarrollo* 53: 89–96.

Hernández Tejeda, T., and L. I. de Bauer. 1986. Photochemical oxidant damage on *Pinus hartwegii* at the "Desierto de los Leones," Mexico, D.F. *Phytopathology* 76, no. 3: 377.

Hernández Tejeda, T., L. I. de Bauer, and S. V. Krupa. 1985. Daños por gases oxidantes en pinos del Ajusco. In *Memoria de los Simposia Nacionales de Parasitología Forestal II and III*, 26–36. Publicación Especial no. 46. Mexico: Secretaría de Agricultura y Recursos Hidráulicos.

Hernández Tejeda, T., L. I. de Bauer, and M. L. Ortega Delgado. 1985. Determinación de la clorofila total de hojas de *Pinus hartwegii* afectadas por gases oxidantes. In *Memoria de los Simposia Nacionales de Parasitología Forestal II and III*, 334–

341. Publicación Especial no. 46. Mexico: Secretaría de Agricultura y Recursos Hidráulicos.

Herrera, I., and A. Cortés. 1989. El sistema acuífero de la cuenca de México. *Ingeniería Hidráulica en México* 4, no. 2 (May/Aug.): 60–66.

Ibarra, V., F. Saavedra, S. Fuente, and M. Schteingart. 1986. La ciudad y el medio ambiente: El caso de la zona metropolitana de la ciudad de México. In *La ciudad y el medio ambiente en América Latina: Seis estudios de caso*, comp. V. Ibarra, S. Fuente, and F. Saavedra, 97–150. Mexico: El Colegio de México.

Jáuregui, E. 1971. La erosión eólica en los suelos vecinos al Lago de Texcoco. *Revista de Ingeniería Hidráulica* 25: 103–118.

———. 1983. Variaciones de largo periodo de la visibilidad en la Ciudad de México. *Geofísica Internacional* 22–23: 251–275.

———. 1990. Algunos efectos antropogénicos sobre el clima de las grandes ciudades. In *Atlas de México*, Map no. V.2.5. Mexico: Instituto de Geografía, UNAM.

Lara, O. 1988. El agua en la Ciudad de México. *Gaceta UNAM* 45, no. 15: 20–22.

Lavín, M. 1983. *Cambios en las áreas verdes de la zona metropolitana de la Ciudad de México de 1940 a 1980*. Informe interno. Mexico: Instituto de Ecología.

Legorreta, Jorge. 1988. El transporte público automotor en la Ciudad de México y sus efectos en la contaminación atmosférica. In *Medio ambiente y calidad de vida*, Proceedings of the "Seminario sobre La Dinámica de la Ciudad de México en la Perspectiva de la Investigación Actual," Tlalpan, Mexico; coordinated by Sergio Puente and Jorge Legorreta, vol. 3, 263–300. Departamento del Distrito Federal, Colección Desarrollo Urbano. Mexico: Plaza y Valdez.

Macgregor, M. T. G., J. González-Sánchez, and E. Cervantes. 1989. Crecimiento espacial de las principales ciudades: Ciudad de México. In *Atlas de México*, Map no. III.3.5. Mexico: Instituto de Geografía, UNAM.

Marsal, Raul J., and Marcos Mazari. 1969. *El subsuelo de la Ciudad de México/The subsoil of Mexico City*. 2 vols. Contribution of the Institute of Engineering to the first Pan American Conference on Soil Mechanics and Foundation Engineering, Mexico City, September 1969 (Congreso Panamericano de Mecánica de Suelos y Cimentaciones). Mexico: Facultad de Ingeniería, UNAM.

Martínez-Palomo, A., and J. Sepúlveda. 1990. *Ciencia* especial: 7–13.

Mazari Hiriart, Marisa. 1992. Potential groundwater contamination by organic compounds in the Mexico City metropolitan area. D.Env. dissertation 153, University of California at Los Angeles.

Mazari, M., and J. Alberro. 1991. Hundimiento de la Ciudad de México. In *Los problemas de la Cuenca de México*, ed. M. Mazari and J. Kumate. Mexico: El Colegio Nacional.

Mazari, M., R. J. Marsal, and J. Alberro. 1984. *Los asentamientos del Templo Mayor analizados por la Mecánica de Suelos*. Mexico: Instituto de Ingeniería, UNAM.

Miranda, Faustino, and Efraim Hernandez Xolocotzl. 1963. *Los tipos de vegetación de México y su clasificación*. Boletín de la Sociedad Botánico de México 28: 29–179. Chapingo, Mexico: Colegio Postgraduatos Nacional de Agricultura.

Monroy Hermosillo, O. 1987. Manejo y disposición de residuos sólidos. *Desarrollo y Medio Ambiente* 2: 2–7.

Murillo, R. 1990. Sobre explotación del acuífero de la cuenca del valle de México: Efectos y alternativas. In *El Subsuelo de la Cuenca del Valle de México y su rela-*

ción con la Ingeniería de Cimentaciones a Cinco Años del Sismo, 109–118. Mexico: Sociedad Mexicana de Mecánica de Suelos.

Negrete, M. E., and H. Salazar. 1986. Zonas Metropolitanas en México, 1980. *Estudios Demográficos y Urbanos* (El Colegio de México, Mexico), no. 1: 97–124.

Niederberger, Christine. 1987. *Paléopaysages et archéologie pré-urbaine du bassin de México (Mexique)*. 2 vols. Etudes mésoaméricaines, vol. 11. Mexico: Centre d'études mexicaines et centraméricaines.

Ortega, A. 1988. Analysis of regional groundwater flow and boundary conditions in the Basin of Mexico. M.Sc. thesis in Earth Sciences, University of Waterloo, Ontario, Canada.

Palerm, Angel. 1973. *Obras hidráulicas prehispánicas en el sistema lacustre del valle de México*. Cordoba, Mexico: Instituto Nacional de Antropología e Historia.

Páramo, V. H., M. A. Guerrero, M. A. Morales, R. E. Morales, and D. Baz Contreras. 1987. Acidez de las precipitaciones en el Distrito Federal. *Ciencia y Desarrollo* 72: 59–66.

Quadri, G. 1990. Una breve historia del ecologismo en México. *Ciencias* no. especial 4: 56–64.

Restrepo, Ivan, and David Phillips. 1985. *La basura: Consumo y desperdicio en el Distrito Federal*. Mexico: Centro de Ecodesarrollo.

Rivera, L., J. C. Sugasty, F. Viniegra, A. Castorena, and R. Benítez. 1980. Efectos sobre la salud pública del reuso de aguas residuales en el Distrito de Riego 03, zona poniente de Tula, Hidalgo. Internal report. Mexico: Escuela de Salud Pública.

Rzedowski, J. 1975. Flora y vegetación en la Cuenca del Valle de México. In *Memoria de las obras del sistema del drenaje profundo del Distrito Federal*, ed. Roberto Rios Elizondo, vol. 1, 79–134. Mexico: Talleres Gráficos de la Nación.

———. 1986. *Vegetación de México*, 3rd edn. Mexico: Limusa.

SAHOP (Secretaría de Asentamientos Humanos y Obras Públicas). 1978. *Diagnóstico de la calidad atmosférica del Valle de México*. Mexico: SAHOP, Subsecretaría de Asentamientos Humanos, Dirección General de Ecología Urbana.

Salazar, S., J. L. Bravo, and Y. Falcón. 1981. Sobre la presencia de algunos metales pesados en la atmósfera de la Ciudad de México. *Geofísica Internacional* 20: 41–54.

Sandbrook, R. 1986. Crisis urbana en el Tercer Mundo. In *La ciudad y el medio ambiente en América Latina: seis estudios de caso (proyecto Ecoville)*, ed. Valentín Ibarra, Sergio Puente, and Fernando Saavedra, 19–27. Mexico: El Colegio de México.

Sanders, William T. 1972. Population, agricultural history, and societal evolution in Mesoamerica. In *Population growth: Anthropological implications*, ed. Brian Spooner, 101–153. Cambridge, MA: MIT Press.

———. 1976. The natural environment of the Basin of Mexico. In *The Valley of Mexico: Studies in prehispanic ecology and society*, ed. Eric R. Wolf, 59–67. Albuquerque: University of New Mexico Press.

Sanders, William T., Jeffrey R. Parsons, and Robert S. Santley. 1979. *The Basin of Mexico: Ecological processes in the evolution of a civilization*. New York: Academic Press.

Sandoval, J. M., and I. Semo. 1985. Los movimientos sociales del ecologismo en México. Mexico: Biosociología Programa Universitario Justo Sierra, Universidad Nacional Autónoma de México (UNAM), October.

SARH (Secretaría de Agricultura y Recursos Hidráulicos). 1985. *Sistema Cutzamala, segunda etapa: Captación valle de Bravo*. Mexico: SARH.

SEDUE (Secretaría de Desarrollo Urbano y Ecología). 1985. *Indice metropolitano de calidad del aire*. Mexico: Corporación Internacional TECNOCONSULT.

———. 1986. *Informe sobre estado del medio ambiente en México*. Mexico: SEDUE.

Serra Puche, M. C. 1991. El Pasado ¿Una forma de acercarnos al futuro? In *Los Problemas de la Cuenca de México*, ed. M. Mazari and J. Kumate, 3–28. Mexico: El Colegio Nacional.

Sigler Andrade, E., V. Fuentes Gea, and C. Vargas Aburto. 1982. Análisis de la contaminación del aire por partículas en Ciudad Universitaria. *Memorias del III Congreso Nacional de Ingeniería Sanitaria y Ambiental*. vol. 2, 1–13. Mexico: Sociedad Mexicana de Ingeniería Sanitaria y Ambiental.

Skärby, L., and G. Selldén. 1984. The effects of ozone on crops and forests. *Ambio* 13, no. 2: 68–72.

SMA (Subsecretaría de Mejoramiento del Ambiente). 1978a. *Desechos sólidos*. Mexico: Secretaría de Salubridad y Asistencia, SMA.

———. 1978b. *Fuentes emisoras en México. Industrias altamente contaminantes*. Mexico: Secretaría de Salubridad y Asistencia, SMA.

———. 1978c. *Situación actual de la contaminación atmosférica en el área metropolitana de la Ciudad de México*. Mexico: SMA.

Soms García, Esteban. 1986. *La hiperurbanización en el Valle de México*. 2 vols. Mexico: Universidad Autónoma Metropolitana.

Stern, C. 1977. Cambios en los volúmenes de migrantes provenientes de distintas zonas geoeconómicas. In *Migración y desigualdad social en la ciudad de México*, ed. Humberto Muñoz, Orlandina de Oliveira, and Claudio Stern, 115–128. Mexico: Universidad Nacional Autónoma de México and El Colegio de México.

Strauss, M. 1986. About wastewater reuse in Mexico. In *Epidemiological aspects of use of wastewater in agriculture in Mexico*, coord. Ursula Blumenthal. Technical Report. London: London School of Hygiene and Tropical Medicine.

———. 1988. Examples of wastewater and excreta use practices in agriculture and aquaculture. In *Human wastes: Health aspects of their use in agriculture and aquaculture. IRCWD News* 24–25: 1–3. Duebendorf, Switzerland: International Reference Centre for Waste Disposal.

Tamayo, L. M., C. Valverde, and A. G. Aguilar. 1989. Desigualdad social en las tres principales áreas metropolitanas. In *Atlas de México*. Map no. III.3.6. Mexico: Instituto de Geografía, UNAM.

Thom, Gary C., and Wayne R. Ott. 1975. *Air pollution indices: A compendium and assessment of indices used in the United States and Canada*. Washington DC: Council on Environmental Quality and the Environmental Protection Agency.

Trejo Vázquez, R. 1987. La disposición de desechos sólidos urbanos. *Ciencia y Desarrollo* 74: 79–90.

Unikel, Luis. 1974. *La dinámica del crecimiento de la Ciudad de México*. Mexico: SEP-Setentas.

Unikel, Luis, Cresencio Ruiz Chiapetto, and Gustavo Garza. 1976. *El desarrollo urbano de México: Diagnóstico e implicaciones futuras*. Mexico: El Colegio de México.

Velasco Levy, A. 1983. La contaminación atmosférica en la ciudad de México. *Ciencia y Desarrollo* 52: 59–68.

Ward, P. 1981. Mexico City. In *Problems and planning in Third World cities*, ed. Michael Pacione. London: Croom Helm.

———. 1990. *Mexico City: The production and reproduction of an urban environment.* Boston: G. K. Hall.

Whitmore, T. M., and B. L. Turner II. 1986. Population reconstruction of the Basin of Mexico: 1150 B.C. to present. Technical Paper no. 1, Millennial Longwaves of Human Occupance Project, Clark University, Worcester, MA.

———. 1992. Landscapes of cultivation in Mesoamerica. In *The Americas before and after 1492: Current geographical research*, ed. Karl W. Butzer, 401–425. *Annals of the Association of American Geographers* 82, no. 3 (September).

Whitmore, T. M., B. L. Turner II, D. L. Johnson, R. W. Kates, and T. R. Gottschang. 1990. Long-term population change. In *The earth as transformed by human action. Global and regional changes in the biosphere over the past 300 years*, ed. B. L. Turner II, William C. Clark, Robert W. Kates, John F. Richards, Jessica T. Mathews, and William B. Meyer, 25–39. Cambridge: Cambridge University Press with Clark University.

WHO (World Health Organization). 1988. *World Health Statistics Annual.* Geneva: World Health Organization.

Williams, Barbara J. 1989. Contact period rural overpopulation in the basin of Mexico: Carrying capacity models tested with documentary data. *American Antiquity* 54: 715–732.

8

The North Sea

Julie Argent and Timothy O'Riordan

The study of critical environmental regions, as noted in chapter 1, addresses the fundamental issue of natural resources and the capacity of the environment to assimilate increasing waste loads. This concept is essentially anthropogenic in application. Some areas of the globe exceed carrying capacity without regard to human needs; such cases are considered elsewhere in this volume but not in this chapter.

Rather, we address growing environmental endangerment in three ways:

- *evident degradation*, where the capacity of the resource base to meet current basic human needs and to ensure survival for those already living in the region is palpably overstretched;
- *potential degradation*, where the resource base is not yet depleted to the point where the life-support requirements of the existing population are being inadequately met, but where the legitimate requirements of a likely expanded population would not be met by the existing resource base, even with known improvements in technology and management;
- *incipient degradation*, where the current demands on a particular resource base are not yet causing significant deterioration, but where the capacity for serious deterioration is possible within the foreseeable future (a state of endangerment, as used in this volume), and where manageable opportunities exist to avoid reaching a state of criticality.

The first of these situations is consistent with the notion of "environmental endangerment" as used in this volume, the latter two with "environmental impoverishment."

In the first case, not even major injections of cash, technology, and skill-training can overcome the overwhelming dilemma of non-sustainability. In the second example, there is scope for technological and managerial innovation to create recovery, though that opportunity will depend upon international aid and long-term investments in promoting self-help. In the third case, criticality is *anticipated* and *avoided* by the injection of effort to create a more environmentally sustainable future for the region.

Of obvious importance is the degree to which the inhabitants of each of the three types of regions have the capabilities to recognize their dilemma, establish appropriate policies to reduce the impact, and invest in suitable alternative strategies to forestall criticality for the foreseeable future. This means:

- *information*: comprehensive environmental data-gathering on the state of resource availability and resource depletion.
- *prediction*: sound and reliable models of likely environmental outcomes following postulated developments, policy changes, or both.
- *adaptability*: the capability to assess and adapt to criticality either within the region or through effective international effort.
- *purposeful adjustment*: the capacity to deploy policy shifts, invest in appropriate technology, and train managers and analysts in the practice of sustainable development.
- *political will*: the political will, backed by informed and supportive public opinion, to embark on a programmed course of action.

The North Sea fits into the category of "incipient degradation," and its relatively wealthy and environmentally concerned surrounding populations have the capability of putting into effect the listed management criteria. The North Sea has been the subject of intensive scientific investigation for more than three decades and is currently undergoing one of the most comprehensive environmental modelling exercises ever undertaken for a specific region, the MANS (management analysis North Sea) study currently being developed by the North Sea Directorate of the Netherlands Ministry of Transport and Public Works. In addition, various natural science research councils of the basin states have embarked upon a cooperative programme of fundamental scientific investigation aimed at tracing the flows and concentrations of all measurable pollutants for land, air, and water to the North Sea. Finally there is the important exercise of the Quality Status Report (QSR 1987), a state-of-the-environment analysis of the North Sea (see below).

The International North Sea Conferences (INSCs) have supported much of this scientific work. Initiated in Bremen in 1984, these have subsequently convened at three-year intervals in London (1987) and in The Hague (1990). Attending the conferences were environment ministers of the eight North Sea basin states (Belgium, Denmark, France, Germany, Netherlands, Norway, Sweden, United Kingdom), as well as other interested parties (e.g. the European Communities and pressure groups). These ministerial conferences provide vital political momentum for promoting the cause of scientific research and for welding ambiguous or indeterminate scientific findings into a pragmatic political framework for action that is truly international. For both the 1987 and 1990 meetings, the conference commissioned major state-of-the-art reviews of the North Sea in the form of a Quality Status Report in 1987 and an Interim Quality Status Report (IQSR) in 1990. Much of the material that follows is based on these documents, together with a critique published by Greenpeace International (Rose 1990) and an assessment of North Sea pollution by various authors (Salomons et al. 1988).

Because the conference is ministerial, it has the moral and political power (but not legal force) to create collective policy for all of the eight states and to ensure compliance. The precise degree of compliance depends on national governments. Generally, much collective pressure exists to act harmoniously in good faith, but this depends on the specificity of the targets that are set. In essence, it is a high-powered politico-scientific forum with the capability of creating binding policy on member governments. But it would be unwise to underplay the future role of the two existing non-political, but scientifically important, pollution-control commissions, namely the Oslo and Paris Commissions. These intergovernmental bodies have responsibility for conducting scientific research, for coördinating data, and for advising governments on the appropriate regulation of wastes entering the air and from the land. Additionally, these commissions are very important for scientific mediation, for information exchange, and for clarifying areas of uncertainty. They also help to set implicit procedures for state-driven regulation, they provide a forum for specialist intergovernmental task forces to thrash out specific problems, and they serve as a focal point for monitoring subsequent actions. In short, the commissions are politico-scientific in nature and act symbiotically with the ministerial conferences, at least for the present.

It is unlikely that the ministerial conferences will ever supplant the work of these two commissions. To begin with, they cover an area much larger than the North Sea, including an important part of the north-east Atlantic. Secondly, the commissions provide a mechanism for ensuring at least a degree of implementation compared with the ministerial conferences, which have no effective power to enforce compliance with their final declarations of intent.

The era of international regulation a decade or so ago was mostly a matter of technical analysis and resolution by compromise, based upon the most workable outcome. In the past the commissions looked for solutions primarily on a substance-by-substance basis and with a sector-by-sector approach. With the adoption of the principles of precaution and best-available technology, particularly with regard to noxious substances that may be persistent and liable to accumulate, the commissions are beginning to adopt a more holistic approach.

This volume is as much concerned with the causes of *transformation*, or the regional dynamics of change, as it is with degrees of criticality. According to Kates, Turner, and Clark (1990, 10–11), the key driving forces for transformation are population growth, technological innovation, and institutional rigidity – all of which can produce adverse outcomes for both humans and nature. In the case of the North Sea, population growth is less of an issue than per capita consumption patterns, which tend to be resource intensive and cause environmental damage far from the point of consumption. They are in turn encouraged by a combination of faulty pricing, insufficient regulation on precautionary lines, and the creation of a false consciousness among consumers. The last arises from a lack of scientific knowledge of cause and effect, an unwillingness to transmit information in ways meaningful for the consumer, and the promotion of personal comfort and status-driven needs of material well-being, all at the expense of environmental systems. In short, the driving forces lie in *institutional failure*, which shows up in pricing, in regulation, in science, in raising awareness, and in the maldistribution of power that feeds the voice of progress at the expense of environmental stability. This chapter examines how this institutional failure is being recognized and overcome, at least up to a point.

The "commons" of the North Sea is still technically a free-access resource. But politically it has become nowadays the property of eight member governments that regard it essentially as a non-sustainable resource that requires safeguarding by the application of the *precautionary principle*. This principle requires appropriate levels of preventive action, by common agreement and hence by obligation in international law, in advance of scientific proof of degradation in situations in which the likely gains of taking measures are reasonably guaranteed to save more costly losses in the future. Under the precautionary principle, certain substances are deemed undesirable in the open environment because their properties are potentially harmful not only to ecosystems and human health, even though absolute scientific proof is not yet available. Currently, much dispute exists about how far the precautionary principle should extend to substances such as nutrients, low-level radioactive wastes, and non-toxic industrial wastes, for which environmental effects are less immediately problematic. Here the scientific case for pre-emptive action is less clear, so precaution takes on more of a political than a scientific hue.

To clarify this point, it should be stressed that the precautionary principle has four important components:

1. *The principle of preventive action.* This applies where a particular environmental change agent is known, on the basis of existing scientific research, to create a hazard, even though the hazard may not yet be fully assessed.
2. *The principle of playing safe.* This applies where the scientific prognosis cannot be proven, but where long-term danger is likely. The persistent and bio-accumulative chemicals are usually controlled on this basis.
3. *The principle of environmental insurance.* Here the workings of environmental systems are not fully understood, so it is regarded as vital to protect the capacity of such systems to cope with further change.
4. *The principle of intrinsic bequest.* Increasingly society wants to bequeath in trust, for future generations, the functioning of integral life-support systems.

In general, however, only the principle of preventive action is applied, and then only to hazardous substances.

The North Sea Conference has, in effect, adopted the mantle of a manager of an international commons regime. In practice the mantle is a little flimsy, since it bears no guarantee of infrastructural political commitment. The issue in point turns on how much scientific consensus on key North Sea environmental changes and their causes and solutions can be reached before political pressure mounts a case for action. In the longer term, the European Union may well take over the role of the INSC, since, by 2000 or earlier, all the North Sea basin states could well be members of an expanded European Union. The INSC should remain as a quasi-political, quasi-scientific working meeting, cooperating with both of the commissions to undertake the scientific and technical assessments.

In this transition, the notion of science itself may require thorough re-examination. What is morally acceptable to an informed and choice-conscious public, well aware of the possible consequences of various possible courses of action, should become the basis for innovative cost–benefit analysis. Ideally, investigating the science of natural systems should encompass wider social, ethical, and political relationships to the point at which the management and articulation of policy options to respond to emerging criticality become the full science of environmental learning. In this regard, the North Sea experience has much to offer for the reformulation of the role of science in environmental management, inasmuch as it can indicate how commons such as the North Sea can be appraised, evaluated, and policed by a collective political entity with supranational, but still democratic, powers.

In summary, for the study of critical environmental regions, the North Sea experience provides a series of lessons:

- Prolonged scientific analysis of resource use and depletion trends can provide a meaningful database for use by the international community.
- Acceptance of the precautionary principle encourages the linkage of scientific prediction to political values and ethics, extending science to the realms of social learning and informed choice.
- International political forums are required to ensure that sovereign states reach and enforce collective environmental agreements, even when individual states may not like the outcome. This supranational democracy may well become a permanent feature of critical-region management.
- Degradation of life-support resources should be set in a global framework and not confined to a particular region. The North Sea may be saved for the moment, but the development and investment of skills and money that make this possible are proceeding at the expense of environmental survivability in various parts of the third world. The developed world, in solving its localized environmental problems, is anyway not paying its full account to those countries

whose environments and societies are in a far more critical condition. The extravagant costs of clean-up of the North Sea cover a programme of action that would not meet a scientifically justifiable cost–benefit analysis in the narrow, "expert" notions of science. This is why the relatively confined "peer group" science of the official institutes and agencies and the more extended "vernacular" science of public concern need to forge a common framework of understanding and action. Only in this way can precious clean-up and precautionary resources be spent in the best interests of the world as a whole.

The North Sea basin

The North Sea amounts to less than 1 per cent of the world's oceans, so, in a very narrow sense, its demise would not undermine the stabilizing properties of the earth's biogeochemical cycles. But the states of the North Sea basin contain large populations of relatively wealthy people (table 8.1), so its viable future is a matter of considerable political and commercial interest. The area of the North Sea with which this report deals is south of latitude 62°N, the Skagerrak, and the English Channel to 5°W. Figure 8.1 displays the littoral North Sea states and some important regions.

The North Sea is an ancient sea with a long history. It is in a constant state of change, as the continental drift, tidal motion, circulatory currents, and human activity continue to modify its character.

Table 8.1 **Population and GNP in the states of the North Sea basin**

Country	Population (mid-1990s) (million)	GNP per capita (US$)
Belgium	10.0	15,540
Denmark	5.1	22,080
France	56.4	19,490
Germany	79.5[a]	22,320[b]
Netherlands	14.9	17,320
Norway	4.2	23,120
Sweden	8.6	23,660
United Kingdom	57.4	16,100

Source: World Bank (1992, 219).

a. Figure is for unified Germany.

b. Pre-unification figure for the Federal Republic of Germany.

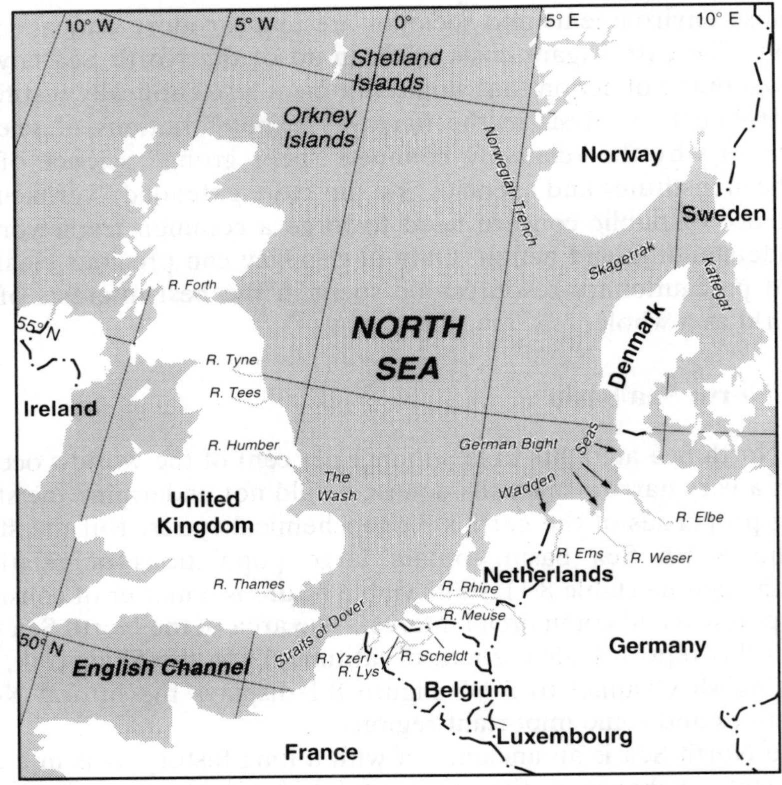

Fig. 8.1 **The North Sea area**

Around 350 million years ago, the land that was to become the North Sea was situated approximately 2 degrees south of the equator, in the location of the present-day Brazilian rain forests. Deposits of mud, covering and compressing the vegetation, gradually engulfed the existing swamp. As the sediments built up, the organic matter gradually changed its form, resulting in the formation of the rich coal seams.

In the Permian era some 240 million years ago, the swamp metamorphosed into a sea, in what is regarded as the true geological birth of the North Sea when the principal basins forming the North Sea came into existence (MacGarvin 1990). The rock under the North Sea began to subside, a process still in progress. This allowed the surrounding seas to resurge, submerging all land except for mountainous and hilly regions. The land mass was still migrating northwards and by this stage was around 20 degrees north of the equator. Some 168 million years ago the land mass rose again, creating an intricate tangle of deltas. Many of the marine deposits created during this age were rich in tiny marine organisms. Compressed under the weight of sediments that began to engulf them, the hydrocarbon substances became sealed, forming the crude oil and natural gas reserves that have subsequently been lucratively exploited by the human race.

By the early Cretaceous period (around 100 million years ago) the region was about 40 degrees north and isolated except for an opening to the north. The water levels rose gradually until most of northwestern Europe lay under a chalk sea. For unknown reasons, and around the same time of the dinosaur extinction, the chalk stopped forming. The emergent land masses were recognizable as those now forming continental Europe (MacGarvin 1990).

Until the ice ages began 2 million years ago, the water levels rose and fell, joining Britain with Europe and then separating the island from the continent. The North Sea basin also continued its drift to its current position.

The succession of ice ages that followed shaped the North Sea basin into what it is today. The most recent ice age, 20,000 years ago, covered the region northwards from the Wash to Jutland with ice over 2 km thick. It was responsible for gorging deep valleys in the sea bed and channelling the rivers of northern Europe along what is now the English Channel. The ice retreated and the water flowed back in to the now familiar shape of the North Sea basin, leaving behind deposits of sand and gravel. Tidal erosion, dredging developments, reclamation, sea defences, and harbour management are continually changing and modifying the finer details of the exact shape of the North Sea.

For analytical purposes the North Sea may be conveniently divided into two parts, the southern and northern North Sea. The northern part is relatively deep, around 50–200 m, and is subject to strong oceanic influences. It has a relatively short turnover time and is surrounded by less populated and industrialized nations, and so receives less waste. Because it is larger in size, however, it receives a greater amount of atmospheric deposition. The southern North Sea is shallower, with depths varying between 20 m and 50 m. It has strong tidal currents and a short turnover time. The southern North Sea carries a large sediment load and includes many areas in which finer sediments are deposited. The water in this area has a notable oceanic component. It is noteworthy that the coasts that flank the southern North Sea are more industrialized than those in the northern sector, and therefore the southern sector receives more in the way of waste inputs (Eisma 1986).

Resources and depletion

The North Sea and its coasts are a vast natural resource, used intensively and in a great variety of ways by the surrounding coastal states and the international community. The heterogeneous nature of the North Sea – its marshes, estuaries, and open waters – provides a wide range of habitats that support a varied and abundant wildlife. This ranges from the smallest unicellular organism to fish, large colonies of seabirds, and mammals (such as seals and dolphins). Several coastal areas that are of exceptional scientific and environmental interest have been designated as nature reserves. The most important is the Waddensea, lying to the north of the Netherlands and abutting the German and Danish coasts. This area is world renowned for its biological productivity, offering habitats for over half the European populations of waders, ducks, and geese (van der Zwiep 1990). This area also contains 21 per cent of all remaining North Sea salt marsh, and provides the nursery for 80 per cent of all plaice and 50 per cent of all sole caught in the North Sea.

Much of the coastline is used for enjoyment and relaxation by the urban population as well as by local communities. The North Sea is one of the most productive fisheries in the world and certain types of the bottom strata are an important source of sand and gravel for the aggregate industry. The Straits of Dover and the southern North Sea are among the most heavily trafficked sea routes on the globe, serviced by large commercial ports and smaller, local ports and harbours dotted along the coasts. The oil and gas fields situated in the central and northern North Sea are a major economic resource. At the same time, the North Sea receives much of the domestic and industrial effluent from the countries surrounding it.

Before the present century, human activity in the North Sea was on such a scale that it had little widespread impact on these resources and no one activity interfered very much with any other. With increased population, growth in industrial activity, and vastly expanded technical capabilities of states using the North Sea, it is becoming increasingly clear that resources, even those that are considered renewable (such as fish stocks), are near the point of over-exploitation and in management terms many are in conflict with one another.

Marine ecology of the North Sea

Plankton

Considerable marine biological productivity emerges from the high input of plankton nutrients spilling in from the north-east Atlantic and some additional nutrients from rivers that discharge into the North Sea. Open waters in the northern North Sea are stratified, for the most part, from late spring to autumn so that vernal and autumnal outbursts of phytoplankton utilize nutrients. These blooms can occur at the fronts that exist between water masses with different characteristics. These phytoplankton populations undergo annual "ploughing," which recycles nutrients in the water column. In addition, because the sea is shallow it has a rich benthic fauna sustained by detritus, and this forms a food supply for fish (Lee 1988).

All the following figures are from De Wolf and Zijlstra (1988). Van den Hoek and colleagues (1979) estimated that there are over 500 species of phytoplankton in the Waddensea alone, though there are undoubtedly more for the North Sea as a whole. The phytoplankton populations in the North Sea are studied in two ways:

1. through the Continuous Plankton Recorder Survey (CPRS), which has recorded spatial and temporal occurrence and variation since 1958 (Glover 1967; Glover, Robinson, and Colebrook 1974); and
2. through the study of phytoplankton dynamics in relation to nutrients, availability of light, hydrographic properties (e.g. salinity, temperature and mixing, grazing of zooplankton).

Data from the continuous survey between 1958 and 1973 indicate significant long-term changes (Reid 1978; Reid and Budd 1979). These changes are thought to relate to the position of the Gulf stream and to climatic change (Garrod and Colebrook 1978; Radach 1982; Reid and Budd 1979). Changes in the phytoplankton were accompanied by a general decline in zooplankton.

The data available for zooplankton are similar to those for phytoplankton, the major data source being the CPRS. Species caught by the CPRS are listed in table 8.2. These species have been regularly observed by the CPRS and only a few appear to be dominant, with the total number of species estimated at less than 300. Variations in

Table 8.2 **Zooplankton in the North Sea**

Species	No.
Branchiopoda (s)	5
Calanoid copepods (s)	22
Cyclopoid copepods (g)	3
Malacostraca (f)	7
Planktonic Gastropods (s)	4
Tunicates (s)	4
Chaetognatha (s)	"few"
Polychaete *Tomopteris* (g)	1

Source: De Wolf and Zijlstra (1988, 130–131).
(s) = species
(g) = genera
(f) = family

Table 8.3 **Numbers of species in infauna and epifaunal macrobenthos**

Area	Polychaetes	Molluscs	Crustaceans	Echinoderms
Infauna				
German Bight (1985)	90	54	52	12
German Bight (1978)	68	38	55	9
Central North Sea	–	–	–	57
Doggerbank	143	–	–	–
Oyster Ground	–	63	–	–
West of Scheveningen	62	16	49	5
Epifauna				
57°20′–54°40′ N and 2°20′–5° E	2	75	56	20

Source: De Wolf and Zijlstra (1988, 134).

their distribution prevail throughout the southern, central, and northern regions of the North Sea.

Benthos

The zoobenthic organisms are usually divided into three categories of micro-, meso-, and macrobenthos. Table 8.3 shows the number of species of infauna and epifaunal macrobenthos.

Fish

The greatest amount of information available on North Sea organisms has been collected on the commercial fish stock. Because of the

Table 8.4 **Data on 11 important fish species in the North Sea fisheries**

Species	Average landing 1965–1969 ('000 tonnes, fresh weight)	% of total landings	Industrial catch 1974 ('000 tonnes)	Habitat	Distribution
Herring	933	30.7	88	Pelagic	All North Sea
Mackerel	618	20.4	230	Pelagic	All North Sea
Haddock	287	9.5	44	Demersal	North, central
Cod	227	7.5	5	Demersal	All North Sea
Norway pout	179	5.9	753	Pelagic	North, central
Sandeel	157	5.2	512	Pelagic	Central, south
Whiting	139	4.6	117	Demersal	All North Sea
Plaice	106	3.5		Demersal	Central, south
Coalfish	86	2.8		Demersal	North
Sprat	77	2.5	243	Pelagic	All North Sea
Sole	25	0.8		Demersal	Central, south
Total	3,036	100.0			

Source: Adapted from De Wolf and Zijlstra (1988, 137).

very intensive fishing of the North Sea, most fish species occur either as the catch or as the by-catch (Tiews 1978). This fishing effort has considerably changed the ecosystem, however, and fisheries are adapting rapidly to these changes.

It is estimated that there are approximately 160–170 fish species in the North Sea (Wheeler 1969, 1978). Although values can vary from sample to sample, it can be concluded that around 25–30 species are very common (table 8.4).

A more detailed explanation of the fishing industry in the North Sea is given later in this chapter.

Birds

Bird populations fall into two groups – coastal and open sea. The littoral populations breed along the coasts, collecting food from the open sea, intertidal mudflats, and inland areas. They usually migrate over the sea at the end of the breeding season. The open-sea birds breed along the coasts, collecting food from the open sea. They normally stay in open sea for six months during winter.

Bellamy and colleagues (1973) list 71 species of coastal and open-sea birds along and on the North Sea. According to Camphysen and van Dijk (1983) many more species live along the coast of the Netherlands. However, only limited data are available on the number of open-sea bird species present in the North Sea, although Evans (1973) lists 19 such species, with a winter population of 21 species.

Mammals

Seals usually occur along or near the coast, spending part of their time on land or on dry tidal flats in the breeding season and the rest of their time in the water. There is a wider knowledge of seals than of cetaceans as they are easier to study. There are six species in the North Sea, of which four are rare or occasional stragglers and two are common (and are discussed here).

Grey seals are mainly found in the west and north-west of the North Sea and are only occasionally located in the eastern regions. Their population in the United Kingdom is thought to be around 29,000–32,000 individuals (Summers, Bonner, and van Haaften 1978). The grey seal used to be common in the German Bight.

The common or harbour seal, as it is sometimes known, lives seaward of the German Bight, the Wash, and the English and Scottish east coast, with estimated populations of around 4,500–5,000, 6,000, and 7,000–10,000, respectively (De Wolf and Zijlstra 1988, 140).

A report from the Food and Agriculture Organization (FAO) of the United Nations in 1978 noted that, over the whole extended range, the seal population seems to be stable. However, there are clear indications that the common seal suffers from the effects of polychlorinated biphenyls (PCBs).

The total food consumption of the seal population in the North Sea is estimated at around 100,000 tonnes per annum, with the common seal requiring 5 kg of fish per day and the grey seal consuming 5–8 kg per day. The favourite fish species of the seals are cod and salmon.

There are known to be 30 species of whales and dolphins in the North Sea: 22 are rare or occasional stragglers, known only because of strandings, whereas 8 occur regularly and in large numbers. These are all dolphins. Whales are extremely rare in the North Sea.

There are two dolphin species with a tendency for coastal distribution that are again better known about because of strandings. These are the harbour porpoise and the bottlenose dolphin (Verweij and Wolff 1982).

Less common species such as the common dolphin, the white-beaked dolphin, the white-sided dolphin, and, in the north, the beluga and pilot whale are hardly known. In the period before the

1960s the minke whale was frequently observed, but there has been a severe decline due to whaling (Zijlstra 1988).

There has been a reduction in population owing to pollution or a reduction in prey, which is thought to be causal in the decline (Andersen 1984). The population is also declining owing to the accidental catching by faster and more powerful fishing vessels (FAO 1978).

Depletion of fish stocks

Fishing is the most established and extensive resource use of the North Sea, yet overfishing is one of the most critical resource issues facing the region today.

Roman merchants in Utrecht conducted active fishing businesses. Small fishing operations, which required relatively little capital outlay, flourished along the east coast of Britain. There are various records of herring fisheries from medieval times. The fourteenth century saw the first conflict between the British and Europeans over territorial fishing rights (Coull 1988). The Dutch were very skilled as a fisheries nation but were unable to meet the demand of the growing European market for fish.

The Dutch were the first to establish a substantial open-sea fishery for herring, and by the fifteenth century had pioneered the basic techniques of catching herring in drift-nets and curing them with salt in barrels, the dominant methods for herring fisheries until World War II. Extensive trading of the barrels, especially in the hinterland of the southern Baltic, provided a source of great wealth to the Dutch.

Up to the nineteenth century the British fishing industry had never been very strong and had declined to a point of danger that the country would lack trained soldiers and sailors to staff ships in times of war. In 1549, Fridays, Saturdays, and Lent were made "fish" days, and in 1563 Wednesdays were added. Although this gave temporary benefit to the industry, food regulations were never popular and were eventually abandoned.

The emergence of the fishing smack in 1830 transformed the British industry, which had previously relied upon the use of hook-and-gill nets (Morley 1968). By the mid-1800s the industry rapidly began to acquire a modern image, mainly because of improvements in fishing techniques and the spread of railways linking ports to large population centres. This shows up in the history of Grimsby town, which grew famous for its fishing trade (table 8.5). The railway allowed the

Table 8.5 **Fish landings in Grimsby, 1854–1958**

Year	Amount of fish landed (tons)
1854	453
1856	1,500
1890	70,000
1900	135,000
1909	175,000
1958	220,000

Source: Adapted from Morley (1968, 123).

transport of Norwegian ice from the port on the Humber to Grimsby, thereby boosting both the fish and lobster trade.

The improved quality of fish reaching the consumer – owing to packaging ice as well as the opportunity for further transportation – led to an unprecedented rise in the demand for fish. This demand in turn necessitated a drastic reorganization of the fishing industry.

By 1900 the British Isles had become the leading fisheries nation of the world at a time when the North Sea was positively abundant with all types of fish species. It has been estimated that British fishing boats caught approximately two-thirds of all herring and nearly all pelagic fish (Morley 1968). During World War I, however, fishing declined dramatically. After the war, the British fishing industry picked up again but never reached its prominent pre-war level.

The inter-war years saw increasing competition from the Germans, whose fish catches after 1925 nearly equalled the British catch. The Germans also competed for the export market and introduced significant changes in fishing methods (e.g. the use of drift-nets with trawlers instead of drifters). World War II again curtailed the fishing industry, but a post-war world shortage of animal oils and the increased use of fish-meal in foodstuffs prompted a change in the fish species sought. These species are known as industrial species (for example, the Norway pout) and included the trawling of areas in search of adolescent 23-year-old herring. The change in demand led to a reduction in the overall British catch, because Britain did not find it economical to engage in industrial fishing.

The current deep-sea-fishing challenge has been met by investment in new high-powered diesel craft and technology in navigation, in methods of locating fish shoals, and in equipment for freezing and processing on board.

Countries of eastern Europe and the former USSR expanded their distant-water fisheries, putting further pressure on the fish resources and increasing the total catches of North Sea herring.

The advent of the revolutionary purse-net in the mid-1960s raised the catching effort to an unprecedented peak. An increase in the strength of the synthetic fibres and the introduction of the power-block meant that purse-nets could now be used in the open sea, not just in sheltered waters to which they had initially been confined. The 1960s also saw the collapse of the surface herring fishery, mainly owing to new technology that enabled the identification of such shoals (MacGarvin 1990). The Norwegians changed fishing grounds from the North Atlantic to the North Sea.

The year 1972 saw the enlargement of the EEC to include two major fisheries nations, the United Kingdom and Denmark, which became influential in the formation of the Common Fisheries Policy (CFP). Norway did not join. In the 1970s there was a worldwide extension of Exclusive Economic Zones (EEZs) to 200 nautical miles, and in 1977 a median line was drawn between the EEC and the Norwegian EEZ.

In pelagic rather than demersal fisheries the diagnosis of overfishing is generally more problematic, and so effective remedies are difficult to formulate. Adult herrings tend to form different shoals from juveniles, which gives greater scope for mesh size controls. Conservation of shoals can be promoted by limiting the length of permissible fishing season or by complete closure. The herring also lays eggs on the seabed rather than letting them drift, a practice that allows ready identification of spawning grounds.

As the capacity and efficiency of fishing fleets increased over the years, concern grew regarding the impact on fisheries and their profits. The monitoring of catches began in the 1950s and was based on the monitoring of fish larvae and the prediction of the amount that would survive to adulthood. It was found that the adult population varied annually, owing to such factors as food availability, the prevalence of disease, and the effect of storms and currents. These unpredictable external factors have led to inaccurate mathematical modelling, which ironically has been used in the setting of fishing quotas. Short-term models have also been used to predict fish stocks but have been too short-sighted to provide an accurate picture of the capability of the stock to regenerate sufficiently (MacGarvin 1990).

With overfishing a reality and spawning stock considerably reduced, it was imperative to impose catch restrictions. The principle of total allowable catches (TAC) was accepted from 1974, though ef-

Table 8.6 **Recommended and adopted total allowable catches (TACs) and total catches for herring in the North Sea, 1974–1976 and 1982–1986 ('000 tonnes)**

	1974	1975	1976		
Whole North Sea:					
Recommended	310–356	136	0		
Adopted	305	183	160		
Catch	331	365	183		
	1982	1983	1984	1985	1986
Skaggerak & Kattegat:					
Recommended	30–40	30–40	30–40	60–80	50
Adopted	61	59	–	117	46
Catch	147	198	205	n.a	n.a.
South North Sea & East Channel:					
Recommended	60	36	49	62	37–42
Adopted	72	73	49	90	70
Catch	69	64	46	n.a.	n.a.
North and central North Sea:					
Recommended	0	62	95	166	235
Adopted	0	72	–[a]	230	500
Catch	167	244	272	n.a.	n.a.

Source: Coull (1988).

a. No agreement.

fective conservation methods were slow to come into action. The United Kingdom used emergency powers of veto to prohibit all herring fisheries beyond its own 12 mile limit after 1977. This was eventually accepted by all countries in 1982. The resultant recovery of the stock has been claimed as one of the few examples of definite and positive results from the new management regime (Coull 1988). Despite the adoption of the principle of TAC, administrators, in the face of pressure from fishing interests, betray a strong tendency to raise the scientifically based advised levels (table 8.6).

It was agreed in 1983 that scientific models should be used to set target catches (i.e. TACs for each species of fish). This required a detailed knowledge of individual life cycles, and, in doubtful cases, species received a "precautionary" TAC (MacGarvin 1990). Not enough is known, however, to define the maximum possible catch consistent with survival.

As table 8.6 shows, economic issues can undermine the TAC principle, as can political pressure. Biologists now recommend that existing TACs should be halved in order to allow for some degree of regeneration (Symes 1990). For example, it is now estimated that over 55 per cent of the total stock (including recruitment age classes) is now caught annually.

TACs and overfishing have again become an important issue of political discussion. The Council of Fisheries Ministers of the European Communities met in 1990 to set annual catch limits and to discuss the preservation of fish stocks and the associated industry. The Council acted on scientific evidence that concluded that an overfishing of more than 90 per cent of fish stocks prevailed in the North Sea. The depletion of cod and haddock, in particular, was considered critical (*Financial Times* 1990a). The Council proposals, which were about half as restrictive as scientists wanted, included reducing the annual cod quota from 98,270 to 85,700 tonnes and the haddock quota from 41,700 to 40,500 tonnes. The Council also ruled that fishing boats near concentrations of cod should remain in port for 10 consecutive days per month, that net mesh sizes should be increased from 90 mm to 120 mm, and that net meshes should be changed from a diamond shape to a square shape.

Although the European Communities reached an unexpected agreement on the reduction of quotas, they did not agree on all conservation measures, in particular net mesh size. Furthermore, coastal states have not yet agreed on planned reductions in boat sizes for the 1990s (Symes 1990).

The total allowable catch for cod was pushed above the EC recommendations, to 93,570 (and not 85,700) tonnes, but it was down on 1990's TAC figure of 98,270 tonnes. The TAC for haddock was set at around 40,500 tonnes. Only "structural conservation measures" were agreed upon – boats near cod stocks were to be kept in port for 8 consecutive days, not 10, per month, and "generous EC funding" was envisioned to encourage the decommissioning of vessels to reduce overcapacity (*Financial Times* 1990b).

The North Sea foodfish decline is serious but not yet critical. The industry is steadily contracting, with much hardship to traditional coastal fishing communities. The politicians are caught in their own trap: TACs are too high and fluctuate annually, as described above. This is no basis for any long-term, controlled reduction in the fishing industry. Furthermore, the reduction in boat numbers is too small, because each quota chosen is politically embarrassing. One solution would be to allocate fishing quotas to the highest bidders, set within TACs. But this would result in a massive shakedown of marginal boats and skippers and is politically unthinkable at present. On balance, the North Sea foodfish industry looks set to remain above the pain threshold for many years to come.

Land reclamation

Land reclamation is a natural process. It usually takes place in sheltered areas such as estuaries, where rich alluvial deposit processes cause gradual accretion. The deposits eventually become colonized by plant species that drain the soil in a process known as soil ripening. The resulting soil can be drained further and is excellent for agricultural purposes, providing a stable, fertile soil for some years.

Gradually man came to the assistance of nature in the North Sea area to speed up the process of accretion. Salt-marshes were embanked to protect them from further inundation. This was the beginning of the operations of land reclamation, started by the demand for fertile farmland and a need for coastal protection, for new space for industry and commerce, and in some cases for building other structures such as roads or railways. Land reclamation in the United Kingdom dates back as far as the eleventh and twelfth centuries. Some areas of the Thames may have been reclaimed by the Romans, with other similar early works around the rivers in Kent and within the Humber estuary. One area that has been well studied is the Wash, where reclamation has been taking place since the Middle Ages. The first significant gain of land reported in this area was in the seventeenth century when around 15,400 ha of salt-marsh were embanked. By 1979 this had reached 31,000 ha.

Land-reclamation works have taken place in many areas along the North Sea coasts of Great Britain and the Continent – for example, at the Firth of Forth, on the banks of the rivers Tees and Humber, on the salt-marshes of the Wash, and in the Wadden area stretching from the city of Den Helder in the Netherlands to Esbjerg in Denmark.

The previously jagged coastline of the Wadden area has been either straightened or shortened artificially, resulting in the loss of tens of thousands of acres of land (including mudflats, salt-marshes, and summer polders) outside the dikes. Only an area of 375 km^2 is left, representing less than 4 per cent of the Wadden area. And even these few areas are threatened by further reclamation.

Mineral extraction

Minerals required by construction industries originate from the ice ages of the Quaternary period. They are extracted on a national basis, as are oil and gas. (All figures are from Sibthorp 1975.)

With regard to the geological environment of the North Sea, only three groups of minerals are likely to be present in quantities sufficient to allow them to be economically worked. These are superficial, unconsolidated deposits, such as sand and gravel and the so-called "heavy minerals" (notably including sources of titanium); bedded deposits such as coal and evaporites (e.g. halite [salt], potash, and anhydrite); and petroleum and natural gas.

The only mineral being extracted on a large scale from sea water is magnesium. Extraction plants are located mainly at Hartlepool in the United Kingdom and in Norway. Current production figures are not available, although it is known that, earlier, 60–65 per cent of world magnesium production (1973 figures) was from sea water. Salt is also being recovered on a small scale at Maldon, Essex (UK).

Difficulty in obtaining sufficient building aggregate on land has led to the increased usage of marine aggregates since the early 1960s. By 1972 this was contributing around 12 per cent of total production in Great Britain. The most suitable deposits are located in the British sector of the North Sea, 7–20 miles offshore at various sites from the Humber to the Thames. The continental side of the North Sea is mainly sandy, with exceptionally rare gravel deposits. As a result, dredged aggregate is delivered from the British areas to Rotterdam, Dordecht, Bruges, Dunkirk, and Calais.

In 1972, about 6 million tonnes of sand and gravel were dredged from the North Sea. Technological developments and the building of very large dredgers now enable areas of lower-grade materials to be worked, but it is becoming clear that many reserves have become exhausted. Strata containing salt, anhydrite (calcium sulphate), and potash extend beneath the North Sea off the Yorkshire and Durham coasts. Salt is extracted near the Tees estuary by controlled pumping of a saturated brine solution through a network of boreholes. Although enormous deposits of salt have been found beneath the North Sea during the search for hydrocarbons, the existence of very large reserves of salt on land in Britain renders it unlikely that salt will ever be extracted from beneath the sea on a large commercial basis.

Potash occurs in an extensive bed at a depth of around 1,000 m over a very large area in Yorkshire, stretching from the Durham border to Scarborough and for a very considerable distance out to sea. Only a small proportion of this area is currently mined because of technical difficulties involved in extraction.

Several coalmines extend beneath the North Sea off the Northumberland and Durham coasts. Usable deposits are located mainly in the southern North sea and are extracted mainly by the United Kingdom, Denmark, the Netherlands, and Belgium. Most of the extraction takes place near the coast, on land, though the United Kingdom disposes of the wastes at sea. The United Kingdom is currently the only country that does this, on the grounds that it is inert material. It is likely that this practice will have to cease by the end of the century if not before (see below on industrial waste).

Oil and gas extraction

The first discovery of natural gas occurred in 1959 and production began in 1967. Since then large-scale production and exploration have been extensive. The search is continuing, with many of the main fields (e.g. the large Stratfjord field) already having been discovered. Gas is a non-renewable resource but it is a very important financial benefit to the economies of the countries (i.e. the Netherlands, the United Kingdom, and Norway) that have jurisdiction of the continental shelf.

Gas fields owned by the United Kingdom are situated mainly in the southern and central North Sea basin, located to the east of Yorkshire, Lincolnshire, and Norfolk. Some of the natural gas fields situated in the northern sector of the North Sea are not extensively exploited commercially. These were formed from the carbonization of flora and fauna in the Carboniferous period, the salt seal that formed above them preventing anaerobic decomposition. They are mostly owned by the Netherlands and the United Kingdom.

Oil fields are found mainly in the northern North Sea, from Jurassic shales. They are predominantly owned by the United Kingdom and Norway. North Sea crude oil is high quality, low in sulphur, and "light," and therefore suitable for the production of petrol and diesel fuel (but unsuitable for heating fuel). Considerable quantities of the mineral have been found in the northern North Sea off the Scottish coast.

The oil and gas reserves are of enormous strategic importance to the North Sea states. They contribute significantly to the wealth of the Norwegian economy and account for more than 10 per cent of the real wealth of the British and Dutch economic output.

With respect to oil, the best estimate for UK reserves is that North Sea oil will begin to decline in annual output around A.D. 2000–2010 and that the effective resource will be viable until around 2040 (BP 1991; *UK Digest of Energy Statistics* 1991–). Much depends on price and technological innovation. Certainly the scope exists for extending existing reserves, given the appropriate incentives.

For gas, the picture is similar to the UK oil reserves, with around 40–50 years of availability at current rates of exploitation (BP 1991). Again, this could be expanded with suitable pricing and regulatory actions. For the Dutch and Norwegian reserves, the expected commercial lifetime is a little longer (about 50–60 years), bearing in mind a growing demand over this time for exports to other North Sea basin states (Kemp 1990).

The oil and gas industries are privately owned in the United Kingdom, and quasi-private in Denmark, Norway, and the Netherlands. Regulatory offices and tax and depletion policies strictly enforce controls over economic exploration. The international price for fossil fuels and the current preference for gas over new coal and oil on the grounds of thermal efficiency, lower carbon-dioxide generation, and lower sulphur-dioxide production influence the management of these resources. Co-generation of gas with oil is likely to increase as a consequence.

Warning signs

Previously, the resources of the North Sea could be used with very little conflict arising among resource users. With increased populations, growth in industrial activity, and vastly expanded technical capability, these resources are nearly overly exploited and are also, in management terms, in conflict with one another.

The fisheries of the North Sea, for example, have visibly declined, and the amount and nature of the wastes that are finding their way into the sea are causing concern regarding possible long-term impacts on food-chains, ecology, and overall human well-being. Waste and pollution enter the North Sea through several pathways.

An element of overfishing is almost an inevitable consequence of a commons resource, where regulation of access tends to await a demonstrable decline in stocks and where international regimes have influence by virtue of the necessity to guarantee fair play. The future of North Sea commercial fish stocks, notably the demanded species of white fish, is problematic, with signs pointing to a contracting industry, higher prices, and only very slow recovery. Either the fish market will have to shift to unpopular species or the industry will have to restructure to a relatively small number of licensed boats, or both. Currently, the Common Fisheries Policy is still in a state of flux, with the politicians erring on the side of optimism and the fisheries biologists leaning towards caution.

There is no prospect of any immediate solution to this dilemma, although the European Union does at least control its own member states, namely Germany, the Netherlands, France, Denmark, Belgium, and the United Kingdom. Norway and Sweden are not yet members of the Union (though both may apply within this decade) and operate through the North East Atlantic Fisheries Commission along with their European Union partners. This is a less satisfactory forum from the viewpoint of sound science and well-adjusted management, but at least it provides a common negotiating arena. The main difficulty lies in rationalizing the industry in those areas in which fishing is still very much part of the local economy and culture – in Scotland, north-east England, and southern Norway. Inevitably, these historic fishing regions will slowly decline – as have other now-exhausted extractive industries – with a slow reorganization of the local economy towards other activities, helped by redundancy payments, job retraining, and the general mobility of job opportunities in the modern post-industrial society.

Pollution of the North Sea

Significant environmental attention is currently being devoted to the pollution of the North Sea. Even though this pollution has less demonstrable impact than the decline of a once-profitable fishing industry, it is a feature of the contemporary environmental scene that harm to food-chains and ecological systems generally now receives weighting equal to damage to human life and property. This is not to say that the modern environmentalist is callous; merely that ecological indicators of natural health are nowadays taken seriously and are protected in law. It is of some significance that the definition of environmental "harm" in European law generally extends to the viability of non-human life-forms.

The most significant areas for concern regarding pollution are the dumping of sewage sludge at sea, the incineration of toxic wastes in the open sea, the discharge of toxic and eutrophic substances in waterways leading to the North Sea, and the deposition of both toxic and eutrophic pollutants from both dry and wet precipitation in the open atmosphere.

The Dutch MANS project is currently attempting to gather a complete picture of the total contribution of pollutants entering the North Sea. This task was initiated by the North Sea Conference in the mid-1980s, but it is still a long way from completion. Indeed, much original research is still being conducted on the pathways of pollution flows, especially in the open North Sea. The regional research of the North Sea Task Force is also contributing to the level of knowledge about the open sea.

An important difference of opinion divides the basin states as to the grounds for controlling pollution in a vast commons such as the North Sea. The British, and to some extent the French, tend to rely on scientific research and estimates of the capacity of ecosystems to assimilate pollutants. Assimilative capacity has two main interpretations, namely rendering harmless by *decomposition* or rendering harmless by *dispersal* and *dilution*. The British line is to try to develop detailed proper scientific audits, estimate rates of assimilation, and take action where likely benefits are offset by predicted costs. This can be a recipe for postponement and may result in unnecessary damage on the basis of insufficient knowledge. It is also a position that invites delaying action by vested interests. Nevertheless, it may also be seen as a pathway to least-cost management.

However, this is not a popular position any more. The continental approach favoured by the Germans, the Danes, and the Dutch is that of *precaution*, taking preventive action ahead of scientific certainty on the grounds of its being better to be safe than sorry. This approach is based more on moral principles of ecological integrity rather than on strict cost–benefit principles. But it is finding favour because it reflects the mood of the modern age, most notably where toxic, persistent, and bio-accumulative substances are concerned. As such, it has now become the dominant approach to North Sea management, though the scientific mode still has its strong supporters. Despite what is discussed below, as far as toxic substances are concerned, North Sea basin states, including the United Kingdom, are committed to the principle of precaution. In practice there is nothing but advantage in trying to combine the two approaches, hence the growth in scientific audits, predictive models, and cost–benefit analyses.

It is interesting to record the shift in position between Britain and its European Union partners over the matter of environmental objectives, based on assimilative capacity and fixed emission standards, linked to fair competition and harmonious application of regulation. At the heart of this dispute lies the distinction between what the British like to regard as environmentally sensitive cost–benefit analyses, in which the consequences of pollution reduction are set against societal gains, and command-and-control regulation, which is increasingly being tied to best-available technology (or techniques). In practice, however, Britain does not use a cost–benefit approach at all seriously. The point is political and rhetorical, designed to sharpen debate and to maintain an important sense of perspective on the role of science in environmental policy-making.

The continentals are apparently less concerned over the possible severe costs of implementing directives aimed at reducing pollution at source. The British like to weigh different options in relation to least overall cost. The precautionary principle is very much the middle course. Eventually some combination of all three approaches is likely to prove the most workable. Meanwhile, the cost–benefit approach to setting emission controls is only slowly becoming recognized (Boehmer-Christiansen 1990).

Behind this argument between science and precaution are important political nuances. In Germany, Denmark, and the Netherlands, the composition of national parliaments is notably more "green" than in Britain and France. The view taken by these "greener" parliaments favours equal treatment: namely, if their country is being forced to clean up expensively, then all countries sharing a common resource should do the same. To begin with, attention was on the obvious "soft" targets of oil and gas production platforms. But they apply only to the United Kingdom and Norway.

In the Netherlands, considerable public alarm attends the decline of fish and mammal species in the North Sea, and general concern prevails over the increase in nutrients from sewage works and agricultural activity. The growth in algal blooms is seen as a consequence of all this, whereas in the United Kingdom the scientific evidence is interpreted much more narrowly. Most blooms are regarded as the consequences of historical fluctuations in growth and productivity, as well as of fluctuations in sunlight, temperature, and the movement of nutrient-rich currents from the north-east Atlantic. The British position is that only a small and localized amount of nutrient build-up, mostly in the shallow seas around Denmark and southern Sweden, is serious.

Just as significant here is the role of the scientist and the scientific model. In some continental countries, scientists tend to be closer to the political centre on account of governmental funding patterns and advisory positions. More important, perhaps, regulations tend to be fairly formal, based on scientific evidence. In the United Kingdom especially, scientists are featured as more independent and are seen as the source of cautious advice. However, the UK government has a policy of acquiring both official and non-official scientific advisers whose role can be very influential. Scientific models are now popular everywhere, but the Dutch build impressive computerized edifices on limited data, unlike the British who tend to build models as the scientific evidence evolves. The result is a tension between the role of science and predictive models in the management of the resource. For toxic substances, and for incineration issues, consensus favours precaution. For nutrients, and to a lesser extent ocean disposal of industrial wastes, far greater divergence prevails.

Atmospheric deposition

It is now estimated that as much as half of all the toxic wastes discharged into the North Sea comes from the atmosphere in the form of aerosols falling as dry matter or precipitated as rain. This has been discovered only over the past 20 years as a result of new monitoring and recording techniques.

It is important to exercise some degree of caution about the accuracy of these values since they are often based on extrapolation and estimation. Usually maximum and minimum values are expressed to give a general idea (table 8.7). Estimates are obtained mainly from measurements of wet deposition and air concentration at coastal stations, although this varies according to which text is consulted. Table 8.7 shows quantities of atmospheric pollutants in the North Sea as submitted for the International North Sea Conference in 1990.

Several recent attempts have calculated atmospheric inputs into the North Sea by means of atmospheric transport models (van Aalst, Duyzer, and Veldt 1983; van Jaarsveld, van Aalst, and Onderdelinden 1986). The models calculate annually or seasonally averaged concentrations and depositions from emissions and meteorological data. However, windspeed, atmospheric stability, mixing-layer depth, and precipitation at sea generally differ from those of the surrounding land (Höhn 1973; Joffre 1985; RSU 1980) and from the different types of water masses in the North Sea (Sibthorp 1975). This will in-

Table 8.7 **Atmospheric pollution in the North Sea (tonnes)**

	Atmospheric input[a]				
	Nitrogen	Cadmium	Copper	Lead	Zinc
Estimates based on 1988 deposition measurements:[b]					
Minimum	326,000	42	1,050	2,570	3,150
Maximum	614,000	84	1,680	4,830	6,090
Estimates based on emission values for various years (1982–1986):[b]					
Minimum	383,000	14	130	2,310	970
Maximum	525,000	18	135	2,600	1,200

Source: IQSR (1990).

a. No information is available on phosphorus, mercury, chromium, nickel, arsenic, hexachlorohexane, or polychlorinated biphenyls.

b. Minimum and maximum estimates result from different calculation methods, calculated for an area of 525,000 km^2 north of the Straits of Dover.

evitably introduce errors additional to the uncertainty of factors such as accurate emission values.

Deposition maps calculated by van Jaarsveld, van Aalst, and Onderdelinden (1986) show a strong north–south gradient in depositional flux and indicate that measurements taken at coastal stations in the Netherlands, Belgium, and the United Kingdom are likely to be higher by a factor of 2–4 than the average flux into the North Sea. Adjusting for the differences, the measured values are comparable with the modelled values.

Knowledge is limited, however, owing to the lack of:

1. adequate and representative measuring data of concentrations in air and precipitation;
2. insight into and quantitative parameters for dry deposition of gases and particles over the sea;
3. accurate data on all European emissions.

Table 8.8 shows the relative contribution of heavy metals from the North Sea states by atmospheric deposition, revealing that the United Kingdom contributes the greatest quantity. The amounts of nitrogen entering the North Sea via the atmosphere from various countries is shown in table 8.9.

Radioactive substances

Considerable quantities of naturally occurring radionuclides, such as potassium 40, rubidium 87, uranium, radium, and nuclides of the de-

Table 8.8 **Calculated relative contribution of some countries to the total deposition in the North Sea (%)**

	Belgium	Denmark	France	FRG[a]	Netherlands	United Kingdom	Other
Arsenic	20	0.6	7	16	1.5	38	18
Silver	27	4	9	9	7	39	6
Cadmium	12	1	13	15	5	39	15
Chromium	8	1	8	10	7	57	9
Copper	15	1	6	14	7	41	16
Nickel	6	3	11	7	5	53	15
Lead	6	1	11	5	8	60	9
Zinc	6	2	14	15	5	45	13

Source: Adapted from van Aalst (1988, 280).

a. Pre-unification West Germany.

Table 8.9 **Nitrogen (reduced and oxidized) entering the North Sea by air, 1988 ('000 tonnes)**

Country of source	Amount
Belgium	26
Czechoslovakia	3
Denmark	28
France	55
GDR	10
FRG	67
Eire	5
Netherlands	51
Norway	4
Portugal	7
Spain	1
Sweden	3
USSR	2
United Kingdom	132
Indeterminate	18
Total	412

Source: Rose (1990, 75).

cayed series of uranium and thorium, exist in sea water and other environments. As a result of the human utilization of the nuclear fission process, so-called artificial or man-made radionuclides are to be found in measurable quantities in sea water.

The principal sources of radionuclide discharge have changed over the past 30 years. Major inputs initially originated via the fallout from nuclear bomb testing in the 1960s, then from the emergence of nuclear power stations and nuclear fuel reprocessing plants during the 1970s, and recently from the accident at Chernobyl in 1986. Other sources, such as the use of radioisotopes in hospitals, science, and industry, contribute relatively small amounts. Since the North Sea is geographically far removed from the major testing sites of the atomic bomb explosions that took place in the Pacific islands in the 1960s, radionuclides from these sources caused only a slight increase in background radiation in the basin states. In the second half of the 1960s, after the practical cessation of atmospheric atomic bomb tests, the introduction of radionuclides from fallout was still only slight and the activity concentrations of those substances decreased markedly in the North Sea (Kautsky 1988, 391).

In 1970 in the southern North Sea and in 1971 in the north-western North Sea, an increase in caesium-137 concentrations was observed (Kautsky 1988). After thorough investigations, it became clear that they had originated from the nuclear fuel reprocessing plants at Sellafield in Cumbria and at Cap la Hague in France. The Sellafield plant was emitting into the Irish Sea waste that followed the oceanic currents and entered the northern North Sea, whereas the French installation was discharging into the English Channel and hence into the southern North Sea. Since this time, a reduction in the concentrations of caesium-134 and caesium-137 from the Sellafield works has been attributed to the installation of the SIXEP (Site Ion Exchange Effluent Plant), which treats water contaminated with radioactive waste from various irradiated fuel storage ponds and other related facilities (BNF 1985).

The most recent large addition of radioactivity to the North Sea came from the disaster at Chernobyl in May 1986. Clouds of radioactive material travelled across the North Sea and also contaminated some areas of the British uplands. As a result, caesium-137 values of 100–205 Bq per m^3 were measured in the German Bight and along the coast of Jutland, Denmark (Becker 1987). Owing to the constant water-exchange process, however, the radionuclides that entered North Sea waters via fallout have in the meantime largely been transported away. Caesium-134 and caesium-137 occur largely in soluble form. Loss of caesium-137 from the sea water by absorption into particulate matter or bottom sediments is, therefore, expected to be in the low range of no more than around 5–10 per cent.

Table 8.10 **Estimated annual inputs of petroleum hydrocarbons to the North Sea, 1980 and 1986 ('000 tonnes)**

Source	1980	1986
Rivers/land runoff	50	40–80
Accidental shipping losses	15	5–12
Refineries	11	6
Coastal sewage	8	3–14
Dumped sewage sludge	5	Not included
Dredge spoils	2.8	Not included
Offshore production	1.68	23
Atmosphere	Not included	19
Natural seeps	Not included	0.3–0.8
Oil terminals	0.61	0.8
Other coastal industrial effluents	Not included	9
Total	94.09	107–165

Sources: Read and Blackman (1980); Bedborough and Blackman (1986); Dicks, Bakke, and Dixon (1988), 525.

Oil discharges

The recent oil exploration and production now under way in the North Sea have inevitably introduced oil into the marine environment. Oil is extracted, shipped throughout the North Sea, and refined at many coastal locations, increasing the risk of spills from these installations as well as from offshore fields. Other sources of oil entering the North Sea and the amounts of petroleum hydrocarbon contained within them are listed in table 8.10, which provides data for 1980 and 1986. During that period, accidental losses decreased by a factor of 2 and offshore activities increased oil-spills by a factor of 10. These statistics are disputed by Greenpeace (Rose 1990), which claims that 72 per cent of oil pollution from shipping is due to deliberate discharges.

The Interim Quality Status Report (IQSR 1990) estimates that illegal oil discharges were between 1,100 and 60,000 tonnes and legal discharges between 1,000 and 1,500 tonnes. States signatory to the Paris Convention have set a limit for oil discharges from oil rigs and other exploration structures of 40 mg oil per litre of sea water. The United Kingdom is well above the other countries in this respect, although it is unclear whether it is exceeding the limit.

The oil-slick resulting from the Gulf conflict in 1991, described by many environmentalists as one of the world's worst ecological disasters, illustrates the great risk that similar oil-spills and accidents could create similar environmental destruction, albeit on a smaller scale, in the North Sea. Except perhaps for the Ekofisk Bravo blow-out in 1977, which spilled 15,000–22,000 tonnes of oil over seven days (Grahl-Nielsen 1978), the North Sea enjoyed a long period free of massive oil-slicks, although many smaller spills have occurred. In January 1993 a supertanker carrying about 25 million gallons of crude oil ran aground off the southern tip of the Shetland Isles (*INER* 1993a). The incident prompted environment and transport ministers to step up ongoing efforts to produce "a common policy on safe seas" (*INER* 1993b, 37).

On the basis of information provided by North Sea states, there are no clear or significant trends in observed slicks that can be detected in the North Sea area since the 1987 Conference (IQSR 1990). Annual surveys show that the United Kingdom achieved a 44 per cent reduction in the number of oil pollution incidents between 1980 and 1987. With regard to other North Sea states, Denmark shows no clear trends, whereas reports for the Netherlands indicate no significant changes in the pattern of oil-slicks during 1986–1988. For the German Bight, results of airborne surveillance operations show a decrease in oil pollution in terms of area covered and quantities involved. The Swedish Coast Guard reports that, compared with 1987, 1988 showed a 49 per cent increase in oil pollution on the west coast of the country. In Norway, the number of recorded oil pollution incidents increased, but the increase was attributed to the introduction of new reporting routines for spills smaller than 1 cubic metre (i.e. they all require notification) and the extended reporting of spills by local authorities and private persons (IQSR 1990).

There was no consensus among North Sea states on estimations of accidental oil discharges from ships, and no information has become available to improve the estimations presented in the 1987 QSR.

Direct inputs and river inputs

Direct inputs are those discharges that come straight into the North Sea, usually via a large effluent transport pipe. These discharges may include concentrations of, for example, heavy metals, nutrients, and organohalogens. The chemicals are discharged into the North Sea from rivers and by direct dumping. The quantities involved are examined below.

The 1987 Quality Status Report gave estimates of inputs from these sources over the years 1984, 1985, and 1986. It is surmised that, of the 400,000 million litres per day of water flowing into the North Sea, 80 per cent is accounted for.

Statistics for the total riverine inputs into the North Sea are somewhat unreliable. This is because not all rivers are included in the assessments, there are no estimates of data reliability, and the French rivers do not discharge directly into the North Sea (but into the Dover Straits).

Data for direct inputs are more diverse and more incomplete than those for rivers. In general, there seems to be an increase in most of the substances in the update of the figures presented at the third international conference in the Interim QSR (IQSR 1990) (see table 8.11).

The major exporters of substances via this route are West Germany, the Netherlands, and the United Kingdom. This is obviously due to several factors, including the geographical position of the rivers, the extent of industrialization on the banks of the rivers, and the countries through which the rivers and their tributaries pass. The IQSR made no estimation of the eastern European contribution.

Disposal of industrial wastes

Direct disposal of industrial waste is now largely controlled through international agreement. In the mid-1980s, West Germany was the principal discharger of such wastes (table 8.12). The largest and most important source was titanium dioxide emanating from both Belgium and West Germany. By the late 1980s, a reduction of 43 per cent had occurred in total industrial wastes discharged into the North Sea, with a corresponding reduction in the disposal of heavy metals (e.g. from 40 per cent for cadmium, 60 per cent for copper, to the nearly total removal of arsenic).

The United Kingdom remains the only North Sea basin state to dispose of solid industrial waste, most of which is associated with coastal coal workings and with fly ash from power-station residues. Despite the agreement of the 1987 North Sea Conference to end all disposal of industrial waste by 1990 (except for materials of natural origin or those that can be shown to produce no environmental harm), Britain continues to dump colliery waste on the grounds that it is an inert material. It is only a matter of time before Britain will be forced to abandon this practice and to come in line with the rest. Again, this

Table 8.11 **Direct river inputs to the North Sea (tonnes)**

	Belgium 1988	Denmark 1986	FRG 1988	Netherlands 1988	Norway 1988	Sweden 1988	UK 1986	Total
Nitrogen	57,400	24,978	255,700	518,510	78,690	20,883	210,406	1,200,000
Phosphorus	8,200	4,195	17,600	42,800	4,670	429	30,425	108,000
Cadmium	4.1	0.4	14	26	0.2	0.3	<28	<73
Mercury	1.8	0.2	16	6.6	0.2	0.02	<7.9	<33
Copper	55	13	420	680	95	44	<480	<1,790
Lead	62	4.3	250	330	17.3	9.5	<320	<994
Zinc	495	44	3,000	3,900	337	210	<2,300	<10,290
Chromium[a]	–	–	–	–	–	–	–	
Nickel[a]	–	–	–	–	–	–	–	
Arsenic[a]	–	–	–	–	–	–	–	
Hexachlorohexane	0.1	–[a]	0.7	1.4	–[a]	–[a]	<0.4	<2.6
Polychlorinated biphenyls	0.05	–[a]	<0.2	0.2	0.09	0.09	–[a]	<0.6

Source: IQSR (1990, 216).

a. No information.

Table 8.12 **Disposal of liquid industrial wastes into the North Sea (tonnes)**

Country of source	Amount dumped	Year	Cadmium	Mercury	Copper	Lead	Zinc	Chromium	Nickel	Arsenic
Belgium	526,269	1988	<0.005	<0.003	0.1	0.7	3.4	95.1	<0.3	<0.31
West Germany	906,159	1988	<0.023	<0.002	0.2	0.7	24.7	177.7	11.5	<0.11
United Kingdom	246,928	1987	0.020	0.006	0.6	0.7	0.5	0.3	0.6	0.02
Total	1,679,356		<0.048	<0.011	1.0	2.1	28.6	273.1	<12.4	<0.44

Source: IQSR (1990, 152).

matter highlights the difference of opinion between UK and continental practice over the appropriate means of protecting the North Sea.

Disposal of dredged materials

Shipping demands minimal water action or currents within harbour basins and therefore creates the optimal conditions for the sedimentation of river- or seaborne materials. It follows that it is necessary to maintain ports and channels in order to keep them accessible to (marine) shipping. Such material is removed by dredging (van Driel, Kerdijk, and Salomons 1984), which also takes place during the construction of new harbours/ports or extensions to existing ones.

A 1979 survey (Förstner and Salomons 1988) based on responses from 37 countries showed that around 350 million tonnes of maintenance dredging occurred that year. It was estimated that approximately 230 million tonnes of this comprised the average annual quantity of dredged materials. The survey showed also that dredged material was disposed of via a marine route, being deposited on wetlands and near-shore areas (Förstner and Salomons 1988).

Of the countries surrounding the North Sea, it is Belgium that dumps the largest proportion of dredged materials into the sea (IQSR 1990). There is concern that the dumping of dredged materials is yet another pathway for pollutants to enter the marine environment. The sediments being removed may well contain large amounts of heavy metals and PCBs, and records document an increase in the cadmium concentrations dredged from the mouth of the Rhine since 1920.

Suspended matter originates from the weathering and erosion of soils and rocks as well as from anthropogenic sources and consists of a variety of compounds (e.g. clay minerals, carbonates, quartzes, feldspars, and organic solids). These are usually coated with either hydrous manganese, iron oxides, or organic substances. The coating affects the interaction process between solids and dissolved components. Depending on the external and internal conditions of the sedimentary environment, the redistribution of trace metals, nutrients, and organic components takes place during the formation of the resulting sediments. Dredging is essentially a relocation of seabed materials, and the amount dumped varies annually owing to hydrological conditions, capital dredging programmes, and maintenance dredging schemes.

It is difficult to draw definite conclusions regarding the extent of contamination, and it is impossible to quantify the impact of dredged material. The amount of contamination released into the marine environment is unknown and depends on a variety of factors, such as local chemical conditions.

Certain dumping operations constitute not an increase in the contaminant load to the marine environment, only a relocation of substances. The IQSR (1990) concludes that dredging as such does not significantly increase the pollutant transport to the North Sea, as, even without dredging and harbour construction, the pollutant load would reach the sea eventually. The environmental impact of dumping dredged materials is difficult to assess as the most problematic constituents tend not to stay in the vicinity of the dumpsite.

In future years, contaminated dredged spoils may show a decrease owing to a relative reduction in the pollution of the North Sea, its rivers, and estuaries. A more systematic monitoring programme, however, is still required to identify the pathways of such pollutants and their environmental consequences.

Disposal of sewage sludge

Until an effective sanitary and sewer system was established, sewage was a menace to public health and unacceptable from an aesthetic point of view. The large, integrated sewage treatment works that we have today are the outcome.

The problems of sewage sludge disposal, however, have become pressing since the nineteenth century when liquid industrial waste was diverted into domestic sewers. Although this allowed the degradation of many substances, it has also added another route by which toxic contaminants can enter established disposal routes.

The choice of a disposal route for sewage sludge varies for each North Sea state (table 8.13) but is related to environmental, social, and economic costs. In densely populated areas, which account for many of the North Sea states, and especially those in the southern North Sea area, marine dumping or incineration is favoured owing to obvious land constraints. The lack of access to relatively short coastlines and sensitive littoral ecologies (e.g. the Waddensea in the Netherlands, West Germany, and Denmark) limits marine disposal in most countries (Parker 1988). Countries such as the Netherlands and the United Kingdom have dense coastal populations, and, in the case

Table 8.13 **Sewage sludge disposal in countries bordering the North Sea and in some other Oslo Convention signatory states**

Country	Sludge production ('000 tonnes/ year)	Disposal routes (% of total) Agriculture	Sanitary landfill	Incinera-tion	Pipeline to sea	Dumped at sea	Unspe-cified	Population density (nos/ha)[a]	Land usage index[b]	Length of coastline (km)	Coastline per unit land area ('000)
Countries bordering the North Sea:											
UK	1,500	41	26	4	2	27	–	5.4	9.8	4,000[c]	50
FRG	2,200	39	49	8	–	–	4	2.5	7.8	563[d]	2
Netherlands	230	60	27	2	11	–	–	4.1	5.9	362	11
Denmark	130	45	45	10	–	–	–	1.2	2.7	1,255[e]	29
Belgium	70	15	83	2	–	–	–	3.2	2.3	62	2
Norway	55	18	82	–	–	–	–	0.1	0.1	3,155	10
Other OSCOM countries:											
France	840	30	50	20	–	–	–	1.0	1.2	2,115[f]	4
Ireland	20	4	51	–	–	45	–	1.2	0.4	1,212	46
Luxembourg	11	90	10	–	–	–	–	–	–	0	0
Spain	1	60	c. 20	–	–	–	–	0.1	0.1	2,259[g]	5
Sweden	25	60	c. 30	–	–	–	–	–	0.5	2,566[h]	6

Sources: Parker (1988, 249); note that Parker cites three additional sources: for sludge production and disposal routes, Vincent and Critchely (1982); for land area, *Whitaker's almanac* (1986); for length of coastline, US Department of State (1969).

a. Population divided by total land area (exclusive of offshore islands and large lakes); this ignores differences in habitability or usage of land.

b. The "land usage index" is derived from (total sludge production x percentage diverted to agriculture and tipping) divided by total land areas (units of tonnes/hectare/year). This provides a very crude measure of the significance of land disposal in terms of usage of land area, ignoring variations in suitability of land for agriculture or tipping. Norway is badly treated by this index because of its very high proportion of mountainous land, but, in association with the population density figures, the index provides a guide to the constraints in other countries.

c. Excluding islands.

d. Of which *c.* 350 km on the North Sea.

e. Of which *c.* 400 km on the North Sea.

f. Of which *c.* 1,600 km on the English Channel/Atlantic.

g. Of which *c.* 900 km on the Atlantic.

h. All in the Kattegat/Baltic.

of the United Kingdom, disposal sites are located approximately 5–10 miles offshore, situated adjacent to major coastal towns, which explains why this route is favoured (Cotter 1988).

Options for the use of sewage sludge as a fertilizer on the land are often impractical owing to the extensive urban areas that may have to be traversed in order to reach agricultural areas. Furthermore, sludge is prone to contamination by toxic residues that render most of it (legally) harmful and thus unacceptable for use as fertilizer. Indeed, the growing prominence of heavy metals in domestic refuse means that the sludge of even small, rural catchments is often not usable as fertilizer. In addition, sewage sludge, if processed incorrectly, smells. The odour is likely to be unacceptable both to local residents and to the public at large. Therefore, where appropriate, disposal at sea is a preferred option, since it involves a single sea trip from a jetty adjoining the works to the dumping site.

Around one-third of the sewage sludge arising in the United Kingdom after treatment is disposed to the sea by ship. The amount dumped in 1987 was around 5,077,000 tonnes, a slight increase as compared with 1985 (QSR 1987). The United Kingdom is the only remaining North Sea country that dumps sewage sludge from vessels into the North Sea. West Germany ceased this practice in 1981 on the grounds that it was damaging the sensitive ecology of the German Bight.

When sewage is dumped into the sea, it usually contains 3–5 per cent solids, a "black milk" that is easily pumpable and readily dispersed at sea. The rationale behind marine dumping is that, because sludge contains primarily organic matter, natural processes will break it down and oxidize it. The same reasoning provides justification for some discharging of raw sewage via outfall pipes running into the North Sea. Sewage sludge contains less than 10 per cent of the toxic materials load currently entering the North Sea and only about 1 per cent of all the heavy metal pollution. Removal of this waste stream cannot scientifically be justified on "narrow" environmental grounds (though it may be on ethical grounds and upon some variant of precaution).

All the same, the 1990 North Sea Conference moved to ban all North Sea sewage sludge dumping by 1998. This example reflects the failure of the assimilative approach to cost–benefit calculation as compared with equal, country-by-country treatment. Politics and a collective inclination to buttress a new morality aimed at protecting the North Sea on precautionary grounds have prevailed. It is highly doubtful that the sludge decision can be justified in terms of economics or natural science, but it may well force a reconsideration of the separation of waste at source and promote the cause of clean technologies.

After putting up a struggle on the basis that the scientific evidence did not warrant such action, the British government reluctantly yielded in order to maintain good relations with its North Sea neighbours. Currently, all sludge-dumping licences are being reviewed with the prospect of early termination. The need to repatriate this sludge has highlighted the dilemma of contamination. About one-half of the total is not disposable on land because it contains a sufficient quantity of residues to be classified as controlled waste and, hence, disposable only at approved sites.

The preferred option for the larger sewage treatment works, such as London, is incineration. This involves no third party for eventual disposal, the technology is deemed satisfactory, and the in-plant production of energy reduces overall costs. The trouble is that local residents are generally of the "Not-In-My-Back-Yard" (NIMBY) disposition and do not want incinerators – regarded nowadays as having a stigma effect similar to that of radioactive waste disposal – in their midst. This means that any proposal for an incinerator is likely to provoke fierce opposition in the form of a local planning inquiry.

At the heart of this dilemma are two issues. One is the need for a proper environmental audit of disposal options, covering comparative risks, energy requirements, and nutrient flows and toxic residues that are genuinely not recyclable, even with the most advanced processes and technology. The other is the application of price-control regulations to force industry to reorganize its waste streams at source so as to minimize the amount and constitution of toxic materials discharged to a sewer. In this way, and over time, it may be possible to create a sludge that is acceptable even for garden use or for land-reclamation purposes, confining incineration to a small quantity of otherwise non-recyclable materials. Currently, these two approaches are receiving only limited examination, since no mechanism exists for ensuring pursuit of the best practicable disposal option. The United Kingdom government has now adopted a policy of applying best available technology to the removal of the so-called "red list" substances as defined by the European Communities' directives. This move means that increasing attention will be given to removing hazardous substances at source rather than waiting for treatment at the end of the pipe.

Incineration at sea

After World War II, the chemical industry grew rapidly and with it the production of organochlorines. It was common practice to dispose of such waste residues (e.g. EDC-tar, which contains 60–70 per cent chlorine) by dumping, especially in the North Sea and in the Gulf of Mexico. After the *Stella Maris* incident and the formation of the Oslo Commission and London Dumping Convention, however, organochlorines were placed on "black lists" and incineration at sea was recommended as an "interim technology" (Compaan 1988).

Sea incinerators do not have stack gas-scrubbing equipment because the hydrogen chloride fumes released are neutralized on contact with the sea. This makes them less expensive to run and offers advantages for the disposal of substances (e.g. chemicals with a high chlorine content or fluoridated and salt-rich wastes) that give off large quantities of highly corrosive fumes.

High-temperature combustion or incineration of wastes at sea began in 1969, mainly to dispose of liquid organochlorines (e.g. vinyl chloride and chlorobenzene), relatively stable compounds that are difficult to deal with by any other method. The waste problem has been made more serious by the necessary destruction of relatively pure organochlorines that are no longer permitted for use in the Western world; these substances include trichlorophenol-based herbicides, PCBs, and DDT. The North Sea has received for incineration more waste than have other seas around the world (Compaan 1988, 259). The total amount of incinerated waste at sea oscillates around 100,000 tonnes per year, though there has been a decreasing trend since 1986 in every country that uses this disposal method.

There are three vessels built specifically to deal with the waste, around 68 per cent of which is loaded at the port of Antwerp. The waste is transported to Antwerp by various means, including road, rail, rivers, canals, and sea.

On the basis of the Ministerial Declaration of the Second International North Sea Conference and in accordance with rule 2(3) of Annex IV of the Oslo Convention, the Oslo Commission decided to reduce and ultimately terminate incineration at sea by 1993 (INSC 1990). The decrease in incineration observed between 1986 and 1988 will, therefore, continue.

Countries such as Norway, Sweden, and the former West Germany have already phased out the use of marine incineration, while the Netherlands and France are very close. Switzerland, the United Kingdom, and Belgium are "progressing well," and expect a 65 per cent reduction by 1991 and termination by the required date. The decision to end the marine incineration practice has led to a new challenge to find alternative methods of disposal, usually meaning land incineration. This, in turn, has sparked vociferous complaints by coalitions of active groups that companies are not doing enough to reduce the residuals as a matter of principle. It is likely that the British government will insist on a sharing approach to waste incineration, in which each major waste-producing area will be expected to dispose of its residues locally, rather than seek external locations. Similarly, the European Commission is seeking to establish a policy by which each member state must have its own waste-disposal facilities, even where it is more economic to export wastes across borders. Beyond this, the Commission of the European Communities is proposing a tough civil liability directive that would require waste producers to be responsible for waste-related contamination, irrespective of good practice and whenever it might occur.

Trajectory and regional dynamics

Compared with some of the other regions examined in this volume, the North Sea is not critical in any non-sustainable sense, in part because the warning signs have been heeded and preventive action duly taken. Nevertheless, the sea is experiencing stress, notably from the accumulation of toxic chemicals and nutrients emanating from the waste discharges of many highly industrialized economies. It receives the outflows of major continental rivers – notably the Elbe, the Rhine, the Meuse, and the Scheldt – into which vast quantities of industrial wastes have been pouring for many years. Just how contaminated the estuarine sediments of all these rivers are is unknown, although dredging of harbour deposits is now controlled where high accumulations of toxic chemicals are evident.

Driving forces, vulnerability, and social equity

The main driving forces for environmental transformation in the North Sea centre on institutional failure, coupled with the popular and politically driven desire for material progress and the pursuit of more profit. As is well known, "the environment" suffers in such circumstances, simply because of a combination of ignorance, cumulative outcomes between individual acts and collective behaviour, and misleading price signals that encourage wholesale externalities and disruption of environmental systems.

This is why this chapter has emphasized both the precautionary principle and international conventions and cross-border binding regulations. Both of these cardinal issues depend in turn on better environmental science, the fundamental building blocks of knowledge that can tell us how much the North Sea environment is changing, who or what is losing and gaining, and what will be the benefits of various courses of action. It is the cost-effectiveness of various economic incentives and other regulatory measures, coupled with the best data, precaution, and cross-border sharing, that will determine the trajectory towards environmental criticality in the North Sea.

Vulnerability should be viewed in terms of those ecosystems most in danger – the global cycles of carbon, nitrogen, sulphur, and phosphorus, the addition of synthetic chemicals into the cycles that are not geared to assimilate such foreign elements, and the disruption of the nutrient status of the south-eastern North Sea. In general, it is eutrophication and toxification on a wide scale that create vulnerability in environmental systems in the North Sea.

But vulnerability has another meaning, namely the impact of remedial measures on those who either are poor or live in peripheral economies highly dependent on depleted natural resources. For instance, some of the many fishing communities affected by depletion of fish stocks and the tough regulation of industry are diversifying into fish farming, but that too carries environmental burdens, many of which are not fully understood.

The issue of cost-effectiveness in environmental management is, therefore, the most revealing. In the absence of good data and a sound knowledge of cause and effect, it is tempting to respond to the obvious cases of crisis, even when it may prove unnecessarily expensive to act on apparent causes. The cases of nutrient removal and sludge dumping are illustrative. As costs mount and as the burden on industrial growth increases, the impact of rearranged prices and diverted economic opportunity falls on those who are poor or who live in areas in which the economy is already moribund. In the case of North Sea communities, this means the isolated zones of the shoreline and the bypassed economies of the poorer or depressed regions – in western Norway, southern Sweden, northern Holland, eastern Germany, upland France, and upland and north-western United Kingdom.

Social-equity considerations are not fully incorporated into the management options for the future of the North Sea. The emphasis lies in environmental restoration and protection. The distributional aspects of the costs and consequences of such action are rarely examined and certainly not in an emphatic manner. The next phase in the programme to safeguard the North Sea will, therefore, have to attend to cost-effectiveness studies and their distributional consequences. These are two areas where institutional failure has not yet sufficiently been addressed.

This chapter indicates that, despite the reductions in recent years, large deposits of wastes still find their way into the North Sea. As the land and river sources are reduced, the contribution from the air becomes more significant. Yet this source of contribution is not easy to regulate, in so far as the sources are fugitive, arising from thousands of diverse emissions. It has recently been discovered, for example, that a potentially large source of nitrogen addition to the open North Sea comes from ammonia released from animal manure stored in heaps in the Netherlands and the United Kingdom (Rendell et al. 1993). This is a function of an overproductive livestock industry that can no longer dispose of its own wastes onto the land. Similarly, it is likely that sizeable proportions of the volatile organic compounds come from minute emissions from motor cars and from certain chemical reactions, again deposited via atmospheric particulates (QSR 1993).

Many of these compounds accumulate in sediment and in food pathways, magnified by concentration. The effects are more chronic than acute, but still poorly documented and understood. Indicators of possible trouble in store include:

- Changes in the species composition of algal populations. These may include species that contain toxins for fish and mammals (though this has yet to be proven) and species that can convert sulphur in the sea into a volatile compound that oxidizes into acid rain (dimethyl sulphide). This biogenic sulphur source could account for up to 30 per cent of acidity in continental Europe.
- A general increase in plankton bloom, indicated by the Continuous Plankton Recorder Survey, although available evidence suggests a climatic cause linked to the movement of nutrient-rich waters from the north-eastern Atlantic rather than anthropogenic factors. This could well prove to be a significant factor in deciding how extensively to regulate future emissions from sewage works. It is likely that the North Sea is becoming steadily eutrophified from entirely natural causes, and human-derived nutrient may be a problem only in shallow waters where the circulation is slow (e.g. the Waddensea

and the German Bight). The Swedish bloom of Chrysocromulina in 1988 was also probably of natural origin, associated with a stable water column and warm, sun-filled summers.

- The disappearance of seals almost to the point of extinction in the Waddensea during the 1970s, a tragedy linked to the increase in PCB contamination. The evidence here is strong – hence the concern to eliminate PCBs entirely.
- The death of seals on a massive scale in 1988 in the southern North Sea and Waddensea owing to a viral disease known as phocine distemper. Up to 60 per cent of the seals died in one year. Currently studies are in process to determine if a link exists between pollution and the immune systems in mammals, although at present the cause is believed to be natural in origin and some historical material exists to suggest that similar "plagues" have occurred in the past.
- The dying, apparently from hunger, of large numbers of sea birds. This may be due to the significant reduction of their fish stocks and may be linked to chlorinated substances and industrial fishing of sandeels. Sea birds also die as a result of oil pollution, though in terms of total population numbers these losses are not excessive.
- The rising incidence of diseases in fish in the German Bight and off the Dutch coast. This is also being attributed to environmental pollution, though the precise cause is still not known. Nevertheless, this is now regarded as one of the more convincing signs of environmental stress. (Lancelot, Billen, and Barth 1990)

This is where the precautionary principle comes into play. Despite the millions of pounds spent on research and modelling, most of the cause-and-effect chains are not proven and may never be conclusively linked in the period during which action should be taken. We are beginning to witness the emergence of a more people-friendly and environment-friendly precautionary science, where ethical values permeate cost–benefit analyses, and where wealthy and technologically innovative societies can afford to invest in preventive action and clean-up. Indeed, in the European Union as a whole, the environmental protection industry is worth about US$180 billion annually – a sizeable component of new economic activity in the region.

One consequence of this more vernacular approach to science is the creation of computer-modelled scenarios of how different policy measures might create particular environmental futures. The Dutch MANS project is not confined to the study of organic, nutrient, and toxic pathways. Nor is it merely a risk-assessment tool. It is explicitly designed to assist economists, lawyers, and policy makers to consider the possible consequences of various courses of action, including regulatory measures to guide industrial activity and consumer behaviour, so that sensitivity can be identified and given weight. The scope for "user-friendly" modelling is considerable.

Management institutions

Commons require collective governance. This is rarely possible to achieve in advance, especially if the alteration of environmental systems is uneven and the countries involved are at different stages of economic development. It is hardly surprising to report that the first moves to control pollution came only in the early 1970s when the problem had already become evident.

The regulation of pollution in the North Sea is largely the work of three important forums:

- *The Oslo Convention*, which came into force in 1974, covers the regulation of marine pollution from dumping by ships and aircraft. The Convention established the Oslo Commission, which consists of representatives of all 14 West European maritime states.
- *The Paris Convention*, which covers the regulation of marine pollution from land-based sources, came into force in 1978. Again, the maritime states are involved in the Paris Commission, although their jurisdiction extends to freshwater sources as well as shore sources. The European Union is a member of this commission. The commission has broad powers for control, including discharge limits, environmental quality standards, and regulations covering the use of substances and products.
- *The International North Sea Conference* (INSC) is not a standing body, but a meeting of environmental ministers of the eight basin states. This is essentially a political initiative that sets the policy framework for national action and specific implementation by the two commissions.

The two commissions, referred to as OSPARCOM, meet annually and tend to act on the advice of expert panels that are vetted by standing scientific and technical bodies. In this sense OSPARCOM provides the regulatory buttress for the INSC proposals, adding legal support for politically inspired positions. The INSC meetings are not in themselves very detailed, so an important measure of scientific and regulatory symbiosis links the two modes of management.

The creation of the North Sea Conferences was a result of a high-level scientific study sponsored by the West German parliament in

1980 (RSU 1980). This brought together for the first time the known scientific information regarding the North Sea and pointed out the gaps in understanding. Above all, it showed clearly that no country acting alone could solve the environmental problems of the North Sea. Such recognition, coming at a time when Europe was becoming politically sensitive to environmental issues, prompted the then most politically powerful country of all, West Germany, to convene the first conference in Bremen in 1984.

The North Sea Conference declarations and the two commissions together find the necessary legal, scientific, and economic bonds to ensure that commitments are made. Thus, the commissions provide the necessary legal and scientific framework to convey ministerial intent into lasting agreement. Following the 1987 London meeting of the conference, the commissions, in league with the International Council for the Exploration of the Seas, established a North Sea Task Force that produced a second Quality Status Report (QSR 1993) for a joint meeting of the conference and the commissions in 1993. Guiding the conference is a Political Working Group that sets the political framework for key decisions. These include the following actions:

- strict control on all "blacklist" chemicals, notably mercury, cadmium, organotin compounds, and new synthetic substances (associated with organochlorine products);
- setting precise targets of all "grey list" substances, including the persistent halogen compounds, PACs (polychlorinated aliphatic hydrocarbons), and dioxins;
- the phasing out, by 1999, of all PCBs entering the North Sea;
- the cessation of sewage sludge dumping by 1998;
- the elimination of all incineration at sea by 1993;
- the cessation of the practice of dumping oil-based muds from offshore platforms;
- the establishment of best available technology for 10 key process industries aimed at process-based discharge standards;
- a review of all nutrient sources with a view to substantial elimination (up to one-half) by 1995 for eastern coastal areas;
- a substantial reduction in pesticides by 1993;
- the cessation of all industrial waste disposal by 1992;
- a reduction of 50 per cent in inputs from estuaries or rivers, and from the air of specified substances, by 1995 (or 1999 at latest);
- a 70 per cent reduction in all substances that cause a major threat to the marine environment, including dioxins, mercury, cadmium, and lead;

- the application of the best available techniques not entailing excessive costs (a variant of the precautionary principle) to all "red list" substances via the implementation of integrated pollution control applied at source in a total management frame of reference (Gibson and Churchill 1990).

All these decisions are set in a framework of both political and scientific backing. The commissions provide the independent scientific authority, whereas the conferences establish the political direction. This includes the prior justification procedure that prohibits any dumping at sea unless no practicable alternative can be found on land and the materials pose no risk as determined by a competent international scientific organization.

This raises the question of whether a single body, along the lines of the Helsinki Commission for the maintenance of peace and security throughout Europe, should be responsible for the North Sea. In essence there is no device that has supranational power both politically and legally that is not forever thwarted by nation-state manoeuvres. In pragmatic terms the current arrangements work well as long as attitudes shift in favour of tough measures and the collective political will is supported by a transfer of knowledge, predictive modelling techniques, technology, and management skills from the advanced to the less advanced nations.

The North Sea is unusual in that every country is sufficiently wealthy and environmentally motivated to reach a surprising degree of common agreement, albeit belatedly. This is not the case for the Mediterranean Sea, where even more formidable problems of resource depletion and environmental degradation abound, yet where the economic circumstances of the most afflicted countries encourage even greater abuse of their precious environmental assets (Haas 1990).

There is no easy solution to such dilemmas. At the heart of the matter is the need to establish a meaningful community of common futures. This needs at the very least:

- adequate monitoring and gathering of comprehensive scientific information;
- sound modelling schemes that can be made policy relevant by simulating outcomes of environmental states based on the proposed impact of possible policy measures. Such models may be used in the classroom as much as in the legislative chamber;
- formal links between political structures, scientific task forces, and the framework for implementing international environmental law;

- agreements to transfer critical resource needs to countries yet unable to establish their own environmental protection programmes. These transfers should be linked to policy performance and policy commitments and delivered through competent international institutions, not by bilateral arrangements;
- commitments to a common protection strategy based on ambient quality standards, emission controls related to best available technology, the application of cost–benefit models related to the most practicable environmental option studies, and the application of the precautionary principle;
- regional compacts to establish localized agreements on management measures to overcome small-scale, yet international problems. These could be based on the principles of critical environmental load based on indicators of environmental sensitivity, and applying the mechanisms of strict liability, best technology, and performance audits.

Restoring an area on a trajectory to endangerment to a semblance of normalcy requires a colossal shift of political attention, resources, and decision-making structures, and prolonged commitment. To bring even more critical regions, such as the Aral Sea (chap. 3) and the Nepal middle mountains (chap. 4), to the bare bones of habitability will require the assistance of the whole globe. It is very doubtful indeed that salvation measures for severe situations can be effectively implemented at the regional level.

Acknowledgements

This chapter has gone through a number of drafts. The authors are particularly indebted to Henry Cleery of the Department of the Environment in London, and to Albert Weale, Seeseana Bateman, Andrea Williams, and Alastair Grant of the University of East Anglia. The usual disclaimers apply.

References

Aalst, R. M., van. 1988. Input from the atmosphere. In *Pollution of the North Sea: An assessment*, ed. Wim Salomons, Brian L. Bayne, Egbert K. Duursma, and Ulrich Förstner, 275–283. Berlin: Springer-Verlag.

Aalst, R. M. van, J. H. Duyzer, and C. Veldt. 1983. *Atmospheric deposition of lead and cadmium in the southern part of the North Sea: Emissions and preliminary model calculations*. Report R 83/222. Delft: TNO.

Andersen, S. H. 1984. Bycatches of the harbour porpoise (*Phocaena phocaena*) in Danish fisheries (1980–1981) and evidence for overexploitation. *Report of the International Whaling Commission* 34: 745–749.

Becker, Gerd Axel. 1987. *Die Auswirkungen des Kenkraftwerkunfalles von Tschernobyl auf Nord- und Ostsee.* Meereskundliche Beobachtungen und Ergebnisse no. 62. Hamburg: Deutsches Hydrographisches Institut.

Bedborough, D., and R. A. A. Blackman. 1986. A survey of inputs to the North Sea resulting from oil and gas development. *Philosophical Transactions of the Royal Society (London)*, Series B 316: 495–509.

Bellamy, D. J., P. Edwards, M. J. D. Hirons, D. J. Jones, and P. R. Evans. 1973. Resources of the North Sea and some interactions. In *North Sea science*, ed. Edward D. Goldberg, 383–399. Cambridge, MA: MIT Press.

Boehmer-Christiansen, Sonja. 1990. Environmental quality objectives versus uniform emission standards. In *The North Sea: Perspectives on regional environmental co-operation*, ed. David Freestone and Ton IJlstra, 139–149. Special issue of the *International Journal of Estuarine and Coastal Law*. London: Graham & Trotman/ Martinus Nijhoff.

BNF (British Nuclear Fuels). 1985. SIXEP, site ion exchange effluent plant. Risley, Warrington, England: Information Services, BNF.

BP (British Petroleum Company). 1991. *BP statistical review of world energy*. London: BP.

Byrne, C. D. 1989. *Community water quality policy for the nineties*. Luxembourg: Commission of the European Communities.

Camphysen, C. J., and J. van Dijk. 1983. See-en kustvogels langs de Nederlandse kust, 1974–1979 (English summary). *Limosa* 57: 81–230.

Compaan, H. 1988. Waste incineration at sea. In *Pollution of the North Sea: An assessment*, ed. Wim Salomons, Brian L. Bayne, Egbert K. Duursma, and Ulrich Förstner, 257–274. Berlin: Springer-Verlag.

Cotter, J. 1988. Sea disposal-licensing and monitoring. In *Chemistry and Industry* 2 May: 290–293.

Coull, James R. 1988. The North Sea herring fishery in the twentieth century. *Ocean Yearbook* 7: 115–131.

De Wolf, P., and J. J. Zijlstra. 1988. The ecosystem. In *Pollution of the North Sea: An assessment*, ed. Wim Salomons, Brian L. Bayne, Egbert K. Duursma, and Ulrich Förstner, 118–151. Berlin: Springer-Verlag.

Dicks, B., T. Bakke, and I. M. T. Dixon. 1988. Oil exploration and production and oil spills. In *Pollution of the North Sea: An assessment*, ed. Wim Salomons, Brian L. Bayne, Egbert K. Duursma, and Ulrich Förstner, 524–537. Berlin: Springer-Verlag.

Driel, W. van, H. N. Kerdijk, and W. Salomons. 1984. Use and disposal of contaminated dredged material. *Land and Water International* 53: 13–18.

Eisma, D. 1986. The North Sea: An overview. In *Reasons for concern: Proceedings of the 2nd North Sea Seminar '86, vol. 1*, ed. E. Hey and G. Peet, 11–28. Amsterdam: Werkgroep Noordzee.

Evans, P. R. 1973. Avian resources of the North Sea. In *North Sea science*, ed. Edward D. Goldberg, 400–412. Cambridge, MA: MIT Press.

FAO (Food and Agriculture Organization of the United Nations). 1978. *Mammals in the sea*, vol. 1. FAO Fisheries Series no. 5. Rome: FAO.

Financial Times. 1990a. Pile of stinking fish fails to spur EC to accept quotas. 20 December: 32.

———. 1990b. Fishing quota reduction agreed. 21 December: 30.

Förstner, Ulrich, and Wim Salomons. 1988. Dredged materials. In *Pollution of the North Sea: An assessment*, ed. Wim Salomons, Brian L. Bayne, Egbert K. Duursma, and Ulrich Förstner, 225–245. Berlin: Springer-Verlag.

Garrod, D. M., and J. M. Colebrook. 1978. Biological effects of variability in the North Atlantic ocean. *Rapports et procès-verbaux des réunions/Conseil international pour l'exploration de la mer* 172: 128–144.

Gibson, John, and Robin R. Churchill. 1990. Problems of implementation of the North Sea declarations: A case study of the United Kingdom. In *The North Sea: Perspectives on regional economic co-operation*, ed. David Freestone and Ton IJlstra, 66–79. Special issue of the *International Journal of Estuarine and Coastal Law*. London: Graham & Trotman/Martinus Nijhoff.

Glover, R. S. 1967. The continuous plankton recorder survey of the North Atlantic. *Symposia of the Zoological Society of London* 19: 189–210.

Glover, R. S., A. Robinson, and J. M. Colebrook. 1974. Marine biological surveyance. *Environmental Change* 2: 395–402.

Grahl-Nielsen, O. 1978. The Ekofisk Bravo blow-out: Petroleum hydrocarbons in the sea. In *The Proceedings of the Conference on Assessment of Ecological Impacts of Oil Spills, 14–17 June 1978, Keystone, Colorado*, 476–487. Arlington, VA: American Institute of Biological Physics.

Haas, Peter M. 1990. *Saving the Mediterranean: The politics of international environmental cooperation*. New York: Columbia University Press.

Hoek, C. van den, W. Admiraal, F. Colijn, and V. N. de Jonge. 1979. The role of algae and seagrasses in the ecosystems of the Wadden Sea: A review. In *Flora and vegetation of the Wadden Sea: Final Report*, ed. W. J. Wolff, 9–118. Wadden Sea Working Group Report 3. Rotterdam: Balkema.

Höhn, R. 1973. On the climatology of the North Sea. In *North Sea science*, ed. Edward D. Goldberg, 183–236. Cambridge, MA: MIT Press.

INER (*International Environment Reporter*). 1993a. Tanker grounded, spilling crude oil off Scotland's Shetland Isles. *INER Current Reports* 16, no. 1 (13 January): 5–6.

———. 1993b. Ministers agree to push through unified policies to curb oil pollution. *INER Current Reports* 16, no. 2 (27 January): 37–38.

INSC (International North Sea Conference). 1990. *Conference proceedings*. The Hague: INSC.

IQSR, 1990. *Interim report on the quality status of the North Sea*. The Hague: Netherlands Ministry of Transport and Public Works.

Jaarsveld, J. A. van, R. M. van Aalst, and D. Onderdelinden. 1986. *Deposition of metals from the atmosphere into the North Sea*. Report RIVM 842015002. Bilthoven, the Netherlands: Rijksinstituut voor Volksgezondheid en Milieuhygiene (RIVM).

Joffre, Sylvain M. 1985. *The structure of the marine atmospheric boundary layer: A review from the point of view of diffusivity, transport and deposition process*. Technical Report 29. Helsinki: Finnish Meteorological Institute.

Kates, Robert W., B. L. Turner II, and William C. Clark. 1990. The great transformation. In *The Earth as transformed by human action: Global and regional changes in the biosphere over the past 300 years*, ed. B. L. Turner II, William C. Clark, Robert W. Kates, Jessica T. Mathews, and William B. Meyer, 1–17. Cambridge: Cambridge University Press with Clark University.

Kautsky, H. 1988. Radioactive substances. In *Pollution of the North Sea: An assessment*, ed. Wim Salomons, Brian L. Bayne, Egbert K. Duursma, and Ulrich Förstner, 390–399. Berlin: Springer-Verlag.

Kemp, Alexander G. 1990. An assessment of the North Sea oil and gas policies: Twenty five years on. *Energy Policy* 18: 599–623.

Lancelot, C., G. Billen, and H. Barth, eds. 1990. *Eutrophication and algal blooms in North Sea coastal zones, the Baltic and adjacent areas: Prediction and assessment of preventive actions: Proceedings of a workshop organised by the Commission of the European Communities Environmental R and D Programme, in Brussels, 26–28 October 1989*. Water Pollution Research Report no. 12. Brussels: Commission of the European Communities.

Lee, A. J. 1988. The North Sea: Setting the scene. In *Environmental protection of the North Sea*, ed. P. J. Newman and A. R. Agg, 1–24. Oxford: Heinemann.

MacGarvin, Malcolm. 1990. *The North Sea*. London: Collins & Brown.

Morley, George. 1968. *The North Sea*. London: Frederick Muller.

Parker, M. 1988. Sewage sludge disposal in the North Sea. In *Pollution of the North Sea: An assessment*, ed. Wim Salomons, Brian L. Bayne, Egbert K. Duursma, and Ulrich Förstner, 246–256. Berlin: Springer-Verlag.

QSR (Quality Status Report). 1987. *Second international conference on the protection of the North Sea: A report by the Scientific and Technical working group*. London: HMSO.

———. 1993. *Quality status report for the North Sea*. London: HMSO.

Radach, G. 1982. Dynamic interactions between lower tropic levels of the marine food web in relation to the physical environment during the Fladen Ground experiment. *Netherlands Journal of Sea Research* 16: 231–246.

Read, A. D., and R. A. A. Blackman. 1980. Oily discharges from North Sea installations: A perspective. *Marine Pollution Bulletin* 11: 44–77.

Reid, P. C. 1978. Continuous plankton records: Large-scale changes in the abundance of phytoplankton in the North Sea from 1958–1973. *Rapports et procès-verbaux réunions/Conseil international pour l'exploration de la mer* 172: 384–389.

Reid, P. C., and T. D. Budd. 1979. Plankton and environment in the North Sea in the period 1948–1977. *International Council for the Exploration of the Sea (ICES)* CM 1979: L26.

Rendell, A. R., C. J. Ottley, T. D. Jickells, and R. Harrison. 1993. The atmospheric input of nitrogen to the North Sea. *Tellus* 45: 53–63.

Rose, Chris, ed. 1990. *Why Britain remains "the dirty man of Europe": A report for Greenpeace by Media Natura*. London: Greenpeace.

RSU (Rat für Sachverständigung für Umweltfragen). 1980. *Umweltprobleme der Nordsee: Sondergutachten Juni 1980*. Stuttgart: Verlag W. Kohlhammer.

Salomons, Wim, Brian L. Bayne, Egbert K. Duursma, and Ulrich Förstner, eds. 1988. *Pollution of the North Sea: An assessment*. Berlin: Springer-Verlag.

Sibthorp, M., ed. 1975. *The North Sea: Challenge and opportunity: Report of a study group of the Davis Davies Memorial Institute of International Studies*. London: Europa for the Institute.

Summers, C. F., W. N. Bonner, and J. van Haaften. 1978. Changes in the seal populations in the North Sea. *Rapports et procès-verbaux des réunions/Conseil international pour l'exploration de la mer* 172: 278–285.

Symes, David. 1990. North Sea fisheries: Trends and management issues. In *The*

North Sea: Perspectives on regional environmental co-operation, ed. David Freestone and Ton IJlstra, 271–288. Special issue of the *International Journal of Estuarine and Coastal Law*. London: Graham & Trotman/Martinus Nijhoff.

Tiews, K. 1978. The German industrial fisheries in the North Sea and their by-catches. *Rapports et procès-verbaux des réunions/Conseil international pour l'exploration de la mer* 172: 230–238.

UK Digest of Energy Statistics. 1991– (annual). London: HMSO.

US Department of State. 1969. Sovereignty of the sea. *Geographic Bulletin* 3: 1–5.

Verweij, J., and W. J. Wolff. 1982. The common or harbour porpoise (*Phocaena phocaena*), the bottlenose dolphin (*Tursiops truncatus*). In *Marine mammals of the Wadden Sea*, ed. Peter J. H. Reijnders and Wim J. Wolff, 51–64. Rotterdam: Balkema.

Vincent, A. J., and R. F. Critchely. 1982. A review of sewage sludge treatment and disposal in Europe. *Water Research Centre Medmenham Report* 442–M: 31.

Wheeler, Alwyne C. 1969. *The fishes of the British Isles and northwest Europe*. London: Macmillan.

———. 1978. *Key to the fisheries of northern Europe*. London: Frederick Warne.

Whitaker's almanac. 1986. London: Whitaker.

World Bank. 1992. *World development report 1992: Development and the environment*. Oxford: Oxford University Press for the World Bank.

Zijlstra, J. J. 1988. The North Sea ecosystem. In *Ecosystems of the world*, ed. D. W. Goodall. Part 27, *Ecosystems of the continental shelves*, ed. H. Postma and J. J. Zijlstra, 231–278. Amsterdam: Elsevier.

Zwiep, Karel van der. 1990. The Wadden Sea: A yardstick for a clean North Sea. In *The North Sea: Perspectives on regional environmental co-operation*, ed. David Freestone and Ton IJlstra, 201–212. Special issue of the *International Journal of Estuarine and Coastal Law*. London: Graham & Trotman/Martinus Nijhoff.

9

The Ordos Plateau of China

Hong Jiang, Peiyuan Zhang, Du Zheng, and Fenghui Wang

The Ordos Plateau is a geographical region demarcated by the Yellow River's elbow section in the north and the Great Wall in the south (fig. 9.1). Administratively, it comprises mainly the Ih-Ju League of Inner Mongolia Region of the People's Republic of China. The sandy and denuded landscape of the plateau contrasts sharply with the adjacent areas – the Yellow River's elbow plain to the north and west, the loess hills and rocky mountains to the east, and the loess plateau to the south.

In 1988, as part of joint research undertaken by the Chinese Academy of Sciences and Clark University, the Ordos Plateau was chosen as a case-study of a potentially endangered zone. Building upon research conducted at the Chinese Academy of Sciences since the 1950s, data collection and field research addressed environmental changes and their human causes within the context of natural variability. Human dimensions of environmental changes in the Ordos, and especially human driving forces and societal responses, received new emphasis.

This chapter examines environmental changes in the Ordos, their effects on society, and the human driving forces of and societal responses to these changes. It concludes with an analysis of the general environmental trajectory of the area and its implications.

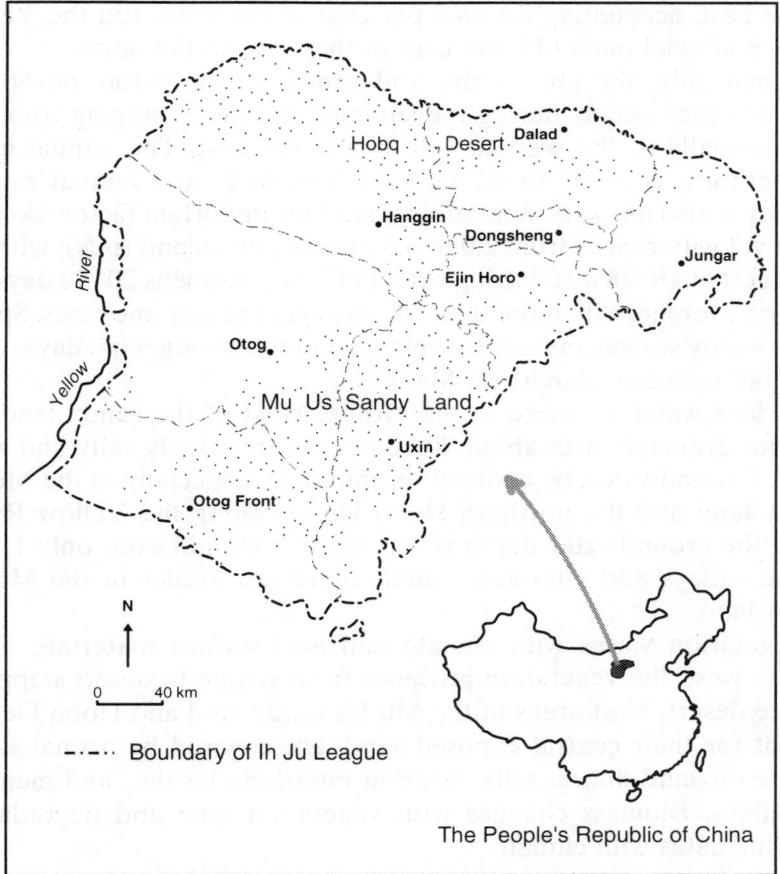

Fig. 9.1 **The Ordos Plateau of China**

Background

Natural setting

The Ih-Ju League of China has an area of 87,428 km^2, most of which is covered by loose Quaternary deposit, easily disturbed and eroded. Sandy land develops easily and occupies much of the area. Base rock predominates in parts of the western high plateau. The Mu Us sandy land and flat valleys cover 28.8 per cent and the Hobq Desert 19.2 per cent of the region. The middle and west are denuded high plateau, accounting for 28.8 per cent of the total area. What is left is the loess hills in the east, accounting for 18.9 per cent of the area, and the Yellow River's alluvial plain (4.3 per cent of the area) in the north.

Climatically, the area is dry and windy. Precipitation, 60–80 per cent of which occurs during the summer, is rare, averaging from 160 mm annually in the west to 400 mm in the east. The annual mean temperature is 5.3°C to 8.7°C, with high daily and annual ranges. Aridity is also marked. Windiness is another important factor: average wind velocity ranges from 2.0 to 4.3 metres per second (m/s), with the strongest at 18–28 m/s. Strong wind (>17 m/s) happens 20–40 days per year on average, with more than 100 days/year in extreme cases. Spring is the windy season and some 40 per cent of the strong-wind days of the year fall between March and May.

Surface water is scarce in the Ordos. Most of the sandy land has interior drainage, with about 70 lakes that are largely salty and alkalized. Groundwater, by contrast, is abundant, especially in the Mu Us sandy land and the northern Hobq Desert along the Yellow River. Here the groundwater depth is less than 10 m, and even only 1–3 m in the valleys and inter-sand, dune-depressed locales in the Mu Us sandy land.

Vegetation varies with climate and land-surface materials. From east to west, the vegetation proceeds from steppe to desert steppe to steppe desert. Vast areas of the Mu Us sandy land and Hobq Desert, except for their central exposed sand, are covered by azonal sandy steppe on sand-dunes, salix shrub in interdune locales, and meadow in valleys. Biomass changes with vegetation type and degradation and fluctuates with climate.

Socio-economic conditions

Administratively, the Ih-Ju League contains seven *banners* (local administrative units), namely Jungar, Dalad, Hanggin, Ejin Horo, Otog, Otog Front, and Uxin banners, and one city (Dongsheng). The terms "league" and "banner," as well as the subunits "sumu" and "baga," suggest the Mongolian origin of the area, whereas city, township, and village refer to Han culture.

Although the area is a Mongolian autonomous region, Han people actually dominate owing to migrations over recent decades. In 1989, of the total population of 1,184,148, 87.7 per cent were Hans and 12 per cent Mongolians. Farmers and shepherds make up 82.7 per cent of the population, and town and city dwellers account for 16.5 per cent.

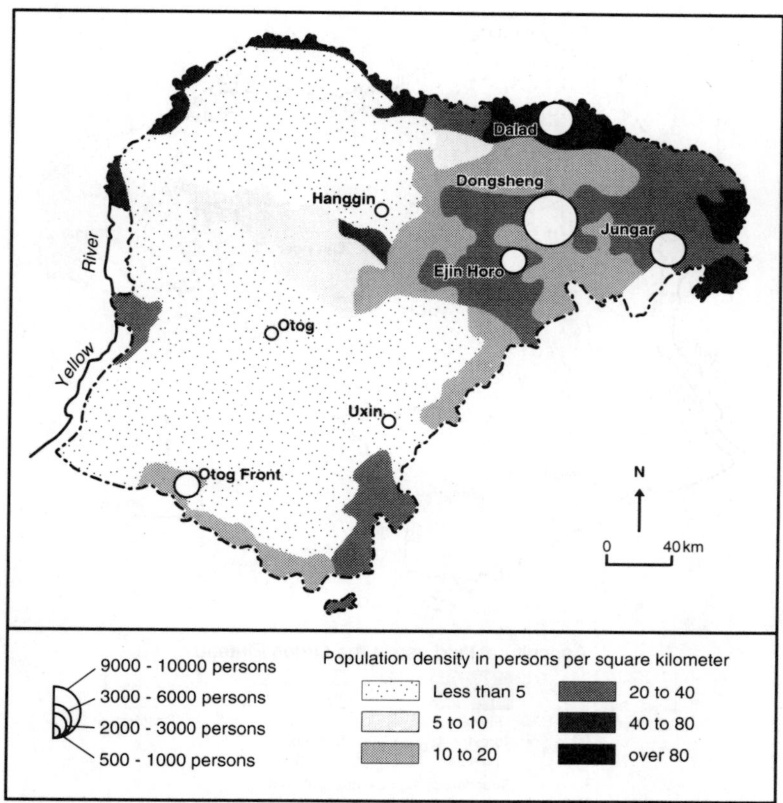

Fig. 9.2 **Population density in the Ordos Plateau (Sources: data compiled from field interviews by the authors and adapted from Ih-Ju League, 1988)**

Population density is highly differentiated (fig. 9.2). In 1989, the average density was 13.5 people/km^2, ranging from 1.4 in the west Otog steppe desert to 148 along the Yellow River north of Dalad. In the western four banners, people live in dispersed settlements over the vast pasture, with several kilometres between households being quite common. Education levels are low, especially for farmers and shepherds. In 1982, 35.4 per cent of the people over 12 years old were illiterate or quasi-illiterate.

The Ih-Ju League is an agricultural area in terms of land use and occupation. In 1985, 76 per cent of the total area and 97.3 per cent of the utilized area were devoted to agriculture. Farming areas occur along the Yellow River alluvial plain in the north, the eastern loess hills area, and the southern river valleys of the Uxin Banner (fig.

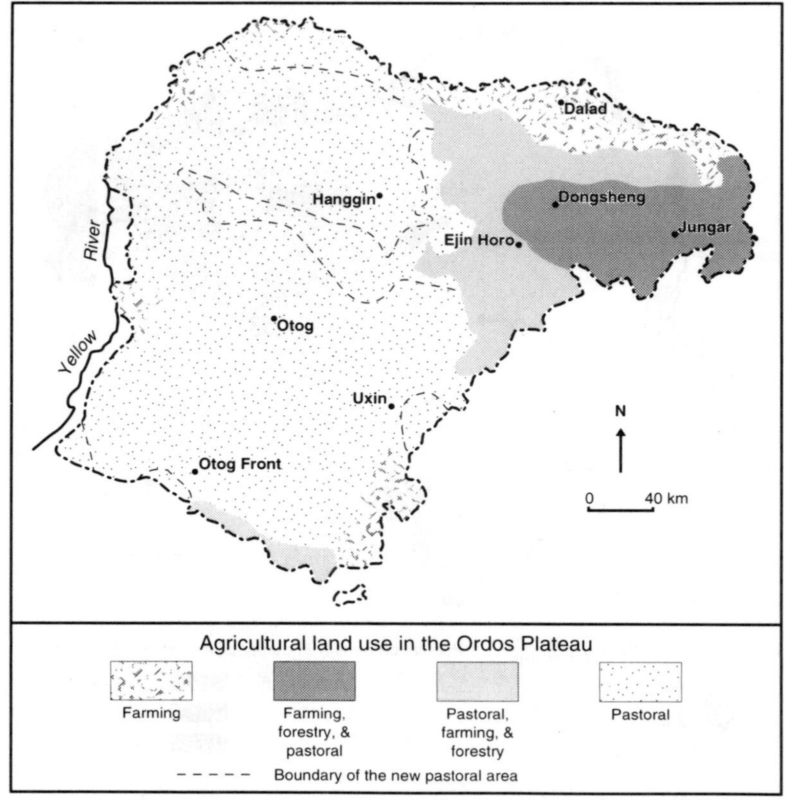

Fig. 9.3 **Agricultural land use in the Ordos Plateau (Sources: adapted from Ih-Ju League, 1988, 1990)**

9.3). Most of the western and south-western parts are pastoral lands linked by a transitional area of combined farming–grazing. Forestry includes the management of trees and shrubs and occurs mainly in the farming and farming–grazing areas.

Of the total agricultural and industrial gross product in 1989, farming, forestry, and animal husbandry totalled 43.4 per cent, of which farming accounted for 37.8 per cent and animal husbandry 45.7 per cent, indicating a generally low level of productivity. In 1989, grain yielded only 1,935 kg/ha and oil-producing crops 1,020 kg/ha. Pasture has a low biomass (1,035 kg/ha in 1989). Agriculture depends mainly on naturally accumulated soil fertility and vegetation resources, and changes significantly with climatic fluctuations.

Industry is strongly oriented to local resources. Although the Ordos has a marginal ecological environment, the Ih-Ju League is rich in coal, salt, and alkali. The three main coalfields – Jungar in the east, Dongsheng in the centre, and Zhuozishanin the west – contain 99.64 billion tonnes of proven high-quality coal deposits and constitute some of China's major coalfields. Coalmining developed very late in the Ordos, however, so that coal is still insufficient even for local power plants. Salt and alkali production and wool textile mills are also small-scale enterprises as reflected in overall current economic production but promise a large future potential for development.

Environmental problems in the area are mainly non-point problems, induced by land exploitation. Therefore, agriculture, involving the overwhelming percentage of land, has provided a key proximate source of environmental change. This has been true in the past and will likely continue to be so in the foreseeable future. Therefore, agriculture will be the focus of this study of environmental changes in the Ordos. Industry, which plays a part in environmental change mainly through its interaction with agriculture, has not yet become a significant source of regional pollution.

As already emphasized, the economy of the Ih-Ju League rests primarily on local resources. Material exchange with other regions is very limited. Output from the area consists mainly of animal-husbandry products and coal, whereas imports from other regions (as shaped by government regulation) are mainly staples (grain) and financial aid. The national government regulates these spatial linkages. According to the national plan, the state is currently investing heavily in coalmining, which is likely to develop rapidly. Another spatial linkage involves the discharge of sand and silt into the Yellow River, affecting its lower reaches.

The Ordos as an endangered area

The Ordos is a naturally marginal and economically backward area, characterized by semi-arid, arid windy, and sandy natural conditions. It has a low-level agricultural economy and a tangential relationship with other regions. Agricultural practices account for environmental erosion and vegetation and soil degeneration in the region. This contrasts sharply with the "modern" environmental problems treated by Ezcurra and colleagues in chapter 7. Although the overuse of fertilizer prevails in many developed countries and has presented a particular problem in the Aral Sea basin (chap. 3), the Ordos has insufficient fertilization. The driving forces of environmental changes in the Ordos come mainly from farmers and shepherds. This is typical of many endangered areas in China and in other developing countries. Therefore, this chapter will explore the relationships between human factors and environmental problems applicable to this type of setting. Economic specialization does, of course, matter in the Ordos. Indeed, abundant mineral resources in the Ordos present a great opportunity for industrial and economic development, although realization of this potential requires economic drive. Other special factors in the Ordos include a long history of human activities, a hierarchical national political economy, and a centralized political system. All these play their roles in the unfolding of environmental change.

The temporal and spatial background of environmental changes

Since the socio-economic forces and regional dynamics of environmental change are the focus of this study, they provide criteria for defining the time-scale of analysis. Therefore, the time-period during which human activities have profoundly affected the present Ordos environment, or, in other words, have formed today's life-supporting ecological system, is the period of primary emphasis. The earlier, less significant periods will be considered largely as context.

In the Ordos Plateau, the period of strong human impact has spanned the last 40–50 years. The year 1949 marks an important turning point, when both the social and economic systems began to change greatly, causing a sudden increase in the intensity of human activity. The existence of economic statistics aside, another reason for choosing the base time of 1949 is the availability of data recording natural factors from that year forward.

Environmental evolution and early human activities

The Ordos is geologically a part of the north China platform. In the Quaternary, it underwent a warm–humid and cold–dry alternating semi-arid climate, with a general tendency toward aridity. Loess deposition and windy sand occurred in dry periods, whereas vegetation covered the land during humid periods. For example, the early Neocene (10,000–7,000 years B.P.) was cold and dry, and moving sand covered much of the area, whereas 6,000–4,000 years B.P. was a warm and humid period, so a steppe emerged, moving sand became fixed, and palaeo-soil developed. In 3,000–1,500 years B.P., a dry climate returned and moving sand spread south of what came to be the Great Wall. Another favourable climatic period spanned 1,500–1,100 years B.P., when moving sand shrank and the steppe expanded. After 1,000 years B.P. the fluctuating climate became slowly drier. Although human activities became more aggressive in the processes of environmental evolution, environmental changes remained largely the product of natural changes, and especially those induced by climatic variability.

Humans first inhabited the area in the era 35,000 years B.P. in the Wuding Watershed. It was the home area of several northern nomadic minorities, such as the Xiongnu (Hun) and Mongolians. Though some scholars believe that farming originated in the area in the Zhou Dynasty, most believe that the area remained nomadic until the Hans began practising cultivation in the Warring States (474–221 B.C.) and the Qin Dynasty (221–207 B.C.; Jiang et al. 1986; S. Zhu 1986).

Having unified China, the Qin Dynasty became strong enough to extend its power to the frontier area, including the Ordos. After conquering the area, the Qin central government moved Han people to reclaim and cultivate the east of the Ordos. The Western Han Dynasty (206 B.C.–A.D. 24) continued the frontier-consolidation policy and cultivation activities. From the Eastern Han (A.D. 25–220) to the end of the Northern Dynasties (A.D. 581), a decline of governmental power led to a loss of control over these marginal areas. The nomadic minorities retook the area and the Han people moved back inland, thereby abandoning croplands and promoting the regeneration of pasture.

In the Sui and Tang Dynasties (A.D. 581–907), the Han government reoccupied the Ordos, settling people, stationing an army, and promoting reclamation. With a policy stipulating that a newly opened field should not be taxed for five years, farmers generally abandoned land and turned to other pastures (Jiang et al. 1986). This had far-reaching environmental effects at the time.

During the Ming Dynasty (A.D. 1368–1644), farming was practised only on the southern edge of Ordos. At the beginning of the Qing Dynasty (A.D. 1644–1911), the Great Wall marked the boundary between farming and grazing, with agricultural activities forbidden in a 25 km strip along the wall, and Han people were not permitted north of the Great Wall. Owing to natural disasters and political decline, however, the people in Northern Shaanxi lived poorly and often migrated illegally to the Ordos to make a living through cultivation. In

1697, Han men were permitted to cultivate north of the Great Wall, but they had to return to their homes in winter (women were still banned from migrating). The corruption of the Qing and Minguo governments sparked a rapid expansion of farming, beginning in the mid-nineteenth century. In order to increase taxation to meet financial difficulties, the Qing government ordered the Mongolian area opened and permitted Han people, including women, to move into the Ordos. A "Reclamation Affairs Company" was set up, and large tracts of pastureland were opened. The Yellow River's elbow plain was also cultivated. In the Minguo period, this reclamation policy continued and caused overt reclamation until 1949.

This very brief history provides some background for this environmental study. Since agriculture originated in China 7,000 years ago, many relevant factors can be traced far into the past in the Ordos. The reclamation activity of the Qing and Minguo had particularly important effects.

Environmental changes and their socio-economic effects

In the Ordos, major forms of environmental change include sandification, vegetation degradation, soil erosion, and soil degeneration. Although these changes are closely interrelated, each has some distinctive properties.

Sandification

Sandification is a process by which utilizable land is converted into or covered by sandy land, indicated by soil coarsening, enlargement of sand cover, and declining productivity. It involves two processes: sand erosion (mainly aeolian) and accumulation. The classification of the Lanzhou Desert Institute of the Chinese Academy of Sciences distinguishes among three grades (serious, medium, and light) according to the percentage of moving and fixed sand, vegetation cover, and soil nutrients.

Most of the Ih-Ju League suffers from sandification (fig. 9.4). Seriously sandified areas occur mainly in the Hobq Desert and northern parts of the Mu Us sandy land. In Uxin-Ju, Gelute, and Ulan-Taolegai sums of Uxin Banner, for example, seriously sandified areas account for as much as 50 per cent of the land. Moderately sandified areas are found mainly adjacent to or mixed with more seriously affected areas. Other parts of the League, owing either to a lack of

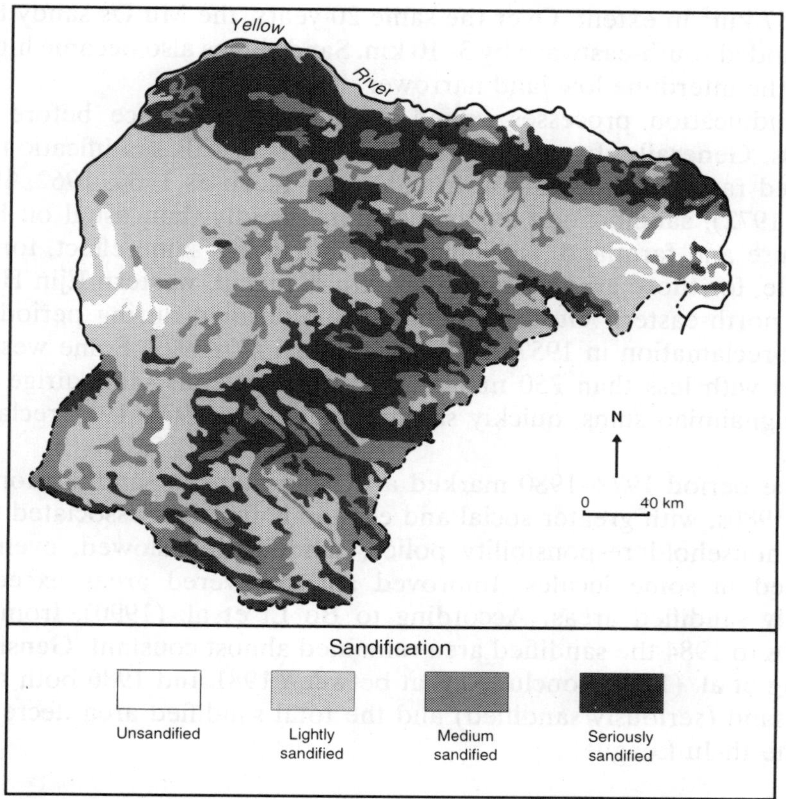

Fig. 9.4 **Sandification in the Ordos Plateau (Source: adapted from Ih-Ju League, 1988)**

sandy material and less strong winds or to less human pressure, are mostly lightly sandified or unsandified. In South Dalad, Dongsheng, and Jungar, more abundant water is the chief reason for the lighter sandification.

Since the classification of sandification is somewhat subjective, data from different sources about sandified areas are not consistent. They all show a general trend, however, toward increasing sandification from 1949 to the end of the 1970s. According to the Lanzhou Desert Institute's aerial photo interpretation (Yang et al. 1991), moving sand increased from 16,446.5 km^2 in 1957 to 27,660 km^2 in 1977 in the Ih-Ju League, the annual increment being 561 km^2. In 1957, the width of the Hobq Desert was 10–40 km, with an area of 16,200 km^2, whereas in 1977 it had increased to 30–65 km wide and

16,757 km^2 in extent. Over the same 20 years, the Mu Us sandy land expanded south-eastward by 3–10 km. Sand-dunes also became higher and the interdune low land narrower.

Sandification processes varied over time and space before the 1980s. Generally, from the late 1950s to the 1970s sandification occurred rapidly. Following a drought year (such as 1960, 1962, 1965, and 1972), sandification expanded more rapidly than usual on both pasture and farmland. Reclamation has had the same effect, for example, for those areas of south-eastern Hanggin, western Ejin Horo, and north-eastern Otog. Sandification intensified during periods of over-reclamation in 1957, 1959–1961, and 1970–1972. Some western areas with less than 250 mm precipitation, such as Gongqirige and Shanghaimiao sums, quickly sandified after the 1970–1972 reclamation.

The period 1978–1980 marked a turning point in sandification. In the 1980s, with greater social and economic freedom associated with the household responsibility policy, sandification slowed, even reversed in some locales. Improved and recovered areas exceeded newly sandified areas. According to Bo Li et al. (1990), from the 1970s to 1984 the sandified area remained almost constant. Gensheng Yang et al. (1991) concluded that between 1981 and 1986 both moving sand (seriously sandified) and the total sandified area decreased in the Ih-Ju League.

Degradation of vegetation

Vegetation changes are characterized by pasture degradation, revealed in a decline in coverage, height, and biomass; simplification of species composition; reductions in high-quality plants; and increases in poor-quality species. According to Bo Li et al. (1990), degraded pasture was 65.6 per cent of the total utilizable pasture area (table 9.1) in 1980, and, of this, 51.79 per cent of the total utilizable pasture was seriously degraded.

Most pasture area has been degraded since 1949, especially from the 1960s to the end of 1970s. From 1966 to 1979, in the whole Ih-Ju League, pasture biomass declined by 26 per cent, and the pasture area, owing to reclamation and sandification, shrank by 17 per cent. Jingye Zhang (personal communication, 1991) estimates that, in the early 1970s, moving sand swallowed 2,000 km^2 of pasture every year.

Regional differences in pasture degradation are apparent. Typical steppe vegetation has become seriously degraded. Second to this in

Table 9.1 **Extent of degraded pasture, 1980**

Location	Degraded		Seriously degraded	
	Area (km²)	As % of total utilizable pasture	Area (km²)	As % of total utilizable pasture
Ih-Ju League	41,389.8	66.8	32,321.5	53.8
Dongsheng	1,000.4	81.3	417.2	33.9
Dalad	4,211.4	81.1	2,708.7	52.1
Jungar	3,377.8	79.3	1,225.8	28.8
Ejin Horo	2,419.6	64.3	2,086.5	55.4
Uxin	7,961.1	93.2	7,195.0	84.3
Otog Front	7,364.6	78.1	6,416.5	68.0
Otog	6,383.3	40.2	5,140.5	32.4
Hanggin	8,599.0	62.8	7,058.9	51.5

Source: Adapted from Li et al. (1990).

importance are the sandy steppe and meadows in the Mu Us and Hobq Desert. Shepherds remember that the *Achnathrerum splendens* was high and dense enough before the 1960s to hide cattle and horses, but by the late 1970s had become so short and sparse that even a running rabbit was visible. In the Hantai valley of the Dalad Banner the *Caragana leucophloea* oasis teemed with wildlife, such as Mongolian gazelle, fox, rabbit, and various migrating birds. With environmental destruction, most of this wildlife has disappeared. Since the early 1980s, measures to protect and recover pasture vegetation have slowed degradation correspondingly and, between 1985 and 1989, biomass declines even halted.

Soil erosion

Water and wind are two powerful forces of soil erosion. Water erosion affects mainly the eastern river catchment, whereas wind erosion affects most other parts. The transitional area between these two parts is affected by both water and wind. In so far as wind erosion, a part of the sandification processes, occurs simultaneously with aeolian accumulation, its extent is relevant to sandification. Strong wind erosion occurs on the high unprotected plateau cropfields, whose average erosion depth is 5–7 cm per year. Moving sand-dunes march 3–10 m along the wind direction every year. Vast areas of sandy land, desert, and high plateau in the Ordos suffer from serious wind erosion. Water erosion dominates in the eastern area.

Western and south-western Jungar Banner are severely eroded. Above the rugged Tertiary silt sand and shale rock is only 20–30 cm of loess layer on average. In many places, the loess has been totally eroded, with bedrock exposed and the land unutilizable.

The total erosion area has increased. The data from the Water Conservancy Centre of the League show that from 1949 to 1983 the area of erosion increased, and even accelerated from 1958 to 1978. Though measures have been taken since 1980 (as described below), soil erosion persists.

Soil degeneration

Soil degeneration results from soil erosion. According to Zhaohua Huang and colleagues (1986), the organic material of dry cropland has decreased by 20–30 per cent since the 1960s, and total nitrogen has declined by 25–46 per cent. In the cropfields of aeolian erosion areas, the topsoil has been stripped away by an average of 5–7 cm every year. Water erosion has stripped some 1–4 cm per year off cropfields. It has been estimated that, even under vegetation protection, the formation of 2.5 cm topsoil will need about 300–1,000 years, or even longer. By comparison, soil depletion in the Ih-Ju League is proceeding even more rapidly.

Erosion measurements have been taken since 1983. Erosion-controlled areas have balanced much of the newly eroded area. The late 1980s witnessed more significant erosion control and land-improvement measures but, owing to the slow speed of soil column building as compared with other environmental changes, soil fertility is recovering only slowly. Therefore, although other environmental problems have been mitigated since the early 1980s, soil depletion still continues.

Environmental changes in perspective

The changing environmental factors discussed above are closely interrelated. Some other factors, such as air, dust, and sand storms, actually accompany wind erosion and sandification. Changes in land surface albedo caused by sandification and soil exposure also exacerbate drought. All these changes combine and interact to degrade the whole ecosystem, the total deterioration of which shows up in declines in productivity and carrying capacity.

Vegetation plays a particularly important role in such deterioration. It not only is the major object of human disturbances but also provides a major medium for human improvements. On the one hand, deterioration begins when vegetation is disturbed. Experiments show that, as compared with sand, when vegetation cover reaches 15–25 per cent, the amounts of transported sand will be reduced to 22–31 per cent. When vegetation cover is 40–50 per cent, the amount will be reduced to only 1 per cent (Yang et al. 1991). On the other hand, controlling environmental deterioration relies principally on the protection and reconstruction of vegetation.

The good news is that the environmental deterioration of the Ordos is retrievable, either by natural regeneration after a halt to exploitation or by deliberate human reconstruction of the vegetation. Unlike the tropical rain forests, the destruction of which may interfere with climatic processes and material recycling so profoundly that regeneration mechanisms may be totally destroyed, environmental deterioration in the Ordos has not ruined the possibility of recovery. Precipitation levels of 160–400 mm provide the necessary conditions for vegetation regeneration or reconstruction. Although it is doubtless true that destruction is easy and recovery difficult, a rapid recovery needs human effort in planting and reconstruction. Generally, environmental restoration is technologically feasible.

As for the causes of environmental changes in the Ordos, competing opinions exist. Using a geological time-scale, some opinion focuses on natural trends of aridity. Disputes over the causes of such environmental changes over historical time are apparent. In his paper on the formation of the Mu Us sandy land, Yongfu Zhao (1981) argues that natural conditions have played a dominant role, whereas human activities have had only slight impacts. Guangrong Dong and colleagues (1983) also believe that human activities are secondary to natural influences. Shiguang Zhu (1986) and Nianhai Shi (1980), on the other hand, put a heavy weight on human factors. Gensheng Yang and colleagues (1991) have even calculated the percentage of human causes, which they set at 87 per cent for sandification changes since the 1960s. On the basis of climatic aridity through historical time, these authors conclude that human activities have accelerated the natural environmental changes more and more significantly. Since too little time has elapsed since 1949 to show any clear trend in a fluctuating ecosystem, the intensity of human activities has played a dominant role in environmental changes. However, no clear boundary emerges between the interwoven factors of natural background and human causes.

Impacts

For a region like the Ordos, whose socio-economic system relies heavily on its natural environment, environmental deterioration directly degenerates the human-support system and can cause profound human dislocations, especially for farmers and shepherds.

According to Bo Li et al. (1990), declines in cropland fertility greatly affect agricultural productivity. From 1949 to the early 1970s, yields averaged 300–530 kg/ha, but some slope land and sandified field yields were only 75–150 kg/ha. From the mid-1970s, crop yields have increased gradually, but productivity has remained low. Although the slow infusion of technology and human interventions have largely compensated for the negative effect of environmental deterioration, farming developments have lagged seriously. Examples include the severely water-eroded areas in west Jungar, where the soil has been so thin as to expose baserock in many places. Cultivation cannot be practised in many lands. As a result, farmers have migrated to other places in search of better land or other economic opportunities (Deshengxi township is one such case).

Wind erosion and sandification impede crop production by eroding topsoil, manure, and seeds (sometimes, a field has to be resowed three, four, or even five times). They also directly destroy crops, causing significant declines in yields. One estimate indicates that fully one-third of cropfields suffers from sandification every year (Huang et al. 1986).

Pastoral degradation and the shrinkage of pasture area directly affect animal husbandry. Given the degradation of pasture, the number of livestock has not increased with population growth. Rather, it has fluctuated with climate change and other natural factors. The per capita level of livestock has actually declined. Meanwhile, pasture area per livestock has fallen sharply, from 3.6 ha in 1949 to 1.1 ha in 1985, and also has one-third less biomass. Overgrazing in the forage period (summer and autumn) has resulted in decreased livestock weight, causing a drop in production. For instance, the average one-year-old sheep in the early 1980s weighed only 72 per cent of one in the 1950s (Zhu et al. 1986). Prior to the establishment of pasture user rights in 1980, some shepherds on degraded pasture were forced to graze their livestock hundreds of kilometres away, causing not only a waste of livestock energy but also pasture degradation.

The effects of environmental deterioration on the regional economy are apparent in the stagnant GNP/per capita, gross social agri-

Table 9.2 **The agricultural economy of the Ordos under environmental deterioration**

Year	Crop area ('000 ha)	Crop yield (kg/ha)	Number of livestock	Economic performance (1980 prices)			
				Per agricultural capita	GNP/ cap.	GSAP/ agr. cap.	ANI/ agr. cap.
1950	64.71	307.5	1,844	4.6	248	310	196
1955	55.03	412.5	3,239	6.5	303	326	204
1960	66.83	345.0	4,404	7.2	372	339	222
1965	49.71	300.0	4,945	7.3	233	273	178
1970	45.95	592.5	4,964	6.4	289	325	213
1975	32.35	802.5	4,655	5.4	327	297	194
1980	24.39	960.0	4,708	5.1	332	284	175
1985	21.68	1,530.0	4,698	4.8	450	326	226
1989	21.61	1,706.3	4,732	4.8	587	395	278

Source: Adapted from Ih-Ju League (1990).

cultural product (GSAP), and agricultural national income (ANI) for the agricultural population (table 9.2). These economic indicators fluctuated, without any general increase, up to the 1980s. The economic gains of the 1980s, which were largely attributable to socio-economic developments, also reflect recent environmental improvements.

Aside from indirect impacts on human well-being, environmental deterioration affects human life directly. Sandification and erosion have damaged human health and private and public properties and impaired daily life. Several examples are relevant:

- The Huqutu Reservoir is a medium-sized reservoir in Jungar Banner. In 1975, when construction began, the maximum depth of water was 25 m. Owing to serious soil erosion in the catchment, it soon became shallow (4 m in 1977 and 1 m in 1980). Before the conveyance irrigation system was completed, the reservoir had silted up, at a cost of about 400,000 yuan in national investment (Shen 1981).
- The Xiliu stream is a short tributary from Dalad running northward to empty into the Yellow River. In ordinary times, cars can cross the stream bed. The sparsely vegetated catchment is, however, seriously eroded. In 1961, over 200 mm rain between 21 and 23 August caused serious flooding and silting, washed away seedlings on more than 26,000 ha, and buried 8,670 ha of cropfield in thick sand. Eleven villagers drowned and more than 8,000 houses collapsed. The amount

of sand carried by the water was so extensive as to form a sandy dam that cut off the flow of the Yellow River for three hours, raising the river level by 405 m and inducing significant effects on both the upper and lower reaches. Similar floods occur about two to three times every 10 years (Shen 1981).

- On 28 April 1983, a sand storm in Ih-Ju League left 4 people dead, 37 people injured, 44,837 livestock dead, 101 houses and 378 livestock shelters destroyed, and 195 wells buried (Yang Gensheng et al. 1991). Sand storms happen on average about 10–25 days per year. Over 200 km of roads suffer from sandification each year, and sand-clearing costs over 1 million yuan annually (Huang et al. 1986).

Spatial linkage

The Ordos Plateau is a major sand deposition area of the Yellow River catchment. The serious sandification and erosion add greatly to the silt discharges, especially the coarse, sandy deposits of the Yellow River. It is estimated that the Ordos accounts for 10 per cent of silt discharges and one-third of the transport of coarse sand for the Yellow River. In short, environmental changes in the Ordos affect deposition in the Yellow River, thereby endangering the lower areas of the river.

Proximate human causes

Human factors, both negative and positive, combine to cause environmental changes in the Ordos. In this section, we focus on the negative effects, leaving the positive effects for the section on human responses. We begin with the proximate activities that serve as direct causes of environmental deterioration. Behind these are the driving forces underlying the demographic, cultural, economic, and political factors. We take them up later.

Land reclamation

Modern farming practice dates back to the middle Ming and especially Qing Dynasty. Dramatic conversion of pastureland into cropland began in the early twentieth century. Songqiao Zhao and colleagues (1958) has identified the major reclamation periods and areas of the Ih-Ju League (fig. 9.5). With the establishment of the Re-

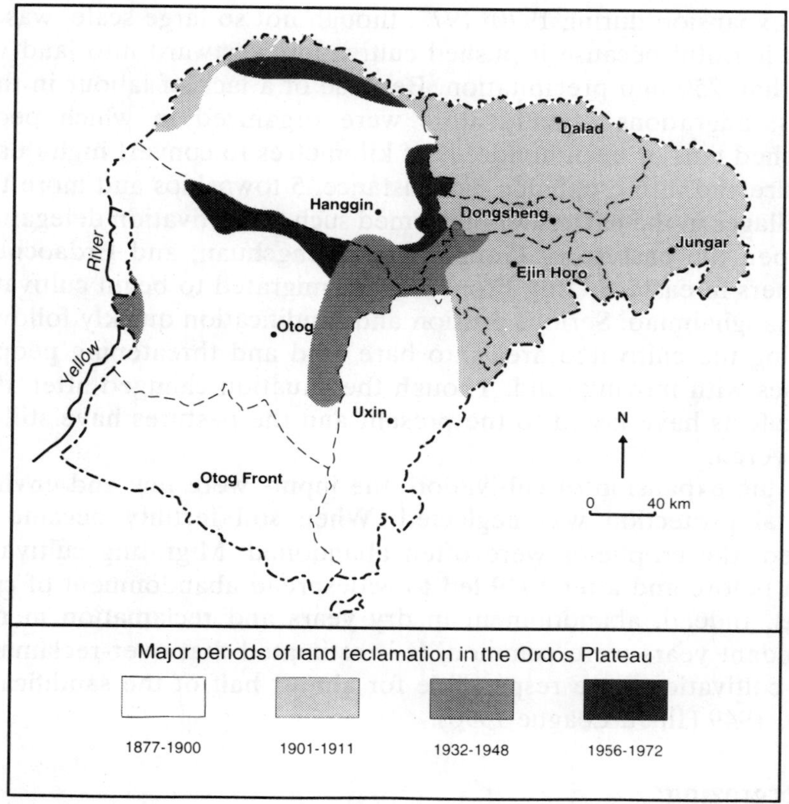

Fig. 9.5 **Major periods of land reclamation in the Ordos Plateau (Sources: adapted from Ih-Ju League, 1988; and Songqiao Zhao et al., 1958)**

clamation Affairs Company, the first stage of active large-scale pasture opening occurred from 1901 to 1911. This continued at a slower rate from 1915 to 1928. Beginning in 1932, the second peak of reclamation occurred under the rule of Guomingdang. According to *Analysis of the Mongolian Economy of Cha-Sui Region* (Sui-Yuan 1934a) and *Report on the Counties of Sui-Yuan Region* (Sui-Yuan 1934b), some 307,533 ha were newly claimed as farming land, with a total 1,880,000 ha devoted to cultivation. By then, the land-reclamation ratio of the Jungar Banner had reached 37 per cent. The third reclamation period extended from 1957 to 1973, during which three expansions occurred as a result of policy changes. The first two took place mainly in areas with precipitation exceeding 250 mm, especially the area between the Hobq Desert and the Mu Us sandy land.

The expansion during 1970–1972, though not so large scale, was the most harmful because it pushed cultivation westward into land with less than 250 mm precipitation. Because of a lack of labour in these areas, migrations of cultivators were organized in which people marched tens or even hundreds of kilometres to convert high-quality pastureland into cropfields. For instance, 5 townships and more than 30 villages in the eastern Otog formed such a "cultivation delegation" to open the pasture of Gongqirige, Chengchuan, and Erdaochuan. Farmers in eastern Otog Front Banner migrated to begin cultivation at Shanghaimiao. Serious erosion and sandification quickly followed, turning the cultivated area into bare land and threatening people's houses with moving sand. Though the situation changed after 1974, the effects have lasted to the present and the pastures have still not recovered.

In the expansion of cultivation, the inputs were few and environmental protection was neglected. When soil fertility became depleted, the cropfields were often abandoned. Migrating cultivation both before and after 1949 led to widespread abandonment of cropfields. Indeed, abandonment in dry years and reclamation in rain-abundant years were common. It is estimated that over-reclamation and cultivation were responsible for almost half of the sandification since 1949 (Ih-Ju League 1990).

Overgrazing

Overgrazing arose from the nomadic grazing tradition under the intensification of expanding human needs and a growing economy. Shepherds, concerned about livestock numbers rather than net production, grazed many livestock (sheep, goats, cattle, horses, and camels) without thinning in cold seasons when forage was scarce and fattening when pasture flourished. This practice wasted much energy and increased pressure on pasturelands. The over-harvesting degraded the soil texture and destroyed the protective crust of the land, exacerbating sandification and vegetation degradation.

Overgrazing, apparent since the late 1950s, has become more and more serious. Table 9.3 shows the trend of over-reclamation and overgrazing of Ejin Horo from the 1950s to the 1970s, as both pasture degradation and overgrazing grew rapidly. From the 1970s to the 1980s, pasture degradation slowed owing to human intervention for conservation, but overgrazing continues to be a serious problem throughout the Ih-Ju League. The Animal Husbandry Department

Table 9.3 **Over-reclamation and overgrazing of Ejin Horo, 1950s–1980s**

Indicator	Early 1950s	Early 1960s	Early 1970s	Early 1980s
Over-reclamation ratio (%)	250	350	200	157
Energy utilization ratio by crop (%)	1.3	0.92	0.69	1.1
Utilizable pasture (ha)	46.0	36.6	39.6	34.1
Pasture biomass (kg/ha)	2,625	2,325	1,650	1,500
Livestock carrying capacity (10 sheep unit)	57.0	40.5	23.3	26.1
Actual livestock (10 sheep unit)	56	65.5	65	80
Overgrazing ratio (%)	−1.8	61.7	179	207

Source: Cao (1988).

of Jungar Banner estimates that the overgrazing rate was 15–25 per cent in the 1970s. Bo Li and colleagues (1990) estimate that, in 1985, overgrazing in the eastern steppe area was a very serious problem. From 1985 to 1990, overgrazing in the eastern area abated, whereas in the western high plateau, and especially in Otog, the number of livestock increased and caused overgrazing.

Climatic fluctuation affects environmental changes in several ways. During drought years shepherds continue to graze most of their livestock, increasing the pressure on pastures. This causes environmental degradation both directly through overexploitation and indirectly through economic decline. For an area like the Ordos, in which environmental management is underdeveloped and human adjustment is weak, drought years were (and are) critical.

Overcollection of fuelwood and medicinal herbs

Prior to the 1980s, farmers and shepherds, a majority of the local population, depended mainly on natural vegetation for fuelwood. In the late 1970s it is estimated that 70 per cent of all households used shrubs for firewood. On average, 1,000 km^2 are sandified owing to fuelwood collection every year (Huang and Song 1981).

Since 1980, with improvements in the economy and in transportation, more and more households have begun to use coal. But there are still households, less than 25 per cent by one 1990 estimate, that continue to collect shrubs from natural pasturelands. The Department of Agriculture (personal interview, 1991) believes that shrub collection in the northern part of the Hobq Desert, where more and more people are harvesting in the central part and destroying the sparsely covered land, is even more serious.

Gathering of medicinal herbs is another serious problem. The Ih-Ju League has rich resources of medicinal herbs totalling 378 species. Of the 112 species purchased nationally, *Glycyrrhiza uralensis* and *Ephedra sinica* are the most important. The problem has escalated since the 1970s as a growing national market has encouraged excessive digging. Since 1982, money has been invested to protect and restore *G. uralensis* vegetation. Although its area has increased (to 415,999 ha in 1985), the situation remains critical. *G. uralensis* is mainly distributed in the western Mu Us sandy land. The annual harvest of 2–4 million kg of *G. uralensis* has caused an estimated 240–480 km^2 of direct destruction and 120–240 million km^2 of land sources exposed to wind. *E. sinica* has experienced a similar destruction. Since it regenerates slowly, the overgathering both in quantity (10 million kg/year) and in manner (cutting of the above-ground stem) has depleted the resource rapidly, and, at the same time, degraded pastureland seriously.

Overhunting

Uncontrolled hunting has sharply reduced the number of predators, such as the fox and the vulture, thus exacerbating the damage caused by harmful insects and rodents. Every year, a fox can kill 1,500–3,000 rats, and a vulture can eat 600–800 rats. Unpublished statistics show that the External Trade Department of the Ih-Ju League purchased 97,600 fox skins between 1965 and 1978 and 4,335 eagles and vultures in 1973 (field interview, 1991).

Road construction

Road construction affects a small area, but the impacts are serious, since 0.06–0.1 km alongside the road is severely disturbed. Coal-mining, the scale of which is fairly small, has been a minor source of landscape transformation in the past, but it will certainly become more important in the future.

Underlying human driving forces

Population

During historical time, the population in the Ih-Ju League has changed tremendously. The Western Han Dynasty saw the first peak, with

Table 9.4 **Population growth in Ih-Ju League**

Year	Total population: Number ('000)	Total population: Growth rate[a] (%)	Agricultural population: Number ('000)	Agricultural population: Growth rate[a] (%)
1950	427.7		402.9	
1955	524.6	4.2	500.3	4.4
1960	661.1	4.7	612.0	4.1
1965	740.3	2.3	679.7	2.1
1970	841.6	2.3	778.5	2.8
1975	966.0	2.8	863.8	2.1
1980	1,043.6	1.6	919.8	1.3
1985	1,133.8	1.7	978.2	1.2
1989	1,184.1	1.1	979.4	0.3

Source: Adapted from Ih-Lu League (1988).
a. Average of previous five years.

a density as high as about 10 people/km^2, representing only some 250,000 fewer people than the present day. With the decline of farming, the population has decreased. The Tang Dynasty was a second peak. From the Song to Ming Dynasties, by comparison, the area was sparsely populated. Before 1912 (from the middle Qing), the population fluctuated around 200,000. By 1949, the Ordos had 411,747 people, engaged mostly in agriculture.

Since 1949, with improving socio-economic conditions, the population has grown rapidly (table 9.4). From 1949 to 1959, the overall population growth rate was 4.3 per cent and that of the agricultural population 4.0 per cent. It was also a time when migration from other areas played a major role (constituting 22 per cent of the total population increase), owing largely to the development of industry. Until the 1970s, although the population growth rate gradually slowed, it remained very high (2.2 per cent for the total population and 1.89 per cent for the agricultural population) in the 1980s. With the adoption of a family-planning policy (one child for the Hans, two children for Mongolians in the countryside, and one child for city couples), the population growth rate has fallen sharply.

Population is the primary driving force of environmental change in the Ordos. From 1949 to the present, population density has increased from 4.7 to 13.5 persons per km^2 (in 1989), and human labour and economic activities have increasingly affected the natural environment. Food needs, fuelwood requirements, and economic growth have all increased roughly proportionally with population growth. To alter or ameliorate these forces of change, more socio-economic improvements, political intervention, education, and technological advances are needed.

The League is composed of mainly Han and Mongolian people. The eastern four banners and the city have been farming and farming–pastoral transitional areas throughout historical time, when the Han people, with a long tradition in cultivation, moved in and occupied the area. The population is dense, with the Han people predominating (over 90 per cent). The western four banners, by contrast, have an economy based upon grazing, and the population is sparse. Many Mongolian people, originally nomadic minorities, have lived there and maintained a traditional style of land use. This differentiation of population shapes the structure of environmental changes. The relatively high population density causes serious environmental deterioration, such as in Jungar Banner. Nationalities also affect the pattern of land exploitation, especially in the past when Han and Mongolian people were more distinct than today. In this sense, the Han people not only introduced new agricultural techniques, modern thoughts, and greater linkage with outside areas, but also triggered environmental deterioration through land reclamation.

It should be mentioned that, compared with other environmentally problematic semi-arid areas, in China and around the world, population density in the Ordos is still rather low. For example, in China, semi-arid sandy land has an average of more than 40 people per km^2. In North Africa, 80–150 people per km^2 inhabit areas with less than 300 mm precipitation and in some desert areas of India more than 50 people/km^2 are found in areas with less than 600 mm rain. The Mediterranean dry belt is also densely populated (with more than 45 people/km^2). For an area like Ih-Ju League, the relatively low 13.5 people/km^2, though a higher density than in the past, presents some opportunities for environmental stabilization and restoration.

Education

The Ordos, as regards its education, ideology, culture, and economy, was a closed and inaccessible area prior to the 1980s. Traditional ideas predominated. Over time, the ideas of farmers and shepherds emerged not from the developing modern sciences and technology but from traditional culture. Formal education did not begin until 1934 when the first primary school was built in the area. Before

1949, it was chiefly the Lama religion that shaped human behaviour. According to the *Report on the Western Four Banners of Ih-Ju League* (Sui-Yuan 1939), the Lama temple was regarded as the highest school at that time, and Lama was considered the most honourable occupation. Some 60–70 per cent of the young men were Lama, leaving only a small percentage of labourers, mostly women, to manage the grazing. Lama doctrine was resistant to the import of outside culture and reinforced the traditional culture. Since 1949, although the educational system has developed rapidly through the actions of the national government, schooling is still not regarded as important by many. Visiting the area in 1991, the authors found that only a small number of farmers and shepherds had ever been to the League capital, Dongsheng. Agricultural research and management institutions, meanwhile, have also developed very slowly in the Ordos.

The illiteracy rate is one indicator of the underdeveloped state of the educational system (table 9.5). The illiterate and quasi-illiterate compose 43.7 per cent of the female population and 23.3 per cent of the male population. Statistics for 1984 show clearly the spatial distribution of education levels; it is clear that farmers and shepherds at-

Table 9.5 **Education levels in the Ih-Ju League (%)**

Year	Place	Univ. or college	Senior high	Junior high	Primary school	Quasi-illiterate or illiterate[a]
1964	Ih-Ju	0.117	0.524	2.404	19.19	43.63
1982	Ih-Ju	0.240	4.68	14.27	26.61	35.40
	China	0.60	6.62	17.76	35.36	23.50
	Inner Mongolia	0.57	7.46	19.30	32.77	22.40
1984	Ih-Ju	0.24	4.67	14.27	26.60	32.86
	Cities and towns	1.30	11.64	19.73	18.47	8.26
	Countryside	0.04	3.20	12.71	26.92	35.81
	Dongsheng	1.15	11.11	21.72	25.74	22.52
	Jungar	0.12	3.93	12.76	25.49	36.85
	Dalad	0.15	4.36	15.27	26.74	32.36
	Ejin Horo	0.12	3.39	12.48	24.08	37.94
	Otog Front	0.04	2.41	9.73	25.95	35.11
	Otog	0.21	4.14	14.30	29.78	30.87
	Uxin	0.19	4.24	12.13	26.43	33.08
	Hanggin	0.14	4.07	13.44	29.42	31.47

Source: Adapted from Ih-Ju League (1988).

a. People aged over 12 years.

tain lower education levels than workers and that females are more poorly educated than males (Ih-Ju League 1990). These low levels of education, particularly for farmers and shepherds, affect behaviour and perspectives on the environment and social change. Many Ordos residents, it is clear, adhere to traditional lifestyles and resist modern ideas and new technology.

None the less, since 1980, the economic opening of the Ordos and its growing linkage with national markets have introduced new ideas and modern technology, which are gradually changing traditional customs. Yet education still lags behind much of China. Primary schools have spread over the Ordos, but few middle schools exist in the countryside. Students must migrate to the city or towns to study. The quality of teachers is also poor. Only 77 per cent of Ordos primary school attenders go on to junior high school, and only 36 per cent of those junior high students eventually enter senior high school.

The market economy and environmental vulnerability

Poverty induces a high vulnerability to environmental changes. From a historical point of view, a high dependence on the environment does not necessarily mean vulnerability for local people. Poverty limits choices for the human utilization of the environment. The lack of suitable management approaches and the human desire for economic growth conspire to produce overexploitation of land, resulting in environmental deterioration, which in turn limits the economy. A cycle or spiral of environmental and economic deterioration takes hold.

A typical example illustrates this. The overcollection of shrubs as fuelwood did not occur as a result of a lack of energy resources. The area is rich in coal deposits, and coal production has occurred since the 1950s. Moreover, wind power is another abundant energy resource. Rather, such overexploitation reflects a shortage of money and transportation. Poverty has also been part of the reason for the overuse of some areas.

Another example is the acceleration of severe overgrazing. Since the 1980s, and especially since 1985, the wool textile industry has developed rapidly, stimulating sheep and goat grazing. In 1986–1988, the price of cashmere and wool rose tremendously, making overgrazing very profitable in the short term. Since 1989, exports of wool products have fallen, causing a sharp drop in cashmere and wool prices. Although many shepherds have reduced their livestock numbers, others have continued to increase their livestock.

For land that is already deteriorated, improvements require money. The Hangpuchuang watershed in Jungar Banner is an example of an improvement induced by heavy investment from the national government. Here investments have ranged from 2,500 to 20,000 yuan per km^2, but only small areas have received such investments. Local governments can deliver only limited funds for environmental improvements. It is clear that the lack of funds, along with other social factors, limits large-scale environmental improvements.

Meanwhile, industrial development, and especially coalmining, while alleviating poverty to some extent, is causing further environmental problems. Since the late 1980s, the national government has invested large amounts of money in industry, especially for the development of mineral resources in middle China. These investments have included coalmining in Dongsheng and the Jungar coalfields. The first stage of the coalmining project began between 1987 and 1992, with open-pit mining as the dominant technology. The most serious environmental effect of coalmining is the potential soil erosion and sandification caused by land-surface disturbance through the construction of houses, mining sites, and roads. The long-term landscape disruption from open mining after the completion of the project is a special concern. The Heidaigou open-cast mine of the Jungar coalfield is an example. The area is covered by sandy loess, with old sand beneath. Li Baoyu (unpublished data) has estimated that the disturbed land surface will produce 11,200–32,500 t/km^2 of erosion, 2–4.5 times that of existing erosion rates. The average loss ratio is 5.22 m for every tonne of coal production (with the mine having a total of 137.3 billion tonnes suitable for open mining). The mine could well generate a total of 1,716.8 billion m^3 of deprived soil mass (Huadong Wang et al. 1991). This is a gigantic potential source of soil erosion and sandification. The Dongsheng and Shenfu (in Shaanxi) coalfields have 24 mining pits and four open coalmines in early stages of development and are likely severely to disturb some 40.3 km^2 of land (Yang et al. 1991). If effective protection measures are not taken, the area will degrade quickly and sand drainage into the Yellow River will increase.

The state and national policy

Among the underlying forces of environmental change, state policy and politics are among the most powerful and effective primary drivers. In historical time, every opening of the Ordos area was induced by a growth in central power and a policy of land expansion in China. Since 1949, the socialist system and public land ownership have turned that area toward the new course of economic development. Liberated from their depressed and exploited positions, people have become more able to benefit from their own labour. Although the period has witnessed great economic improvements, it has also experienced accelerated environmental deterioration. The rapid growth of population and intensifying pressure on the environment have accompanied economic growth. The "Great Leap Forward" and the "Cultural Revolution" caused real environmental disasters in the area from the late 1950s to the early 1970s. The direct effect was land expansion under a national "grain-dominating" agricultural policy. Indirect effects, even more damaging, arose from the application of science and an overemphasis on class struggle. Driven by these state political interventions, the Ordos, like most other regions in China, lost control over population growth, economic development, and the exploitation of natural resources. Overcentralized economic policies denied choice and flexibility to local governments and peoples.

In the 1950s and 1960s, the pasture-protection policy of local government was not powerful enough to counter the national policy of grain purchase. As a result, the expansion of cultivation could not be stopped. And in the 1970s, although the Gongqirige people believed that their land was more suitable for grazing than for cultivation, they were unable to change the government's classification of the township as a farming one. The national government collectively purchased at low prices designated targets of agricultural products. The market economy, of course, was banned. Economic decline followed, while alternative adjustments in resources exploitation were prohibited. Moreover, the lack of local autonomy and increasing environmental deterioration destroyed the morale of farmers, shepherds, and their leaders. Weak social organization and environmental protection efforts made it easy for environmental deterioration to proceed unimpeded, even though some local people recognized the need for environmental countermeasures.

Since the 1980s, economic reforms have corrected many of these damaging state policies and established a market economy. The Ordos economy has developed rapidly, and an emphasis on environmental control and improvement has contributed to some general mitigation of environmental problems. State policy has been both a source of environmental improvement and a cause of continued damage to the environment. A typical example is the destruction caused by the collection of medicinal herbs. Though regulations on the utilization and protection of pastureland were set forth in 1979, they were undermined by the herbs collection policy. For the significant economic benefits of processing *Glycyrrhiza uralensis* and *Ephedra sinica*, the medical departments of the League and adjacent regions have established administrative targets for banners, townships, and villages without regard for the pressure on the regeneration needs of the pasturelands. Some places even use the fulfilment of these production goals to evaluate the performance of local leaders. Researchers on the Pasture Survey Team of the Animal Husbandry Department of Ih-Ju League estimate that the targets have exceeded resources and pasture capacity every year in recent times. In some years, the targeting has even exceeded the total above-ground biomass of *Ephedra sinica*. Administrative imperatives and cash-crop prospects (these herbs fetch high prices) have been more powerful than the pasture-utilization conservation regulations.

For the Ordos, with a depressed economy and a context of embryonic national environmental legislation, human awareness of environmental problems does not lead directly to environmental protection policies, especially since economic development is still very important in orienting human behaviour.

Human awareness and societal responses

Human awareness and measures for environmental protection are positive aspects of the human dimensions of environmental change. They can slow down, stop, or even reverse environmental deterioration.

Human awareness and attitudes to nature

The Chinese people have long believed that human beings are part of the environment. The Mongolian people, originating in nomadic tribes, link their life even more closely to the fate of nature. Harmony is pursued ideally, however, not by seeking intervention but by acceptance. The attitude of "what will be will be" about nature is also a part of the Chinese conception. For the Ordos Plateau, much of the population holds Buddhist beliefs, which emphasize a passive acceptance of "the present life" while projecting hope into "the next life." What nature does to people is thought to be the result of their morality. This cultural orientation deeply affects environmental perception and behaviour.

Generally, local people first became aware of environmental changes during the 1950s and 1960s owing to the enlarged sandy land, increasingly sparse pasture, and soil erosion. From their experiences, they understood the harmful effects of environmental deterioration both on everyday life and on the agricultural economy. But that does not mean they would take active action to counter it. Prior to the 1980s, owing to their low economic status and the weakness of social forces, Ordos people were not sanguine about the possibility of environmental improvements. The overcentralized social system afforded little choice, thereby encouraging passivity. It is ironic that, during the Cultural Revolution, a "man-over-nature" concept was imposed and even politicized, but it did not enhance rational human environmental action.

Since 1980, environmental awareness has arisen quickly in the scientific community, in governmental agendas, and in the popular media. Different levels of government in the Ordos have strengthened public policies and programmes on environmental protection. The local newspaper, *Er Duo Si Ri Bao* (*The Ordos Daily*), and local broadcast media have covered environmental protection events extensively. Local government has also conducted revegetation demonstrations. These actions have enhanced local environmental awareness, partly owing to administrative incentives and partly owing to the evident beneficial economic results. Confidence about environmental improvements has grown and strengthened. The integration of centralization and privatization, beginning with the household responsibility system (i.e. land ownership is still public, but user rights are distributed to each household), promotes both collective security and enthusiasm for private interests.

All the same, long-term environmental protection is still of secondary importance in the Ordos. Overgrazing of livestock and overcollection of medicinal herbs continue, for example, and these practices may well be reasonable considering economic conditions in the area. Environmental deterioration is still considered to be chiefly an *economic* problem and not a source of major harm to human health and well-being or a moral issue. Local government has recognized the importance of pasture protection since the 1960s. The Inner Mongolia government has promoted revegetation and measures to control moving sand. From 1952 to 1955, with land reform and cooperative transformation of agriculture, the development of animal husbandry and the protection of pasture were the foci of Ih-Ju League governmental policy. This policy banned land development and overcollection of fuelwood and promoted rotational grazing, the planting of trees, shrubs, and herbs, the designation of fuel-collection areas, and other countermeasures. In farming–grazing areas, grazing was recognized as the dominant preferred activity. Soil and water conservation were first recognized in the Ih-Ju League agricultural plan of 1953, and massive closing of pastures and protecting of steep slope were undertaken. Despite heavy emphasis by the local government, however, these policies were not paid much heed by the local populace. Influenced by national policy and the political atmosphere, and lacking a full understanding of the importance of environmental protection for the local economy, local governments permitted deviations from their own policies.

With the slow infusion of science into policy-making, national government came rather late to understanding environmental problems. Since 1978, national policy has emphasized pasture protection, prohibition of land clearances, and pastoral needs. Environmental measures, meanwhile, have become more and more powerful.

In academic circles, the earliest attention to sandification in the Ordos appeared in the 1930s. Since 1949, many research programmes have been carried out in the Ordos. In the late 1950s and early 1960s, a geographical survey occurred, followed by sandification studies in the late 1970s (Beijing University Geography Department et al. 1983). The 1980s saw the establishment of an Inner Mongolia remote-sensing survey programme as well as the launching of a study of the loess plateau. Scientists recognized the problems of sandification, soil erosion, and pasture degradation during the 1950s and early 1960s. Those studies revealed the widespread over-reclamation and fuelwood collection. Since the late 1970s, scientific research has revived after 10 years of stagnation, with further investigations into the causes, processes, and impacts of environmental problems. With increasing environmental awareness and activity in China, these environmental problems are now viewed as largely human induced.

Environmental protection measures

Before 1980, human responses were mostly adaptive. Prior to the 1960s, since population was sparse, land area per capita was large. When one cropfield was depleted, farmers abandoned it and turned to others. When one pasture was degraded, shepherds moved their households and livestock to other places. They avoided degraded areas and looked for higher-quality land. In the 1970s, with population increases and growing human interference with nature, adaptation strategies were not allowed for seriously eroded and sandified areas, such as Jungar and north Uxin. Therefore, in the movement of "Learning from Dazhai," terraced and dammed basic cropfields were built in Jungar to reduce erosion and to increase yields. The enclosure of pasture and the removal of poisonous herbs helped to restore degraded vegetation in Uxin-Ju township. These activities illustrated the positive effect of a political movement during the Cultural Revolution. Generally, environmental control efforts existed only for small areas, without consideration of the total ecosystem. In Jungar, for example, dammed lands and reservoirs at the outlet of gullies were not coordinated with gully vegetative measures. As a result, the land was destroyed by flooding and the reservoirs filled with deposits. In Uxin-Ju township, only a small area of pasture was enclosed, whereas others continued to be overgrazed and sandified.

Since 1980, purposeful adjustments have become more widespread, except for very small and restricted areas such as in parts of western Jungar, where capital scarcity and environmental conditions do not permit improvement efforts. Specific measures for environmental control and improvement include several different initiatives. Some cultivated land has been returned to natural or man-made pastures.

With the three expansions of cultivation, farming–grazing transitional areas and even some original grazing areas have been turned into cultivation regions. The eastern farming area has expanded onto steep slope lands. In the 1980s, an improved land-use policy reclassified 15 townships as a new grazing region. Slope land of over 20° and with thin soil layers was reallocated from cultivation to natural or man-made pastures.

In the 1950s, the Ih-Ju League government promoted pasture enclosure in valley meadows. But, owing to funding shortages for fencing and mismanagement of collective pasture utilization, it was not applied widely. Since the 1980s, with economic growth and the allocation of pasture-utilization rights, pasture enclosure has increased rapidly. In 1985, enclosed pasture accounted for fully 10.3 per cent of the total utilizable area; in 1989, the proportion increased further to 18.7 per cent.

Aerial sowing of vegetation and herbs began in the Ih-Ju League in 1979. This labour-saving and highly efficient way to improve pasture is suitable for sandy land where sand-dunes are not very high and for large interdune lowlands. Experiments show that, in the total aerially sown area, vegetation cover has increased by about 40 per cent, turning moving sand into fixed sand within five years (Yunzhong Wang et al. 1983).

Sand-dune improvement first appeared in the 1950s, and local people have rich and lengthy experience with such dunes. Vegetative measures have been chiefly conducted on windward slopes and in interdune low areas. On the lower third of slopes, *Artemisia ordosica* and *Salix psammophila* are planted to hold the sand. Wind barriers are built on the upper slope. With the growth of these plants, surface (0–30 cm) wind speed is reduced by 60 per cent, and sand transportation by 85 per cent (at a wind speed of 3.7–6.4 m/s). As the slopes are gradually flattened, planting continues toward the top of the sand-dune. Within four years, the sand-dune can be completely flattened and covered with vegetation. On the low area in front of the leeward slope, several rows of *Salix psammophila* are planted to block the moving sand. Multilayer pasture is built on interdune low areas (Huang et al. 1982).

The principal intervention for cropfield protection has been to plant shrubs perpendicular to the wind direction. *Salix psammophila* and *Caragana Korshinskii* have been used frequently. The protective shrubs not only help to control wind erosion but also protect crops from sand attack, so that yields can be raised by as much as 20 per cent. Rotational cultivation of crop and leguminous herbs and green manuring are effective in increasing soil fertility and combating salinization and alkalinization. As a result, yields have increased by as much as 20–80 per cent.

Regional developmental policy

Environmental deterioration in the Ordos, as noted above, is more the result of economic and political policies than of natural processes. Policies that address environmental problems are certainly important, but those promoting regional social and economic development are even more significant. The relationship between environmental changes and socio-economic factors is close. On the one hand, environmental control is of decisive importance to economic growth; on the other hand, the potential of environmental control depends strongly on socio-economic development. In regional development policy, environmental and socio-economic factors are intertwined.

Since 1980, regional development policies have evolved with the implementation of the household responsibility system (involving the equal distribution of land-use rights to each household). From 1980 to 1982, user rights for cropfield and pasture were distributed, with the stipulation that they would not change in the short run. In 1984–1985, the distribution of five kinds of cleared land – range, gully, slope, valley, and sand – gave user rights to households that improved them. These policies greatly encouraged intensive cropland management, pasture enclosure, and land revegetation. All farmers and shepherds know that such initiatives are the only ways to gain a better livelihood for themselves. Even so, people actively claim the more remote and seriously degraded land. Nevertheless, environmental improvements by households have become more common, although, owing to a lack of labour and integrated planning, only small patches show real improvement.

Recognizing this problem, the Ih-Ju League and some banner governments in 1989–1990 re-amalgamated the cleared land into large-scale management units, requiring that each household and each labourer devote certain labour days to land improvement. Recently, to address overgrazing, some banners have evaluated and recorded pasture grades for each household. Increases or decreases in quality elicit financial and other rewards or punishments. Means to adjust livestock according to available forage are identified and promoted. Some other measures have included strengthening the basic fields, increasing fruit and timber trees, and improving livestock breeds. Some programmes (sponsored by either the national or local governments), such as the national government's North China Green-Belt Construction, Uxin Banner's Family Pasture Programme, Otog Banner's Livestock Hazard-Resistant Programme, and the Man-Made Pasture Building Programme in salinized and alkalinized land along the Yellow River plain, have also been instituted.

Science and technology have received new emphasis. In 1990, an Act of Agricultural Development established a network of services and leaders for banners, townships, and villages. Leaders for technology applications contract to help farmers and shepherds with cultivation techniques, family pasturing, the improvement of livestock breeds, and revegetation. Education, both traditional and vocational, is emphasized. Training in agricultural technology is especially popular.

It is apparent that the Ih-Ju League has undertaken environmental improvement as part of its overall approach to economic development. Regional policies have addressed both environmental problems and human driving forces. Environmental policies and also enforcement (such as the distribution of degraded land to each household) have become more effective. From practices in the Ih-Ju League, it is clear that environmental policies are not sufficient in themselves; the close coordination of environmental improvement and economic development is a powerful way to convert environmental awareness into actual improvements. Agricultural economic policies are now better coordinated with environmental goals. Thus, an emphasis on forestry (shrubs, trees, and fruits) in the eastern loess hills and forage cultivation in the pastoral lowlands, and the restriction of cashcrop grain production to river valleys and plains have emerged. These policies have been very effective in improving the regional economy. Although they do not directly address environmental problems, they do serve as environmental countermeasures, and the resulting economic growth has provided the necessary conditions and potential capacity for environmental improvement. Other policies promoting technological application, education, and population control are also effective in addressing the basic driving forces of environmental deterioration. What remain inadequate are the means of implementation, such as overgrazing. Efforts now under way are seeking such means, and the future appears promising.

The trajectory of environmental changes

Designations of endangerment and criticality, as used in this volume, rely on an assessment of the total sustainability of the environmental–socio-economic system now and in the near term. Different approaches to evaluation can, of course, provide different results. Geocentric approaches emphasize the ecosystem, with the natural environment as the basic criterion. Anthropocentric approaches emphasize human livelihood and well-being. This volume seeks an integrative approach to understanding environmental changes as well as changes in human livelihood. The trends and rates of environmental change are important, and the possibility of sustaining socio-economic development over the longer term is essential. In the case of "criticality," environmental deterioration has become so serious as to pre-empt continued economic development and improved social well-being.

Another issue is the terminology. "Can sustain" and "cannot sustain" are key judgements; however, they are very subjective. Here we emphasize the standards and perspectives of local people. For some people, the wind storm accompanied by wind erosion in the Ordos would indicate a vicious threat to human health, and this factor alone could result in the whole system's being judged as "critical." For local people in the Ordos, however, it is not so important; rather, it is a background condition taken for granted. In other words, we adopt the relatively low living standard of local people as the basis for judging their environmental–socio-economic system and for evaluating its degree of endangerment or criticality. Both criticality and sustainability, then, refer not to static situations but to trends toward man–nature harmony (or disharmony) and social development. Judging whether the situation is static or dynamic is also difficult and requires an in-depth understanding of local circumstances.

From our analysis, we conclude that environmental deterioration became more and more serious from 1949 until the early 1980s, and, correspondingly, greatly affected the economy and human life. Since 1980, with the measures taken for environmental protection and improvement, the situation has begun to change. The environmental trajectory of the Ordos falls into four periods:

1. *The pre-1949 period.* Few data exist to assess the situation before 1949. The literature suggests a long stagnant period during which population was low and did not change much. The economy was stable at a low level of development, living conditions were poor, and the environment was slowly deteriorating. Generally, it was a situation that could have been maintained for a long time with a sparse population and low levels of socio-economic development.
2. *Endangerment during the 1950s.* In 1949, drastic changes in the socio-economic and political systems prompted a substantial increase in incentives for economic development and exploitation of nature. With increasing human interference with the environment, environmental deterioration gradually accelerated. People began to become aware of the economic impacts of environmental deterioration and to engage in well-intentioned but largely ineffective action aimed at prevention and restoration.
3. *The critical period of the 1960s and 1970s.* During this period, the population increased rapidly, while social development and human well-being stagnated. The economic situation worsened and morale was low. The environment was seriously exploited and degraded, which in turn impeded socio-economic development. Local people were aware of the problems but saw no effective means for

environmental control. Only limited and small-scale measures were taken, producing few concrete results. Meanwhile, economic production and lifestyle suffered.

4. *The post-1980 period.* The period 1978–1980 was a turning point in the environmental trajectory, induced by the household responsibility system and the new land-use policies, which emphasized economic development and environmental control and implemented new national policies and programmes. The regional economy has grown and human well-being has improved greatly, thereby increasing the social capacity for environmental improvement. Government policies have stimulated effective environmental responses by addressing both environmental problems and human driving forces. Local people have adopted environmental measures as the basis for regional economic growth. Large-scale environmental actions, under governmental sponsorship, have integrated spatially linked areas and coordinated environmental protection with economic growth. As a result, environmental deterioration has slowed and perhaps even been reversed. The overall trend is toward greater environmental protection, restoration, and improvement.

The periods both before 1949 and since 1980 could have been sustained over long time-periods. They contrast in economic level, human life, social restriction and choices, and possibilities for further development. The year 1949 was not a totally catastrophic turning point, although since then the environmental–socio-economic system has marched toward economic development and greater environmental endangerment.

The third and the fourth periods may typify changes in human driving forces and responses. During the third stage, population increases, traditional ideas, and poverty were the driving forces of environmental changes, although they in some sense provided latent conditions. What drove much of the change was political forces. For instance, under the slogan "more people, more strength," population increased without control. Education was replaced by "cultural revolution" and economy by "class struggle." Social institutions became so weak that only traditional land-use styles, working almost instinctively, allowed people to survive. Poverty reflected the accumulation of past policy. In a word, it interacted with driving forces in the system.

In the last stage, it was state policy that changed the whole environmental trajectory of the Ordos from endangerment to stabilization. Policy replaced other driving forces in the society, and either changed or minimized them. For example, family-planning regulations controlled population increases; market policy afforded the Ordos the chance for economic growth; new environmental policies strengthened local environmental protection. The combination of publicization and privatization had far-reaching effects on every aspect of social life. In short, political forces have played a decisive role in the environmental changes of the Ordos over the past 15 years.

Future trends

Current regional policy, the potential for economic growth, socioeconomic developments, possible natural changes, and potential policy regulations combine to define possible future scenarios of environmental change. Future natural variability, mainly climatic, will probably not be dramatically different from the scale of past fluctuation in the near term (although potential climatic change could prove important over the longer term). Peijun Shi (1991) predicted a 12–15 per cent variation in precipitation from the present (1955–1980) over the next 50 years. Therefore, possible human actions and policy regulations are likely to be decisive in the future trajectory of environmental changes. Coalmining development may be particularly important.

Over the next 10 years, it seems clear that, although the household responsibility system is working well and has greatly increased productivity, collective management could become more and more important. Individual households cannot manage improvements in crop variety and livestock breeds, fertilizers, and agricultural technology. Government, both national and local, has realized this problem in China and is trying to increase the collective service system in order to coordinate further publicization and privatization. Economic development and environmental protection continue to be major political objectives and to represent criteria for evaluating the performance of public leaders.

Most of the coalmining and power generation industry in China is run by the state. The profits and products (coal and electricity) will go mostly to other areas of China; some of the coal will even be exported abroad. Industrial development of the Ordos will increase the material and money fluxes to other areas, and regional linkages will become more and more important. With these fluxes will come other interactions, such as road and railway construction linking the

Ordos to east China. Information exchange will be important. Given growing regional linkages, it is difficult to see the Ordos remaining a politically and economically marginal area. Although the benefits of industrial development may accrue mostly to the state, it will still provide a great opportunity for the Ordos to develop service enterprises and to increase economic growth.

With national governmental policy for the development of coalmining and other related industry (such as power generation), soil erosion and sandification caused by open-cast mining could become more serious in the future. Rapid population growth, air pollution, and wastewater contamination are other threats attendant on coalmining.

The potential effects of coalmining have attracted great attention from both national and local governments. Policy makers are well aware that such mining could determine future environmental trends in the Ordos, and they have conducted environmental impact assessments for these projects and proposed technological countermeasures. Local governments have also explored possible environmental taxes on coalmining. Since these newly developing large-scale coalmines are run by the national government, coordination between national and local governments will obviously be very important in future efforts to protect the environment.

Conclusion

As a dry, windy, and sandy area, the Ordos Plateau is a fragile region. Under the pressure of human activities since 1949, the area has experienced several stages of environmental change: endangerment in the 1950s, growing threats in the 1960s and 1970s, and progress toward environmental sustainability since 1980. Each stage is indicated by certain types of environmental deterioration and socio-economic situations, which are themselves closely related. Given the high human dependence on the environment and the great vulnerability of local people, environmental changes have greatly affected the Ordos people. Land-use styles, traditional ideas, population growth, and the education levels of the local people have all played a major role, although national policy and the state have been most important, as both negative and positive responses to environmental changes. Future scenarios may well continue to strengthen the current trend toward sustainability, but that will depend very much on the course of national policy and on the implementation of measures as well.

Acknowledgements

The authors are extremely grateful to Mr. Jia Jong, a young geographer at Beijing Normal University, for his generous help in field research. Ms. Zhen Shuping also deserves our warm gratitude for her assistance.

References (in Chinese)

Beijing University Geography Department, et al. 1983. *Natural conditions and amelioration of the Mu Us sandy land.* Beijing: Science Press.

Cao, Lihe. 1988. Discussion on land desertification and rational utilization. *Journal of Desert Research* 8, no. 4: 59–65.

Dong, Guangrong, et al. 1983. Change of the Mu Us since the late Pleistocene, as seen from the Salaus River strata. *Journal of Desert Research* 3, no. 2: 9–14.

Huang, Zhaohua, et al. 1982. Utilization and improvement of the Ordos Steppe, *Memoir of Institute of Desert Research, Academia Sinica, Lanzhou, China* 1: 19–37.

———. 1986. Desertification and its control in Ih-Ju League, Inner Mongolia. *Memoir of Institute of Desert Research, Academia Sinica, Lanzhou, China* 3: 35–47.

Huang, Zhaohua, and Bing Kui Song. 1981. Sandification and its prevention in the Ih-Ju League, Inner Mongolia. Unpublished report.

Ih-Ju League. 1988. Planning Committee. *Land resources of the Ih-Ju League*. Huhehaote: Inner Mongolia People's Press.

———. 1990. Agricultural Regionalization Editing Committee. *Ih-Ju League agricultural regionalization*. Huhehaote: Inner Mongolia People's Press.

Jiang, Dingsheng, et al. 1986. Soil erosion history and control measures in the area along the Great Wall. *Journal of Soil Conservation* 8: 38–43.

Li, Bo, et al. 1990. *Natural resources and the environment of the Ordos Plateau in Inner Mongolia.* Beijing: Science Press.

Shen, Yongling. 1981. Causes and control of soil erosion in the Ih Ju League. *Journal of Soil Conservation* 3: 33–38.

Shi, Nianhai. 1980. Distribution and changes in agriculture in the Ordos and the elbow plain over the past 2,300 years. *Journal of Beijing Normal University* (Philosophy and Social Sciences) 6: 1–14.

Shi, Peijun. 1991. *Theory and practice of geo-environmental change study*. Beijing: Science Press.

Sui-Yuan (Regional Government). 1934a. Analysis of the Mongolian economy of the Cha-Sui region. Beijing: Commercial Publishing House.

——— (Department of Mass Education). 1934b. Report on the counties of Sui-Yuan region. Sui-Yuan: Department of Mass Education.

——— (Regional Government). 1939. Report on the western four banners of the Ih-Ju League. Sui-Yuan: Regional Government.

Wang, Huadong, et al. 1991. *Environmental impacts of industry, mining, and urban development on the loess plateau and countermeasures*. Beijing: Science Press.

Wang, Yunzhong, et al. 1983. Experiment of aerial sowing of sand-fixing plants in the Mu Us sandy land of the Ih-Ju League. *Journal of Desert Research* 3, no. 1: 36–41.

Yang, Gensheng, et al. 1991. *Integrated improvement of land desertification in the sandy area north of the loess plateau.* Beijing: Science Press.
Zhao, Songqiao, et al. 1958. *Preliminary study of farming and pastoral distribution in Inner-Mongolia.* Beijing: Science Press.
Zhao, Yongfu. 1981. Change in the Mu Us sandy land in historical time. *Historical Geography*, first issue: 34–47.
Zhu, Shiguang. 1986. Comments on the discussion of the formation and change of the Mu Us sandy land. *History and Geography of Northwest China* 4: 17–27.
Zhu, Zhenda, et al. 1986. Approach of desertification control in the farming–pastoral transitional area in northern China. *Memoir of Institute of Desert Research, Academia Sinica, Lanzhou, China* 3: 1–18.

10

The eastern Sundaland region of South-East Asia

Lesley Potter, Harold Brookfield, and Yvonne Byron

The analysis in this chapter covers all Borneo and the east of Peninsular Malaysia, but for reasons of space we focus principally on Borneo, both Indonesian and Malaysian, and make only brief reference to the Malay Peninsula. In a larger sense, Sundaland, the partly submerged continental spur extending south-eastward from Asia to the Wallace line, also includes Sumatra and Java, and all of it was dry land during the low-sealevel periods of the Pleistocene. Our area of focus, together with much of Sumatra, has for 30 years been the "resource frontier" of Indonesia and Malaysia. This role is undergoing change as the old-growth timber resource that has been heavily exploited nears exhaustion, leading to a new phase that will have to depend more on oil and gas, agriculture, forest management, and industry.

We focus principally on four of the questions posed by the authors of chapter 1. First is the change in the resource base. Clearly, the timber resource is declining rapidly, but the agricultural land resource, however defined, has increased, though the increase may be approaching limits. We have to try to place values on this shift, and to do so in global, regional, and quite local contexts. The second question involves the thresholds of criticality, an issue of continuing concern in this volume. For much of the original forests, any such threshold has long since passed, and we do not think that merely to lament this fact is productive. Criticality has to be assessed in terms of the present transitional economy and its effect on people and on the environment. The third question addresses poverty. National governments see their policies as reducing a pre-existing condition of poverty rather than as creating new poverty. In asking, who are the poor, we need also to ask, who are the rich? Moreover, change in any environment creates biophysical vulnerability, but how much is this transitory? What is the role of tropical deforestation in increasing global vulnerability through climatic interference? Each of these questions needs to be disaggregated and considered at different levels of scale. We deal with them through the text, then bring the issues together in conclusion.

To approach these problems we first review eastern Sundaland as a whole, to determine what about its present condition might be regarded as critical, both in terms of how the world sees it and in terms of its own transitory situation. We then describe the changes and the current conditions on the island of Borneo. Because it is the central issue, we concentrate almost wholly on the changes arising from deforestation, timber extraction, and conversion to agriculture. These issues underlie all others. Although oil and gas, mainly extracted offshore, will be of major future importance, the land and forest resource issues are our vehicles for discussion of criticality in Sundaland.

Sundaland as a "critical environmental zone"

A region of rapid change

The 1990 population of Borneo was 12.7 million people – 3.3 million in East Malaysia, 0.3 million in Brunei, and 9.1 million in Kalimantan (see fig. 10.1 for locations). Table 10.1 shows the distribution of population. In addition, between 0.5 and 1 million people, most of whom are illegal but tolerated immigrants in Malaysian Borneo, are unrecorded in census data. Peninsular Malaysia has 14.7 million people, plus up to 1 million illegals. The island of Sumatra has a further 33 million people, and over 107 million now live on Java, with a land area about the size of the former Czechoslovakia. Together with almost 3 million in Singapore, there are over 170 million people in the whole of greater Sundaland. Only 7.5 per cent are in Borneo. Growth is rapid, but in most of Borneo the density of population is still low. Except for the oil and gas fields, the major element in the recent exploitation of our part of Sundaland has been the clearance of for-

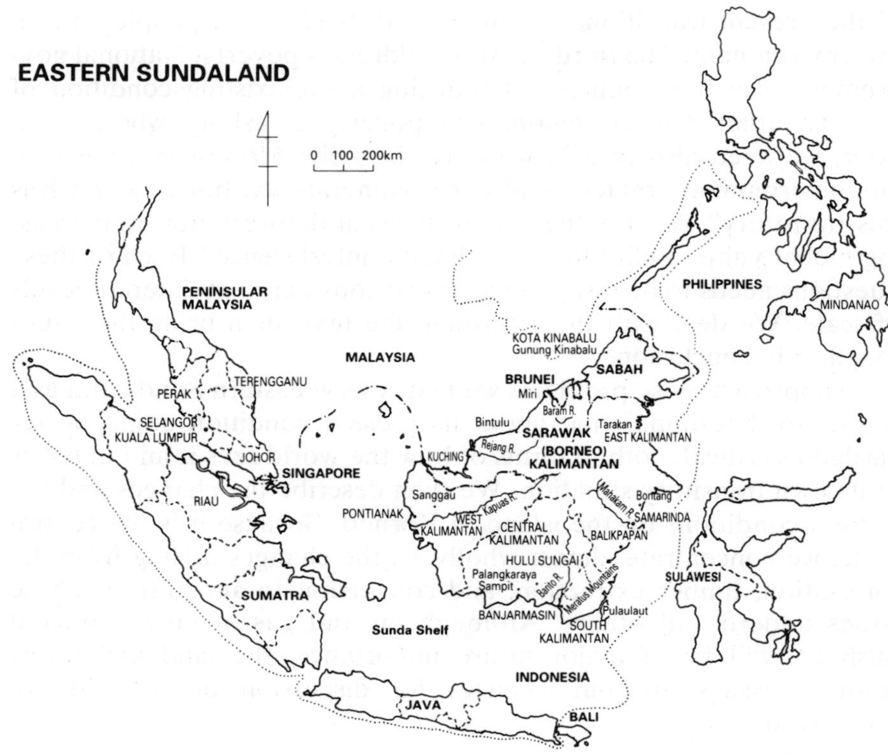

Fig. 10.1 **Sundaland and adjacent areas, showing places mentioned in the text**

Table 10.1 **Population densities on the island of Borneo, 1990**

State	Population (million)	Area (km^2)	Population density (persons/km^2)
Indonesia			
E. Kalimantan	1.88	211,440	8.9
W. Kalimantan	3.24	146,807	22.0
C. Kalimantan	1.39	153,800	9.0
S. Kalimantan	2.59	36,985	70.0
Malaysia			
Sarawak	1.77	124,449	14.2
Sabah	1.54	74,398	20.7
Brunei	0.30	5,765	52.0

Sources: Census of Indonesia (1990); *Asian Yearbook 1990*.

est, both for planned and unplanned land settlement and for timber extraction. The island of Borneo alone has provided at least one-half of the world's total exports of non-coniferous tropical hardwoods since the early 1970s and 60 per cent in 1987 (Brookfield and Byron 1990). After the United States and Canada, Malaysia is the world's third-largest exporter, almost entirely from its Borneo territories, of all solid woods (hardwood and softwood together) (Vincent 1988); Indonesia, principally from its Borneo (Kalimantan) provinces, produced 58 per cent of all world exports of tropical plywoods by 1987.

Equatorial South-East Asia is both the most populous and the most rapidly developing part of the low-latitude tropics. Singapore and Malaysia, though not yet Indonesia, have attained levels of per capita national income above or comparable with those of the lesser-developed countries of Europe, and the GDP growth rates of all three countries over the period 1965–1989 were consistently high, though more spectacular in the 1970s than in the 1980s (World Bank 1991, 206–207). The people of both Indonesia and Malaysia, and of all ethnic groups within them, are proud of their national achievements since independence and impatient for further development. It would be folly to disregard this essential part of the total environment.

Deforestation as a critical issue

The rate of deforestation, and its consequences, are now recognized as serious issues in both Indonesia and Malaysia, but this recognition is rather new and its origins are more economic than ecological. In the eyes of the powerful world conservationist movement, on the other hand, deforestation alone makes this area a "critical environmental region." The issue rose to international prominence in the late 1970s out of a growing realization that rates of clearance and harvesting were both unsustainable and ecologically damaging (e.g. Eckholm 1976; Myers 1980, 1984). In the United States, a series of official inquiries conducted around 1980 brought concern about tropical deforestation into US aid and foreign policy (Stowe 1987). The International Tropical Timber Organization (ITTO), initially proposed as a trade organization in 1977, became also a body charged with sustainable use and conservation by the time it was formed in 1983. It is argued that, in the long run, the high rate of forest reduction both for timber extraction and for agricultural land settlement will have been unsuccessful in establishing any sort of sustainable future even for agriculture. The latter claim, the evaluation of which is central to any review of "environmental endangerment or criticality" in this region, is found mainly in the more popular literature and seems to derive largely from extrapolation of tropical American experience to South-East Asia. Yet the view gains support in relation to South-East Asia from Gillis (1988), who joins more forcefully with Repetto (1988, 1990) and many others in maintaining that neither Indonesia nor Malaysia will have gained much lasting benefit from the rapid depletion of their forest resources. Conservationists see the rate of deforestation as critical for two further reasons: it is destroying a "global" resource of inestimable value and great genetic diversity, and in the process is also wiping out the basis of livelihood of the forest-dwelling people; it is contributing substantially to carbon dioxide emissions into the atmosphere, and hence to global climatic change. An immense literature covers both these aspects; the former is mainly a regional issue that we take up below, but the latter is of global concern.

The global significance of deforestation

The issues involved have been complex from the outset. Estimates of deforestation (usefully reviewed by Brown and Lugo 1982; Lugo and Brown 1982; and Allen and Barnes 1985) are now being refined on the basis of improved information. Some problems of interpretation, and the policy implications, were recently assessed by Wood (1990). The World Resources Institute (1988, 1990) has raised its former estimate of Indonesia's annual deforestation rate from 6,000 to 9,000 km^2 per year, putting this country third in rank after Brazil and India; the estimate for Malaysia remains unchanged at 2,550 km^2 per year. Revisions are said to be based on satellite information, a data source criticized as full of "ambiguities and impossibilities" by Blasco and Achard (1990); apart from the problems of low resolution and lack of synchroneity in cloudy regions such as Sundaland, there are inconsistencies in interpretation through time. In addition to complete clearance for land development, generalized deforestation data may or may not include the effects of shifting cultivation and the consequences of selective logging. It is widely held that tropical deforestation is an important source of CO_2 inputs into the atmosphere. Tropical Asia as a whole is estimated to provide 25 per cent of the world's contribution from biotic sources (World Resources Institute 1988). This is a view hotly disputed in some quarters in the developing countries, most recently by the Indian Centre for Science and Environment (Agarwal and Narain 1991).

A review of data on greenhouse gas emissions at national levels put Indonesia in seventh rank among contributors in carbon equivalent, ahead of West Germany and the United Kingdom and behind only the United States, the USSR, China, Brazil, India, and Japan (Hammond, Rodenburg, and Moomaw 1991). Malaysia, being much smaller, comes a long way further down the list, but lies well above Indonesia on a per capita basis. Two principal elements contribute to the high rank of Indonesia: the quantitatively small but effective interceptor, methane, and carbon. The former is produced largely from wet ricefields and swamps. The review pays more attention, however, to the carbon released by forest-clearing and from the soil exposed in consequence of deforestation. A principal authoritative source on carbon flux is Richard Houghton (1991; Houghton et al. 1987; Palm et al. 1986), whose work is used by Hammond, Rodenburg, and Moomaw (1991). The estimation of carbon flux from tropical forests undergoing change has improved enormously since the time of some initially very high estimates made in the 1970s, but it remains an area in which increasingly sound methodology is applied to very unsound data. What can be described only as "heroic" extrapolations from very limited measurements are necessary.

Three main elements are involved. First is estimation of change in the forest area and its rate. Second is calculation of forest biomass. Third is evaluation of the effects of interference other than complete conversion to non-forest uses, that is, of shifting cultivation and logging. This last element is complicated by uncertainty about the net effect of initial destruction and subsequent recovery during which new growth takes up carbon at a higher rate than occurs in dynamically stable forest. It is also necessary to take account of carbon removed, but not destroyed, in the form of wood products. Calculations based on land-use change alone yielded a carbon release from all the non-fallow forests of the Asian tropics equal to only 7 per cent of that from global fossil-fuel consumption (Houghton et al. 1985).

Subsequent work has both modified results and provided important new bases for quantitative estimation of the effects of forest interference (Dale, Houghton, and Hall 1991). Brown, Gillespie, and Lugo (1989) revised the basis for conversion of forest inventory data to biomass, using expansion factors applied to stand tables. Hall and Uhlig (1991) further refined biomass estimates by using these new expansion factors with data on commercial tree volumes per hectare, for undisturbed, logged, unproductive, and managed forest. They applied the results to FAO data on 1980 land use, with allowance for shifting cultivation, to obtain new estimates of carbon flux, but the lack of good data on shifting cultivation reduces the value of their effort to refine estimation on this basis.

Other researchers (Brown, Gillespie, and Lugo 1991) made use of the two national forest inventories of Peninsular Malaysia, carried out in 1972 and 1981 (FAO 1973; Malaysia 1987), to introduce the concept of "degraded" forest, meaning forest reduced in biomass from its original state, principally by logging or shifting cultivation. Comparing area and calculated biomass for different forest types on the Peninsula at the two dates, they found a statistically highly significant reduction in mean biomass per hectare on the much-enlarged area of partially logged hill forest and the very small area of shifting-cultivation forest. For no very evident reason, biomass in the small area of partially logged swamp forest had increased. They noted that degradation as well as decrease in the forest area implies loss of carbon, and derived a "degradation ratio" from the ratio of biomass lost to area lost, relative to the initial average biomass. For Peninsular Malaysia in 1981 this ratio was 1.6.

The data on which all these estimates rely are a good deal less than satisfactory, though the authors have worked very hard to improve on them. The effect, however, is to enhance the role of tropical deforestation and degradation as an important contributor to global carbon emissions, so long as we accept at least the median level of estimates. The Scientific Assessment Report of the Intergovernmental Panel on Climatic Change (IPCC) notes, however, that one of three possibilities that might explain the imbalance in the global carbon cycle could be, just possibly, that inputs from tropical deforestation are at the low end of the range (Houghton, Jenkins, and Ephraums 1990, 17). A comparison of maps of carbon emissions from terrestrial ecosystems and from fossil fuels, on an equivalent tonnes/km^2 basis (Houghton and Skole 1990, 399), places tropical South-East Asia in a class with the industrialized countries. The new data on forest degradation would add to this calculated contribution. Even though the total area concerned, and hence the total quantity, is far smaller than that supplying high levels of carbon from fossil fuels, the addition to atmospheric carbon by forest conversion and degradation in Sundaland could, therefore, be a significant, though uncertain, element in global atmospheric pollution. Methane from the ricefields and wetlands, and the growing flux of carbon from fossil fuels burned in the region, might already be as important.

Borneo

The island

The large island of Borneo is occupied by the two eastern states of Malaysia, Sabah and Sarawak, by the independent country of Brunei, and by the four Indonesian provinces of East, West, South, and Central Kalimantan. Two-thirds of the total area of 753,644 km^2 is in Kalimantan, one-third in Malaysia and Brunei. Borneo has long been famous for its forests: current estimates give Indonesian Borneo 51 per cent of Indonesia's standing stock in forests of all types, and 75 per cent of the commercially valuable dipterocarps (FAO and GOI 1990). With the rest of "Sundaland," including Sumatra and Malaysia, Borneo forms the important forest belt of West Malesia, with a uniquely rich and varied flora and fauna (Whitmore 1984).

Borneo has considerable physiographic complexity, the landforms generally descending from a north–central mountainous spine. The geology of the Malaysian part is better known than that of Kalimantan, though a recent survey of a potentially mineral-bearing swath across northern Kalimantan helps rectify this imbalance (Pieters and Supriatna 1990). Palaeozoic basement rocks and Mesozoic volcanics and meta-sediments form a central and south-western core related to that of Peninsular Malaysia, onto which Mesozoic mountains have been attached in the south-eastern Meratus range (Katili 1974). Most of northern and eastern Borneo is also added to the original Sunda plate. Oceanic basement sediments in eastern Kalimantan contain Devonian corals. Some of the highest north–central mountains are younger than the pre-Tertiary core. The Crocker range of Sabah, rising to 4,100 m in Gunung Kinabalu, is a mass of igneous intrusives less than 2 million years old. Late-Tertiary volcanic plateaux cap older formations, to rise to between 2,000 m and 3,000 m in eastern parts of Sarawak and western East Kalimantan. Tertiary limestone formations are widespread, with cave systems of great size in Sarawak that hold important evidence of human prehistory.

Most of Sarawak plus Brunei forms a geosynclinal belt of Tertiary and Quaternary sedimentaries, still actively subsiding, and comparable Tertiary basins lie in northern and central East Kalimantan. These basins and their offshore extensions contain large oil and gas pools, and Kalimantan has extensive coal deposits. Extensive Quaternary deposits occupy the lower valleys of numerous large rivers, the most important being the Kapuas, Mahakam, Rejang, and Barito (fig. 10.1), and there is considerable Holocene peat swamp development along and behind the aggrading southern, western, and northwestern shores. Except in some alluvial areas, the soils of Borneo are generally of low quality and deeply weathered. However, the volcanic plateaux in Sarawak and East Kalimantan, though remote, possess favourable soils, and similar volcanic soils exist at low altitude in the east of Sabah.

The dipterocarp forests are most richly developed in the non-swampy lowlands and the foothills, particularly in Sarawak, Sabah, and East and Central Kalimantan, whereas swamp timbers, such as Ramin (*Gonystylus bancanus*), have also been utilized commercially. Following two decades of continuous exploitation, East and Central Kalimantan still have 69 per cent of their land under forest. This declines to 54 per cent and 44 per cent, respectively, in the more heavily populated western and southern regions (FAO and GOI, 1990). On the Malaysian side, Sarawak retains a forest cover of about 68 per cent and Sabah 60 per cent of their respective areas (Thang 1990).

Kalimantan

Administered as two districts by the Dutch, and as one large unmanageable unit after independence in 1949, Kalimantan received its current subdivision in 1957. The old cities that had served as the seats of colonial administration, Banjarmasin (South) and Pontianak (West), are now the largest urban centres in Borneo, with roughly 500,000 and 400,000 inhabitants, respectively, and their provinces are also the most populous (table 10.1). East Kalimantan already had two towns, Balikpapan and Samarinda, to act as foci for its resource extraction, begun in a limited way during colonial times (Potter 1988). Balikpapan developed solely to serve the nearby oil wells from its inception in 1898, but Samarinda, with an extensive hinterland up the Mahakam river, was a gateway to the interior and its timber. The new province of Central Kalimantan was most remote, with its capital, Palangkaraya, far inland with no road access. Despite much recent road construction in all provinces, one finds a network only in the more populous areas.

Before the logging boom commenced in the late 1960s, both Banjarmasin and Pontianak derived much of their small industrial income from the processing of rubber, the principal peasant cash crop since the early 1900s. Timber and other forest products have provided the impetus for recent growth, from large plywood mills to small hand-operated sawmills and furniture factories. The influence of the forest remains pervasive, despite the existence of important hinterland agricultural activities. South Kalimantan leads in wet rice production, West Kalimantan in tree crops, especially smallholder rubber. The bulk of the logging is carried out in East and Central Kalimantan. The value of East Kalimantan's lowland dipterocarp forests was recognized early, and a forestry office was established at Samarinda in 1923. Almost all of the forests in East, Central, and South Kalimantan had been mapped after a fashion by 1933, and published figures recorded the volume and extent of valuable species. These early maps and statistics, although approximate, were still in use by Indonesian foresters and concessionaires in 1975. The entry of Japanese interests to East Kalimantan in the 1930s prompted attempts to organize and regulate concessions. All the logs cut on the Japanese concessions were exported directly to Japan, but there was also an effort to establish a large-scale sawmilling industry. The swampy coast near Sampit in Central Kalimantan, which had seen a boom in the wild rubber, *jelutung* (*Dyera* sp.), around 1910 was, in 1941, selected as the site for the development of *Agathis bornensis*, intended for plywood and pulp. Production was overtaken by World War II, but resumed during the late 1940s, when it became the leading timber export from Kalimantan for a few years.

Samarinda and Balikpapan now have 300,000 people each; with Tarakan and the new industrial centre at Bontang, with its large liquefied natural gas plant, they constitute a typically immigrant, "enclave" economy based on timber and oil; 49 per cent of East Kalimantan's population is urban. Samarinda has one of the world's largest concentrations of sawmills, plywood factories, and other timber industries (Schindele and Thoma 1989). Much of Central Kalimantan's timber, on the other hand, is produced in the thinly peopled north of the province and rafted down the Barito river for processing in Banjarmasin. The up-country areas, away from the coastal urban agglomerations and alluvial agricultural land, remain regions of low population density, with no roads apart from logging tracks, where scattered Dayak groups practise shifting cultivation along the rivers. It is in these districts that recent changes have been most rapid – from the timber industry itself and accompanying government resettlement schemes; and from the influx of new arrivals, both government-sponsored and spontaneous, intent on converting the logged-over lands to alternative uses. It is not surprising that, with 28 per cent of the area of Indonesia and, in 1990, still only 5 per cent of its total population, Kalimantan has been perceived as an "empty" land and a suitable location for new settlers, mainly officially sponsored government transmigrants from the crowded islands of Java and Bali.

Sabah and Sarawak: Two semi-independent states

The Malaysian part of Borneo has a very different history. Sabah and Sarawak joined the Federation of Malaysia only in 1963. Oil-rich Brunei, the third territory in the former British area of Borneo, opted to retain its independence. Brunei is the small remainder of the ancient sultanate, which lost most of its territory to British colonial entrepreneurs during the nineteenth century. It permits little timber extraction and is not discussed here. Sarawak was under the private rule of the Brooke family until World War II, after which it became a British crown colony. Sabah was the fief of the British North Borneo Company until the same time. In joining the Federation, Sarawak and Sabah retained a greater degree of independence in relation to central government than did the 11 states of Peninsular Malaysia; they have far more autonomy than the provinces of Kalimantan. Each maintains full control over immigration (even movement within East Malaysia) and over the use of its land and forests.

Most of the 1.5 million people of Sabah and the 1.8 million people of Sarawak live in the western parts of the two states, in the lowlands west of the Rejang delta in Sarawak, and on the western coastal strip of Sabah. Large areas in eastern Sabah have been almost without population for at least two centuries, and in the interior of Sarawak people now live mainly along the rivers. Throughout north-western Borneo, large movements of population have occurred since the seventeenth century as Iban people have expanded from an original homeland in present West Kalimantan, driving others before them. Later, people moved to the rivers to gain easier access to trade. With the exception of formerly powerful Brunei, northern Borneo had no towns of significance before the colonial period, and the modern capitals, Kuching and Kota Kinabalu, remain much smaller than the cities of Kalimantan. They are still populated largely by the descendants of immigrant Chinese. The oil and gas centres of Bintulu and Miri are smaller, but rapidly growing. As in most of Kalimantan, Sabah and Sarawak have substantial indigenous, or "Dayak," populations, most of whom practise various forms of shifting cultivation, while a few are hunters and gatherers. These indigenous, mainly non-Muslim people, form 44 per cent of the population of Sarawak and are the majority in Sabah. Like their cousins in Kalimantan (and many groups are found on both sides of the international border), they have for centuries been linked to regional networks through the trade in forest products such as rattans, resins, and edible birds' nests, mediated through the coastal Malays and Chinese.

Early commercial development was limited. The North Borneo Company sought to promote tobacco plantations in early cash-cropping efforts along the sparsely peopled east coast of Sabah but met with only limited success. Rubber plantations became established on the west coast, and the focus of economic activity shifted there. Activities along the east coast focused on timber extraction following the founding of the Forest Department in 1915. Timber soon became an important export (Avé and King 1986; Naval Intelligence Division 1944). After World War II, some large timber concessions were allocated. Mechanization was introduced for the extraction of dipterocarp timbers, and by 1960 Sabah was the principal exporter of sawlogs in the Indonesia–Malaysia region (Brookfield and Byron 1990). The Brooke government in pre-1941 Sarawak was more concerned with keeping the peace than with development, though happy to receive revenues from the mining of antimony, gold, coal, and the oil discovered at Miri in 1910. Only four estates were established, but smallholder rubber was planted quite widely, even well inland (Jackson 1968; Lian 1987); for some years it was the principal export, although, from 1948 on, the main thrust was with timber. The pioneers developed the extensive swamp-forest stands of Ramin (*Gonystylus bancanus*) as sawn timber for the British market. Although no mechanization of timber extraction occurred for more than a decade, production expanded rapidly and, by 1960, the swamp forests were almost all under timber concessions. Only toward the end of the 1950s did logging commence in the dryland dipterocarp forests in response to the rising Japanese demand for hardwood sawlogs. The introduction of mechanized extraction followed in the early 1960s, with capital from abroad (Jackson 1968).

Formation of the Federation in 1963 was expected to signal a new period of development, based on agricultural diversification. From the outset, however, there was a shortage of labour for new enterprises, especially in Sabah, where unsuccessful attempts were made to recruit migrants from the Peninsula (Ongkilli 1972). The rising Japanese demand for sawlogs soon came to dominate the economies of both states, but in different contexts. In Sabah, a major part of the forested area has, from the outset, been intended for conversion to agriculture. The declared Permanent Forest Estate (PFE) came eventually to occupy 45 per cent of the land (Collins, Sayer, and Whitmore 1991). In Sarawak, the main non-timber use of the forests is for shifting cultivation. The area "assumed to be available for timber production" covers 59,300 km^2, only 48 per cent of the state (ITTC 1990, 30), but the actual timber-production area is larger. Sarawak has experienced more diversified development than Sabah, with some significant expansion of petrochemical and other industries, including even car assembly.

As in much of Kalimantan, a basic problem of development in East Malaysia is lack of infrastructure. The river systems have been the main arteries of transport in Sarawak since the Brooke period. Today, hawkers still travel their navigable length, buying produce and selling retail goods and fuel, and the reach of river communication extends as far as longboats and canoes can be paddled and pushed over the rapids. Penetration of the interior by roads is, however, increasing rapidly. A trans-Sabah road was opened in the early 1970s, and a road from Kuching to eastern Sarawak in the early 1980s, and all towns are now linked by at least dry-weather roads. In Sarawak, the lower reaches of the river systems are already being bypassed as transport arteries.

Forestry in Borneo since the 1960s

Deconstructing the rainforest issues

Considerable uncertainty remains about the dynamics of the forests themselves, especially after disturbance, fire, and cataclysmic destruction (Whitmore 1984, 1990, 1991; Wirawan 1993). With the new understanding of the role of disturbance in forest ecology that has arisen, especially since the Borneo fires in 1982–1983, it is no longer possible to think of the forests in terms of simple dynamic stability. Woods (1987, 1989) noted that, in 1983 in Sabah, many trees died from drought rather than from fire, and that drought is a frequent hazard, with a return period much shorter than the recovery time of a species-stable climax forest. In nearby Papua New Guinea, Johns (1986, 1989) has suggested that fire, occurring almost only in drought, has been an important factor in the ecology of large areas of the rain forest.

"Management" means different things to different people (Gomez-Pompa and Burley 1991). So does "conservation," be it of an intact and unchanging forest – which is an unattainable goal, since forests are in constant change – or of its rare species rather than the widespread or common species among which they are contained. Good forestry practices might attain the latter while yielding a harvest, though with important changes in species composition through time. The literature betrays a degree of confusion between the policies and practices of forestry, with the former often held up as environmentally sound and sustainable. Burgess (1990) provides a regional summary of both policies and the large deviations from them in practice. In fact, there is really "little knowledge of the extent to which rain forest ecosystems are resilient and recover from logging" (Whitmore 1991, 84). Light-demanding species, including many of the 72 *Shorea* spp. known in Malay as *meranti*, certainly grow rapidly in gaps, whether natural or anthropogenic, and can yield a new harvest in only a few decades. The slow-growing species, however, which include some other dipterocarps growing in the shade created by the light-demanding trees, are much more rigorous in the conditions required for regrowth and re-establishment (Woods 1989). Unlike the quickly regenerating nomads, many of them will seed only a short distance from their parent trees.

The literature both minimizes and exaggerates the large deviations in practice from the paper policies, depending on the viewpoints of the different writers. "Selective" systems, now policy in both Indonesia and Malaysia, require that only trees that exceed a certain girth be harvested, so that an immature generation will replace them in as little as 25–35 years (Potter 1990; Salleh 1988). It would always be difficult to ensure that this restriction is observed; often it is not (Burgess 1990; Leslie 1977). Great damage is often done to immature trees in extracting the mature timber, whereas compaction and disturbance of the soil reduce the chances that seedlings will survive. Elsewhere we have summarized the literature on damage caused by logging operations (Brookfield et al. 1990). Some official commentators write as if selective systems were in successful and conservationist operation. Other commentators, including Schmidt (1991), Salleh (1988), and Burgess (1990), describe elements of good management, potentially leading toward a sustainable silviculture based on managed natural regeneration, but a reality that falls short of this ideal.

These considerations have, or should have, a bearing on economic evaluations of present practices and on the development of downstream woodworking industries in both countries, a now-critical issue, as we shall see below. Here, it will be useful to take account of a debate on the employment-generating capacities of a truly sustainable forest industry, in comparison with that of the agriculture that has often replaced the forests. Burbridge, Dixon, and Soewardi (1981) for Indonesia, and Kumar (1986) for Malaysia, have argued that, on a per hectare basis, a forestry industry could support a larger workforce than could a tree-crop agriculture, when account is also taken of jobs in downstream woodworking industries. Kumar supports this claim with a model that incorporates elasticities, capital, labour, and land intensities. His calculations support conclusions in favour of forestry, by showing that, whereas logging alone used three times the area per employee of the rubber and oil-palm industries, the addition of downstream processing brought the area per employee below that for the agricultural industries. For Indonesia, however, an unpublished World Bank study has argued that tree-crop estates are a better employment-generating option than forest plantations (World Bank 1989). In the absence of data, it is simply not possible to choose between these views, and the question of social benefit from different uses of forest land has to remain open. The conservationist literature, we note, virtually ignores this consideration. The question, therefore, falls back on the sustainability of forestry itself, whether on a selective cutting basis, with all its present inefficiencies, or on some other basis. If forestry itself proves to be unsustainable, then the option of wood-based industry becomes unsustainable with it. A second question, that of the sustainability of the new agricultural economies created in place of the forest, then becomes central. These two questions, and others associated with them, are now treated through the empirical evidence of recent development and environmental history. We take up the story in the 1960s, when the modern boom began.

Forestry in Sabah and Sarawak

Though quickly overtaken by Kalimantan, Sabah remained the largest exporter of timber from Borneo until the early 1970s (tables 10.2 and 10.3). Whole areas are cut over, despite the official adoption of a "minimum girth" criterion in 1971 (Aten Suwandi n.d.). Between

Table 10.2 **Tropical timber exports: Kalimantan, Sabah, and Sarawak (roundwood equivalents), 1965–1988**

	Kalimantan				Sabah				Sarawak			
Year	Total exports ('000 m³)	Plywood (%)	Sawn timber (%)	Sawlogs (%)	Total exports ('000 m³)	Plywood (%)	Sawn timber (%)	Sawlogs (%)	Total exports ('000 m³)	Plywood (%)	Sawn timber (%)	Sawlogs (%)
1965	143	0.0	0.0	100.0	3,808	0.0	0.3	99.7	1,614	0.0	25.2	74.8
1966	229	0.0	0.0	100.0	5,332	0.1	0.1	99.8	2,531	1.0	10.4	88.6
1967	53	0.0	0.0	100.0	4,863	0.0	0.1	99.9	2,275	0.4	14.6	85.0
1968	651	0.0	0.4	99.6	5,809	0.1	0.1	99.8	3,478	0.7	13.4	85.9
1969	2,413	0.0	0.7	99.3	6,209	0.1	0.2	99.6	3,553	1.0	12.9	86.2
1970	4,865	0.0	1.0	99.0	6,177	0.1	0.3	99.6	3,616	0.4	13.1	86.5
1971	6,877	0.0	0.7	99.3	6,578	0.2	0.1	99.7	2,999	0.9	14.1	85.0
1972	9,424	0.0	1.7	98.3	7,741	0.3	0.2	99.6	2,472	1.1	18.4	80.4
1973	13,042	0.0	3.2	96.8	10,184	0.2	0.2	99.6	2,301	1.5	16.8	81.7
1974	12,060	0.0	3.4	96.6	9,761	0.2	0.1	99.7	2,027	1.2	15.9	82.8
1975	9,351	0.0	5.6	94.4	9,044	0.5	0.1	99.4	1,644	1.7	22.1	76.2
1976	12,161	0.1	6.4	93.5	12,123	0.3	0.2	99.5	3,406	0.9	12.6	86.4
1977	14,464	0.0	4.9	95.1	12,412	0.3	0.4	99.3	3,839	0.8	9.0	90.2
1978	15,804	0.2	5.6	94.3	12,449	0.1	0.4	99.5	4,513	0.7	6.3	92.9
1979	13,812	0.8	9.6	89.7	9,862	0.3	1.2	98.5	6,332	0.5	4.1	95.4
1980	9,722	2.2	12.3	85.6	8,611	0.5	4.1	95.3	6,979	0.4	3.7	95.9
1981	5,893	13.3	20.6	66.1	9,310	0.4	6.2	93.4	7,182	0.2	3.4	96.4
1982	4,552	29.3	25.9	44.8	10,822	0.3	8.9	90.8	9,464	0.1	2.9	97.0
1983	4,707	49.4	5.5	45.2	10,896	0.3	12.9	86.8	9,332	0.2	2.5	97.3
1984	5,526	65.4	17.4	17.2	8,960	0.7	14.3	85.0	9,435	0.3	2.1	97.6
1985	5,808	77.7	21.9	0.4	9,791	0.5	15.1	84.4	8,746	0.3	2.4	97.2
1986	6,177	78.0	22.0	0.0	7,791	1.1	17.7	81.2	10,577	0.3	2.6	97.0
1987	8,227	82.2	17.8	0.0	11,727	2.0	11.6	86.4	12,951	0.3	2.0	97.6
1988	8,957	80.2	19.8	0.0								

Sources: Annual volumes, 1965–1988, of *Statistik perdagangan luar negeri Indonesia: Ekspor*; *Kalimantan Barat dalam angka*; *Kalimantan Selatan dalam angka*; *Kalimantan Tengah dalam angka*; and *Kalimantan Timur dalam angka*. See also quarterly issues of *Timber Trade Review* for the same period.

Table 10.3 **Tropical timber exports: Peninsular Malaysia, Brunei + Indonesia + Malaysia, and the world (roundwood equivalents), 1965–1987**

	Peninsular Malaysia				Brunei + Indonesia + Malaysia				World			
Year	Total exports ('000 m^3)	Plywood (%)	Sawn timber (%)	Sawlogs (%)	Total exports ('000 m^3)	Plywood (%)	Sawn timber (%)	Sawlogs (%)	Total exports ('000 m^3)	Plywood (%)	Sawn timber (%)	Sawlogs (%)
1965	1,751	1.2	39.6	59.2	7,336	0.3	15.3	84.4	23,227	3.0	13.6	83.3
1966	2,151	1.4	33.4	65.2	9,593	0.4	11.1	88.5	25,624	2.9	12.2	84.9
1967	2,540	2.4	39.6	57.9	10,946	0.8	11.8	87.4	27,277	3.0	12.3	84.7
1968	3,128	4.3	40.4	55.3	13,771	1.2	12.8	86.0	33,151	3.5	12.2	84.3
1969	4,281	5.3	51.2	43.5	17,757	1.4	15.3	83.3	38,317	3.0	11.0	86.0
1970	3,925	7.8	39.3	52.9	21,621	1.5	9.7	88.7	42,566	3.4	10.7	85.9
1971	3,971	10.1	38.5	51.4	24,495	1.8	8.5	89.7	44,551	3.4	10.4	86.2
1972	4,650	12.4	46.8	40.9	28,380	2.2	9.9	87.9	47,683	4.0	11.6	84.4
1973	4,446	17.1	63.7	19.1	35,932	2.3	10.4	87.3	59,313	4.0	12.6	83.4
1974	3,912	12.0	68.6	19.4	32,971	1.5	10.4	88.1	50,188	2.9	13.5	83.6
1975	3,285	14.1	69.2	16.7	27,101	2.0	11.9	86.1	41,245	3.3	14.5	82.2
1976	5,429	15.9	75.0	9.0	39,660	2.4	13.9	83.7	53,405	3.9	16.0	80.0
1977	5,004	14.6	79.2	6.2	40,900	2.0	13.2	84.7	54,618	3.9	15.6	80.5
1978	4,870	18.4	79.0	2.6	42,328	2.6	12.6	84.8	56,356	4.6	15.2	80.2
1979	6,492	15.6	73.2	11.3	42,682	3.1	16.5	80.3	56,918	5.0	20.1	74.9
1980	5,358	19.0	76.4	4.6	38,200	4.3	17.1	78.6	52,190	6.2	20.4	73.4
1981	4,519	22.6	71.9	5.5	30,718	9.2	19.0	71.8	43,223	10.2	21.3	68.5
1982	4,732	23.5	70.5	6.0	32,560	11.5	19.7	68.8	44,888	11.0	21.6	67.5
1983	4,776	21.9	72.7	5.4	35,532	16.7	21.9	61.3	49,997	19.8	22.8	57.4
1984	3,725	22.2	73.2	4.7	33,091	23.8	22.7	53.6	46,191	20.2	23.6	56.2
1985	6,178	12.2	39.2	48.6	36,695	26.0	20.1	54.0	48,400	22.8	22.5	54.6
1986	6,153	14.9	46.0	39.1	39,107	29.8	21.6	48.6	49,891	26.2	23.5	50.3
1987	5,522	23.4	76.0	0.6	46,975	30.2	21.2	48.6	58,041	27.2	23.6	49.1

Sources: Annual volumes, 1965–1987, of *Yearbook of forest products*; and *Buku tahunan perangkaan*; annual volumes, 1973–1980, of *Siaran perangkaan tahunan*. See also quarterly issues of *Timber Trade Review* for the period 1965–1987.

1973 and 1983 the area of undisturbed forest was halved (Collins, Sayer, and Whitmore 1991). Although there were early plans to set up sawmilling, the remoteness, lack of infrastructure, and small population of eastern and central Sabah inhibited processing until about 1980, and the whole timber industry became geared to the export of logs. Log-export royalties represented 32 per cent of the average log price up to the mid-1980s, as against only 11 per cent for Sarawak and 9 per cent for Peninsular Malaysia (Vincent 1990). Together with minor charges on the timber industry, they came to generate at least 50 per cent of state revenue by and right through the 1980s. Sabah has also shifted belatedly to processing and was to phase out log exports altogether within three years from 1993 (*New York Times*, 18 April 1993).

Once timber extraction from the inland dipterocarp forests of Sarawak began in the early 1960s, use of the rivers was the means by which rapid expansion was possible. Timber concessions were awarded along the rivers, and access roads were constructed up to 100 km into the forests from riverside timber camps, ultimately established up to the highest points seasonally reachable by barges to bring machinery and supplies and carry away the heavy logs that do not float. When Peninsular Malaysia and Indonesia restricted and then banned log exports to create domestic downstream industries, the comparative advantage of Sarawak and Sabah as log exporters was enhanced. Their combined share in the total world export of tropical sawlogs grew from 37 per cent in 1978 to 80 per cent in 1987 (Brookfield and Byron 1990). Sarawak's share, much smaller than that of Sabah in the 1970s, grew rapidly to become the world's largest from 1984 onward (tables 10.2 and 10.3).

Development of timber extraction in Kalimantan

Following the achievement of full Indonesian independence in 1949, the state attempted to develop Kalimantan's forest resource directly, since the left-wing Sukarno government mistrusted involvement of private capitalists. "Production-sharing agreements" between the government instrumentality (Perum Perhutani) and Japanese firms, however, have been notably unsuccessful. The establishment of the "New Order" Suharto regime in 1965 led to a change of strategy, which encouraged private interests, both local and foreign, to take up timber concessions on 20-year leases. An expanded demand for tropical timbers in North-East Asia ensured the success of this approach, with Indonesian timber partly taking the place of already declining Philippine supplies in the Japanese market. Of the 561 concessions in operation in Indonesia in 1992, 298 were in Kalimantan; most of these were issued after 1969 and were due for renewal before 1993.

Toward the end of the 1970s, Indonesia's government began to insist on more local processing. The decision was made to concentrate on plywood, with concessionaires being forced to construct plywood plants and large sawmills, as the export of raw logs was gradually phased out between 1980 and 1985. After a few years of lower production while the new industry became established and markets were aggressively penetrated, Indonesia soon reached a position of world dominance in tropical plywood (tables 10.2 and 10.3). Kalimantan has become a leading supplier of plywood products from 65 mills, 27 of which are in Samarinda alone. Most plywood producers are now members of large cartels, with control over log supplies from several sources. They form a powerful political lobby.

Land-use change and agricultural settlement

Land-use allocation in Kalimantan

In the early years after the opening of the Kalimantan forests, provincial authorities granted many small concessions, sometimes to contractors using traditional hand methods. This did not suit the Japanese buyers, who provided credit for mechanization and refused to accept hand-logged timber after 1971. A rationalization of production occurred, with the central government assuming responsibility and setting minimum sizes for concessions. More foreign capital was attracted in partnership with Indonesian firms. At the same time, regulations were drawn up to protect watershed areas. Initially these were defined as all land above 500 m, broadened in 1974 to include all hillsides with slopes of 20 per cent or more. Such regulations, however, were scarcely policed, and it was common to see timber being winched from extremely steep hills.

Beginning in 1980, a further effort attempted to place logging activities under tighter control and to designate zones for timber production, for protection of watersheds, and for conservation. Although steepness of slope and likely erodibility served as the criteria both for fixing the "protected forest" boundary and, to a lesser degree, for differentiating between "limited" and ordinary production forest, it has been the production/conversion forest divide that has caused the most argument. The conversion forest encompasses most of the accessible lands along coasts or rivers. Clear felling is permitted and all transmigration and other government settlements are supposed to be located in these areas. Local people, however, already occupy many such lands. The transmigration agency, seeking locations with reasonable soils as settlement sites, would often stray into the production forest and propose "swaps" of land from one category to another. Yet a piece of land unsuitable for forestry is not necessarily ideal for farming, a point made by Ross (1984) after several years' experience with transmigration settlements in East Kalimantan.

In many areas, the land-use zones bear little relation to conditions on the ground, particularly vegetation. Some "protected forest" is pure grassland. By definition, it is illegal for settlements to exist in protected forest, so people whose village lands fall within that boundary face problems and will meet with pressure to resettle (Potter 1990). The forest inventory under way in Indonesia is incomplete, but studies under the Regional Physical Planning Programme for Transmigration (RePPProT), carried out by a British team around 1985–1987 but based largely on 1982 data, provide a baseline on which to assess the extent and condition of the forested area. As their terms of reference were to analyse all existing land systems with a view to finding areas suitable for transmigration, these studies favour agriculture over forestry as a potential future land use.

The RePPProT team has provided a revision of the land-use zones, expanding the areas of both protected and conversion forest while considerably reducing that allocated to timber production (RePPProT 1985, 1987a,b; Potter 1990). Three series maps at 1:250,000 cover the whole of Kalimantan and provide information on land systems, current land use, forest status, and suggested future development, often in areas previously lacking accurate data. These maps, and accompanying descriptive volumes, are vital sources when examining the possibilities for sustainable land use, of whatever type. A constant warning throughout is that, despite the theoretical and "conditional" recommendations given for tree-crop development, soils everywhere tend to be low in nutrients, strongly weathered so that they are unable to yield fresh minerals or to retain added fertilizer, prone to erosion on slopes, and highly acid, especially in the swampy areas (RePPProT 1985).

Transmigrants in Kalimantan

Kalimantan's present population of 9.1 million people has grown from 5.2 million in 1971 (Census of Indonesia 1990). Above-average rates of increase in East and Central Kalimantan testify to the impact of net in-migration, both sponsored and spontaneous. In the other two provinces, outward movements partly offset settler arrivals, some of them to new opportunities on the forest frontier. Intakes of transmigrants were particularly high between 1980 and 1985, when nearly 400,000 went to Kalimantan (World Bank 1988), but they have since declined (*Statistik Indonesia* 1990). Over the 1980–1985 period, transmigration accounted for 41–65 per cent of the population increase in three of the provinces, but for only 14 per cent of that in East Kalimantan, which has been more affected by spontaneous movement (World Bank 1988).

Unlike settlers on official schemes in Malaysia, which from the outset have been based on tree crops such as rubber and oil-palm, the bulk of transmigrants entering Kalimantan have come as food-crop farmers. Whatever the quality of land available, they have been given 2 hectares, one near the house to function in part as the house yard, the other further away, intended for permanent tree crops or extension of the food-crop area. Often this second hectare remains uncleared because of a household labour shortage. Not all of the land was originally under dipterocarp forest; tidal swamp and grassland locations were common. Wet rice growing has been practised where feasible, since this is the type of agriculture most familiar to settlers who come overwhelmingly from Java, but was possible on only a minority of sites, especially in the tidal swamps. There, yields are low because of problems with water control and development of acid-sulphate soils. In the uplands, dry rice yields usually decline after a couple of years. The use of fertilization to prolong cropping periods, especially when cash crops are introduced, poses a severe risk of erosion. Studies of individual transmigrant settlements (e.g. Levang and Riskan 1984) have concluded that incomes are too low for migrants to live from their farms alone. In accessible districts, most farmers (both local and transmigrant) are involved in off-farm work (Arman 1987). Many settlements are in remote areas, however, and often settlers end up practising shifting cultivation, ironically under the tutelage of the very locals whose farming system they were supposed, by example, to improve (Hidayati 1990; Hidayati, personal communication).

Transmigrants who arrived in Kalimantan in the early 1980s faced additional problems of severe drought, leading to crop failure. Two very dry years, 1982 and 1983, were followed by further droughts in 1987 and 1991. Even without these extra difficulties, transmigrant smallholder food-crop agriculture, as practised on the soils of Kalimantan, is likely to lead at best to poverty, probably also to erosion or other environmental problems and in some cases eventual abandonment. A list of the 37 least successful transmigration projects as of April 1983 included 10 from Kalimantan. One description reads: "The working areas and gardens consist of quartz sand. The plants are stunted. Vegetation growth is not good and has no production. Topsoil is eroding. A large portion of the land slope exceeds 8 per cent so it is easily eroded" (IIED and GOI 1985, Annex D).

This particular project was in West Kalimantan, where 20,000 people were struggling with an obviously unsuitable site. At a location in the swamplands of Central Kalimantan, the soil was thick peat (4–5 m) with a pH of only 3.8. Plant growth was abnormally small, and chlorosis was present. Almost all of the recommendations for new transmigrant sites in the RePPProT reports are prefaced by warnings that only tree-crop projects are suitable. Recent years have finally seen a shift away from food-crop schemes toward the tree-crop alternative. A number of PIR (Perkebunan Inti Rakyat) smallholder cash-crop schemes have been established around a central processing facility or existing government estate. Settlers are given 2 ha of tree-crop and 0.5–1 ha of food-crop land for subsistence, and earn money both as labourers on the estate and by working their own holdings. Although rubber projects have been most common in Kalimantan, coconut, oil-palm, cocoa, and even sugar cane have also been introduced, and there are plans for rattan. All these projects carry the possibility for much better income levels than in the food-crop schemes, as well as greater environmental protection (World Bank 1989). Nevertheless, the prices received for these products are notoriously variable on the world market. Such developments are also much more expensive than food-crop projects.

Spontaneous settlers

Especially in East Kalimantan, many settlers arrive independently, not as participants in any government-assisted scheme. The most famous of these are the oft-described Bugis pepper-growers from Sulawesi, who have settled along the Balikpapan–Samarinda road in East Kalimantan. Vayda and Sahur (1985), who studied some of these farmers in Sulawesi and in Kalimantan in both 1980 and 1984, maintain that this production, which began in 1961, is essentially transitory, as are the growers. They claim that pepper production without fertilizer on these ultisols is unlikely to last more than 10 years before declining yields necessitate abandonment. Inoue and Lahjie (1990) suggest that the cycle may be 15 years and hint that fertilizer may now be applied. Potter has seen serious erosion in the sloping, clean-weeded fields. There is little obvious sign of retreat by the settlers, although abandoned fields are interspersed among the healthy crops. Several suggestions have been made for improvement in practices, and the situation is better in some areas than in others (Hadi, Hidayat, and Udiansyah 1988; Seibert 1990).

Criticism has focused on the impact of spontaneous migrants who follow the timber contractors and settle along the logging roads, destroying forest as they go. We believe this to be exaggerated, in so far as these roads are often quite empty of settlers and in some cases are actually broken up by the departing contractors. Nevertheless, there is no doubt that such settlers do open forest in the more accessible districts. Logged-out forests are easier to clear, especially if illegal loggers have also been active. Kartawinata and Vayda (1984) reported 50–60 illegal logging teams along the Balikpapan–Samarinda road in 1980. Hidayati (1990) quotes (from Franz 1988) figures of 400 km^2 of forest being cleared by 25,000 spontaneous migrants in East Kalimantan.

Land development in Sabah and Sarawak

Eastern Sabah contains substantial tracts of unoccupied, but potentially good, arable land. The developmental efforts of the former British North Borneo Company have been expanded by the Sabah Land Development Board (LDB), set up in 1969, and then by the Peninsula-based Federal Land Development Authority (FELDA), invited to extend its activities to Sabah in 1978. Land is prepared and planted by contractors before settlers arrive, and blocks of 4–6 ha, a figure much larger than in Kalimantan, are allocated. Settlers are expected to repay the large costs over time. Initially, oil-palm was the principal crop planted, and by 1978 Sabah already had 780 km^2 under this crop. Subsequently, FELDA land in Sabah has increasingly been planted to cocoa. By 1987–1988, over 52,000 ha had been planted with oil-palm and cocoa, principally in the east, where the large Sahabat Complex, which will cover 1,000 km^2 if it is ever fully developed, is larger in size than any of the newer settlement complexes of Peninsular Malaysia.

The pace of settlement has, however, never kept pace with the increase in the area cleared and planted. In 1987, the 34 LDB schemes housed only 2,748 settler families on 52,289 ha, fewer than on a smaller area of land in 1980. The indigenous people of Sabah are reportedly unwilling to accept discipline on the Peninsular model (Sutton 1989). Few of the Sahabat schemes had attracted settlers by the end of the 1980s, and three whole groups of schemes were almost without settler families; a production much smaller than that of the private sector was sustained only on a plantation-estate basis, using immigrants from the Philippines and Indonesia as the principal source of labour. By 1986, foreign workers formed 90 per cent of labour in Sabah agriculture as a whole and almost half the workforce in forestry (Pang 1990). A blanket termination in 1991 of all new land development by FELDA in the Peninsula, discussed below, applies also in Sabah (Malaysia 1991a). Hopes of developing large new agricultural areas by land settlement seem to be at an end.

In Sarawak, land settlement has been of small importance. No core organization promoted tree-crop development. A need to resettle people away from the insecure border with Indonesia, in the 1963–1965 "confrontation" mini-war, initiated new settlement on the FELDA pattern (Jackson 1968). A Land Development Board began to create oil-palm estates on state land. Since 1976, more resources have gone into land consolidation and rehabilitation, sometimes on existing cultivated land, but often on new blocks right away from the former longhouses. A Sarawak equivalent of the Peninsula Federal Land Consolidation and Rehabilitation Authority (FELCRA), named SALCRA, was set up for this purpose. Most of its activity has been among impoverished farmers in the more closely occupied areas of western Sarawak but, despite constrained resources, recent innovation has progressed further east in areas made sensitive by conflicts over land rights (King 1988). Few SALCRA schemes have been truly successful, but a new drive is being undertaken in the 1990s (Hatch 1982; Malaysia 1991a).

Impending crisis in forestry and the timber industries

Problems of logging in Kalimantan

Critics have asserted that unsustainable logging practices are causing permanent degradation of a unique resource, and are likely to jeopardize future timber-related employment, including downstream industrial processing in the urban centres. The Indonesian selective-cutting system, similar to that now also used in most of Malaysia, theorizes a return period of 35 years after the first logging cycle. To permit this, however, only trees with a minimum diameter at breast height (DBH) of 50 cm may be logged, while on each hectare at least 25 trees of marketable species, with DBH 35 cm, should remain to secure the next cut. Field studies have revealed that such a number of medium-sized trees is rarely available (Marsono 1980; Soekotjo 1981). Criticisms of logging activities have emphasized the damage done to surrounding trees by mechanized selective cutting, with an average of 50 per cent of the stands being destroyed or damaged, although only 30 per cent is removed (Hamzah 1978; Kartawinata 1978). Thang (1990) has argued for Malaysia that a second cut in as few as 35 years will be possible only if residual damage is not greater than 30 per cent. The compaction of soils, which impedes regeneration of dipterocarps and favours nomad species, and the similar effect of the large gaps often left after logging are other reasons cited for inadequate regrowth of desirable timber types (Kartawinata 1990; Whitmore 1991). A recent study in one district of East Kalimantan has noted that the proportional areas of "primary" and "secondary" forest have shifted dramatically toward the latter (Sukardjo 1990). A further problem is that of fire, which we discuss separately below.

A recent Indonesian study, using information from Malaysia and the Philippines as well, has now admitted that, even with enrichment planting and good seedling regeneration, it would be more likely to take 60–70 years than 35 years for the next crop of timber to be available (FAO and GOI 1990). The authors agree with earlier writers that the area logged could be reduced through an increase in the number of species designated "commercial," so that smaller sections of forest could be worked more intensively, and with less waste (FAO and GOI 1990; IIED and GOI 1985; Ross 1984). In addition to problems that seem to apply even if the selective system is followed, many concessionaires (or their multiple contractors) do not operate within the rules. Each year they are supposed to cut only in a carefully designated area, but instead evidence abounds of haphazard cutting all over the concession, or the re-logging of parts of it within the 20-year lease period. Inadequate marking of boundaries may lead to the felling of protected forest, or even of timber belonging to a neighbouring concession, as in a 1991 case that has inspired much comment (*Jakarta Post*, 17 July 1991; *Tempo*, 27 July 1991). It is sometimes suggested that more flexible management systems be adopted, bearing local conditions in mind. Extended concession periods would be necessary, since one of the biggest problems has been to interest concessionaires holding 20-year leases in any form of long-term planning.

In 1990, Kalimantan was estimated still to have 22.7 million ha of forest with "management potential" (i.e. outside protected areas, national parks, etc). Of this, nearly 6 million ha (26 per cent) were classified as "conversion and unclassed forest" (eventually to be cleared for agriculture and other activities) and 16.7 million ha were production forest. Of the production forest, 10.8 million ha were classed as "unlogged," 4 million ha as "logged," and 1.9 million ha as "heavily logged" (FAO and GOI 1990). Although it is noteworthy that much of the unlogged forest was in inaccessible districts, there is obvious scope for several more years of continued production. Between the 1982 RePPProT studies and the 1990 FAO report, however, the total area forested is calculated to have declined from 72 per cent to 63 per cent. East Kalimantan experienced a drop of almost 16 per cent, the largest decline of the four provinces, partly a result of the 1982–1983 fire.

Supply constraints in the wood-based industries of Kalimantan

We have noted that the banning of log exports brought about no lasting reduction in the pressure on the forests of Kalimantan. The Indonesian plywood industry, which draws all its raw material from natural forests, has been warned not to exceed an annual capacity of 10 million m^3 through the 1990s; otherwise, real shortages of raw materials could arise by 2000. Some say this shortfall will arise sooner, by the mid-1990s (MOF and FAO 1991). Until now, however, only the plywood mills of West Kalimantan need to bring in supplementary supplies of logs from Sarawak (Dinas Kehutanan, Kalbar 1990). Since shortages of higher-quality logs will soon be likely in Sumatra, it is suggested that Kalimantan's mills begin to diversify their equipment, so that they can supply some of Sumatra's needs and begin to process lower-quality logs at the same time, instead of simply sending them to the sawmiller (FAO and GOI 1990).

The rapid growth of the Indonesian plywood industry has been possible largely because of low local prices for both logs and labour, which have resulted in a cheaper finished product. Such prices have, however, militated against care and efficiency in all stages of the industry. There is certainly room for improvements in efficiency; wastage is sometimes very high, in both the forest and the mill, and, on the basis of international comparison, mill workforces might be cut 25 per cent without loss of production. The milling of smaller and lower-quality logs is recommended, as well as, conversely, development of some specialization in high-quality veneers following the pattern of Peninsular Malaysia. Most telling is that recent publications emanating from the government (FAO and GOI 1990; MOF and FAO 1991) suggest an increase in the local price of logs, and even a partial lifting of the logging ban for high-quality, but high-priced, timber. This recommendation is seen as a way of improving logging conditions and protecting the remaining forests.

In a move that appears contradictory to that discussed above, recent years have witnessed an imposition of export bans on raw and semi-processed rattan and the introduction of a high export tax on sawn timber. The purported aim was to encourage internal processing, but the result has been a catastrophic decline in local prices, since the local rattan industry cannot develop fast enough to absorb the quantities of raw material collected originally for export. The impact has been very severe on the small producers. Rattan-growing has been encouraged to provide a cash crop for shifting cultivators and is recommended in agro-forestry systems. Both rattan carpets and rattan furniture have proved to be difficult to sell on export markets, necessitating centralized quality control that has essentially cut out many small manufacturers, especially those from rural districts.

It is the same for sawmillers. The newspaper *Kompas* (20 and 24 October 1989) estimated that small regional mills employ 200,000 people; Kalimantan must have had at least one-half of these. Whereas the large sawmillers attached to the concessions have a high-quality product and will survive, the medium-sized mechanized mills have had a difficult time. In South Kalimantan, they have disappeared from rural areas, forcing the people of whole villages to move to town. Moreover, in the city, a gap separates the very large producers and the tiny, hand-operated sawmills (wantilan), which use off-cuts from the bigger mills and cater to the bottom end of the market (field survey, July 1991). These two commodities – sawn timber and rattan – provide examples of the tendencies in the Indonesian economy for centralization and large-scale activity, which greatly exacerbates inequalities and reduces local opportunities.

Toward a "post-timber" future in Sabah

Much of the foregoing discussion about Kalimantan applies with equal force in Malaysian Borneo, but there are differences owing to the long-continued specialization in the export of unprocessed round timber. Sabah already faces a serious crisis that foreshadows what may happen elsewhere in the island. Estimates of the area annually cut over in Sabah fell from 3,640 km^2 in 1978 to not more than 2,000 km^2 a decade later (*Malaysian Business*, 1 August 1988; Country Profile 1991). Most of this is now hill forest; estimates of the remaining timber resource have been declining sharply. With imposed quotas, log exports fell by over one-half between 1987 and 1990 and, although sawn timber production increased by over 40 per cent during the same period, the total volume of exports has fallen by almost one-third (Country Profile 1990; *Buku tahunan perangkaan* 1990). A debate, if this is the right term, between official and commercial apologists for the high rate of logging in Malaysian Borneo, on the one hand, and critics on the other, is well presented and analysed by Hurst (1990). At least in Sabah, the debate is resolved by events.

The change in Sabah from apparent surplus to perceived deficit has been sudden and demonstrates the extraordinary measure of self-delusion about the achievement of sustainability that has characterized responsible officials and their publicists, not only in Sabah but throughout the region. Hurst's comprehensive discussion uses sources to 1988 and even 1989 but reveals only that logging was up to four times the estimated rate of regeneration (Hurst 1990, 141). In 1989 a Forestry Department study, however, foresaw a drop in productivity by almost an order of magnitude between 1988 and 1998, leading to the prediction that "from 1992 onwards, timber production from natural forest would not be able to meet [even] local demand" (Pang 1990, 10). Belatedly in the late 1980s there was a serious attempt to develop a wood-based industry in Sabah, principally simple sawmilling, imposing quotas and higher export royalties to restrict log exports. Sawmills and veneer and plywood mills all increased sharply in number.

Sustainability in Sarawak?

In Sarawak, official circles have perceived no supply constraint, so log exports have continued to expand, taking up, in Japan, Korea, and

Taiwan, the market share vacated by Indonesia and increasingly also by Sabah (Asean Focus 1989; Logging and Resources 1989; Sarawak Update 1990). The rate of cutting is virtually out of control in a system in which the whole timber operation, including sale, is frequently let out to contractors by the concessionaires, and the contractors themselves further subcontract (Hurst 1990; Lian 1987). Making use of estimates of timber density in relation to data on log production, Hong (1987, 128–129) estimated the area logged between 1963 and 1985 as 28,217 km^2, about 30 per cent of the whole forest area. The rate, however, was rising, with 60 per cent of the forest area under concession in 1984. More recently, a careful external review has concluded that:

> if harvesting of the hill forests continues as at present (13,000,000 m^3/yr +/–), all primary forests in PFE [Permanent Forest Estate] and State land assumed to be available for timber production, including those of more than 60 per cent slope, would have been harvested in about 11 years. At that time only cutover forests would remain. There could then ensue a sharp decline in yield, employment and revenue until the cutover forests mature. (ITTC 1990, 35)

However, harvest levels reached a record 20,000,000 m^3 in 1990, and it remains to be seen if a decision to halve this coup will be capable of implementation (Primack 1991).

Yet good management principles are in place in Sarawak. A selective-cutting system is supposedly in use, and in the Permanent Forest Estate (PFE) concessionaires should lodge working plans showing the area to be cut in each year. Similar but less restrictive regulations apply on the equal area of state land outside the PFE, from which most timber is currently cut. The 1989 International Tropical Timber Organization mission found most of the policies good but implementation inadequate (ITTC 1990). In particular, the concession system frustrated rather than facilitated sustainable management, the Forest Department needed greatly to be strengthened, catchment protection called for major improvement, and, above all, the area cut annually had greatly to be reduced. They concluded that "utilization and management cannot maintain the forest based economic structure at its present level and, at the same time, sustain it indefinitely into the future" (ITTC 1990, 60). Primack (1991) interprets the report and its findings to suggest that a reduction of harvesting levels by at least two-thirds is the only way to achieve a sustainable industry.

The mission was also doubtful about the drive to build a woodworking industry to absorb 50 per cent of the cut by 2000, pointing to market uncertainties. The new drive has had limited success, with about 10 per cent of timber domestically processed, much less than in Sabah (Asean Focus 1989; Country Profile 1991). Many problems exist, including the woodworking industry's heavy dependence on illegal immigrant labour. Strong federal pressure on the state government calls for more extensive bans on log exports, currently applied to only a few species. Yet proposals from Peninsular wood manufacturers that certain species of logs be reserved in their interest, or that domestic rates of royalty be applied to timber sold to the Peninsula, have encountered strong resistance (Vincent 1988). This continued through 1991. Both East Malaysian states prefer to try to develop their own timber-working industries, in spite of high costs, and to attract timber-starved Peninsular sawmillers to relocate in East Malaysia.

As interpreted by the Sarawak authorities, the ITTC mission report offered encouragement that firm government support for its recommendations would achieve sustainable forestry (Sarawak Update 1990; Primack 1991). If more conservationist policies are in fact implemented, if the market problems can be resolved, if infrastructure can be improved, and if the labour shortage can be overcome (Asean Focus 1989), there might yet be some hope of developing in Sarawak a vertically integrated timber industry with a sustained future, using dipterocarp and other indigenous timbers. But these "ifs" are of a large order. Dependence on natural regeneration is clearly still the aim. Enrichment and "silvicultural treatment" of dipterocarp forest is planned for 370 km^2, but this contrasts with 2,000 km^2 in Sabah and 3,931 km^2 in Peninsular Malaysia (Malaysia 1991a).

Plantation forestry as a solution?

Timber shortages are now real in both Peninsular Malaysia and Sabah, are imminent in Sumatra, and are a longer-term prospect even in Kalimantan and Sarawak. Given a low rate of success with "enrichment planting," greater emphasis is now being placed on plantation forestry, which began seriously in Sabah in 1983. Initially, this was with pines, but other fast-growing exotics are now mainly used, principally *Acacia mangium*, *Paraserianthes falcataria*, *Gmelina arborea*, and, sometimes, *Eucalyptus deglupta*. The method is to clear the site completely, but without destumping, and weeding is required until the seedlings become young trees and develop a shading canopy. In Peninsular Malaysia, where major plans now exist for the expansion of plantation forestry, a sustainable yield on a 15-year cycle is anticipated. Apart from *Gmelina arborea*, which makes reasonable furniture, the fast-growing timber is suitable only for constructional purposes and as pulpwood or as fillers in plywood. Sabah Softwoods, the pioneer in the region, still regards plantations as high-risk ventures that require a considerable degree of skill in monitoring and management (Golokin and Cassels 1988). Moreover, a risk of disease and pest invasion is attributable to the narrow genetic base; it is reported that the whole stock of *Acacia mangium* in Sabah comes from a single Australian parent (Salleh and Hashim 1982).

Indonesia has stepped up its reforestation efforts, now using mainly *Acacia mangium*. The industrial-plantation programme in Kalimantan looks to the future establishment of pulp and paper mills. Experimental plantings date back more than a decade on one huge concession in East Kalimantan and off the south-east coast at Pulaulaut, where problems of insect infestation and inappropriate varieties have been encountered and overcome. Supposedly, reforestation is practised on a part of every concession, but little has been developed. The selective logging system has now changed its name to the "selective logging and planting system" and, in a new move to encourage private investment, the government has permitted the leasing of land areas quite separate from the concessions for plantation forestry for 35 years (FAO and GOI 1990).

In Sabah, where the situation is most critical and where there is also the greatest fund of experience, plans for 1991–1995 allow for 3,200 km^2 of new forest plantations (Malaysia 1991a). This is in addition to the large area designated for enrichment planting. It is likely that a significant part of the new effort will be in areas burned in 1983, most of which had been logged. Since drought is a recurrent hazard in Sabah, as in East and South Kalimantan, important questions arise regarding the drought-tolerance of the planted species. Most have little fire resistance and this is more serious, especially where the pre-existing vegetation was not forest but grassland. This grass burns readily in the dry season and, even in normal years, some of the new plantings have been lost. Where local shifting cultivators perceive the plantations as taking over their lands, the rates of burning are likely to increase. In one such area in South Kalimantan during July 1991, tensions were high between forest police, protecting the plantation, and villagers, not allowed to burn as their usual method of field preparation. In Sarawak, forest plantations hardly exist, and plans for the coming five years include only 200 km^2, less than the 420 km^2 planned for Peninsular Malaysia. Yet some badly degraded areas in western and west–central Sarawak are at least at risk from drought, and forest plantations could be a very suitable use of the land.

The state, the timber industry, and shifting cultivators

A problem of high visibility

The Indonesian and Malaysian governments, like many others in the tropics, are committed to eliminating shifting cultivation in all its forms. Large areas lying fallow at any one time form an essential component of the system and offend those who wish to see resources, whether of land or of timber, in commercially productive use. Yields of basic food crops, especially rice, tend to be less reliable than those in other forms of agriculture, and it is widely believed that shifting cultivators are not only inefficient but also among the poorest of the rural poor. Elimination of the system would, therefore, meet social as well as developmental goals. Persuasion has been applied for many years, but the timber boom has created a new urgency that blames shifting cultivators for eating into primary and late-secondary forest that could yield timber revenues to the state – even so much so that, for every log felled, "another goes up in smoke" (Lau 1979). No government in the region has given its indigenous peoples inalienable rights to all the land they use.

The issues in Sarawak

Although collisions of interest between logging entrepreneurs, state land-settlement agencies, and indigenous shifting cultivators have also developed in Kalimantan and in Sabah, it is in Sarawak that the sharpest conflicts have arisen and have achieved by far the widest notice. The Sarawak Land Code does not recognize customary rights to land under forest, unless it was occupied and used before 1958. Even this has been applied conservatively, and only some 15 per cent of all land has registered title under systems initiated under the Brookes and codified in the colonial period (Cramb and Dixon 1988). Little of this belongs to shifting cultivators, although they claim an estimated 25 per cent, and in fact more, customary land. This compares with 19 per cent of the state estimated as used for shifting cultivation by Hatch (1982), and 28 per cent by Kavanagh, Rahim, and Hails

(1989) using an estimate based on 1985 Landsat imagery by Majaran and Dimin (1989).

In fact, probably many fewer than one-half of the 570,000 indigenous people of Sarawak practise shifting cultivation in anything like its classic form. In the more densely occupied western areas, the pioneering stage made famous, or infamous, by Freeman (1955, 1970) is long past. Many communities occupy land first cleared from forest more than 300 years ago. Their forests are all secondary and contain many trees planted or conserved for their edible fruit or other useful produce. Areas of semi-permanent swamp rice supplement hill-rice swiddens (Cramb 1988; Padoch 1982a; Sather 1990). The true swiddeners, who occupy the more sparsely populated eastern parts of Sarawak, are composed of several ethnic groups, and most have a history of recent migration (Lian 1987; Padoch 1982a). They live and cultivate along and close to the rivers, penetrating only a limited way into the surrounding forests. Although their basic methods of cultivation are the same as those of the more densely settled areas, practices are less intensive, with smaller areas of selectively managed forest and much larger areas of natural regrowth. These, principally, are the people against whose "wasteful" methods generations of administrators and agriculturalists have railed, and who – together with the few thousand hunter–gatherer Penan – are now most closely affected by the timber industry.

Three main prongs of criticism address the shifting cultivators, about whom little agreement prevails. The question of poverty and insecurity of livelihood, implicit or explicit in almost every relevant planning document, may have some truth. King (1988) reports his own estimate that 40 per cent of Sarawak's population live below the poverty line, overwhelmingly in rural areas but probably largely in the west. Lian (1987) and Cramb (1989a) question the lack of self-sufficiency in basic foods, the more so when foods supplementary to rice are taken into account. Yields are low, and a great deal depends on skill in timing activities in relation to the weather, but there is often a surplus. The argument that the system is extremely destructive of natural resources has an extensive literature, spearheaded in Sarawak by Freeman (1955), and challenged by a large number of writers including Cramb (1989b), Padoch (1982a,b), and others. Much seems to depend on the area described by particular writers, for, while there are no vast tracts of *Imperata cylindrica* or other grassland in Sarawak, grasslands, erosion, and badly degraded forests all exist. The third argument – that shifting cultivation consumes annually large areas of primary forest – is orthodoxy (Hatch and Lim 1978), but critics have argued that Lau's (1979) estimate, mentioned above, relied on erroneous data concerning the area under shifting cultivation at any one time. They have shown that in specific cases only quite small areas of primary forest are used, most swiddens being made in secondary growth of from 7 to 20 years (Hong 1987; Lian 1987; Sather 1990). Cramb (1990) has produced data purporting to show that shifting cultivators annually increase the area cut by only 0.2 per cent – about as much as is logged each week. The debate continues, with no resolution in sight.

Lian (1987) studied a longhouse community adjacent to a timber camp, and detailed the effects of the new and temporary source of employment and income on the people. Although employed only in the lowest jobs and at low wages, the indigenous people gained important new cash income, causing them temporarily to neglect other cash crops and to reduce the area farmed to that which would principally be maintained by the women. One effect, however, was to shorten the swidden cycle. This community had received private compensation from the contractor for access over its land close to the river. Moreover, they received free electricity from the timber camp. Changing sources of income had a levelling effect on class structure. None the less, the community was looking beyond the timber period and considering future options that might include hitherto-resisted resettlement.

"Confrontations" and the environment

Confrontations between shifting cultivators and loggers supported by the Malaysian authorities became common in the 1980s, starting some years before the better-known blockades of logging roads by small groups of Penan. They are often interpreted as a desperate defence of livelihood and environment, and in this context have gained very wide publicity (e.g. World Rainforest Movement and Sahabat Alam Malaysia 1990). There are, however, those who maintain that the confrontations have been misunderstood. Lian (1993) points out that only 5 per cent of the fewer than 10,000 Penan are still hunter–gatherers and that the sago on which they rely is in areas that do not attract logging. He points out that food shortages preceded logging by some years and that land sales from Penan to other groups have exacerbated the problem. Kavanagh, Rahim, and Hails (1989), following a State Planning Department report of 1987, agree that few Penan are now wholly nomadic, but say that up to 70 per cent still spend a part of each year hunting and gathering, away from the shifting cultivation settlements made since the 1950s. Lian (personal communication) argues that the confrontations involving Penan and other peoples have had more to do with the distribution of rewards from logging than with safeguarding the rain forest or the environment generally. Hurst (1990) and Primack (1991) agree that this is true in at least some cases. Whether to do with cash rewards or with protection of food resources, the motivation would, with this interpretation, be primarily economic. The partial resolution now proposed by the government is to create some reserve areas within which Penan can obtain their traditional food supplies.

Most certainly, however, the inland people are concerned about damage to their environment, especially to their rivers (Aten Suwandi n.d.). They are resistant to resettlement, but they seek the benefits of development. They are taking advantage of the network of roads now being created by the linking up of the better-constructed logging roads. They like the resulting drop in the cost of imported goods. It is their survival as a distinctive people, not as a population, that is under threat from development. Present indications are that their response to this challenge is to take a more active role in politics, which their numbers make possible. Given the probability that Sarawak's forests will continue to be heavily logged, albeit with efforts to develop tighter management control that will support the growth of industry, further major changes must be anticipated in the coming decade. The ITTC mission strongly urged that confrontation be replaced by discussion and compromise when areas claimed under customary tenure are to be logged (ITTC 1990). Lian's (1987) evidence of mutual accommodation, from a valley in which the loggers are about equal in number to the local people, suggests that this would be possible.

The problem in Kalimantan

Kalimantan at present lacks the degree of confrontation encountered in Sarawak, even though shifting cultivators are no more considered to be legal occupiers of the land they use than are those in Malaysian Borneo. Much of their land is being cut over, and in Kalimantan there is the additional problem of transmigrant settlement. The farming systems themselves are changing. People from remote districts in East Kalimantan, sometimes under government direction, are moving closer to Samarinda and reducing fallow periods; possessing or hiring chainsaws, they clear larger areas for cash crops. This has led observers to query whether forest recovery is likely still to occur when areas cleared by several adjacent families reach as much as 300 ha, as compared with 30 ha in the more remote villages (Inoue and Lahjie 1990; Kartawinata et al. 1984).

The total area under shifting cultivation in Kalimantan is almost certainly larger than in Sarawak (about 5.5 million ha against 3.5 million ha by the best estimates). Data are very uncertain, however, and estimates of over 1 million individuals depending on the system are questionable. The RePPProT studies provide the most reliable information. In terms of land occupied, shifting cultivation is most important in West and Central Kalimantan, where it takes up 24 per cent and 22 per cent of the forest area respectively. Overall, 61 per cent of shifting cultivators are located in conversion and unclassed forest (i.e. areas already marked out for permanent clearing) but, whereas 72 per cent are on such land in East Kalimantan, in West Kalimantan the figure is only 56 per cent. The authors of the West Kalimantan study warn: "Pioneering shifting cultivation penetrates far into the ... forest areas and threatens to fragment and consume all remaining non-swampland lowland forests in the short to medium term" (RePPProT 1987b, 1, 30).

It is not clear whether locals or migrants are the alleged culprits here, but such a sweeping statement necessitates fieldwork, to check both its veracity and the reasons for the situation. The view expressed is redolent of the debates about the "forest-consuming" propensities of the Iban in Sarawak, recalling that some of the Dayak groups in West Kalimantan are of Iban origin (Freeman 1955, 1970; Padoch 1982a,b). It is, however, also true that intricate agro-forestry systems have arisen in parts of West Kalimantan, even incorporating planting of the long-maturing Borneo ironwood (*Eusideroxylon zwagerei*), as well as rattan, rubber, durians, and a wide range of other useful trees. Particularly important are the nuts from the *tengkawang* trees (*Shorea* spp.), important sources of edible oils (Padoch and Peluso 1991). Collection of these products from managed forest, plus tapping of planted rubber, supplements and partly replaces rice swiddens as a means of livelihood.

Government policy and the shifting cultivators

The governments of both countries seek positive ways of overcoming the problems perceived as being associated with "pioneering" shifting cultivation in East Malaysia and Kalimantan. Whatever the defence of the system in its classic form, a real problem exists where numbers increase and where commercial crops are grown by swidden methods. Unfortunately, most current solutions involve resettlement and a complete change, rather than adaptation, of farming methods. With the stated aim of reducing poverty, the government of Sarawak has sought to resettle shifting cultivators in managed cash-crop blocks for over 20 years. SALCRA was set up for this purpose. The Indonesian authorities have been even more determined in moving indigenous people to what are seen as better-located sites, usually in conversion forest, where they can, supposedly, learn more intensive agriculture. East Kalimantan has been most active in promoting such resettlement schemes, which have been criticized as culturally insensitive and often economically unviable (Appell and Appell-Warren 1985; Avé and King 1986). These have usually been food-crop schemes, resembling transmigration projects. Indeed, transmigration schemes always include reserved places for locals, partly in order to dampen accusations of favouritism towards Javanese and other newcomers. After a few years, some of these resettlement projects are simply abandoned and the people drift back to their old lands; the government-provided houses are then re-used for another group of transmigrants.

More positive approaches could involve extensions of the indigenous agro-forestry systems described above from West Kalimantan, perhaps also adopting Davis's suggestion that all shifting cultivators be given tenure to a reasonably large area of land, say 20 ha (World Bank 1990). Another idea is that of community forests, which would be a kind of buffer zone around the edge of protected areas or national parks, controlled by local villagers, who would have the right to use all produce from the zone without encroaching on the clearly demarcated boundary of the park. Leighton and Peart (1990) have suggested enrichment planting of useful species, such as harvestable fruit trees and rattan, in the fallow. Other proposals call for making more effective use of traditional systems of land tenure in the management of consolidation and rehabilitation (Cramb and Wills 1990).

Lessons for the future from Peninsular Malaysia

A greater and more rapid transformation

Before drawing the argument together, we digress briefly to draw lessons from the experience of Peninsular Malaysia. Much of what is now happening in Borneo has already transpired on the Peninsula. By 1989, the forested area was reduced to only 42 per cent of the land (Thang 1990). The unpublished land-use survey of 1982 showed 31 per cent of the Peninsula as already under rubber and oil-palm, and almost all this was formerly forest. Problems for the sustainability of forestry as an industry were foreseen early (*Malayan Forester* 1967), and the warning was frequently repeated (e.g. Kumar 1986). Peninsular Malaysia already faces a shortage of timber supply for its downstream woodworking industries, based mainly on sawmilling. Between 1973 and 1981 the value of output in the whole group of timber industries grew by 12.9 per cent per year and employment grew by 5.7 per cent (MIDA and UNIDO 1985). A much greater increase has since boosted the production of 681 large sawmills, 43 veneer and plywood mills, and more than 1,200 small woodworking plants, furniture factories, and other small wood-using enterprises (Country Profile 1990). The consequence of expansion has been an increasingly severe shortage of timber for the mills, for the building industry, for exporters of sawn timber, and for the downstream factories (*Malaysian Business*, 16–30 September 1989, 1–15 August 1990; Country Profile 1990).

Yet efforts at management have been stronger in the Peninsula than in Borneo, guided by what is certainly the best forestry service in the region (Burgess 1990). A National Forestry Policy was formulated in 1977, and its provisions included the creation of the PFE and also of conservation forests. Although illegal logging still occurs, management has clearly improved as resources have grown scarce. The permitted coup was reduced by 12.5 per cent between 1985 and 1990 (Malaysia 1991a). Both enrichment planting and plantation forestry are now required on a greatly increased scale to supplement improved management.

The fate of the new rural economy

Most of the land cleared from forest since 1960 has been converted into land-settlement schemes, particularly by FELDA. Mechanized forestry and land clearance have reduced the agricultural capability of the land through compaction, loss of topsoil, destruction of soil structure, and exposure to erosion (Mohd. Nor Zakaria et al. 1985). Yet, with the use of fertilizers, yields have remained satisfactory, even though increasing areas of steepland have come into agricultural use. Now, however, the expansion of agricultural land has encountered limits. The larger problems are economic and demographic rather than ecological. The cost of land preparation has risen as clearance has moved into hilly land, so that, according to two sources, the mean cost of establishing a family rose by 73 per cent between 1976 and 1985 (Drury 1988) and by 41 per cent between 1980 and 1985 (Chamhuri and Nik Hashim 1988). Depressed prices have hit rural incomes, and a shortage of labour now affects most parts of the Peninsular rural economy. The estates depend largely on illegal immigrants from Indonesia, estimates of whose total number in the Peninsula range from 100,000 to more than 1 million. In an interview, the Minister of Primary Industries has stated that if immigrant labour were to be "done away with, my whole estate sector will collapse" (Logging and Resources 1990).

With growing difficulty in attracting settlers to the raw environment of remote areas, FELDA terminated all new land development in 1991, after completion of ongoing work. All those schemes that have not recruited settlers are to be managed through the formation of plantation companies (Malaysia 1991a). This will be implemented in 222 FELDA schemes in the Peninsula, covering a total area of 300,000 ha, about 40 per cent of all FELDA land. What is being created de facto is a major extension of the estate sector. The crisis of land settlement is no greater than that in Sabah, but the reasons are different. Labour shortage in Peninsular agriculture is a product mainly of the rapid industrialization and urbanization of the national economy, and of the drift against agriculture in the terms of trade and comparative labour pricing. The apparent solution is the same as in Sabah however, involving reliance on abundant supplies of illegal immigrant labour from the less developed and more populous countries of the region.

Implications for Borneo

The Peninsular economy is increasingly dominated by urban and industrial development, and the "resource frontier" period is over. Conversion of forest to agriculture will cease even before it has reached its potential high-cost limits, some of the cut-over land will become tree plantations for higher-density timber farming, and the rest of the forest will be subject to much more stringent management controls. It may be that some cleared land, especially on the hills, will never undergo profitable development and will join considerable areas of older rubber in returning to secondary forest.

Management of Peninsular forestry has been better than that of any part of Borneo and log-export bans began sooner. Land preparation for tree-crop plantation has improved significantly since research and the major floods of 1971 revealed the heavy erosion of earlier years. This is not to say that environmental damage is fully under control, but, if anything like Peninsular management had been applied in Borneo, the situation there would now be less alarming than it is. Peninsular Malaysia is now acquiring a managed environment, both in forestry and in agriculture. But the essential difference lies in the urbanization and industrialization that have become established in the two national heartlands, in western Malaysia and in Java, leaving Borneo the acknowledged resource frontier. Lessons for management are available, but the fundamental changes in the national economies do not readily cross the South China and Java seas.

Questions of criticality in Borneo

Problems of the environment: Critical lands

We now return to some of the issues of criticality, starting with the land. The question of who is responsible for the most environmental damage, the loggers or the cultivators and settlers, is close to the heart of much of the dispute between conservationists and the authorities. Despite a dearth of hard data, there can be little doubt that erosion and sediment transport are quite substantial under natural conditions in the forest, but are increased with cultivation and increased much more with logging. In nearby Mindanao, Kellman (1969) reported an 18-fold increase in soil loss from forest after logging. An identical increase has recently been established in Sabah by an Anglo-Malaysian project (*New Straits Times*, 26 September 1990, 1). After rain, rivers quickly become turbid, but the opaquely high turbidity of rivers in the logging areas is a modern phenomenon. How fast the load travels downstream is unknown, but navigation difficulties are experienced on some rivers (Aten Suwandi n.d.). Douglas (personal communication), however, reports work from Sabah showing that, because logged areas very quickly revegetate, erodibility falls to modest levels in as little as a few weeks.

The same is certainly also true of shifting cultivation clearings that revert to forest rather than to grassland, which applies to most of them. Badly eroded grasslands exist in Borneo, however, and, in Kalimantan, watersheds in which soil erosion has become severe are designated "critical land" (*Tanah Kritis*). A recent estimate by the Worldwide Fund for Nature of 20 million ha for the whole of Indonesia has been reduced to 13.1 million by reforestation and rehabilitation work carried out, mainly in Java, by the Ministry of Forestry (MOF and FAO 1991). These new studies have, however, resulted in an upward revision of critical lands in Kalimantan to almost 3 million ha, or 23 per cent of the total area; two-thirds of these lands are in West and Central Kalimantan (*Statistik Indonesia* 1990). Previous estimates had always emphasized the West and South, attributing very low figures to the two less-populated provinces. Now both these are acknowledged to have an erosion problem, although no information designates its location.

In West Kalimantan the main problem area appears to lie in the hilly districts north of the Kapuas river. The RePPProT report describes "large areas of barren land" in this region. A further statement is more explicit: "Very steep ridge systems of the Western Plains and Mountains and the Middle Kapuas Basin have been degraded to grassland and scrub by over-intensive shifting cultivation. The erosion of these areas is excessive. Present reforestation activities should concentrate on these areas first" (RePPProT 1987b, 38). Though little is visible from the Pontianak–Sanggau road, extensive tracts of *Imperata cylindrica* grassland may be seen from the air. Since this zone lies within easy access of Pontianak and the coast, it would seem to have been under pressure for many years. There are also extensive grassland areas in the middle Melawi basin.

Similar recommendations are made for steep ridge systems in the Meratus mountain foothills of South Kalimantan that are also said to be eroding excessively as a result of shifting cultivation (RePPProT 1987a, 15). These latter areas, also under *Imperata cylindrica*, have largely been cleared during the past century, though some of the grassland may be older (Potter 1987). About 16 per cent of South Kalimantan has a cover of grassland, which government authorities have been attempting for many years to reforest; dry-season fires have been a recurring problem for at least a century.

Drought and fire

Since the major fires in East Kalimantan and Sabah in 1982–1983, it has been recognized that substantial evidence exists of earlier fires in parts of the east Borneo forests (Wirawan 1993). This is not surprising, since all modern reports of large forest fires to be found in the literature correspond with periods of unusual drought associated with major ENSO (El Niño–Southern Oscillation) events, and several major episodes have occurred in the past 120 years of records. Moreover, there can be no doubt that they have continued over a very long time (Brookfield and Allen 1991; Nicholls 1991). In the Malesian region, normally a principal focus of deep convection in the troposphere, ENSO events see this convection moved out into the central Pacific and its replacement with persistently descending air. The effect in these year-long events is to extend and intensify the dry season where it exists and greatly to weaken the wet season. Even in Borneo, severe drought of several months' duration can be a consequence.

Although there are reports of forest fires in 1902 and 1914, the conflagrations of 1982–1983 were almost certainly without recent historical precedent in their scale. Studies conducted by German experts in the 32,000 km^2 of East Kalimantan burned in 1982–1983 concluded that it was largely the impact of recent logging that led to the size of the fire, by changing the composition of the forest towards more inflammable secondary species (Schindele, Thoma, and Panzer 1989). They also pointed out that in the more severely burned areas it could be hundreds of years before some of the valuable species reappeared, for they would be suppressed by competitive vegetation. The same set of fires destroyed a further 10,000 km^2, 85 per cent of which had been logged, in Sabah (Woods 1987). There is some risk that such large gaps, subjected to new droughts, may never revegetate with forest and could become grassland.

Considerable new burning occurred from August to November 1991, during an ENSO event of wide scope in the western Pacific. Estimates at mid-October put the total area burned at about 90,000 ha, of which 50,000 were in Kalimantan (*Kompas*, 12 October 1991; *Tempo*, 19 October 1991). In the absence of survey, these estimates may entail more than an element of guesswork; one television broadcast around the same time put the area in Central Kalimantan alone at 76,000 ha! Large areas were covered with smoke, airplanes could not land at Palangkaraya, Pontianak, and various locations in Sumatra, and haze affected aviation as far afield as Singapore and Peninsular Malaysia. Although some of this was related to burning underground coal seams in East Kalimantan, a good deal more is attributable to deliberate clearing of local swamp forest, with small farmers taking advantage of the dry conditions to extend cultivation into swamps. The burn near Palangkaraya in Central Kalimantan was said to be started by shifting cultivators and, as it was almost entirely in swamp forest, this is probably the explanation. In South Kalimantan a line of fire was observable from the air all along the mountain foothills, the approximate location of the *Acacia mangium* plantations. These fires were less severe than those of 1982–1983, but they were a warning of how widespread and disruptive conflagrations can be whenever a drought occurs.

Apart from fire, other serious consequences of the 1991 drought were the widespread crop losses, the large numbers of deaths from cholera and other waterborne diseases (148 in Central Kalimantan), and the disruption to transport caused by the low volume of water in the rivers, which seriously interrupted log-rafting to plywood factories in the lower reaches of the Mahakam and Barito. Low river levels also interfered with logging in Sarawak.

Poverty and wealth

The beginning of this chapter posed the question of the effect of rapid change on human welfare. It is not simply answered, since the evidence is equivocal. If the incomes from oil and its products are included, East Kalimantan is Indonesia's richest province, providing on its own more than 5 per cent of the nation's GDP (*Statistik Indonesia* 1990), or a per capita income in 1988 of US$2,626, which is closely comparable to that of Selangor in the Malay Peninsula (about US$2,700 in 1990), which ranks third among the states of much wealthier Malaysia. Even excluding oil, the remaining income (US$819) was twice the national average, whereas that of West Kalimantan, the poorest of the four provinces (US$317), was below this. Within Malaysia, Sabah ranks fifth in per capita GDP, at about US$1,800 in 1990, some way below the wealthier urban states and oil-rich Terengganu, whereas Sarawak, at about US$1,550, is on a level comparable with the more developed rural states of the Peninsula (Malaysia 1991b). Small Brunei, with a per capita GDP of US$14,076 (*The Far East and Australasia* 1991) is among the world's richest countries.

These gross comparisons do have some meaning, and the generally higher level in Malaysian than in Indonesian Borneo is reflected in greater provision of infrastructure, especially in the urbanized areas. We have already noted, however, the extent of rural poverty in Sarawak, at least on a statistical basis. Poverty in Malaysia is measured by monthly household cash income and, on the basis of a "poverty line" that has varied somewhat through time, 1989 survey data showed 34 per cent of the population of Sabah and 21 per cent of that of Sarawak as poor, levels much higher than in the Peninsula (Malaysia 1991a). Most poverty-level households are rural in both states.

Poverty in Indonesia is largely measured by levels of household expenditure on essential foodstuffs, considered more accurate than income figures, and probably correctly so for rural families. In the most popular method, that of Sayogyo (1975), the poverty line is drawn at the cost of purchasing 20 kg of rice per person in the rural areas, 30 kg in the cities. Measured in this way, poverty has been at quite moderate levels in Kalimantan. However, much of the off-farm employment has gone to Javanese in-migrant workers, even in the large plywood factories. There has been concern that the transmigration programme will transfer poverty out of Java to rural parts of the outer islands where transmigrants are numerous (World Bank 1989). Some provisional results from the most recent National Socio-Economic Survey (SUSENAS), held in 1987, lend credence to this belief. A study carried out in South Kalimantan, using the detailed SUSENAS results (BAPPEDA/Kantor Statistik, Kalsel 1987), revealed 10.2 per cent of the urban population and 12.4 per cent of the rural population as falling below the poverty line. Yet an examination of data at the district and regency level found that some particular areas stood out as being much poorer. These were sections of the tidal swamps with many transmigrant settlements, where poverty was over 30 per cent in 7 of the 14 regencies, and parts of the east coast, where the more inaccessible regencies with large transmigrant populations showed similar poverty figures.

Pockets of poverty also exist among settled agricultural populations in the inland Hulu Sungai area of South Kalimantan. Although soils are good by Kalimantan standards, agriculture has remained risky because of problems with water control. Droughts, floods, and, more recently, low rubber prices have triggered waves of migrants seeking new land. They have travelled to Perak and Johore in Malaysia and to Riau on the east coast of Sumatra; they have also opened tidal swamps nearer home. Those away have usually retained their landholdings, which now results in high levels of sharecropping and low returns to growers, despite widespread use of high-yielding rice varieties. Multiplying occupations, rather than intensifying existing production, has been the preferred strategy, with recent migrants heading for the cities rather than seeking new rural land. West Kalimantan, with the lowest per capita incomes and household expenditures, still has 73 per cent of its labour force engaged in agriculture, the highest of the four provinces; less than 5 per cent are in manufacturing and 17 per cent in services and trade. For highly urbanized East Kalimantan, agriculture (including forestry) occupies only 43 per cent of the workforce, with 7 per cent in manufacturing and a high 39 per cent in services and trade. Income levels from farming, when not combined with other cash-earning activities, fall inevitably below the poverty line. Even though farmers in West Kalimantan, and elsewhere, may attempt to diversify, yields are low, the resource base poor, and transport undeveloped.

Wealth, on the other hand, is not conspicuous in most of Borneo, with the striking exception of Brunei. It is visible in urban areas, as in the superior housing of oil company executives in Balikpapan, Bintulu, and other oil towns, and the "palaces" of a few merchants or industrialists in Banjarmasin. Nevertheless, the timber royalties that have been available to local governments have resulted in improved urban facilities, especially in Samarinda and Palangkaraya in Kalimantan and in all the towns of Malaysian Borneo. Timber is now worth 16 per cent of Indonesia's GNP, and benefits have "trickled down" in the form of village schools and health centres. Oil incomes produce more concentrated spin-offs in the oil towns of north and east Borneo. Pangestu (1989) points out that local benefits from the oil industry have been quite substantial in East Kalimantan. The refinery at Balikpapan and the large liquefied natural gas and fertilizer plants to the north provide useful employment, and the companies have supplied schools, medical services, electricity, and water to the new communities.

There are, however, differences between the two parts of Borneo. The wealth that has flowed from the forests and the oil wells of Kalimantan has largely left the island for Jakarta, or has been transferred overseas. In Sabah and Sarawak, more of this income stays within the state. Road construction, land development, education, and other social services, and, most clearly in Sabah, the construction of glassy towers in the capital, Kota Kinabalu, all depended primarily on timber income, together with a smaller but rising income from oil and gas in the South China Sea. The Kalimantan provinces are only 4 out of the 26 that constitute Indonesia, and are subject to centralized policies emanating from Jakarta. Forces for change are nationwide, and particular regions of Indonesia, other than Java itself, are seldom at the forefront of consideration. The greater degree of economic independence in the states of Malaysian Borneo is reflected in development policies that are only in part encapsulated in the national plans, and, moreover, these plans are always careful to stress the interests of the Borneo states.

The welfare of one group of people is missing from all the statistics. These people are the illegal immigrants – almost all in the Malaysian part of Borneo and in Brunei – from Indonesia and the Philippines, with a few from other places. Where they work as agricultural or construction workers, or in other manual tasks, most are poorly paid yet they still find it advantageous to have moved. Some, however, have become tenant farmers, and still others engage in various entrepreneurial activities. There are peri-urban settlements around the towns of northern Borneo within which at least a few illegal immigrants have certainly prospered. Though they are less numerous than their counterparts in Peninsular Malaysia, the illegals constitute a significant minority, which is large in Sabah. Very little is known about them.

A changing resource frontier

A basic problem

A period may now be approaching in which timber and the timber-based industry will decline in both absolute and relative importance in most of Borneo. Energy and other minerals, especially the large offshore oil and gas resources now being developed in the seas to the north and east, are likely to increase in significance. The rate of expansion of "non-oil exports," of which plywood occupies a major share, has been declining in Indonesia over the last three years (Nasution 1991; Parker 1991). Both in Malaysia and in Indonesia, oil and gas are expected to remain important energy sources well into the next century. New reserves discovered recently off the Mahakam mouth in East Kalimantan have countered predictions that both reserves and production were set to fall (OPEC 1991). Indonesia is now the world's largest exporter of liquefied natural gas (LNG), about one-half of it coming from the East Kalimantan field, and mainly destined for the Japanese market. New oil and gas fields are also being developed off Sarawak and Sabah, the former linked to the LNG plant at Bintulu, the output of which will almost double by 1995 (Malaysia 1991a).

These developments will give greater value to the mineral-rich parts of Borneo in the two national economies, but they may also put off the day when dependence on a resource-extraction strategy of development has to be relinquished. Byron and Waugh (1988) suggested that "Ricardian" limits, approached through rising economic and social costs, would bring resource depletion to a tapering end rather than a sudden "Malthusian" exhaustion. Despite signs that this is true, the delusion of inexhaustible resources has persisted well into the "Ricardian" period, so that where an end has come it has done so suddenly.

Economic criticality and resource criticality have arrived together in Sabah and threaten to do the same in parts of Kalimantan and Sarawak within a few years. Thus, these areas are clearly endangered, in the terms discussed in chapter 1. This is the consequence of basing rapid economic growth on a resource that is mined to quick exhaustion. It is the consequence also of treating all seemingly vacant land as though it were equally available for agricultural development; success, where achieved at all, has often been brief in the absence of large subsidies on imported fertilizer. Moreover, rising costs may trigger a sudden decision to halt large programmes. The basic problem has, in all cases, been a careless approach to the sustainability of resources.

Institutional weaknesses

The national and state institutions that have either spearheaded the development drive or provided massive support to its private agents have begun to change tack in the face of partial exhaustion of resources. A period of more careful and conservative management may now be ushered in, with less licence to greed and corruption than has occurred in the past. Even in the national heartlands of Malaysia and Indonesia, however, the institutions of environmental management are not strong. Across just a narrow sea they become very much weaker. Barber (1989) remarks, of a much wider area, that its institutional frameworks for environmental and resource management are a patchwork rather than a system. Both in Malaysia and in Indonesia the environmental ministries and agencies created in the 1970s are without line responsibility and have very limited professional staff. Malaysia has fewer than 100 professionals charged with a huge range of duties over the whole country and lacks both equipment and funds (Sham 1987, 64). Meanwhile, in Indonesia:

> The State Minister of Population and the Environment, who does not head a department, lacks the competence to make, let alone enforce, ultimate judgements on land-use and development proposals. Government Regulation No. 29 of 1986 concerning Environmental Impact Analysis, with its forty clauses that include reference to various interdepartmental commissions at different levels, has not helped to simplify a complex problem, especially since it makes no mention of legal consequences for those who ignore its stipulations. (Hardjono 1991, 13)

Actual responsibility for environmental management is widely dispersed among ministries and agencies, the centre, and the states and provinces. Their primary goals are not centrally concerned with the environment, and they are not legally or administratively obliged to accept direction from the environmental ministries. Coordination is difficult to achieve, and great scope exists for interested persons and organizations to subvert outcomes in their favour. This remains a major problem in both parts of Borneo, where state officials and ministers can face charges of corruption over the issue of timber licences without losing position or power, and where inspection to ensure compliance with regulations on the ground is minimal. Good policies may be in place, but good enforcement and even the political will to encourage enforcement are ill developed.

Conclusion

Even an interim balance sheet cannot rest in Borneo alone, for Borneo is but part of two countries. The benefits gained by society in Borneo have been reduced by the considerable flow of wealth outside the immediate region, but national revenues gained from Borneo have brought important benefits in the form of more rapid development to the two nations as wholes. The severest pressures arising from development have been felt by the indigenous people of Sarawak and Kalimantan, yet the impacts have not been wholly negative. The indigenous societies of Borneo are adaptable, not fragile, and though their interests have received low priority in national decision-making, they have gained diversity of economic and social opportunity and are in no danger of being destroyed. Some of the migrant settlers and workers have done well, but others find they are little better off than they were at home.

Notwithstanding rapid industrial development in the South-East Asian region and the growth of insecure employment opportunities for South-East Asians in North-East Asia and the Middle East, population growth alone makes it likely that both legal and illegal migration to resource-frontier regions will continue to be a major factor in regional development through the coming generation. Oil, gas, other mining, and resource-based industries will produce a geographical pattern of opportunity different from that created during the boom based on timber, but will not of themselves change the basic status of the Borneo provinces and states within the two countries. This requires a sort of development that is not yet in sight, yet the whole environmental future of the island depends on the evolution of a more integrated set of economies in Borneo.

East and Central Kalimantan, and Sarawak, still have a considerable portion of their forests though large areas have already been logged once; only Sabah is already at the end of a period based on the exploitation of old-growth timber. Land settlement is in difficulties, and major decisions are needed about the agricultural future in all parts of Borneo. There is opportunity for change. For the forests themselves, the future is uncertain. Better management and less rapacious cutting, if they come about, will help. Replanting of cut-over and degraded areas will probably improve the condition of the land and the economy, but the loss of biodiversity creates risk, and the rich diversity of the Malesian rain forest will survive only in quite limited areas, few of them in the lowlands. Perhaps the main hope for the forests will, after all, be Ricardian. As costs rise, demand for all but specialized woods may shift back from tropical forests to the temperate lands (Vincent 1988). The now very probable "opening up" of the eastern Siberian forests for the North-East Asian market (*Australian Financial Review*, 20 September 1991) will be of no benefit to the global environment but could yet be the saving of what remains of the rain forests of South-East Asia.

References

Agarwal, Anil, and Sunita Narain. 1991. *Global warming in an unequal world. A case of environmental colonialism*. New Delhi: Centre for Science and Environment.

Allen, J. C., and D. F. Barnes. 1985. The causes of deforestation in developing countries. *Annals of the Association of American Geographers* 75: 163–184.

Appell, G., and L. Appell-Warren. 1985. Resettlement of peoples in Indonesian Borneo. *Borneo Research Bulletin* 17, no. 1: 4–31.

Arman, Syamsuni. 1987. Off-farm work in three coastal communities of West Kalimantan, Indonesia. Ph.D. dissertation, Rutgers University, New Brunswick, NJ.

Asean Focus. 1989. Sarawak: A cautious approach. *Asia Pacific Forest Industries*, September: 26–28.

Asian Yearbook 1990. 1990. Hong Kong: Far Eastern Economic Review.

Aten Suwandi, Ir. H. n.d. Draft project report: Rehabilitation of logged-over forests in Asia/Pacific Region. Annex II. Indonesia and Malaysia. Prepared for International Tropical Timber Organization by Japan Overseas Forestry Consultants Association.

Avé, J., and V. King. 1986. *People of the weeping forest: Tradition and change in Borneo*. Leiden: National Museum of Ethnology.

BAPPEDA/Kantor Statistik, Kalsel [Regional Planning Office/Statistical Office, South Kalimantan]. 1987. *Pengkajian perkembangan tingkat ketimpangan pendapatan dan kemiskinan di Propinsi Kalimantan Selatan 1981–87* [Development of understanding of the levels of inadequate income and poverty in the province of South Kalimantan, 1981–87]. Banjarmasin: South Kalimantan Statistical Office.

Barber, Charles Victor. 1989. Institutional issues in environmental and natural resources management for the Asia/Near East region. Manuscript prepared for the Bureau for Asia and the Near East, US Agency for International Development. Washington DC: World Resources Institute.

Blasco, F., and F. Achard. 1990. Analysis of vegetation changes using satellite data. In *Soils and the greenhouse effect: The present status and future trends concerning the effect of soils and their cover on the fluxes of greenhouse gases, the surface energy balance and the water balance: Proceedings of the International Conference on Soils and the Greenhouse Effect, August 14–18, Wageningen, Netherlands*, ed. A. F. Bouwman, 303–310. Chichester: Wiley.

Brookfield, Harold, and B . Allen. 1991. Environmental and human responses to climatic variability in the west Pacific "maritime continent" region. In *South Pacific environments: Interactions with weather and climate. Proceedings of a Conference organized by Environmental Science, University of Auckland, 2–7 September 1991*, ed. John E. Hay, 71–82. Auckland: Environmental Science.

Brookfield, Harold, and Yvonne Byron. 1990. Deforestation and timber extraction in Borneo and the Malay Peninsula: The record since 1965. *Global Environmental Change: Human and Policy Dimensions* 1, no. 1: 42–56.

Brookfield, Harold, Francis J. Lian, Low Kwai-sim, and Lesley Potter. 1990. Borneo and the Malay Peninsula. In *The earth as transformed by human action. Global and regional changes in the biosphere over the past 300 years*, ed. B. L. Turner II, William C. Clark, Robert W. Kates, John F. Richards, Jessica T. Mathews, and William B. Meyer, 495–512. Cambridge: Cambridge University Press with Clark University.

Brown, S., and A. E. Lugo. 1982. The storage and production of organic matter in tropical forests and their role in the global carbon cycle. *Biotropica* 14: 161–187.

Brown, S., A. J. R. Gillespie, and A. E. Lugo. 1989. Biomass estimation methods for tropical forests with applications to forest inventory data. *Forest Science* 35: 881–902.

———. 1991. Biomass of tropical forests of south and southeast Asia. *Canadian Journal of Forest Research* 21: 111–117.

Buku tahunan perangkaan [Yearbook of statistics]. Annual. Kuala Lumpur, Malaysia: Government Printing Office.

Burbridge, P., A. Dixon, and B. Soewardi. 1981. Forestry and agriculture: Options for resource allocation in choosing lands for transmigration. *Applied Geography* 1: 237–258.

Burgess, P. F. 1990. Asia. In *No timber without trees: Sustainability in the tropical forest*, ed. Duncan Poore, 117–153. London: Earthscan Publications.

Byron, N., and G. Waugh. 1988. Forestry and fisheries in the Asian–Pacific region: Issues in natural resource management. *Asian Pacific Economic Literature* 2, no. 1: 46–80.

Census of Indonesia. 1990. *Penduduk Indonesia, hasil sensus penduduk 1990*. Jakarta: Biro Pusat Statistik (Central Statistical Office).

Chamhuri Siwar, and Nik Hashim Nik Mustapha. 1988. *Integrated rural development in Malaysia: An assessment*. Fakulti Ekonomi Monograph 4. Bangi (Selangor): Penerbit Universiti Kebangsaan Malaysia.

Collins, N. Mark, Jeffrey A. Sayer, and Timothy C. Whitmore. 1991. *The conservation atlas of tropical forests. Asia and the Pacific*. New York: Simon & Schuster.

Country Profile. 1990. Malaysia: Coping with diminishing resources. *Asia Pacific Forest Industries*, June: 12–21.

———. 1991. Sabah, Malaysia: Timber industry at a crossroad. *Asia Pacific Forest Industries*, April: 10–20.

Cramb, R. A. 1989a. The use and productivity of labour in shifting cultivation: An East Malaysian case study. *Agricultural Systems* 29: 97–115.

———. 1989b. Shifting cultivation and resource degradation in Sarawak: Perceptions and policies. *Borneo Research Bulletin* 21, no. 1: 22–49.

———. 1990. Reply to John Palmer. *Borneo Research Bulletin* 22, no. 1: 44–46.

Cramb, R. A., and G. Dixon. 1988. Development in Sarawak: An overview. In *Development in Sarawak: Historical and contemporary perspectives*, ed. R. A. Cramb and Robert H. W. Reece, 1–19. Monash Papers on Southeast Asia, no. 17. Oakleigh South, Victoria, Australia: Centre of Southeast Asian Studies, Monash Universily.

Cramb, R. A. and I. R. Wills. 1990. The role of traditional institutions in rural development: Community-based land tenure and government land policy in Sarawak, Malaysia. *World Development* 18: 347–360.

Dale, V. I., R. A. Houghton, and A. C. S. Hall. 1991. Estimating the effects of land-use change on global atmospheric CO_2 concentrations. *Canadian Journal of Forest Research* 21: 87–90.

Dinas Kehutanan, Kalbar [Forestry Department, West Kalimantan]. 1990. *Laporan Tahunan, 1989–90* [Annual report, 1989–90]. Pontianak, West Kalimantan.

Drury, B. 1988. The limits of conservative reform: Agricultural policy in Malaysia. *ASEAN Economic Bulletin* 4: 287–301.

Eckholm, Erik P. 1976. *Losing ground: Environmental stress and world food prospects*. New York: Norton.

FAO (Food and Agriculture Organization of the United Nations). 1973. *Forestry and forest industries development, Malaysia: A national forest inventory of West Malaysia, 1970–1972*. FO:DP/MAL/72/009. Technical Report no. 5. Rome: FAO.

FAO (Food and Agriculture Organization of the United Nations) and GOI (Directorate-General of Forest Utilization in the Ministry of Forestry, Government of Indonesia). 1990. *Situation and outlook of the forestry sector in Indonesia*. 5 vols. Jakarta: GOI for FAO.

The Far East and Australasia 1991. 1991. London: Europa Publications.

Franz, J. 1988. Effects and consequences of spontaneous settlement activities (an East Kalimantan case study). In *Settlement concept as integrated part of regional and rural development*, ed. A. Birowo et al., 193–201. Jakarta: Mercu Buana University.

Freeman, Derek. 1955. *Iban agriculture: A report on the shifting cultivation of hill rice by the Iban of Sarawak*. Colonial Research Studies no. 18. London: HMSO.

———. 1970. *Report on the Iban*. London: Athlone Press.

Gillis, M. 1988. The logging industry in tropical Asia. In *People of the tropical rain forest*, ed. Julie S. Denslow and Christine Padoch, 177–184. Berkeley: University of California Press in association with Smithsonian Institution Traveling Exhibition Service.

Golokin, S., and P. Cassels. 1988. An appraisal of Sabah Softwoods Sdn. Bhd. twelve years after establishment. In *Future role of forest plantations in the national economy, and incentives required to encourage investments in forest plantation development: Proceedings of a seminar held at Kota Kinabalu, Sabah, November 30 to December 4, 1987*, ed. Hon Tat Tang, Cyril C. Pinso, and Clive Marsh, 107–114. Ede, the Netherlands: Tropenbos.

Gomez-Pompa, A., and F. W. Burley. 1991. The management of natural tropical forests. In *Rain forest regeneration and management*, ed. Arturo Gomez-Pompa, Timothy C. Whitmore, and Malcolm Hadley, 3–18. Man and the Biosphere Series, v.6. Paris: UNESCO.

Hadi, S., R. Hidayat, and Udiansyah. 1988. Perbandingan antara nilai harapan murni *Acacia mangium* dan tegakan campuran *A. mangium* dengan lada (*Piper nigrum*) [Comparisons between levels of output of pure stands of *A. mangium* and when mixed with pepper (*Piper nigrum*)]. In *Agroforestry untuk pengembangan daerah pedesaan di Kalimantan Timur* [Agroforestry for the development of village districts in East Kalimantan]: *Proceedings of a Seminar held at Universitas Mulawarman, Samarinda, East Kalimantan, 19–21 Sept. 1988*, ed. A. Lahjie and B. Seibert, 207–222. Samarinda: Fakultas Kehutanan, UNMUL and German Forestry Group, German Agency for Technical Cooperation (GTZ).

Hall, A. C. S., and J. Uhlig. 1991. Refining estimates of carbon released from tropical land use change. *Canadian Journal of Forest Research* 21: 118–131.

Hammond, A. L., E. Rodenburg, and William R. Moomaw. 1991. Calculating national accountability for climate change. *Environment* 33, no. 1: 11–15, 33–35.

Hamzah, Z. 1978. Some observations on the effects of mechanical logging on regeneration, soil and hydrological conditions in East Kalimantan. In *Symposium on the Long-Term Effects of Logging in Southeast Asia, June 24–June 27, 1975, Bogor, Indonesia: Proceedings*, ed. S. Rahardjo, I. Soerianegara, Z. Hamzah, H. Haeruman Js., S. Hadi, S. Manan, H. Basjarudin, and W. Sukotjo, 73–87. BIOTROP Special Publication no. 3. Bogor: BIOTROP.

Hardjono, Joan. 1991. The dimensions of Indonesia's environmental problems. *Indonesia: Resources, ecology, and environment*, ed. Joan Hardjono, 1–16. Singapore: Oxford University Press.

Hatch, T. 1982. *Shifting cultivation in Sarawak: A Review*. Technical Paper no. 8. Kuching, Sarawak, Malaysia: Soils Division, Research Branch, Department of Agriculture.

Hatch, T., and C. P. Lim. 1978. *Shifting cultivation in Sarawak: A report based on the Workshop on Shifting Cultivation held in Kuching on 7–8th December 1978*. Kuching, Sarawak, Malaysia: Soils Division, Research Branch, Department of Agriculture.

Hidayati, D. 1990. Effects of development on the extension of agricultural land in East Kalimantan, Indonesia. Paper presented to Asian Studies Association of Australia 8th Biennial Conference, Griffith University, Queensland, 2–5 July 1990.

Hong, Evelyn. 1987. *Natives of Sarawak: Survival in Borneo's vanishing forest*. Pulau Pinang, Malaysia: Institut Masyarakat.

Houghton, John T., Geoffrey G. Jenkins, and J. J. Ephraums, eds. 1990. *Climate change: The IPCC scientific assessment*. Cambridge: Cambridge University Press.

Houghton, R. A. 1991. Releases of carbon to the atmosphere from degradation of forests in tropical Asia. *Canadian Journal of Forest Research* 21: 132–142.

Houghton, R. A., and D. L. Skole. 1990. Carbon. In *The earth as transformed by human action: Global and regional changes in the biosphere over the past 300 years*, ed. B. L. Turner II, William C. Clark, Robert W. Kates, John F. Richards, Jessica T. Mathews, and William B. Meyer, 393–408. Cambridge: Cambridge University Press with Clark University.

Houghton, R. A., R. D. Boone, J. M. Melillo, C. A. Palm, G. M. Woodwell, N. Myers, B. Moore, and D. L. Skole. 1985. Net flux of CO_2 from tropical forests in 1980. *Nature* 316: 617–620.

Houghton, R. A., R. D. Boone, J. R. Fruci, J. E. Hobbie, J. M. Melillo, C. A. Palm, B. J. Peterson, G. R. Shaver, G. M. Woodwell, B. Moore, D. L. Skole, and N. Myers. 1987. The flux of carbon from terrestrial ecosystems to the atmosphere in 1980 due to changes in land use: geographical distribution of the global flux. *Tellus* 39B: 122–139.

Hurst, Philip. 1990. *Rainforest politics: Ecological destruction in South-East Asia*. London: Zed Books.

IIED (International Institute for Environment and Development) and GOI (Government of Indonesia). 1985. *A review of policies affecting the sustainable development of forest lands in Indonesia*. 5 vols. Jakarta: GOI.

Inoue, M., and Lahjie, A. 1990. Dynamics of swidden agriculture in East Kalimantan. *Agroforestry Systems* 12: 269–284.

ITTC (International Tropical Timber Council). 1990. *Report submitted to the International Tropical Timber Council by Mission established pursuant to Resolution I (IV): The promotion of sustainable forest management: A case study in Sarawak, Malaysia*. Den Pasar, Bali: International Tropical Timber Council.

Jackson, James C. 1968. *Sarawak: A geographical survey of a developing state*. London: University of London Press.

Johns, R. J. 1986. The instability of the tropical ecosystem in New Guinea. *Blumea* 31: 341–371.

———. 1989. The influence of drought on tropical rainforest vegetation in Papua New Guinea. *Mountain Research and Development* 9: 248–251.

Kalimantan Barat dalam angka [West Kalimantan in figures]. Annual. Pontianak: Kantor Sensus and Propinsi Kalimantan Barat.

Kalimantan Selatan dalam angka [South Kalimantan in figures]. Annual. Banjarmasin: Kantor.

Kalimantan Tengah dalam angka [Central Kalimantan in figures]. Annual. Palangka Raya: Propinsi Kalimantan Tengah.

Kalimantan Timur dalam angka [East Kalimantan in figures]. Annual. Samarinda: Propinsi Kalimantan Timur.

Kartawinata, K. 1978. Biological changes after logging in lowland Dipterocarp forest. In *Symposium on the Long-Term Effects of Logging in Southeast Asia, June 24–June 27, 1975, Bogor, Indonesia: Proceedings*, ed. S. Rahardjo, I. Soerianegara, Z. Hamzah, H. Haeruman Js., S. Hadi, S. Manan, H. Basjarudin, and W. Sukotjo, 25–34. BIOTROP Special Publication no. 3. Bogor: BIOTROP.

———. 1990. A review of natural vegetation studies in Malesia, with special reference to Indonesia. In *The plant diversity of Malesia: Proceedings of the Flora Malesiana Symposium commemorating Professor C. G. G. J. van Steenis, Leiden, August 1989*, ed. Pieter Baas, Kees Kalkman, and Rob Geesink, 121–132. Dordrecht: Kluwer Academic Publishers.

Kartawinata, K., and A. Vayda. 1984. Forest conversion in East Kalimantan, Indonesia: The activities and impact of timber companies, shifting cultivators, migrant pepper farmers, and others. In *Ecology in practice, part 1: Ecosystem management*, ed. Francesco Di Castri, F. W. G. Baker, and Malcolm Hadley, 99–126. Paris: UNESCO.

Kartawinata, K., H. Soedjito, T. Jessup, A. Vayda, and C. Colfer. 1984. The impact of development on interactions between people and forests in East Kalimantan: A comparison of two areas of Kenyah Dayak settlement. *The Environmentalist* 4, Supplement no. 7: 87–95.

Katili, John A. 1974. *Geological environment of the Indonesian mineral deposits: A plate tectonic approach*. Geological Survey of Indonesia, Publikasi Teknik-Seri Geologi Ekonomi no. 7. Jakarta: Direktorat Jonderal Perjanbargan.

Kavanagh, Mikkaail, Abdullah Abdul Rahim, and Christopher J. Hails. 1989. *Rainforest conservation in Sarawak: An international policy for WWF*. Kuala Lumpur: World Wildlife Fund Malaysia.

Kellman, M. C. 1969. Some environmental components of shifting cultivation in upland Mindanao. *Journal of Tropical Geography* 28: 40–56.

King, V. T. 1988. Models and realities: Malaysian national planning and East Malaysian development problems. *Modern Asian Studies* 22: 263–298.

Kumar, Raj. 1986. *The forest resources of Malaysia: Their economics and development*. Singapore: Oxford University Press.

Lau, B. T. 1979. The effect of shifting cultivation on sustained yield management for Sarawak national forests. *Malaysian Forester* 42: 418–429.

Leighton, M., and D. Peart. 1990. Research on enrichment planting for forest and conservation management. Paper presented to International Conference on Forest Biology and Conservation in Borneo, Kota Kinabalu, Sabah, 30 July–3 August 1990.

Leslie, A. 1977. Where contradictory theory and practice co-exist. *Unasylva* 29: 2–17.

Levang, P., and Marten Riskan. 1984. *Sebamban I, agro-economic survey of a transmigration center on South Kalimantan*. Indonesia–ORSTOM Transmigration Project PTA-44. Paris: Institut français de recherche scientifique pour le développement en coopération (ORSTOM).

Lian, F. J. 1987. Farmers' perceptions and economic change: The case of Kenyah swidden farmers in Sarawak. Ph.D. thesis, Australian National University, Canberra.

———. 1993. On threatened peoples. In *South-East Asia's environmental future: The search for sustainability*, ed. Harold Brookfield and Yvonne Byron, 322–340. Tokyo and Kuala Lumpur: United Nations University Press and Oxford University Press.

Logging and Resources. 1989. Sarawak: A matter of perspective. *Asia Pacific Forest Industries*, September: 37–40.

———. 1990. Export bans, tax increases and quotas. *Asia Pacific Forest Industries*, March: 18–22.

Lugo, A. E., and S. Brown. 1982. Conversion of tropical moist forests: A critique. *Interciencia* 7: 89–93.

Majaran, E., and A. Dimin. 1989. The practice of shifting cultivation in Sarawak: A menace to forest management and conservation. Paper delivered to the Malaysian Forest Management Conference, Kuantan, 24–29 July.

Malayan Forester. 1967. Forestry and conservation in the lowlands of West Malaysia. 30: 243–245.

Malaysia. 1987. Inventori hutan nasional II Semanenanjung Malaysia 1981–1982 [Second national forest inventory of Peninsula Malaysia 1981–1982]. Kuala Lumpur: Unit Pengugurusan Hutan, Ibu Perhutan, Semanenanjung Malaysia.

———. 1991a. *Sixth Malaysia plan 1991–1995*. Kuala Lumpur: National Printing Department.

———. 1991b. *The second outline perspective plan: 1991–2000*. Kuala Lumpur: National Printing Department.

Marsono, D. 1980. The effect of Indonesian selective cutting (TPI) on the structure and regeneration of lowland tropical dipterocarp forests in East Kalimantan, Indonesia. Ph.D. dissertation, University of the Philippines at Los Banos.

MIDA (Malaysian Industrial Development Authority) and UNIDO (United Nations Industrial Development Organization). 1985. *Medium and long-term industrial master plan, 1986–1995: Executive highlights*. Kuala Lumpur: National Printing Department.

MOF (Ministry of Forestry, Government of Indonesia) and FAO (Food and Agriculture Organization of the United Nations). 1991. *Indonesian tropical forestry action programme: Country brief*. 3 vols. Jakarta: MOF.

Mohd. Nor Zakaria, P. K. Yew, E. Pushparajah, and Bahtiar A. Karim. 1985. Current programmes, problems and strategies for land clearing and development in Malaysia. *Land Development Digest* 7, no. 2: 10–22.

Myers, Norman. 1980. *Conversion of tropical moist forests*. Washington DC: National Academy of Sciences.

———. 1984. *The primary source*. New York: W. W. Norton.

Nasution, N. 1991. Survey of recent developments. *Bulletin of Indonesian Economic Studies* 27, no. 2: 3–44.

Naval Intelligence Division. 1944. *Geographical handbook series: Netherlands East Indies*, vol. 2 (Appendices VI–IX). London: Naval Intelligence Division of the Admiralty.

Nicholls, N. 1991. The El Niño-Southern Oscillation: Recent Australian research.

Paper presented at the ENSO/Climatic Change Workshop, Tara Hotel, Bangkok, Thailand, 4–7 November (mimeo).

Ongkili, James P. 1972. *Modernization in East Malaysia, 1960–1970*. Kuala Lumpur: Oxford University Press.

OPEC. 1991. *Bulletin* 22, no. 10 (Nov.–Dec.).

Padoch, Christine. 1982a. Land use in new and old areas of Iban settlement. *Borneo Research Bulletin* 14, no. 1: 3–14.

———. 1982b. Migration and its alternatives among the Iban of Sarawak. Verhandelingen van het Koninklijk Instituut voor Taal-, Land- en Volkenkunde 98. The Hague: Martinus Nijhoff.

Padoch, Christine, and Nancy Peluso. 1991. Managed forests and resource rights in West Kalimantan. Paper presented to the conference on Interactions of People and Forests in Kalimantan, New York Botanical Garden, New York, 21–23 June.

Palm, C. A., R. A. Houghton, J. M. Melillo, and D. L. Skole. 1986. Atmospheric carbon dioxide from deforestation in southeast Asia. *Biotropica* 18: 177–188.

Pang Teck Wai. 1990. The making of a development plan for Sabah: Issues, problems, solutions. Paper delivered to the Borneo Research Council Seminar on Change and Development, Kuching, 4–9 August.

Pangestu, M. 1989. East Kalimantan: Beyond the timber and oil boom. In *Unity and diversity: Regional economic development in Indonesia since 1970*, ed. H. Hill, 151–176. Singapore: Oxford University Press.

Parker, S. 1991. Survey of recent developments. *Bulletin of Indonesian Economic Studies* 27, no. 1: 3–38.

Pieters, P., and S. Supriatna. 1990. *Geological map of the West, Central and East Kalimantan Area*. Bandung: Geological Research and Development Centre.

Potter, Lesley. 1987. Degradation, innovation and social welfare in the Riam Kiwa valley, South Kalimantan, Indonesia. In *Land degradation and society*, by Piers Blaikie and Harold Brookfield with contributions by others, 164–176. London: Methuen.

———. 1988. Indigenes and colonisers: Dutch forest policy in South and East Borneo (Kalimantan), 1900 to 1950. In *Changing tropical forests: Historical perspectives on today's challenges in Asia, Australasia and the Pacific*, ed. J. Dargavel, K. Dixon, and N. Semple, 127–153. Canberra: Centre for Resource and Environmental Studies, Australian National University.

———. 1990. Forest classification, policy and land-use planning in Kalimantan. *Borneo Review* 1: 91–128.

Primack, R. B. 1991. Logging, conservation and native rights in Sarawak forests from different viewpoints. *Borneo Research Bulletin* 23: 3–13.

Repetto, R. 1988. Needed: New policy goals. *American Forests* 94, no. 11/12: 59, 82–86.

———. 1990. Deforestation in the tropics. *Scientific American* 262, no. 4: 36–42.

RePPProT (Regional Physical Planning Programme for Transmigration). 1985. *Review of Phase Ib Results, Central Kalimantan*. London and Jakarta: Land Resources Development Centre, Overseas Development Administration (ODA), Foreign and Commonwealth Office, and Government of Indonesia (GOI).

———. 1987a. *Review of Phase I Results, East and South Kalimantan*. London and Jakarta: Overseas Development Administration (ODA) and Government of Indonesia (GOI).

———. 1987b. *Review of Phase I Results, West Kalimantan*. London and Jakarta: Overseas Development Administration (ODA) and Government of Indonesia (GOI).

Ross, M. S. 1984. Forestry in land use policy for Indonesia. Ph.D. thesis, Oxford University.

Salleh Mohd. Nor. 1988. Forest management. In *Key environments: Malaysia*, ed. Earl of Cranbrook, 126–137. Oxford: Pergamon Press in collaboration with the International Union for Conservation of Nature and Natural Resources.

Salleh Mohd. Nor, and Hashim Mohd. Nor. 1982. Plantations: Are we creating a sterile system? In *Ecological basis for rational resource utilization in the humid tropics (1) South East Asia: Proceedings of a workshop at Universiti Pertanian Malaysia, January 1982*, ed. Kamis Awang, S. S. Lee, F. S. Lai, Abdul Rahman Mohd. Darus, and Shellah Ali Abud, 140–144. Paris: UNESCO/MAB-UNEP.

Sarawak Update. 1990. Sustainable forest management: A demonstration of cooperation. *Asia Pacific Forest Industries*, December: 8–17.

Sather, C. 1990. Trees and tree tenure in Paku Iban society: The management of secondary forest resources in a long-established Iban community. *Borneo Review* 1: 16–40.

Sayogyo. 1975. *Usaha perbaikan gizi keluarga: ANP evaluation study, 1973* [Efforts to improve family nutrition: ANP evaluation study, 1973]. Bogor, Indonesia: Lembaga Penelitian Sosiôlogi Pedesan, Institut Pertanian Bogor.

Schindele, W., and W. Thoma. 1989. *Investigation of the steps needed to rehabilitate the areas of East Kalimantan seriously affected by fire*. GTZ–ITTO, Proposal for a pilot project for forest rehabilitation after fire in East Kalimantan. FR-Report No. 10.

Schindele, W., W. Thoma, and K. Panzer. 1989. *Investigation of the steps needed to rehabilitate the areas of East Kalimantan seriously affected by fire*. GTZ-ITTO, The Kalimantan Forest Fire 1982–3 in East Kalimantan Part I: The Fire, the Effects, the Damage and Technical Solutions. FR-Report No. 5.

Schmidt, R. C. 1991. Tropical rain forest management: A status report. In *Rain forest regeneration and management*, ed. Arturo Gomez-Pompa, Timothy C. Whitmore, and Malcolm Hadley, 181–207. Man and the Biosphere Series, v.6. Paris: UNESCO.

Seibert, J. 1990. Aspects of agroforestry for lowland humid areas with low population densities, the example of East Kalimantan, Indonesia. In *Symposium on Agroforestry Systems and Technologies, Bogor, Indonesia, 19–21 September 1989*, ed. Junus Kartasubrata, Sitti Soetarmi Tjitrosomo, and Ruben C. Umaly, 147–156. BIOTROP Special Publication no. 39. Bogor, Indonesia: SEAMEO BIOTROP, Southeast Asian Center for Tropical Biology.

Sham Sani. 1987. *Urbanization and the atmospheric environment in the low tropics: Experiences from the Kelang valley region, Malaysia*. Bangi, Selangor: Penerbit Universiti Kebangsaan Malaysia.

Siaran perangkaan tahunan [Annual statistical bulletin]. Annual. Kuala Lumpur, Malaysia: Government Printing Office.

Siaran perangkaan tahunan-Sabah [Annual statistical bulletin: Sabah]. Annual. Kota Kinabalu, Malaysia: Jabatan Perangkaan.

Siaran perangkaan tahunan-Sarawak [Annual statistical bulletin: Sarawak]. Annual. Kuching: Jabatan Perangkaan.

Soekotjo. 1981. Diameter growth of residual stands in logged over areas in East Kalimantan tropical rain forest, Indonesia. Ph.D. dissertation, Michigan State University, East Lansing, Michigan.

Statistik Indonesia [Statistical yearbook of Indonesia]. 1990. Jakarta: Biro Pusat Statistik.

Statistik perdagangan luar negeri Indonesia: Ekspor [Indonesian foreign trade statistics: Exports]. Annual. Jakarta: Biro Pusat Statistik.

Stowe, R. C. 1987. United States foreign policy and the conservation of natural resources: The case of tropical deforestation. *Natural Resources Journal* 27: 55–101.

Sukardjo, S. 1990. The secondary forest of Tanah Grogot, East Kalimantan, Indonesia. In *The plant diversity of Malesia: Proceedings of the Flora Malesiana Symposium commemorating Professor C. G. G. J. van Steenis, Leiden, August 1989*, ed. Pieter Baas, Kees Kalkman, and Rob Geesink, 213–224. Dordrecht: Kluwer Academic Publishers.

Sutton, K. 1989. Malaysia's FELDA land settlement model in time and space. *Geoforum* 20: 339–354.

Thang, H. 1990. Forest conservation and management practices in Malaysia. Paper presented at the workshop on Realistic Strategies for Tropical Forests, in conjunction with the 18th session of the IUCN General Assembly, Perth, 28 November–5 December.

Thompson, G. P. 1985. New faces, new opportunities: The environmental movement goes to business school. *Environment* 27, no. 4 (May): 6–11, 30.

Timber Trade Review [Warta Perdagangan Kayu]. Quarterly. Kuala Lumpur.

Vayda, A., and A. Sahur. 1985. Forest clearing and pepper farming by Bugis migrants in East Kalimantan: Antecedents and impact. *Indonesia* 39: 93–110.

Vincent, J. R. 1988. Malaysia: Key player in international trade. *Journal of Forestry* 86, no. 12: 32–35.

———. 1990. Rent capture and the feasibility of tropical forest management. *Land Economics* 66: 212–223.

Whitmore, Timothy C. 1984. *Tropical rain forests of the Far East*. 2nd edn. Oxford: Oxford University Press.

———. 1990. *An introduction to tropical rain forests*. Oxford: Clarendon Press.

———. 1991 . Tropical rain forest dynamics and its implications for management. In *Rain forest regeneration and management*, ed. Arturo Gomez-Pompa, Timothy C. Whitmore, and Malcolm Hadley, 67–89. Man and the Biosphere Series, v.6. Paris: UNESCO.

Wirawan, N. 1993. The hazard of fire. In *South-East Asia's environmental future: The search for sustainability*, ed. Harold Brookfield and Yvonne Byron, 242–262. Tokyo and Kuala Lumpur: United Nations University Press and Oxford University Press.

Wood, William B. 1990. Tropical deforestation: Balancing regional development demands and global environmental concerns. *Global Environmental Change: Human and Policy Dimensions* 1, no. 1: 23–41.

Woods, P. 1987. Drought and fires in tropical forests in Sabah: An analysis of rainfall patterns and some ecological effects. In *Proceedings of the Third International Round Table Conference, Samarinda, 16–20 April 1985*, ed. A. J. G. H. Kostermans, 367–387. Jakarta: UNESCO.

———. 1989. Effects of logging, drought and fire on structure and composition of tropical forests in Sabah, Malaysia. *Biotropica* 21: 290–298.

World Bank. 1988. *Indonesia: The transmigration program in perspective, Country Study*. Washington DC: World Bank.

———. 1989. Indonesia: Strategies for sustained development of tree crops (rubber, coconut and oil palm). Unpublished.

———. 1990. *Indonesia: Sustainable development of forest, land and water*. Bangkok: Country Dept V, Asia Regional Office, World Bank.

———. 1991. *World development report 1991*. Washington DC: World Bank.

World Rainforest Movement, and Sahabat Alam Malaysia. 1990. *The battle for Sarawak's forests*. 2nd edn. Penang, Malaysia: Sahabat Alam Malaysia.

World Resources Institute. 1988. *World resources 1988–89: An assessment of the resource base that supports the global community*. New York: Basic Books.

———. 1990. *World resources 1990–91: An assessment of the resource base that supports the global community*. Washington DC: World Resources Institute.

Yearbook of Forest Products. Annual. Rome: Food and Agriculture Organization of the United Nations.

11

Comparisons and conclusions

B. L. Turner II, Jeanne X. Kasperson, Roger E. Kasperson, Kirstin Dow, and William B. Meyer

The original impetus for this volume was the exploration of the concept of environmental criticality in a series of regional case-studies across the globe. During the exercise, the concept of criticality was refined by adding the categories of sustainability, impoverishment, and endangerment. Guiding our study were several central questions: (1) do critical environmental regions exist, as defined in chapter 1, and do certain regions popularly supposed to be in a state of environmental crisis meet the definition? (2) can we characterize and explain the human–environment interactions that have led to growing criticality; and (3) how have societies responded to emerging environmental degradation, and with what success? In addressing these questions, the various contributors to this volume have focused on environmental changes largely internal to each area (in our usage, "cumulative" change) and not on "systemic" global changes (such as climate change or stratospheric ozone depletion) that might, over the longer term, affect ecosystems and human life in the regions (Turner et al. 1990b). Eschewing narrow "geocentric" and "anthropocentric" approaches (see chap. 1), we have sought a more integrative assessment of the unfolding threats posed by environmental change over time. Attention to historical and regional contexts has been central in such assessments. The analyses that follow focus on changing regional trajectories in nature–society relationships and the "regional dynamics" of change that shape such trajectories.

Several aspects of this enquiry require clarification. Human use invariably alters an environment, an alteration that from a purely ecological or "geocentric" perspective may be interpreted as environmental degradation. But such human use often, perhaps even usually, increases the value of the environment, at least over the short run, by harnessing it for economic returns. Environmental degradation may follow, but so may a growing ability of the users to repair damage and sustain the environment. Thus, the capacity of society to respond, either through substitution in the productive system or through additions to the buffering capacity of the ecosystem, is a key consideration in judging the health of the nature–society relationship. Sustainable uses are those in which the environment can meet and absorb the human demands placed on it over the long run. Degradation and sustainability in this perspective are functions of economics as well as of the biophysical environment.

These considerations are not easy to apply in practice because of several complicating factors that qualify our assessments of the trajectories of and prospects for the nine regions dealt with in this volume. The growing role of interregional and international trade, and of external political control over local uses of the environment, geographically separates the human driving forces of change from their environmental impacts. The more "open" the use–environment system in our regions, as illustrated in figure 11.1, the more difficult it is to assess long-term trajectories of change and their ultimate consequences, in part because of the ability to change the regional use system, to substitute critical inputs from elsewhere, or to export degradation to other regions. (Such transfer of demands and impacts is possible, of course, only so long as other regions exist that are capable of absorbing them; the development of regionally unsustainable pressures in many areas simultaneously could conceivably accumulate to a global threat.)

Every region studied in this volume has experienced significant environmental alteration through increased human use, but almost every region (with the glaring and recent exception of the Aral region) has also enjoyed overall improvements in per capita wealth and well-being for most inhabitants. This result is not surprising; it is a pattern recurrent in history (see the regional studies in Turner et al. 1990a). The important considerations in judging the state of each region are the sustainability of the present use–environment relation-

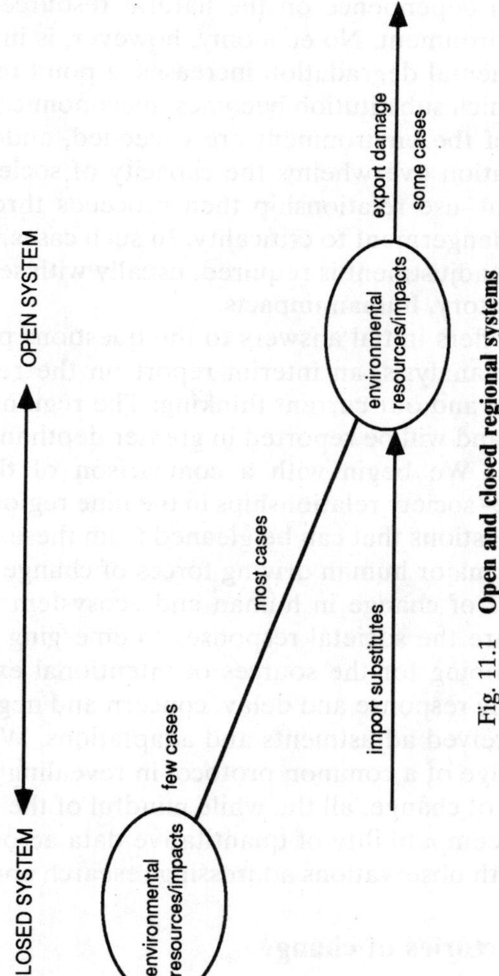

Fig. 11.1 Open and closed regional systems

ship and the range and diversity of options available to current and future human occupants. These options vary, of course, with both the physical and the political–economic environment. The resource base can continue to be severely degraded if the regional economy is sufficiently robust to provide substitutes or if it becomes increasingly disengaged from dependence on the natural resources and sinks of the regional environment. No economy, however, is infinitely robust, and, if environmental degradation increases, a point must eventually be reached at which substitution becomes uneconomical, the assimilative capacities of the environment are exceeded, and/or the rate or scale of degradation overwhelms the capacity of society to respond. The environment–use relationship then proceeds through impoverishment and endangerment to criticality. In such cases, major restructuring or human adjustment is required, usually with severe, although sometimes transitory, human impacts.

This chapter offers initial answers to the questions posed above. It is a preliminary analysis, an interim report on the results from the nine case-studies and our current thinking. The regional analyses are still in progress and will be reported in greater depth in a forthcoming series of books. We begin with a comparison of the patterns of change in nature–society relationships in the nine regions and the generic issues or questions that can be gleaned from these patterns. Next, we consider the major human driving forces of change in each region and the patterns of change in human and ecosystem vulnerabilities. Then we compare the societal responses to emerging environmental degradation, probing for the sources of intentional exploitation and mitigation, timely response and delay, concern and neglect, and effective and ill-conceived adjustments and adaptations. We go on to discuss the advantage of a common protocol in revealing broad patterns and trajectories of change, all the while mindful of the constraints imposed by the incompatibility of quantitative data across case-studies. We conclude with observations addressing research and public policy.

Regional trajectories of change

Although lacking thorough and comparable quantitative data, the nine case-studies do provide information about broader human–environment trends threatening the human occupation or use of the regions. They permit estimation of general aggregate trends in environmental change, per capita well-being, and the sustainability of the current human–environment interactions for each region.

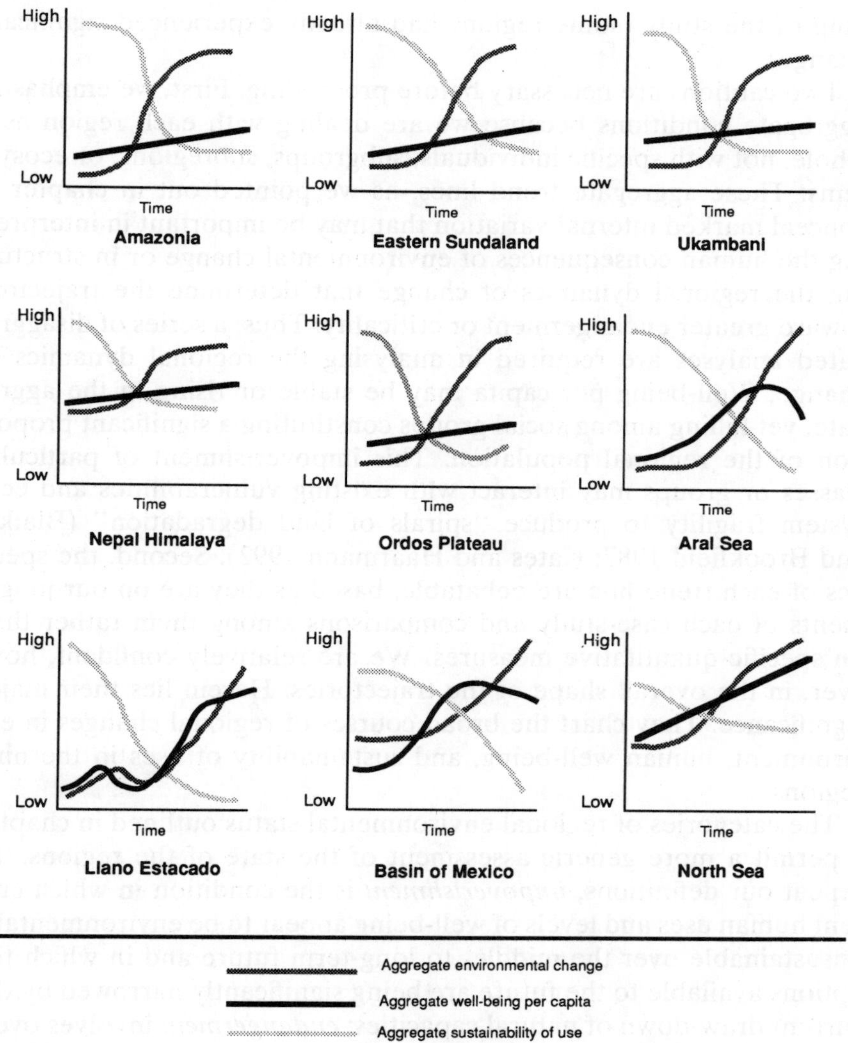

Fig. 11.2 **Regional changes in environment, human well-being, and sustainability of uses**

These aggregate trends are graphed in figure 11.2, where the X-axis is the time-period of the trend lines (approximately 50 years ago to present), and the Y-axis is the amount of environmental change, the level of per capita well-being, and the judged long-term sustainability of human uses. The height at which the trend lines begin along the Y-axis indicates the relative position of each at the time of the beginning of the study (some regions had already experienced significant change).

Two cautions are necessary before proceeding. First, we emphasize aggregate conditions because we are dealing with each region as a whole, not with specific individuals, subgroups, subregions, or ecosystems. These aggregate trend lines, as we pointed out in chapter 1, conceal marked internal variation that may be important in interpreting the human consequences of environmental change or in structuring the regional dynamics of change that determine the trajectory toward greater endangerment or criticality. Thus, a series of disaggregated analyses are required in analysing the regional dynamics of change. Well-being per capita may be stable or rising in the aggregate, yet falling among social groups constituting a significant proportion of the regional population. This impoverishment of particular classes or groups may interact with existing vulnerabilities and ecosystem fragility to produce "spirals of land degradation" (Blaikie and Brookfield 1987; Kates and Haarmann 1992). Second, the specifics of each trend line are debatable, based as they are on our judgements of each case-study and comparisons among them rather than on specific quantitative measures. We are relatively confident, however, in the overall shape of the trajectories. Herein lies their major significance. They chart the broad courses of regional changes in environment, human well-being, and sustainability of uses in the nine regions.

The categories of regional environmental status outlined in chapter 1 permit a more generic assessment of the state of the regions. To repeat our definitions, *impoverishment* is the condition in which current human uses and levels of well-being appear to be environmentally unsustainable over the middle- to long-term future and in which the options available to the future are being significantly narrowed by the current draw-down of natural capacities; *endangerment* involves overall human uses of the environment that appear to be unsustainable over the near term (this and the next generation) in the absence of radical adjustments in their scale or composition; *criticality* is the condition in which the environment has been so seriously degraded that the human condition (wealth and well-being) is already deteriorating as a direct consequence of environmental changes. Any condition not categorized as one of the above is judged to be *sustainable*. No representatives of this last category occur among our nine regions, which is not surprising given that they were selected because they showed strong indications of unsustainability. As these definitions suggest, the imminence of consequences is a central consideration in this analysis, whereas the steepness of, and possible non-linearities in, the trajectory of human–environment relationships are key factors in an assessment of such imminence.

Human uses of a regional environment require certain inputs and offer certain returns. A human use becomes unsustainable if the cost of the inputs rises or the value of the returns falls to a sufficient degree and if the deficit is not made up from some other source. A region is environmentally threatened if human-induced environmental changes have made the current use unsustainable either at present or in the likely near- to medium-term future and if no alternative use exists that would sustain the same level of wealth and well-being. In this relational view, the maintenance of a region over time depends primarily on two factors: (1) the return available from the use of the environment, and (2) the availability of subsidies to make up the difference if the net return of the use is inadequate. (Such "subsidies" can include the externalization of costs to marginal groups that have little say in decisions.) We term the first factor "environmental recoverability" and the second "sustainability of use costs." Changing nature–society conditions (impoverishment, endangerment, criticality) can result from a decline in "environmental recoverability" as a result of the draw-down of the environmental resource base, possibly exacerbated by a decline in the "sustainability of use costs" for any of a number of reasons (such as decline in the political power of the region, decline in regional wealth, or change in terms of trade). The three states of increasing environmental threat (impoverishment, endangerment, and criticality) are characterized by different trajectories and relationships in the two trend lines. Figure 11.3 illustrates the movement of a hypothetical region from sustainability to criticality through deterioration in both recoverability and sustainability of costs, whereas figure 11.4 suggests how these trends relate to emerging environmental criticality. Figure 11.5 depicts our judgements as to these trends in our nine regions and their trajectories toward greater endangerment and criticality. Table 11.1, in turn, provides an overview of our judgements concerning the current states of nature–society trajectories in the nine regions and the degree of confidence we have in the probable accuracy of our judgements.

It may be that all nine of the regions in this study (and perhaps almost every inhabited region in the world), if recent past or current trends were to continue unabated, would soon enter some stage of

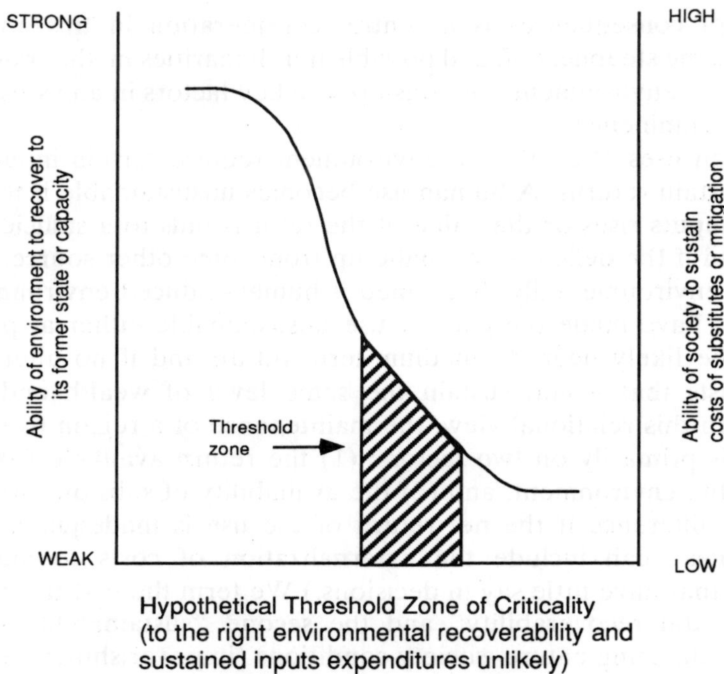

Fig. 11.3 **Regional movement to environmental criticality**

impoverishment or endangerment. In this sense, every region is one in which some level of long-term endangerment exists. In assigning a regional case to one of our categories of impoverishment–endangerment–criticality, we have judged the likelihood that recent trends will continue, whether they can be altered by feasible adjustments, and whether such human adjustments are possible in a time-frame to prevent the onset of severe consequences. Obviously, such judgements are debatable and our analyses envision them as heuristic and suggestive rather than conclusive. Ideally such assessments should move from these subjective assessments to more quantitative expressions of particular indicators.

Human adjustments, often leading to partial recovery from the environmental damage and to total recovery or even improvement in human well-being, have been common throughout human history. Viewed over the short run, the trajectories of environmental and social change may appear to be inexorable, but, over the long run, regions typically display a fluctuating long-wave path in which

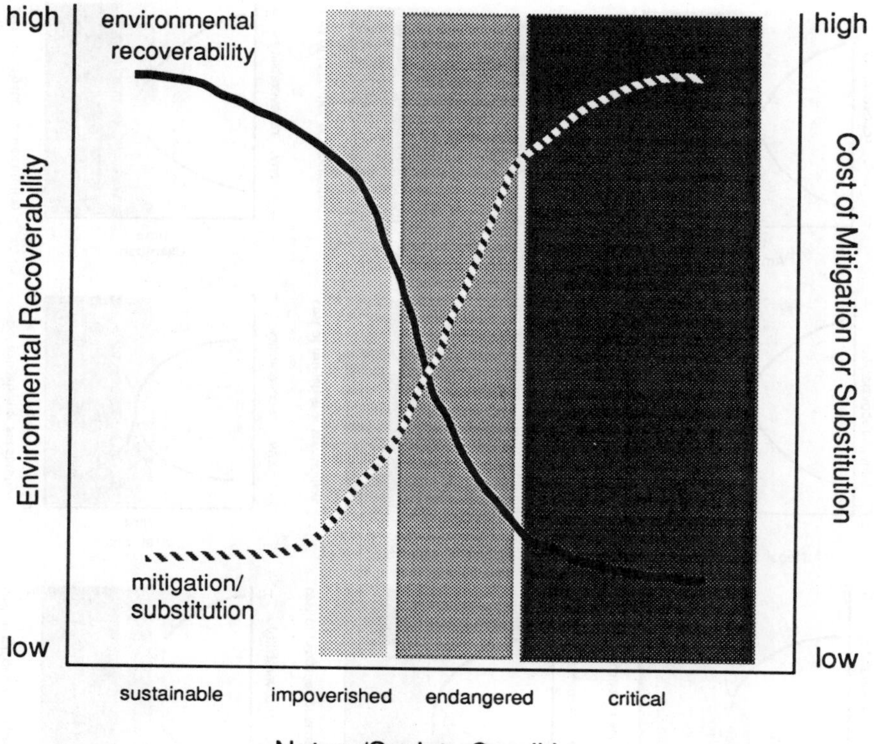

Fig. 11.4 **Regional trajectories and emerging criticality**

environmental deterioration and social well-being are linked, only to be followed by a social rebound (e.g. Berry 1991; Whitmore et al. 1990).

The studies in this volume, it should be emphasized, assess regional, not global, environmental implications. This regional emphasis can lead to assessments that differ from some conventional wisdom about the planet as a whole. For example, we do not consider the possible contribution of deforestation to global climate change, or the cutting of tropical old-growth forests in terms of potential long-term economic losses resulting from a decrease in biodiversity. Local users rarely make decisions in terms of global environmental implications, and evaluating long-term potential losses from decreased biotic diversity is a highly speculative exercise at this time. On the other

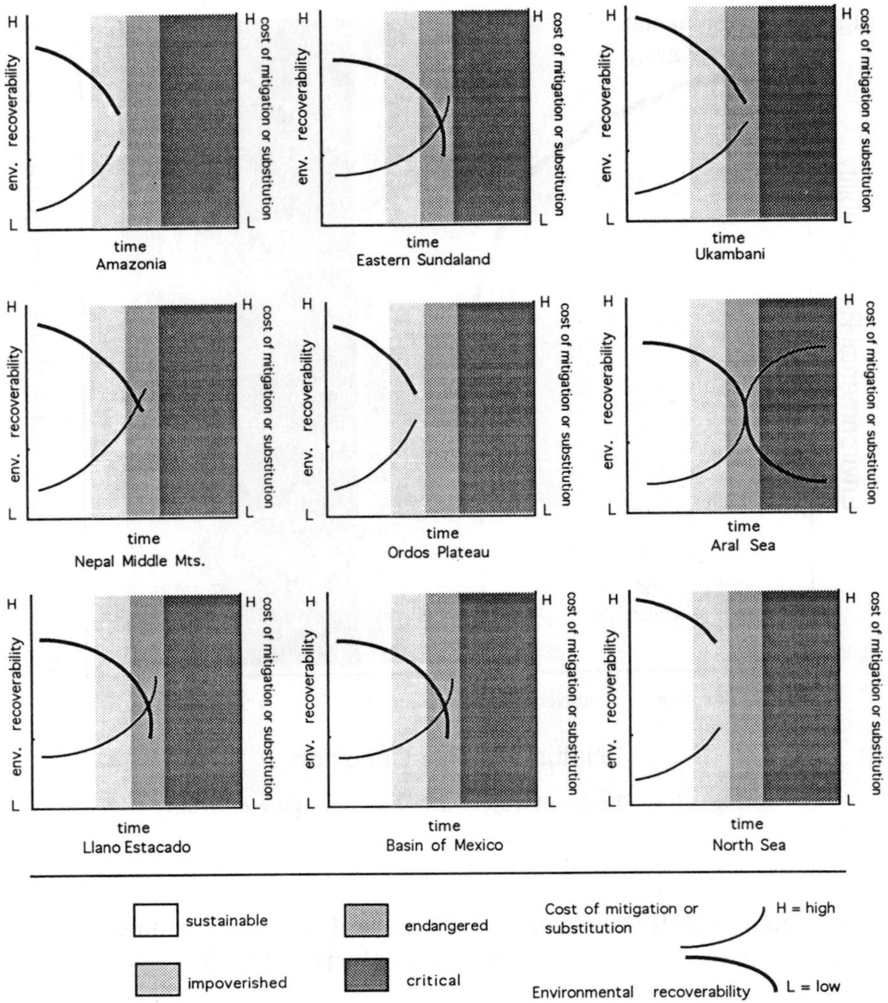

Fig. 11.5 **Regional trajectories of environmental recoverability and the sustainability of use costs**

hand, we are concerned with the long-term implications associated with the rapid draw-down of nature that is so common in our regional cases and the associated impacts on the security and well-being of future generations. With these considerations in mind, we turn to our individual regional studies for brief characterizations by which to interpret figures 11.2 and 11.4 and table 11.1.

Table 11.1 **Comparison of the status of the nine regions**

Region	Status: Impoverished	Endangered	Critical
Amazonia	√√**		
Sundaland	√√	√***	
Ukambani	√√*	√*	
Nepal middle mountains	√√	√√**	
Ordos Plateau	√√**		
Aral Sea	√√	√√	√√***
Llano Estacado	√√	√*	
Basin of Mexico	√√	√√*	
North Sea	√√***		

√ = partial √√ = broad-based
*** = high, ** = medium, * = low degree of confidence that classification is correct
Note: a low level of confidence implies that the evidence is sufficiently inconsistent or uncertain to lead to different outcomes.

Amazonia

Environmental change has been rapid and significant indeed in Amazonia. The foremost impact has been deforestation as a result of cropland and grassland/pasture expansion, timber extraction, and flooding for hydroelectric power reservoirs. The rate of land-cover change may, however, be slowing. In addition, mining (largely small-scale gold prospecting) has released toxic chemicals into the drainage system, affecting water quality and, potentially, the health of downstream populations.

Consequent changes in human well-being are difficult to assess because most of the region's inhabitants are recent in-migrants, many of whom are fleeing poverty elsewhere, and because of the differing economic situations of large landowners, smallholders, and indigenous peoples. For these reasons, and considering the rapid population growth in this region, a low-growth trend in human well-being is appropriate. The sustainability of use decreased markedly in the initial rush to develop the region, but it may now be approaching stabilization in some production activities (e.g. agriculture and livestock-raising). Given the demonstration that ecologically and economically sustainable systems of production are possible and the potential slowing of the pace of deforestation, Amazonia may prove a classic case of a frontier that experiences a transition to more settled and sustainable conditions. Much depends upon interventions that are only beginning. Also, as Smith and his colleagues indicate, multiple trajectories are at work within the Amazon, some leading to greater and some to less environmental degradation, whereas overall well-being, except among indigenous groups, continues to increase.

Based on these findings, we assign Amazonia to the environmentally impoverished category. The pace of deforestation (which recent information, e.g. Bonalume 1991, suggests may in any case have been much slower than previously thought) appears to have slackened and uses have emerged that appear better attuned to the environment. It remains to be seen whether the slower pace of change, improvements in land management, and an enhanced ability to sustain the costs of inputs for land-use development will continue.

Eastern Sundaland

Like Amazonia, eastern Sundaland has witnessed rapid environmental change and considerable variation in the associated consequences for different social groups. The primary environmental impacts are substantial deforestation and associated soil degradation (from compaction); the cut-over forest also becomes highly susceptible to fires (from both human and natural sources) and the loss in biodiversity is notable.

The immediate sources of deforestation are timber extraction and agricultural development. The former as it is currently practised (especially in Borneo) appears to be unsustainable; its scale and pace far outstrip replanting or natural regeneration. The bountiful economic rewards derived by the timber companies, local loggers, and timber mill workers from the "mining" of the forest cannot long continue. Much of Borneo (except Sabah) is endangered, but a caveat is in order. Deforestation is taking place in sparsely occupied areas (to the detriment, certainly, of the native inhabitants) that are likely to reforest. Of course, the new-growth forest will not be the same as the old, but it is not clear that the future environment will be significantly more hostile to human use than it was before logging, save locally where some soil degradation is bound to occur. Agricultural development activities suggest another story. Systems being adopted, especially tree estates, appear to be ecologically suitable, although more time is needed to determine if they will be economically sustainable as well.

Overall, therefore, our trend line for the sustainability of uses in the region internalizes two very different cases: logging and agriculture. Both activities have led to considerable environmental change, although the change attributable to agriculture is considered benign compared with that of logging. The latter, in terms of its pace, magnitude, and management, is devastating, with two caveats: much of the population appears to benefit from a significant "trickle down" of economic gains, the ultimate impacts of which are not known, and much of the deforestation is taking place in relatively remote areas that may regain forest, albeit not the mature growth that has been and is being cut. The loss of biodiversity, however, could have long-term regional implications, removing a significant environmental asset for the future. Meanwhile, societal responses to halt the depletion of these old-growth forests are dilatory and still quite ineffective. Finally, it is uncertain whether the agricultural systems that are emerging will be economically sustainable.

For these conflicting reasons, we consider the region as a whole to be in an early stage of partial endangerment. By this we mean that the pace, magnitude, and management of timber extraction – widespread as it is throughout the region – appear to be creating conditions ripe for a large-scale future collapse or ultimate decay of the regional environment and economy.

Ukambani (south-eastern Kenya)

Ukambani has witnessed a major shift in land uses from those based largely on pastoralism to increasingly intensive cultivation. Farmers have increasingly moved down-slope from the wetter highlands into semi-arid Ukambani seeking land and livelihood. The accumulation of land pressures has made it impossible to continue the multiple uses practised in the past, including the use of different niches at different times of the year. It has increasingly forced resource-poor farmers to sustain themselves on fixed portions of semi-arid land, with mixed results. On the better land, some farmers have prospered, becoming successful large-holders with improved, intensive cultivation. Other farmers, on more marginal land, have been less fortunate, lacking the resources and labour to make land improvements. Their lands display numerous indicators of environmental degradation – soil erosion, deforestation, overgrazing, and loss of soil moisture and biodiversity. Given the variability in rainfall, periodic famines have been recurrent (1946, 1951–1952, 1961, and 1984–1985). Owing to these mixed results, we characterize this region also as in early endangerment, but it appears to be at a crucial juncture from which it could move in its trajectory either toward greater stabilization or to greater endangerment.

The Nepal middle mountains

Recent environmental changes in the Nepal middle mountains have been significant, but geographically variable. They have largely been those associated with land-use intensification lacking adequate inputs: cropland and pasture degradation, deforestation, and (probably) increased irregularity of water flow through drainage systems, an important impediment to irrigation.

Unlike Amazonia and eastern Sundaland, the middle mountain zone of the Nepalese Himalayas has had a substantial and growing population for over 100 years. Until recently, production was principally for consumption rather than for the market. The environmental impacts of the past several decades reflect changes in the agricultural system: a shift to market production on improved land, and intensified and expanded consumption production by marginal farmers and herders on less productive and more fragile land. The economic consequences of commercialization, of course, have not been uniform and, because much of the wealth generated ends up highly concentrated in Nepal or outside the region (especially in India), material well-being has not kept pace with the scale of production changes. The predominantly rural population remains in desperate economic straits but probably better off in several respects (e.g. health, social services) than in previous periods. Many of these changes are marked by environmental degradation, but as yet no indication exists of an impending overall collapse of the regional human use–environment system. Meanwhile, conflicting evidence points to both continued environmental degradation and some adjustments that are lowering the rate of degradation. This case, therefore, is one of endangerment.

Ordos Plateau

The Ordos Plateau region has witnessed significant changes in human–environment relations in a sensitive environment. The expansion and intensification of agriculture have caused a decline in grassland cover, which, in turn, has promoted soil degradation. Large-scale gully erosion dominates the landscape. The loss in sustained annual vegetation (and especially grassland cover) has contributed to wind erosion and increased "sandification" (the spread of sand-dunes), which, in turn, threatens livestock and agricultural land. The introduction of woollen industries has intensified livestock production and grassland degradation throughout the region. Industrial and population growth have depleted groundwater supplies, while coalmining has generated surface water pollution in parts of the eastern Ordos. Central state policies have intentionally promoted migration, cultivation, and industrial development in the Ordos but have been less successful in dealing with environmental impacts or their immediate human causes.

Although the human forces of change have slowed since 1978, and various measures have been adopted to combat degradation, it is not clear that the loss of key resources (soil and grass cover) has yet abated sufficiently, or that enough will be done in the near term to offset the trajectory of these losses and to put the system on a more sustainable path. Owing to this uncertainty, and the facts that some indicators of well-being (health, education) are improving and that some effective societal responses are occurring, we classify the Ordos Plateau as an impoverished zone, though a greater degree of endangerment is likely unless recent trends of environmental response, better land management, and economic growth continue.

Aral Sea

The Aral Sea case is one of criticality by any measure. Massive environmental degradation has taken place in land cover, water discharge, and water and soil pollution, mainly through the desiccation of the sea itself and the associated devastation of the human population and regional economy. The environmental impacts have been documented in detail. The irrigation system overtaxes the availability of water, leading to losses in irrigated land and to major shortfalls in the amount of fresh water entering the Aral Sea (virtually none at certain times of the year). Much of the sea has dried up, and its once lucrative fishing industry has been destroyed. With the sea's moderating influence on the local climate diminished, less precipitation falls and more sand storms occur, with wind-blown salts from the exposed sea floor degrading regional grasslands and contaminating water as far away as the drainage headwaters. Meanwhile, the chemical-based agricultural system has severely polluted soil and drinking water and, along with wind-blown salts, has apparently produced major health problems, increased infant mortality, and even premature deaths. In face of these major problems, however, the region has grown significantly in population and in material infrastructure (e.g. urban areas, buildings, roads).

The massive irrigation systems that have brought on these impacts cannot be sustained, and a scaling back of cultivation must ultimately occur. Per capita well-being has been dropping, particularly in terms of severe health problems associated with pollution. Whereas adjustments are necessary and are likely to occur eventually, they will have to be of a major magnitude (even, perhaps, an international rescue effort) to arrest the rapid movement to regional catastrophe. Meanwhile, the societal capability to respond to the situation, in view of the breakup of the former Soviet Union, the disarray of the regional economy, and political disintegration within the region, has plummeted in relation to the rapidly accumulating disaster.

The Aral Sea case, therefore, meets the criteria of a critical region in our terminology. The environment has been devastated; much of the environmental damage cannot be repaired save at prohibitive cost or over the long run; the well-being of the region's population has been dropping precipitously owing to the environmental changes; and no solutions to rectify these conditions appear on the horizon. It should be noted, however, that these conditions have emerged after 30–40 years of sustained economic growth.

Llano Estacado

During this century, the semi-arid Llano Estacado has witnessed at least one and a half boom–bust cycles: expansion of agriculture, dust bowl, and return of agriculture. In the first cycle, rainfed cultivation and livestock-raising predominated. The draw-down of the regional aquifer largely supported the second boom, making possible an expansion of irrigated agriculture with substantial economic rewards. The major consequence of the change in land use has been severe stress on the southern Ogallala aquifer and on soils. Groundwater is being depleted at an increasing pace, and soil erosion has increased on exposed or degraded agricultural lands.

Aquifer depletion, the most significant form of environmental change in the region, raises issues of the longer-term sustainability of rural land use. It is obvious that the current mode of mining of the aquifer is not sustainable over the long run, and adjustments in the use of groundwater and other agriculture/livestock activities are already under way. Without changes in market conditions, however, new land-use practices may not be as economically rewarding as those of the recent boom. For this reason, we judge this region as partially endangered, with a growing overall risk of eventual regional collapse of the current rural land management practices. We add the "partial" qualifier because this region is part of a wealthy society that subsidizes it and because the regional population possesses substantial technological, institutional, and economic resources to engineer favourable outcomes in the face of serious environmental stresses.

Basin of Mexico

With a long history of modification, even transformation, the Basin of Mexico has been radically altered still further since the middle of this century by the growth of an industrial mega-city. The consequences of this massive urban–industrial development in an enclosed basin are ominous. Industrialization, including energy production and transportation, has created such extensive pollution that the air of the basin is literally unsafe to breathe and serious health problems have emerged. Surface water is widely contaminated. Water demand long ago exceeded the supply available within the basin, so much so that continuing and costly inputs are required to meet daily needs.

Owing to the extraordinary pace of in-migration and growing density of settlement, aggregate human per capita well-being in the basin is already dropping, even if it represents an improvement for many over the poverty from which they have migrated. Growing health problems represent an important dimension of environmental "biteback" and may portend the fate of many other emerging world megacities. Only radical adjustments will rectify these trends. Meanwhile, societal responses have been ineffective in that they have largely concentrated on mitigation rather than alteration of basic human driving forces or have sometimes even inadvertently accelerated the trajectory to criticality. For these reasons, one must consider the Basin of Mexico as at an advanced stage of endangerment, nearing criticality.

North Sea

Human actions have long transformed the rimlands of the North Sea. The major process of environmental change today is marine pollution from industrial and consumption activities. These activities threaten the age-old fishing industry and may also adversely affect health and recreation. It is clear that the sea as an ecological unit cannot much longer sustain the trajectory of human uses associated with advanced industrialization and urbanization. Ultimately, oil and gas under the sea will be depleted, with significant economic consequences for the rimlands (but consequences for which proven substitutes exist).

What makes this case somewhat different from the others is that the ecological degradation experienced does not fundamentally threaten the regional economy. The fishing industry and other productive uses of the sea, excepting oil and gas extraction, are not fundamental to the livelihoods of most inhabitants. The region has very high societal capability to respond to the degradation, and social mobilization in behalf of environmental issues is at a mature stage of development. Because of this wealth of the rimlands and the high overall societal capability to respond to the degradation, the North Sea is at most a case of environmental impoverishment. Indeed, the strongest implications of current trends are for future peoples rather than for current generations.

Human driving forces

The human causes of environmental change are numerous and interrelated. The extent to which any cause is present and the precise ways in which causes interact vary by location and through time. The search for cause is influenced by the way questions are posed and the "depth" of explanation sought. A single event of deforestation, for example, can be variously attributed to burning, agricultural expansion, population and market-driven land pressures, government policies towards population and markets, or international leverages on governments. What is a fundamental human cause in one analysis becomes merely a proximate or mediating cause if the question or level of analysis is redirected (Stern, Young, and Druckman 1992; Turner 1989).

Leaving aside this conceptual problem, the literature points to recurring sets or clusters of human driving forces – those facets of individuals and societies that significantly and directly influence the decisions that, intentionally or not, lead to actions that change the environment (e.g. Palo and Mery 1990). Various analysts and committees addressing the subject have synthesized these driving forces into several major clusters: population, technological capacity, affluence/poverty, political economy/structure, and beliefs/attitudes (Clark 1988;

Stern, Young, and Druckman 1992; Turner and Meyer 1991; WCED 1987).

The nine case-studies illustrate some of the variety in the relationship between driving forces and environmental change. Each case describes a particular set of variables (see table 11.2) that have interacted to create local and regional environmental change, as well as linking in some cases to systemic global change through greenhouse gas emissions or albedo change. Here we distill each case, using summary diagrams for illustration. The specific variables identified are associated with the clusters of driving forces that appear in table 11.2. Each case is treated in terms of the broad human forces of change identified. The case-studies do not treat all such forces; rather, attention is directed to those that most significantly affect the environment and the human occupance of the region. The discussion that follows first summarizes each of the cases, then assesses more general issues.

Amazonia (fig. 11.6)

The countries of the Amazon Basin suffer from poverty and foreign debt and seek the means to alleviate both. Amazonia is a region of immense mineral and biotic riches and its "frontier" development offers one means to improve the national economy and generate wealth for international and national investors (markets). Save for some local market demands, almost all of the forces of change lie outside the basin. They affect Amazonia primarily through governmental policy, which has promoted industrial and agricultural growth as well as migration into the region. The commercialization of agriculture and the agglomeration of landholdings outside Amazonia have promoted migration into the region, rapidly increasing its population. This population increase and exogenous investments have led to major increases in the use of land for livestock production, agriculture, mining, generation of hydroelectric power. and (more recently) extraction of timber.

Amazonia, therefore, is a case of a frontier invaded by forces of production and consumption partly in response to directly or indirectly state-created incentives and subsidies. Historically, extractive and environmentally damaging activities characterize such frontier invasions in the short run, but they often shift through time to activities that have less immediate extractive consequences. From a regional perspective, the forces of change may be slowing and their consequences moving toward less overall damage.

Table 11.2 **Human driving forces of environmental change: Association of specific variables from the case-studies with clusters of driving forces**

Cluster of human driving forces				
Population[a]	Technological capacity[b]	Affluence/poverty[c]	Political economy/structure[d]	Beliefs/attitudes[e]
Population growth	Irrigation development	Urbanization	International market	Frontier development
Migration	Mechanization	Poverty	National market	Ethnic/religious views
Natural growth	Fertilization		State policy	Mass-consuming view of nature
	Pasture improvement		Shift to commodity production	Acceptance of corruption
	Industrialization infrastructure		Foreign debt, balance of trade	
	Agricultural intensification		Resource allocation rules & institutions	
			Capital extraction	
			Political corruption	

a. Population: increase or decrease in number of people per unit area.
b. Technological capacity: movement to a different technology, including shifts in suites of technology.
c. Affluence/poverty: level of wealth of an area, generally measured by per capita consumption and well-being.
d. Political economy/structure: economic, political, and social institutions that govern resource and environmental use.
e. Beliefs/attitudes: ideas and norms of behaviour that underlie formal institutions.

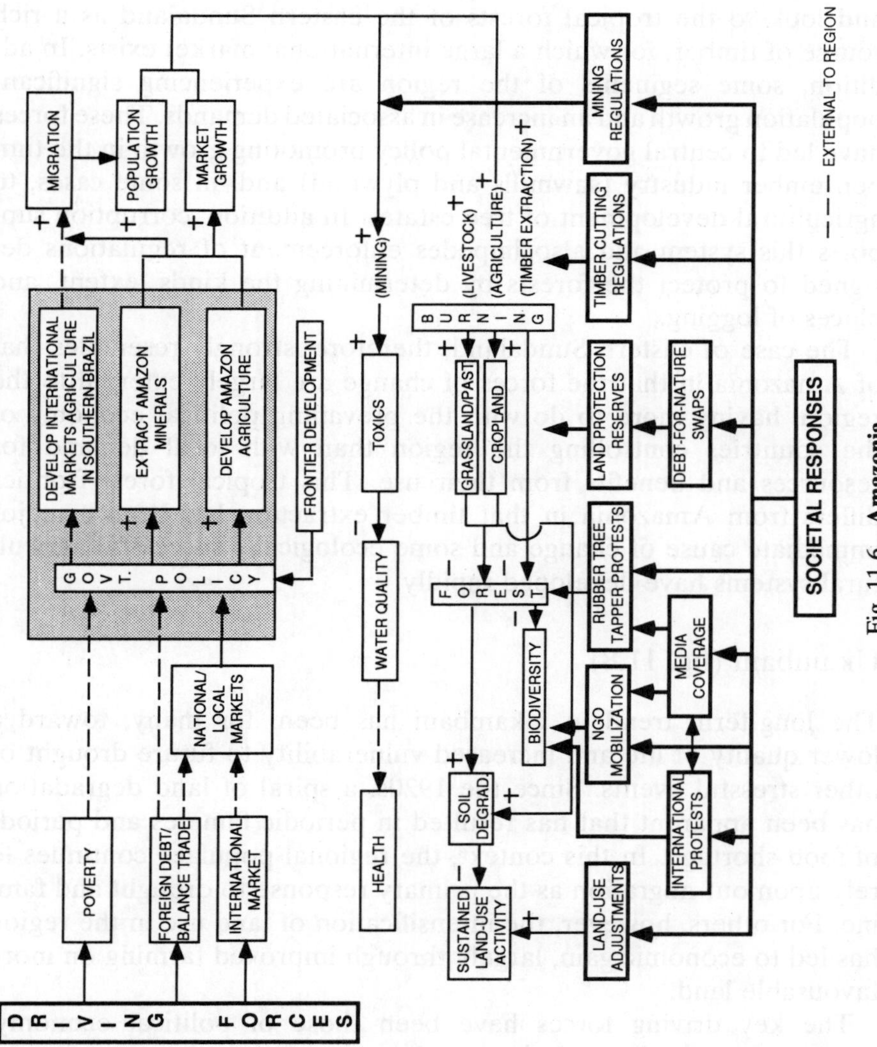
DRIVING FORCES
POVERTY
FOREIGN DEBT/ BALANCE TRADE
INTERNATIONAL MARKET
NATIONAL/ LOCAL MARKETS
GOVT. POLICY
DEVELOP INTERNATIONAL MARKETS AGRICULTURE IN SOUTHERN BRAZIL
EXTRACT AMAZON MINERALS
DEVELOP AMAZON AGRICULTURE
FRONTIER DEVELOPMENT
MIGRATION
POPULATION GROWTH
MARKET GROWTH
(MINING)
TOXICS
WATER QUALITY
HEALTH
BURNING
(LIVESTOCK)
(AGRICULTURE)
(TIMBER EXTRACTION)
GRASSLAND/PAST
CROPLAND
FOREST
BIODIVERSITY
SOIL DEGRAD.
SUSTAINED LAND-USE ACTIVITY
LAND-USE ADJUSTMENTS
INTERNATIONAL PROTESTS
NGO MOBILIZATION
MEDIA COVERAGE
RUBBER TREE TAPPER PROTESTS
LAND PROTECTION RESERVES
DEBT-FOR-NATURE SWAPS
TIMBER CUTTING REGULATIONS
MINING REGULATIONS
SOCIETAL RESPONSES
EXTERNAL TO REGION

Fig. 11.6 **Amazonia**

Eastern Sundaland (fig. 11.7)

The forces of change in eastern Sundaland are variable, showing differing degrees of impact and intensity in different parts of the region. All countries controlling the region espouse development strategies and look to the tropical forests of the eastern Sundaland as a rich source of timber, for which a large international market exists. In addition, some segments of the region are experiencing significant population growth and an increase in associated demands. These forces have led to central governmental policy promoting growth in the timber/lumber industry (sawmills and plywood) and, in some cases, to agricultural development of tree estates. In addition, corruption supports this system and also impedes enforcement of regulations designed to protect the forests by determining the kinds, extent, and places of logging.

The case of eastern Sundaland, therefore, strongly resembles that of Amazonia in that the forces of change are largely external to the region, having more to do with the prevailing political economy of the countries controlling the region than with local demand for resources and benefits from their use. This tropical forest frontier differs from Amazonia in that timber extraction has been a major immediate cause of change and some ecologically successful agricultural systems have developed rapidly.

Ukambani (fig. 11.8)

The long-term trend in Ukambani has been, for many, toward a lower quality of life and increased vulnerability to future drought or other stressful events. Since the 1920s, a spiral of land degradation has been apparent that has resulted in periodic famines and periods of food shortage. In this context, the regional populace continues to rely upon out-migration as the primary response to drought and famine. For others, however, the intensification of land use in the region has led to economic gain, largely through improved farming on more favourable land.

The key driving forces have been those of political economy. Changes in state intervention, land tenure, and settlement arrangements, and legal and policy initiatives for land use and management have largely guided the spiral of land degradation and food shortages. While population increase has been a factor, its contribution has largely been to exacerbate the effects of these other driving

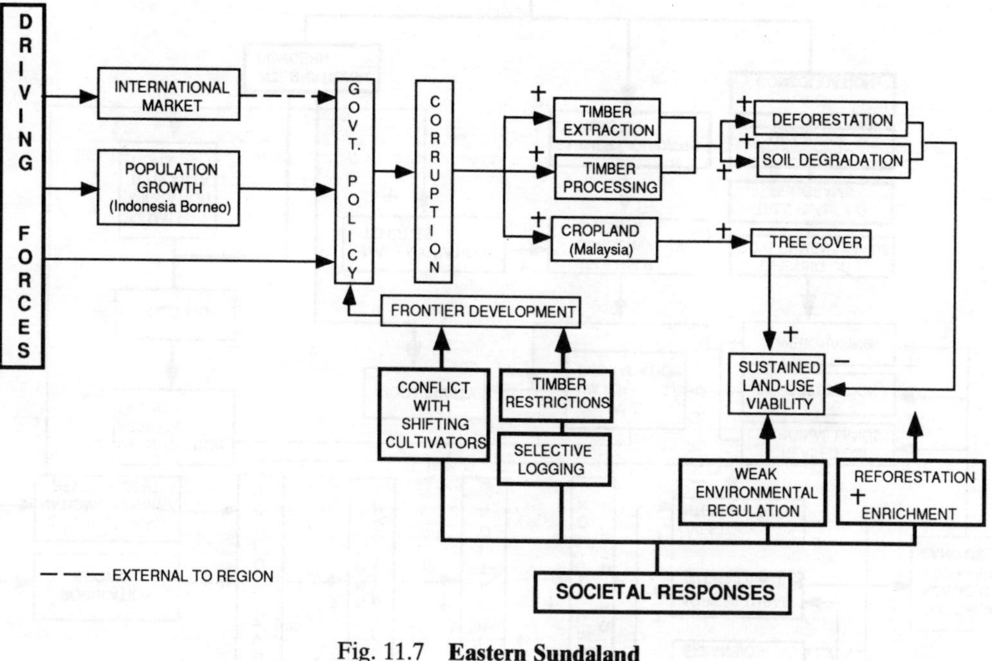

Fig. 11.7 **Eastern Sundaland**

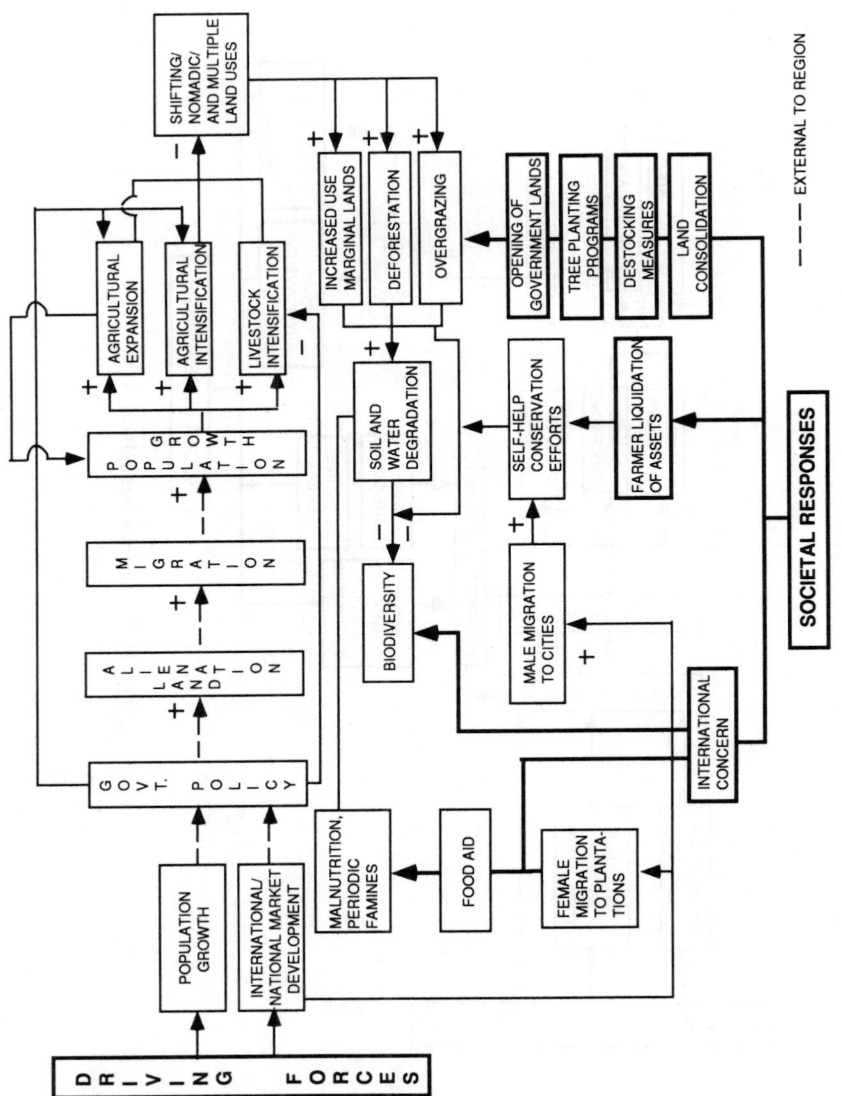

Fig. 11.8 Ukambani

forces. Land alienation to conserve resources for future use by the state or commercial interests has underlain much of the societal response to land degradation and propelled the trajectory to greater endangerment.

The Nepal middle mountains (fig. 11.9)

The middle mountains of Nepal, unlike the two frontier cases described above, have a long history of significant traditional occupance and use based on cultivation and pastoralism. Population and poverty have grown at the same time that the country has sought to develop markets to alleviate foreign debt and promote development. These forces have combined to influence a government policy of market-oriented development aided by subsidized infrastructure and technical inputs, as well as changed rules of resource allocation. Perhaps most important in this policy has been the dramatic shift from traditional rules of allocation (common property) to private ownership (cropland) and state control (e.g. protected forests), and the behavioural changes associated with the increasing commodity production (Ives and Messerli 1989; Jodha 1992). Concurrently, such services as health-care facilities have promoted rapid population growth.

The situation in the middle mountains of Nepal resembles that of many other regions experiencing a transition from traditional to capitalist economies. The disruptive impacts of this change are heightened here, however, by the high-energy environment of the Himalayas, as in other mountain environments (Jodha, Banskota, and Partap 1992).

Ordos Plateau (fig. 11.10)

The Ordos Plateau is an arid sandstone environment that has been a focus of development within a centrally planned economy. The goals of development have been to generate capital income for national development goals, to redress an unfavourable international balance of trade and foreign debt, and to settle farmers from the more crowded areas to the south. National strategies have promoted agricultural and industrial growth as well as in-migration. Population increases have led to significant land stresses, particularly through cropland expansion on natural grasslands and fuelwood harvesting. Agricultural and industrial growth has promoted intensive livestock

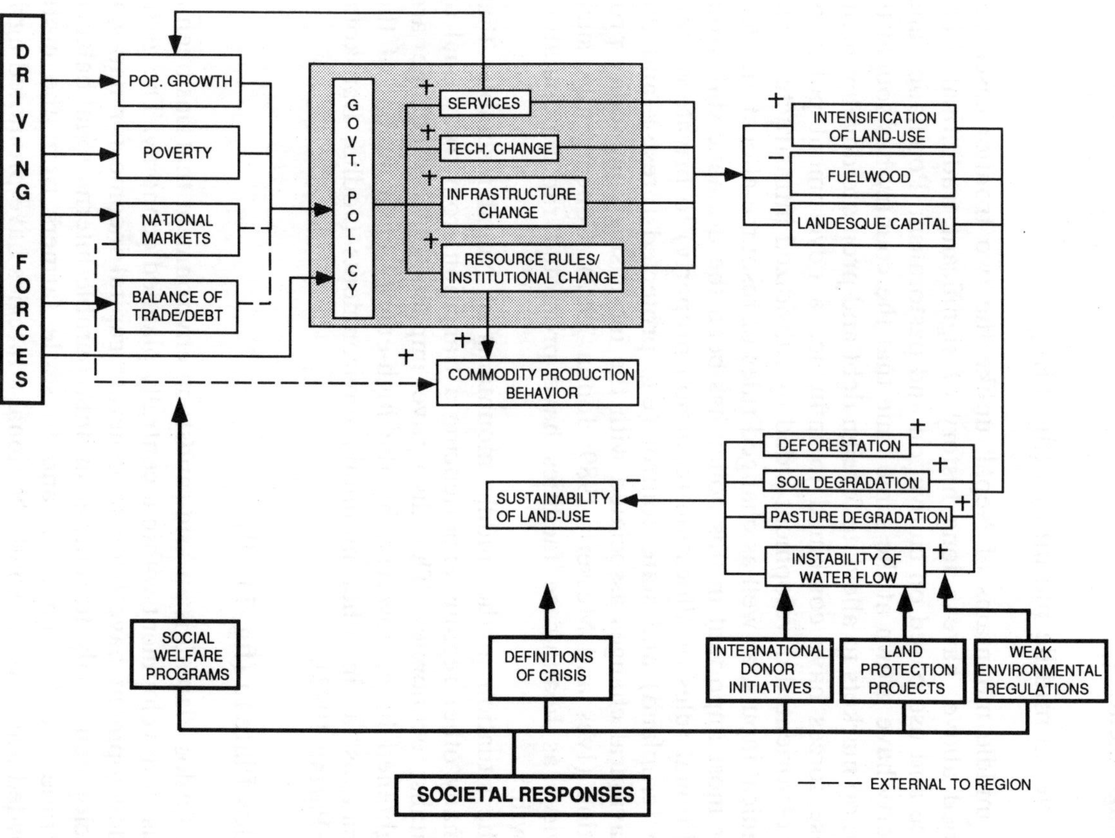

Fig. 11.9 **The Nepal middle mountains**

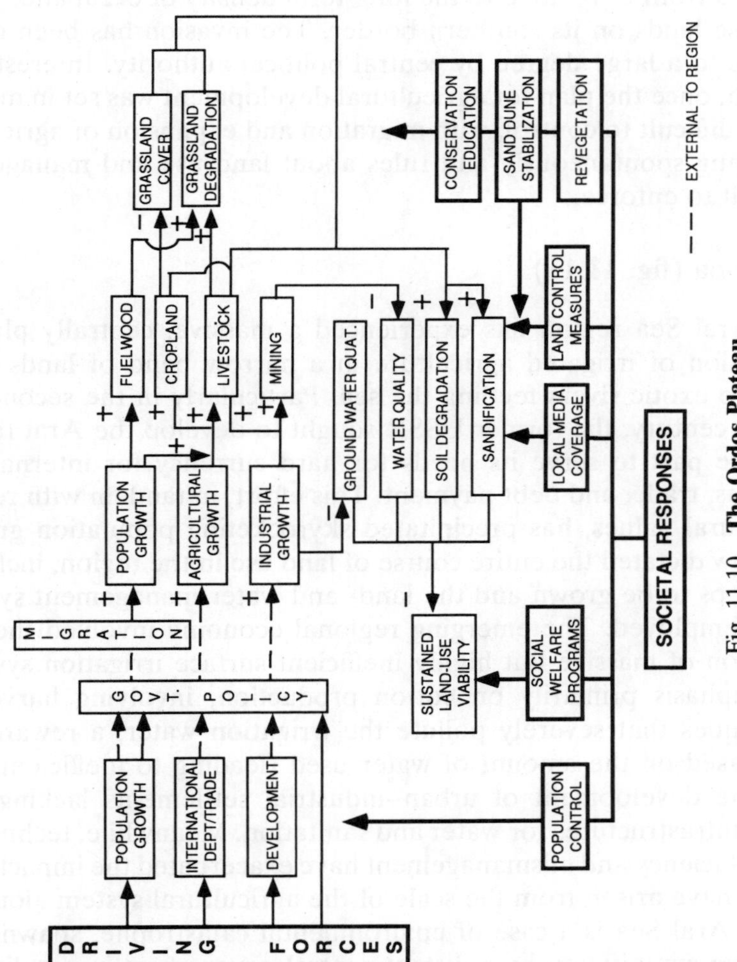

Fig. 11.10 The Ordos Plateau

production, particularly of sheep for the new wool industries. In addition, extensive coalmining has begun in various sections of the region, largely serving the needs of the Chinese state outside the Ordos proper.

The Ordos Plateau is a case of the invasion of an arid frontier region – a frontier relative to the long-term density of occupance of the Chinese lands on its southern border. The invasion has been orchestrated to a large degree by central political authority. Interestingly, though, once the plan for agricultural development was set in motion, it was difficult to control, with migration and expansion of agriculture occurring spontaneously and rules about land use and management difficult to enforce.

Aral Sea (fig. 11.11)

The Aral Sea region has experienced a massive, centrally planned expansion of irrigated agriculture in a narrow band of lands along the two exotic rivers feeding the sea. Particularly in the second half of this century, the former USSR sought to develop the Aral region, in large part to serve its needs for hard currency for international markets, trade, and debt payment. This effort, in tandem with regional cultural values, has precipitated skyrocketing population growth. Moscow dictated the entire course of land use in the region, including the crops to be grown and the land- and water-management systems to be employed. The emerging regional economy involved the construction of massive but highly inefficient surface irrigation systems, an emphasis primarily on cotton production, involving harvesting techniques that severely pollute the irrigation water, a reward system based on the amount of water used (leading to inefficient use), and the development of urban–industrial settlements lacking adequate infrastructures for water and sanitation. Meanwhile, technological inefficiency and mismanagement have exacerbated the impacts that would have arisen from the scale of the agricultural system alone.

The Aral Sea is a case of environmental catastrophe, spawned by knowing exploitation by a distant central government in a politically marginal region. It suggests the kinds of problems that can occur in marginal areas of a political economy considered expendable by the centre. It is unique among our regions in that the main locus of change – exploitation by the central government in the USSR – has evaporated. The process of environmental degradation that it set in motion, however, remains uncorrected.

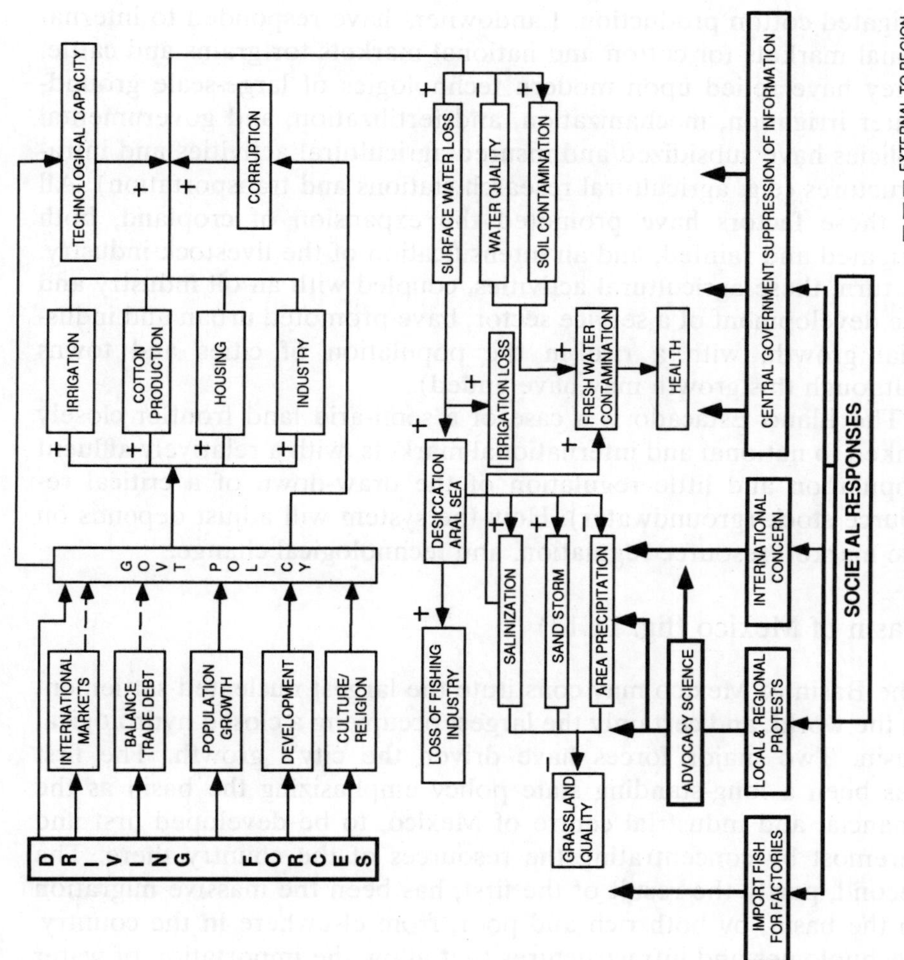

Fig. 11.11 The Aral Sea

Llano Estacado (fig. 11.12)

The semi-arid Llano Estacado region of the Southern High Plains of the United States, situated mostly in the Panhandle of Texas, has been significantly transformed over the last century from an extensive to an intensive agricultural economy, with an emphasis on irrigated cotton production. Landowners have responded to international markets for cotton and national markets for grains and cattle. They have relied upon modern technologies of large-scale groundwater irrigation, mechanization, and fertilization, and governmental policies have subsidized and insured agricultural activities and infrastructures (e.g. agricultural research stations and transportation). All of these factors have promoted the expansion of cropland, both irrigated and rainfed, and an intensification of the livestock industry. In turn, these agricultural activities, coupled with an oil industry and the development of a service sector, have promoted urban and industrial growth, with a rise in the population of cities and towns (although this growth may have ended).

The Llano Estacado is a case of a semi-arid land frontier closely linked to national and international markets, with a relatively affluent population and little regulation of the draw-down of a critical resource stock (groundwater). How the system will adjust depends on the market, resource regulation, and technological change.

Basin of Mexico (fig. 11.13)

The Basin of Mexico may constitute the largest nucleated settlement in the world, and certainly the largest occupying a closed hydrological basin. Two major forces have driven the city's growth. The first has been a long-standing state policy emphasizing the basin as the financial and industrial centre of Mexico, to be developed first and foremost by concentrating the resources of the country there. The second, partly the result of the first, has been the massive migration to the basin, by both rich and poor, from elsewhere in the country. Technologies and infrastructures that allow the importation of water from, and the export of wastes to, adjacent basins have largely sustained these developments.

The current use of the basin requires enormous subsidies drawn from Mexico at large. If these subsidies were diminished, the system would collapse. At the same time, the continued use of these subsidies has contributed to trajectories of change that threaten dire

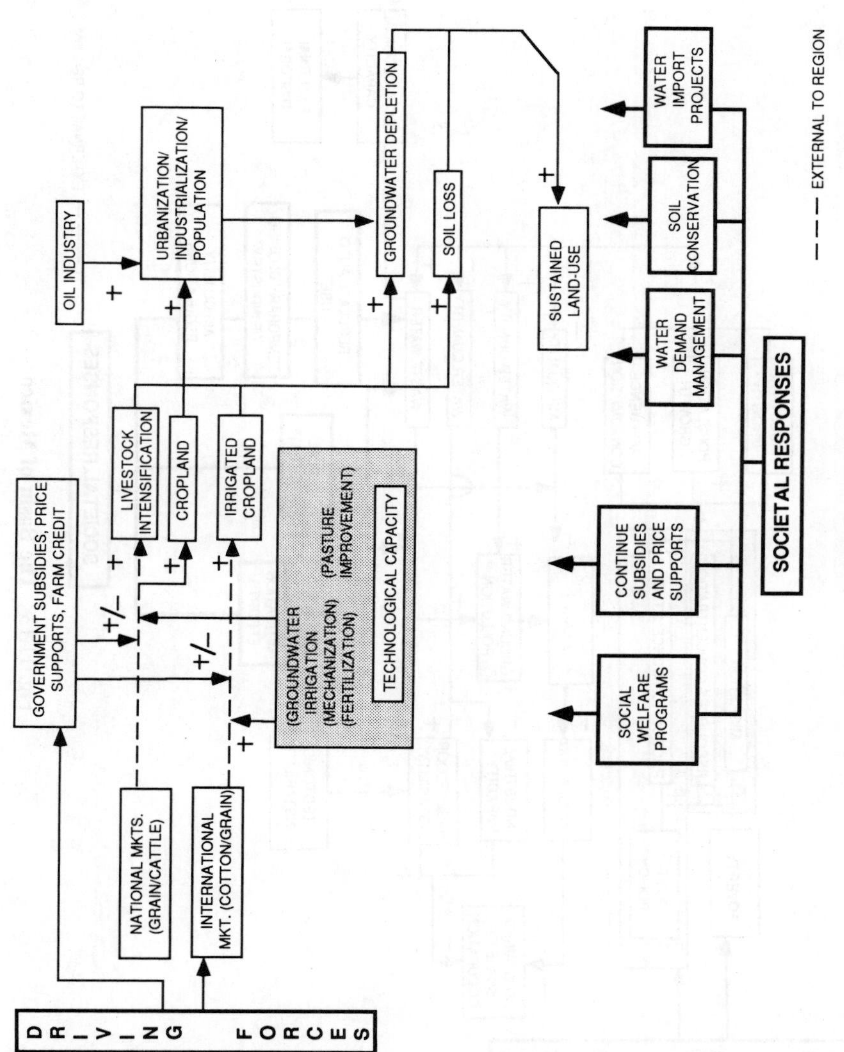

DRIVING FORCES
GOVERNMENT SUBSIDIES, PRICE SUPPORTS, FARM CREDIT
NATIONAL MKTS. (GRAIN/CATTLE)
INTERNATIONAL MKT. (COTTON/GRAIN)
+/–
+/–
+
+
+
+
LIVESTOCK INTENSIFICATION
CROPLAND
IRRIGATED CROPLAND
(GROUNDWATER IRRIGATION) (MECHANIZATION) (FERTILIZATION)
(PASTURE IMPROVEMENT)
TECHNOLOGICAL CAPACITY
OIL INDUSTRY
+
+
URBANIZATION/ INDUSTRIALIZATION/ POPULATION
+
GROUNDWATER DEPLETION
+
SOIL LOSS
+
SUSTAINED LAND-USE
SOCIAL WELFARE PROGRAMS
CONTINUE SUBSIDIES AND PRICE SUPPORTS
WATER DEMAND MANAGEMENT
SOIL CONSERVATION
WATER IMPORT PROJECTS
SOCIETAL RESPONSES
– – – EXTERNAL TO REGION

Fig. 11.12 **The Llano Estacado**

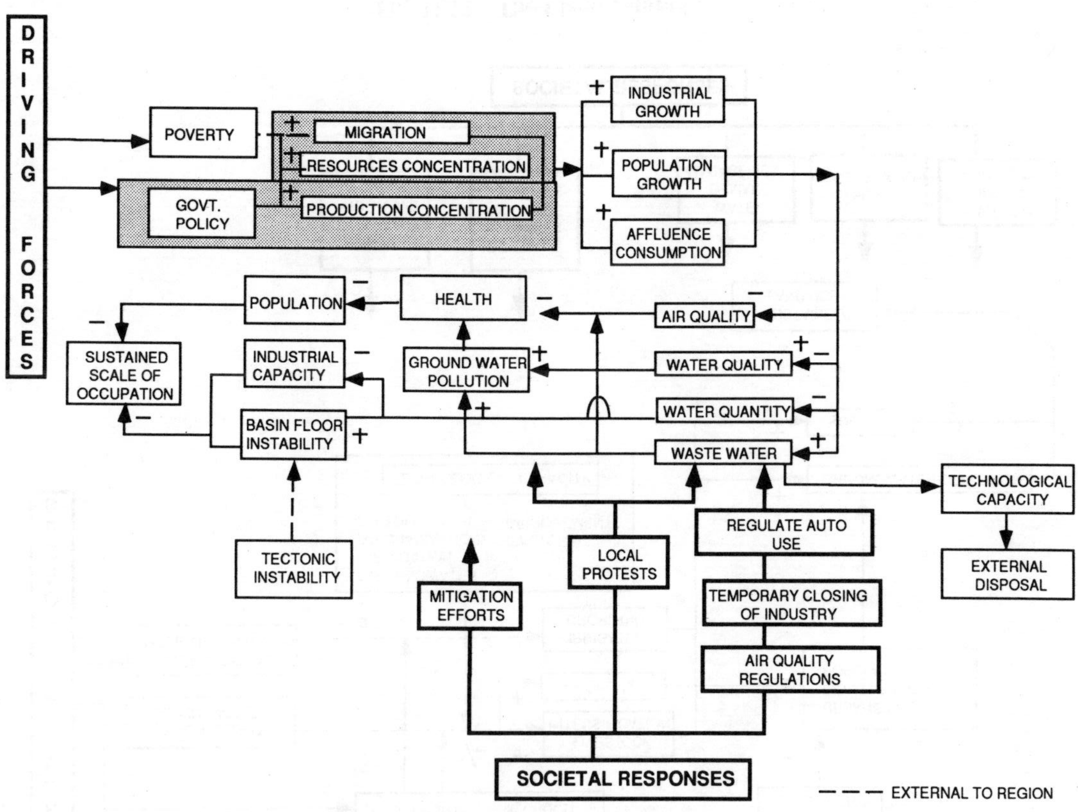

Fig. 11.13 **The Basin of Mexico**

long-term consequences and possible collapse. The Basin of Mexico represents the problems of concentration of all kinds within an environment that is capable of immediately "biting back" (enclosed air inversions and a basin floor sinking from a lack of water). The problems of groundwater have been abated at high cost by engineering solutions; those of air pollution have not.

North Sea (Fig. 11.14)

The North Sea case has two distinctive aspects: it involves a common-pool resource (and an oceanic one at that), surrounded by a very large, affluent, and urban–industrialized society on its rimland. Since this rimland has long sustained a large population, and this population is not growing at a substantial rate (at least by world standards), population change *per se* is not a critical driving force; high per capita consumption (affluence) of the large population, however, is. As important as the urbanized population and industrialized economy are, both are predicated on international markets. These factors coalesce to create demands for North Sea resources. These demands are mediated by: a high technological capacity that facilitates fishing, oil and gas extraction at sea, heavy sea-borne traffic, and waste disposal and marine pollution (from both sea and land activities); variable intergovernmental regulation of this common-pool resource (subsidies for certain activities, non-regulation of others); and a "false consciousness" among the population about its impacts on the sea (what Sack, 1990, refers to as "a myth of mass consuming societies," an unrealistic view of the environmental associations of modern consumption).

The North Sea exemplifies the impacts of industrialized society on an unregulated common-pool resource. Change can be swift. The affluence and technological capacity of the region, however, provide an enormous ability to address this degradation, assuming that society continues to judge the benefits of doing so to be worth the cost.

Driving forces in perspective

Each case displays different clusters of the driving forces identified above, operating in different contexts. Here we focus on what each case says about these clusters.

Population growth within the region was a major driving force in six cases (Amazonia, the Nepal middle mountains, the Ordos Plateau,

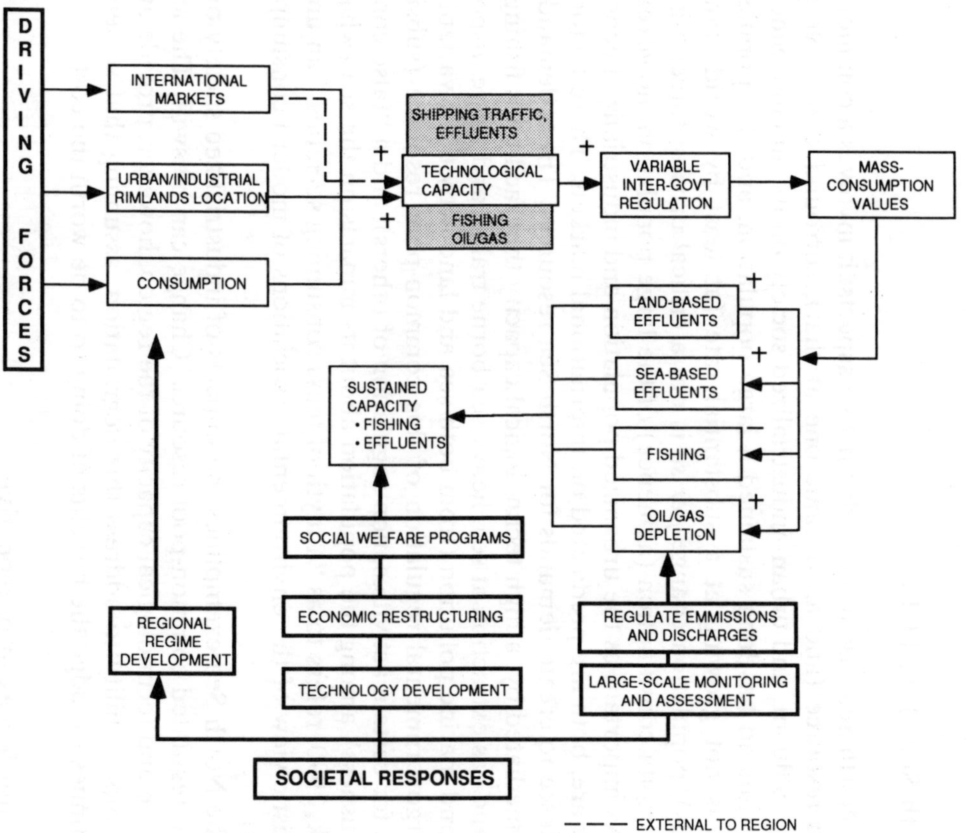

Fig. 11.14 **The North Sea**

the Aral Sea, the Basin of Mexico, and part of eastern Sundaland), all involving regions or regional systems of underdevelopment. Such growth, of course, was usually the product of other forces (largely those of political economy and structure) that stimulated migration into or natural growth within the region.

Technological capacity entered in two ways: changes in technology permitting new uses of the region and enhancing the overall level of technology available to users. Technological innovation supported the introduction of modern infrastructures and enlarged means of production, usually to frontiers or sparsely inhabited areas (Amazonia, eastern Sundaland, the Nepal middle mountains, the Ordos Plateau, and the Llano Estacado). Damage initially followed from technologies unsuited to specific environments, in some cases producing initial impacts that were reduced over time by the adoption or development of new techniques (as in Amazonia). At least three broad types of interactions occurred: (1) poorly constructed, inefficient, and highly polluting technologies (the Ordos Plateau, the Aral Sea, the Basin of Mexico), (2) state-of-the-art technologies that exacerbate impacts, intended or not (the North Sea, the Llano Estacado, the Basin of Mexico), and/or (3) technologies that abate problems through substitution, such as water transfers or changes in fuel types (as in the Basin of Mexico).

Affluence was directly identified as a driving force only for the North Sea case, where high per capita consumption has had obvious impacts, and in the Basin of Mexico, where high per capita use of cars, for example, contributes to major pollution problems. It was implied for the Llano Estacado in the sense that local producers who are seeking to sustain and improve an already very high standard of living drive economic activities there. Increased per capita consumption, of course, is occurring in several other cases (especially in rural, developing areas), but its contribution as a driving force has been relatively small.

The opposite of affluence, or *poverty*, appears as an important driving force in four cases (Amazonia, the Nepal middle mountains, the Basin of Mexico, and Ukambani). In each of these cases, poverty drove inappropriate resource use that exacerbated resource consumption or loss. In rural areas, this involved the intensification of land use without appropriate inputs (as in the Nepal middle mountains) and, in the case of Mexico, was a "push" stimulus for migration. Finally, if poverty is expanded to country-scale "underdevelopment" or imbalance of trade and debt, then all of the cases, save the Llano Estacado and the North Sea, had this force operating through its influence on the policy of use.

Two broad *political–economic forces* operated in all cases through state policy and the character of the economy. The role of state policy was obvious and direct in centrally planned economies (the Aral Sea, the Ordos Plateau, the Basin of Mexico), but it was also important in poorly developed marginal areas and frontiers having little power *vis-à-vis* the national government (Amazonia, eastern Sundaland) or seeking state assistance to develop (the Nepal middle mountains). In the developed-world cases, the state operated through more individually directed policy, such as subsidies for farming in the Llano Estacado or the lack of regulation in the North Sea.

The economy operated as a driving force in several major ways. First, the region provided a desired resource that would not necessarily have been exploited without external intervention (eastern Sundaland, Amazonia). Related to this was resource use predicated on external demands regulated through the market or government controls (the Aral Sea, the Llano Estacado, the North Sea). Second, shifts from a pre-capitalist (traditional) toward a capitalist (market) economy heightened environmental change because of the transaction costs of changing the rules of resource allocation (the Nepal middle mountains). Finally, two regions – the North Sea and the Ogallala aquifer (Llano Estacado) – suffered from inadequate or improper valuation of environmental impacts on a common-pool resource. (Air pollution in the Basin of Mexico may also reflect a common-pool situation.)

Beliefs and attitudes are usually difficult to identify as autonomous forces of change. Nevertheless, the case-studies identified three forces that qualify for consideration here. The first is a "frontier" outlook, prevalent in the Amazonia and eastern Sundaland (and once prevalent in the Llano Estacado), that emphasizes rapid development. This orientation is not purely economic, but takes root as part of a new world-view. The second is ethnic identity and associated religious beliefs that serve to increase natural population growth and hence resource demands (as in the Aral Sea region). This same force may also operate, though less directly, in the case of the Basin of Mexico. Finally, the underestimation – perhaps denial – by mass-consuming, industrialized, and urbanized societies of the environmental consequences of their activities was apparent in the North Sea and Basin of Mexico cases.

Toward a synthesis

The different emphases in the case-studies and the absence of standardized quantitative data for the major driving forces preclude any statistical explorations of their roles (singly or interactively) in inducing environmental change. The case-studies do, however, provide qualitative evidence of the role of certain characteristic clusters of driving forces, showing (save for the category of beliefs/attitudes) rather marked consistency among the specific variables identified or implied. As expected, these regional studies identified the cluster of driving forces in political economy and structure as particularly significant. These forces were important in all cases and perhaps dominant in a number (the Basin of Mexico, Amazonia, the Aral Sea, eastern Sundaland, Ukambani, and the Llano Estacado).

This result stands in contrast to global aggregate assessments (e.g. CEQ 1980; Meadows et al. 1972; WCED 1987), which typically emphasize the triad of population, affluence, and technology (e.g. I = PAT assessments). Such differences are not necessarily irreconcilable, given that the spatial and temporal scales and the mode of analysis used affect the findings. At the global scale, the I = PAT formula sums up the human pressures on resources in a closed system, but it says nothing about where within the system those pressures will be felt or how they will be mediated. Regions are not closed systems, and, as our cases show, the export of demands and degradation from their source areas to distant points (or distant generations) is a common occurrence.

Indeed, driving forces external to the region affected were typically more important than internal forces. These external forces tended to be those of resource extraction or production for distant national and international markets and those causing in-migration from densely settled areas. In every case, resource extraction or production for external consumption was an important factor, and only in the highly urbanized–industrialized cases (the North Sea and the Basin of Mexico) was consumption internal to the region a major force of change. Also, in every case, state policy and institutions affecting resources and environment were key forces of change, and, with the exception of a few regions totally controlled from afar, external demands operated in the context of state policy and institutions, illustrating the confluence of external and internal forces of change. One institutional force that stood out was legal and institutional structures affecting common-pool resources, in which minimal or no rules of allocation or use operated.

The I = PAT formula can also be criticized for treating only affluence, or high levels of consumption, as a driving force, while neglecting the ways in which poverty may drive environmental degradation (Leonard 1989; Kates and Haarmann 1992). Our two cases of agglomerated environmental stressors (the North Sea and the Basin of Mexico) represent the I = PAT scenario of relatively high levels of consumption taxing the capacities of the regional environment. As noted above, however, in at least as many cases (e.g. Amazonia, the Nepal middle mountains, and the Basin of Mexico) poverty rather than affluence has driven unsustainable resource use. Overall, the fact that regional population, affluence, and technology did not predominate compared with external forces suggests that some rethinking of the conventional wisdom of the relationship between human driving forces and environmental change may be needed.

Vulnerability

The nine cases explore the vulnerability of the environment–human use relationship in less depth than they do the human driving forces of change. None the less, they do indicate several common features, mostly involving the social dimensions of vulnerability. Ecosystem fragility receives less systematic attention. The case-studies deal with multiple changes that pose multiple threats. In general, the discussions focus not on differential abilities to respond to a specific threat but on a general regional ability to respond to a broad spectrum of changes and variability in the environment.

Our concern here is with the vulnerability of the environment–human use relationship, not with the vulnerability of the human-use system to other types of social and economic threats. Some socio-economic processes that threaten to lower regional wealth and well-being can at the same time lead to ecological recovery. In the Llano Estacado, for example, competition from other cotton producers in the world economy is one non-environmental source of downward pressure on regional wealth. To the extent that it leads to land being taken out of production, it reduces soil erosion and aquifer draw-down. A past case of regional economic and demographic decline (resulting in reduced environmental stress) stemming from similar external competition is that of Amazonia, which grew wealthy from rubber exports but experienced a dramatic and long-lasting collapse in 1912 when the successful cultivation of rubber in South-East Asia undercut its profits.

The nine regions illustrate some obvious ways in which vulnerability has declined over time. Technological interventions have reduced the vulnerability of some regions to fluctuations in the physical environment. In the North American High Plains, of which the Llano Estacado is a part, the widespread adoption of groundwater irrigation has insulated productive activities against the droughts that caused several major collapses of regional population and economy in earlier decades. Advanced pumping technology delivers water to a water-stressed Basin of Mexico, as well as removing pollution from the basin. (It should be noted, however, that these technological solutions bring with them potentially greater environmental vulnerability – to the loss of irrigation water in the Llano Estacado and the sustained growth of Mexico City in the basin.) A different form of reduced vulnerability appears in the North Sea and Llano Estacado cases. The increased wealth of the societies in which the regions are embedded has expanded the ability to mitigate environmental degradation and its consequences. Finally, improved access to the world market expands the range of options for use and response in a variety of ways: creating new uses and demands for regional resources once little valued, allowing resources to be imported as substitutes for ones locally exhausted, and making possible the adoption of innumerable technologies (developed elsewhere) to mitigate problems or increase the efficiency of resource use.

In the nine case-study chapters, however – perhaps because they represent a sample weighted toward failure rather than success – processes that have increased vulnerability or made it manifest in actual impacts appear more prominently. The two major types of change identified as increasing vulnerability result from human uses that (1) immediately alter the physical characteristics of the environment, and (2) link the use–environment system more closely with a highly variable, unreliable, or exploitative political economy.

Our regional case-studies suggest that environmental degradation involves such fragile or vulnerable settings as (1) extensive old-growth forests (Amazonia, eastern Sundaland); (2) arid lands or water sources in arid lands (the Ordos Plateau, the Aral Sea, the Llano Estacado, Ukambani, and, partly, the Basin of Mexico); (3) high-energy environments (e.g. the Nepal middle mountains); and (4) common-pool resources (the North Sea, the Llano Estacado, the Aral Sea, and the Basin of Mexico). The Basin of Mexico dramatically illustrates the significance of the biophysical environment and regional ecology. Here an enclosed basin and thermal inversions exacerbate air pollution, aridity accentuates water delivery problems, an ancient lake-bed subsiding because of groundwater depletion creates basic problems of land-surface stability, and steep slopes provide a high-energy source for erosion and other degrading processes. These environmental or resource characteristics do not in themselves create environmental change or degradation, which is a function also of the nature of the human uses. In an earlier agrarian era, the Basin of Mexico responded positively to use.

Such physical changes may increase the potential for surprise and disruption of an environment–use system, reduce the options and the buffering and regenerative capacity of the land, or deplete resources so that the ability to meet human-induced stresses erodes. The degree of regional dependence on the particular environmental uses undergoing change is a key dimension of vulnerability in all of the cases. Regional vulnerability to management initiatives and the long-term biophysical vulnerability created by losses of genetic resources are specifically treated in the North Sea and the eastern Sundaland cases.

In Amazonia, Smith and colleagues suggest that, as humans increasingly alter forest and aquatic environments, their activities could become increasingly vulnerable to ecological surprises. In addition, to the extent that increased reliance on development and technology accompanies alterations in resource-use patterns, vulnerability to production failure increases with development. This increased potential for biophysical surprise is a key dimension of vulnerability, given the growing linkage of regions with the global economy, fluctuations in world markets, and the impacts of such fluctuations on regional livelihood systems.

In the Nepal middle mountains, Jodha identifies several types of vulnerability that relate to the resource endowments of subregions. He also describes social and ecological processes that create vulnerabilities. The first type occurs in an economically stagnant area that is reliant on subsistence agriculture, where vulnerability appears in:

1. the reduced range, dependability, and payoffs of production or resources use options, because of (a) the breakdown and infeasibility of traditional diversified, resource-regenerative practices, and (b) a degradation of the resource base;
2. the slackening or disruption of collective risk-sharing institutions and resource-management systems (such as common-property re-

sources) and the introduction of more formal, legalistic arrangements to regulate people's relationship to their natural resources. The second type involves rapidly commercializing areas in which potential vulnerability reflects changing linkages with distant markets. On a macro level, in this case a nation, uneven trade also is a source of vulnerability, which is expressed in widespread food deficits and the state's inability to implement effective development policies (as in the Ukambani case).

In the Llano Estacado, various social supports have propped up an economy based on agriculture and little else. Here cotton operates at its biophysical margin. The land use is vulnerable to groundwater depletion and rapid erosion under cropping (whereas grazing would provide a more ecologically sustainable alternative). A situation has developed with a high dependence on agriculture, an increasingly restricted range of regional options, and a dependence on volatile agricultural commodity markets. Ukambani exhibits a similar dependence on commercialization of agriculture and on agricultural commodity markets. But here state policies restricting access to land and pushing poorer farmers onto more marginal lands have increased vulnerability to droughts and to market shifts. Meanwhile, the subsidies and safety nets that support agriculturalists in the Llano Estacado are unavailable, so that periodic famines and food shortages occur.

The Basin of Mexico is also increasingly precarious. Indeed, it represents strikingly a situation of resource use supporting urbanization that is reaching its ecological limits. Some of these limits are set by the biophysical characteristics of the basin, as noted above, whereas others involve technological and social abilities to substitute or to import needed resources. Pollution and deforestation are reducing some capacities to self-regulate the water supply and to maintain the requisite self-sufficiency, whereas the political–economic structures that subsidize the basin's water and waste disposal may also be approaching their limits.

The final two cases provide a somewhat different perspective on vulnerability. In the North Sea, environmental changes undoubtedly have had particularly severe impacts on the fishing industry and some other users of the sea. In eastern Sundaland, by contrast, the picture of vulnerability among social groups is more mixed. There, the biophysical dimensions of vulnerability raise several broader issues. First, considerable uncertainty surrounds the future consequences of environmental changes; insufficient knowledge renders it difficult to determine which forest systems will recover quickly. Second, irreversible losses in biodiversity are occurring, and the lack of alternatives to these species places those losses in a unique category that is difficult to evaluate over the near term and for the region. Similar long-term problems of biodiversity loss are apparent in Ukambani.

All nine cases address changing vulnerability primarily in terms of changes in the overall vulnerability over time as a region copes with a myriad of threats and environmental change. The internal vulnerability of different social groups or genders generally receives less attention (but see chaps. 5 and 6). The severity of the impacts on local peoples of changes supported by national and international policies does appear repeatedly, particularly where local groups are marginal to the political process. In the Nepal middle mountains, Amazonia, the Aral Sea region, eastern Sundaland, and Ukambani, the people with an established history of resource use in the area seem almost always to lose more, gain less, and receive less compensation from the environmental changes that have accompanied development.

On a regional level, three aspects of changing environmental and socio-economic conditions suggest an increasing potential for higher or catastrophic losses and merit further scrutiny.

1. *Vulnerability and overshoot.* In the Basin of Mexico, increasing demands are overwhelming finite sources of non-substitutable resources, such as clean air and water. The momentum of growth is outpacing the ability both to procure other supplies of necessary resources and to limit demand or mitigate damage. Meanwhile, the scale of the problems is growing relentlessly, suggesting an "overshoot" type of vulnerability.
2. *Market conditions and overcapitalization.* Several regions confront narrowing options and growing demands in more flexible global markets. The capital investments involved in the unsustainable production levels of cotton products (the Aral Sea region, the Llano Estacado) and timber products (Amazonia, eastern Sundaland) for the world market create livelihood systems dependent on those markets yet vulnerable to their fluctuations. Growing regional economic dependence on these environmental resources portends higher risks; transitions to other options and greater diversity, meanwhile, are increasingly painful. The difficulties faced by the fishing industry in the North Sea illustrate this case for a narrow portion of a regional population.
3. *Loss of options and safety nets.* For part of the Nepal middle mountains, environmental degradation has narrowed agricultural options, and changes in the production system have eroded the

capabilities of existing risk-management systems while failing to replace them with new systems. Environmental changes in Amazonia hold an increased potential for environmental surprises, and the extent to which the new productive systems will provide new buffers and sources of security is uncertain. Meanwhile, failures are likely to have far-reaching consequences because of the lack of entitlements and of back-up societal and livelihood options.

Societal response

The final cluster of analysis in our regional case-studies concerns societal responses to emerging environmental degradation. Such responses are central to the environmental futures of the regions as the trajectories of change, as noted above, depend heavily upon the capabilities of society to respond to deteriorating situations and on the actions that are undertaken to mitigate damage and to alter the trajectory. Such corrective interventions can occur at various levels and scales, ranging from individual resource managers to the state and international governance regimes. Further, the interventions may be "downstream," aimed at reducing exposure or ameliorating consequences; "midstream," aimed at reducing environmental stresses or vulnerability to damage; or "upstream," involving interventions into the more fundamental driving forces that generate environmental stresses or shape social and economic vulnerabilities (Kates, Hohenemser, and Kasperson 1985).

Many issues are involved in characterizing and interpreting societal responses to environmental change, and they are described at length elsewhere (Kasperson and Kasperson forthcoming). Suffice it to note here that societal interventions to alter trajectories toward greater endangerment or criticality are typically preceded by growing awareness of the threat and assessment of the causes of environmental degradation (Brooks 1986; Stern, Young, and Druckman 1992). Assessments will need to unravel the complex of natural variability and human causes to identify the bases of the threat and possible corrective actions. Important to such assessments will be "signals" of long-term threat in the midst, catalysts that stimulate action, and the social memory to fashion appropriate responses (Clark 1990; Kates, Ausubel, and Berberian 1985). Issues of political economy will also be central, since many of the most severely affected regions and regional groups may lack the resources and political power to alter the forces that are driving degradation, structuring vulnerabilities, and controlling management systems (Blaikie 1985; Smith 1984). The nine cases amply suggest the multitude of obstacles to more timely and effective response.

Amazonia

State objectives lie at the heart of both the driving forces of environmental change (as noted above) and the societal response in Amazomia. Since the Brazilian state has seen the Amazon as a "frontier" area for development, as an area that needs to be "integrated" into the state as a whole, and as a safety-valve for migration from poverty-prone areas, state concern over deforestation and pollution of waterways has been very muted until recently. And the building of roads through Amazonia will certainly continue to drive the developmental processes that are altering the environment.

Early concern focused on indigenous groups in the Amazon, on the movement to protect rubber trees, and on non-governmental organizations. More recent concern over global climate change and biodiversity has sparked international pressure for remedial measures. The central government has begun to respond, balancing opportunities for debt reduction and remediation of some of the worst damage with protection of its national sovereignty and development goals. The net effect has been to pull down the steepness of the trajectory of change and to begin to ameliorate damage, though the driving forces remain largely intact. Yet, how much of this slowdown is attributable to government policy and how much to longer-term market forces is not documented.

Eastern Sundaland

The patterns of societal response apparent in other frontier areas are also apparent in Sundaland. As in Amazonia and Ukambani, the state is committed to the development of a frontier area (Borneo) for the benefit of the state and the national political élite. The presence of a ready international market and the opportunity to generate revenues support the ongoing timber boom that will soon deplete the remaining primary forests of Borneo. This resource-development thrust is also supported by a central government's policy of eliminating shifting cultivation, based in part on the recognition that shifting cultivators and loggers are in continuing conflict.

Peninsular Malaysia, where industrialization and urbanization have dominated, is increasingly becoming a managed environment. Enrichment planting and plantations are proceeding on a greater scale. Many of the worst environmental problems are being addressed and often ameliorated. The government has also sought to resettle shifting cultivators in reserve areas, with only partial success. While central government policy in the region incorporates greater recognition and more determined response to environmental problems, the policy and institutional infrastructure is still emerging and implementation is still weak. Meanwhile, the conflict between local shifting cultivators and loggers and the growing international concern over deforestation in Borneo are centring greater attention on the trajectory of regional change; nevertheless, restructuring of the pattern of economic gain and the political institutions that support the trajectory is yet to occur.

Ukambani

The state has also been a key shaper of societal response in the Ukambani "frontier" area of Kenya, which too has suffered from many of the problems associated with political marginality. But, unlike Amazonia, the Aral Sea, and the Basin of Mexico, Ukambani has witnessed a continuing series of relatively rapid state responses aimed at mitigating what has been seen as a series of environmental crises. Interestingly, these responses have been driven by the perceived threat that these crises pose to central objectives of the state for the sequestering of land for the social élite and for support of the national economy. Unlike the generally superficial and delayed responses in these three other regions, the responses to environmental degradation in Ukambani have often been broad-based and have addressed such basic elements of driving forces and "proximate" causes as land tenure, enclosure, privatization, type of agricultural system, and livestock numbers. So the "reach" into the structure of causation has been deep.

Unfortunately, these responses have both exacerbated and ameliorated problems. Amelioration of environmental degradation has been closely intertwined with other state objectives, notably those associated with economic development and land allocation. Accordingly, the "problems" of degradation or low productivity have been defined as "overgrazing," "poor cultivation," or an "inadequate cash-crop focus." Predictably, such problem definitions have led to responses that have sometimes compounded problems or created new ones.

As their integration with and dependency upon national and international markets have grown, the Akamba people have sought to maintain livelihood diversity and forms of traditional resilience in the face of the new vulnerabilities produced by top–down changes. The variable effects of these changes, with both winners and losers, raise questions as to the direction of the trajectory of change. Yet, as Mortimore (1989) and Tiffen and Mortimore (1992) note, sombre forecasts by earlier analysts of regional collapse have not been realized.

The Nepal middle mountains

The state has acted as both a driving force of environmental change and a locus of efforts to mitigate environmental degradation and its effects in the Nepal middle mountains. As in Amazonia, the Aral Sea region, and Eastern Sundaland, the primary objective over the past several decades has been resource extraction. State interventions have alienated land and reduced the access of mountain inhabitants to natural resources through the nationalization of forests, the building of roads and industries, and the privatization of common property. Meanwhile, the state has sought, through public investments and subsidies, to intensify production and to increase public revenues. The net effect of such policies and their supply or production orientation, despite emerging national and international concern with environmental degradation, has been to increase the vulnerability of mountain farmers and to cause further environmental degradation.

Various ameliorative efforts have been undertaken in the form of watershed development, forestation, and pasture development. Achieving greater equity in land ownership has ostensibly been a state goal. But vested economic and political interests and ineffective implementation have conspired to continue the problems of landlessness and ownership inequities, to add to the growing proletarianization of the rural peasantry, and to intensify pressures on small and often marginal landholdings. Meanwhile state efforts, and patronage, to provide relief and cushion the human impacts of environmental change have maintained pressures upon mountain resources without enlarging the available resource base. Thus, as in Amazonia, Sundaland, and (even) the Basin of Mexico, environmental mitigation is submerged into basic state policies aimed at a complex of development, growth, resource extraction, and continued concentration of wealth. As a consequence, the region continues to operate close to the limits of the ecosystem.

The Ordos Plateau

Until recently, the attractiveness of the Ordos Plateau as a peripheral area in the Chinese state had been limited. The extensive grazing and cultivation economy attracted little central government intervention until 1978. This is not to say that the region was not significantly affected by national policies, such as the grain-purchasing programmes of the 1950s and 1960s, which extracted food production from the Ordos and produced significant adverse environmental effects, or the settlement programmes of the same period, which resulted in damaging increases in cultivated areas. Most environmental response occurred at the individual farmer level, and it consisted principally of adaptations to climatic variations and the increased pressures arising from national development programmes. The pasture-protection and afforestation programmes undertaken by local governments in the Ordos were too weak and sporadic to have any major role in mitigating environmental degradation in the region.

Since 1980, the state has undertaken more concerted efforts to arrest the rapid course of soil erosion and sandification in the Ordos. In particular, plans have sought to integrate regional development with new programmes of environmental protection aimed at halting overgrazing and restricting the spread of cultivation in marginal areas. Various mitigative measures have been undertaken at the local level. Looming over the Ordos is the prospect of a rapid development of coal resources, with substantial uncertainty as to the controls that will be implemented for environmental protection.

The Aral Sea

Just as the Aral Sea is the clearest case of criticality among the nine regions, it also is the archetypal example of state exploitation of a marginal area and people. As Glazovsky makes evident in chapter 3, the ecological impacts of the diversion of waters from the Aral Sea have been a very secondary consideration behind the objectives in Moscow to develop irrigated cotton production that would generate export earnings and provide cotton for the clothing industry. As warnings appeared from scientists during the 1970s of the dire threats posed by water diversions, the state response was to suppress such reports. Even during the past decade, as the magnitude of the unfolding catastrophe has become clear, effective intervention has not been forthcoming. Indeed, the collusion between the local political corruption involved in the administration of the regional irrigation system and the unwillingness of the state fundamentally to alter the trajectory to criticality has proved too powerful for regional protests to overcome.

Such protests have none the less grown rapidly in number and determination over the past 20 years. Beginning about 1970, scientists pointed out the emerging devastating effects upon the natural systems of the sea. In the 1980s, comprehensive plans appeared for saving the Aral. At the same time, local protest groups carried the fight for heading off the emerging disaster to the media, to regional political authorities, and to government officials in Moscow. Late in the 1980s, the Aral catastrophe was attracting international concern, and the United Nations Environment Programme sent a delegation to the Aral to diagnose the situation and propose remedial actions. By now, however, the scale of needed interventions and the declining societal capacity to respond in the face of the political fragmentation of the region suggest that the regional collapse may be difficult to avert.

The Llano Estacado

The Llano Estacado displays many of the problems of resource depletion characteristic of the frontier regions treated in this volume. A major difference, however, is that this region is of limited economic importance to the state, so that its role in the pursuit of national policies and goals has been relatively minor. At the same time, the regional inhabitants have benefited from various subsidy systems that have propped up the regional economy and in significant measure have accelerated the trajectory to endangerment and (perhaps) eventual regional collapse.

During this century, a broad array of responses has arisen to the long-term depletion of groundwater and soil erosion. The Dust Bowl period in particular stimulated federal studies and interventions. More recently, states have established groundwater management institutions aimed at solving water-allocation conflicts and mitigating depletion rates. For their part, local inhabitants have adapted by shifting occupations or, in periods of great stress, migrating to other areas. Governmental interventions have thus far been largely mitigative in nature. Proposals for more basic changes in economy and nature–society relations, meanwhile, have been debated sporadically but have failed to gather the requisite political support. On the other hand, it is clear that the region and the political system of which it is part have a strong capability for economic substitution, technological change, and mitigative efforts.

The Basin of Mexico

State policy has also played a central role in the emerging societal responses to the growing contamination and precariousness of the Basin of Mexico environment. With continuing rapid in-migration, chronic water shortages, an increasingly unhealthy atmosphere, mounting waste problems, and disappearing open spaces, warnings have abounded of the basin's trajectory toward environmental criticality. Despite the lengthy time-period and numerous warnings, governmental recognition of the seriousness of the environmental problems and the long-term threat posed by the trajectory of change has come only recently. Indeed, the long-standing governmental response, given the established state policy of promoting growth and concentration of wealth in Mexico City, has been either to deny that problems exist or to assert that technology provides ample means for responding to them.

Thus, the story of societal response to emerging criticality in the Basin of Mexico has been one of problem evasion – since confronting the issues would have interfered with other state objectives – and more recently of tentative, delayed, and ineffective responses to a trajectory rapidly heading to criticality. Growing political pressure from environmental groups and concerned inhabitants is now stimulating more vigorous governmental responses, including some emergency measures. Demonstrable health effects have provided the most persuasive, and legitimate, evidence. Despite strong scientific capability and societal capacity to respond, problems have grown rapidly worse. Where state responses have occurred, they have focused on mitigating the worst of the damage rather than decisively engaging the driving forces of urbanization, economic growth, economic concentration, and affluence. Indeed, the state has continued to subsidize the causal forces of environmental degradation. The current recognition of the severity of the issues and the substantial national resources provide some reason to believe, however, that increasingly determined efforts may be forthcoming.

The North Sea

Among the nine regions, the North Sea is distinctive in the pattern of societal response as well as in its international, common-pool resource setting. In the midst of a constellation of affluent societies with a well-developed environmental awareness and ethic, the North Sea has been the subject of intensive scientific investigations for over three decades. A series of International North Sea Conferences now appears to be growing into a collective policy-setting institution in which an innovative international regime is emerging – one that capitalizes on the high capability and homogeneity of the rimland countries to explore the limits of existing policy instruments for collective environmental management. Its holistic approaches draw together scientific assessments and "vernacular" science, precautionary principles of intervention that wed science and values, and approaches that push technology in the interest of abating environmental damage. While clearly indicating future pathways for international response to global and regional environmental problems, the North Sea experience also indicates how different the capabilities of societal response to trajectories of endangerment are in the developed and the developing world.

Generic patterns and issues

Ideally, comparative regional assessments, particularly if they involve data collection and analyses at different scales, provide a means by which to discern broad patterns of relationships and trajectories of change. This ideal requires a common protocol among the case-studies, such as the one drawn up for this project, as well as the availability of common data to all groups of researchers. For a variety of reasons, these common data sets were not available for each case-study, and the different case-study authors had to address various parts of the protocol with evidence that was not quantitatively comparable. This limitation makes statistical comparisons unsuitable (as they would be in any case because of the small number of studies), but the rich array of evidence and the understanding of how that evidence fits together suggest broader lessons.

Specificity and context

No single set of regularities emerges from comparison of the regional trajectories of change and associated case-study interpretations that explains the diversity of the regional cases and the complexities implicit in the slopes and shapes of the trajectories. Although most regions revealed similar long-term decreasing sustainability, each must be examined within its particular historical, landscape, and societal context for a satisfying interpretation. The observations that follow suggest some cross-cutting issues worthy of further attention but do not point to one or several factors that dominate the dynamics of change or the "smoking guns" of global environmental change within these areas.

Environmental degradation and improved regional well-being

It has long been recognized that environmental change is an inevitable outcome of human occupation and use. How this change is best examined and characterized, however, has been a source of contention. Change that constitutes "ecological degradation" may improve the productivity, sustainability, and quality of the land as judged by its human users. Indeed, notions of what constitutes "environmental degradation," like concepts of "pollution," are themselves scientifically and culturally contentious (Douglas 1966; Douglas and Wildavsky 1982; Krimsky and Golding 1992). Our case-studies were selected from areas where environmental change was thought be of a kind that was harmful to the occupants or the particular use; it is this sense of environmental degradation that we address here (this is consistent with Blaikie and Brookfield 1987, 7).

The nine case-studies suggest that environmental degradation often proceeds in parallel with rising human well-being. Only one of our case-studies, that of the Aral Sea, involves a broad decline in human well-being in the aggregate that has occurred following several decades of increase in the material standards of life in the region. The other regional cases involve aggregate improvement in wealth and well-being, though in some cases with significantly different results for a substantial minority of the regional population (e.g. Ukambani, Amazonia, the Nepal middle mountains).

The complexity of the relationship between environmental change and human wealth and well-being has been widely discussed, particularly by economists and technologists (Ausubel and Sladovich 1989). Land and its "natural" stocks offer resources that, under certain economic, political, and technological systems, are used to increase the well-being of some or most of the users. Where this use involves resource extraction (e.g. large-scale clear-cutting of forest or mining of water), inadequate replacement (e.g. agricultural intensification without requisite inputs), or diminishment (e.g. pollution), environmental degradation occurs. As particular resources are exhausted, substitution allows regional populations to move to the exploitation of other resources and environmental components. Technology and management play critical roles in such continuing adaptation, maintaining or even increasing the stream of livelihood opportunities over time. Environmental sinks set certain limits, of course. When they are exceeded, even technology may not be able to sustain continued well-being. Nevertheless, it is apparent that the interactions among technology, adaptation, substitution, spatial linkages, and mitigation of damage allow regions to continue to improve their well-being over long periods of time in the face of evident environmental degradation. This dynamic averts regional economic collapses or, after a period of adjustment, permits regional regrowth, according to the "technological fix" or "optimist" perspective on the use–change–outcome relationship (Simon and Kahn 1984).

The Llano Estacado and the North Sea are the best positioned of our regions to make these kinds of adjustments, owing to their position within advanced industrial economies. The other cases are more difficult to assess, but, because of growing linkage to and dependence on a global political economy that reduces options, decreasing well-being and increasing risk are possible outcomes (e.g. Ukambani, the Aral Sea, the Llano Estacado).

Symptoms of emerging criticality

Since environmental change is ubiquitous throughout the world, identifying and diagnosing symptoms of emerging environmental criticality in the overall "noise" of environmental change are essential (however perplexing). Most current attention in discussions of global environmental change focuses on rapid land-cover change (especially deforestation), on global climatic change and ozone depletion, and on loss of biodiversity. At the regional scale, however, it is not at all clear that these are the dominant problems. Rapid land-cover change is characteristic of many of our cases and, more generally, occurs in many regions throughout the world undergoing intensive human occupation. While such changes often lead to short-term losses, regeneration and shifts in human uses allow continuing adaptations and productive use of the regional environment in the face of dire predictions.

It is perhaps instructive that, of the nine regions, those with the steepest trajectories to criticality are arid or semi-arid areas where water-resource depletion threatens continued human occupancy and well-being. The Aral Sea, with its extensive mismanagement of regional water resources, is the most striking case. But two other more prosperous situations – the Llano Estacado in the United States and the Basin of Mexico – reveal long-term trends of water depletion and dependence that are unsustainable over the long term and that involve a rising potential for erosion in life-support systems and for eventual regional collapse. This pattern seems to reflect the distinctive qualities of water as a resource: its indispensability for many human activities combined with the tremendous, almost prohibitive cost of importing it over any substantial distance when local supplies prove inadequate, and its central role in many human conflicts (Falkenmark 1986; Gleick 1991, 1992).

The indicators of human impacts that appeared to elicit most public concern involved human health, as in the case of the Aral Sea and the Basin of Mexico. In both cases it has been environmental contamination and the overwhelming of environmental sinks that have precipitated these impacts. Emigration or economic decline were not yet apparent in any of the regions, at an aggregate level, although several regions seem poised to witness such declines. The observation about the sink-health path to criticality may suggest that it is the more difficult one for human societies to respond to inasmuch as sinks have long fallen outside the control of the market and have proved difficult to regulate through other institutions.

Spatial and temporal export

It is clear that distant regions and generations often bear the costs of environmental "draw-downs" or impoverishment of nature. Our studies suggest that two types of spatial separation are involved. In the first, exogenous agents control the extraction of resources or surplus from the region, as in the case of international logging in eastern Sundaland and mining in Amazonia, or agricultural production in the Aral Sea region or the Nepal middle mountains. In the other, effluents from production and consumption in one place are physically exported to another. Such is the case in our industrial regions:

in Mexico City's dumping of its metropolitan waste into adjacent drainage outside the basin, in the air and marine contaminants from the North Sea region that affect air and water quality elsewhere in Europe, and in the toxic contamination of the Aral Sea region and the desiccation of the sea itself.

Where such "sinks" are overloaded, the resulting costs may be passed on to future generations. The same can be said of extractive "draw-downs," such as the mining of forests and water, with a caveat. Historically, the loss of resources through extractive activities has been countered by adjustments in use (Ausubel and Sladovich 1989), so that the loss *per se* may not have an obvious impact on the well-being of future generations.

Categories of environmental change

Examination of the nine trajectories and associated regional dynamics suggests that eight of the nine cases can be grouped into two major contrasting situations – those involving peripheral or marginal situations and those involving agglomerated environmental stressors.

The *peripheral or marginal situations* involve rapid environmental (especially land-cover) change accompanying the extraction of resources in relatively sparsely settled regions that are marginal in national political economies. In one common pattern, the needs of the national economy (poverty, debt, balance of trade) drive the exploitation of specific resources within the region. A powerful central government or external power uses or develops the area for its benefit, often with the collusion of local élites. Specific means used include resource concessions to external parties, encouragement of in-migration from more densely settled or poverty-prone areas elsewhere in the country, or production targets necessitating intensification. The environmental resource base of the extractive or development activities is often rapidly and severely degraded. Six of our regions – eastern Sundaland, the Nepal middle mountains, the Ordos Plateau, the Aral Sea, Ukambani, and Amazonia – typify this situation. A seventh, the Llano Estacado, represents a variant situation: a region that is marginal to the national economy in which it is situated and vulnerable to the world market for cotton on which it has come to depend, but rather than being exploited is subsidized by national agricultural and trade policies.

The situations of *agglomerated environmental stressors* are typically the inverse of the cases of peripherality and marginality. These regions lie in the economic cores of states, global industrialization, and the world economy. Here environmental degradation is the product of relative success rather than of powerlessness. The environmental threat takes the form of contamination and the overwhelming of sinks by concentrated population, industrialization, and affluence rather than the depletion of local natural resources to support productive systems and extraregional needs. The Basin of Mexico typifies this problem in its mega-city expression, where state policies favouring the expansion of the basin have largely created the trajectory toward criticality. The North Sea example is an international, common-property expression, where successful capitalist economies and the concentration of wealth and affluence threaten to overwhelm common-pool sinks and resources.

These two situations do not, of course, exhaust the spectrum of human–environment relations or trajectories of environmental change and associated regional dynamics. They simply reflect broad but common situations in the nine regions examined here. Variants within these two situations can be detected even in a pool of only nine case-studies, and we are confident that other common situations will emerge if a broader spectrum of cases is examined.

Delay and overshoot

In their seminal work *The Limits to Growth* and the subsequent *Beyond the Limits*, Donella Meadows and colleagues (1972, 1992) argue that human society has a tendency toward overshoot, in which environmental changes occur rapidly, signals of such changes are late, distorted, or denied, and responses are slow. As a result, environmental degradation overshoots responses, creating the potential for collapse of some kind. We call this pattern – akin to Malthusian themes – one of delay and overshoot.

The nine regional cases provide sufficient evidence for this argument to be disturbing, while adding new perspectives to the interpretation of causation. In all of the nine regions (chosen, to be sure, because they were candidates for endangerment or criticality), societal responses have been delayed and ineffective, often badly so. This is particularly the case with the seven marginal regions, where signals of environmental endangerment have typically been ignored, suppressed, or devalued and environment–society relations have been allowed to continue to deteriorate. The widespread nature of delay and half-hearted, often symbolic or unimplemented, responses provides little basis for optimism that, in the decades to follow the 1992 Earth Summit in Brazil, existing national policies, programmes, and institutions will prove adequate to the task of meeting mounting environmental change in many regions of the world. To put it another way, most of our regions appear to be in trajectories headed toward endangerment or criticality, with diminishing time for creating effective responses if deteriorating situations are to be stabilized.

It is further evident that societal responses in most of the regions have focused on "downstream" measures, mitigative effects designed to ameliorate damage and cushion the impacts of environmental deterioration on human health and well-being. The reason, as we have noted elsewhere in discussion of hazard management (Kasperson, Kates, and Hohenemser 1985), is that "upstream" intervention unavoidably interferes with the driving forces of change and, by inference, interferes with other desired societal objectives. So, even in the Aral Sea and the Basin of Mexico, where environmental degradation has reached advanced stages or approaches criticality, with human health impacts already apparent, interventions aimed at altering the basic driving forces have yet to be implemented with determination.

The sources of delay

Delays in societal response to hazards and threats of various kinds often stem from inadequacies in the signalling and knowledge base or the high levels of associated uncertainty. Thus, the lengthy emergence of response to global warming and the loss of global biodiversity is connected in no small part to the large uncertainties and long time-spans associated with potential impacts in the former and the scant database for the latter. Hazards research attests to assessment failures as a recurring source of delayed or even maladaptive responses (National Research Council 1983; Royal Society 1983). Indeed, Meadows, Meadows, and Randers (1992) argue that information is the key to the transformation involved in a sustainability revolution.

But not in our cases, apparently. While it is clear that alerting systems and knowledge bases to support well-fashioned societal responses have often been incomplete or even seriously deficient, in none of our cases has this been decisive. Despite the suppression of scientific studies to detail the Aral Sea catastrophe, for example, deliberations at the 1990 International Conference on the Aral Sea revealed a relatively high level of documentation of causes and natural system impacts as well as a well-reasoned programme of needed corrective measures among local officials and independent scientists. A core, albeit incomplete, understanding of the causes and ongoing effects of environmental change is widespread in the nine regions.

Rather, the decisive impediments to effective response typically lie in the domain of political will and political economy. Distant élites or consumers who exercise control over driving forces often accept the environmental price exacted by the ongoing exploitation of a peripheral region. A particularly common pattern of impediment is the linkage between state policies aimed at revenue generation in a distant region, implemented and sustained through political corruption involving the local élite. The Aral Sea and the eastern Sundaland are perhaps the most notable cases, but the phenomenon is a generic one found to some degree in many of the regions.

Types of environmental change and societal concern

A key factor in societal response is public awareness of emerging environmental degradation and the ecological and human threats that such degradation poses. Such awareness is obviously essential to resource managers if they are to undertake interventions to alter trajectories of change but also for governments in the allocation of scarce resources among competing objectives and demands.

It has long been noted that public perception of environmental and technological threats is highly variable and often episodic and that extreme events involving extensive media coverage (botulism, nuclear plant accidents, toxic wastes, airplane crashes) stimulate much greater public concern than ubiquitous chronic hazards (smoking, diet, automobile accidents) that are familiar but carry high societal tolls in mortality (Freudenburg 1988; Slovic 1989). Global warming has generated far more public concern and governmental attention than the accumulated toll of widespread water and soil depletion or extensive contamination of the urban environment in the third world (Louis Harris and Associates 1989).

Accordingly, it is not surprising that public awareness has been highly variable among our nine cases. Rapid deforestation appears to have attracted the greatest concern at the international level. Thus, the cutting of tropical forests in Amazonia and Borneo has received extensive media coverage and attention from environmental groups throughout the world despite the fact that the changes do not appear to pose the level of human threat apparent in a number of other regions. Certainly the drama accompanying the destruction of the primary forest and the loss of species, together with the vividness of those changes in television depictions, is an element in the high levels of public concern. Local concern in these areas, meanwhile, has tended to focus more on the economic issues and the pattern of gains and losses associated with resource depletion.

A second source of concern has been environmental degradation leading to demonstrable harm to human health and well-being. Accordingly, although the Aral Sea and Basin of Mexico situations are the most critical of our nine regions, neither generated extensive national and international public concern until the magnitude of the human health threat to the local populace became apparent. Even in 1994 the degree of human impacts was still poorly documented in the Aral Sea and is only now becoming well publicized in the case of Mexico City.

Meanwhile, the serious soil erosion in the Ordos Plateau and the growing vulnerability of agriculturalists in Ukambani and the Nepal middle mountains receive relatively little international attention. It is apparent, as was very evident at the 1992 Earth Summit in Brazil, that global attention to environmental change proceeds along a highly skewed agenda.

Problem construction

The threat associated with environmental degradation must, if it is to elicit societal response, be constructed into a "problem," a mental construct of the threat, its causes and pathways to harmful consequences, and who (if anyone) is to blame for its occurrence. Cultural factors, as Douglas and Wildavsky (1982) and Thompson et al. (1990) have extensively demonstrated, shape pervasively which threats are "selected" as problems and which are relegated to minor concern, and how the problem is culturally constructed. Recent studies have provided further insight into the "mental model" of environmental and technological hazards (e.g. Kasperson and Stallen 1991). These constructions define the terms on which blame is allocated and remedial responses are fashioned.

Two of our cases shed light on problem construction. In eastern Sundaland, Indonesian and Malaysian authorities have made a determination that shifting cultivation is the source of many of those countries' agricultural, economic, and environmental problems. In this view, shifting cultivation causes large areas of land to remain fallow and unproductive, while the basic food crops involved are less reliable (and, of course, provide fewer export earnings for the state) and deliver lower yields than commercial agriculture, ultimately keeping its practitioners in a state of poverty. It also, in this view, eats into primary and late-secondary forest and thus detracts from timber revenues to the state. This problem definition is often erroneous or invalid in particulars, but fits broader state objectives and provides a supporting policy rationale. As such, it is not an independent source of causation (i.e. a driving force or even proximate source of change) but is part of the hazard construction and rationalization in which collective societal responses are lodged.

In Ukambani, colonial officers, drawing in part on the US "Dust Bowl" experience, defined land degradation as a problem of soil erosion and overgrazing in the 1930s. Subsequently, this mutated to the belief that "low agricultural productivity" and "poor cultivation practices" were the culprits. These notions supported the view that agricultural intensification, crop commercialization, and land-tenure reform were the needed corrective measures. This problem construction became important to perceptions of crisis in Ukambani and to the broad-based state programmes of agricultural reform that have occurred. Interestingly, these problem constructions have survived independence in Kenya and continue to underlie state responses to environmental degradation in this region.

The cases suggest that how environmental degradation is socially constructed is an important part of the fabric of societal response, particularly that by the state. It is also apparent that such problem constructions are tightly intertwined with political objectives and the structure of the political economy within these regions.

Capacity to respond

The nine case-studies speak persuasively to the political power of the state, not only as a driving force but also as the major repository of societal response for mitigation. Unfortunately, this inextricable mixture underlines the insight long apparent in social science and policy studies – that government, like industry, is not an effective independent source of intervention to intercept growing environmental degradation in a political economy geared to production objectives. Yet it is clear that the state is the level at which the constellation of resources and capabilities exists for responding to the trajectories of change evident in our nine regions. Correspondingly, the ability of subnational regions to undertake environmental mitigation in the nine regions, with the exceptions of the North Sea and the Basin of Mexico, has been highly limited because the control over driving forces is lodged at scales beyond the region. Societal response, then, is a matter of the possible, and that is often mitigative, ameliorative, or adaptive responses. While these are frequently underestimated in their short-term effectiveness, as we note below, they also have only limited impact on the long-term course of nature–society trajectories.

Many human factors are involved in the societal capacity to respond to growing environmental degradation, including such diverse attributes as scientific and technological resources, wealth, legal and regulatory regimes, degree of national indebtedness, institutional infrastructure, public environmental values, degree of militarism, and democratic development. The Agenda 21 initiatives that seek to implement and further the initiatives adopted at the 1992 Earth Summit emphasize the development of national scientific and institutional capabilities (United Nations 1992). But our cases suggest that, important as these issues are, the capacity to respond rests more centrally on political will and the ability to bring state objectives and environmental protection into greater consonance.

Of course, at some juncture in the trajectory toward environmental criticality, the sheer scale and rate of change of the problem and the growing urgency (and time limitations) for response threaten to eclipse even the state's resources and ability to mobilize needed efforts and capabilities within the time-frame of potential stabilization. This is the situation in the Aral Sea region and, albeit at an earlier stage, the Basin of Mexico.

Common-property regimes

The growing importance of the global economy, the emergence of international legal and institutional regimes for the environment, and increasing concern over human alteration of natural fluxes in the earth's biosphere have focused greater attention on the potential societal responses in common-property regimes (Berkes 1989; McCay and Acheson 1987; Ostrom 1990). The studies of the Nepal middle mountains and the Ukambani region of Kenya suggest the increasing vulnerability of regional populations that may accompany the transformation from traditional common-property arrangements to privatization and commercialization. But only the North Sea case explores the emergence of common-property arrangements to address the misfit between the international scope of many environmental problems – in this case the overwhelming of natural sinks by contamination – and the political patterning of the globe.

There is much that is encouraging in the North Sea case. After three decades of scientific investigations, the North Sea is now the subject of an emerging governance system for the sea commons, in the form of the International North Sea Conferences. The emerging institutional responses promise to define new management principles and structures for responding to the growing internationalization of environmental challenges. At the same time, the case suggests how important affluence, relative international equality, developed environmental capabilities and values, and political will are likely to be for such governance systems. These are exactly the attributes that are in precious short supply in all of our third world cases and in global environmental tensions more generally.

With these comparative observations about trajectories, driving forces, vulnerability, and societal response, we now turn to some conclusions about the more general questions suggested by this nine-region study.

The larger issues

In this chapter we have noted many of the specific cross-cutting findings and issues relevant to understanding environmental change in various endangered or critical regions of the world. We conclude with several broad implications for global response.

Global environmental change through a regional lens

Discussions of global environmental change abound with long-term world population growth, aggregate loss of global biodiversity, world energy use and non-renewable resources, and international summit conferences and institutions to combat these large-scale changes. Environmental problems take on a different hue at the regional scale. It is not, of course, that the issues and their causes so apparent at the global scale are not present in the world's regions; they are. But the change depicted in the smooth averaged curves that portray global trends is placed in much sharper relief in the world's regions. And the mosaic and processes of change often appear very different from the averaged or even dominant global trends. The regional landscape, economies, and cultures reappear and can provide new insights or challenges to broader assumptions and interpretations.

The picture of environmental change in the nine regions treated in this volume is one in which regions have been selected because they are widely regarded as environmentally threatened to some degree. Thus, they may not indicate the more general nature–society situation prevailing in the diversity of the world's regions. But the trajectories of change in these threatened areas provide a warning, one that supplements those recent discoveries or events such as stratospheric ozone depletion or mounting levels of carbon dioxide in the atmosphere at the global scale. In nearly all these regions, trajectories of change are proceeding to greater endangerment, sometimes rapidly so, while societal efforts to stabilize these trajectories and to avert further environmental deterioration are lagging and are generally only ameliorating the damage rather than intercepting the basic human driving forces of change.

This is not to say that disaster is imminent in most of these regions, although we judge the Aral Sea already to be an environmental catastrophe and the Basin of Mexico as rapidly nearing criticality. It is to say that the trajectories of change in most of these regions are rapidly outstripping societal responses, that the future populations who will occupy these regions are being environmentally impoverished by these trends, and that the trajectories suggest growing long-term costs of regional substitution, adaptation, and remedial measures. At some indeterminable point in the future, these trends will also eclipse regional societal capabilities to respond.

A rich tapestry of human causation

At the regional level, the pattern of human causation is richly variegated. Rarely can a single dominant human driving force be discerned that explains the historical emergence of environmental degradation or that captures the complexity of change. Nor do the various grand theories, whether they arise from welfare economics, political economy, neo-Marxist thinking, global dependency models, or development theory, provide satisfying broad interpretations, although all have elements to contribute. So what we term the regional dynamics of change – the interplay among the trends of environmental change, vulnerabilities and fragility, human driving forces, and societal responses – must be examined within their cultural, economic, and ecological contexts. And the most satisfying interpretations invariably recognize the shifting complexes of driving forces and responses over time, tap diverse social science theory, and are firmly grounded in careful empirical work.

Increasing global integration

The mosaic of global change is increasingly the product of the growing linkages between regional productive systems and the global economy, between small states and international financial and development institutions, between local aspirations and the value systems and lifestyles of advanced industrial societies, and between the exporters and importers of technological change. Global markets facilitate increasing agricultural specialization in the Aral Sea region, in the Nepal middle mountains, and in Ukambani in Kenya, while international markets for timber facilitate the cutting of the Amazonian and Borneo forests. But, just as these global market opportunities are a key ingredient in the complex of driving forces and, along with state policies of resource extraction and revenue production, the shapers of regional dependency and vulnerability, they are also the levers for restructuring and the sources of more promising environmental futures.

Accordingly, regional trajectories of change and associated regional dynamics can be understood only in the context of changing extra-regional linkages. Simultaneously, changes in the global economy and trade policies, such as GATT, have a major environmental fallout for the world's regions.

Needed focus

These issues raise basic questions about whether emerging international efforts to combat global environmental degradation have the necessary focus to be effective. The interim results reported on in this volume suggest that substantial regional tailoring of initiatives will be required. To this end, the regional structure emerging under the Global Change System for Analysis, Research, and Training (START) programme is promising, for only a strongly regionally based structure of programmes and development efforts is likely to succeed.

Beyond this, several other elements for the required focus in global initiatives, such as START and the World Environmental Facility of the World Bank, may be suggested:

- The problems of *systemic global environmental change* (e.g. climate change, ozone depletion) so dominant in media attention and public concern in the North and at the 1992 Earth Summit may not be the dominant problems immediately confronting the environmentally endangered regions of the world. Rather, *cumulative global environmental change* involving land degradation, localized environmental contamination, water depletion, and so on are the ongoing changes that most imperil the people living in these endangered areas and the priority, therefore, for early interventions for international mitigative efforts.

- Frontier areas that are marginal to state economies and polities and/or that are strongly dependent on the global economy appear particularly vulnerable to environmental change and often powerless to intervene in driving forces whose sources frequently lie outside the affected region. Five of our nine regions fall into this category. These are likely to prove particularly difficult to stabilize as often they either are of low priority in the political units in which they are located or are expendable for other state objectives. In either case, outside intervention, as the cases of Amazonia and Borneo suggest, is likely to be strongly resisted.
- Areas of agglomerated stress, such as mega-cities, bring together in dramatic concentration many of the traditional driving forces of population and economic growth and affluence with the complex of contributing factors in spatial linkage and political economy. Typically, the rates of change are proceeding at an extraordinary pace that challenges capabilities of assessment and societal response. The threats involved include both the ongoing depletion of regional and more distant natural resources to support these vast population agglomerations and the overwhelming of local environmental sinks. While urbanization and industrialization are often subsidized by the state, the appearance of metropols of 20 million or more people, continuing to grow very rapidly and increasingly dependent on imported resources and technological change to combat ongoing environmental degradation, involves a relentless increase in the risk of eventual collapse from unanticipated futures.

Discrepancies in rates of change

As noted above, the regional dynamics of change in the nine regions reveal a recurring disjuncture between the fast rate of environmental change and the slow pace of societal response. Interestingly, the global scale reveals a much more mixed picture where societal responses to such changes as stratospheric ozone depletion, global warming, and industrial accidents have often been quite rapid, if less than totally effective. Still, signals of environmental threat have been processed with considerable speed and coping actions undertaken. But the trajectories of change in the nine regions provide considerable confirmation of the argument of overshoot put forth by Donella Meadows and her colleagues (1972, 1992). Only in Amazonia, the North Sea, the Ordos Plateau, parts of Sundaland, and perhaps Ukambani do responses appear to have some potential for stabilization or at least a significant "flattening" in the trajectory toward greater endangerment or criticality. But the dominant situation is one of divergence in the rates of environmental change and societal response, promising increasing environmental impoverishment of future populations and ascending costs of the substitution and mitigative efforts that must eventually occur. And the primary causes for disjuncture lie less in inadequacies in scientific understanding than in socio-political structures, institutions, and processes.

Global capability inequity

The 1992 Earth Summit addressed with determined attention the broad issues associated with capacity-building in developing countries (United Nations 1992). Agenda 21 calls for national assessments of capabilities and for specific initiatives and programmes needed for strengthening such capabilities. Involved are not only scientific and financial resources, but the infrastructure of institutions required to formulate and implement national programmes of sustainable development.

The nine case-studies in this volume underscore the importance of these initiatives. Among the various inequities that cause and structure the global pattern of environmental degradation and associated human harm, two stand out. First is the array of human driving forces in which inequalities in wealth, differential stages of development, patterns of debt, world poverty, and a global economy shape a continuing unequal distribution of environmental impoverishment, endangerment, and criticality. Second is the highly variable capability to anticipate, assess, and respond to this degradation (Agarwal and Narain 1991; South Commission 1990). Early and effective efforts to bring trajectories of economic development and long-term environmental protection into consonance are highly cost-effective as well as protective of generations yet to be born. But such efforts are also an outcome of levels of minimal well-being, requisite institutional and scientific capabilities, and political will. The North Sea case, when placed in the context of the eight developing-country regions, suggests that the differential capability to respond to emerging environmental degradation is no less important than the levels of degradation found throughout the South. Such differences are likely to widen rather than narrow and will require major initiatives if differential response is not to exacerbate rather than ameliorate other global inequities.

References

Agarwal, Anil, and Sunita Narain. 1991. *Global warming in an unequal world*. New Delhi: Centre for Science and Development.

Ausubel, Jesse, and Hedy E. Sladovich, eds. 1989. *Technology and environment*. Washington DC: National Academy Press.

Berkes, Fikret, ed. 1989. *Common property resources: Ecology and community-based sustainable development*. London: Methuen.

Berry, Brian J. L. 1991. *Long-wave rhythms in economic development and political behavior*. Baltimore, MD: Johns Hopkins University Press.

Blaikie, Piers M. 1985. *The political economy of soil erosion in developing countries*. London: Longman.

Blaikie, Piers M., and Harold C. Brookfield. 1987. *Land degradation and society*. London: Methuen.

Bonalume, R. 1991. Deforestation rate is falling. *Nature* 350: 368.

Brooks, H. 1986. The typology of surprises in technology, institutions, and development. In *Sustainable development of the biosphere*, ed. W. C. Clark and R. E. Munn, 325–348. New York: Cambridge University Press.

CEQ (US Council on Environmental Quality). 1980. *The global 2000 report to the President*. Washington DC: Council on Environmental Quality.

Clark, William C. 1988. The human dimensions of global change. In *Toward an understanding of global change*, ed. National Research Council, 134–200. Washington DC: National Academy Press.

———. 1990. Toward useful assessments of global environmental risks. In *Understanding global environmental change: The contribution of risk analysis and management*, ed. Roger E. Kasperson, Kirstin Dow, Dominic Golding, and Jeanne X. Kasperson, 5–22. Worcester, MA: Clark University, The Earth Transformed Program.

Douglas, Mary. 1966. *Poverty and danger: Concepts of pollution and taboo*. London: Routledge & Kegan Paul.

Douglas, Mary, and Aaron Wildavsky. 1982. *Risk and culture. An essay on the selection of technological and environmental dangers*. Berkeley: University of California Press.

Falkenmark, Malin. 1986. Fresh water: Time for a modified approach. *Ambio* 15, no. 4: 194–200.

Freudenburg, William. 1988. Perceived risk, real risk: Social science and the art of probabilistic risk assessment. *Science* 242: 44–49.

Gleick, Peter H. 1991. Environment and security: Clear connections. *Bulletin of the Atomic Scientists* 47, no. 3: 17–21.

———. 1992. *Water and conflict*. Occasional Paper no. 1 of "Environmental Change and Acute Conflict," American Academy of Arts and Sciences and the University of Toronto. Cambridge, MA: American Academy of Arts and Sciences.

Ives, Jack D., and Bruno Messerli. 1989. *The Himalayan dilemma: Reconciling development and conservation*. London: Routledge.

Jodha, N. S. 1992. *Common property resources: A missing dimension of development strategies*. World Bank Discussion Papers no. 169. Washington DC: The World Bank.

Jodha, N. S., Mahesh Banskota, and Tej Partap, eds. 1992. *Sustainable mountain agriculture*. 2 vols. New Delhi: Oxford and IBH Publishing Company.

Kasperson, Jeanne X., and Roger E. Kasperson. Forthcoming. *Global environmental risk*. Tokyo: United Nations University Press.

Kasperson, Roger E., and Pieter-Jan M. Stallen, eds. 1991. *Communicating risks to the public*. Dordrecht: Kluwer.

Kasperson, Roger E., Robert W. Kates, and Christoph Hohenemser. 1985. Hazard management. In *Perilous progress: Managing the hazards of technology*, ed. Robert W. Kates, Christoph Hohenemser, and Jeanne X. Kasperson, 43–66. Boulder, CO: Westview Press.

Kates, Robert W., and Viola Haarmann. 1992. Where the poor live: Are the assumptions correct? *Environment* 34, no. 4 (May): 4–11, 25–28.

Kates, Robert W., Jesse H. Ausubel, and Mimi Berberian, eds. 1985. *Climate impact assessment*. SCOPE 27. Chichester, UK: John Wiley.

Kates, Robert W., Christoph Hohenemser, and Jeanne X. Kasperson, eds. 1985. *Perilous progress: Managing the hazards of technology*. Boulder, CO: Westview Press.

Krimsky, Sheldon, and Dominic Golding, eds. 1992. *Social theories of risk*. Westport, CT: Praeger.

Leonard, Jeffrey H. 1989. *Environment and the poor: Development strategies for a common agenda*. New Brunswick, NJ: Transaction Books.

Louis Harris and Associates. 1989. *Public and leadership attitudes to the environment in four continents: A report of a survey in 16 countries*. New York: Louis Harris and Associates.

McCay, Bonnie, and James M. Acheson, eds. 1987. *The question of the commons: The culture and ecology of communal resources*. Tucson: University of Arizona Press.

Meadows, Donella H., et al. 1972. *Limits to growth*. New York: Universe Books.

Meadows, Donella H., Dennis L. Meadows, and Jørgen Randers. 1992. *Beyond the limits: Confronting global collapse, envisioning a sustainable future*. Mills, VT: Chelsea Green.

Mortimore, Michael J. 1989. *Adapting to drought: Farmers, famines, and desertification in West Africa*. Cambridge: Cambridge University Press.

National Research Council. 1983. *Risk assessment in the federal government: Managing the process*. Washington DC: National Academy Press.

Ostrom, Elinor. 1990. *Governing the commons: The evolution of institutions for collective action*. Cambridge: Cambridge University Press.

Palo, Matti, and Gerardo Mery, eds. 1990. *Deforestation or development in the Third World? Volume III*. Metsäntukimuslaitoksen tiedonantoja 349; Scandinavian Forest Economics no. 32. Helsinki: Finnish Research Institute.

Royal Society. 1983. *Risk assessment: A study group report*. London: The Royal Society.

Sack, R. D. 1990. The realm of meaning: The inadequacy of human-nature theory and the view of mass consumption. In *The earth as transformed by human action. Global and regional changes in the biosphere over the past 300 years*, ed. B. L. Turner II, William C. Clark, Robert W. Kates, John F. Richards, Jessica T. Mathews, and William B. Meyer, 659–671. Cambridge: Cambridge University Press with Clark University.

Simon, Julian L., and Herman Kahn. 1984. *The resourceful earth: A response to Global 2000*. Oxford: Basil Blackwell.

Slovic, P. 1989. Perception of risk. *Science* 236: 280–285.

Smith, Neil. 1984. *Uneven development: Nature, capital, and the production of space*. Oxford: Basil Blackwell.

South Commission. 1990. *Challenge to the South*. New York: Oxford University Press.

Stern, Paul C., Oran R. Young, and Daniel Druckman, eds. 1992. *Global environmental change: Understanding the human dimension*. Washington DC: National Academy Press.

Thompson, Michael, Richard Ellis, and Aaron Wildavsky. 1990. *Cultural theory*. Boulder, CO: Westview Press.

Tiffen, Mary, and Michael Mortimore. 1992. Environment, population growth and productivity in Kenya: A case study of the Machakos District. *Development Policy Review* 10: 359–387.

Turner, B. L., II. 1989. The specialist-synthesis approach: The case of cultural ecology. *Annals of the Association of American Geographers* 79: 88–100.

Turner, B. L., II, and William B. Meyer. 1991. Land use and land cover in global environmental change: Considerations for study. *International Social Science Journal* 130: 669–679.

Turner, B. L., II, William C. Clark, Robert W. Kates, John F. Richards, Jessica T. Mathews, and William B. Meyer, eds. 1990a. *The earth as transformed by human action: Global and regional changes in the biosphere over the past 300 years*. Cambridge: Cambridge University Press with Clark University.

Turner, B. L., II, Roger E. Kasperson, William B. Meyer, Kirstin M. Dow, Dominic Golding, Jeanne X. Kasperson, Robert C. Mitchell, and Samuel J. Ratick. 1990b. Two types of global environmental change: Definitional and spatial-scale issues in their human dimensions. *Global Environmental Change: Human Dimensions and Policy* 1, no. 1 (December): 14–22.

United Nations. 1992. *Agenda 21, Rio Declaration, Forest Principles*. New York: United Nations.

WCED (World Commission on Environment and Development). 1987. *Our common future*. New York: Oxford University Press.

Whitmore, T., B. L. Turner II, D. Johnson, R. W. Kates, and T. Gottschang. 1990. Long-term population change. In *The earth as transformed by human action*, ed. B. L. Turner II, William C. Clark, Robert W. Kates, John F. Richards, Jessica T. Mathews, and William B. Meyer, 25–39. Cambridge: Cambridge University Press with Clark University.

Contributors

Adrián Guillermo Aguilar
Senior researcher, Institute of Geography, Universidad Nacional Autónoma de México (UNAM)

Paulo de T. Alvim
President of Fundação Pau-Brasil, Ilheus, Brazil

Julie Argent
Served as research assistant to Professor Timothy O'Riordan, University of East Anglia, Norwich, UK

Patricia Benjamin
Graduate student in geography, Clark University, Worcester, MA, USA; currently conducting dissertation research in Tanzania

Harold Brookfield
Professor emeritus, Department of Human Geography, Research School of Pacific Studies, the Australian National University, Canberra

Elizabeth Brooks
Is completing a Ph.D. in geography, Clark University, Worcester, MA, USA

Yvonne Byron
Research assistant to Harold Brookfield, Research School of Pacific Studies, the Australian National University, Canberra

Alex Diang'a
Research associate, African Centre for Technology Studies (ACTS), Nairobi, Kenya

Kirstin Dow
Ph.D. candidate, Graduate School of Geography, Clark University, Worcester, MA, USA; currently an associate for JK Research Associates

Jacque Emel
Assistant professor, Graduate School of Geography, Clark University, Worcester, MA, USA

Exequiel Ezcurra
Senior researcher, Centro de Ecología, Universidad Nacional Autónoma de México (UNAM); currently head of the planning directorate at Mexico's Ministry of Social Development (SEDESOL)

Italo C. Falesi
Soil scientist, Brazilian Agricultural Research System for Eastern Amazonia, Belém, Eastern Amazonia

Teresa García
Is completing a Master's degree in ecology, Faculty of Sciences, Universidad Nacional Autónoma de México (UNAM)

Nikita F. Glazovsky
Deputy director of the Institute of Geography, Russian Academy of Sciences, Moscow

N. S. Jodha
Heads the Mountain Farming Systems Division, International Centre for Integrated Mountain Development (ICIMOD), Kathmandu, Nepal

Hong Jiang
Ph.D. candidate, Graduate School of Geography, Clark University, Worcester, MA, USA

Jeanne X. Kasperson
Research associate professor and research librarian, George Perkins Marsh Institute, Clark University, Worcester, MA, USA, and senior research associate, World Hunger Program, Brown University, Providence, RI, USA

Roger E. Kasperson
Professor of government and geography, Clark University, Worcester, MA, USA; currently university provost

Marisa Mazari Hiriart
Associate researcher, Centro de Ecología, Universidad Nacional Autónoma de México (UNAM)

William B. Meyer
Research assistant professor, George Perkins Marsh Institute, Clark University, Worcester, MA, USA

Professor Timothy O'Riordan
Associate director, Centre for Social and Economic Research on the Global Environment (CSERGE), School of Environmental Sciences, University of East Anglia, Norwich, UK

Irene Pisanty
Associate professor, Biology Department, Faculty of Sciences, Universidad Nacional Autónoma de México (UNAM)

Lesley Potter
Senior lecturer in geography, Department of Geography, University of Adelaide, Australia

Dianne Rocheleau
Assistant professor, Graduate School of Geography, Clark University, Worcester, MA, USA

Emanuel Adilson S. Serrão
Scientific director, Brazilian Agricultural Research System for Eastern Amazonia, Belém, Eastern Amazonia

Nigel J. H. Smith
Professor of geography, University of Florida, Gainesville, USA

B. L. Turner II
Professor of geography and director of the George Perkins Marsh Institute, Clark University, Worcester, MA, USA

Fenghui Wang
Institute of Geography, Chinese Academy of Sciences, Beijing

Peiyuan Zhang
Institute of Geography, Chinese Academy of Sciences, Beijing

Du Zheng
Institute of Geography, Chinese Academy of Sciences, Beijing